DATE DUE

WORKS BY LIN YUTANG

In English (except the last seven titles, the following are published in Shanghai by the Commercial Press)

LETTERS OF A CHINESE AMAZON

READINGS IN MODERN JOURNALISTIC PROSE

THE LITTLE CRITIC: FIRST SERIES (1930-1932)

THE LITTLE CRITIC: SECOND SERIES (1933-1935)

CONFUCIUS SAW NANCY (*A Drama*) AND ESSAYS ABOUT NOTHING

A NUN OF TAISHAN AND OTHER TRANSLATIONS

KAIMING ENGLISH BOOKS

KAIMING ENGLISH GRAMMAR BASED ON NOTIONAL CATEGORIES

A HISTORY OF THE PRESS AND PUBLIC OPINION IN CHINA (*University of Chicago Press*)

MY COUNTRY AND MY PEOPLE (*John Day*)

THE IMPORTANCE OF LIVING (*John Day*)

MOMENT IN PEKING (*John Day*)

THE WISDOM OF CONFUCIUS (*Modern Library*)

In Chinese

PHILOLOGICAL ESSAYS (*Yüyenhsüeh Lunts'ung*)

SKIRMISHES (*Chienfuchi*)

THE LONE WAYFARER (*Tahuangchi*)

IT SEEMS TO ME (*Woti Hua*), 2 vols.

MOMENT IN PEKING

MOMENT IN PEKING

A Novel of Contemporary Chinese Life

by Lin Yutang ～ ～ ～

THE JOHN DAY COMPANY · NEW YORK

★

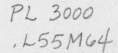

TO

THE BRAVE SOLDIERS OF CHINA

WHO ARE LAYING DOWN THEIR LIVES

THAT OUR CHILDREN AND GRANDCHILDREN

SHALL BE FREE MEN AND WOMEN

THIS VOLUME WRITTEN BETWEEN

AUGUST 1938 AND AUGUST 1939

IS HUMBLY DEDICATED

PREFACE

*W*HAT is a novel but "a little talk," as the name *hsiaoshuo* implies? So, reader, listen to this little talk awhile when you have nothing better to do. This novel is neither an apology for contemporary Chinese life nor an exposé of it, as so many recent Chinese "dark curtain" novels purport to be. It is neither a glorification of the old way of life nor a defense of the new. It is merely a story of how men and women in the contemporary era grow up and learn to live with one another, how they love and hate and quarrel and forgive and suffer and enjoy, how certain habits of living and ways of thinking are formed, and how, above all, they adjust themselves to the circumstances in this earthly life where men strive but the gods rule.

L. Y. T.

CONTENTS

THE CHARACTERS

Brackets indicate families, grouped by generations, and including maidservants important in the story.
Names in *italics* indicate maidservants.
Names followed by "!" indicate illicit relationships.
Names followed by * indicate concubines.

HOW TO PRONOUNCE THE NAMES

Pronounce the Chinese names like Italian names, as a general principle, i.e., pronounce *a, e, i, o, u* as *ah, ay, ee, o, oo*. For instance, pronounce MULAN as "Milan," but with the MU- as in "Mussolini." Chinese names have no stress, but only tones, but those who must stress one of the syllables would do well to stress the last, as in "Milan." TAO is pronounced like "tah-ō" as a diphthong.

(Lifu)	FU as in Cor*fu*			(Chen)	EN as in B*urn*et		
(Sunya)	UN as in br*un*ette			(Feng)	ENG as in b*ung*alow (nearly)		
(Lihua)	UA as in Pad*ua*			(San)	AN as in K*ahn*		
(Ailien)	AI as in Nikol*ai*			(Wang)	A as in *are*		
(Paofen)	AO as in P*ow*ell			(Hsieh)	IEH as in *yea*		
(Mochow)	OW as in L*ow*						

The point to remember is that a name like SUN is pronounced like "sŏŏn," while a name like FENG is pronounced like "ferng," or nearly like "fung(-us)."

In addition, there are four sounds, for which only approximate equivalents will have to serve.

Pronounce   SZE (Sze-an) as *see*
    and   TSE (Tse-an) as *tsee*
Pronounce   IH (Shihcheng) as *ee* or *er*
Pronounce ERH (Huan-erh) as Huan-*erl*
Pronounce   HS (Hsieh) as *sh*

SZE is the English sound "s" prolonged and vocalized, and TSE is the English sound "ts" prolonged and vocalized. IH is the English sound "sh" prolonged and vocalized. ERH at the end of names is always unaccented, so that HUAN-ERH can be read almost as one syllable, "Huan-erl," the ending resembling that of "Powell." HS resembles "ch" in German "ich." Pronounce HS as "sh," and disregard all "h's" at the end of syllables and one cannot go very far wrong.

In the spelling of Chinese names, all aspirate marks and diacritical marks have been omitted.

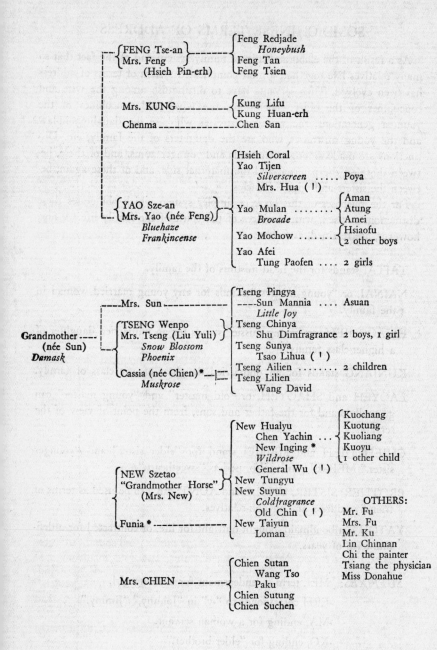

FENG Tse-an, Mrs. Feng (Hsieh Pin-erh) — Feng Redjade / *Honeybush*, Feng Tan, Feng Tsien

Mrs. KUNG — Kung Lifu, Kung Huan-erh
Chenma — Chen San

YAO Sze-an, Mrs. Yao (née Feng) *Bluehaze* *Frankincense* —
Hsieh Coral
Yao Tijen
Silverscreen ..... Poya
Mrs. Hua (!)
Yao Mulan *Brocade* .... Aman, Atung, Amei
Yao Mochow .... Hsiaofu, 2 other boys
Yao Afei
Tung Paofen .... 2 girls

Grandmother (née Sun) *Damask*

Mrs. Sun — Tseng Pingya, ----Sun Mannia .... Asuan, *Little Joy*

TSENG Wenpo, Mrs. Tseng (Liu Yuli) *Snow Blossom* *Phoenix* —
Tseng Chinya
Shu Dimfragrance 2 boys, 1 girl
Tseng Sunya
Tsao Lihua (!)
Tseng Ailien .... 2 children

Cassia (née Chien)* *Muskrose* — Tseng Lilien, Wang David

NEW Szetao "Grandmother Horse" (Mrs. New) —
New Hualyu
Chen Yachin ... Kuochang, Kuotung, Kuoliang, Kuoyu, 1 other child
New Inging* *Wildrose*
General Wu (!)
New Tungyu
New Suyun *Coldfragrance*
Old Chin (!)

Funia* — New Taiyun, Loman

OTHERS:
Mr. Fu
Mrs. Fu
Mr. Ku
Lin Chinnan
Chi the painter
Tsiang the physician
Miss Donahue

Mrs. CHIEN — Chien Sutan, Wang Tso, Paku, Chien Sutung, Chien Suchen

SOME CHINESE TERMS OF ADDRESS

As a result of the elaborate Chinese family system and of the fact that so many relatives live together, a most complicated system of terms of address has been evolved. Thus servants have to distinguish among the wife and concubines of the older generations, the wives and concubines of the younger generations, the young mistresses who are the daughters-in-law and the young mistresses who are the daughters of the family, etc. Distinctions are made among elder aunts and younger aunts, and of these, between those on the paternal and the maternal side, and of these again, between the sisters and wives of uncles.

For the purposes of this book, a simpler system which obliterates these distinctions is used, with sacrifices of the spirit of the family life. A few, however, are retained, as follows:

TAITAI stands for the head mistress of the family.

NAINAI, or "young mistress" stands for any young married woman in the family.

HSIAOCHIEH, or "young missie" stands for an unmarried daughter of a higher-class family.

KUNIANG stands for an unmarried daughter of any class of family.

LAOYEH and SHAOYEH, or "old master" and "young master" can generally stand for the father and sons, from the point of view of the servants.

CHIEHCHIEH and MEIMEI stand for "elder sister" and "younger sister." MEIMEI can be also used as "sweetheart."

BROTHER, SISTER, UNCLE and AUNT, can also be used as terms of friendly address among non-relatives.

YATOU is a bondmaid, bought outright for life, or contracted for a definite term of years.

SUFFIXES: -MEI, term of endearment for a young girl.
　　　　　　-ERH corresponds to "-y" in "Johnny," "Jimmy."
　　　　　　-MA, ending for a woman servant.
　　　　　　-KO, ending for "elder brother."

Book One

THE DAUGHTERS OF A TAOIST

To Tao, the zenith is not high, nor the nadir low; no point in time is long ago, nor by lapse of ages has it grown old.

From the essay on "The Master" by Chuangtse.

CHAPTER I

*I*T WAS the morning of the twentieth of July, 1900. A party of mule carts were lined up at the western entrance of Matajen Hutung, a street in the East City of Peking, part of the mules and carts extending to the alley running north and south along the pink walls of the Big Buddha Temple. The cart drivers were early; they had come there at dawn, and there was quite a hubbub in that early morning, as was always the case with these noisy drivers.

Lota, an old man of about fifty and head servant of the family that had engaged the carts for a long journey, was smoking a pipe and watching the drivers feeding the mules; and the drivers were joking and quarreling with each other. When they could not joke about each other's animals and the animals' ancestors, they joked about themselves.

"In such times," said one, "who can tell whether one comes back dead or alive after this journey?"

"You are well paid for it, aren't you?" said Lota. "You can buy a farm with a hundred taels of silver."

"What is the use of silver when you are dead?" replied the driver. "Those bullets from foreign rifles don't recognize persons. *Peng-teng!* It goes through your brain-cap and you are already a corpse with a crooked queue. Look at the belly of this mule! Can flesh stay bullets? But what can you do? One has to earn a living."

"It's difficult to say," rejoined another. "Once the foreign soldiers come into the city, Peking won't be such a good place to live in, either. For myself, I'm glad to get away."

The sun rose from the east and shone upon the entrance to the house, making the leaves of the big colanut tree glisten with the dew. This was the Yao house. It was not an imposing entrance—a small black door with a red disc in the center. The colanut tree cast its shade over the entrance, and a driver was sitting on a low stone tablet sunk into the ground. The morning was delightful, and yet it promised to

3

be a hot day with a clear sky. A medium-sized earthen jar was standing near the tree, which provided tea in hot summer days for thirsty wayfarers. But it was still empty. Noticing the jar, a driver remarked, "Your master does good deeds."

Lota replied there was no better man on earth than their master. He pointed to a slip of red paper pasted near the doorpost, which the driver could not read; but Lota explained to him that it said that medicines against cholera, colic, and dysentery would be given free to anybody.

"That's something important," said the driver. "You'd better give us some of that medicine for the journey."

"Why should you worry about medicine when you are traveling with our master?" said Lota. "Isn't it the same whether you carry it or our master carries it?"

The drivers tried to pry out of Lota information about the family. Lota merely told them that his master was an owner of medicine shops.

Soon the master appeared to see that all was in order. He was a man of about forty, short, stumpy, with bushy eyebrows and pouches under the eyes, and no beard, but a very healthy complexion. His hair was still perfectly black. He walked with a young, steady gait, with slow but firm steps. It was obviously the gait of a trained Chinese athlete, in which the body preserved an absolute poise, ready for a surprise attack at any unsuspected moment from the front, the side, or behind. One foot was firmly planted on the ground, while the other leg was in a forward, slightly bent and open, self-protective position, so that he could never be thrown out of his balance. He greeted the drivers and, noticing the jar, reminded Lota to keep it daily filled with tea as usual during his absence.

"You're a good man," chorused the drivers.

He went in, and soon appeared a beautiful young woman. She had small feet and exquisite jet-black hair done in a loose coiffure, and wore an old broad-sleeved pink jacket, trimmed around the collar and the sleeve ends with a three-inch broad, very pale green satin. She talked freely with the drivers and showed none of the shyness usual among higher-class Chinese young women. She asked if all the mules had been fed, and disappeared again.

"What luck your master has!" exclaimed one young driver. "A good man always is rewarded with good luck. Such a young and pretty concubine!"

4

"Rot your tongue!" said Lota. "Our master has no concubines. That young woman is his adopted daughter and a widow."

The young driver slapped his own face in fun, and the others laughed.

Soon another servant and a number of pretty maids, from twelve or thirteen to eighteen in age, came out with bedding, packages, and little pots. The drivers were rather dazzled, but dared not pass further comments. A boy of thirteen followed, and Lota told the drivers it was the young master.

After half an hour of this confusion, the departing family came out. The beautiful young woman appeared again with two girls, both dressed very simply in white cotton jackets, one with green, the other with violet trousers. You can always tell a daughter of a well-to-do family from a maidservant by her greater leisureliness and quietness of manner; and the fact that the young woman was holding their hands showed the drivers these two were the daughters of the family.

"*Hsiaochieh,* come into my cart," said the young driver. "The other's mule is bad."

Mulan, the elder girl, thought and compared. The other cart had a smaller mule, but his driver had a more jovial appearance. On the other hand, this young driver had ugly sores on his head. Mulan chose by the driver rather than the mule.

So important are little things in our life, perfectly meaningless in themselves, but as we look back upon them in their chain of cause and effect, we realize they are sometimes fraught with momentous consequences. If the young driver had not had sores on his head, and Mulan had not got into the other cart with the small and sickly-looking mule, things would not have happened on this journey as they did, and the course of Mulan's whole life would have been altered.

In the midst of the hustle, Mulan heard her mother scolding Silverscreen, a maid of sixteen in the other cart, for being overpainted and overdressed. Silverscreen was embarrassed before everybody; and Bluehaze, the elder maid of nineteen, assisting the mother into her cart, was silently smiling, being secretly glad that she had known better than to overdress for this journey and had listened to the mistress's instructions.

You could see at a glance that the mother was the ruler of the family. She was a woman in the middle thirties, broad-shouldered, square-faced, and inclined to be stout; and she spoke in a clear, commanding voice.

5

When everybody was well seated and ready to start, a little maid of eleven, whose name was Frankincense, was seen crying at the door. She was utterly miserable about being left behind to stay alone with Lota and the other servants.

"Let her come along," Mulan's father said to his wife. "She can at least help fill the tobacco for your water pipe."

So, at the last moment, Frankincense jumped into the maids' cart. Everybody seemed to have found a place. Mrs. Yao shouted to the maids to let down the bamboo screen at the front of their covered cart, and not to peep out too much.

There were five covered carts, with one pony among the mules. The maternal uncle, Feng, and the young boy led the party, followed by the mother, riding with the elder maid, Bluehaze, who was holding a baby two years old. In the third cart were Mulan and her sister Mochow and the adopted daughter, whose name was Coral. The three other maids, Silverscreen, Brocade, fourteen, and little Frankincense, were in the next cart. Mr. Yao, the father, sat alone and brought up the rear. His son Tijen had avoided riding in the same cart with him, and had preferred the uncle.

A manservant, Lotung, who was the brother of Lota, sat on the outside in Mr. Yao's cart, one leg crossed on the shaft and one left dangling.

To the people who had gathered to watch the departing family, Mrs. Yao loudly announced that they were going for a few days to their relatives in the Western Hills, although actually they were going south.

Whatever their destination, it was obvious to the passers-by that they were fleeing from the oncoming allied European troops who were marching upon Peking because of the Boxer uprising.

And so with a *waddle-ho!* and *ta . . . tr!* and crackings of whips, the party started. The children were all excited, for it was their first trip to their Hangchow home, about which they had heard their parents speak so often.

. · .

Mulan greatly admired her father. He had refused to flee from Peking until the evening of the eighteenth; and, now that they had decided to seek safety in their home at Hangchow, he had made extremely cool and unperturbed preparations for the departure. For Mr. Yao was a true Taoist, and refused to be excited.

6

"Excitement is not good for the soul," Mulan heard her father say. Another argument of his was: "When you yourself are right, nothing that happens to you can ever be wrong." In later life Mulan had many occasions to think about this saying of her father's, and it became a sort of philosophy for her, from which she derived much of her good cheer and courage. A world in which nothing that happens to you can ever be wrong is a good, cheerful world, and one has courage to live and to endure.

War clouds had been in the air since May. The allied foreign troops had taken the fort at the seacoast, but the railway to Peking had been destroyed by the Boxers, who had grown in power and popularity and swarmed over the countryside.

The Empress Dowager had hesitated between avoiding a war with the foreign powers and using the Boxers, a strange, unknown, frightening force whose one object was to destroy the foreigners in China and who claimed magical powers and magic protection against foreign bullets. The Court issued orders one day for the arrest of the Boxer leaders, and the next day appointed the pro-Boxer Prince Tuan as minister for foreign affairs. Court intrigue played an important part in this reversal of the decision to suppress the Boxers. The Empress Dowager had already deprived her nephew the Emperor of his actual power, and was planning to depose him. She favored Prince Tuan's son, a worthless rascal, as successor to the throne. Thinking that a foreign war would increase his personal power and obtain the throne for his son, Prince Tuan encouraged the Empress Dowager to believe that the Boxers' magic actually made them proof against foreign bullets. Besides, the Boxers had threatened to capture "one Dragon and two Tigers" to sacrifice to heaven for betrayal of their nation, the "Dragon" being the reformist Emperor whose "hundred days of reform" two years earlier had shocked the conservative mandarinate, and the "Tigers" being the elderly Prince Ching and Li Hungchang, who had been in charge of the foreign policy.

Prince Tuan forged a joint note from the diplomatic corps of Peking, asking the Empress Dowager to restore the Emperor to actual power, thus making the old woman believe that the foreign powers stood in the way of her plan to depose the Emperor, so that she decided to throw in her lot with the Boxers, whose secret of power was their war cry of "driving out the Oceanic People." Some enlightened cabinet ministers had opposed the Boxers on account of the burning of the

7

European Legations, advocated by the Boxers, which was against Western usage; but these opponents had been killed by the power of Prince Tuan. The Chancellor of the University had committed hara-kiri by disemboweling himself.

The Boxers were actually within the capital. A lieutenant colonel who had been sent out to fight them had been ambushed and killed, and his soldiers had joined the Boxers. Highly popular and triumphant, the Boxers had captured Peking, killing foreigners and Christian Chinese and burning their churches. The diplomatic corps protested, but Kang Yi, sent to "investigate" the Boxers, reported that they were "sent from Heaven to drive out the Oceanic People and wipe out China's shame" and secretly let tens of thousands of them into the capital.

Once inside, the Boxers, under the covert protection of the Empress Dowager and Prince Tuan, terrorized the city. They roamed the streets, hunting and killing "First Hairies" and "Second and Third Hairies." The "First Hairies" were the foreigners; the "Second and Third Hairies" were the Christians, clerks in foreign firms, and any other English-speaking Chinese. They went about burning churches and foreign houses, destroying foreign mirrors, foreign umbrellas, foreign clocks, and foreign paintings. Actually they killed more Chinese than foreigners. Their method of proving a Chinese to be a "Second Hairy" was simple. Suspects were made to kneel before a Boxer altar in the open street, while a piece of paper containing a message to their patron god was burned, and the suspect was pronounced guilty or not guilty according to whether the ashes flew up or flew down. Altars would be set up in the streets toward sunset, and the people who showed obedience to the Boxers would burn incense while they danced their monkey dance, the Monkey Spirit being one of the most popular of their patron gods. The smell of incense filled the streets, and one could believe oneself living in the magic land of *Hsiyuchi* once more. Even important officials had set up altars and invited the Boxer leaders to their homes, and servants had joined the Boxers to tyrannize over their masters.

Mr. Yao, being a well-read man and in sympathy with the reformist Emperor, thought the whole thing silly and dangerous child's play, but kept his convictions to himself. He had his own good reasons to be "antiforeign" in a sense, and hated the church as a foreign religion protected by a superior foreign power; but he was too intelligent to

8

approve of the Boxers, and was grateful that Lota and his brother Lotung had kept away from the rabble.

There was fighting in the city. The German Minister had been fallen upon and murdered by Manchu soldiers. The Legation Quarter was under siege, and the Legation Guards had been holding out for two months, waiting for relief from Tientsin. Yung Lu, one of the most trusted men of the Empress Dowager, who was put in command of the Imperial Guards to attack the Legations, was not in favor of the attack and secretly gave orders for their protection. But whole blocks of the city near the Legation Quarter had been razed to the ground, and whole streets in the South City burned down. The city was truly more in the hands of the Boxers than of the Government. Even the water carriers and toilet cleaners were not allowed to pursue their business unless they had red and yellow turbans wound around their heads.

All through this period Mr. Yao had refused to consider moving. All he consented to was to destroy a few big foreign mirrors in his home and a collapsible foreign telescope that he had bought as a curiosity. His house was a little out of the zone of great destruction. To his wife's pleadings for flight from the killing, looting, and turmoil, he did not reply; he refused to consider them. The country around was swarming with troops, and Mr. Yao thought that it was better to sit still than to make a move. He believed that men contrive, but the gods decide; and he was willing to take things as they came.

His calm and nonchalance exasperated his wife. She accused him of intending to live and die with his curios and his garden. But when the allied troops were actually approaching there was a real fear of a sack of the city, and she said, "If you don't care for your life, you must think of these little children."

This argument drove home, although he said, "How do you know it will be safer on the way?"

So on the afternoon of July 18 they decided to go. He thought that if they could get mule carts and go straight south to Tehchow, the first city in Shantung, an eight- or nine-day journey, they would then be safe. The new governor of Shantung had driven the Boxers out of his province by force and so preserved peace and order. The Boxers had originated in Shantung, because it was there that several "religious incidents" had taken place, including the one which caused the leasing

9

of Tsingtao to the Germans and the dismissal of the previous governor, Yu Hsien, who had encouraged the Boxers.

One day the new governor, Yuan Shihkai, had asked a Boxer leader to come to him to prove their magic powers. He ordered ten Boxers to stand in line and face a firing squad armed with modern rifles. At a signal, his men fired and, marvelous to behold, the ten Boxers were unhurt; the rifles had not been loaded. The Boxer chief was elated, and cried, "You see . . . !" Before he had finished the governor himself drew a revolver and killed the Boxers one by one. That had finished the Boxers in Shantung, and after a brief campaign they all drifted over to Chihli.

Flight through Tientsin was impossible. If Peking was in a state of pandemonium, Tientsin was in a state of hell; and the route to it was in the direct line of battle. Refugees from Tientsin to the capital said that traffic on the Grand Canal was jammed for miles, and boats had been known to make only half a mile advance in a whole day. So they were to go by land south to Tehchow, on the Shantung border, before taking a boat on the Grand Canal; and because there were *hunhun,* or bandits, outside Yungtingmen Gate, they must go by way of the Marco Polo Bridge, and follow the route to Chochow before they struck southeastward.

The journey from Tehchow down the Grand Canal to Shanghai and Hangchow would be safe also, because the governors in southeast China had signed an agreement with the foreign consuls to preserve peace and protect foreign lives and property, so that the Boxer conflict had been strictly localized in the north.

"When are we leaving?" asked Mrs. Yao.

"The day after tomorrow," replied her husband. "We have to arrange for the mule carts. Then we have to do a little packing."

Now that she had won her point, Mrs. Yao was dismayed at the thought of packing.

"How can I do it in a day?" she exclaimed. "There are all the trunks and carpets and furs and jewels—and your curios."

"Never mind about my curios," said Mr. Yao curtly. "Leave the house entirely as it is. There's nothing to pack, except some summer clothing and some silver for the journey. We are not taking a pleasure trip; we are fleeing in war. I shall leave Lota and a few servants to guard the house. It may be looted by the Boxers. Secondly, it may be looted by the soldiers. Thirdly, it may be looted by the foreign troops.

And fourthly, the whole house may be burned down, whether you roll up your carpets and pack your trunks or not. If we escape all these, we escape; and if we lose, we lose."

"But all our furs and treasures?" said his wife.

"How many carts are we going to take? The men and women alone will need five carts, and I am not sure we can find even that many."

Later, he called Lota to the hall. Lota had been with the family for years, and was himself a distant relative from Mrs. Yao's village. The master knew he could trust his entire fortune to his hands.

"Lota," he said, "tomorrow I shall pack up a few things with you, the porcelain and jade and the best paintings, and store them away. But we will leave all the cabinets and stands as they are. If any looters come, offer no resistance but ask them to help themselves. Do not risk your old life for these trash and rubbish! They are not worth it."

He instructed Feng, his wife's brother, who was managing the business of the household and looking after their medicine shops and tea firms, to go next day for some silver and gold for the journey, in ingots and broken pieces. Feng was also to call on the Imperial Physician and see if he could get some sort of official protection on the journey.

∴

In the dead of the night, Mr. Yao, who was sleeping alone in his studio in the southwest court, got up and woke Lota. He told Lota to light a lamp and follow him to the back garden, bringing a hoe and shovel, and to make no noise whatsoever. So they went out, old master and old servant, with six Chou and Han bronzes and several dozens of jade pieces and seal stones, that he had himself packed up carefully in sandalwood boxes, and buried them under the date tree in the garden. There they worked for over an hour under the light of the lamp and the summer stars.

Cheerful and really excited, Mr. Yao came back into the house before anyone was up. The dew was heavy, and Lota, coughing a little, suggested that he should go and make a pot of hot tea.

Mr. Yao often slept alone and he had no concubines. As head of a wealthy family, he had no great interests outside his books and curios and his children. He had no concubines for a double reason. First, because his wife would not permit it. Second, because there had been an abrupt change in his life at his thirtieth year, when he married Mu-

11

lan's mother. Then a sensuous, adventurous rogue and playboy became a Taoist saint. His life before then was a complete dark chapter to his family. He had drunk, gambled, ridden on horseback, fenced, boxed, philandered and kept a sing-song artist, had traveled widely and known the best society. Suddenly he changed. His father died a year after his marriage and left him a huge fortune in medicine shops and tea firms in Hangchow, Soochow, Yangchow, and Peking, with regular service of herbs from Szechuen, and tea from Fukien and Anhwei, and a few pawnshops besides. The spiritual history of this man in that period was so hidden in mystery that even his wife did not know whether he had reformed after marrying her or before. He stopped not only his gambling and the reckless drinking, for which he had enormous capacity, his philandering and otherwise abusing his magnificent constitution, but he also stopped attending to business, leaving the management to his wife's brother, Feng, who was a thoroughly able businessman.

In those days between 1898 and 1900, "new thought" was in the air, advocated by those who for a short period led the reforms which ended with the disastrous *coup d'état* when the Emperor was imprisoned in the Palace. Mr. Yao read and absorbed the new ideas in the current books and magazines.

While Lota went to make tea for him, old Yao, instead of turning to his wife's court, where the children slept, went to his own studio in the front western court. He lay on the covered earthen bed and thought about the things he had to do that day. Whenever he started a period of physical regimen for himself, he always slept in his studio. He would get up at exactly midnight, cross his legs and sit in position, perform the regular number of rubbings on his forehead, the sides of his head, his cheeks and chin, then his palms and feet, and begin to control his breath and practice deep abdominal breathing and regulate the swallow of his saliva. Thus with his circulation stimulated and breathing controlled he could hear, in the deep silence of the night, his own intestinal fluid circulating and nourishing the lower abdomen where the whole center of spiritual force lay. He would do this for about ten minutes, or sometimes fifteen or twenty minutes, for the purpose of nourishing his *ch'i,* or simple nervous energy. At regular intervals he would repeat the regular rubbings of his palms and feet. But he would never tire himself out, and would stop when he reached a state of excellent well-being, his body glowing with the blood coursing down his legs, a sweet exquisite sensation. Then he would relax and lie down and sleep a perfect sound sleep.

Lota lifted the screen and entered with a tea pot in his hand, and, pouring a hot cup, brought it to the bed. Old Yao gargled with the tea and spat it into a spittoon.

"*Laoyeh,* the journey will be strenuous," Lota said, "and you should rest yourself today. I do not know whether we can find drivers and carts. The man is coming in to report this morning."

He poured another cup for his master.

"I have thought over the matter," he continued. "It is better that Second Master Feng stay behind. The responsibility is too great for me. But take Bluehaze, Brocade, Silverscreen, and Frankincense. At such times as these, girls only bring trouble."

"That is right," said Yao. "Ask Ting and Chang to come and guard the house with you. But Second Master will go with us." Ting and Chang were old employees of the medicine shop on Morrison Street, which lay a distance south of the house. Because Yao's shop selling Chinese medicines and tea leaves clearly had nothing to do with the foreigners, it had thus far been spared by the looters.

"I will. But nobody else," replied Lota. "The fewer people in the house, the less cause for trouble. But the shop?"

"The Chen brothers will remain there. There is nothing to steal except some grass roots and pepper and herbs. What do they want these for? We have no foreign mirrors for them to smash, and in any case the shop will be closed until things improve. Several days ago the foreign shop Powei was looted. They smashed all the watches, clocks, and glasses. Someone took a bottle of foreign perfume for foreign wine and drank it. He turned white and fell on the floor and shouted that he had been poisoned by foreign concoctions. A boy working in the firm said they smashed the electric talking machine (telephone) and cut the wire because they thought it was a devilish land-mine to blow them up. Someone caught up a foreign mannikin, tore off the dress, and carried the naked foreign woman across the street. The crowd cheered and had the greatest fun out of that lady. Children ran and scrambled for her golden hair and started to fight among themselves. . . ." Lota and old Yao laughed together.

It was now broad daylight, and there were noises in the courtyards. Lota rolled down the paper on the window, remarking that it would be a hot day. Summer nights in Peking are always cool, and during the hot days, the rooms all being on the ground floor, the inhabitants roll down the tissue paper on their windows to keep the rooms cool like a cellar. This year Yao did not have a mat shed built thirty or forty feet high over the roofs and courtyard, as in other summers, which gave a perfect shade to the whole house like a big tree, yet permitted the movement of air. There were too many fires in the city during the May troubles, and such a mat shed made of wooden poles and a roof of bamboo matting would have made a perfect trap for fire to spread to the house.

Lota lifted the screen and went out. After sitting still a while to collect his thoughts, Yao heard his favorite daughter, Mulan, calling, "Father, are you up already?"

Mulan was a slim little child then, and small for a girl of ten. She had very bright eyes and dark hair coming down in a queue across her shoulder, and her light summer dress made her seem unusually small. She had always come to her father's studio and listened to him about all sorts of things, and her father liked to talk to her. Every morning when her father had not been sleeping in her mother's room in the inside court, she would come and say "early" to her father in the front court, the first thing after she got up and washed.

"Is your mother up yet?" asked her father, as she came in.

"They are all up, except Tijen and Sister," said Mulan; and then she asked, "Why did you say last night that all the curios are trash and rubbish?"

"If you consider them trash and rubbish, then they *are* trash and rubbish," he said. This was too profound for Mulan.

"But are you really going to leave all those things? At least hide away the little jade and amber animals for me. I want them."

"I have done so, my dear child." Then he told her as a great secret what he had done and enumerated to her the things he had buried, and Mulan knew them all by name.

"What if somebody should find them and dig them up?" she asked.

"Listen, child," said her father. "Everything has its destined owner. How many hundred owners do you think those Chou bronzes have had in the last three thousand years? No one ever permanently owns a thing in this world. For the time being, I am their owner. A hundred years from now, who will be their owner?"

Mulan felt very sad, until he added, "If someone who is not their

14

destined owner should dig up the treasure, he will find only jars of water."

"And the jade animals in the box?"

"They will fly away as little birds."

"But if *we* dig them up on our return?"

"The jade will be jade, and the bronze will be bronze."

This made Mulan happy. But it was also a lesson to her. Luck, or *fochi,* was not something that happened to a man from the outside, but was within him. To enjoy any form of luck or earthly happiness, a man has to have the character to enjoy and keep it. For one qualified for luck, jars of water will turn into silver; and for one who is not qualified, jars of silver will turn into water.

Bluehaze, the elder maid, now came to say that her mistress was asking if he had got up, and if so she would ask him to go over and discuss matters.

"Is the second master up yet?"

"He is already there."

Mr. Yao went in with his daughter and, passing through a moon door, came to the inner yard, where he saw Coral busy moving leather trunks which littered the floor of the central hall. Coral, his adopted daughter, was a woman over twenty. She was the orphan child of his best friend, Hsieh, and since her parent's death Yao had brought her up like his own daughter and had married her off at nineteen to a good husband. But her husband had died the year after, without leaving a child, and she had preferred to come back and had been living with them the last four years. She was a great help to Mrs. Yao in running the household and looking after the servants; she was like an elder sister to Mulan and Mochow. Sorrow had left no mark on her face; she never thought of marrying again and she was perfectly happy as she was. Apparently she had no sex consciousness, and she was not shy toward men. Like Mulan, she called Mr. and Mrs. Yao Father and Mother. Mulan called her *Tachieh* (eldest sister) and so Mulan herself, although the eldest daughter, was called *Erh Hsiaochieh* (number two daughter), and Mochow was called *San Hsiaochieh* (number three daughter) in the household.

Coral made herself so useful that Mrs. Yao came to depend on her a great deal, and she had a great influence in making decisions at the family council.

"You are early, Father," Coral greeted him, and hurriedly moved the trunks for him to pass.

"You haven't combed your hair yet. Do it after breakfast," he said.

She stood up and smiled. She had made a braid of her hair for the night, and looked almost a young girl in her pajamas.

"It will be hot after breakfast. I'd rather do it now," she replied.

Yao went into the western room and passed on to the inner chamber, while Coral followed him. Mrs. Yao was sitting on the bed while her brother occupied a chair beside it discussing the preparations for the journey with his sister. Feng Tse-an, a young man of thirty, was dressed in an old long gown of rich white gauze. Brocade was making the braid for Mochow. All but Mrs. Yao got up to greet the father, as he walked to his seat opposite the mother. Mulan had quietly slipped to her mother's side and seated herself, ready to listen. There is a point in the life of Chinese children when they suddenly behave like grown-ups, while retaining all their childishness of spirit. Girls reach that point at about nine or ten, while the boys, if not pampered, reach it at about twelve or thirteen. They aspire to be like the grown-ups, to know the ways of the grown-ups and to imitate them—they are proud to know how to behave, to know the manners and rules of life; and they lose face when they do not. And those who know the proper manners are treated as grown-ups, rather severely. But Mulan had not yet grown afraid of her mother, who tended to be naturally severe; for, since the death of her invalid child, she had softened toward the remaining daughters, Mulan and Mochow.

It may be remarked here that Mr. Yao had a peculiar way of naming his children. He eschewed all the conventional, overused literary words of which Chinese girls' names are usually composed, such as autumn, moon, cloud, musk, verdure, clarity, intelligence, delicacy, luster, orchid, peony, rose, and all sorts of plant names. He took instead classical names from Chinese history, which was very seldom done. Mulan (magnolia) was the name of a Chinese Joan of Arc, celebrated in a well-known poem, who took her father's place as a general in an army campaign for twelve years without being recognized and then returned to put on rouge and powder and to dress as a woman again. Mochow, meaning "don't worry," was the name of a lucky girl in a rich family, after whom a lake outside the Nanking city wall is still named today. Mulien, the third daughter, had been a sickly child from infancy and was given the name of the Buddhist saint in a religious drama, who tried to save the saint's mother (an unbeliever) suffering in hell—a drama picturing vividly hell torments and very popular because it combines the motives of religion and filial piety. Though she had been given this name and adopted as godchild by a nun at a temple in the Western Hills, this unfortunate child had died.

Turning to Feng, Mr. Yao said, "You had better go early and see the Imperial Physician."

"Who is ill?" asked Mulan.

Her mother cut her short. "Children should have ears and no mouth." But turning to her brother, "What are you going to see him for?"

"To see if we can obtain, through his influence, some sort of official protection on the way."

"Why not get Boxers to protect us, since it's the Boxers who are in power now?" suggested Mulan, forgetting again to check herself.

Silence fell upon the company with the dawn of a new idea. Feng looked at Yao and Yao looked at Feng, while Mrs. Yao looked at both.

Mr. Yao looked at the child and, beaming with pride, said, "She has an idea. The best would be to get a safe conduct from Prince Tuan; the Imperial Physician knows him."

"Look at this child," said Coral. "She is only ten, but you must not misjudge her. I shall be afraid of her when she is grown up. She will have to marry a dumb husband and do the talking for the two of them for life."

Mulan was both delighted at her unexpected triumph and embarrassed by the approval of grown-ups.

"The child simply says what comes to her mind. What does she know about it?" the mother said in an effort to discourage her pride. It was always the correct thing to do.

Bluehaze came in to say that breakfast was ready.

"Where is Tijen?" asked the mother, concerning the son.

"He is watching Silverscreen feed his hawk in the east garden. I have told him to come."

The family went to the dining room on the east of the courtyard. Before they had finished their breakfast, Lota announced that the cart driver had come. Feng thrust his bread in his mouth and went out to see him.

The cart driver said that there were many soldiers and bandits outside the gates, that mules and horses were difficult to get, that few

17

drivers were willing to risk the journey, and that, in consequence, they must pay a price to make it worth his while. He named a price that was shocking, five hundred taels for five carts. That, he said, was a small sum for about ten days' journey at great risks. After long haggling, the driver refused to yield an inch, all the time claiming that he might lose his mules and carts and all. Feng explained to him they would have official protection, but could not get him to reduce the price. Since the driver seemed an honest man, Feng was at last satisfied, though no doubt this would be the costliest journey they ever made.

When Feng came in and told of the arrangements, Mrs. Yao said the price was unheard-of, but there was nothing else to do. The children were excited to learn that there were five carts to go in, and began to talk of how they were going to pair off. Tijen wanted to ride with Silverscreen, the maid, while both Mulan and Mochow claimed Coral. For the children it was all fun and excitement; and for Mulan and Mochow it was their first journey either in carts or in canal boats, and they yearned to see Hangchow, about which they had heard their mother and Coral speak so much.

Feng went to call on the Imperial Physician, who was a great friend of the Yao family, and the Imperial Physician promised to bring him the safe conduct and whatever escort he could obtain. An order from Prince Tuan would be protection for them against both soldiers and Boxers on the way.

The business of packing seemed so much lighter after Mr. Yao said they were to take only the summer clothing, but there was enough to keep the entire household busy the whole day, except Tijen, who continued to play in the eastern garden with his hawk, interrupting Silverscreen at her other duties.

That evening there was a brilliant sunset, promising a hot day for the morrow. After supper the family sat in council and decided how they were going to divide up for the riding in the different carts.

To each one Mrs. Yao explained clearly that they were going to Tehchow to take a boat, and gave the address of their home at Hangchow—just in case any one should get lost. Then all were told to go to bed early as they were to get up at dawn.

CHAPTER II

ULAN, seated with crossed legs on the hard blue cotton cushion with her eight-year-old sister and Coral, first learned the jolting sensation of a Peking mule cart. She was excited and distinctly felt she was adventuring in the wide world.

Soon she and Mochow and Coral were talking with the driver, who was a jovial fellow and told them about the Boxers and what they did and what they did not do, about his chats with them, about war in Tientsin, about the Emperor and the Empress Dowager and Ta Ako (heir presumptive), and about their prospective journey.

After they had passed into the Southern City, they saw many charred houses in ruins, and while following the city wall westward along that deserted section they came to a crowd standing on a vacant lot around a Boxer altar, covered with a red cloth and with pewter candlesticks and red candles on it. Several Chinese suspected of being Second Hairies were kneeling on the ground on trial.

The driver pointed out some Boxer girls and women, dressed in red jackets and red trousers. Their tiny bound feet showed beneath the broad trousers, and their hair was tied up into broad bands on top of their heads. Like the men Boxers, who were also in red shirts or red shirt fronts, they had broad girdles around their waists, which gave them a martial look. The driver told them the women were the so-called "Red Lantern Shades" and "Black Lantern Shades." They were supposed to carry red fans in the daytime, with even the skeletons painted red, and red lanterns at night. The Red Lantern Shades were young girls, while the Black Lantern Shades were widows. Those without bound feet were recruited from the boat women. Their chief, whom they called "Holy Mother," was herself a boat woman working on the Grand Canal, but, the driver said, she had been taken to the governor's yamen in a yellow sedan chair and received by the governor himself. Some of these girls could "box," but most of them could not.

19

It was magic power they had. They had to learn the incantations, and after short practice they could wave their red fans and fly up to heaven if they wanted to; but they could certainly climb up walls, for the driver had seen them on housetops.

Had the driver seen the Boxers at work?

Yes, he had seen them many, many times. They would arrange an altar, burn candles, and start mumbling things in their mouths. Soon they would fall into a paroxysm, talking the magic language. That meant they were possessed of the spirit, and their eyes would stare straight and open. Then they started brandishing their broad knives and would chop hard at their own bellies, but the knives would not cut.

The spirit that possessed them and entered their bodies was the Monkey Spirit, Sun Wukung, celebrated in the religious epic *Hsiyuchi*.

All this was romance become reality for Mulan.

Before the story was over, they had long passed the Hsipienmen Gate and come outside the city into the open country.

∴

The first three days of the journey were comparatively easy and uneventful, except for the heat and the jolting of the carts. Everybody complained of his legs. But they traveled by starting very early, would go ten or twenty *li* before the breakfast hour, and covered the most ground in the early mornings and late afternoons, with a long rest for the men and mules at midday. Tijen and Feng would often get down and walk for a mile, when their legs were cramped; but after the fourth day the body seemed to tune itself to the jolting sensation.

Tijen was a most restless boy, and he changed his cart many times, demanding to sit now with his mother, now with the maids; and his mother, being overindulgent to the boy, allowed him. He was always happy when in the company of Silverscreen, who was three years his senior; and he loved to chatter and make fun of Brocade, until Brocade could not stand it any longer and came over to the mother's cart and helped carry the baby for a change.

On the fourth day, two days after they had left Chochow on the main road to Paoting and turned southeastward, all did not seem well. Rumors flew about that the allied troops had entered Peking and disorderly soldiers and Boxers were retreating south. One rumor had it that both Governor Yu Lu and General Li Pingheng had committed suicide and the Kansu troops were retreating in that direction.

There was sporadic fighting between the Boxers and the soldiers; and the Boxers, armed only with knives and pitchforklike weapons, had the worst of it. At the sound of gunfire the Boxers would start to run pell-mell in all directions. The people and soldiers did not know what to think of the Boxers. In the same company half the soldiers said they ought to fight them, and half thought not. The Boxers were popular with the people; they were burning churches and exterminating the much-hated foreigners. By imperial order, they had been commanded in the spring to organize Boxer bands; now the soldiers were supposed to arrest and destroy them; recently once more the Imperial Court seemed to favor them and adopt their antiforeign policy.

As more and more soldiers and Boxers retreated across the countryside, looting increased. The road was flooded with refugees, on foot and in mule carts, wheel carts, on donkeys and ponies. Peasants carried two baskets suspended from a pole on their shoulders, with piglets in one basket and a baby in the other. But the Yaos were ahead of most of the retreating soldiers, and the country they passed through was comparatively peaceful. The women began to be worried, and Tijen was no longer restless. Mr. Yao gave orders to hurry as much as possible and not take longer rests than were necessary, in the hope of reaching Tehchow before they were overtaken by the soldiers. He had already destroyed the official paper issued by Prince Tuan's yamen, as it no longer meant anything, and in fact might implicate them with either the Boxers or the soldiers.

They reached Jenchiu before sunset that afternoon, as they had only a short stop at midday. Stopping at an inn, Mr. Yao asked the innkeeper if there were soldiers in the city, and was considerably relieved when he was told that the commander of the Sixth Brocade Banner Regiment of Tientsin was stationed at the place and preserving order. The Catholic Church here had been burned a month ago but, as Commander Hsu entered the city and arrested and beheaded dozens of these "elder brothers," the bands had dispersed into the countryside.

A traveler with his family, two women and three children, also refugees, who arrived later at the inn, brought a disconcerting story. He had left Paoting that morning and fled direct toward Jenchiu, having heard that Commander Hsu was able to preserve order at the city. The story was this:

A family of a well-to-do official was traveling on the road to Paoting. There was a woman in the group who had a golden bracelet on her arm. A roving band of soldiers approached and, seeing the golden bracelet, demanded it. The woman was slow about it, and one of the soldiers cut off her arm and ran away with the bracelet. Another party of soldiers came up and learned of what had happened and, seeing that the golden bracelet was somewhere in the hands of the soldiers ahead, pursued and shot them. Some of the soldiers in front who had escaped hid themselves among the tall grain on the roadside, and shot down the soldiers who had robbed them as they came up. Thus a single bracelet had cost seventy or eighty lives.

The fellow-travelers told the story in whispers, and Mr. Yao kept it to himself. He ordered his family to go to bed immediately after supper, and forbade the maids and children to go outside their room. They had only one room for twelve people, but the family refused to be separated into different inns. The arrival of the other family made the situation worse. The room had only an earthen bed fifteen feet wide, and the maids had to sleep on the floor. Mr. Yao was not the man to stand on his rights when other people were in need, and he consented to have the two women from the other party sleep in the room, while he and Feng and Lotung and the rest of the other party had to sleep in the outside room, which was a combination of kitchen, sitting room, and dining room.

While the children were sleeping peacefully in the inner room and Lotung was snoring heavily in his sleep, Mr. Yao did not feel he required sleep at all, nor wanted it. He was thinking that if they started early the next day, they should be able to reach Hochienfu before sunset.

For a while yet there was peace. A little oil lamp was burning on the stove, pretty and peaceful. He took out his pipe and meditated. It was to be the last night for a long time he could meditate with peace in his heart. He later recalled it and thought it was heaven—the feeling of having one's dear ones safe sleeping in the next room, while he smoked his pipe and an oil lamp burned on a kitchen stove.

Toward midnight, Mr. Yao thought he heard his wife utter a scream in her sleep, followed by a stirring in the room. He went to the stove and picked up the oil lamp and looked in at the door. Mrs. Yao, with the baby at her side, had sat up and was patting Mulan's face and smoothing her hair.

"What are you doing there at this time of the night? You haven't gone to bed yet?" asked the mother.

"I thought I heard you scream in your sleep," said the father.

"Did I? It gave me such a fright. I had an awful dream of Mulan calling to me from a great distance in some valley. I shivered so and woke up. I am so happy it is only a dream." And she stared at Mulan and looked about at her other children.

"It's only a dream," he said. "Go to sleep again."

The father retired.

Soon there came a shower and the steady patter of rain made Mr. Yao drowsy and sent him to sleep without his knowing.

∴

On that morning of July 25, Mr. Yao was awakened by noises in the room and found that most of the family had got up and already washed their faces. The mule drivers were at the door, and said it was a delightful, cool day after the rain. The sky was cloudy and promised to remain so for the day. It was only sixty *li* to Hochienfu, and they should be able to cover the distance easily. Mules could easily go a hundred *li* a day without heavy burden: for a long journey, with all the cart burden, they could go sixty or at most seventy *li*. Moreover, one of the mules had stepped into a ditch and nearly fallen on its knees and upset the cart, and one of its forelegs seemed sprained. Consequently, the going had to be slower.

At about eight the party started, Mrs. Yao asking Bluehaze to come over to her cart and hold the baby. The mule in Mulan's cart limped.

After going about fifteen *li,* it showed signs of increasing irritability and often stopped dead, its sides panting. The mule is an animal with the body of a horse and the mind of a donkey, as powerful as the former and as stubborn as the latter. The driver said it was unwell and would die if they didn't go slow. "Animals are just like men; when they are ill, they lose their appetite and won't eat. This one only sniffed at the hay and nibbled a little this morning. You can't make a journey on an empty stomach. Aren't they just like men?"

It took them three and a half hours to cover the next twenty *li* before they reached Hsinchungyi. It was about half-past one when the party alighted, hungry for a meal. Hsinchungyi was an old courier station, where horses were kept for imperial couriers running in relays. By such a system of relays, urgent official messages could be sent to the capital from Hochienfu—a distance of a hundred miles—within twelve hours. There was a stable near by, and three or four horses were tied to trees in a grove.

Since they expected to change some of the mules at Hochienfu for the remaining part of the journey, the owner of the sick mule decided he would try to secure one of the horses, at least for the day's journey. The driver knew the man at the courier station, and the arrangement was made.

After lunch the party had a rest in the pavilion, while Mulan and Mochow and Tijen strolled to the grove to watch the horses. Tijen went too near a white horse and it started to kick, which sent Mulan flying and screaming, pulling her sister with her. These courier horses were powerful animals, and Mr. Yao shouted across the field impetuously to Tijen to come back.

Mr. Yao was in an irascible temper. His wife had been telling him last night's dream. She was walking in a valley with a wide stream running in the middle and forest on one side. She was holding Mochow by her hand. She thought she heard Mulan's voice calling her, and she suddenly realized Mulan was not near her and she seemed to have not seen her for days. At first the voice seemed to come from the treetops and, as she was turning into the heavy forest, with all paths blocked, and didn't know what to do, she heard Mulan's call again, faintly but distinctly, from the other side, across the river. "I'm here, I'm here," said the voice. The mother turned and saw the figure of her child picking flowers in the meadow across the river. She saw no bridge or ferry and wondered how the child had got across. She left Mochow on the bank, and started to wade the shallow rapids, when a big torrent arose and swept her off her feet, and she woke up to find herself lying on the *kang* in the inn.

The story made everyone uncomfortable, although none said a word after she had finished.

So the lame mule was left at the station, to be picked up by the driver on the return journey. At about three they started again, with the new horse pulling the cart containing Coral and the two sisters. The horse was constantly rushing ahead; and the driver, not knowing its temper and ways, had difficulty in holding it back.

Toward five, when they had reached within twelve or thirteen *li* of the city, they saw bands of soldiers coming across the country at a distance on the left. Mr. Yao said he would ride at the front, but the road

24

lay three or four feet below the ground level, and until they came up to the level there was no way of passing the other carts. There were parties of refugees in front of them and behind at a distance of a hundred yards.

Suddenly they heard a shot. The near-by fields were covered by tall *kaoliang* fifteen feet high, and they were deep on the road below, so that they could not tell where the soldiers were, although they heard voices coming nearer. More shots followed. They could not turn back, nor would they know which way to turn, as the shots and voices seemed to come both from in front and behind. As they came up to the level seven or eight fleeing soldiers ran past them at the crossroads, and they could see bands of soldiers fifty yards away on the left. All the carts stopped dead, and Mrs. Yao shouted to Coral to bring the sisters over to her cart.

Getting down from a mule cart was a difficult business for Coral with her bound feet, but she did it. When she had alighted on the ground, she stretched her arms toward Mochow and lifted her down. She brought Mochow to her mother's cart, intending to come back again for Mulan. The interruption had completely stopped the traffic at the crossroads, blocking the refugees at their rear, and there was a great deal of cursing and shouting from the drivers behind.

At this moment, shots were heard again and some soldiers on horseback dashed across right in front of the party. The courier horse took fright and started to gallop, and Mulan's cart was swept along with the crowd of soldiers and horses.

In the confusion nobody knew what had happened. The soldiers seemed to be more bent on fleeing than on robbing. The Yao party, after being held back by more groups of passing men and horses, were literally pushed onto the road straight in front by the carts behind, and all animals flew off at a gallop. With the confusion and the clouds of dust it was impossible to discern anything. Coral, who hastily got into the mother's cart when the mounted soldiers swept past them, took half a second to realize that Mulan was alone in the other cart. "Mulan!" she screamed. Mulan's mother instinctively wanted to jump down, but in the twinkling of an eye all carts had swung around. She could see only a confusion of men and carts and horses' hoofs before her. Then her cart dashed ahead with the rest. To direct those animals by shouts, once they started going, was like preaching to a locomotive engine. There were dozens of carts before her, and she could only hope that

25

one of them contained her child. Mr. Yao did not even know that Mulan was alone. He thought the worst was over since the soldiers had not stopped to rob them.

While all the carts were dashing ahead, Mr. Yao's instinct was to get away from the soldiers as fast and as far as possible before they stopped to take stock of what had happened, assuming that everybody was going in the same direction. Mrs. Yao's mind was torn between two impulses: to get ahead and recognize Mulan's cart or the driver among those in front, or to slow down and round up anyone left behind. Actually she could do neither. The road was broad enough for one-way traffic only. Several times she would have jumped down from the cart, but Coral held her back.

After seven or eight minutes of this madness, the animals began to slacken their pace. No soldiers were in sight. They had already left the crossroads at least two miles behind. A cart crashed into the roadside ditch, and a woman who fell was nearly run over by the carts behind. Another cart came up, and a passenger who knew the woman jumped down and the cart was drawn up in the middle of the road. Perforce the Yao carts were also stopped. Feng ran around to inquire. Mrs. Yao was in hysterics. Coral and Bluehaze were crying. Pointing to those carts still going in front and disappearing into the distance, Mrs. Yao shouted that Mulan might be in one of them and they had to follow and not stop at this place.

"Mulan is alone!" shouted the mother.

The awful realization penetrated into the father's mind. It was no time for questioning why Mulan was left alone. He snatched the pony, untied it from his cart, mounted, and galloped past the crowd after the refugees going in front. It was a futile chase.

The maids had come down, too, pale with fright and struck dumb by the news. Coral had now literally rolled down from the cart; how that cart contained three women and two children in the last quarter of an hour, nobody could explain. The mother held Mochow fast on her lap, while Bluehaze was carrying the baby. Mochow, at first dumb with terror, now started to cry. Refugees gathered and passed. Some stopped to watch the woman fallen on the ground; it appeared her mule had been shot in the leg and it was difficult to disentangle it from the harness of the overturned cart. Some stopped to hear the news of a girl of ten lost. Some expressed sympathy and others passed on unconcerned.

Tijen said he had seen the courier horse of Mulan's cart running to the right with the soldiers, but he could not see clearly. If so, Mulan had gone off their road and probably was carried along with the crowd of soldiers and horses. But the driver was with her, and he would drive it to Hochienfu and might catch up with them and rejoin them on the way.

While they did not know exactly what to think or do, they saw Mulan's cart driver running up from behind with a whip in his hand and shouting to them. Everybody's countenance fell to see him appear without the cart.

"Is the child safe?"

"Who knows? We were swept along, and the courier horse took fright and could not be stopped . . ."

"Where is she?"

"Which way has she gone?"

"How did you lose the cart?"

The driver was as incoherent as the questioners. He had swung to the right with the soldiers and the horses, then into a road on the right to get out of the way of the soldiers; and, seeing that he had lost the company, he got down to hold the horse. The horse was too powerful for him and he lost hold of his reins, and the horse dashed ahead.

One thing was certain: Mulan was still in the cart. Moreover, it was traveling away from Hochienfu and going back north when the driver last saw it turn and disappear into the *kaoliang* fields. He was sure the courier horse would find its way back to Hsinchungyi. In his simplicity of heart, he had rushed back to inform the parents.

After what seemed hours of desperation, Mr. Yao came back on his pony. He had looked into every cart, had made detours, and had even come within sight of the city itself, before he gave up.

The driver's suggestion seemed right to Mr. Yao; the horse would find its way back home to Hsinchungyi.

It was nearly sunset. Mr. Yao would go back in his cart with the driver to Hsinchungyi, the driver to recover his cart and the father to recover his daughter. The rest of the party had to go on to the city, as the city gate would soon be closed. The drivers told them of an inn to stop at for the night, where they would await the news.

· ·

Mulan's mother did not sleep the whole night, but shed silent tears.

27

At dawn, she asked Lotung and her brother to get up and go to the North Gate and look for Mulan.

About nine the next morning, the father arrived at the city inn. The horse and cart had returned, but without the child. He had retraced the route and scoured the country at the crossroads but had found nothing.

The news struck like thunder. Mulan was then definitely lost. The mother fell to weeping aloud, "My child Mulan, you should not leave me now like this, and follow your sister Mulien. If you leave me now, I do not care to live this old life any more!"

"Mother," said Coral, "all things are determined from above; no one can be sure whether they will turn out good or bad. It's better that you do not grieve so much as to injure your health. The journey is still far ahead, and all these lives depend upon you. If you are in good health, the burden of all us children will be made lighter to bear. We don't know yet surely that Mulan is lost; we are going to search for her. It was all my fault; I shouldn't have left her alone . . .!"

Mrs. Yao controlled herself and replied, "It's not you, Coral, but my bad luck that caused this. I shouldn't have asked you to bring your sisters over. But who could have foreseen it would have happened like this? If something should happen to Mulan, or she is kidnaped and sold . . ." She broke down again.

Mr. Yao stood by not saying a word. Mulan was his favorite child, and the loss cut too deep into his heart. At the word "kidnap" he walked away like a wounded animal.

Brocade, who had been silently standing against the wall, suddenly broke down completely. Fourteen years old, she had almost grown up with Mulan. She had taught her to play all the children's games and sing all the nursery songs, and they had played together as children and Mulan had treated her as her own sister. The mention of "kidnap" reminded her of her own fate and her lost parents. She threw herself on the bed and wept uncontrollably. Seeing her crying, Tijen and Mochow also cried, and there was a hubbub in the room. Bluehaze approached and pulled Brocade up, saying:

"*Taitai* has just composed herself and here you start howling so that even Master Tijen and Miss Mochow are crying."

Brocade sat up, ashamed of herself, but still rubbing her red eyes. Silverscreen, who never liked Brocade, remarked sarcastically, "Since this morning she has sat alone. Miss Mochow had neither washed nor combed her hair, until I had to help her dress. They are so fond of each other and it is natural that she feels very badly about it."

Brocade walked out of the room, crying out with the voice of one injured: "I shed my own tears. What business is it of yours if I feel like crying? What business is it of yours if I am fond of Miss Mulan?"

"We are all serving *Taitai,* young master and young mistresses, and nobody is interfering with anybody else," replied Silverscreen heatedly.

"This is a rebellion!" shouted Mrs. Yao.

Coral hurried over to the next room. "Is this the time to make more trouble? Haven't we had enough?"

"I didn't want to cry," said Brocade between her sobs. "But I thought of Miss Mulan and, when *Taitai* mentioned kidnaping, I thought of myself. Oh my parents, if you were living, I shouldn't be bullied like this."

"Of course we are all sorry, and it's all right to cry, because you can't help it," said Coral, trying to calm her.

"See if she doesn't cry if Master Tijen is lost," said Brocade wickedly.

Silverscreen, who had been listening outside, came in. Coral turned around and pushed her out, and forbade both to open their mouths again.

The horrors raised in the imagination of the parents, of what might happen to a lost girl of Mulan's age and beauty, were worse than death. The uncertainty, the haunting fears, the inability to tell what she was doing, the outstanding hope that she might still be found in this city or elsewhere, almost paralyzed their minds.

That morning Mrs. Yao did not speak again, except to say, "I'll search for her dead or alive." She was transformed into an automaton, governed by a single idea, seeing nothing and hearing nothing.

At noon, when dinner was served, she walked automatically to the table. She ate, but did not know she was eating. Again, while Brocade was quietly eating her rice, all of a sudden she dropped her bowl and sobbed and left the table.

Terrified by Mrs. Yao's calm, Coral said, "Mother, you must rest. You did not sleep last night. This search will probably last a few days. We must keep ourselves well." Mechanically Mrs. Yao allowed herself to be led to bed, without a word.

· ·

Hochienfu was a prefecture city of fifty thousand inhabitants, in the middle of a low-lying plain, surrounded by river tributaries running northeastward to Tientsin. Thirty miles to the east lay Tsangchow on the Grand Canal. Forty miles to the south Tehchow formed the apex of a triangle, with almost equal distances to the two points on the north, Hochienfu by land route and Tsangchow by the Grand Canal.

They would search for Mulan by posting placards in all inns and city gates and approaches to the city, giving the address of their inn and offering rewards for persons helping to find her. The reward was one hundred taels. The women were to stay strictly at the inn, while the father, Feng, the servant Lotung, and the drivers (with offers of reward) were to search the entire city and the surrounding country. Mulan's mother, transformed into a tremendous, silent force, prowled the streets and alleys and looked into rivers night and day, searching for her child.

But Hochienfu was full of refugees and stray children. Mulan was not the only child lost. There were several false reports. Mulan's mother even went outside the West Gate to look at a girl's corpse on the bank of a river.

Mr. Yao scoured the countryside on horseback, and others went off east as far as Shaho Bridge and west as far as Shuning.

But there was no trace of Mulan.

The child might have fallen into the hands of a gang in the child-slave traffic. Nothing was more probable. Mulan would be worth a hundred taels, although no one dared to say so. Feng came home one night with the story that the slave traffickers operated on the Grand Canal with boat women. Brocade, who had herself been kidnaped, confirmed the story and said the boat women had treated her very well. In those days the Grand Canal was the main route of travel between the capital and the south. The Green Gang operated on the canal with a perfect system. It was after the Tsinpu Railway was built that the canal lost its trade and the Greens joined with the Reds on the Yangtse and became the "Green-Red Gangs," which even today, in the Shanghai French Concession, control all the thieves, opium dealers, and brothels. They are famous for their kidnapings and robberies and for their philanthropy as well. Their leaders act as advisers to the municipal authorities and head every flood and famine relief, and their birthdays are celebrated with felicitations from the highest officials of the Government. The gangs were self-protective and mutually co-operative secret societies for the social riffraff and unemployed, guaranteeing a living, faring and sharing alike, extremely generous among themselves, observing a high code of honor, and tracing their origin to secret societies a thousand years ago. Legendary heroes were the gods they worshiped, loyal generals, righteous bandits who robbed the rich to give to the poor, popular heroes all.

The Boxers, known as *Yihotuan*, or "Union for Peace and Justice," were also a secret society. They were a branch of the White Lotus Society, which in the eighteenth century was plotting the overthrow of the Manchus. Historical circumstances merely had turned this force into one of antiforeignism, against the West and supporting the Manchus, which gave it an international significance.

On the theory that Mulan had been kidnaped, after days of fruitless search it was decided that they would strike for the Grand Canal. Feng offered to go straight east to Tsangchow, which was only a day's journey, and work his way down the Canal, stopping at towns and ferries to pick up any clues, while the main party was to continue its cart journey directly and wait for him at Tehchow.

There were only two signs of hope. On the third day Mrs. Yao called in a blind astrologer and asked him about a lost child. She gave him the "eight characters," consisting of the hour, day, month, and year of Mulan's birth, each being represented by two characters of the Celestial and Terrestrial Cycles. The astrologer said that Mulan had a group of "eight lucky characters," with twin stars shining in her destiny, that it was expected she would meet with some accident in her tenth year, but that her luck would carry her over it and "change the evil into luck." Moreover, her romantic destiny would begin early and, though she would not be *kuei* or become wife of a high official, she would be without worry for food and drink her whole life. Asked whether they would find the child, he said oracularly that "unknown forces were protecting her." On the whole, it was such a good combination of "eight characters" that he demanded the unusual fee of one dollar, and Mrs. Yao gave him two dollars. This put her in such a good mood that she went to burn incense at the City God's Temple. Strange to say, three times the wooden blocks were tossed before the god and three times they turned out favorable.

That night the mother had a dream similar to the one she had had before. She heard Mulan distinctly calling, "I'm here, I'm here!" and again she saw her child picking flowers on the meadow across the river, and with her was another girl whom she thought she had never seen before. The mother asked Mulan to come, and she shouted across,

31

"You come over to me. This side is our home. You are on the wrong side." The mother tried to find a bridge or ferry, but could not; and then she seemed to be walking easily on the river surface, down, down, down, at a tremendous speed, having already forgotten about the child. She passed cities and hamlets and towers and temples on hilltops on the bank and was approaching a bridge when she saw an old man trudging on the bridge, and recognized him as her husband. And she saw he was being assisted by a young woman, and the young woman was no other than Mulan. She shouted to them from the river, but they did not seem to hear her, and went on and on over the bridge. She was so absorbed looking at them that she knocked herself against a bridge pole, and she lost the power to float on the water and sank and woke up.

She told her husband the dream the next morning, and it gave both parents greater strength.

CHAPTER III

WHAT happened to Mulan was this, as far as her parents could make out of her story later:

When she found she was alone, she was very frightened, but did not cry. She thought she must get down somehow from the cart and she did, when the horse came to a bridgehead and hesitated as if to make up its mind which road to take. Nobody was near, but she saw some soldiers a long distance away, and she knew that was the direction from which she had come. So she ran that way until she came to the crossroads. Everybody had gone, and then, overcome and dazed with fear, she sat on the roadside and wept. A group of soldiers came along and a fat, jolly fellow stopped to ask what was the matter.

"Good uncles, take me to my parents," she begged.

"Where are your parents?"

"I don't know. We came from Peking. Good uncles, help me to find my parents. They have money and will reward you," said Mulan.

Then a woman came up with some more soldiers. She wore a red girdle, and Mulan knew that she was a Red Lantern Shade such as she had seen in Peking. She was a big, brown-faced woman and her feet were not bound. It appeared that these were Boxers and the woman was their commander.

"Good auntie, bring me to my parents," Mulan begged.

"Where are you going?" asked the woman kindly.

Mulan could not remember the name of the next city, Hochienfu, so she answered, "We are going to Tehchow."

"Why, Tehchow is my home. You shall go with me."

Mulan felt afraid of the Boxer woman, but after all she was a woman and the only help in sight.

"If you will take me to Tehchow, my parents will reward you," Mulan said.

The woman turned to the fat soldier and ordered him to carry the

33

child. This man was so jolly that Mulan lost her fear, although she disliked his rough and dirty hands, which seemed to press hard on her and hurt her, and he smelled of garlic. Soon they saw a stray horse, and the woman told the soldiers to catch the horse, and the fat man was ordered to ride with the child. This gave Mulan a queer feeling because she had never been on horseback before. The fat Boxer asked her many questions, and, at first guarded in her replies, she soon overcame her fear. He told her that his name was Laopa and she told him that she was Mulan and her family name was Yao. The fat man laughed and said since she was Mulan, she must have been in the army for twelve years and asked her if she liked it.

After an hour's journey, Mulan still saw no city and asked Laopa why, for she knew they should have come to a city soon. Laopa said, "You must be thinking of Hochienfu." Mulan remembered the name now and said that was it. But Laopa told her they could not go there because the soldiers in the city would attack them.

Mulan now was really frightened. The sun was setting and it was the hour when every child's instinct is for rest and security. But Mulan's parents were far away and she was with strangers. She began to cry and then fell asleep, and waked in fear and cried herself to sleep again.

When she waked the next time, they were making camp for the night in a village temple.

The woman offered her a bowl of congee with salted turnips, but Mulan was not hungry. The woman made her lie down beside her on the floor, and Mulan, exhausted, fell soundly asleep.

In the morning, as soon as Mulan waked, she began to cry, but the woman was very severe and stopped her.

"Good auntie, take me to Hochienfu to my parents," Mulan wailed.

"You said you were going to Tehchow, and I am taking you to Tehchow. If you cry again, I shall spank you," the woman replied.

Laopa offered to take the child to Hochienfu, but the woman said sharply, "You will go there and get shot!"

After breakfast, the party set out again. There were now between thirty and forty persons in all.

Mulan learned that they were Boxers who had fought east of Peking and retreated across the country when it was rumored that the foreign devils were advancing on the capital. Several days afterward they learned that the Empress Dowager and the Emperor had fled, that

Peking was in a state of terrible looting and pillage, and that moreover the white soldiers were coming southward.

"Why is it that we are defeated and why can foreign bullets kill us?" asked Mulan.

"Because foreigners also have magic and their magic is better than ours. That's how," Laopa had replied. "The Monkey Spirit never saw such red-haired, blue-eyed monsters before, and he is powerless to protect us because it is a different system of magic that the foreigners use. They have a devilish thing that they put to their eyes and can see a thousand miles."

Now that the capital was captured and the Emperor had run away, the Boxers were thinking only of going home. Most of the village people were, if not friendly, at least not hostile to them, for they were natives of this district and spoke the dialect. Some threw away their Boxer turbans. They complained that the Government had no business to organize them and then fight them and then again send them to fight the foreigners. Many regretted that they had joined the Boxers at all, and wished they had stayed to till their fields at home. Each day the party grew smaller as more and more dropped out, each going to his home village.

It now appeared that Laopa and the woman chief were lovers, but were going to part soon. For he was returning to his own village and not going on to Tehchow. Mulan began to be afraid to be left alone with the woman and wanted him to stay with her.

Curious as it may seem, Mulan had her first English lesson from Laopa, a Boxer. Laopa told her many things about the foreigners that he had seen, and taught her a rhyme about English words that he had learned. The song was this:

> *Lai* say "come"
> *Ch'u* say "go"
> *Niensze* "twentyfo" (twenty-four)
> *Shanyao* "potato"
> "Yes! Yes! No."
> *Malapatse! chualai fanghuo!*

The last sentence meant "Damn them, we'll catch them and set them on fire!" The funniest words were "Yes! Yes!" which Laopa said sounded like "deadly hot" in Chinese. Every time he came to these words, he said them energetically and roared with laughter.

Mulan began to feel like a Boxer herself. She thought she hated

35

the foreigners, too. They had no business to come to her country and preach a foreign god. The Chinese Christians, or Second Hairies, relied on their foreign friends to bully their own people. She had heard her father say so; she had heard him say that in lawsuits between Christians and other Chinese, the magistrate must let the Christians win, or he would be dismissed from his office.

Now, it was true that it was the policy of missionaries to protect Chinese Christians and themselves by their superior foreign power, which set the Chinese Christians as a race apart, more allied to foreigners than to their own country and their own people. There had been a series of "religious incidents," where missionaries were killed, and the magistrates were dismissed. For the killing of two foreigners, they had to give Tsingtao to the Germans and the Governor of Shantung was dismissed. That was why he was so bitter against the foreigners, and why he was one of the prime movers in influencing the Empress Dowager to favor the Boxers. The missionaries were thorns in the cushions of the magistrates' seats. The magistrates were more afraid of an incident involving missionaries and Christians than of thunder from heaven. It nearly always meant the end of their office, no matter what they did.

Moreover, Mulan had been told by her father that the "Oceanic People" did everything upside down. Their writing went from left to right, instead of from right to left, and horizontally in "crab-walk" fashion instead of from top to bottom. They put their personal names before their family names, and strangest of all, in writing addresses, they began with the house number, then the street, then the city, then the province, as if purposely to be contrary. They had to begin from the bottom if they wanted to know to which city a letter was going. And their women had large feet, a foot long, and talked in a loud voice, and had curly hair and blue eyes and went about arm in arm with men when walking.

All in all, the foreigners were the strangest imaginable sort of people.

∴

They had been some days on the journey and still Tehchow was not in sight. They were avoiding the main cities which were in the hands of other troops. One day they had a brief encounter with some soldiers in which they lost four or five men, which terrified Mulan. There were still about twenty persons left in the party.

36

At a place where they tarried for several days, the woman chief and Laopa had a quarrel. He wanted her to go with him to his home village, and she wanted him to go to Tehchow, which he refused to do. Mulan could hear them swearing at each other. There was no more of the Boxer titles of "Elder Brother" and "Honored Mother." They were now just ordinary people, going back to their old work. Mulan was torn between her desire to reach Tehchow and her fear of the woman. Laopa had grown very fond of Mulan and wanted to take her with him, but the woman had the stronger will, and he could not make her give up the child. In the heat of the argument, Laopa began to call the woman every sort of name, "thief's wife," "Shantung whore," "big-footed witch," "swindler," and "child snatcher."

"I know you are going to sell this child, you child snatcher! I know your business!" he threw at her.

To Mulan he said, "I can't keep you. It can't be helped. But you look out for this woman!" And then he went away.

Mulan stared with big eyes at the woman, but dared not utter a sound. She had heard of child snatchers from her father and from Brocade, and she was struck with terror. She made up her mind that she must try to escape as soon as she got to Tehchow, but now she said not a word.

It was terrible to go with this woman. She had to walk now and keep up with the woman. She was told not to talk with any man on the road and to pretend that she was the woman's daughter.

Luckily it was less than a day's journey, and at nightfall they reached Tehchow. At sight of the city, Mulan tried to slip away, but the woman pulled her back and struck her on the head and face and threatened her with a scorching iron if she tried to escape again. From that moment the woman did not relax her hold on Mulan. They went into the city, but after a few streets passed out of another gate and went on to a deserted village and to a house surrounded with trees, near a little stream barely ten feet wide. There was a big man about forty in the house. Mulan was so tired that she did not care what happened now. They locked her in a dark little room, and while the woman talked with the man in the hall outside her door, she fell asleep.

In the morning Mulan woke to find herself in that little cell, with only a high window above her reach. The woman came in with a red-hot poker and said: "Would you like a taste of this? If you try to run away, I will burn your eyes out."

37

Mulan, dazed with fear, promised to obey and never to go away.

On the third day, a girl about six years old was thrown into the same room.

The rest was terror and suspense.

.·.

For two days Mulan did not hear the woman's voice although men's voices were to be heard from time to time.

Then one day the woman came in, laughing happily.

"It's done!" the woman shouted.

Mulan heard the key turn in the door.

"*Hsiaochieh!*" she said, all smiles. It was the first time for many days that Mulan had been called *Hsiaochieh*. "You are lucky! I have found your family, and you are going to them today. Didn't I tell you I would bring you to your family? Haven't I been good to you?"

Excited beyond measure, Mulan shed tears of happiness.

The woman drew Mulan out into the hall, where there was an altar with candlesticks, and a little wooden shrine with a faded, red-faced idol without a beard, the image of "Tsitian Holy Ruler," the crazy monk-magician.

"Where are my parents?" Mulan asked.

"Be still," the woman said. "We will take you to the city."

"Many thanks to you and Buddha will bless you!" cried the child. "When do we leave?"

"As soon as you are dressed."

"How about Dimfragrance?" asked Mulan. Dimfragrance was the other girl who had shared her cell all these days.

"Nobody has come for her yet. It is her parents' business."

"Can I take her with me?" Mulan asked.

"If your people will pay for her," the woman said.

Mulan rushed back to the door and called, "Dimfragrance, I shall ask my parents to come and get you."

But she was forcibly pulled away. "Who told you to bother about other people's business?" the woman scolded sternly.

The woman now insisted on combing and braiding her hair for her, and tied the braid with a new pink tape at the lower end, and poured on her hair "tea oil" which had a strong smell. She also wanted to daub on Mulan's face a coating of powder and rouge, but the child refused, saying that she had never used rouge, which annoyed the woman.

A man brought several bowls of congee cooked with dates and sweetened with black sugar, and Mulan was offered a bowl. These gangs were a superstitious people and there was a ceremony about parting with one of their hostages. The child must be dressed as prettily as possible before being returned, and everything must appear auspicious for the future.

Mulan, being impatient to start, said she was not hungry, but she had to taste a few mouthfuls of the congee. "I am going home, and I am not hungry," she said. "Can I give this bowl to Dimfragrance?"

The woman looked at the child and then at the bowl of good congee, and she took it in and gave it to Dimfragrance herself. "Your luck!" Mulan heard her shouting.

They had then to go through a ceremony. A man lighted three incense sticks and bowed to the shrine three times, then went outside the hall into the back garden, and facing southeast bowed with incense sticks in hand three times to Heaven and Earth.

"Say you will bring us good luck!" Mulan was told, when they were through with the ceremony and about to leave.

"I will bring you good luck, and Old Father Heaven will bless you and you will live a hundred years," said the child.

"That's it!" cried the woman, greatly pleased.

They went down to a small boat on the little stream. Mulan could hear Dimfragrance wailing inside and felt deeply sorry for her.

They rowed down the stream to the Grand Canal, and approached a big canal boat with a red flag on its cabin. Mulan, who could read, saw that the boat belonged to an official of some sort from Peking, and the big character read "TSENG," which was the family name.

A woman was sitting at the bow of the boat, anxiously watching Mulan's boat, and several boys were beside her, staring with curiosity and fear. Mulan stared at her, not knowing how to greet or meet her. To her great disappointment, she saw that she was not being taken to her parents. Was this woman her parents' friend? She knew she had never seen her before.

Trembling and blushing, half excited and half afraid, Mulan was taken aboard the big boat. The woman extended her hand. She seemed kind and well-bred and motherly. Mulan instinctively liked her.

"My dear child, you must have had a terrible time," said Mrs. Tseng and drew her close to her breast. Mulan burst out crying. She knew that this was the breast of a good woman, like her own mother.

Now a strange thing happened. A middle-aged austere-looking gentleman came forward. He had a high forehead and wore spectacles and a slight beard. He was in a white pajama dress for underclothing, topped by a vest of pale-blue satin, and he held a water pipe in his hand. He was standing in his white cloth socks, for on such river boats, though the women kept their shoes on, the men took off theirs so as not to soil the well-scrubbed varnished boards that formed the cabin floor.

The gentleman came toward Mulan with a reassuring smile. Mrs. Tseng said, "This is Tseng *Laoyeh*. He wonders if you know him."

Mulan, all confused, could not say either "yes" or "no" but performed the usual ceremonial bowing and muttered in a trembling voice, "Tseng *Laoyeh*! Ten-thousand fortunes! I greet you!"

"You are of the Yao family, aren't you?" asked Mr. Tseng.

"Yes, sir." Mulan thought she had heard this voice somewhere.

"Where is your home in Peking?" he asked.

"Matajen Hutung, at East-Four Pailou."

"Is your name Mulan, or your sister's?"

"My name is Mulan. My sister is called Mochow," replied the child.

Slowly Mr. Tseng took from his sleeve a small package wrapped in a handkerchief and unfolded it with a curious smile. Lying on his palm in the open handkerchief were two little pieces of musty-looking old bones, each about an inch wide and eight to ten inches long. They were such unimpressive pieces of old animal bones as anyone might pick up on the ground in an old garden or in a ruin.

"What are these?" asked Mr. Tseng.

Mulan's eyes brightened as she said, "Aren't they bones with ancient inscriptions?"

"There you are! She is Yao Mulan, the only girl in the world who knows about these old bones!" Mr. Tseng shouted with enthusiasm in a voice that startled not only Mulan, but also his wife and the boys.

Mulan was confused and embarrassed. Suddenly she remembered. He was the man whom she and her father had met one day at the Lungfusze Temple Fair, picking up some of those inscribed bones.

"You are Tseng *Laoyeh*!" she cried. "You have been to our home!"

"You think I have been collecting rare treasure," said Tseng, speaking to his wife. "Today I have found a real treasure for you. It is she," pointing to Mulan.

Mrs. Tseng thought she had never seen her husband so enthusiastic, so completely relaxed, so undignified.

It is true that in 1900 Mulan was perhaps the only girl who had heard of these inscribed bones dating back to the eighteenth century, B.C. These things, containing the earliest examples of Chinese writing and now well-known because of their importance, were then just beginning to appear from an eroded river bank in Honan, at the site of the old Shang capital, and only a few collectors took an interest in them. Mulan's father was one of these, and one day when she accompanied him, they had met Tseng and the two men had begun to talk to each other. Mulan's father was proud of his child and had spoken of Mulan, and of how she loved these things because they were so old. Mr. Yao had also, after they had met again at the fair, asked Mr. Tseng to come to his studio and look at his pieces, and again Mulan was summoned by her father to appear and sit in their company. By rescuing Mulan, Mr. Tseng was now doing a service to his friend, Yao, both because he knew how her father valued her, and because he himself had been charmed by this vivacious, intelligent child. He was very proud of what he had done today.

The woman chief and her man companion had stood and witnessed this mystifying scene. Mr. Tseng went into the cabin at the back of the boat and came out with pieces of silver and a scale. After weighing a hundred ounces of taels, he wrapped them up and turned them over to the man.

"Here's your payment. You can go."

The man and the woman took the money, crossed over to their boat, and rowed away. Mulan wanted to speak of the other girl, Dimfragrance, but she was afraid. Later she spoke of it, but Mr. Tseng did not think it his affair.

The boys were standing apart, looking at Mulan with great curiosity, wondering and admiring and afraid to speak to her. The mother turned round and, holding Mulan's hand, introduced her boys one by one. "This is Pingya, my eldest. This is Chinya, my second boy. And this is Sunya, my third boy. How old are you, Mulan?"

Mulan said she was ten. Pingya was sixteen. Chinya was thirteen. Sunya was eleven.

Pingya was polite. Chinya was noncommittal. Sunya, the fat boy, smiled a broad smile, and his eyes glittered. Mulan was shy. Later she was to find that she would have enough to stand from this mischievous and straightforward fat boy.

Now that the first bewilderment had subsided, and Mulan knew she was among friends, she drew a deep breath and asked, "Where are my parents?"

"They are not here. They must have gone ahead. We will get in touch with them. Meanwhile, you will stay with us."

"Are you traveling also? Where are you going?"

"We are going to Tai-an, where our home is."

"Did you see my parents?"

"No. We did not even know you were leaving for the south."

"But how did you know I was lost, and how did you find me?"

"Come inside, and have some food, and I'll tell you."

Mrs. Tseng was a woman of about thirty, of very fine features and small in build, a contrast to her tall husband, who was ten years her senior. She came from an official family in Shantung that had lived for generations in Peking, and like the daughters of good families of the scholar or official class, she could read and write. She was Mr. Tseng's second wife, the first having died after giving birth to Pingya, whom she had brought up like one of her own children. These things were easy for a well-bred woman who knew exactly the right thing a good wife was supposed to do. For in her quiet, unobtrusive way, Mrs. Tseng had calm and dignity. Brought up in a high-class home, Mrs. Tseng had the grand style of Chinese womanhood, decency, orderliness, generosity toward servants, competence in family matters, knowing when to stand one's ground and above all, when to yield, what to overlook or ignore. Overlooking things was as important as supervising in running a household or a husband. For the rest, Mrs. Tseng, small and fine-featured, was of the nervous type, and this and her weak constitution combined to make her susceptible to illness and ailments of all kinds. At this period her skin was unusually fair and she was young and pretty.

Now her first thought was of Mulan. "You wash first, and I will give you a dress to change to presently," said Mrs. Tseng.

A girl brought forward a basin of water and a towel. When Mulan had washed, Mrs. Tseng had a bowl of pork and noodles ready for her. Mulan politely said she was not hungry, but really she was famished and Mrs. Tseng insisted, saying it was early yet and it would be some time before they had their lunch. It was the first bowl of good, clean food Mulan had tasted for days. She had never eaten anything better in her life. So important are the trivial things which are a woman's duty to attend to.

But Mulan was a sensitive girl. Although she was hungry and the soup was delicious, she ate slowly for fear of being laughed at. Mrs. Tseng was sitting at the table while the boys stood at a distance.

"Was it good?" asked Mrs. Tseng when she had finished.

"Very good, thank you. Now tell me about my parents. When can I see them?"

"I really don't know," said Mrs. Tseng. "We didn't see them."

"Then how did you find me?"

"I did find you, didn't I?" said Mr. Tseng, triumphantly. The boys were delighted to see their father was in such a gay mood.

"The child is asking, and you ought to answer properly," said his wife. "My dear child," she said to Mulan, "we have spent the last four or five days trying to find you."

. . .

Mr. Tseng had reason to be proud. Finding Mulan was very simple and yet it was very ably done. He had the usual feeling of a man who had done a job successfully and well, and he was sentimental about finding this young child who, at the age of ten, appreciated antiques.

The Tsengs had been on their way to their home near the foot of the Taishan Mountain in Shantung. They had left Peking five weeks ago, and had been held up for nearly three weeks in Tientsin. As they reached a village on the Grand Canal below Tsangchow, Mr. Tseng went ashore and while at a teashop saw a handwritten poster on yellow paper on the wall. He was attracted by the name and address of the signer of the poster. Mr. Feng, Mulan's uncle, had chosen to walk down to Tehchow on foot along the bank of the Canal so that he could stop freely to pick up any clues about the lost girl, and in tea houses at different ferries and hamlets, he had put up these posters.

REWARD FOR LOST GIRL

LOST—A girl, Yao Mulan, ten years old, dressed in white jacket and red trousers, eyes clear and eyebrows delicate, hair jet-black in a braid, feet unbound; face small and skin white, body height three feet; speaking perfect Peking accent. Girl

43

was lost on the way between Hsinchungyi and Hochienfu. Any kind person giving information leading to location of the child will be rewarded with FIFTY TAELS of silver, and anybody returning the child in person will be rewarded with ONE HUNDRED TAELS. The Blue Heaven is my witness, and I will not eat my own words.

PEKING, MATAJEN HUTUNG, YAO SZE-AN

HANGCHOW, THREE-EYED WELL, DOUBLE-DRAGON TEA FIRM

(Temporary address: Tehchow, Changfa Hotel).

When he read this, Mr. Tseng had cried, "It is my old friend, Yao Hueitsai and his little daughter!" The street address corresponded, and he had heard that Mr. Yao had medicine shops and tea firms in Hangchow. The unusual name of the girl was also unmistakable. He went back to his boat and spoke to his wife about it and told her how intelligent this child was. Mrs. Tseng remarked how remarkably lucky they themselves had been to get through those harassing days near Tientsin with all members of the family safe and unharmed.

As Mr. Tseng was a native of Shantung, in which province Tehchow was situated, he had a simple way of going about finding the child. Moreover, he had the advantage of being an official from Peking and could bring his influence to bear on the local authorities, if necessary. He knew that there was a complete system of kidnaping, as well as petty thievery, among the Green Gangs on the Canal. If one lost a watch and went to the right source immediately, he could have it returned in five minutes. The Shantung bandits were as well organized as the Shansi bankers, and in those earlier days, the bankers could send carts containing silver across the bandit-infested mountainous regions with perfect safety, provided they had the stamp and signature on a safe conduct permit issued by the gang's Peking office. The bandits on the road would honor the signature. Unlike the government, it was the bandits' principle never to collect transit levies twice on the same goods. Their word of honor was their word of honor.

Now if the girl had been kidnaped by the gangs, she would be sure to be sent down the Canal and most probably shipped to the south where there was a good market for young girls. Tehchow was a principal center of the gang's operations.

As soon as they reached Tehchow, Mr. Tseng went straight to the Changfa Hotel, hoping to find his friend Mr. Yao there. The hotel owner told him that Mr. Yao's party had gone six or seven days ago,

44

but had left behind twenty taels of cash and a letter of credit with a bank in the city, to be paid after identification of the child when found. He had also left at the bank a family photograph.

Next, Mr. Tseng went to a wine shop, quietly showed his card to the head of the shop, and told him what he wanted. Soon the man was able to bring to him a member of the gang. Partly by threat and partly by bribe, Mr. Tseng made this man take him to the house of a minor chief to whom he gave the name, address, and description of the child.

"If you don't bring her in a few days," said Mr. Tseng, "I'll tell the magistrate and have you put in jail for a Boxer."

The man pleaded that he also had seen the posters, but had no knowledge of the child's whereabouts or whether she was held by their gang at all. He promised to investigate and as soon as he heard any news, he would report to His Honor. Mr. Tseng promised to pay him well for his trouble.

For two days on two successive visits to the wine shop, Mr. Tseng could learn nothing. But he would not give up.

On the third day there was definite news that Mulan was within the neighborhood of Tehchow.

The rest was simple. He gave the man five taels and promised to give a hundred taels when the girl was delivered. The man hesitated, but he thought he would be lucky to get out of this without trouble, and he would be thankful indeed for a hundred taels, although that was no more than the advertised reward.

. ˙.

To Mulan listening, it was like being told a fairy tale with herself as the heroine in distress. While Mrs. Tseng was telling it, with corrections from her husband, a tall young woman, well-shaped and rather full-bodied, came on the boat from the bank, leading a child of about six. She had very small feet, neatly bound, but she stood quite erect. She wore a violet dress, broad-trimmed in green, and no skirts, but only green trousers, trimmed with broad, horizontal bands of a continuous swastika design in black. Beneath the trousers showed a pair of red bow shoes, three and a half inches long, beautifully embroidered and topped by ankle bands of white cloth.

A well-bound, well shaped pair of dainty feet was a delight because most bound feet were not well bound with regard to proportion and

45

angle. The principal thing, apart from perfect harmony of line, was "uprightness" so that the feet formed a perfect base for the woman's body. This young woman's feet were almost ideal, being small, upright and neat, round and soft and tapering to the point gradually, and not flattened as many common feet were. Mulan's heart leaped when she first saw that pair of red shoes through a door near the rear of the boat, for she had always desperately admired such small feet. Her mother had wanted to begin to bind her feet, but her father, having read the "Essay on Natural Feet" by Liang Chichao and being caught with new reformist ideas then making their stir in Peking and elsewhere in China, strongly opposed it. It was one of those questions of the times affecting one's personal life, brought about by the contact with Western ideas. Mulan listened to her father, but her heart wished otherwise.

This young woman, Cassia, happened to be a provokingly beautiful example. Of course it was not the bound feet alone; her whole figure emphasized their beauty, like a good statue on a harmonious base. Her "upright" feet supported her body delicately yet firmly, so that at any time the line was perfect. The effect of the bow shoes in which a woman walked essentially on her high heels was exactly like that of Western high-heeled shoes, which change the walking gait, throwing the hips backward and making it almost impossible for a woman wearing them to assume any but an erect position, or to walk slovenly as in low-heeled shoes. Cassia was rather tall, with a good head and neck, the line of her body gradually flowing out until below the waist it tapered in, with the round, carefully balanced trousers, and ending at the two small tips of the slightly upturned shoes—like a perfectly proportioned vase that one can examine for days and feel its perfection without being able to tell why it is perfect. A pair of big unbound feet would have completely ruined this harmony of line.

Such was the fleeting impression of beauty that Mulan felt on first seeing Cassia. With a girl's instinct, she gasped. Later, she discovered that when Cassia began to talk, or to smile, her mouth was slightly too large, and this was a defect. Her voice was also naturally broad and clear.

Cassia was the concubine of Mr. Tseng. Her name of address in the household had been *Kueichieh* or "Sister Cassia" before she was raised from maid to concubine. Now, although as concubine she should be addressed by the children as *yima* or "aunt," some of the children still called her "Sister Cassia" and she did not mind. The servants of the house, however, had to call her "*Yima*" or "Chien *Yima*," Chien being her family name. She was a maid from Mrs. Tseng's maiden home, who had accompanied her at the wedding and joined the Tseng home. Since Mrs. Tseng had given birth to two boys and since she was often ill, and Cassia was always obedient, the promotion of the maid into concubine was perfectly natural. It did not make the slightest change in their relationship, for to the wife she was always maid. When Cassia was twenty-one, Mr. Tseng fell sick at a time when his wife was suffering from loss of blood and stomach pains, and it had been necessary for Cassia to nurse the master during his illness, helping him to get up and to lie down, and bathe him and change his underwear. The twenty-one-year-old Cassia was shy about such intimacies, which the Chinese girl had the idea of reserving for the man she was going to serve for life. The line was very rigidly guarded, and only definite arrangements about the man she was going to "belong to" could break it. So the wife suggested that after her husband's recovery, Cassia should be his concubine. This made it easy for Cassia and she tended him throughout his illness, to his great delight. After his recovery, they had a feast, inviting the family relatives, and red candles were burned on the hall altar, and Mrs. Tseng was very happy.

Now Cassia was companion and chief assistant to Mrs. Tseng, and wife to her husband as well. What a combination of usefulness in different roles a woman could be!

A wife is like a flower, which may either be enhanced in beauty and dignity or completely spoiled by the vase that goes with it. Mrs. Tseng felt dignified by the arrangement and completely secure, because she was a well-bred woman, sure of her own ground. She could read and write, while Cassia could not, and the distinction between wife and maid-concubine was protected by a feeling of status and character. The wife could wear skirts, but the concubine must wear trousers. For her part, Cassia knew better than to challenge Mrs. Tseng's position and the respect due her as mistress. Originally a slave girl, she was far too happy to want to change the position.

The whole thing was decent and healthy because it was so open. The difficulty in keeping a mistress is not personal, but social; not what the husband thinks of it, but what the wife thinks of it, what the mistress thinks of herself, and, most important of all, what society thinks of them all.

There is a dignity about being useful to people with whom one eats one's daily bowls of rice, and Cassia felt herself very useful in many ways.

She had also given birth to two girls, Ailien, now six, and a baby just six months old. She was busy with the household duties and the children, like any wife and mother. But there was this difference: she had to stand at meals and to serve the mistress and the family, while her own children sat at table. This was not unusual, for in large official families in other times, the daughters-in-law, even though not concubines and coming themselves from official families, had to keep up the fiction of serving at dinner while the parents-in-law were eating, in order to emphasize personal service. With Cassia, the rule was not rigidly kept. She usually sat down at table and ate after the others had finished. There would be occasions when other servants were there and she was not needed, when she would be ordered by the mistress to sit down. Then she would pull up a stool and sit obliquely on it, behind Ailien, and busy herself helping the children with their food, so that she was not really eating herself. This was firstly, to show that she knew the rules, secondly, to be helpful, and, thirdly, to show that she was not greedy. The mistress would say, "You must eat yourself, for after the meal you have other things to do." Then Cassia would nibble a little food, and start all over again helping the children with their soup and seeing that all were well fed. When the other members of the family had nearly finished, then she would set to and eat from what remained of the dishes. Probably her early training as a maid had made her used to this; but women always know how to control themselves at table, out of regard for table manners or the desire to be slim, and no mother needs to eat when her children are being fed. The saying is, "To look at her child eating makes the mother filled."

. ˙ .

Mulan watched Cassia as she came through the small corridor barely two feet wide leading from the stern of the boat to the center of the main cabin. These boats were so constructed that there were one or two small compartments, about ten feet deep and four or five feet wide, separated from the main center of the boat and opening on a narrow passageway on one side. As she came, Cassia called in a rich voice, "Is Miss Yao already here?"

48

"Come and see her," Mrs. Tseng replied. "She has been here for half an hour."

Mulan noticed that Cassia had to bend slightly while coming through the passage. She emerged into the main cabin, a look of interested curiosity upon her face.

"Is this Miss Yao? What a pretty child! No wonder *Laoyeh* was so crazy about finding you, unable to sleep for three days and three nights."

She came very close and put her white, plump hands on Mulan's shoulders and said, "You are here now, and this is our home. Anything you want, you must tell me."

"The child doesn't know who you are yet," said the wife. "Mulan, this is Chien *Yima*."

"Call me Sister Cassia, *hsiaochieh*."

"That she also can do," said Mrs. Tseng, "but you need not call her Miss Yao; just call her Mulan."

"Mulan, you are going to have a little sister. Her name is Ailien," said Cassia. Turning around, she looked for Ailien who was peeping from the compartment door. Ailien was extremely shy and hung back and her mother literally dragged her to Mulan.

"This is Mulan *Chiehchieh* (elder sister)," she said to Ailien. The little six-year-old girl smiled and hid her face in her mother's dress.

Now Cassia looked at Mulan closely and opened a paper package.

"Have you found anything suitable?" asked Mrs. Tseng. There being no girl of Mulan's age in the family, she had sent Cassia to see what she could find in the shops selling ready-made dresses.

"I went into several shops," said Cassia, opening the package, "but the dresses were all made of the cheapest material, and it was hard to find her size. This is the best I could find."

It was a country girl's dress of cotton in duck's-egg green and two sizes too large. Mulan looked ridiculous in it.

"Why not try one of Sunya's old dresses?" said Cassia. "He is about her height, and it really doesn't make any difference for boys and girls of this age."

So Cassia went and found an old dress of Sunya's, made of a luxuriously rich *fangchou* silk, that with successive washings, had become heavier and softer and had changed from its original pale greenish-white to cream color. Mulan tried it on after some persuasion, and was shy because the boys were looking on. The length would do, but it

49

was much too ample for her small frame and an inch too loose around the collar. The effect was comical and the boys laughed and Mulan was ready to die with shame.

Then the table was laid, and they had lunch, Mulan sitting next to Mrs. Tseng.

In the afternoon Mr. Tseng took Mulan to the bank and told the people that the child had been found. The banker was willing to reimburse Mr. Tseng for the money, but Mr. Tseng said there was no hurry and he would wait till he got in touch with her parents. He wrote a letter at the bank and asked Mulan to add a few words in her own handwriting. The letter informed her parents that Mulan was to stay at the Tseng home at Tai-an until they should come and fetch her, and they were not to worry. The letter was to be sent to the bank's own Hangchow office by the hotel couriers who traveled from place to place, and forwarded to Yao's tea firm in that city.

And so the Tsengs set out the next day for their home. Mulan was fairly happy, having found playmates in the boys and little Ailien, and in Cassia and Mrs. Tseng understanding elders who were very kind and fond of her. Cassia, in spite of all her duties and the care of her baby and the hot August weather, bought a piece of Shantung silk pongee and cut and made a new dress for Mulan in less than two days. She was made to tell them all of her experiences with the Boxers, and Sunya listened with wide-open eyes and thought Mulan a very brave girl.

After the first excitement of the recovery of Mulan, Mr. Tseng retired into his shell of dignity. Mulan was afraid of him, as she never was of her own father.

CHAPTER IV

THEY left the Canal at Tung-o and took sedan chairs, striking straight east for Tai-an. Mulan spent an enchanting night watching the moon near the Tungping Lake on the night of Mid-Autumn. The next afternoon at about three, they arrived at the Tseng mansion in Tai-an city. Mr. Tseng's two menservants had gone ahead on foot to inform the people of their coming, and even the county magistrate and the prefect magistrate came to receive them at the West Gate. Street urchins, half or completely naked, swarmed around them at the gate, staring at them, announcing the sensational event of the arrival of "an official from Peking." Mulan shared in the glory. Not until the Tsengs were back in their home city, did she realize how important the family was, and how good one felt to be in an official family. For, although Mulan's family was wealthy and well-connected, her father and grandfather were never officials.

The Tseng mansion was near the East Gate, close to the city wall. Although not comparable in grandeur to some of the Peking officials' residences, it was finely designed and solidly built. In front of the house gate, flanked by long white walls, was the customary pair of stone lions, and a green-painted four-paneled wooden screen directly inside the entrance cut off the view from the outside. A charming little garden with a stone-paved road in the center led to the first hall, with massive red and green painted beams. Mulan smelled an exquisite fragrance when she entered behind the screen, and saw two gorgeous cassia trees in bloom. She had a curious sense that she belonged in this house. It was so homelike and so congenial.

Standing in the center of the open hall was a well-dressed, short old woman, leaning on a red-lacquered stick, and wearing a black band on her head, sloping toward the sides, with a piece of green jade in the center. It was the grandmother. Mr. Tseng hastened up the steps and made his formal greeting, by bowing low from the waist.

51

"Hai-ah! I have been worried to death for you." Speaking with the characteristic memory for dates of a country woman, she said, "Since I got news on July the eighth of your coming, I have been waiting for you every day and this is one month and nine days."

Each of the women went up to greet the grandmother. First of all the new grandchild was presented to her for inspection. The grandmother said it was a very pretty baby, although a girl, and Cassia was proud.

The grandmother was all excited. Her brood had come back and she was living once more. She remarked that the boys had grown, especially Pingya, and hugged the fat Sunya close to her breast. She said she never thought the Cassia maid would become such a beautiful young mother, and reminded her that she was a tiny, pale child only such a short time ago.

Grandmother was doing all the talking and everybody listened, anxious to hear what she said, firstly, because she was the head of the family, and secondly, because she was a woman and the affairs of family reunion are the natural monopoly of women, about which men have little to say. Mr. Tseng stood correctly by with the rest. However, he introduced Mulan to the grandmother, briefly saying that she was the daughter of a friend and had been lost on the way. Mulan was led up to the grandmother, who said, surveying her:

"Such a pretty child, with such delicate eyes and eyebrows, will make a good daughter-in-law for the Tseng family!"

"If you will be the matchmaker, Old Ancestor," said Cassia.

Everybody laughed, and Mulan was embarrassed and dared not raise her eyes.

"I ought to send for Mannia tomorrow," said the grandmother again. "She will be a good playmate for Mulan. She has grown a good deal, too. She was here only half a month ago. . . . You will see, in a few years, I shall be a great-grandmother," she added.

Everybody looked at Pingya and smiled, and it was his turn to be embarrassed. Mannia was a cousin of the Tseng children, the daughter of one of the grandmother's nephews, with the same family name, Sun, as the grandmother. Her father was a scholar and her family was poor, but the grandmother liked Mannia's beauty and her ways and had already decided to marry her to Pingya as the eldest boy. Although not strictly a "child daughter-in-law," she often came to live with the Tsengs whenever they asked for her and her own family could spare

52

her. The Tsengs being the most distinguished family in the city and their house and garden being so grand and spacious, Mannia willingly spent many days there, and so had grown up intimately with her cousins.

Sunya pinched Mulan and led her to the second hall, across a big stone courtyard, paved with stones, very old and worn smooth, cut from the near-by mountain. Mulan saw that the second hall was even grander, but built of simple, massive woodwork in contrast to the ornateness of the first hall.

Turning toward the west, they passed through a covered corridor, bordering on the inner courtyard, with rooms on the north, which excited and dazzled Mulan. At the end of the corridor, a door opened on the west and led into a garden, with many pear trees and a few very old cypresses. In the distance across the roofs and the city wall they could see the sacred mountain.

"That is Taishan!" said Sunya.

"Is that it—so small?" asked Mulan.

"Why do you say 'so small'? That is Confucius' own Taishan!"

Mulan saw that Sunya was injured, and hastily said, "I meant only it looks so small in the distance, like the Western Hills of Peking. Of course it will be bigger, I suppose, when one gets nearer."

"Oh, you will see. Our mountain is much bigger than the Western Hills. You can see the ocean from its top. You cannot see the ocean from the Western Hills."

"But you haven't seen our Western Hills." Mulan's father had a country house in the Western Hills and she felt called to defend them. But she added, "Can we go and see your mountain one day?"

"I'll ask my father," said Sunya, pacified. "You will see for yourself."

And so what threatened to be their first quarrel ended peacefully. Sunya climbed up his favorite pear tree, and Mulan watched and admired him from below.

Mulan thought it a wonderful place. They stayed there until a servant came to call them.

．·．

The next day Mannia came.

Mannia was a simple small-town girl. Brought up by her Confucian father, she had a complete girl's education of the classical type. By classical education is not meant her knowledge of books, which was only a minor part of it, but knowledge of manners and proper behavior, as embodied in the well-established four phases of woman's training: "woman's character, woman's speech, woman's appearance, and woman's accomplishments." These represented the solid, unchallenged tradition of well-bred, educated womanhood, for which girlhood was an important preparation, a tradition that girls in ancient times accepted and aspired to live up to, especially those who could read. There was an ideal, definite, vivid, well-established, and well-illustrated by stories of famous wives and mothers, and there was a conveniently clear code of conduct and of manners. Probably manners were the most important, because it was impossible for a good woman to have bad manners, and nearly impossible for a woman of good manners to be a bad woman. "Woman's character" was to be industrious and thrifty, to be soft, submissive and yielding, and to live in harmony with all relatives; "woman's appearance" was to be neat and orderly; "woman's speech" was to be soft and low, and to avoid gossip and carrying tales, and to refrain from complaining to her husband about his brothers and sisters; "woman's accomplishments" included primarily good cooking, neat sewing, fine embroidery, and if she was born in a scholar's family and taught to read, then also the ability to read and write, always a little poetry, but not enough to distract her mind and senses, a little history, and if possible, a little painting. Certainly none of these bookish things were to overshadow the other more ladylike pursuits, and such learning was to be looked upon as helping toward a more intelligent understanding of the principles of living; but otherwise not to be taken too seriously. Literature as such was strictly a luxurious pastime, an ornamentation upon a woman's character. There was also some insistence on the woman's not being jealous, so much so that a wife's broad-mindedness was a test of her goodness. Husbands who had such "good wives" usually appreciated them and thought themselves lucky by comparison with their friends. Chastity was taken for granted as inviolable for the girl, although she never expected the impossible of the man. The ideal of chastity, generally speaking, was rigidly lived up to by more than nine out of ten of the family girls, perhaps altogether in certain classes, while it might be as low as four out of ten among the maids of rich households. Chastity was a passion; girls were taught to regard it as a sacred possession and to consider their body as practically untouchable by men, or as it is said, to "guard their bodies like jade." Sexual idealism, which plays an important role in a girl's religion during puberty, played also a direct role in this desire to live up to a feminine ideal. A girl literally glowed with the sexualism to prepare her for her mate.

Mannia was a fair example of this type of classical womanhood, so much so that later, in the first years of the Republic, she seemed an antiquated rarity, like a picture that leaps out of the pages of an ancient book. Hers was a type that apparently could not or did not survive in these modern days.

Mannia was beautiful for her eyelashes, her smile, her even teeth, and her sweet appearance. When Mulan first saw her, she was fourteen and had bound feet. While Mulan herself was vivacious, she appreciated Mannia's quietness and gentleness. They slept in the same room in the inner courtyard, and in a few days Mannia was like an elder sister to Mulan.

It was the first real friendship that Mulan formed, and the more she knew Mannia, the more she worshiped her. Mulan was capable of great love. She had never so unreservedly loved another person before, except her sister Mochow and her father and mother.

Mr. Tseng complained that the children had missed their lessons ever since the Boxer outbreak and asked an old scholar to come and teach them at home in the morning and afternoon. The teacher was one Mr. Fang, sixty years old, married but childless, and he stayed in a room in the outer eastern court, next to the school room. He had a small queue, wore glasses, and was stern and never seemed to like children, although his tone always softened when he spoke to the girls. The classes began after breakfast, and the girls finished at about eleven, while the boys continued till lunchtime. The boys and girls studied together *The Book of Poetry* and the *Five Kinds of Inherited Teachings,* which was a collection of essays on proper living, school discipline, children's duties to parents, and methods of study, and the girls of course beat the boys, except Pingya who could always recite well. The girls were almost invariably called upon to recite first, and the teacher would start in fairly good humor and get into a worse and worse mood as the day wore on.

All the children conspired to cheat the teacher by helping any one who faltered.

The method of recital was for the pupil to go up to the teacher's desk and, surrendering her book, turn about with her back to the teacher and start repeating the lesson by memory, as fluently as possible, while swaying the whole body sideways and balancing its weight alternately on the left and right legs. The teacher being thus more or less covered, the pupil had full opportunity to receive help from the others, who whispered or turned their books around for the reciter to see.

Mannia would often grow confused and skip her lines. She was timid and did not have so good a memory as Mulan. Also, she was reciting in the presence of her fiancé. Yet when Pingya tried to help her, she grew all the more embarrassed. Actually she cared more to put on a good appearance before him than for the approval of the teacher.

Mulan seldom had difficulties, so that at night, when the two girls lay in the same bed, and Mulan was questioning her on her experiences with her bound feet, Mannia would suddenly ask her what followed a certain line, and they both had the liveliest time discussing passages in the *Book of Poetry* that the teacher had refused to explain, passages about girls eloping with boys, a gentleman "tossing in bed" for love, and about a widow with seven sons who still wanted to remarry. The teacher had passed over this poetry as sacred text, and demanded merely memory of the words by rote. Chinya, in order to embarrass the girls, had purposely asked the teacher why the mother of seven sons was still "not contented with her home," and the teacher had reprimanded him by curtly saying it was a satire against disloyalty of ministers.

Mannia was plainly both excited and uncomfortable at school. When the teacher had left them and retired into his own room, and the children were supposed to be either studying the new lesson or practicing penmanship, the boys would say things which made her blush. She was always glad to come away at about eleven with Mulan. The girls had a shorter period because the grandmother had insisted that girls should not study too much, or they would be too learned and lose their simplicity, and, besides, they had so much needlework to do. So Mannia and Mulan would go into the inner court and do their needlework either in Mrs. Tseng's room or in the grandmother's. There while they worked they would listen to all that was happening in the household.

Mannia was happy because she felt that was exactly the thing a girl should do. But Mulan loved embroidery because she loved color and was fascinated by the many subtle or brilliant shades of the silk threads.

56

She loved colors of all kinds—rainbows, sunsets, clouds, jades and precious stones, parrots, flowers after rain, ripening corn. She loved the translucent color of amber, and she often peeped into a prism that her father had given her. The spectrum of the prism held for her an inexhaustible mystery.

. ˙ .

One day Sunya slunk away from school and joined the girls in the mother's room. When his mother asked him why he had left, he replied that he had a stomach-ache.

"He is so small," said Cassia, "and shouldn't be studying the whole day. I don't see why a child of eleven should try to finish reading all the books in the world."

"Good sister," said Sunya, "will you speak to Father about it? I usually finish my lesson by this time, and it is so dull sitting there in school. I don't study the *Yuhsueh Chiunglin* and *Mencius* which Eldest Brother and Second Brother are studying."

"Really what you want," said Cassia smilingly, "is to play with Mulan."

Now Sunya was very fond of Mulan, though she did not like him especially, because he was so mischievous. Seeing that Mulan was working on a tiny tobacco pouch, he came and said he wanted to embroider also. Mulan would not give it to him, but he snatched it and the silk thread slipped from its needle.

"There!" said Mulan, "since you've slipped it out, you must put it through the needle again."

Sunya tried and tried and failed, and the girls and the mother laughed.

"Good sister-in-law," said Sunya to Mannia, "do it for me, and I won't bother you again."

Chinya and Sunya often teased Mannia by calling her sister-in-law, as Pingya's fiancée.

"I have never seen boys like you brothers," said Mannia, biting her teeth. But she secretly liked that term of endearment, which defined her position in the Tseng family.

"Sister-in-law, do it for him," said Mulan. This was a mistake, for Mulan had no relation to the Tseng family.

"You, too!" said Mannia to Mulan. "I may really be your sister-in-law one day."

57

"Perhaps one day you will. Won't she become a member of our Tseng family?" said Cassia.

Mulan blushed all over. The joke was now on her, and Mannia was triumphant. She took the thread and needle from Sunya and put it through and returned it to Mulan. But Sunya, not to be deterred, snatched the tobacco pouch and insisted on trying it himself. Mulan threw the needle and thread at him with a pout.

"This pouch is for Grandmother. You will spoil it." After a while Sunya gave up.

"This is not boy's work," said Cassia. "If he wants to do something, he had better learn to make knots and tassels."

That was the beginning of joint work by Mulan and Sunya. The tassels were lovely things, with as much color as embroidery itself. There were tassels for fans, tassels for tobacco pouches and water pipes, tassels for bed-curtain hooks, tassels for embroidered cases for the spectacles that old ladies carried, suspended by a string to a jacket button near the right shoulder. There were threads of all shades of green, pink, blue, red, yellow, orange, white, violet, and black to match and choose from, as well as special threads of golden and silver luster. In tying the different patterns, often the fine embroidery threads would be used, while for the tassels, stronger and heavier threads were used, which were easier for the children to manipulate. Mulan and Sunya learned to make the different kinds of knots which consisted of embroidery threads tied around special wires. These were of many patterns—the butterfly knot, the plum-flower knot, the happy-union knot, consisting of two characters for "happiness" joined together, and the "eight treasures," which were the wheel of the Law, the conch shell, the umbrella, the canopy, the lotus, the jar, the fish, and the mystic knot which has no beginning and no end. Mulan and Sunya liked especially the ancient coin tassel, because it was so simple and so pretty. It was made by winding differently colored silk threads around a copper coin in such a way as to give a definite pattern, and to afford an opportunity for matching colors. The knot would then be attached to a bunch of tassels. Each would make one and present it to the mother, competing in neatness and beauty of color.

To Sunya, the youngest boy of the family, the mother was indulgent. She watched the boy and the girl innocently playing together and working on the knots and tassels, and thought Mulan decidedly more clever than her son. Thus an idea entered her head, and she became particularly motherly and attentive to Mulan.

. ·. .

After lunch, Mannia was taking up her embroidery again, when Mrs. Tseng said, "Mannia, you must not do that directly after lunch. You will sit yourself ill. It is the day of Cold Dew today. Go out to the garden and take your little sister and little brother out to see the storks and gather the feathers they have shed. You and Mulan have not been to the garden for days."

Although the garden was surrounded by high walls, Mannia had learned a point of manners not to go out into it unless with others. And since she had heard from her father that practically all Chinese dramas and stories associate the downfall of girls or the beginning of romance with the "back garden," she also disliked to go to the garden when the boys were playing in it, and especially if Pingya was alone there.

"Do you want to go?" she said to Mulan. "I'll go if you will."

"Go, Mulan," said Mrs. Tseng. "And ask the boys to go along. But don't any of you catch crickets again, or, if you do, don't bring them into the house."

Something had happened the previous day to make Mr. Tseng angry.

When he had returned home some weeks before, he had at once put on his official hat and gown to take part in the worship of the God of the Soil on the god's day. This day sometimes came before, and sometimes after, the Autumn Equinox, which is in the eighth moon. The proverb said that if the Autumn Equinox came before the god's day, the year would have good harvests, and if it came later, it meant bad harvests. This year the god's day came very late, and there was great rejoicing among the people.

After the worship, Mr. Tseng had come home and put away his mandarin hat and gown. Now if there was anything sacred in the Tseng household, it was that hat and gown. The children had been forbidden to touch them. Mrs. Tseng used to take care of them herself, allowing no one else to do so, because they were symbols of authority and of the status of the family, and furthermore represented the gift of the Emperor. They were always placed, together with the official dress boots and some good fans, in a special cupboard, which held also such relics of the grandfather, who had also been a vice-

59

minister in the Ministry of the Interior. The children looked upon all these things with awe and piety and never thought of touching them.

When an Imperial Inspector was passing through the city Mr. Tseng took out his hat and gown again. To his dismay, he found that the peacock feather on his hat had evidently been bitten by insects. It was frayed at the sides and quite ruffled and the ridge at the center was bent. Mr. Tseng demanded how this had happened, and his wife was miserable and could not tell the reason, because it had never happened before. Then Mr. Tseng heard a chirp and caught a cricket right beside the cupboard. A hole was discovered in the shelf which had permitted the cricket to get through from under.

"How did this cricket come to be there?"

"It was mine. I don't know how it escaped," answered Sunya, quite terrified. Instead of running away, Sunya had stayed, and watched his father throw his cricket to the floor and crush it beneath his mandarin boots. It was a good fighter and had won a match with Chinya's cricket. He was too frightened to cry, although his heart was ready to break. How the cricket had got out of its cage in the lower shelf, he could not understand.

"Have you no better place to keep crickets than to bring them into this room?" said the father. Had it been one of the elder boys, the culprit would have had more than a mere scolding. But Sunya was small, and the father was somewhat partial to him.

The affair had passed, but Mr. Tseng was still angry the following day, because he had felt uneasy and ridiculous about being seen at the dinner by his fellow officials with the ruffled peacock feather, although naturally no one had said anything about it.

So Mannia and Mulan went to the garden with Sunya and Ailien. They went straight over the bridge to the further end of the garden where two storks were kept. After watching the storks, they walked about in the wild grass. Mannia was looking for touch-me-nots, whose juice could be used as red dye for the fingernails. Sunya did not care for the stork's feathers or the flowers they were looking for, for he was anxious to catch another cricket, and wandered on alone to the other side of the bridge, listening for chirps near the wall and under the rocks.

Suddenly the girls heard a loud bird call. They turned and saw that the boys Pingya and Chinya were coming; for it was an artificial bird call made by Pingya, and Sunya had answered with a whistle. The boys rushed toward them, calling that it was a holiday because the teacher was ill with dysentery and had gone home. Sunya hushed them, thinking he was on the point of finding a male cricket with a healthy, ringing chirp. You could tell a good or bad cricket by its chirp alone, and if it had a powerful head and legs it was a good fighter, called a "general."

The girls kept on in their search for touch-me-nots. Mannia found one, and Mulan asked how she was going to dye her fingernails with it. "We must collect a number of these flowers. Then we pound them into pulp and add a little alum, and rub it on the 'nameless finger' (third finger) and the little finger for several mornings, with the dew, after which the red will stay on." Mulan admired Mannia because she seemed to know every little thing of women's lore. Though she had seen Bluehaze dye her fingernails, she had never been told how the dye was made. Coral was a widow and would never use it, and Mulan's own mother being thirty-five, disdained such vanities.

Soon the girls heard a triumphant shout. They rushed over to Sunya. He had captured a fine cricket, with a big, well-poised head and powerful legs, and unusually long, straight whiskers. It was of a reddish brown tint. Pingya, who said it was a "red bell," the kind that both sang and fought lustily, immediately challenged it and rushed into the house to get his own fighter. Sunya did not want his cricket to fight at once, but he had to take up the challenge, so he held the cricket and let it crawl from one palm to another for a long time in order to madden it. Its whiskers stuck up straight in the air, its eyes glowered, and its fangs opened and closed with rhythmic ferocity.

They cleared a spot on the dry ground and set the fighters opposite each other, but held them back and let them threaten each other for a while before letting them go. It was a clearly unequal match. In professional fights, this would not be allowed, for fighters had to be weighed and matched against opponents of equal weight. But Pingya's "general," though smaller and black like varnish, was a well-built insect and had a great deal of fight in him. After the first few encounters, Pingya's cricket broke one of his whiskers.

Now to Mulan's sensitive mind, this was horrible slaughter. In her childish imagination, these were real beasts of gigantic size, armored and equipped with powerful jaws for devouring one another, and legs armed with deadly teeth for cutting the enemy. She seemed to be watching the combat of lions. The bodies were so perfectly fashioned, the heads so smooth, the shading of color on the armored backs so delicate and so perfect, and their legs were like Foochow lacquer. She did not want to see either of them hurt, yet she felt sure the smaller one would be killed. So she asked Ailien to come away.

Mannia was different. She was so timid that she could not touch worms or butterflies. But she watched because Pingya's cricket was losing. She wanted to stop the fight and pleaded with Pingya. But his insect had put up a brave fight, and the other big cricket already had a bruised head and seemed to have lost its temper. Pingya wanted to see it through, and the game went on. The boys pricked the insects on with grass stalks frayed at the end. At last, Pingya's cricket broke one of his hind legs and rolled on the ground, and before he could recover his position he was pitilessly bitten. Mannia clutched Pingya's arm in fear and pity.

The little cricket got up again, but he was quite finished and in a few moments he was pecked to death by the massive fangs of the enemy, standing triumphantly over him.

Mannia cried out and held Pingya fast, her eyes moist. Pingya got up from the ground, crestfallen, and then he raised his eyes and saw Mannia looking at him, sharing his sorrow.

"I told you to stop it and you wouldn't. It was unfair," she said.

Then for the first time he realized how beautiful Mannia was, her eyes dark and expressive with youthful ardor, and shadowed now by her long, moist lashes.

"It is a little thing," he said to her. "Do you cry for that?"

"You should have listened to me," said Mannia.

"I will, next time," said Pingya.

He stretched out his hand and held hers, which he should not have done. The gentle pressure of their two hands awakened an emotion that lasted a lifetime.

At that moment, a voice awakened them out of their dream. They turned and heard Ailien shouting that Mulan had fallen. They all rushed to the place and saw Chinya run away and disappear into the house.

Now when Mulan left with the little Ailien, the second boy, Chinya, had joined them because he himself had no cricket worthy to fight with such generals. Chinya had a fair intelligence; but he was not frank and at ease and sociable like his elder or younger brother; he was naturally hesitant and cautious, and this showed itself in his speech. He was often silent and he spoke hesitantly and sometimes would repeat his sentences as if to see if what he said sounded right. His fear of his severe father only helped to repress him and made him less self-confident than ever. The world for him was already difficult, presenting him with hard decisions to make. His mind worked like this:

"I have not a good cricket, have I? A good cricket like Sunya's is difficult to find. I don't think I can find it. I can find one, but most probably I can't find one so good. Perhaps I can, but most probably not. There is no use trying to find one, and if I find one, it won't be so good. Still . . ." The mind automatically locked itself up, and leaving the question unsettled, tried to find a change.

Joining Mulan among the trees in the orchard, Chinya thought they might try to find the skin of a cicada. The cicada shed its skin about this time and walked out of its shell as a lady steps out of her dress, through a slit in the back, leaving the dry, empty shell with head and body and legs intact resting on a branch, like a real insect, except that the shell was transparent. Sighting such a shell on a date tree, he climbed up, and the idea struck him that he might play Mulan a trick. The lowest branch was seven or eight feet from the ground, but Mulan was persuaded to climb up.

She had never been up a tree and the suggestion attracted her fancy. Chinya helped her up, led her out on a branch, then climbed down suddenly, and Mulan was left alone.

She was thoroughly frightened and helpless. Her feet slipped. She clutched a higher branch for support and tried to find the lower branch with her feet again, but could not. While she hung thus precariously Chinya clapped his hands in glee because he could see from the ground part of her body under her short jacket, and thought it funny. Losing her control with fright, Mulan let go and fell to the ground twelve feet below.

Her head struck a jagged rock and she lay unconscious. Ailien screamed for help, and when Chinya saw her bleeding at the temple, he fled.

Pingya, Sunya, and Mannia were frightened to find Mulan stunned, her face smeared with blood which reddened the ground. Ailien cried in terror and the boys rushed into the house screaming that Mulan had "fallen killed."

Menservants rushed into the garden, followed by Mrs. Tseng and maidservants. Mr. Tseng, who was taking a nap, was awakened and appeared next. Cassia happened to be away in the front court and was the last to hear the news. She was feeding the parrots, and when she heard, she thought Ailien was killed and the bowl of water dropped from her hand, splashing her dress and trousers, and she came hurrying on her dainty feet, "taking three strides in two," leaning on walls and veranda posts for support.

Mulan was carried into the mother's room, where the grandmother was anxiously waiting, and laid on the *kang*, or earthen bed. The boys, dumb with terror, followed. Mannia was crying. Cassia began to wash the wound. The room was choked full with people.

"If anything untoward should happen to this child, how can we ever face the Yao family?" said Mrs. Tseng.

"How did this happen?" Mr. Tseng asked the boys.

"We didn't see her fall. Chinya and Ailien were with her," said Pingya.

"Where is Chinya?"

"We saw him running away."

Mr. Tseng gave orders that Chinya be brought immediately.

"You saw it," said Mr. Tseng to little Ailien.

"Second Brother asked Mulan to go up the tree to get a cicada shell, and then he came down himself and left her alone there. Mulan was frightened and he clapped his hands and laughed at her, and then she was still more frightened and screamed and fell down."

"The little 'bad-goods'!" snorted Mr. Tseng.

Cassia was greatly concerned at what her child had said.

"Don't listen entirely to what the child says. It may or may not be true."

"Bring me the *chiafa!*" was Mr. Tseng's answer. The *chiafa*, meaning "family discipline," was a birch rod.

Silence fell in the room.

"You must also listen to what Chinya has to say when he comes," pleaded Mrs. Tseng.

"He is guilty. If not, why is he hiding himself?"

Chinya was already crying when he was dragged in, having been told that his father was in a fit of anger.

The first greeting was a couple of hard blows on his right and left cheeks. The father dragged him by his ear into the court and made

64

him kneel on the ground. The head servant interceded, but Mr. Tseng would not listen.

The *chiafa* was brought, and the mother heard three lashes of the rod and the moans of the boy on the ground. She rushed into the courtyard and threw herself over the boy's body.

"Flog me to death first before flogging him to death! Such a young child and you flog him with a hard hand!"

The grandmother also ran out and commanded her son to stop.

"Are you crazy? If the child has done anything wrong, I am still here and you can tell me. You don't have to kill my grandson for the sake of a child of another family."

The father threw away the rod and turned around. "Mother," he said respectfully, "if such a boy is not taught now, what will he become when he grows up?"

At this moment, Cassia shouted, "*Laoyeh,* calm your anger. The child has recovered and there is nothing to worry about."

The maids clustered round to help Mrs. Tseng to her feet and bring her in, while menservants carried the boy inside, still moaning. Cassia, lifting his dress, saw on his back several welts of red and blue. Mrs. Tseng's heart melted at the sight and she cried, "My child! Bitter fate! How could he flog you like this?"

Turning round to her own child Ailien, Cassia gave her a few whacks on the head, which was for the mistress' benefit, because Chinya's punishment was due to what Ailien had said.

"It is all the fault of your tongue!" said Cassia.

"I didn't tell lies," said Ailien, crying and confused. "The others were catching crickets."

Cassia was horrified.

"If you say another word, I'll pinch your mouth," she said, stopping the child from adding to the story.

"Don't be too severe with her," said the mistress.

Mulan heard faintly all this noise. She remembered the fall and opened her eyes and said, "Why do you beat Ailien?" She wanted to sit up, but was kept down. Mannia bent close over her, in tears of happiness because she was conscious again.

Mr. Tseng disappeared into the front of the house, thinking that he had been somewhat too severe with his son. The other boys had fled to the kitchen when the "family discipline" was being brought. When they heard their father was gone and everything was over, they came back into their mother's room to find Mulan and Chinya both stretched on the *kang,* Chinya lying on his side, and Ailien crying, to add to the confusion. Pingya and Sunya came to see their brother and ask how he was, but Mrs. Tseng shouted to them, "Are you still poking around? Go and study!" So they stealthily walked away, not knowing what to study, but vaguely aware that studying was the best way to keep themselves safe for the rest of the day.

The grandmother ordered a medicinal stew to calm the hearts of both Mulan and Chinya. Mrs. Tseng said Chinya was to stay with her that night, being anxious lest her boy had had a serious fright, which as everyone knows, might develop into further trouble. Mulan had suffered loss of blood, but her case was really the lighter, and it was decided she could sleep with Mannia as usual. And so there was no peace in the house that day, and Cassia was busy the whole evening changing the plaster on Chinya's back.

There was no school for three or four days after that. The teacher was still unwell. Chinya was kept in bed, and Mannia would not go to school without Mulan. By the time Mulan and Chinya could go to school again, there was already frost in the garden and the autumn wind had set in and leaves were turning golden. The grandmother said that in accordance with ancient custom, this was the season for girls to do needlework and for women to spin at night, and that the crickets appear at this time of the year to remind women of weaving, by their chirp, which sounds like the clatter of the loom.

Thus ended for Mulan the short school life in Shantung. She still saw the boys daily at table and after school, but Chinya was always sullen. He was at that age when boys hate girls and his experience had taught him that girls were a nuisance. Mulan tried to make up with him, but he showed no response, and this attitude became fixed for life, so that he never liked Mulan afterward.

. .

Mulan never went to that garden again, for Mannia would not go there and it was getting cold.

Except for the trip to Taishan on the ninth day of September the girls did not go out at all. That day the whole family went up to the mountain, except Mrs. Tseng and Cassia's children. Mrs. Tseng wanted Cassia to go, and offered to stay at home to look after the baby, as with the onset of the autumn weather she was not feeling well in her

66

legs. Even the grandmother went, because she was so happy with the family around her this year, and because she was religious. The children had recovered their spirit of fun together, and Mulan never forgot her first journey up to the South Gate of Heaven, being carried up the last stretch of almost perpendicular steps in the same sedan chair with Sunya, hanging out, it seemed to her, in the mid-air, and hugging very close to him. She was later to visit the same mountain with him in quite different circumstances.

After the staggering climb at the approach to the South Gate of Heaven, Mulan had to admit to Sunya that his mountain was higher; and he, trying to imitate grown-ups, became apologetic, expressing the hope that his "miserable mountain" would satisfy her as the distinguished visitor.

Cassia had heard this bit of conversation between the two children and told the grandmother about it while they were at the Temple to the Jade Emperor. "Such little children, already learning to talk mandarin!" she said.

The grandmother laughed and said to Sunya, "Little Number Three, you are talking the official language before becoming an official. If you become an official, I shall arrange that Mulan becomes a titled lady." It was a pleasantry that an old, privileged woman could allow herself.

"And I'll come and pay my respects to the lady of rank," said Mannia, at Mulan's expense.

The thought touched old Tseng. There in the court of the Jade Emperor's Temple at the top of Taishan, he thought of his ancestors, and planned and wished he could see his three sons grow up to be officials. He thought he could already see them in the official dress of the mandarins. He felt that Pingya, the noble and good boy, would make a better scholar than an official. Sunya, the youngest, would get along, with his easy ways; but Chinya, the second one, would succeed best as an official because he did not talk much, and behind his silence there was a great deal of cunning. But he would have to be severely disciplined, and his intelligence guided into proper channels. This reminded Mr. Tseng that there was Mannia to help Pingya; he was satisfied with her as a daughter-in-law. He probably would not have great difficulty in arranging a match between Mulan and Sunya, and Mulan seemed very intelligent. After what he had done for Mulan, it would be ungrateful of her parents not to accept the proposal. What had happened seemed to indicate that the match was destined by Heaven. He looked at Mulan in that light and felt fatherly toward her, as if he were going to entrust a great responsibility to her and place the future welfare of his son in her hands. That would seem like a prosperous household by the time he was sixty and retired. Then he thought of Chinya and saw that his dream picture was incomplete, and he wished he knew who was going to be his second daughter-in-law and what she would be like.

So, he was tender toward Chinya, and at lunch in the Temple he did a very unusual thing, one that he never did at home. He lifted a piece of meat with his chopsticks and gave it to Chinya. Chinya felt touched by this unusual favor, and the grandmother and Cassia silently watched, and knew he had been forgiven, although the father had not said a word.

It was Mr. Tseng's habit never to praise or encourage a boy in his presence. They were uniformly "bad eggs," when nothing was wrong, and "seeds of sin" when something was wrong. He never said yes to a request even by his wife; when he did not oppose or was silent, his wife knew that he had consented. He would rather speak to Mannia, for she was not his son and he did not have to use the dignified fatherly voice. So after lunch, he said to Mannia:

"Go out with the brothers and play. But don't go near the *Shehshenai*." This was the precipice where some people had committed suicide.

For the children, this was the final writ of pardon, and they thought their austere father was unusually kind that day. It had been a perfect outing for them. Going down did not seem to take more than an hour. They could see the city lying on the plain, a square enclosure, but it was dusk when they reached the streets and they could already see lamps in people's homes.

To crown the day, a telegram was waiting, from Mulan's father. It was dated only a week before at Hangchow, and was forwarded by mail from the provincial capital. Telegrams were such a novelty then that the whole family thought it unbelievable for a message to come from Hangchow in seven days, and all wanted to see what a telegram looked like. The message expressed profuse thanks to Mr. Tseng for this great favor, never to be fully requited even if Mr. Yao became a dog or horse in the next incarnation to serve him; and it stated that he did not worry at all, because he was sure Mulan was as well off as in her own home, and said that around Slight Snow, that is, about the middle of October, he would come in person to offer his gratitude to Mr. Tseng and his family. To Mulan, it added that her family had arrived safely in Hangchow on September 1, that they were all well, and that she should worship Mr. and Mrs. Tseng as her "parents of a second life" and obey and listen to them.

．∴．

That night, Mulan was so excited she could not sleep. She talked about going back with her father to Hangchow or to Peking. She kept Mannia enthralled with stories of Peking city, and Mannia like any provincial girl yearned to go there.

"You shall see Peking," said Mulan. "There will be people who will come to welcome you to Peking in a red wedding chair."

"Lanmei, let us be sworn sisters," cried Mannia.

It was a simple children's agreement. They did not burn incense, nor worship Heaven in the courtyard, nor exchange the respective "eight characters" of their birthday and hour. They held each other's hands and swore before the light of the vegetable oil lamp that they would be sisters for life and would help each other in poverty and distress. Mannia gave Mulan a small jade peach, but Mulan had nothing to give in return.

This secret pledge made it possible for Mannia to bare to Mulan the intimate secrets of her thoughts. The first thing that Mannia said to Mulan after this pledge was: "If you marry Sunya when you grow up, we can be sisters-in-law and live in the same family for life."

"I want to be your sister-in-law, but I don't want to marry Sunya," said Mulan.

"Chinya, then."

"No, certainly not," replied Mulan.

"Then how can you be my sister-in-law, if you don't marry a son of the Tseng family?"

"I just want to live forever with you, but I don't want to marry any of them."

"Don't you like Sunya?"

Mulan, too young to understand love, was merely amused at the thought of marriage. She smiled.

"I like only Pingya. He is so gentle."

"I will let you marry Pingya, and I'll be his concubine," said Mannia.

"How could I? You are older than I," Mulan paused and added, "I don't like boys anyway. I want to be a boy myself."

"Why, Lanmei, what are you saying?" Mannia was so wholly feminine that she could not understand any girl wanting to be a boy. "These things are predetermined by our previous incarnation and cannot be changed."

"I want to be a boy," said Mulan again, letting her thoughts flow. "They have all the advantages. They can go out and see the visitors. They can take the examinations and become officials, and ride on horseback and be carried in blue velvet sedan chairs. And they can travel and see all the famous mountains and read all the books in the world. Like my brother Tijen—my mother lets him do anything and he gives orders to me and my sister. He always says 'you girls' which makes me angry."

It was the first time Mannia had heard her speak about her brother. "Is Tijen a good boy?" she asked.

"No, he is bad. My mother pampers him, because he was the only son until my younger brother came two years ago. He has fits of temper and threatens to break things and once he actually kicked Brocade, the maid, and overthrew the tray she was carrying and splashed the things on her whole body."

"Does your father allow that?"

"My father doesn't know. My brother is afraid of my father, but my mother always shields him. She is very severe to us girls. I am afraid of my mother, but I am never afraid of my father."

"You said your father wouldn't let your feet be bound."

"Yes. My mother wanted to, but my father reads many new books, and he says he wants to bring me up as a new girl."

"These things are all predetermined," said Mannia. "It is like my meeting you. How could I have met you if you had not been lost? There are unseen forces governing our lives. But I don't understand what it is to be a new girl. How are you going to get married without bound feet?"

A whim shot across Mulan's mind.

"*Chiehchieh,* I should like to try. Will you bind my feet for me?"

It was a suggestion that Mannia could not resist. They closed the door to make sure that no one could see them. Mulan, giggling with excitement, stretched out her feet. And Mannia took off Mulan's shoes and stockings and bound her feet with long bands of strong white

70

cotton cloth, folding all the toes except the great one under the soles as tightly as she could, so that Mulan felt her feet stiff and useless.

The next day she decided that she would not have her feet bound and wanted all the more to have the feet of a boy.

CHAPTER V

Mr. Yao came in mid-October. The journey back to Hangchow was so long that he decided to take Mulan to Peking.

The Empress Dowager and the Emperor were still in flight, but Prince Ching and Li Hungchang had been empowered to conduct peace negotiations with the foreign powers. The war had been localized in the North by a special understanding with the foreign consuls at Shanghai, while Yuan Shihkai had continued to keep the province of Shantung out of the conflict, so that Mr. Yao was able to travel back and forth in peace.

Peking had been saved from much bloodshed and looting, and order was gradually restored, thanks to a sing-song girl, Sai Chinhua. In 1887, Sai Chinhua, at the age of fourteen, had become concubine to the Chinese Ambassador to Russia, Germany, Austria, and Holland, and had gone with her husband to Berlin. Her husband, who was thirty-six years older than she, had died in 1893, and she had come back to China to become a very popular sing-song girl. She went to Peking at the beginning of the Boxer trouble. After the German Minister had been murdered, some German soldiers had discovered in the sing-song district this artist who could understand and talk German. They reported her to General Waldersee, who was the chief of the allied troops, and she came to be a great favorite with the German commander. She persuaded Peking merchants to sell food to the foreign soldiers and she saved many Chinese civilians from killing, looting, and rape at the hands of the foreign troops. The people were so grateful to her that she actually came to be known as Sai Erh-yeh, although that is a man's title.

The day after Mr. Yao's arrival at Tai-an, he again ordered his daughter to "worship" Mr. and Mrs. Tseng as her "parents of a second life." He personally placed two chairs in the center of the hall for Mr. and Mrs. Tseng to receive the kowtow of the child, and put a red cushion on the floor for Mulan to kneel upon. Mr. and Mrs. Tseng took the ceremony seriously, and put on formal dress for it. Mr. Yao himself bowed to them and recognized them as his *tungchia* friends, a condition of friendship which permitted the women of one family to see the men of the other family. Then he gave a dinner. As the Tsengs had already given a dinner on the previous night to "wash the dust" of Mr. Yao's traveling feet, they did not return the dinner until Mr. Yao was ready to depart three days later.

The grandmother also received Mulan's worship, and thenceforth Mulan was to call her "Grandmother" and call Mr. and Mrs. Tseng "Father" and "Mother" like the other children. Mulan never felt so important in her life.

Parting was very hard for Mannia and Mulan. Mulan had asked to be taken to visit Mannia's own home and Mannia had at first politely apologized, telling her that her home was a very humble one. But when Mr. Tseng went to Tsinan to pay his respects to the Governor on the occasion of the autumn maneuvers, she had taken Mulan to meet her parents, introducing her jokingly as her "little sworn sister," although their pledge of sisterhood was a secret between them. Mulan had seen that it was a very simple, dignified, poor scholar's family and had stayed for a simple lunch, with a thousand apologies from Mannia's mother for the food.

Now at the parting, though the boys watched Mulan get up into the sedan chair, Mannia refused to go out to the gate, for she was already breaking into tears. The boys cried out to Mulan that they would see her again in Peking in the spring.

Mannia knew that she was not going to Peking with the Tseng family when they went back there in the spring. She was not a "child bride," but a cousin, and she was reaching that age when she would have to avoid seeing too much of the grown-up boys, as far as was practicable for cousins living so closely together. That day of Cold Dew in the garden had wrought a change in Mannia. She had become sex-conscious, and the more she loved Pingya, the more reserved and remote she kept herself from him. Pingya complained about this to her when he could find her alone, which was seldom. Once meeting her in a covered corridor alone, he stopped to talk to her and took her hand, but she snatched it away. "What will people say if they see us like this?" she said and she ran away, and Pingya stood transfixed. He came to value every glance of her eyes, every note of her voice, and

73

every approach to her presence. She was growing naturally into the classical pattern of the ancient *hsiaochieh,* the woman born to attract and then retire, bestowing her favors only rarely, artfully, and sparingly, a woman beautiful, remote, elusive, unattainable, artfully concealed as well as artfully revealed, exercising her feminine instinct of attraction by evasion, of hiding in her boudoir and watching from the inside the pursuing male outside, hearing all that was going on in the household by remaining in her room, peeping through latticed screens and in company seeing a great deal with furtive glances, never directly gazing at any male face.

. ·.

Mulan's father, who had always been fond of her, now found her doubly dear, as if she had come back from death. The months which they spent together alone in Peking, before the family returned, and their long talks together, deepened their relationship. Their house had escaped looting and was intact, probably because of its location in the middle of the East City, for it was the South and Southeast City that suffered the greatest ravages. The date tree under which the bronzes were buried had died. Only their country home on the Western Hills had been thoroughly robbed. Of tales of suffering and horror there was no end. Mulan saw with a shock the charred houses and fallen walls, and the Chienmen Tower scorched and riddled with bullet holes.

Mulan was made into a heroine when her mother and family came back from Hangchow in March. Her mother had changed toward her. Instead of leaving it to Brocade to help dress her and play with her, her mother began to dress her herself and to have her sleep with Mochow in the same room with her. Coral, apologetic for having left her alone on that fatal day, was more than ever anxious to please her. She was made to tell her experiences again and again. She told about the woman Boxer and Laopa and the English song she had learned, which was the only thing Tijen liked and learned quickly, and about her fall from a date tree and her school and the visit to Taishan Mountain. Most of all, she told them about Mannia, so that the whole household, from Mr. and Mrs. Yao down to Bluehaze and Lota and the *amahs,* knew there was a Mannia in Shantung. Mochow listened to her sister's story with wonder and excitement, showing her new front teeth, and thought Mulan a wonderful elder sister. Thus Mulan

74

began to be accepted as the responsible grown-up daughter of the family, while Tijen's position as eldest son gradually grew less important. Mulan began to look after Mochow and the little Afei. By the time she was fourteen, her mind was fully mature, and she learned ways of putting up with injustices and insults from her elder brother which were so essentially a part of a girl's education. "To yield, to yield" must be the girl's attitude; to be sober and not expect too much from life, always to expect men to have more freedom and to indulge in mischief.

The Tseng's came back in early April, and thenceforth the families came to know each other well, and the children often visited each other. At every festival, there was an exchange of presents, and Mulan's father insisted that the Tseng family were to get their medicines free from his shop, and the Tsengs accepted. Mrs. Yao presented Mrs. Tseng with the best variety of ginseng on the Beginning of Winter every year. As the Chinese medicine shop dealt not only in medicine, but also in tonics and delicacies of all kinds, such as swallows' nests, sharks' fins from the South Seas, ham from Yunnan, tigers'-tendon-and-quince wine from Canton, and wined crabs from Soochow, which all came by the same system of transport as the medicinal herbs, there was a fairly regular stream of presents to the Tseng family. The present baskets never came back empty, because the Tsengs always sent in return presents of the season. It was comfortable and easy to cement friendship with gifts when both families were well-to-do.

One day Mulan and her sister were invited to luncheon with the Tseng family and they went accompanied by a woman servant, Chaoma. They were asked to stay for tea, and, as Chaoma had been sent for by her husband, she said she would come back for them at five. Mulan told her not to come back, as they were quite familiar with the way home; it was only fifteen minutes' walk through a broad avenue of shops, where nothing could happen.

On the way home, Mulan and her sister saw a crowd around a professional boxer-and-medicine-man performing on the broad dirt sidewalk of Hatamen Street. The man was half-naked, the upper part of his body entirely bare, and he was offering to cut a sandstone four or five inches thick with the edge of his bare palm.

He cut the stone and then began to sell his medicine for knife wounds and boxing wounds. After that he took a piece of green cloth and, turning it in and out to show to the crowd, spread it on the ground

75

and produced from beneath it a bowl of steaming hot noodles and shrimps.

Now, the girls of higher families were not supposed to be out in the streets unchaperoned. But Mulan was only fourteen and her sister twelve, and they could not resist the stolen pleasure of wandering about free and alone. Delighted with the boxer-magician's show, they went on, and saw a seller of sugared crab apples, which had just appeared for the winter season. Their mouths watered and they each bought a stick of five sugared apples and ate them, as happy as children could be. Further on there was a peep show, with pictures of the Boxers and the foreign gunboats, and the girls paid for a peep, with their mouths still full of sugared crab apples.

At that moment of intense delight, Mulan felt a hand clutch her arm. Her stick of candy fell to the ground. She turned around and saw Tijen. Before she could say anything, he slapped her on the cheek.

"What are you doing here?" he demanded.

"We are on our way home," said Mulan, angrily. "Why do you slap me?"

"Of course I should slap you," replied Tijen. "You girls are going to be 'street-running women.' Once you are let out of the home, you have no sense of decency."

"Why can you go out, and we cannot?"

"You are girls, that's all. If you don't like it, I'll tell mother about it."

"Go ahead and tell mother." Mulan was really angry. "You have no right to slap me. You haven't! Our parents are still living!" To defend herself, Mulan added, "I'll tell father about what you do, too."

Her brother walked away, and the sisters were left alone. Angry and injured, they picked their way home. The more they thought about it, the more they felt incensed at the injustice. What made it unbearable was to be slapped and admonished by Tijen, who they knew was so far from being good that he was the last person to have the right to admonish them.

Was Tijen going to tell Mother about it or not? What they had done was something not quite right, but not very improper. They hadn't gone far out of their way. Children always saw peep shows. They had eaten candies at home.

They decided they would wait for Tijen to make the first move. At dinner, he said not a word. Mulan's threat of telling their father about what he had done might mean telling about slapping her, but it might mean much more, for there were many things that he had done that should not be told. His one fear in his life was his father. He thought it was the part of discretion to hold his tongue.

Such little persecutions from their brother united the two girls and set them thinking about the difference between men and women. It made Mulan listen more gladly to what her father said about the "new girl"—with natural feet, equality with men, and a modern education. Such fantastic, Western ideas were already stirring China.

. **.**

Tijen was not only being pampered and spoilt, but was actually losing his proper place in the family.

Tijen, was in fact, a love-child, having been born five months after his mother's wedding. The latter was the daughter of the owner of a fan shop in Hangchow, an ordinary middle-class merchant. When she met Mr. Yao he was already thirty, and she was twenty-two. After he became involved with her, his old father came to know about it and insisted that his son should marry her, because she was a good family girl. There was some talk that the wife's family had stipulated that there was to be no concubine, but this could not be verified for both families were anxious to hush up the scandal. As we have told, Mr. Yao, having sowed all the wild oats he wanted to, had not only reformed, but had also ceased to take an interest in business and had begun to study Taoism. During one period he squandered a small fortune on a swindler who promised him the secret of transmuting gold. Mrs. Yao, although she was completely illiterate, began to look after the business accounts and collect rents, and soon her brother was put in charge of the business.

She had married into a wealthy family, living in a spacious home in the city, with more servants and maids than she ever could use. She was not used to such luxury, and wanted her son to enjoy all the things she had missed. But she did not have the educated woman's sense of how a son in even a wealthy family should be brought up. From childhood Tijen was surrounded with maids and he was even allowed to slap them in her presence. He was a handsome boy, as so many love-children are, fair-skinned like his father, and brilliant and entertaining when he cared to be. He was allowed to ride a spirited horse and dash through the streets of the city. In general he came to think of himself as a very unusual person. Instead of observing the

77

manners required of other boys, he would leave the room in the middle of a feast at a friend's house, and go out and talk with servant maids. His mother made him feel that he was the sole heir of the family and that his life was worth those of ten common men. By the time he was fifteen, Mrs. Yao realized that he was completely spoiled, and there was nothing to be done about it.

His father's attitude was quite different. He realized that Tijen was like himself when he was young. He knew that he himself had been pampered, which got him into much trouble. But the more a father tries to be severe with his son, the less he sees of him, because the son avoids him the more; and Mr. Yao got Tijen into a state of thorough fear of his presence.

Only a few months before they fled from the Boxer trouble, Tijen had taken a knife and cut another boy's face near the neck, so that it bled terribly. His father tied him to a tree in the courtyard and beat him till he was half dead. It only made him more afraid of, and resentful against, his father. The boy was in bed for ten days after the punishment, and Mrs. Yao told her husband, in his presence, "I know that he must be taught. But if anything should happen to him, what am I to live for, and whom can I depend upon in my old age?"

Thus the father and mother were working at cross purposes in regard to Tijen, and he began to be thought of as a "seed of sin," to be allowed to run his course and ruin the family if necessary. Either alternative was bad, letting him have his way, or reforming him by drastic means which might injure him physically or mentally. The traditional idea was that fear was a bad thing for the body and that a person could develop all sorts of troubles if his system of fluids was upset, and if the gall bladder, which represented courage, was "broken." In time, the mother began soon to look upon Tijen as a *yuanchia* "a predetermined enemy," as quarrelsome or fickle lovers fondly say, or as a son sent by fate to exact repayment of a debt that she had owed somebody in a previous incarnation, or, in plain terms, a son destined to squander the family fortune.

The mother was fatalistic about it from circumstances, and the father was fatalistic about it from philosophy.

Mulan also was pulled in two opposite directions. While Tijen became less and less important, she was being taken more and more seriously, through her own merits.

Mrs. Yao was as severe toward her daughters as she was lenient toward her sons. She was giving them the traditional training that all daughters of China should have. In this she was quite logical. The girls were born and brought up in a rich family, but they were not going to remain forever in the family and live off its fortune. They would be married into different families with different means. Hence they must have the mainstay qualities of womanhood: thrift, industry, sobriety, good manners, a yielding temper, obedience, knowledge of household management, and the domestic arts of nursing, cooking, and sewing.

But the difference in treatment between the sons and the daughters of the Yao family was much more than in other families.

Mulan and Mochow learned at the age of eight or ten, to sit erect, with their legs close together, while Tijen never sat in a chair but tilted it and put his legs on top of a table. With maids idling about, Mulan and Mochow washed their own underclothing (sunning it, of course, in out-of-the-way places entirely out of the possible sight of male visitors), helped in the kitchen, made pastries, rolled pancakes, made their own shoes, cut and made their own dresses. The only things they did not practice were pounding rice and grinding rice flower by the hand mill, which would have coarsened the skin on their palms. They had to learn all about the social usages and customs of womanhood—the sending of presents, tips to servants bringing presents, names and special foods for different festivals, rites and rituals of weddings, funerals, and birthday parties; and the complicated science of nomenclature for different gradations of kinship among the paternal and maternal uncles and aunts, paternal uncles' wives, maternal uncles' wives, paternal aunts' husbands, maternal aunts' husbands, sisters and sisters-in-law of the aunts both paternal and maternal, children of the sisters of the aunts, both paternal and maternal, and every possible variation of cousins and nephews and nieces and nieces' husbands. The girls' feminine intelligence absorbed all this complicated scheme without difficulty. Mulan, at fourteen, could tell at a glance at a funeral, how many sons, daughters, daughters-in-law, sons-in-law, and grandchildren the deceased man had following his coffin by noting merely their different signs of mourning. Mulan knew when a bride was to return to her home after a wedding and when the bride's younger brother was to return the call, and exactly what four bowls were to be served when the bride's younger brother paid the call to the husband's home. She knew that the bride's brother was to taste, but

79

not eat up, the four different delicacies. This was living knowledge, interesting and useful.

Mrs. Yao gradually came to discuss many things of the household with Mulan, and ask her to write things down, like things packed away, as an aid to memory. The child thus helped her mother greatly, such as remembering what presents were sent to and received from a certain family at the last Dragon-Boat Festival.

In addition, Mulan learned how to stew Chinese medicinal herbs, and by sheer experience came to have some knowledge of the principles of Chinese medicine. She knew that crab and persimmons did not go together, that crab was "cold" and eel was "hot" for the body. She knew the Chinese medicinal herbs by their sight and smell, and she was fully familiar with the essentials of Chinese home medicines and their important relation to food.

In spite of all this, Mulan had several unwomanly accomplishments: first, whistling; second, singing Peking opera; third, the collection and appreciation of curios. The first she learned from Sunya in Shantung and perfected in Peking. The latter two were encouraged by her father.

Mulan's father was generally regarded by her mother as a corrupting or disrupting influence. When the mother found on Mulan's return from Shantung that she was beginning to whistle, she was shocked. It was so unwomanly. But her father said, "What is the harm?" It was nothing very serious, and she perfected it and taught it to her sister in the rear garden, and the mother did not bother about it again. Brocade learned it also, but being a maid she never dared to whistle in the presence of the mistress.

But the father's corrupting influence was most clearly shown in teaching Mulan to sing Peking operatic selections. Imagine a father teaching his daughter such singing! Music, dancing, and the theater were entirely in the hands of sing-song girls and the actors and actresses—both belonging to a social class considered low, if not downright immoral, by the Confucianists, who loved them. But Mr. Yao was not a Confucianist. He was a free-thinking Taoist, and he was unconventional. And though he had given up gambling and reckless drinking, he kept his love of the theater. For that matter, there was not a soul in that household, from the father down to the servants, who did not love the theater, which was in its nature essentially opera. Mrs. Yao herself went regularly to the public theater with Coral and the children, occupying a box on the gallery, spending a whole afternoon there, accompanied by their personal maids, who poured tea and guarded things and filled the water-tobacco pipe for Mrs. Yao, while they drank tea and chewed melon seeds and chattered.

Many amateur singers learned the favorite airs and passages just by listening to these operas again and again. Women, however, generally abstained. But Mulan's father *taught* her these tunes, as if purposely to defy her mother and society in general. Such was Mr. Yao's broad-mindedness that it made him among the first to seize the ideas that were beginning to change Chinese society. And up to the age of sixteen, Mulan still often accompanied her father to the Lungfusze Temple Fair in search of antiques.

So Mulan grew in wisdom and knowledge, her mother giving her the wisdom and her father giving her the knowledge, if such a line could be drawn. And Mochow quickly took after her sister, but made faster progress in the wisdom than in the knowledge.

CHAPTER VI

THE girlhood of Mannia was like the blossoming of the plum flower in cold January, growing on hardened, twisted branches without leaves, thriving in the cold air between the end of winter and the coming of spring, solitary and without its flower companions, and destined to retire and enjoy its own fragrance and dream its hours away within the hard bark of its branches when the peaches and pears and other spring flowers begin to bloom.

The two months' visit of Mulan had been like an exquisite dream to her. It came when she was fourteen and could bestow on Mulan all her budding instincts of motherhood and the unexpressed instincts of an elder sister. For Mannia never had sisters. She had never before slept in the same bed with another girl and talked at night as girls talk. She was naturally timid and not at ease with boys. She was brought up as a lone child until she was ten when her younger brother appeared, but the brother died at the age of five, a year after Mulan returned to Peking. Mannia's uncle had no child, either girl or boy, and had adopted one. Her grandfather, a younger brother of Grandmother Tseng, had spent his fortune and died poor, leaving two sons, Mannia's father and uncle, to struggle along with the help of their aunt. Families are like trees: some are prolific, and others gradually die in spite of all human care. This Sun family seemed to be dying out, its blood running thin.

As fate would have it, a year after her brother died Mannia's father died also, in the early spring. This made the grandmother think of what was to be done to carry on the family name of the Suns.

Mannia was the only blood descendant to continue the incense and candle offerings in the ancestral temple. The grandmother was worried and was unusually kind to Mannia.

Mannia and her mother were asked to move into the Tseng home and keep the grandmother company. They had a few farms and a house of their own, which, with taking extra work in embroidery, could easily keep the mother and daughter alive. But there was the spacious Tseng home, and the grandmother had no other company than Li Yima, a protégé who was now shriveling up into a nervous old maid.

For the grandmother had refused to go to Peking with her son's family. She had in her own time seen the splendors of the court, but now that her son was so successful as an official, she was thankful for her lot and had turned into a devout Buddhist, believing in doing good deeds to accumulate merit for her future life and "shadow" or bring blessings upon her progeny. She donated four front pillars to Yenlo's Temple on a hill outside the southwest of the city at the foot of the mountain. She was a great friend of the monk there and when he suggested "rebuilding the temple," the common excuse for soliciting contributions, she gladly gave the pillars. These pillars were carved with encircling dragons in high relief, in the style of the Confucian Temple at Confucius' birthplace, only a few miles away. The name of Yenlo's Temple fascinated her, and she was bent on currying the favor of the King of Hell. Below the Temple, there were the Golden Bridge and Silver Bridge and the Bridge of Sorrow over which everybody had to pass when he died and went to Hell. It was good to familiarize oneself with the way there.

So the grandmother insisted on staying at home with Li Yima, while her son's family lived in Peking. Although they pleaded with her to come and stay with them, Mrs. Tseng was secretly glad, as all women are, to live without her mother-in-law, and as the sole mistress of the house in Peking.

But what pleased her more was leaving Li Yima behind. Behind the grandmother's back, the whole family down to the servants, regarded Li Yima as a plague. Li Yima's position was illogical, but she made it provocative. She was one of the beneficiaries of the family system, but she would not be gracious about it. She was now about fifty, but she had had a strange childhood. As an infant, during the Taiping Rebellion, she had fled with her parents from Anking to Shantung, and her father had acted as bodyguard for the grandmother's father and once risked his life to save his master. When he died, the grandmother's family promised to bring up the child out of gratitude. Later, when the grandmother was married into the Tseng family, she managed to get Li Yima, then a widow, to come and live with her and help look

83

after her son, now Mr. Tseng. She remained as a sort of institution in the family long after her services were needed, lower than a relative, but higher than a servant.

Mrs. Tseng early found that Li Yima adopted a protective attitude toward her husband and she had to put up with more interference from her than from the grandmother. Still later, after Mr. Tseng became a successful official, Li Yima took the attitude that now she was entitled to be supported for life, because she had "kneaded" him up since he was a tiny tot. On Mr. Tseng's part, he could not be other than tolerant toward her without being accused of ingratitude, and he could well afford to feed one extra mouth.

As time went on, Li Yima had less and less to do, and demanded more and more attention from the servants. She constantly imagined she was being insulted or was being shown lack of respect, and she would complain about the servants on trivial matters. Mrs. Tseng would have to say that the servants were in the wrong, else Li Yima would fly into a fit and say that she was not wanted any more. The grandmother also protected her as a matter of habit, and out of a desire to be generous toward a dependent, as was correct in a prosperous family of scholars. The grandmother found in her also a talking companion in her old age. But Li Yima would too often talk about the Taiping Rebellion and her father's exploits until the children were sick of the Rebellion and its brave generals.

. .

The grandmother decided to solemnize Mannia's engagement to her eldest grandson, on the occasion of the death of Mannia's father. Pingya was summoned back to Shantung, for according to the grandmother's plan, the engagement was to be a very formal ceremony and to be combined with the funeral of Mannia's father, in which Pingya was to take part.

Pingya's studies were upset for that spring, because the whole educational system of China was being changed. The defeat of the Boxers meant also the defeat of the ultra-conservative party, and the coming into power of the more enlightened Chinese ministers. Intermarriage between Manchus and Chinese was permitted, and foot-binding was prohibited. Orders were issued that the old civil examinations were to be entirely remodeled, and all old colleges were to be changed into modern colleges, high schools, and primary schools; and graduates

84

who passed the examinations were to be given the old academic degrees of *kungsheng, chujen,* and *chinshih.* Curricula were changed and at the civil service examinations the conventional "eight-movement" essay was to be replaced by essays on current politics. Schools were just springing up and were in utter confusion as to what to teach their pupils, and Mr. Tseng himself was in doubt as to what his children were now supposed to learn in order to enter officialdom. So he let Pingya return to Shantung, and the boy's mother went with him.

The grandmother thought it would be more convenient for Mannia's family to observe the forty-nine days of mourning in the Tseng home before the funeral, and so Mannia and her mother moved in at the beginning of the period. The grandmother ordered a special courtyard on the east to be set aside for the Sun family and the coffin; and in front of the hall where the coffin lay in state, there were two huge oil-paper lanterns marked with a big character "SUN" in black, partly covered by two crossed white paper bands, to show that this was a funeral of the Sun family and that it was held in a Sun home. The grandmother also assigned a few men and women servants to attend to the funeral arrangements, which made everything much easier for the widow and daughter. The funeral was socially known as that of an "external relative," that is, a relative of a woman married into the family, and all local officials and gentry paid their respects. The grandmother also had altars set up in the courtyard and asked monk-priests to say the number of masses requisite to save the soul of the deceased from Hell.

Mannia was dressed all in white during the "seven times seven" days, and at night she and her mother had to sleep behind the curtain in the hall to keep vigil over the coffin. At first, the black curtain and the coffin and the candles in the dark night made her shudder and shrink close to her mother. During the daytime, she and her mother had to attend to the food for the monks and tips to servants bringing friends' funeral gifts and a thousand and one things, so that she was thoroughly worn out. But she was truly in sorrow, and the whole routine of ritual and the atmosphere of the forty-nine days made her feel the loss of her father the more keenly.

Now the grandmother, with the consent of the Pingya's mother, did an extraordinary thing. Pingya was at best a fiancé and Mannia technically had not yet "crossed the threshold" of the Tseng family. But the grandmother's whole idea was that her nephew's funeral was to be celebrated with a "son-in-law." On the day of *kaitiao,* or receiving guests who came to pay respects to the deceased, there would have to be a man to receive the guests, and what was more important, to stand at the side of the coffin and return the low bow when the guests bowed three times to the coffin. At night, when Pingya saw the mother and daughter were tired out, he offered to take turns with them at keeping the vigil, or guarding the "soul," as the coffin was euphemistically called.

Mannia was grateful for a hundred reasons. She was grateful that with the help of her cousin's family, the funeral could be celebrated with so much style, which the soul of the deceased should appreciate and Mannia appreciated on behalf of her family. She was grateful that during the funeral procession Pingya was going to wear the proper mourning of a son-in-law, and that he already was mourning and keeping vigil over the coffin at night to relieve them. She was grateful for the good and comfortable feeling that there was a man in her family, after the loss of her father, when the widow and daughter were helpless. She was grateful that, in obedience to the grandmother's wish, Pingya had called her mother "Mother" instead of "Maternal Aunt"—a very unusual thing to do, and ordinarily embarrassing even for a married son-in-law. She was grateful that he was so decent about it all, so young and handsome and gentle. And so when the two of them, the boy of eighteen and the girl of sixteen, both clad in white cotton, met in the morning or at night in the dusk of the candle-lighted hall, her eyes were often moist, and no one could have said whether they were tears of mourning or tears of gratitude, tears of sorrow or tears of happiness. She did not know, herself.

Above all, she was touched to the bottom of her heart to hear him call her *Meimei,* or younger sister, and she called him "Pingko," or elder brother Ping. As an "external" cousin, one of a different family name, she could not have ranked with the daughters of the Tseng family and be called "eldest," "second," or "third younger sister" according to relative age, as might be done with "internal" cousins in the family system, and it would not sound well to call her "Manmei" (or Mannia the younger sister), and so Mannia's mother herself suggested the address *Meimei.*

Under the circumstances, it would have been easy to throw discretion to the winds and for the two young cousins to become familiar. But

86

Mrs. Tseng was a strict mother and had cautioned her son about decorum.

"Ping-erh" she said, "you are daily seeing your *Meimei*, and I like her for being so well brought up. But there must be no transgression of the rules of decorum, if you value your future wife. Between husband and wife respect comes first." Mrs. Tseng came from a learned family and she had these phrases at her tongue's tip.

The result was that the boy and the girl tended to keep aloof, and that each therefore seemed more desirable to each other.

. ˙.

Once, however, Pingya made an advance which was rejected by Mannia. One evening they were alone before the altar, when Mannia's mother had temporarily gone to the kitchen. They were talking again of Mulan and that short period of school life together, and Pingya told her he had seen Mulan, who was now growing a little taller. He could not understand why a woman in sorrow was more beautiful than a woman in gaiety, and he wondered why Mannia in her white mourning cotton dress had a ghostly beauty. It seemed to him she was like a Goddess of Mercy, she was so remote from him. And yet her voice was familiar and human and because she had wept so much she spoke with a nasal sound, which certainly was of the present world.

"*Meimei*," said Pingya, "you too have grown in these two years since I last saw you."

She avoided his glance.

"Why are you so distant and cool toward me?" he asked.

Mannia cast her eyes up. It was a challenge. There was so much she wanted to say, but she did not know how to begin. "Pingko," she said after a pause, "do not be unjust. After what you have done now for my deceased father, Mother and I can never repay you."

"But you are distant," protested Pingya. "At this moment you are still talking the polite language of gratitude! Is it not clear enough that I am doing this all for you, that in my heart there is no difference beween your family and mine? For you I am willing to wear a three-year mourning, not merely a hundred days. If you would only not be so cool and distant from me, we could be so good to each other!"

Mannia's resistance was broken within her, but she only said with a smile, "There is a whole lifetime for us to be good to each other."

The tone and the smile satisfied Pingya for the moment and he felt he had wooed and won a goddess.

Mannia tried to change the topic by talking about Mulan again. She confided to him that Mulan and she were sworn sisters and went inside to bring out the jade pendant that Mulan had sent her in return for the jade peach she had given her while in Shantung.

"Close your eyes," she said as she went in. "Don't move until I come back."

When she came out, she came close to Pingya's side and told him to open his eyes and see her treasure. The jade was extraordinarily beautiful for its sheer luster and fine carving.

"Isn't it lovely?" she said.

"Yes," said Pingya. "Indeed, but you should see Mulan's whole collection of jade miniatures—tigers, elephants, rabbits, ducks, boats, pagodas, candle stands, shrines, bodhisattvas—the best I have ever seen."

As Pingya received the jade he took the occasion to hold her hand, but Mannia quickly withdrew it, so that the jade almost fell to the ground.

"You shouldn't do that," she chided quite flushed.

"You let me hold your hand that day of the cricket match, when my cricket was killed," he protested.

"Then was then and now is now," said Mannia.

"Why is it different?"

"We are grown up. I should not hold hands with you now."

"Don't we belong to each other now?"

Mannia drew away a little distance and said, "Pingko, there is a rule for everything. Really, my whole body belongs to you, but this is not the time. Do not be impatient. There is a whole lifetime."

The speech was like a homily. Pingya felt here was a girl who could admonish him and he admitted to himself that she was right. But thereafter, in the morning, in the afternoon and at night, whether in Shantung or Peking, Pingya continued to hear this whisper in the air, "There is a whole lifetime," as if it came from an invisible spirit hovering around him.

So does "Nature play pranks with human beings" and create from a girl's whispered phrase or the slight pressure of a soft hand life-long emotions, which have momentous consequences. No one could say whether a life of love and suffering was not better than a life without

love and suffering at all. In the case of Mannia, one is inclined to think
that it was worth it.

. : .

Three nights later, something occurred which drew Mannia and
Pingya irrevocably closer. It was the eve of the thirty-fifth day of
mourning, or the Fifth Seventh Day as it was called, when an important mass would be held. Among the priests invited, there was a young
man about twenty whose roving eyes Mannia did not like. While saying the mass with the others, with his eyes supposed to be closed and
his palms joined before his chest, this young monk constantly stole
glances at her. It was a thing that a girl can instantly feel and notice,
and she had told her mother about the "thievish eyes" of the monk.

Now it happened that after supper that night, Li Yima had an
unusual fit of hysterics. Mrs. Tseng had been managing the entire
course of the ceremony alone, and if any questions came up she directly
consulted the grandmother, who loved these funeral affairs which
broke the monotony of her life, so that Li Yima felt she had been left
entirely unnoticed with nothing important to do. She had been fasting,
as she often did, and about the time the others had finished supper,
she fell on the floor, and her eyes rolled and then looked straight ahead.
After screaming and tearing her hair, she began to talk in the fashion
of one possessed of a spirit. Assuming the role and voice of the deceased Mr. Sun, she called the grandmother *Taku* or "Big Aunt" and
cried, "*Taku*, help! help! I am rolling down the Valley of Burning
Sands! It is hot. I am suffocating. Help! Help!" Then addressing herself to the younger Mrs. Tseng, she asked, "Why doesn't my cousin
come to my funeral?"

Upon this, Mannia's mother broke out wailing, "Ah, my husband,
why did you leave us mother and child alone?" Mrs. Tseng thought at
once of the monks who were staying over for the night and sent for
them to come and exorcise the spirit by incantations. She comforted
the widow, while the grandmother, who thoroughly believed she was
talking to her deceased nephew's spirit, comforted the possessed Yima
by saying that they were doing their best in saying prayers for his soul.
On being asked whether "he" had seen his little son who died a year
ago, the possessed woman replied, "I have already asked a few small
devils about him, and they have replied that Hell is a big place and it
would take much time to look for him by description." All the small

devils wanted money and "he" had to bribe them, and they must burn plenty of paper money for his use. The grandmother then asked if he were thirsty, and offered a drink of water, which the woman took, and then her spasms gradually ceased and she lay unconscious, her mumblings gradually becoming stilled.

Now Mannia and her mother usually had their meals in their own rooms, but tonight there had been a special dinner in the grandmother's courtyard and they had come over, leaving a woman servant to keep watch over the coffin. Immediately after supper, Mannia had left to go back to their courtyard, which was on the southeast corner, and she had to pass through several corridors in the dark. About halfway a servant came running to overtake her, saying that "Li Yima was possessed of a ghost," and hurrying on to get the monks who were staying in the southern rooms. Frightened, though not knowing exactly what had happened, she went on, until she reached the moon door which led into the eastern section of the house. Here she saw the monks coming toward her, and she hesitated a moment whether she should turn back with them, but decided that it was more important to go to the coffin. She stood aside to let the monks pass.

Passing by the covered promenade corridor after turning south from the moon door, she came to the double turn which separated her from the rear entrance to her courtyard by an enclosed alley forty feet long. At that entrance she saw a shadow and there was the young monk peeping out. Immediately she withdrew and hid herself at the turn of the corner, her heart palpitating with fear. What was the monk doing or going to do? She was afraid to go ahead and equally afraid to turn back lest he should come after her. She waited breathlessly and after a few minutes looked again, and again the young monk was peeping at the other end. After waiting a few minutes, she looked once more and did not see him. She assured herself now that he had turned back, and that it was nearer and safer to hurry the short distance to her own rooms. But just as she had gone halfway through the narrow enclosed passage, she saw the young monk rush toward her through the back entrance. He seemed surprised to find her there and stopped short, his small thievish eyes now wild and terrible to see.

She screamed and ran back. It seemed to her that the young monk was coming after her, but she did not dare turn her head to look. In the darkness, she ran and ran, and the faster she went the more afraid she became.

Suddenly she heard a voice calling to her, "*Meimei*, what has happened?" Pingya was standing ten feet in front of her. Before she knew it she was in his arms. "Pingko, I'm afraid! I'm afraid!" she cried.

"What is it?"

"The young monk! Is he behind me?"

Pingya looked over her shoulders.

"There is no one," he said. "Anyway, don't be afraid, *Meimei;* I'm with you." And he bent over her tenderly and his voice was soft and reassuring.

Now that her fear was gone she realized what she had done. How she found herself in his arms she did not know. She felt guilty and ashamed and began to draw away. For permitting a man to hold her body so close was an intimacy as decisive as to permit a kiss.

But Pingya would not let her go. "Come, we will go together. I was worried that you might be afraid without your mother, and when I saw that the young monk had not come with the others I slipped away to come to you."

They turned toward her courtyard, and he was still holding her hand, and she was still so excited that she let him. She felt that after she had thrown herself into his arms, holding a hand did not matter much; it gave her a stolen pleasure, and if she blushed no one could see her in the dark. So they went along and she told him what she had seen.

"Oh, you foolish little *Meimei*, you are so easily frightened. I shall always be with you, for life," said Pingya, and she drew a little closer to him and felt that it was exciting and wonderful.

When they reached the courtyard everything was as usual. The young monk evidently had retired to his room. Only the woman servant remarked with relief, "So you've come at last! All the priests have gone and I saw a man several times peeping in through the window lattice."

Soon the priests returned, followed by several servants holding lanterns, and Mrs. Tseng and Mrs. Sun. Li Yima had come back to consciousness after a few incantations, and professed not to know anything of what she had said and had been sent to bed. The priests suggested that prayers should be said before the coffin especially early that night, and more candles were lighted so that the whole room was brilliantly illuminated. The "wooden fish" was beaten and the priests began their drowsy chants, and the place was full of noise.

Mrs. Tseng sat in the room for over an hour to keep Mrs. Sun company.

"It is a wonder," Mrs. Tseng said, "that we have passed these five weeks so peacefully already. I never saw an important occasion in the family but that there was some unexpected trouble. When spirits possess a living person's body, there must be a good reason, something to complain about. While I do not boast, there has been nothing lacking in our arrangements for Cousin's funeral. Had it not been for Grandmother's generosity, everything might not have been done so well. Now there is nothing which is not done properly, from erecting an altar and saying mass to burning paper money and guarding the coffin and even Ping-erh wears the mourning of a son-in-law. I think Cousin's spirit should be more than pleased." Thus she partially implied Li Yima's hysterics were not genuine.

The widow hastened to express her deep appreciation of all they had done for them, but being a careful woman, she did not say anything about Li Yima.

Pingya told his mother about the young monk's conduct, and Mannia and her mother and the *amah* added to the story. "That is nothing difficult," said Mrs. Tseng. "Tomorrow, I shall tell the head priest to send the young monk away on some pretext," and Mrs. Sun thought she spoke like a mistress of an official family and admired her dignity and composure. Before she went away with Pingya at about eleven o'clock, Mrs. Tseng asked two extra servants to sleep in the hall near the door.

Mannia could not sleep that night, and her mother thought it was merely due to her fear, but deep in Mannia's heart she felt a great confusion of feelings which were deep and strange and wordless. She was not thinking. She was sensing life with the thoughtless language of the instincts of awakened womanhood. Life seemed to her wonderful and terrible, beautiful and tragic, all at the same time.

To a girl brought up in the strict classical tradition, permitting a man to hold her was to commit herself to him for life. Technically, according to Confucian puritanism, she was no longer immaculate. Her body was like a photographic plate, and once she exposed it to one man, she could not belong to another. This might not be so with peasant girls and waitresses at tea houses, but Mannia, brought up as an educated girl by her Confucian father, knew better. And she said silently to herself, "Pingko, I am yours!"

By the time Pingya and his mother went back to Peking, it was already the end of spring. Pingya went back without further intimacy than what had happened by pure accident on that eve of the Fifth Seventh Day, for Mannia again became self-conscious and shy. The boy and the girl met each other on the tantalizing level of half-familiarity and half-aloofness, so that Pingya's mind invested Mannia with the spiritual beauty of the unattainable, and he loved her with an un-quenchable ardor. No, Mannia was not perfect, was not divine to him; she was human and timid and thin and she had coughed a little for two weeks. She was so much better that way. She was also jealous; this he had noticed. At times when Pingya talked about the splendors of Peking and the many feasts and festivals and exchange of visits, if any strange girl's name was incidentally mentioned, Mannia would ask, "Who is that?" and her lips would quiver and her eyes would glance sharply at him and then look far away. She thought of herself as a provincial girl; she was his poor cousin; she believed he loved her, and she was educated enough to be his wife; but it made her tremble to think of all the well-dressed girls of rich families in the capital that he had met or might meet. While he was in Peking in that society, she would still remain a small-town girl back at home.

Outwardly, so far as that went, she had nothing for which to re-proach Pingya. He had taken part in the funeral procession after the forty-nine days were over. He walked in front of the coffin and wore the formal mourning dress of a son-in-law, in white *kweihsing* cap and gown, with a knot of red stuck around the girdle because his own parents were living. What pleased her most and made her doubly secure was the fact that when the ancestral tablet was installed at the ancestral hall, on the left of the name of the spirit were inscribed the words: "Daughter Mannia and Son-in-law Tseng Kang jointly offer worship"—"Kang" being the regular personal name of Pingya. This was the grandmother's wish and it made his relationship as son-in-law legally valid, even if the grandmother should die before their wedding and if the question should ever come up.

The great obstacle in their way was that they were not supposed to correspond with each other. Mannia thought there would be times when she would be asked by the grandmother to write letters to the family at Peking, but certainly she should not think of writing a per-sonal letter to Pingya. Her letters were to be strictly businesslike and impersonal. They talked about this and Mannia said that she might secretly send letters through Mulan. She also said that Pingya might suggest to his parents that she come to Peking to attend school with Mulan. But nothing came of this, and she stayed at home, separated from Pingya for two whole years. She had hoped that the following spring Pingya could return to Shantung on the pretext of "sweeping the grave" at *chingming* Festival, at the beginning of the third moon, but his parents did not approve, because it was too long a journey and would interfere with his studies. That summer only Cassia came alone with her three-year-old baby, and from her Mannia eagerly gathered all the news she could about the Tseng boys and their friends and the names of the new maids.

CHAPTER VII

*I*T HAS been necessary to tell in detail the episode of Mannia and Pingya in Shantung, for in the spring of the year after Cassia's return, Pingya fell seriously ill, so that Mannia was sent for to be married to him in Peking.

Pingya was normally a healthy boy, not robust, but doing well for an official's son, neither strong nor suffering from any ailment, but shut up a little too much during the period of adolescence because of the studies to which he was fairly devoted. The better a boy was at his studies, the paler and weaker he usually became. In February of that year, Pingya had had an attack of intermittent fever or some form of influenza. When Mannia heard the news, she knew that all hope of his visit to her father's tomb at this year's *chingming* was again dashed to pieces.

Since Pingya had gone away two years ago, Mannia was much changed. The two months of his delicious presence had left in her a feeling of strange loneliness, and she became unusually quiet. The circumstances of their silent and impassive love-making somehow created in her mind a fused picture of love and sorrow, so that she came to associate love definitely with wearing the mourning dress. She made several suits of the white cotton cloth, and often changed and had them washed and pressed and kept neat and began to love them. It also made her desire to hear Buddhist chants, and she watched with fascination other people's funerals passing their house. To her mind a funeral now suggested love. Others might believe that the loss of her father made her pensive, but her mother knew, because when a letter from Mulan brought news of Pingya, or indeed when any letter came from Peking, she would become livelier for a few days before settling back to her forlorn silence. Her mother saw that when she opened Mulan's letters a flush crept into her cheeks and her small lips quivered in a way quite characteristic of her. Li Yima suggested that Mannia was in love, but the grandmother would never admit that she had gone too far in bringing Mannia and Pingya together before their marriage. The grandmother became quite used to Mannia's mother's company, so that moving to live in Peking was out of the question. All that Mannia was doing was waiting to go to Peking and be married, when her three-years' mourning should be over and she would be nineteen. And now she was already eighteen.

So at this year's *chingming* she cried at her father's tomb unusually bitterly, so much so that she caught a cold. She was in bed when the news of Pingya's recovery reached her, and then her cold left her quickly.

Pingya's fever at that time had been quickly cured by his drinking a medicinal stew of sickle-leaved hare's ear and other plants much relied upon for all kinds of colds, and when he was convalescent he had pills made of various ingredients from cardamon, Szechuen varnish, and nutgrass, which drove off the illness definitely. But he had lost strength and vitality; he felt sleepy in the daytime and his limbs were weak for a month, and it was six weeks before he went to school again.

Toward the end of April, he was sent to bed again, with fits of shivering and headache, and soreness of the neck. His parents thought it was the influenza returning and gave him the same stew of hare's ear. A week passed before they called any doctor. Through Mulan's family, they had made the acquaintance of the Imperial Physician. He came and felt Pingya's pulse and would say nothing but prescribed a stew of *ephedra*, cinnamon barks, fried licorice powder and almonds, to induce perspiration.

Mulan was then already fourteen and had read a few books on medicine, and had been encouraged by her unusual father to have many talks with their friend the Imperial Physician. So when she went to the Tsengs' home and learned of the prescription, she recognized it as the characteristic treatment for the beginning of *shanghan*, and told her parents so on her return.

Now *shanghan* was the disease which the doctors most dreaded: the most debated, the most written about, the most obscure and least understood, and the most complicated disease in Chinese medicine. It combined a variety of illnesses, with alternate spells of chills and fever, under the typhus category, being known as *chuanching shanghan*, or a type of fever that passed from one system to another. The modern term for it is "intestinal fever." It was supposed to attack first the three

96

yang systems, and might pass on to any of the three *yin* systems or all three. The three *yang* systems are regarded as the alimentary or nourishing systems, being the small intestine, the large intestine, and the entrances to stomach and bladder and the pylorus; at times we speak of the "six *yang* systems" including the bladder, the gall bladder, and the stomach. The lungs, the heart, and the membranes around the heart with the pancreas, the kidneys, and the liver, form the *yin* group, responsible for respiration, circulation, and elimination. The terms *yin* and *yang* are regarded as relative and complimentary, and not as absolute and mutually exclusive. The nourishing systems (*yang*) support and build up body heat and strength while the other exchange systems (*yin*) regulate and secrete liquids for lubricating the body. The kidney, the liver, and the pancreas in particular are regarded as secreting important fluids for balancing the system.

Everything depended upon care and attention in the first stage, when the disease was still confined to *yang* intestines. Soon Pingya felt his throat and lips dry without thirst, and his eyes were dizzy, his ears tingled and his chest was full. The doctor told the family the case was serious, but Mrs. Tseng thought it was also psychological, and an adolescent trouble. Her mother's instinct told her that the grandmother had gone too far in bringing the boy and the girl together. When half a month had passed and the fever did not subside, and his pulse, which had always been "on the surface" or easily noticeable, began to sink, she was really frightened. She thought at once of sending for Mannia, for two reasons. First, because she still largely thought of the origin of his illness as due to love, or a case of "love-sickness" for which the sure cure was the sight and touch and voice and presence of the beloved. Second, because she believed in *tsunghsi*, or confronting an evil by a happy event, in short, having the wedding while the boy was ill. She was willing to wait and see whether it would be necessary to take that step, but it would certainly be convenient to have Mannia near if it should be necessary. The doctor, being more or less helpless or at least never sure of himself in a case of *shanghan*, greatly encouraged this proposal, which modern doctors now describe as combined psychological treatment.

The mother asked Pingya if he wanted Mannia to come and see him, and he said yes.

Mr. Tseng therefore sent a telegram to Shantung. He was then, in addition to his old office, a vice-director of the government telegraph bureau, under Yuan Shihkai. Yuan was at this time one of the most powerful men at the court, having been made Governor of the metropolitan province, Tupan of Railways and Mines, Tupan of Telegraphs, and most important of all, Chief of the Military Training Headquarters, which was training a "new" army with modern rifles. Mr. Tseng had made the acquaintance of Yuan through Mr. New, a fellow-official and fellow-provincial of Shantung, and Yuan had given him the vice-directorship of the government telegraphs. He therefore sent a rather long message, asking his mother to let Mannia and her mother come without delay, and stating that Pingya was seriously ill.

To Mannia the telegram was like a thunderbolt and there was not the slightest question in her mind that she should go. The grandmother and Mannia's mother discussed the matter together, and the grandmother whispered that it must be for a hurried wedding in sickness for *tsunghsi*, otherwise the mother would not be explicitly asked to accompany Mannia. But Mannia's mother did not tell her this, for she could not. Although the boat voyage would be more comfortable, Mannia brushed aside all such considerations and told her mother they must go by carts and sedan chairs, which would take them to the capital in about a week's time. The grandmother was also much shocked by the news, for Pingya as her eldest grandson held a very important position in the family scheme. She wanted to go also, but she said she would come with Li Yima by boat a few days later, and sent the mother and daughter ahead with a man servant, an *amah*, and a personal maid for Mannia, called Little Joy, whose real name was Four-Joy.

The Tseng family received by a return telegram the news of their departure, and thought the journey might take them ten days at the quickest. Pingya was already in a critical stage. He was considerably emaciated, his fever still ran high, his pulse was weak, he occasionally vomited, his limbs were cold, and he complained of "cold pain" in the abdomen which was tender and full. By all signs, the *yang* systems had "collapsed within" and the disease had "spread to the *yin* systems." It seemed that his body was being dried up, and his throat became parched and his eyes dull. The doctor no longer tried to "bring out" the fever by ephedrine and cinnamon bark and licorice, but recognized the necessity of "conciliatory medicine" to tone up or "warm up" the *yin* systems, for it was now recognized that it was a kind of *yin* cold and the secreting organs were not functioning properly. For this, a stew of autumn roots, dried ginger, the white of small onions and pig's gall were used. Then, as the patient steadily grew worse, a more drastic medicine was used, consisting of rhubarb, thorny limebush, *magnolia officinalis*, and even *manghsiao*, a product of saltpeter in fine crystals.

Mannia's arrival was anxiously awaited, and her first meeting with the sick boy had to be carefully arranged. A great deal was being expected of her, for she was to be the patient's doctor and savior. Pingya had several times asked his mother if Mannia was coming and when she would arrive. At times when he had high fever and his mind was not clear, he would mumble Mannia's name. Once Cassia, attending to him alone, heard him say distinctly, "*Meimei*, why did you run away?" and "There is a whole lifetime." Scandalized, she secretly told the mother about it, and it convinced the mother all the more that Mannia's presence would make a great difference to the boy's recovery.

Yet there was a problem which bothered Mrs. Tseng and Cassia and their husband. Pingya had become considerably worse than when they decided to send for Mannia. This put a new complexion upon their original idea of counteracting the sickness by a wedding. There was Mannia to consider. In a less critical illness it would not be so difficult, but since Pingya's life was hanging in the balance, it was a little too much to ask of Mannia. "How can I open my mouth and speak to cousin-in-law about it when our son is so ill?" said Mrs. Tseng. She hoped that with Mannia's arrival and presence, her son would take a turn for the better. But it was too much to expect without *tsunghsi*, and this was the last resort, since the doctor was already doing all he could. Mrs. Tseng could of course gently suggest the idea, but it would be less embarrassing if the initiative came from Mannia's mother, who must have thought of it, she reasoned, because it was so obvious under the circumstances, and otherwise Mrs. Sun's presence would not have been explicitly asked for. Mannia was formally engaged and it was unimaginable she would marry anybody else. But would she and would her mother consent? For *tsunghsi*, though often practiced, could not be done without the absolute consent of the other family; this was true of all marriages, but here particularly the bride-to-be must be consulted.

For the idea of wedding a girl to a man critically ill, possibly on his deathbed, was a kind of voluntary offering, and was not something that money could buy. He might not recover, although the presumption or the hope was that he would. And so sacred was widowhood regarded in Confucian families, that it must not be undertaken lightly. Even ordinary widowhood could not be forced or enforced by the strictest of families, and a widowhood of this kind was doubly appreciated and held as unusual. While the former was *chieh*, or meritorious widowhood, the latter was *tseng* or meritorious virginity. No power on earth could force a widow to be *chieh* or a virgin to be *tseng*, if she did not choose to do so. It was like a vow to enter a convent for life—a strictly personal matter.

Mannia might be placing an offering on the altar of love, like so many girls who have chosen to remain unmarried and refused all offers because their lovers died.

. .

Mannia and her mother arrived in Peking about three in the afternoon of the twenty-second of May, in the midst of a sandstorm in the air. That is to say, there was no storm near the earth's surface, but the entire sky was overcast by an unbroken sheet of yellow dust moving somewhere in the upper strata. The sun was barely discernible as a blue disc, giving a queer, quiet effect to the city, like a premature and prolonged twilight.

Mannia was excited, because she was coming to the city of her dreams and to Pingya's home. She had not yet learned how ill he was, and she was all impatience. She watched the streets and especially the way Chinese and Manchu women dressed. Her mother, her maid, Little Joy, and the *amah*, were equally excited, for none of them but the manservant had ever been to Peking before.

Mannia thought too of Mulan, who must certainly have been told of her coming. How would she look now, she wondered, after these four years? And she thought of the embarrassing situation she was in: as a cousin, she could very well stay in the Tseng home, yet she was now a fully grown girl, and the Tseng boys were more or less grown-up—even the little Sunya must be now fifteen—and how was she to meet and talk with all of them? And she was the fiancée of Pingya, and fiancés were not supposed to see each other! Yet why was she asked to come if not to see him, and how was she to avoid being laughed at by all the boys and grown-ups and maids and servants?

While she was musing over these vexatious questions, the cart pulled up in front of a big house. The white walls stretched over a hundred feet in length, and at the entrance was a raised pavement over twenty-five feet wide, with the walls on both sides slanting inward toward the gate, which was shining red with golden knobs. On the top of the gate was a black-varnished signboard, bearing in golden characters a foot high the inscription, "The Air of Luck Brings Blessed Peace." Beside the gate hung a vertical signboard in white and sprinkled gold, bearing cabbage green characters which read, "Residence of the Vice-Director Tseng of the Government Telegraph Bureau." In front of the raised pavement were a pair of maliciously grinning stone lions, and the road at that point widened with "screen walls" facing the gate and receding in the opposite direction, giving a large space for parking carriages. Mannia had never seen anything like this in Shantung.

The Tseng family had been fully prepared for their arrival, but had not expected them so soon. When the gatekeeper reported that they had come, there was a flurry in the house. The boys Chinya and Sunya were away at school, but Mr. and Mrs. Tseng, the two daughters born of Cassia, and the servants and maids came out to receive them at the second gate, leaving only Cassia to stay with the sick boy.

Pingya was dozing in his sleep and Cassia dared not leave. She heard the hubbub of women's voices and servants' noises outside. Soon Ailien, her daughter, ran in to tell her how beautiful Mannia looked and how she had grown and how she was dressed. Cassia pressed her finger to her lips to hush the child, but at the sound of Mannia's name, Pingya's eyes opened and he said, "Is she here?" Cassia rushed to his side and said gently, "Ping-erh, Mannia is here. You are very happy, aren't you?" Pingya still had high fever and smiled feebly, and closed his eyes, then opened them again and said, "Is she *really* here? You are not deceiving me? Why does she not come in to see me?"

"You are impatient," said Cassia. "They have just arrived. She is in mourning and cannot come into the sickroom as she is."

"How many days were they on the way? It seemed so long."

"Only six or seven days. Do not bother your head about such questions. They have come very fast. You were very sick and didn't know anything."

"Can I get well now?" said Pingya. The sick boy of twenty spoke like a child.

"Of course you will. Keep your mind calm and rest yourself and when the lilacs bloom, I will go with you and Mannia to Shihshahai to see them. Isn't this good?"

She gave him a drink of a warm stew which was kept ready and asked a servant to stay with him while she went out to see Mannia and her mother.

The Tseng mansion was a spacious house, four-court deep, with a narrow but long patch of vacant space lined with tall elm trees on the east of the main courts, and a number of rambling, zigzag promenade corridors leading to well-concealed courtyards on the west. Pingya had been removed to the innermost rear court on the west, separated by a wall from the parents' rooms in the back middle courtyard. His room looked out on a courtyard thirty feet wide, with a rockery, a fish pool and great pots of pomegranate trees. He had been taken to this court because of its extreme quiet, and also because his illness was becoming critical, and if something untoward should happen the main rooms would not have such a bad association.

Cassia had to go from this rear court and through a hexagonal door to the main back court before she came to the third hall where the guests were still talking with Mr. and Mrs. Tseng.

Mannia was wearing a simple blue jacket and green trousers, for she was no longer in heavy mourning. On her braided hair were a knot of black and a black flower. She was never tall but she seemed to have grown considerably since Cassia had seen her last year. They were talking about the journey and Pingya's illness, but as yet, Mrs. Tseng had not dared tell Mannia's mother the real situation. When the guests saw Cassia appear with Ailien, they immediately rose from their seats, and Cassia said "ten thousand fortunes" to greet them.

"I must crave your pardon for appearing late, Auntie Sun," Cassia apologized. It was the habit of mothers to address their relatives as their children would do, and so Cassia addressed Mrs. Sun as aunt. "The journey must have been hard for you, mother and child. I was keeping Ping-erh company, and he was asleep, and woke up only when Ailien came in to tell of your arrival. He is asking about you and asking why Mannia *meimei* had not come in to see him."

Mannia blushed slightly and her mother replied, "Ask him to be at ease. We are in mourning and should not go in without washing ourselves and making a change of dress."

This brought to Mrs. Tseng's mind the question of the proper arrangement for Mannia to see Pingya.

"That is quite right," she said. "We have troubled you this time, mother and child, because we could not help it. We thought the illness came from the heart, since Ping-erh is a grown-up boy, and he was

102

used to Mannia's company, and so perhaps when they see each other, his heart will be happier and his illness will pass the more quickly. I was talking at lunch with Cassia about your coming and we thought the hour must be properly chosen. According to the almanac, this evening at the period of seven to nine would be a propitious time. By and by, *Saotse,* you can go in to see him first, after you have washed and rested, and Mannia can go and see him this evening. You must be tired and I will show you your rooms."

Mrs. Tseng's speech implied that she set greater store by Mannia's visit than by that of her mother, but she was also showing a great courtesy to the mother, for usually she would have entrusted to Cassia the work of showing her to her rooms. Mrs. Sun protested, but Mrs. Tseng insisted that she must go herself, for she had a great deal to say —she did not know what—to the mother and child. So she told Cassia to go back to Pingya, and Mannia and her mother said good-by for the time being to Mr. Tseng and Cassia.

Their luggage had already been taken to their rooms in the Calm-Heart Studio, in a separate court west from the main hall, with a side door opening on Pingya's court on the west. The different courts in this house were so designed and constructed that each itself was a complete enclosed unit, which made the living together of relatives in the same house possible. These courts usually looked out upon a small yard, quiet, secluded, simple and perfect in itself, with no suggestion of its connections with the other courts. As Mannia went through the latticed corridors and small doors, she thought she would never be able to find her way out again.

Theirs was a small quiet court of three rooms with southern exposure, and a corridor on the east leading to the servants' rooms. Against the white southern wall enclosing the court stood a thin, sparse bush of bamboo, keeping company with a tall, slender perforated stone slab of pale blue about eight feet high. The place was the incarnation of the spirit of simplicity and dignified seclusion. Yet the courtyard was so designed that it offered a perfectly open view of the sky, with nothing to obstruct the view of the moon when it came up.

On the west side was the ancestral hall of the family, situated in vacant ground partly wild with some fruit trees, an old pavilion, and piles of débris, and behind the ancestral hall was the courtyard now occupied by Pingya.

This was one of the most select courts available in the house for a separate family, being removed from the main halls, and would be enviable for a scholar's apartment, or that of a courtesan. It was the sort of place where one could bury oneself, consumed in some great passion, academic or sensuous, and forget that the outside world existed.

Mrs. Tseng showed them the most unusual courtesy. She looked over the rooms, the beddings, the cupboards, the dressing table and fittings, and personally conducted Little Joy and the *amah* to the kitchen. Dragon's-eye tea and almond soup were served, and Mrs. Tseng told them that soon noodles would be ready for their afternoon refreshment.

A servant brought in a pair of new sitting cushions, a new spittoon, a white-copper water pipe for smoking and a new embroidered table cover for a side table. "Why haven't you had everything prepared instead of leaving it until this minute?" scolded Mrs. Tseng. She knew that the guests had arrived earlier than was expected, so that it was not the servant's fault; but she said this to show the greater respect to the guests.

"If there is anything you lack, just send Little Joy over to tell Mistress Cassia about it," she said.

"We have come this time in such a hurry that we have not brought any worthy gifts from the country, but on the contrary are overwhelmed by your hospitality," Mrs. Sun replied. "Such rooms are good enough for fairies, if only we had the luck to deserve them."

"Deserve!" replied Mrs. Tseng. "We were only afraid you would not accept our invitation. I think it must be our cycle of bad luck this year. Since the spring, there has been no peace in the house; one or another of the household has been ill. I hope that with the presence of you, mother and child, our fortunes will improve. This Ping-erh of mine has now been sick for almost a month, and there seems to be no turn for the better."

"How is he now?" asked Mrs. Sun.

"How can a young body stand the daily stewing of abdominal fire for so long?" Mrs. Tseng said, thinking that she would prepare her guests for the true situation and continued, "He is constipated and his urine is free and he complains of cold pain and fullness of the stomach. His limbs are all cold and weak, and yesterday when changing his underwear I saw his shoulder bones stuck out. A thousand and ten-thousand regrets that we did not send for the doctor in the beginning, thinking it was the old influenza! Now the doctor is prescribing the

Big Sustaining Stew and says it is used for attacking organic fever or substantial fever, which as you know differs from functional fever. The saltpeter is not used unless there is real poison in the blood. But I have been thinking how much saltpeter can such a young body stand? Every illness comes from the disturbance of some vital force and is only brought on by some external cold or heat. It is like a plant; if the root is strong the branches will prosper, and if the root is affected the branches dry up. Being thus helpless, Pingya's father and I thought that if you came, Ping-erh's heart would be happier and the spring of vital force in him would be opened. That was why we sent for you. This poor child of mine. . . ." Mrs. Tseng broke down.

"Put your heart at ease," said Mannia's mother. "Such a good boy will not come to an ill end so young. Our hope is that the bodhisattvas will protect him, while we human beings do all we can. There is nothing that we mother and child would not do to help his recovery."

Mrs. Tseng, in tears, said, "If you mother and child can save my son's life, you will be great benefactors of the Tseng family."

Then she lost her control and turned to Mannia, pathetically saying, "Mannia *hsiaochieh*, I beg you to save my son's life."

She was no longer speaking as the aunt and authoritative future mother-in-law, but as the distressed mother of a sick boy to the possible savior of his life.

At the description of Pingya's real condition, the tip of Mannia's heart had felt a twinge, and tears welled forth and rolled down her face like a broken chain of pearls, though she dared not weep aloud. But when Mrs. Tseng used the word "beg" to her, she could stand it no longer, and she turned and went into the next room and fell sobbing on the bed.

Mrs. Tseng hearing the muffled sobbing from the other room was all alert again and interpreted nicely the abrupt retirement without reply to her appeal.

Now controlling herself, she said, "If Father Heaven has eyes, He ought to protect this young couple and make them united in wedlock." Yet she could proceed no further. She felt like a mother to Mannia and went inside and seating herself on the bed, tried to comfort her. Mannia sat up, ashamed of herself, and Mrs. Tseng hugged her closely. This made it worse for Mannia, and she fell sobbing on Mrs. Tseng's breast.

So an understanding was reached between the woman and the girl without words.

. · .

Now Muskrose, Cassia's maid, had been standing beyond the door screen all this time, not daring to come in. When Mrs. Tseng looked up and saw her shadow outside the bead screen, she called, "Isn't that Muskrose? Come in. What do you want?" Mannia, ashamed, turned completely the other way, bending her head and not making a sound.

"I am sent to ask," said Muskrose, "whether Mistress Aunt would have the noodles now or a little later. If it's wanted now, it will be brought in immediately."

"We are not hungry," replied Mrs. Sun, who had followed Mrs. Tseng into the room.

Mrs. Tseng asked Mrs. Sun again, but Mrs. Sun said she was not in the mood for eating at this time. To the maid, Mrs. Tseng said, "Go back and report that there is no need now. After another hour, she can have it brought here, when they have rested a little." Turning to Mrs. Sun, she said, "You have just arrived, and I ought not to have disturbed you with my own troubles. I must be going now."

Mrs. Sun said she wanted to go over to see the sick Pingya as soon as she had washed, and put on a new dress, and taken the black knot from her hair. In respect to her mourning this was all right, as two years had now passed, black being the color of the third year of mourning. A maid would be sent in half an hour to bring her to Pingya.

"You should persuade Man-erh to calm herself," said Mrs. Tseng. Somehow the name "Man-erh" (with the diminutive of endearment) came to her lips quite naturally without any forethought. "She ought to have a good rest, and this evening when she goes to see Ping-erh, you should dress her up a little. It will make him all the happier to see her."

Muskrose offered to go back with Mrs. Tseng. Her rooms were not so far away, but there were some promenade corridors running along the wall on one side and open on the other, which were designed to make the passage as labyrinthic as possible, with many windings and ups and downs, very fine for a leisurely stroll but inconvenient for hurried business. They both went to Cassia's room. Mr. Tseng was taking a nap inside and Cassia came outside to tell Mrs. Tseng how Pingya was getting on. "Since he woke up, he has not slept well again, asking again and again why Mannia has not come in yet."

"I never saw a young boy and girl so attached to each other. Mannia has been crying like a 'doll of tears.'"

"Did you say anything about *tsunghsi*?"

"I couldn't do it, so soon after their arrival. I don't know whether the mother will be willing."

"But their lives are already tied together anyway," said Cassia. "Can man untie the knot of red strings that was tied in heaven above? I shall speak to Mannia; if she is willing, I think her mother will not object. I get along with her very well, since my return to Shantung last year, and she will speak her real mind to me. Of course a girl is always shy in speaking of her marriage."

"That is a good idea," said Mrs. Tseng. "Her mother will come to see Pingya in a little while, and you can go in and talk with her alone."

Mrs. Tseng then went to Pingya, to be there when Mannia's mother should come. Coming out, she met her sons Chinya and Sunya, just returned from school, all excited and wanting to see their sister-in-law, but the mother told them that she was resting now and they could not see her until she sent for them.

Within Muskrose, the maid, was describing to Cassia what she had seen, with many giggles. "I saw them mother-in-law and daughter-in-law weeping in a heap together."

"Did Mannia cry a great deal?" asked Cassia, much interested.

"How was I to see her? She turned her back completely toward me when I went in, and I only saw her shoulders shaking and heaving and a white handkerchief covering her face."

. .

Now Mrs. Sun and Mannia were alone for the first time since their arrival. In a mood of exquisite sadness Mannia walked about the rooms. The place seemed so quiet and homelike, so comfortable and familiar. A great jar, about four feet in diameter, containing gold fish, stood in the yard. She was embarrassed to see how beautifully even the maids were dressed; the gatekeeper, she thought, was better dressed than her own father had been.

The big bed was of hard, carved black wood, the bedposts were in black and brown designs, the bed curtain of greenish-blue gauze, and the curtain hooks exquisitely shaped in gilt. The top of the bed canopy was in three sections, framing three colored drawings on silk, a pair of mandarin ducks swimming among lotus leaves and flowers in the middle section, a few swallows above gorgeous peony flowers on the right, and a cuckoo crying spring on the left. She smelled a strange perfume and discovered two silk bags containing musk suspended on each of the front bedposts inside the curtain. She sat on the bed, and saw the spot on the cushion which her tears had wetted and felt ashamed.

This was the western room, stretching south so that its southern end flanked the courtyard on the west, and the soft light of the late afternoon permeated that end through the window papers and serried shells. On that afternoon it looked like eternal twilight in a strange land. A flat redwood desk stood against the window there, with a section of very old bamboo, almost leather-colored from age, used as a holder for paint brushes. On the south wall was a bookshelf, and on the western wall some scrolls of writing in running script intertwined in rapid rhythm. This room evidently had been used as a study.

The whole room caught her imagination. Sitting on the bed, she could see beside the bookshelf in the southwest corner a porcelain Goddess of Mercy, almost two feet high, exquisitely modeled in pure white. Upon the face shone a smile of kindness and peace, utterly imperturbable. Now every woman knew the *Kuanyin*, or Goddess of Mercy, by her longer title "The Great Spirit of Great Kindness and Great Mercy, Saving the Afflicted and the Distressed." Mannia's feet carried her to the statue, and she stood before it praying silently in humble adoration. It was a girl's prayer of helpless dependence on one who was kind and merciful, asking for an occult answer to an unrevealed mystery and an unfulfilled destiny.

Mannia's mother was used to these silent moods of her only daughter, and left her alone while she herself was washing and changing and waiting for Little Joy to come back and help with the unpacking. Little Joy was a fat and rather stupid country girl, with a broken tooth in front, and she had been all in a flurry ever since she had come into such a mansion as this. She had been sent to get a new broom and borrow a hammer, but it was twenty minutes before she returned. When she appeared Mrs. Sun asked, "Where have you been? There are all these things to do."

"*Taitai*," said the maid, "I have never seen a house like this. I lost

108

my way completely and found myself at the front gate—I don't know how—and the gatekeeper asked me what I wanted, and I told him I was going to the back kitchen, and he burst into a big laugh. Then he told me to go straight in and turn east at the third court, but on coming back, I again went all round before I could find my way here."

"Now we are in Peking and in this big house and garden," said Mrs. Sun, "you should be careful what you say. When people ask you things, think before you reply, and don't talk too much. Say half of what you want to say, and swallow the other half. It isn't like the country, you know. Observe others and try to learn the manners and rules."

Mrs. Sun then called Mannia to come and wash, which she did, using the foreign soap of which she would not have known the use if she had not lived in the Tseng home in Shantung.

A maid named Snow Blossom who served in Pingya's room entered by the side door, and instead of coming straight in, went to the servants' quarters on the east to report that she was come to bring the mother over when she was ready. When Little Joy came in to report this, Mrs. Sun immediately told her, "You see, this is the rule of manners. When you go to the other courts, you should not go straight in to see the mistress or the children, but you must speak to their maids first."

Mrs. Sun then asked Snow Blossom to come in, and she came and said, "Our *Taitai* greets you and says when you are ready, I am to bring you."

Mrs. Sun then went and Mannia was alone again. Soon a servant brought a bowl of chicken noodle soup, saying that her mother would be served inside. Mannia was still half-dazed, and her legs were still tingling from the journey, but after the hot chicken soup, she felt warmed, and went and lay down on the bed in the western chamber.

A strange drowsiness came over her, and hardly had she closed her eyes when she saw an old, deserted temple, in a field covered with snow. She was walking in the snow, which was still falling in big flakes, and she wondered why she was alone and where her companions had gone. She looked at the signboard across the entrance, and saw it was an ancestral temple, but the signboard was so old that the name of the family was almost illegible. She went in and found the place completely deserted. It was dusk, and she was cold and afraid, and thought she would build a fire. She found some straw on the ground but could not find a match. As she was wondering what to do, she heard a voice calling from the outside. She turned around and saw a girl in black, carrying a basket of charcoal and saying with a smile, "Mannia, look here, see what I have brought you." The girl looked like Mulan, and she remembered she had not seen her for years. The girl in black came in and as she was saying to herself, "But where is the match?" the girl in black seemed to have read her mind, and said, "Look, isn't there a light in the everlasting lamp?" She looked up and indeed she saw the oil lamp suspended in front of the altar, and together they took some straw and lit it from the lamp and made themselves a beautiful fire. Then they went inside, but she was afraid when she saw several coffins lying in the long, narrow passage. Suddenly a woman in white was standing at the other end of the passage and her face was beautiful, because she resembled the Merciful One. "Mannia, come over!" the woman called to her. Mannia was still afraid to go through the passage, but she wanted to go nearer to see that kind face. She asked the girl in black to go with her, but the other said, "No, I will stay here and keep the fire going for you and wait until you come back." A strange force of fascination seemed to draw her along through the passage lined with coffins. The way was dark, and she hesitated, but still the Merciful One smiled and called to her not to be afraid, and that she would show her her palace. She went on, and at the end of the passage there was a deep ditch, with only a coffin top serving as the bridge, and the woman in white was now on the other side of the ditch. "I can't come over," she said to the Merciful One. "Yes, you can. You must." The coffin top was barely one foot and a half wide and curved downward, and she had bound feet. She could not do the impossible. "You must and you can," said the voice. Unbelievable as it seemed, she went across the bridge, and lo! she was on a fairy island of jade trees and pearl flowers, painted girders and golden roofs and vermilion towers and treasure pagodas and winding latticed corridors. The deserted temple behind her had vanished and all around the fairy palace was a stretch of snowy white; she found herself clad in white mourning, and white seemed to be so beautiful. Icicles hung on the silvery trees and the atmosphere was thin and rare. "See what I have shown you," said the woman; the nearer she came the more she was like the Goddess of Mercy. They passed over marble terraces and went into a palace. It was, she knew, the Palace of Eternal Light. In the great hall there were boys and girls carrying baskets of flowers and others tending the incense on the altar, and the boys and girls seemed to talk and mingle with each other without any shyness. Among them was one in green dress who came to greet her and said how glad she was to see her come back. And it suddenly seemed that she had been here before, and the palace was familiar, and she herself lost all shyness and talked and mingled with the boys freely. The girl in green asked, "Where is the companion who went down with you?" Mannia stopped and wondered and could not even remember who it was. "It was all your fault," said the girl in green, "that you both went away and left this place." Now all came back to Mannia. She had once been a fairy maid in an orchard and had loved a young gardener, which she should not have done, and on that account they had both been banished from the place, to love and to suffer. She understood now why she had to suffer more than her companion.

The woman in white then came and led her away, saying that her friend would be waiting for her. And so they came back to the gate and, with a light touch of her finger, the Merciful One thrust her out, and she seemed to fall far down in space and she heard a voice calling, "Wake up, wake up, Mannia!" She looked around and found herself once more in the deserted temple. And the girl in black was still there guarding the fire, while she was lying sleepily on the floor.

"Where am I?" asked Mannia.

"You have been here all the time. You must have been dreaming. You have slept for half an hour. Look at the fire; it is almost going out."

Mannia looked at the fire, and it was so real that she thought indeed she had been dreaming.

"I dreamed I was in a strange beautiful place, after I passed through that passage lined with coffins and over a bridge made of a single coffin top, and you would not come with me."

"What passage?" asked the girl in black.

"There!" Mannia replied, and she got up to look for it.

"You were dreaming, there is no passage—only a courtyard."

"It is unbelievable. *You* are dreaming. I shall go and see."

The girl in black drew her back, and said, "Nonsense, you are excited about a foolish dream. We are here and it is still snowing outside."

As the girl pulled harder, she heard again "Mannia, you are dreaming," and she woke up and found Cassia standing by her side in her bedroom in the Tseng house, pulling her sleeves and smiling.

"You must be all tired out," Cassia said.

Mannia sat up, perplexed. "When did you come? Did I keep you waiting long?" she asked.

"Not very long," answered Cassia, still smiling. She sat down by her side and pressed close on her arms.

"Don't press me so hard," said Mannia, "or I shall fall out of this dream, too."

"What are you talking about?" asked Cassia. "Have you or have you not waked up?"

"Pinch me," said Mannia, and Cassia pinched her. Mannia felt a slight pain and said to herself, "This time perhaps I am really awake."

"What were you dreaming about? You were talking and arguing with some one that you weren't dreaming, and that the other person was dreaming."

"I was dreaming that I had a wonderful dream. . . . Then I woke out of the second dream into the first dream, and the fire was still burning, and there was snow on the ground. . . . Oh, I am all confused!"

Then her eyes fell upon the Goddess of Mercy at the corner of the study and there was the face of the woman in white who had spoken to her in the dream, and she remembered that she had looked closely at that face before she fell asleep, and the mansion she was now in was like the palace in the dream to her.

. ˙ .

Cassia had come alone, without her maid, in order that she might talk with Mannia quite in private, and since the topic was very delicate, she groped for a place to begin.

"You have not re-combed your hair yet," she said. "You must dress up a little when you go to see him this evening."

"See whom?" asked Mannia, pretending not to understand.

"See *him*," replied Cassia, with a wicked smile. "Whom else have you come to the capital to see, if not your Pingko?"

No one else so far had directly spoken to Mannia about seeing her fiancé. She knitted her eyebrows in embarrassment. "How can I?" she said. "You are making fun of me."

"No, I am serious. The whole purpose of asking you to come is for you to see Pingko. Otherwise we would not have sent the telegram. It is not usual for fiancés to see each other, but there was nothing else to do."

"But if I do not see him?"

Cassia knew that Mannia was parrying merely out of shyness. "When your father died, a certain person was willing to wear mourning and to have his name carved on the ancestral tablet as son-in-law. And now that person is ill, and you will not even see him?"

"It is not that I am ungrateful. But I should be laughed at," replied Mannia. "The engagement was arranged by our parents, according to the rules, and what will people say if now I brush aside all modesty and see him in bed? I should die of shame."

"You need not worry about that. This is not like a secret meeting. Of course the men will not be there, but only his mother and your mother and myself. Nobody then can laugh at you. Get up and I will braid your hair."

Mannia said she would not dare to trouble her, but Cassia insisted and led her to the dressing table and made her sit down before it. Cassia opened the little black-varnished cabinet which stood on the table and lifted the top which had a mirror inside and propped it up in position. She stood behind Mannia, feeling that thus they were in an easier position to talk about the topic she had in mind, while she could watch Mannia's expression in the mirror. She loosened the girl's hair and it fell over her shoulders, forming a black background for her small white face and delicate lips. Mannia's eyes were slightly red.

"You need not try to deceive me," said Cassia. "You have been crying."

Mannia, annoyed, turned around to snatch at the comb. *"Nainai,* if you want to make fun of me, I won't let you comb for me. Give it to me."

Cassia forced her to sit still and turn toward the mirror again. "If we don't hurry, there will not be time to finish. Chinya and Sunya have returned from school and are waiting to see you, too."

Mannia submitted. When the braid was done, Cassia looked at the face in the mirror and said, "See! I don't blame Pingya. For a face like that, I would fall ill, too, if I were a man. And I would get well too, when such a face came to visit me in my illness."

Cassia saw Mannia's eyes in the mirror look up at her.

"What do you think I am? I am not a grass root that can cure people's sickness."

"More than that. You can be the good fairy," said Cassia, pressing Mannia's hair smooth with two of her fingers. "I have told nobody, but I don't know how many times Pingya has asked about you. Several days ago I was in his room alone when he had high fever and he called your name and said, '*Meimei,* why do you keep away from me?'"

Mannia blushed all over, and her small lips quivered again. In her heart, she wished she could rush in to see him that very moment.

"Honestly, I tell you," Cassia pressed on, "the whole Tseng family look upon you as the good fairy to save Pingya's life. You alone can make him happy and when he sees you, he will suffer less."

Mannia's face dropped into her hands.

"I know it is hard for you," said Cassia, sitting behind her and holding her shoulders. "But you are not strangers to each other, you grew up together as cousins. And this thing is the wish of the elders, and in the third place, Pingya is very ill and it is not the time to cling to the conventional rules."

Mannia raised her head and her eyes were moist. "But we are not married and what can I do when I see him? How can I attend upon him and nurse him even if I want to?"

Cassia saw that it meant a great deal for Mannia to talk not only of seeing him but of actually serving and nursing him.

"I think," said Cassia, "for the present it is not necessary for you to look after him morning and night. All he wants is to see you and talk with you. The Tseng family will be greatly in your debt if you will help to cure Pingya. At present, of course, it is inconvenient. *Taitai* was saying that to me last night. If you and Pingya were already married, you could see him all the time, and people would not say anything, but as it is, we others have to be there when you see him and it will be like a formal visit." Mannia was listening attentively and Cassia continued, "You know, Mannia, when we first sent for you by telegram, *Taitai* thought of a quick wedding for you to *tsunghsi,* and that was why we asked for your mother to come also. But now Pingya's illness is so much worse and we don't know how it will turn out, and *Taitai* dares not ask this of you. If something untoward should happen—and you are so young."

"If something untoward should happen, do you think I would marry some other person?" said Mannia without a moment's hesita-

114

tion. "They have been so kind to me, and if I did not know my gratitude, I should not be a human being." Her face was grave as she went on, *"Nainai,* I'll tell you what is in my mind. Living, I shall be a Tseng family person; dead, I shall be a Tseng family ghost."

It was a simple, dignified, and sincere sentence, and she had said it without any emotional display, as if there had never been any question in her mind that this was the thing to do.

"Of course, I never doubted that you would be willing," said Cassia, "and we all hope that after the *tsunghsi,* Pingya will be so happy that he will quickly recover. But the parents naturally have to consider your future and they would not do it unless you yourself were willing. There is not much else that we can do now. That is why it is so hard to decide."

"Anything, anything that will help him to get well!" said Mannia, sobbing.

"If something unfortunate should happen, I would shave my head and enter a convent," she said, after a moment.

"Don't talk nonsense," said Cassia. "Things are not as bad as that, and besides, the parents would not let you and there is your mother. You are indeed already a Tseng family person and as far as I can see, your destiny and Pingya's are tied up together. We shall wait and see— who can tell but next year *Laoyeh* and *Taitai* will carry a grandchild and we shall eat red eggs?"

"Now you are making fun of me again," said Mannia with a sigh and rose and turned aside.

Muskrose was standing outside the door and announced that the Second and Third Young Masters wanted to see Mannia. Cassia whispered to Mannia, wiping her tears. "It was all my fault. Don't let them see you with your red eyes. Sunya is quite naughty yet, you know— still full of childish ways."

Mannia went to dry her face before the mirror, while Cassia told Muskrose to bring the boys to the central room which was the parlor. This reminded Cassia to tell Mannia that Mulan had been sending servants to inquire when she would arrive, and she said she would have to let Mulan know about her arrival that evening. As Mannia powdered her face, she felt that the day's happenings were all like a dream. Then she heard Sunya's voice calling outside "Mannia, we've come to see the celestial spirit, and the celestial spirit is still powdering her face."

Looking into the mirror, she saw Sunya standing right at the door. Cassia cried out in reproach. "How can a younger brother-in-law peep into the chamber of an elder sister-in-law? If you don't go to your seats, I shall tell Mannia not to see you."

In spite of Mannia's timidity, which made her heart jump at the slightest excitement, it was still so good to hear Sunya's voice again, and it reminded her of Mulan and of her happy days four years ago. When she came out, she was smiling, and Chinya and Sunya saw her dark eyes twinkling under her eyelashes. Daintily she walked forward and stopped just outside the door, while they greeted each other. Chinya had grown considerably, and his face was thinner and longer, but Sunya was still plump and short and had a much ruddier complexion and he was smiling a broad smile that was almost a grin. They were both wearing light grayish-blue crepe gowns for house wear. Sunya was certainly the handsomer boy; his eyes were big and direct, though his lips were somewhat thick, and he had a dimple when he smiled like that—as if to say, "Now what are you going to do?" Chinya, being seventeen, was more self-conscious and his smile was restrained.

"All are grown up now," said Cassia, "and all don't know the laws of manners, but just stare at each other, speechless. Quickly bow to your Elder Sister!"

The boys did so, and Mannia returned the courtesy, but they did not know how to begin the conversation. Muskrose, standing by, watched them with amusement. In a soft, hardly audible voice, Mannia asked them to sit down and then took a seat herself by the door. Sunya was still grinning and looking at Mannia as if she were a curiosity or a stranger.

"Chinya, Sunya," said Mannia, "we have not seen each other for four years, and now you have all grown up so." Her voice was affectionate in speaking to Pingya's brothers as it had never been before. "You have just come back from school, haven't you? Is your teacher good, and what are you studying now?"

"Oh, we study astronomy and geography and mathematics," replied Chinya.

Though Mannia had heard of these, they were subjects she knew she never would have to study and were therefore quite remote and vague to her. Her father had damned these queer and much advertised new sciences, astronomy, geography, and others like physics and chemistry, as belonging to the foreign devils and the wretched group of moderns who were denouncing foot-binding.

Mannia, trying to picture for herself what Pingya had been studying, asked "Don't you study Chinese things any more?"

"We are studying *Tsochuan*," said Sunya, "but we have a teacher who says it is all antiquated and useless. We have not gone on with the *Book of Songs* since we left Shantung. Do you remember the mother of seven sons who still wanted to remarry? How we loved them! Now we are not even supposed to read our books aloud in class."

It all came back to Mannia, their school days together, the nights she had spent with Mulan, exquisite in memory, the *Book of Songs* that they had chanted together. The very sounds and tones of those verses tingled now in her ears.

"You are still the naughty Sunya," said Mannia, but Sunya sprang up and interrupted her.

"Oh and we are studying English! *Goote morning, Father. Mather. Brather. Sister. You are may sister. I ime your brather. One, two, tree, four, fav. . . .*" Sunya, like a northerner, could never make a good short *a* and confused *am* with *ime* and *five* with *fav*. Chinya was chuckling. Mannia laughed aloud.

"What is this? What is this?" she asked.

"*One, two, tree, four, fav,*" said Sunya again, bending his out-stretched fingers one by one. "*You—are—may—sister. You—you are— may—sister. Pingya—is—may—brather.*"

Sunya laughed and Chinya chuckled, and Mannia could not make it out. She heard only the word "Pingya" and was embarrassed.

"Well, you are studying a foreign language to malign people," said Mannia.

"I am not maligning you. I say you are my *SIS-TER!*" said Sunya.

"What is *se-se-ter?*" asked Cassia of Chinya. "I'm sure he's talking of Mannia." But Chinya would not reply and only burst out in a fit of laughter, and Mannia was annoyed and blushed.

At this moment, Mannia's mother came in, ushered by Snow Blossom. The boys, who had already met Mrs. Sun in the other court, all stood up as she came in. She saw them laughing and Mannia miserable and about to cry, and said to Cassia, "What is all this?" and turned to the boys. "She has just arrived, and you shouldn't bully her."

"I don't know what it is all about," replied Cassia. "You ask Sunya."

Chinya replied, "We do not mean to bully our Elder Sister. Sunya was telling her how we study English at school."

"I heard him saying. . . ." said Mannia. She wanted to say the word "Pingya" and checked herself.

"What word?" demanded Sunya.

"Never mind. When you talk a foreign language, I know you are maligning me," said Mannia, evading the question.

Turning to Chinya, Cassia asked, "What was Sunya saying?"

"Well," explained Chinya, "he was saying that Pingya was his brother and Mannia was his sister-in-law."

"That was nothing very bad," said Mannia's mother, but Mannia pouted her lips and stamped her foot, and Sunya came close to Mannia and said to her tenderly, "Do not be angry. You see I wasn't maligning you."

Mannia could neither cry nor laugh, for she liked Sunya in spite of his naughtiness and mischief.

Cassia went away with the boys to their apartments. But after that the English word "sister" was Sunya's mode of address to Mannia whenever he was in a playful mood or wanted to tease her. But neither Sunya nor any of them made any progress in English beyond those elementary words.

CHAPTER VIII

THAT night, there was a special dinner in honor of Mannia and her mother. Mannia appeared flushed and so resplendent that even the austere Mr. Tseng could not help glancing several times at her. Cassia as usual was busy helping others with food and she paid such attention to the guests that Mrs. Sun was quite overwhelmed. Sunya was in apologetic mood and constantly talking to his "cousin-sister." Chinya was quiet because he was older and was afraid of his father.

Mannia almost felt like a bride. Actually it was better than that, for she was about to have what was to her a lover's reunion after a two-year separation. She barely touched the food. The halo and glamour of a girl in love were upon her. Her eyes were unusually bright and her cheeks above her small, white teeth were hot and rosy, while her legs were shivering at the joints. The thing her heart wanted so much to do she was now going to do by order of the parents. The table of food, the conversation, Sunya's voice, the maidservants attending them —all floated around her in a world of heightened gaiety. One thought alone dominated her being, "Am I or am I not the good fairy to help Pingya get well?" Every one of the thirty-six thousand pores in her body was exuding a supernatural energy, ready to assist, and she felt a strange, intoxicating desire, shaking her whole body, to finish the dinner at once and see him. Other forces than her conscious mind had taken hold of her being, and waves of crimson rushed to her cheeks, and her stomach gurgled and little beads of perspiration formed on her forehead.

Of the conversation during the whole dinner she could not remember a single thing the next day. She was conscious only that all eyes, including those of the servants, were centered upon her.

The dinner ended with fruits for dessert, and after taking a great many slices of pear she felt better.

Now Pingya's courtyard was on the west of the back row where Mr. and Mrs. Tseng lived. But while the rooms of the main court were connected and fronted by a common long porch two feet above the courtyard, Pingya's rooms were in a building separated from the main court by a wall with a hexagonal door, with a peach tree on either side. The court was paved with very old and thick tiles two feet square, with winding paths of paved pebbles in various designs. It had a rockery and a small pool, and three long stone steps led up to the porch. There were three rooms in the main building, with servant quarters on the east separate from it.

Cassia hurriedly left before the dessert to prepare Pingya for the auspicious visit. She was greeted by Snow Blossom who asked her if the new young mistress was coming. Snow Blossom's reference to the "new young mistress" or the "bride daughter-in-law," was in fun and Cassia merely said smilingly, "Don't talk nonsense."

Pingya had had a good sleep. The bowl of hot silver fungus cooked in chicken soup had done him good, and he had waked up by himself with perspiration on his head. A foreign oil lamp was already lighted and turned low, standing on the table. He had asked Snow Blossom what time it was, and she had told him that they were having dinner and Miss Sun would soon come over to see him. He told Snow Blossom to turn the light up so that the room would be bright when she came, and asked for a towel, wrung in very hot water, and Snow Blossom brought it and washed his face with it. Snow Blossom was a very intelligent and responsible girl, which was why she had been assigned to attend to Pingya during his illness. Her original name was Pear Blossom, but in order to avoid the taboo in Mrs. Tseng's personal name (Jade Pear), it was changed to Snow Blossom.

When Cassia came she found the room brightly lit as it had never been before during the last week.

She sent Snow Blossom to look out for the guests at the steps, while she talked with Pingya. Before five minutes had passed, Snow Blossom was heard shouting in the courtyard, "They have come!" She ran forward to assist Mrs. Tseng while Mannia followed with her mother, assisted by Little Joy. Cassia was waiting at the chamber door to receive them. The three women blocked the entrance and Mannia lagged behind. She stood at the threshold, waiting, excited.

Suddenly there was an open space. Pingya's bedcurtain had been hooked up and through the open door Mannia saw his thin face and great eyes looking at her. Instinctively she lowered her eyelashes.

Now Mrs. Tseng came and took her hand and led her to the bedside. To her son, she said, "Ping-erh, your cousin-sister is here."

It was a most awkward situation for a girl of eighteen, but Mannia said courageously, in a shaky voice:

"Pingko, I have come."

"*Meimei,* you have come," said Pingya.

That was all. But it meant a world to Pingya.

Afraid that Pingya might say something improper or embarrassing, Mrs. Tseng now led Mannia away and seated her by the table at the end of the bed, and the soft lamplight cast a red glow over her face and her green jade earrings, and set the profile of her hair and her straight small nose in a strong relief. Mrs. Tseng showed Mannia's mother to a chair and sat herself on the edge of the bed, while Cassia remained standing.

To Snow Blossom, Cassia said, "You can wait outside with Little Joy."

Pingya stretched his arm from beneath the satin quilt, and Mrs. Tseng tried to put it back, saying he must not catch cold.

"I am feeling very much better now," he said. The mother leaned to feel his forehead. It was true that the fever had gone down. Mrs. Sun also said that indeed he was better than when she saw him this afternoon. Cassia in turn came to feel his pulse, and said,

"It is true, indeed. I did not believe the fairy medicine was so marvelous. The coming of you, mother and daughter, is better than ten imperial physicians. Mannia was protesting this afternoon that she was not a grass root, and I said she was better than all grass roots because she was the lucky star in Ping-erh's fate. When the lucky star descends and shines, the demon of illness leaves of itself."

Mannia was finding it hard to conceal a smile of happiness, but when Cassia said all these things about her, she said to her mother, "She loves to make fun of me."

"All things are determined from Heaven," said Mannia's mother. "A disease runs its natural course, and the patient will get well if Old Father Buddha protects him. It is not the merit of human beings, and we, mother and daughter, dare not take the honor."

Mrs. Tseng said happily, "The doctor came this afternoon and said if he kept on like this, he would be able to take old, unhulled rice in a few days. A human body must have the grain principle for nourishment, and when he can take congee, progress will be rapid. All these grass roots and herbs merely attack the system and cannot be relied upon to restore the energy."

Pingya lay silently hearing the good news about himself. His outstretched left hand lay exposed and resting upon the green satin quilt, and Mannia saw it white and gaunt, and was fascinated by it.

Mrs. Tseng was so satisfied that she rose and said to Mannia's mother, "You must be tired after today's journey and should retire early." Mannia's mother also rose. Pingya was surprised and Mannia was distressed and she rose also. But Cassia said, "Mannia has just come. The cousins have not seen each other for two years and you ought to let them talk a little longer. You can go and I will stay to keep them company."

"That is well, also," said Mrs. Tseng. It was evident that this had been prearranged.

When Cassia returned to the room after seeing the ladies off, Pingya said to Mannia, "Come and sit here on the bed, Mannia," but Mannia would not. Cassia said, "If cousin-brother wants you to sit nearer, then sit nearer. It will be easier for him to talk to you."

So Mannia moved shyly and felt that she was doing something terribly improper and exciting. She sat obliquely on the edge of the bed, at the very end, and in spite of herself, her hands gently fondled the satin quilt. Pingya told her to come nearer and she protested, saying, "Pingko, what is the matter with you?" but she did come nearer. Gently, instinctively, her hand fell upon his outstretched hand and he grasped it happily and she let him.

"*Meimei,* you have grown so, so beautiful. I shall get well for your sake," he said.

Mannia looked imploringly at Cassia and said, "What am I to do?"

"*Meimei,* I have waited so long for you to come, and waited all afternoon today. I thought I wanted to say so many things to you, but now I cannot say a thing. It does not matter; you have come." He was panting a little already, but he went on, "It is so good to see you and hear your voice. I am very weak."

"Pingko," said Mannia, "you must not talk too much. I have come and you must get well quickly."

Her sharp eyes saw that he was perspiring.

"He is perspiring," she said to Cassia. "I think we should give him a hot towel."

Cassia went to the back room where medicines were kept and stewed, and where a small earthen stove was kept going with a kettle always standing upon it. She wrung a hot towel and brought it to Mannia.

"What do you mean?" said Mannia.

"You wipe his face for him," said Cassia.

"I want you to," said Pingya to Mannia.

So Mannia, excited, leaned over to wash his face and thought she had never been happier. She would not mind nursing him for life if she had to do it.

Cassia held Pingya's head up and the three heads were very close together. Mannia lightly whispered, "Is anybody outside? What would this look like?"

"I have sent them away," Cassia whispered. Cassia loosened Pingya's collar and Mannia was desperately courageous and finished by washing his neck and wiping it with a dry towel from the rack above the bed.

"You see how thin he is," she said. Pingya caught her hand and said, "Thank you, *Meimei*. You won't leave me again?"

Mannia drew back a little and said, "Ease your mind," and rose to extricate herself from an extremely compromising position. She took the wet towel to the back room and stood looking around for a few seconds, before she came out and sat on the chair.

"Sit here," said Pingya, and again she yielded and went to sit on the bed.

"You are perspiring, too," said Cassia, and Mannia took a dry towel and wiped her own forehead with it. Pingya watched her every movement, and when she leaned over to put the towel back on the rack, he smelled the fragrance and her dress almost brushed against her face, and he saw against the lamplight a magic profile of her hair, her nose, her earrings, and, for the first time, the swelling outline of her breast, usually so well concealed. Pingya was held by a strange, new fascination, and he lay still, not saying a word.

Mannia heard a footstep in the courtyard and went back to her seat near the table. Pingya protested, but she pointed silently outside. Snow Blossom lifted the curtain and beckoned to Cassia and whispered that she would accompany Mannia back to her court when she wanted to go. Now Mannia thought it was time for her to leave, yet somehow she could not do so and wished to stay for a few more minutes. She had wanted very much to make a better acquaintance with Snow Blossom, and especially now she envied her job. So she said, "Why not ask Snow Blossom to come in?"

Snow Blossom was glad to have this chance to have a more intimate meeting with one whom she considered the "new young mistress" and besides she had been struck by her beauty and her gentleness.

"Sit down," said Mannia.

"I am not worthy," replied Snow Blossom. "You must pardon my rudeness. You have come to our place and I have not even offered you a cup of tea."

"We are all one family," Mannia replied, "and you do not have to observe all the rules."

Snow Blossom passed on to the back room and soon brought a cup of tea, and while Mannia was drinking it she went again to get some charcoal for the stove from the servants' quarters. Coming in with a small bamboo basket of charcoal, she said, "You see, servant people, if you don't ask them, they never make a move by themselves."

"You must rest a little yourself," said Mannia.

"Oh, it is nothing. I'll just go in and keep the fire going. Soon he must have his silver fungus soup before he goes to sleep."

"Who keeps him company at night?" asked Mannia, while Snow Blossom was inside.

"Oh, it's not certain," said Cassia. "*Taitai* and I take turns at night to keep him company until he goes to sleep, but several days ago when he was not so well, we all sat up the whole night and went to sleep by turns. Sometimes Muskrose comes to relieve Snow Blossom, or sometimes, it is the maid Phoenix, and they sleep in the western room. We rely most upon Snow Blossom and she has never stolen an hour of idleness throughout his sickness."

"Did you hear that?" said Mannia to Snow Blossom when she came back again. "She was praising your good service."

"Is that something worth talking about?" asked Snow Blossom in a matter-of-fact tone. "It is my duty and I am used to it and, besides, he has got to be attended to, and if you see he is not attended to properly by some one else you can't just leave him. If people do not say things behind my back when they see that *Taitai* trusts me and often listens to what I say, I shall be quite satisfied."

"Any time you need help," said Mannia, "come over and ask Little

124

Joy to help you. She is a stupid girl from the country, but she is thoroughly honest and willing to learn. I have a great mind to ask her to come and learn the rules and manners from you if you are willing to teach her."

Snow Blossom thanked her and felt that Mannia was humble and kind. Mannia saw Pingya was tired and said that she must leave, but Pingya said, "*Meimei,* don't go."

Cassia came to the bed and asked if Pingya would have his soup now, but he said, "Ask *Meimei* to stay. If she goes, I will not take anything."

"Mannia," said Cassia, "You had better stay until he has had his soup."

Mannia could not refuse. So again Snow Blossom went to the back room, and Mannia, fascinated by the sound of water and spoons and bowls, followed to help with the preparation. Snow Blossom was too intelligent either to refuse her help or to laugh at her for helping. Mannia let Snow Blossom bring the silver fungus soup out, and when she was still looking round inside, she heard Pingya suddenly cry out, "*Meimei!* where is *Meimei*? Is she gone?"

She rushed out and stood before him.

"If you go, I won't take anything any more," said Pingya.

"*Meimei* is still here," said Cassia. "But she has to go to sleep. She just arrived this afternoon after such a long journey and you ought to allow her to go and rest."

"But you are not going away, are you?" asked Pingya.

"Pingko, ease your mind," Mannia replied. "I am staying at this house. And I will come and see you again."

Thus Mannia soon left, accompanied by Snow Blossom who held the lantern for her to show the way. On the way, Mannia privately thanked Snow Blossom for what she was doing for Pingya and then thought it was foolish of her to have said it, but Snow Blossom, completely won over by Mannia's sweet manner, cheerfully said good night to her.

When Snow Blossom came back, Cassia immediately went over to tell Mrs. Tseng of the last scene and what Pingya had said about not taking anything if Mannia went away. What were they to do? It certainly would not do to let Mannia attend upon Pingya as he desired, nor indeed would Mannia consent to throw aside all rules of etiquette. It was an extremely confusing situation. More and more they thought that a wedding would set everything right, and they decided to consult Mannia's mother about it the next day.

For Mannia, it had been a completely successful meeting. She had been privileged to do more, to say more to Pingya, and to hear more from him about his feelings toward herself than she had ever dared to expect from the first visit. She lay for hours recalling everything she had seen that night, every word he had said, every gesture he had made, one by one.

.·.

Events moved very fast the next morning. Mannia had hardly finished her breakfast and taken a short stroll through that section of the house as far as the vacant land south of the ancestral hall, when a woman servant came to the side door to tell her that Mulan had come to see her, and she hurried in with Little Joy.

Mulan was sitting in the parlor in her court, talking with Mannia's mother. Mulan had changed so much that she could hardly recognize her, for not only was she grown a great deal, but she was dressed more richly than she had ever seen her in Shantung. She seemed so digni- fied, so at home in these surroundings, and she had the easy, pleasant accent and manner of a girl brought up in Peking. She was no longer the refugee child that Mannia had known. The eyes, yes, they were unmistakably Mulan's, and when Mannia came into the room, looking at her full in the face, she was half biting her lip as if, while surveying her friend, she were restraining the impulse to rush to her and embrace her. Mulan, too, was quite as much struck by the change in Mannia. After a wavering moment Mulan burst out: "You predetermined enemy, I almost died thinking of you and waiting for you."

Mulan could assume that jesting vein, but Mannia could not. She merely exclaimed warmly, "Mulan!" She really was half afraid of Mulan's style and manner.

They came close to each other, and Mannia said, "Are you really Mulan?" and seized her hand and led her into her bedroom.

"I heard you had arrived and I could not sleep a wink last night," said Mulan, "and this morning I got up so early to dress that mother asked me if I was going to elope with somebody."

Gradually Mannia recovered from her first fear of Mulan and felt like an elder sister to her once more. Mulan was still shorter than she, and she was the one person in the world to whom she could open her heart. Her presence was a great source of strength and comfort in this new and strange Peking environment. "We have waited a long time to meet, but I never thought we would meet in circumstances like these," said Mannia.

"How is Pingko?" asked Mulan.

Mannia blushed all over, and hesitated before she said, "This morning my mother sent Little Joy to inquire, and Snow Blossom said he had slept well."

"You did not know how afraid we all were last week. . . . You have seen him, haven't you?" asked Mulan, but Mannia remained silent, as if she had not heard.

"Soon we will go in together and see him, shall we?" Mulan went on.

"You have to ask the *Taitai* first. You see in what an embarrassing situation I am. I can not go and see him without permission—that would not be proper and what would people say?"

Cassia burst into the room, crying, "Mulan, your good friend is here at last and I can see that you are happier than if the moon had dropped into your lap from heaven."

Mannia's and Mulan's hands fell apart.

"Cassia *Nainai*," asked Mulan, "I am going in to see Pingko by and by, and may Mannia go in with me? She has come such a long way and you ought to let them see each other."

Cassia was taken by surprise and then burst into such a laugh that both girls were greatly embarrassed.

"I didn't say that I hadn't seen him," explained Mannia, and Mulan turned her eyes suspiciously toward Mannia. "So you have seen each other already!" Smilingly, she asked Cassia again if it was all right for them to go in and see Pingya.

"It must be all right, but we have to let *Taitai* know first. I must go now. *Taitai* is asking Mannia's mother to go over and discuss things."

Mulan's eyes rested on Cassia's retiring figure, and when she was gone, she asked, "What are they going to discuss?"

Eventually, Mannia told her friend what Mrs. Tseng had said to her and what Cassia had said about the *tsunghsi* idea. She told her most of the story of her visit with Pingya but without telling what were to her the really dramatic scenes. She spoke of Sunya's naughtiness, and of Snow Blossom's good service, which was confirmed by Mulan, except that Mulan added that she had heard that Snow Blossom was very much maligned by the other servants as wanting to become Pingya's concubine at some future time. And Mannia told of her strangely beautiful dream and said that the girl in black who had brought charcoal to her during the snow storm in the ancient temple was Mulan. And Mulan wondered greatly at the dream and its meaning. "Who can say but that you and I haven't really awakened from the dream, and we are all dream creatures?"

"At least," said Mannia, "all that has happened in the last twenty-four hours is just like a dream to me."

Hand in hand they went, Mannia and Mulan, to stand before the Goddess of Mercy in the study and they gazed at the statue of pure beauty and asked no questions.

"This statue has fascinated me ever since my eyes lighted upon it yesterday," said Mannia. "It seems to have great powers. I have a mind to burn incense and worship it."

"It is Fukien porcelain of the Ming Dynasty," said Mulan. "It is very unusual to find one of this size. It is a treasure." Mulan moved thoughtfully back toward the bedroom, and then she suddenly turned back, saying, "You are right. Here is a tripod at the corner. We will do it."

She ran out to ask the woman servant to bring some sticks of incense while they carefully moved the porcelain Goddess of Mercy with its hardwood pedestal to a side table against the western wall of the study. Mulan brought some ashes and filled the bronze tripod with them, and when the woman servant came with a red package of incense sticks, she took them and told the servant to go away.

"Shall we renew the oath of sisterhood we made together years ago?" asked Mulan. Mannia agreed eagerly, and they lighted the incense sticks and held them in their hands and bowed three times and placed the sticks on the tripod. Then joining hands, before the eyes of the Goddess, they pledged themselves again as sworn sisters, and that they would be true to each other for life and help each other in adversity and trouble. Silently Mannia said another prayer for the rapid recovery of Pingya and for their united happiness.

Soon the maid, Phoenix, came with Ailien to say that Pingya was changing his dress and that after a while, they could go in and see him.

"Mother is talking to auntie," said Ailien, "about the 'happy event' for sister Mannia and whether they should wait for the grandmother's arrival to celebrate the wedding."

"Is it to be so soon?" asked Mulan, and she turned to congratulate Mannia, but Mannia remained silent.

. .

When they went in to see Pingya, Mannia noticed that the scene had changed. The glamour of the night before had faded; there was not the glow of the lamplight and Pingya looked more gaunt and pale than she had thought him. His breath was short, his voice was weak and halting and his hands and fingers seemed very bony. Mulan asked what medicine he was having, and Snow Blossom replied that it was the same stew, except that thorny bush and magnolia were omitted; that is, he was having rhubarb and saltpeter and licorice, and the rhubarb had to be soaked in wine. She said that last week when he was very ill and talked incoherently in his fever, the Imperial Physician had changed the prescription.

It was a short and more formal visit, the last visit of Mannia before her wedding although Mannia did not then know it. When they went outside, Snow Blossom told Mulan that the wedding would be very soon, for the news had spread incredibly fast among the maidservants. Mannia heard it with perfect composure as if she had been fully prepared for it and even welcomed it.

"I congratulate you, Miss Sun," said Snow Blossom. "Pingya will have one more person to attend to him and my responsibility will be lighter. I hear that it will be in only one or two days."

"*Taitai* was saying," said Phoenix, "that Miss Sun will not be seeing him now until the wedding."

Mulan did not go in to say good morning to Mrs. Tseng because she knew that they were discussing "affairs of grown-up people," so she went back with Mannia to her court, while Phoenix went away with Ailien.

"Tell me," asked Mannia, "What do you think of this illness? Isn't saltpeter what they make gunpowder from?"

"Of course, it is," replied Mulan, who had followed Pingya's case in her talks with the Imperial Physician. "It is used only for substantial fever in the blood and then only in extreme cases, to remedy dry heat in the body and to soften hard formations. It is so powerful that it softens metals and dissolves stones. When there is substantial fever you have to clean the blood with it. But it must be used sparingly, otherwise it injures the system."

"How can that be?" Mannia said, shocked by the idea of a man eating gunpowder. "I still don't understand."

"It is like this," said Mulan. "When there is poison in the body, the poison receives the effect of the purgative, but if there is no poison, then the bodily system itself is injured."

While they were talking Mannia's mother returned looking troubled and excited.

"Mannia, my child," said her mother, and then she stopped. Mulan thought she was in the way, and said, "I am going to see my adopted mother and you, mother and child, can talk together." But Mannia would not let her go, and turning to her mother, she said, "Mulan is like my own sister. Say what you wish to say before her."

Mannia's mother looked at the two girls and felt that her daughter leaned very much upon Mulan for help. She herself was troubled, because, being of the bride's family, she could seek no counsel from the Tsengs, and now she seemed to speak to Mulan more than to her own daughter. "The idea of the Tseng family is to have the wedding in a few days to ward off the evil of Pingya's illness. It will be also easier for Mannia to look after him until he is well. The Tseng family have been very kind to us, and I could not refuse. But I have told them that Mannia herself would have to be consulted, and Auntie Tseng said Man-erh would put her under a great obligation if she consented, and Cassia said she was certain Mannia would be willing, and that the earlier the wedding takes place, the better it will be for Pingya. . . . Mannia, this is an affair affecting your whole life, and I, as the mother, cannot force you. Your father is dead, and I am a woman, and we are in a strange city. How can I bear this great responsibility?" At the thought of her deceased husband, Mrs. Sun wept a little and wiped her eyes with a handkerchief.

Mannia had listened in silence to what her mother was saying, although she knew what was coming. Now she did not weep with her mother, but said without hesitation and simply: "Mother, you decide." This was the same as saying that she was willing.

"When is it to be?" asked Mulan.

"They are thinking of the day after tomorrow," said Mrs. Sun.

"Why, there is not time for all the preparations!"

"We cannot follow the usual customs now. At first they thought they should wait for the grandmother, but she might not be here until a week hence, and they decided it would be better to hurry the wedding. We are not going to let the friends and relatives know, nor have the usual celebrations and dinners; and, since we are strangers and practically guests here, *Taitai* said they would undertake all the arrangements. In such a large family, with plenty of money and so many servants, it would not be difficult to get things done. I am all lost and do not know what to do."

"I have an idea," said Mulan. "A wedding after all is a wedding and should not be too casual. It would not look well to marry Mannia into the Tseng family by having her go into the red sedan chair in one court and carrying her to another. After all, Mannia is a bride now and should not stay in the Tseng home. She is like my own sister, and I have already had the idea of inviting her to stay in our home for a few days and told it to my mother, and she said she would be delighted to have you. Now I should love to have you both mother and child come and stay with us and start for the wedding from our home. My parents would be very glad. If you don't think our place unworthy, I shall tell my parents and they will send for you this afternoon."

Both Mannia and her mother were pleased by the idea, and the mother said, "Mannia, what do you think? People are so kind to us."

"I am only afraid of going about and troubling others," said Mannia. "*Meimei,* I want also to see your home. I only saw your father years ago, and have never met your family. But how can we impose this upon you?"

"Don't talk so," said Mulan. "My sister Mochow also wishes very much to see you. She wanted at first to come with me this morning, but I said you had just arrived. My father and mother wish to invite you both to dinner tonight. We were so excited I didn't tell you about it." To Mannia's mother, she repeated the request and added, "Auntie Sun, you must not refuse. I want Mannia with me a few nights before she becomes somebody's bride. You will see that Auntie Tseng will approve of the idea. Really, there is no better way. We and the Tseng family are like one family, and as this wedding is not to be announced to other friends it will be strictly a matter among ourselves. Nor will the Tseng family be afraid that we will secretly let the bride run away."

"You see, mother, how well this sister of mine talks," said Mannia.

So Mulan went to see Mrs. Tseng who thought it a very good idea. And Mulan returned to say good-by to Mannia and her mother, saying she would come in the afternoon to take them to her home.

CHAPTER IX

THANKS to Mulan, the wedding of Mannia was more like a wedding than it might have been. No announcements were sent to friends and relatives and none but Mulan's family and one other family, the News, came to know about it. To those who learned of it afterward, Mr. and Mrs. Tseng apologized on the ground that the bridegroom was ill and no dinners were given. Still the fact that the bride was living in a different house made it possible to have the form of a bridal procession and have the exchange of gifts made with some show of formality.

Mulan came in the afternoon in a carriage accompanied by her sister Mochow and her mother's own maid Bluehaze. Mrs. Tseng accompanied Mrs. Sun to the very gate and Cassia accompanied Mannia. The maids and servants of the whole household turned out to see Mannia, and she felt she was already being stared at as a bride.

At the gate, Mrs. Tseng profoundly thanked Mrs. Sun, for now they were in the relationship of parents of bride and groom, besides their old relationship as cousins-in-law. Mrs. Tseng apologized beforehand for any deficiencies in the hasty arrangements and said that they were unfair to Mannia in having such a hasty wedding, but that she would make up for it in future, and Mannia would be the eldest daughter-in-law of the family, no matter what happened.

Cassia said to Mulan and Mochow at parting, "We are entrusting the bride to you. If she disappears, I will catch one of you to fill the bride's place."

"That might be all right for you, but it is a question whether it would be all right for Pingya," retorted Mulan, and laughingly seized Mannia's hand and led her into the carriage. Mannia jerked her hand away and got in silently.

"I love you and I hate you," she said, as they were seated and the carriage rolled off. The maid, Little Joy, was riding with them while Mochow went in the other carriage with Mrs. Sun and Bluehaze.

"There are substitutes for some things," said Mulan. "But there is no substitute for the Star of Salvation in one's fate." Mannia did not know how to retort and said, "*Meimei,* are you really making fun of me? Why does your tongue never rot?"

"What unlucky words for a bride to say!" said Mulan.

"I think your sister Mochow is more simple and honest than you are," said Mannia.

"It is true," said Mulan. "She is a better girl than I am. I had rather be a boy, but she, never!"

Little Joy thought she ought to say something, and she said, "It seems to me Mrs. Tseng and Cassia need have no worry. How could my mistress want to run away? If she ran away she would run back to the Tseng house, wouldn't she?"

Mulan burst into laughter. "There's a simple and honest girl for you! It was I who was not simple and honest. If you run away, I am sure your little feet will carry you back *tock, tock, tock* to the Tseng home even in your dreams!"

Mannia was at first ready to laugh at Little Joy's simple remark, but she was exasperated at what Mulan said, and she bit her lips and said, "None of you is simple and honest. I won't talk with you."

Mulan brought out the jade peach which Mannia had given her and which she wore suspended at her breast inside her jacket and said, "Good Sister, forgive me this time. I only want to make you happy." She pressed Mannia's hand and said, "Why are you so beautiful when you are displeased?" For Mulan desperately admired Mannia's beauty, her small mouth and her bright fawnlike eyes. Mannia pressed her hand in return, and said, "I thought you were the little girl in black who brought charcoal in snow, but you are adding fuel to the fire."

"What a good couplet! The tones are perfectly balanced," said Mulan, and they both smiled.

. . .

Mannia and her mother were put in Mr. Yao's study, and Mulan's father for the time being slept in her mother's room.

While the front of the Yao house was unpretentious, it was only a subterfuge to hide the luxury within. The house in no way compared with the Tseng mansion in grandeur, yet it was solid, well-proportioned, and exquisitely furnished and had none of the features of shabby gentility. Mannia began to understand the atmosphere from which Mulan derived her style and self-confidence. The ceilings, the woodwork, the hangings, the beddings, the curio cabinets, the scrolls, the low hardwood tables, the flower stands with gnarled roots, and the many little objects of fine workmanship and beauty of design, obviously but so beautifully superfluous, testified to their ease and comfort. Although Mannia had no idea how much an old vase or a little jade seal was worth, the feeling of the Yaos' wealth was a kind of barrier between her and Mulan, and she wished that either she had been born as rich as Mulan, or Mulan born as poor as herself.

The study consisted of three rooms, a room being in Peking a standard unit of width in a house; the eastern end was an enclosed bedroom, while the other two rooms were actually one large room separated by a fretwork partition. At the back of the central room stood a hardwood screen, six or seven feet wide, concealing the back entrance. It was of an inlaid Sung palace design, with curved roofs of towers reaching into the clouds, and wild geese flying against distant hills in the background, and palace women with high coiffures and low-necked dresses in the towers playing flutes or standing on a covered terrace looking at fish swimming amidst lotus flowers in the foreground. The whole was in a delicate design of translucent white, green, and pink against the black varnish background, and the inlaid pieces were of amethyst, carnelian, and pink tourmaline for the ladies' dresses, moss-green jadeite for the lotus leaves, rose-tipped for the lotus flowers, and mother-of-pearl for the fish scintillating in the water, while on the right side of the screen was a mass of cream-colored soapstone for the tassels of the rushes on the bank, signifying autumn, with the rushes bent in such a way that one could almost feel the cold autumn air. This screen was like a man's dream of happiness on earth.

Somehow Mannia found a different atmosphere in Mulan's home, in which she could act and behave more freely than in the Tseng home. It was more a woman's place. Mulan's mother seemed to rule the place, and next to her was Coral, the widowed adopted sister. Mulan's younger brother Afei was a child of six; Tijen, her elder brother, did not count and was always absent from home; there were only Coral and Mochow. In the second place, there was not the feeling of constraint between parents and children, and it was a shock to Mannia to see Mr. Yao joking with his children and chatting familiarly with Coral.

Mrs. Yao was a more assertive character than the cultured and

134

physically small Mrs. Tseng, but Mr. Yao seemed to be perfectly contented to rule by not ruling, in accordance with his Taoist philosophy, to let Mrs. Yao take care of the house and home, while insisting on certain rights of his own, which included undermining the discipline of his wife over the children. Thus he let his wife imagine she was the master, while Mrs. Tseng let her husband imagine he was the master. Actually Mr. Yao had more influence over his children than his wife did, and so had Mrs. Tseng over her children as against her husband. Such is the interplay of personalities in a close household that no one is actually master, but it was true that in the old family life, the men always played a ridiculously insignificant role, whether it was like that of the Yaos or like that of the Tsengs.

The excitement of living in the new environment and meeting Coral and Mochow and Mrs. Yao made Mannia almost forget her situation, and Pingya seemed far away. When Mannia and her mother were finally left alone in their room for rest, a maid brought in a bowl of chicken soup cooked with *tangkuei* especially for the bride. Mannia had finished it and taken off her ornaments and was in her room when Lotung lifted the screen and announced that Tsiang, the Imperial Physician, had come. Lotung, who had just come back from an errand, had not known that Mannia's party had arrived and had shown the doctor to Mr. Yao's study. On hearing the name of the Imperial Physician, Mannia came out, and mistaking her for a maidservant, the doctor asked where Mr. Yao was. Mannia replied that he was inside, but it puzzled the doctor that she remained standing in the room. If she were a guest she would not have come out, and if she were a maid she should have gone in to announce his arrival. He felt that probably she was a guest and not a maid, and avoided talking with her by going to the western end of the room, and sitting down pretending not to see anything. But in a moment, he was conscious that the young girl was coming toward him.

"Imperial doctor," she said, "may I ask you a question?"

He looked up through his spectacles in amazement, at a beautiful face which he had never seen before in this house.

"Certainly," he said in his professional manner. "Is any one ill here?"

"No, it is about the son of the Tseng family."

The old doctor was greatly puzzled. He knew that the bride-to-be had arrived in Peking, but she was staying with the Tsengs. Was this after all a maid or some one in love with Pingya?

"How is he and will he get well?" Mannia went on.

"He is making good progress. Probably he will recover now."

"Do you think so?" asked Mannia, and her voice quivered. Such a concern about the sick boy was not exactly good form. The doctor liked talking to a pretty face, and he said, with the idea of testing her, "A case like this half depends on men and half depends on Heaven. It half depends on the power of medicine and half upon the patient's vitality. He has been sick for so long." Then noticing that the girl winced at the remark, he had a queer feeling that he might be talking to the bride herself.

"Are you a relative?" he asked, smiling.

Mannia blushed and hesitated and said, "Er—yes."

At that moment, Lotung came in to serve tea and was astonished to find the young girl talking with the old doctor.

"Aren't you Miss Sun?" he asked. "So you have arrived, and I didn't know! I congratulate you."

The doctor stood up, excited. "So you are Miss Sun!" he said. "We were waiting for you like waiting for the moon from heaven. Now that you have come, your elder cousin will get well. You are better than any physician. Isn't it only a few days before the wedding?"

Mannia was embarrassed and did not know what to do and called to her mother, "Doctor Tsiang is here," and then she slipped into her own room as a fish dives into the depths of a pond.

...

Coral and Mulan and her sister came over early the next morning to discuss with Mannia and her mother the preparations for the wedding. Coral came to pluck the hair on Mannia's face, as was done for every bride, while the others looked on and chatted merrily along. No razor was used, but the fine hair on the girls' face was lifted, or rather screwed off, by means of a coarse cotton thread dipped in water. A loop was made of the thread, held distended by two fingers of the left hand, while one end of the thread was held between Coral's teeth and the other end in her right hand. The place where the threads crossed was laid close to the bride's face, and as the right hand moved, the thread twirled and twisted at the crossing and screwed off the fine hair at its root. Coral was so skillful that Mannia felt no pain at all.

It was unbelievable that they could get the bride's dresses ready and Mrs. Sun was greatly worried. How was Mannia to dress as a bride, what type of bridal headdress and jacket and skirts? How was she to get a dozen new pairs of shoes as part of her daughter's trousseau? What about her jewels and hair ornaments? In how many trunks were her things to go in the procession, and how could she fill them all? How many sets of bedding were to be shown? The groom's family had promised to undertake all arrangements, but what part of all this could they expect from the bridegroom's side?

Soon Mannia's bedroom was like a jeweler's shop, with trays and cases of jade and pearl and gold ornaments, for Mulan and her sisters were selecting wedding presents for the bride. Mannia had very little jewelry of her own and she never dreamed of all this. Much less did she expect to find Mulan's family so generous towards her. Mulan and Mochow each gave her a pair of earrings and a gold hair brooch, inlaid with pearls. One pair of earrings was of old silver inlaid with sky-blue kingfisher's feathers, and one was of old gold in a heavy, intricate design of solid gold rings cleverly arranged and interlocked. Coral also gave her a hair brooch of pearls tied into the form of the mystic knot on a kingfisher blue background, as token of a beginning friendship. They were sure that the bracelets would be provided by the bridegroom's family. Everybody came to lunch after this as pleasantly exhausted as if they had attended a theater, and Mannia felt for the first time like a member of a rich family.

After lunch, Cassia came bringing her daughters with her, and accompanied by her maid Muskrose and a manservant, who brought four brand new gold-sprinkled red leather trunks with shining copper locks. These were the gifts of the bridegroom's family.

"Our *Taitai* says that everything is incomplete owing to the hurry," said Cassia, "but the important thing is the bride's own outfit. The rest can be made up gradually."

She took out of her jacket a package of silver and turned it over to the bride's mother and said this was the *menpao,* or presents of silver for the servants of the bride's family which in this case meant the servants of the Yaos. Next she gave a red envelope containing a bank check for six hundred taels, which constituted the *pingli,* usually given months before the wedding by the bridegroom's family for the bride to buy her trousseau with, apart from the actual dresses. Then she asked Muskrose to untie a red scarf which covered a toilet case with drawers. This was opened, and Cassia took out jewelry and hair decorations in the presence of Mrs. Yao and Mrs. Sun. Cassia was being received in the inner main hall, and Mannia had hidden herself in her own court, but Mulan flew over to bring her out to see the jewels. These included a pair of solid gold bracelets and a pair of bright green jade bracelets of extreme luster; a ring of diamond, a ring of Persian turquoise, a ring of sapphire, and a ring of beryl; an exquisite pair of earrings of small pear-shaped, brilliant rubies; a pair of "pearl flowers" for hair decoration, and a jade hair brooch, with carving in fine relief of two entwined hearts; and a pair of small gold anklets with tiny, jingling bells. This was considerably more than was usual for the bridegroom's family to present to the bride, but it was understood that Mannia's mother as a guest in the city was unable to provide all for the bride.

Then in a special red cardboard box was the bride's diadem of small pearls and an ornament of pearls mixed with small emeralds, in the design of the Great Dipper constellation, with down-hanging strings of colored stones. There was also a jade *juyi,* a purely ornamental but important formal wedding gift, usually placed on the table for display as a symbol of good luck, although the original purpose of the queer-shaped *juyi* was obscure, it being too cumbersome even to serve as a baton for giving directions. And in the trunks were the bridal jacket in Chinese red silk with fine-colored embroidery of twin lotus flowers, a bridal shoulderpiece of varicolored cloud design, and a deep navy-blue "hundred-pleated" satin skirt with a simple but wide embroidered trimming in undulating waves, broad lines of pale green alternating with blue. There was also a new dress for Little Joy. The toilet case, the *juyi,* and the trunks would usually be carried through the streets in open exhibit cases specially made for the purpose of a wedding procession, but they had arrived in this manner because Mr. and Mrs. Tseng were anxious to keep the wedding a secret for the time being.

But Mannia's happiness did not last long. Leaving her mother to attend to the gifts, she slipped away with Ailien to her own room, saying she would show her the gifts of Mulan and Mochow.

"How is Pingya?" she asked the little girl.

"I hear he is not very well today. This morning *Taitai* hurriedly sent for the physician."

"What did the physician say?"

"I don't know," said Ailien.

Cassia was discussing arrangements with Mannia's mother and Mrs. Yao. The time of the wedding was to be about five o'clock the following afternoon. Coral and Mrs. Yao decided that as the bride was not tall, the best coiffure would be that known as "encircling dragons" consisting of intertwining multiple coils on top of the head. Little Joy was to accompany the bride as her personal maid, with Snow Blossom assisting. Then came the question of the bride's mother, and her part during the wedding.

"I think in this case, all usual rules can be put aside," said Cassia. "The bride's mother can come along."

"How can that be?" said Coral. "Mrs. Sun as the bride's mother is not supposed even to be in the bridegroom's home at all."

"But they are relatives and are only adding a new relationship to an old one. We should do whatever is best for the bride," said Mulan.

"But certainly you don't mean the bride's own mother is going to conduct the bride out of her sedan chair on arrival," said Mochow.

"What Mochow says is right," said Mrs. Sun. "I think I have to be there, and if I stay over here my mind will not be at ease. But I have this idea: Mannia's wedding still lacks a formal go-between, and there is no better person than Mrs. Yao, and she can accompany and guide Mannia at the ceremony."

"I shall be delighted to do it," said Mulan's mother. "As for Mrs. Sun, we don't know really how many days it is possible for her to stay away. It depends also on how well the bridegroom is progressing."

"How is he now?" asked Mannia's mother, and everyone waited anxiously for the answer.

"Not so well," Cassia slowly replied, anxious not to deceive them and yet not to cause them undue worry. "Last night he could not sleep, and this morning he complained of dry throat. His eyes were dull, and we sent for the doctor to see him."

Silence fell upon them, and Cassia added. "But it is best not to let Mannia know about it."

"I think we will not stand on ceremony at such a time," said Mannia's mother. "I should accompany her. We had better get Mannia's own opinion."

Little Joy was sent to bring Mannia in and when she came, her eyes slightly red, no one mentioned the topic of Pingya's illness again. It was Mannia's opinion that her mother should accomany her, if not with the procession, at least separately.

"After all you are relatives," said Mulan's mother. "Whatever is natural is good form."

Thus the matter was settled.

Throughout that afternoon Mannia was pensive. In this conflict of emotions and incongruous events and anticipation she felt more than ever that she was playing a role at the command of Destiny itself, knowing that she could not do otherwise and welcoming what to-morrow had in store for her. She had forgotten all about the jewels. The picture of the wedding had been completely altered in her mind, and it seemed to her she was going on duty as a nurse, rather than as a bride. But if she was not excited as a bride might be, she was also not afraid.

That night Mulan insisted that Mannia sleep with her in her own room, and in bed the bride said to her:

"*Meimei,* you have done so much for me this time. Without you and your parents, my mother and I would be all lost. Who would not want to have a grand wedding? But this time the forms must be laid aside, and thoughts of happiness must wait. Do you think I am going to be dressed up like a doll for three days, like a regular bride to be stared at and to amuse people? The minute I am married I shall change from the bridal outfit and attend to him and serve his soup and medicines. That was why I wanted my mother to be near, and I have thought that we two and Snow Blossom and Little Joy can take turns watching him at night. If he gets well, there will be time for happiness. If he does not get well, I shall burn incense and say prayers for him and eat only vegetarian food and embroider Buddhas until the end of my days, and the parents will certainly not let me starve."

And Mulan, who had never heard of anything so amazing from the lips of a bride, greatly admired her.

. .

The next day, May the twenty-fifth, was Mannia's wedding day. While her mother was getting things ready with the assistance of Coral and Mulan, and they were waiting for the sedan chairs to come at the proper hour, the Tseng house was in a great turmoil. There were a thousand things to prepare for the bride, and red sashes and colored festoons of silk and big lanterns to be hung up, and the bridegroom's rooms to be decorated. Everything had to be new, tables, candle stands, wash basins, spittoons, commodes, even the curtains and bedding on Pingya's bed—practically everything except the bed itself on which he was sleeping. The leeks and mint herbs hung above the door by every family on the Dragon-Boat Festival at the onset of summer, had to be taken down, and red festoons hung in their place above the door and along the door jambs. A disinfection, to drive away evil air, was usually done by burning mint herbs in the house on the Dragon-Boat Festival and children carried beautiful colored silk pendants on their breasts, containing fragrant powder from herbs to ward off disease for the summer, which was the usual season for epidemics. In this way Pingya's room had been fumigated before he was moved in. The idea now however, was to make as great a change of atmosphere in the sick-room as possible, showing everywhere the red color of happiness to drive away any lurking evil air.

On top of all these preparations, Pingya had taken a turn for the worse. He complained that he could not see clearly, and his bowels would not function. His tongue showed a thick coating, and his limbs were cold while he felt hot inside. His pulse was weak and sluggish. The doctor had to press all three fingers on his wrist to feel the pulse beat, and this was a sign the volume of blood was decreasing. Upon the varied nuances of the pulse beats and their undertones, the *yun,* the old doctor relied as the modern doctor relies upon the temperature chart; but it was something finely felt, to be recognized only by experi-ence and impossible to state in figures. Although Pingya's mind was clear, he was too weak to talk, and all morning and afternoon, he lay half-dormant, vaguely conscious that this was his wedding day.

Although there was no sign of a wedding outside, there was an air of gaiety within. All the servants and maids wore new dresses and even Snow Blossom's hair was decorated and she had on earrings. Mr. Tseng did not go to his office and Chinya and Sunya did not go to school, but were sent on shopping errands, including the buying of fire-crackers. There was to be a band of drums and brass pipes in the first court to welcome the bride's arrival, but in Pingya's court there was to be only a band of flutes and stringed instruments. A master of cere-mony and a professional bride's companion were engaged. The bride's companion was to act as the bride's guide and adviser at every step of the complicated ceremonies.

. . .

They had lunch early, as the dressing of the bride's hair and head-dress would take hours. When the sedan chairs arrived, Mannia's bridal diadem was put on and a red silk veil hung before her face which completely hid it from onlookers. Her mother went unofficially a little ahead, and Mulan's mother went in the procession in the sedan chair of the official go-between, and the bride's sedan chair was carefully covered and closed so that she could not see anything in the street or know where she was being carried, nor could any one in the streets see the bride.

At the bridegroom's house, the whole family including the servants waited for the bride's arrival in the first hall. The room was full of women and there were some from the New family, Mr. New being a close fellow-official of Mr. Tseng.

Ailien went to the gate with her little sister Lilien to be on the lookout. Soon she saw the procession coming, preceded by players of drums and brass pipes and bugles. At this, firecrackers were set off, and the little band inside the gate stood ready to play. Long strips of red cloth, three feet wide, had been laid on the bride's path from the gate, through the court and up the steps to the hall. Ailien could not see the bride, but only the bridal chair, enclosed by covers of red velvet embroidered with golden threads. Such a rush of children and women of the neighborhood were following the bridal chair that Ailien and her little sister were almost crowded out.

The bridal chair was carried straight to the second court, where it was lowered, and the bamboo poles were taken out and shorter wooden poles were put in. Mrs. Yao, as the go-between, came out first and was served a cup of *kueiyuan* tea, while the bride remained hidden in the dark chair, hot and dizzy and not knowing where she was. Mrs. Yao was informed that the ceremony would take place in the ancestral hall directly in front of Pingya's court. As it was impossible for the bridegroom to take part in the ceremony, it was deemed desirable to emphasize all the more the ceremonial worship before the ancestral tablets. They had therefore to go round a long way to the ancestral hall, on account of the bridal chair, which had to be carried with the bride in it through a side door, and along various corridors, while the women rushed across by a shorter way, and the neighbors' children were pushed outside.

The crowd of women and maids and children were there long before the bridal chair appeared and stopped before the steps of the hall. The band of chamber music struck up and the master of ceremony, who was wearing a mandarin hat with artificial flowers in golden leaves, shouted a verse of four lines and then chanted: "Let the bride descend from the sedan and lift her steps, step by step, climbing high! *Ching!*"

At this signal, Mrs. Yao and the bride's companion went to the sedan chair and untied the front and taking off the arm rest led the bride out. Mannia, half suffocated with her headdress heavy upon her head, now breathed more easily, but still the red silk was hanging over her head and face and she could see nothing. Supported on the right and left by Mrs. Yao and the bride's companion, she stepped out slowly, her head bent.

She was led up the stone steps while the music played and more fire-crackers were set off. Mulan came close and whispered to her, "*Chieh-chieh,* both my mother and I are here." All that Mannia could see were women's feet on the floor, and she thought she could recognize Mulan's unbound feet.

Mulan was conscious of the eyes of women and girls and maids and boys looking at her. It was one of those situations where the usual restrictions between the sexes broke down and strange men could stare at girls usually secluded, and maidens could look at strangers near at hand. Accordingly, Mulan's every sense was alert. She felt and saw the crowd not only with her eyes, but with her ears, her nose, her skin pores, with every nerve ending on her body. And what Mulan felt, Mochow and every one of the other girls and maids was feeling also. That women's faculty of sensing who is in the room and who is hostile and who is friendly without apparently raising their eyes, which Westerners mysteriously call the "sixth sense," is a perfectly normal function. Women in such situations can hear two persons talking at the same time and take in completely the dress and shoes and earrings of other women from head to foot, in the same way that clever scholars are reputed to be able to read ten lines at one glance on a page. This is why weddings and even funerals are so exciting to women's instincts.

Among the whole crowd, Mulan was most conscious of the eyes of Mrs. New, a square-faced old woman with a narrow, low forehead, a long upper lip, and a wide, sensitive mouth. The whole face had a dominating look and was what is called a "horse face," being proportionately long between the eyes and the mouth. Faces like that are said to belong to able mothers-in-law and administrators such as the Empress Dowager. Men with such "horse faces" are also good administrators, but in women the combination of uncanny sense and practical realism and strong love and hatred often produces a frightening result. Such persons are usually able and pleasant-mannered and smooth, but once they set their minds on acquiring power or money, there is no stopping them. How many palace beauties, more beautiful than these, have been outwitted and eliminated, and how many young princes have been murdered by women with such faces!

Mannia had no such enjoyable sense of the company. To her it was one big booming sensation of going somewhere, of performing things beyond her control, yet not without a touch of high solemnity, of sacred resolve, of fulfilling a destiny for which she had been born, a destiny indeed probably fixed in heaven long before she was born. Everything had been inevitable—everything seemed to belong to a high plan in heaven. The rest of the plan not yet unrolled was unclear, but in her mind there were no doubts or perplexities.

The bride's companion came forward and raised a corner of the red silk over the bride's face and, in the absence of the bridegroom, the mother, Mrs. Tseng, held a brand new steelyard wrapped in red paper, and with the end of it gently lifted the red silk from the bride's face. The steelyard with its horizontal beam and sliding weight was used for luck because its name had the meaning of "to have everything according to one's wish." There was a moment of silence through all the company present, followed by quick whispering of admiration, as though a marble statue of perfect beauty had been unveiled.

Mannia kept her head bent and she still felt and moved like an automaton performing what was indicated for her. Her knees bent to the ground without her control when the master of ceremony shouted, "Kneel! Kowtow! Again kowtow! A third time kowtow! Rise! Kneel! Kowtow! Again kowtow! A third time kowtow!" She was vaguely aware that she was doing this before the ancestral tablets, and although she was doing it alone, without the bridegroom, she was not standing in the middle, but a little to the right, with a "knee cushion" on the ground to the left for the absent bridegroom.

It was then that two ceremonial chairs were placed in the center of the hall and the bridegroom's parents were asked to go up and take their seats and receive the obeisance of the bride. Both wore the official mandarin dress and hat and shoes, with squares of colored embroidery of dragons and serpents at the chest, making them look unusually large and dignified, but both were smiling widely. The master of ceremony chanted again for the bride to kneel and kowtow, and Mannia fell on her knees again and kowtowed and was commanded again to rise.

She rose and was told to stand at the west side facing the guests and relatives. As the bridegroom was on his sickbed, the ceremony of mutual obeisances between husband and wife was omitted. She was told to bow low with her hands holding the two sides of the lower ends of her jacket, first toward the go-between, Mrs. Yao, and then toward Cassia and the brothers and sisters-in-law, and they returned the courtesy.

The master of ceremony then chanted flowery, conventional, "lucky" verses to the effect that the couple would live married until a hundred years old and would be blessed with children and grandchildren, like a vine producing whole trailing strings of gourds, and that the bride known as a "new person" was to be escorted to the bridal chamber.

The band struck up again and more firecrackers were let off as the bride, escorted by the bride's companion and followed by Snow Blossom and Little Joy as her personal maids, was led through a door at the back over a marked path of red cloth into the court behind. Thus far, the bride's mother had watched unofficially and now she withdrew to her own court. Mannia went with slow steps through the court where only three days ago, on a quiet evening, everything had been so magical to her. She felt that ages had passed since then.

As she went up the steps a blazing mass of red and gold met her eyes. The walls of the hall were covered with scrolls of red silk with great characters cut out of golden-colored paper; the tables and chairs were covered with embroidered cloth of scarlet; the doors were decorated with red and green festoons; and the floor was covered with red cloth over the carpets. A pair of bright red candles, three feet long, with painted silver characters, stood in silver candle stands upon the central table, flanked by vases and tripods of cloisonné. The candles were lighted although it was still daylight. In the center against the wall hung a red scroll containing a double character three feet high, which consisted of the word *hsi* for "happiness" written double, signifying "united happiness." The smell of sulphur from the firecrackers which filled the air seemed intoxicating to Mannia.

Now while the wedding ceremony was taking place, both Pingya's mother and Cassia had had to come away from Pingya's room, and Snow Blossom also had a little part to play as the bride's personal maid. When the bridal chair arrived, therefore, Snow Blossom, who was beautifully dressed and decorated, had hurried to the front courtyard, leaving a woman servant to attend to Pingya. The moment the bride stepped into Pingya's court, she went ahead to make sure that everything was in order for the bride. Usually the crowd of women guests would rush into the bridal chamber with the bride, but Mrs. Tseng and Cassia had arranged for only a few to go in, explaining to the relatives that too many persons would disturb the bridegroom, although she studiously avoided the word "illness" on that day. First to be admitted of necessity were the bride's companion and Little Joy and Snow Blossom, and it had been agreed that Cassia should go in next and then Mulan and Mochow. But Mulan's mother also insisted on taking the occasion to see Pingya, and was not refused. Mrs. Tseng herself accompanied the other guests to the main third hall where refreshments were served.

Pingya lay in bed covered with new pink quilts. He knew it was his wedding, and was conscious that everything in the room was red and that a pair of tall red candles were burning on the table, the reed wicks in the candles occasionally giving a splutter. The noise of arrangements outside had tired him and they had not even attempted to change his dress since the morning. The arrival of the bridal chair and the playing of the stringed instruments and firing of crackers had waked him from his doze, and Snow Blossom had come in to warn him that the ceremony was beginning and she would be gone for a moment. After ten minutes had passed and nothing had happened, he felt listless and dozed off until he heard the music again, and took some time to realize that he was awake and the music was for his wedding, and wondered how long ago Snow Blossom had gone and how long he had slept, and why the bride still had not come. Then the woman servant came to touch him gently and tell him the bride was coming, and only now he began to be fully awake.

He saw his bride come in with her escorts. Her red bridal veil was off and she could see the room, so transformed that she could hardly recognize it. The bride's companion led her straight to the bedside, for it was the custom to let the bride sit on the bed. Pingya made an effort to move, but Cassia stopped him and he lay back panting. The bride's companion who had many lucky phrases and verses for such occasions at her tongue's tip said something about the blessed harmony of the male and the female phoenix, and said since the mutual obeisances of bride and groom had been dispensed with, the bride should now bow to the groom, and Mannia did so with her hands holding the ends of her bridal jacket. Then she was turned around and seated on the edge of the bed, so that her back was not completely turned toward the bridegroom.

The bride was not supposed to speak, nor could the bridegroom find anything to say. As Mannia sat on the bed, she had a feeling of having reached some end, whatever it might be. Strange to say, she was less afraid than she had thought she would be, now that she had gone through it. She was glad to see in the room only familiar and friendly faces, the most comforting of which was that of Mulan, who was looking full at her and smiling, and she smiled in return. She felt it wonderful that she had stayed in this house before, had seen this room and had known Cassia and Snow Blossom, which made everything less strange to her than it would be to the average bride. Mulan came forward to congratulate the bride and groom, and the others followed.

Mulan's mother asked how the bridegroom was, and Pingya was clear-headed enough to recognize her, and feebly spoke to her by name. Everybody was pleased he spoke it clearly.

"Pingya, I congratulate you on your happiness," said Mulan's mother. "You have such a good bride, and by her luck you will quickly get well."

All this time it had not been proper for Mannia to look at the bridegroom; but now that he had spoken she had an opportunity to glance toward him. She saw lying before her the person who mattered most in her life, and whose quick recovery it was her duty to bring about, and felt strangely at peace and well-rewarded. He was in her hands, and if he did not recover, it would be through no fault of hers.

"Thank you," said Pingya in reply to Mrs. Yao. "When I get up, I shall come and thank you all for the trouble." His arms groped and he said, "Can I sit up a little?"

"You must not," they all cried.

Now it was the custom for bride and groom to have a ceremonial small wine meal together, consisting of a cup of wine and a bowl of pig's heart and other vital parts, so that the couple having eaten it might have the "same heart" or harmony of mind. While other customs could be put aside, this one could not, and the "union of wine cups" was to be performed when the bride and bridegroom were left alone. A low table was therefore brought in by Snow Blossom and put on the bed, and when the preparations were made every one retired. The bride's companion wanted to stay to help, but Cassia told her to come out, and came to tell the bride that this was done for the sake of form and that she should let Ping-erh take only what he could.

After the door was closed upon them Mannia sat for a while now, looking shyly at Pingya. Her heart beat fast but she could not speak. Pingya stretched his hand toward her and she gave her hand to him, and he took it feebly and said, "*Meimei*, henceforth you cannot escape from me."

"I shall not even if you drive me away, Pingko," said Mannia. "I have come to serve you. For my sake you must get well. I will do anything. I can even go without sleep till you are well."

"I am sorry I could not stand up and go through the ceremony with you. You see I am so weak," said Pingya, his voice very thin.

"You should not even think of such a thing," said Mannia.

"Was everything all right?"

"Yes, everything was all right," she replied.

"*Meimei*, it is hard for you."

"You lie quietly and all will be well."

Mannia stood close to him, but there was the table and she was wearing the high headdress, full of pearl hangings and tassels, and she found it very inconvenient to move.

"We must do this," she said, and took up the two cups of wine. She gave one cup to him and said, "Can you hold this?" and he took it, though his hand shook. Mannia took the other cup and touched his quickly, and before he spilled it, she quickly withdrew both cups and put them on the table. For she could not take the wine.

Then she took a spoon and lifted a little slice of the heart and some soup from the bowl and tried to feed him, holding the bowl close to him. But he was lying down and her headdress was heavy, and she could not do it. Her hand shook with excitement, but barely had he taken a little sip when the soup ran out of his mouth, and she hastily tried to put the bowl down, and the soup was spilled on the new quilts. She set the bowl on the low table, and took a towel from the rack over his head to dry his face and neck and then discovered that her own dress also was spoiled.

"Give me just a little bit of the heart," said Pingya.

"That is what I should have done," said Mannia. And she took up a piece with the ivory chopsticks and gave it to him, but Pingya said, "No, you bite it first," and Mannia bit off a little herself and gave the rest to Pingya, and he ate it.

"No one but you shall serve me hereafter," he said.

Thus the wedding ceremony was completed.

CHAPTER X

While the others were sitting in the central room, Mulan took the occcasion to look about the place. Behind the wooden partition of the central room was a narrow strip of a room barely four or five feet deep, connected with the central room by two side doors, and leading into a quiet, stone-paved courtyard with stone benches, a stone table and a pavement of stone slabs. Pots of flowers and dwarf yews on stone stands, and some porcelain stools, shaped like barrels or drums, were set about. Over the wall Mulan saw a very tall tree a hundred yards away in a neighbor's house. It was a beautiful and quiet corner. From this backyard, Mulan looked in through barred windows to the back room behind Pingya's room. There she saw Mannia wiping her dress and said, "Have you finished?" Mannia looked up and saw Mulan and said "Come in." So Mulan went through the narrow rear hall and found that this back room was fitted with a small new bed and new furniture as the bride's own bedroom.

"You have such a beautiful courtyard," said Mulan and wanted to drag her out to see it, but Mannia came only to the threshold and peeped out upon the court that was to become completely her own and where she was to spend so many of her days and evenings.

At this moment Snow Blossom opened a door and asked the bride's companions to go into the other room where noodles and *popo* with the "united happiness" marks were served.

Then she brought in chestnut pudding, noodle soup, *chiaotse,* and "united happiness" *popo* for the young ladies. Mannia declined to eat and Snow Blossom said, "You must eat a little now and for dinner tonight they will send things over to you."

"Isn't she going to be at the wedding dinner tonight?" asked Mulan. "The bride has to present the wine."

"It is true," replied Snow Blossom. "But according to the rules, she has not yet formally 'met' the parents and will not until tomorrow, and

149

she is not supposed to leave the bridal chamber tonight. Usually the wedding feast is given on the third day, but we are doing away with the forms. There are only three tables including the children. It is only the Yao family, the New family, and the Imperial Physician and his wife, and our own family. You are lucky; there will be no teasing the bride tonight, since this is just a family party."

And so Mannia was persuaded to take a bowl of noodles and some *chiaotse* which she loved as all northerners do. The bride's companion now told her to take off her formal dress and said that very soon she would have to change and get ready for the evening.

Mannia heard sounds in Pingya's room and said to Snow Blossom, "He is calling you." Snow Blossom went into the front room to ask what he wanted, and Pingya said in a feeble voice, "I have called to you so many times. Where is the bride?"

Snow Blossom came back quickly, smiling. "The bridegroom is asking for you," she said. "We all deserve death. He called many times and none of us heard until after all the bride heard him."

Mannia therefore went in, and Mulan thought of something and went out to the central room and asked her maid Brocade, "Where is Silverscreen?"

"She said she had stomach-ache and went home immediately after the ceremony," said Brocade.

"Have you seen Tijen?" asked Mulan.

"No. I think he has gone home, too," said Brocade.

Mulan said nothing, but sent word to Mannia that she was going to join her mother, and took Mochow and Brocade with her.

They now went to the inner court where Mrs. Tseng's room was and found the four ladies, her mother, Mannia's mother, Mrs. New, and Mrs. Tsiang talking together, while Cassia was talking with Mrs. New's daughter Suyun, in another corner. The sisters went in and bowed. Mrs. New said, "Mrs. Yao, I congratulate you. How did you bring up two such pretty daughters? It makes one happy to look at them."

"My husband often praises them at home," said the physician's wife. "I have heard that they are both accomplished in household arts and in literary matters, and understand astronomy, geography, mathematics, and medicine, besides sewing, cooking, and embroidery."

"It isn't true," said the girls' mother modestly. "It is all because you and your husband love them and are indulgent toward them."

"Mulan and Mochow, come and let me look at you," said Mrs. New. "Don't they look like the talented beauties that we see on the stage? The family that gets them for daughters-in-law will be lucky. They have such good manners. In these modern times it is difficult to bring up daughters. Even girls go into schools and write essays, and when they come out, they talk of 'free marriage' and learn new ways but they don't know manners. What is the world coming to?"

She spoke in a clear, easy voice and in the tone of one used to ruling, and no one contradicted her. She continued. "As the saying goes, 'stupid girls are virtuous,' and the important things for girls to learn are how to manage a home, serving superiors and controlling inferiors, and giving birth to sons and bringing up daughters. Some of them can study but some of them can't and how can you compel them to study? But now the fashion is changed, they all want to go to school, they all want to study, and when they come back, they marry just the same. All the things they have learned at school are useless. There are lots of people who know only that four fives are twenty and five fives are twenty-five and who still make a lot of money and become high officials."

All this time she was looking closely at Mulan and Mochow, and turning to their mother she said, "You have never bound their feet?"

"It is their father who would not allow it," said Mrs. Yao.

"Unbound feet are coming into fashion," Mrs. New said. "I had Suyun's feet bound at ten, and now she will not have it any more and I have to let it go, because the government has forbidden it. All Chinese girls are going to have big feet like the Manchu girls."

When Suyun heard her mother mention her name, she turned to listen, and her mother commanded, "Come over, Suyun, and talk with the Yao *meimei*."

Suyun rose and came over daintily, as was becoming to the daughter of a high official. She dressed daintily, moved daintily, and talked daintily. She was not pert and saucy, but superior and reserved; not wanting in feminine charm, but somewhat overrefined and conscious of it; in short, she was the product of an artificial society. She had a way of holding her perfumed handkerchief to her nose as if she thought that she might be contaminated at any moment by the company. Somehow she suggested one of the favorite poses of the ancient beauty Hsishih—either having a heartache or having a toothache, but in any case showing the famous "knitted brow."

The ladies were comparing the girls' feet. Each of Suyun's feet had an awkward hump above the arch, because they had once been bound, but they were also smaller than the others. One of the things that made Mulan dissatisfied with herself was that she had rather large feet.

"Miss Yao's feet are bigger and better," said Suyun. "No matter how I unbind mine now and try to make them bigger, they won't grow big enough."

"Don't say so," remarked Mulan. "Even among unbound feet, the smaller ones are the better."

That was Suyun's first triumph over Mulan. Suyun knew she had triumphed but Mulan did not know it yet. Suyun went on:

"I was at Vice-Minister Tan's home yesterday, and the eldest Miss Tan was also having her feet unbound, and she said the daughters of the Vice-Director Hsu of the Military Training Headquarters were also letting their feet alone." The official titles rolled off Suyun's lips like well-greased water-wheels. Mulan did not know the daughters of officials and could not say anything about them. This was Suyun's second triumph over Mulan.

Still, Mulan rather liked and admired Suyun for she liked a pretty girl when she saw one. It was her sister Mochow who was more practical and who saw that this was snobbery and later, at home, told Mulan she did not like Suyun a bit.

. .

Mrs. New had that clairvoyant sense of fact and situation which some women possess. Perhaps it was merely the clear thinking of a mind that knew what it wanted, simply and definitely, without being embarrassed by details. She was now calculating the future of the young people in the three families, the Tsengs, the Yaos, and her own. She had two sons, Huaiyu, nineteen, and Tungyu, seventeen. Huaiyu was already engaged to a girl of a Chen family. Tungyu was still young, and her scheming mind hoped to make a more important alliance for him with an official family. The Yaos were not officials. She desired, however, a match with the Tsengs, and there was her daughter Suyun, who was fifteen and who might marry either Chinya or Sunya. She knew of the close relationship between Mulan and the Tseng family, and that probably Mulan would marry one of the boys. In that light she paid great attention to Mulan and mentally surveyed the characters of Chinya and Sunya.

Ordinary people would perhaps choose the younger and more active Sunya, but Mrs. New was not ordinary. She wanted a son-in-law who would be an official, and she knew exactly the qualities that made an official, which were completely different from the qualities that made a man. As matters were in those days, a good man could not be an official; an active man could not be an official; an impatient man could not be an official; an honest man could not be an official; a scholarly man could not be an official; a too intelligent man could not be an official; a sensitive or conscientious man could not be an official; a man with too much courage could not be an official. Officialdom, even the corrupt mandarinate of those times, was not of one pattern, because officialdom drew from too many sources, being like a sea into which were dumped all the children of official families and all who could not make a living otherwise, and there were naturally some who were honest, some who were scholarly, some who were active and some who were conscientious. But, in this big "sea of officialdom," as we say, there were many winds and waves, and some sank and some swam, and only those who had a combination of active spirit and intelligence, plus a touch of ruthlessness, rode on the tides of success. Among the myriads who filled the posts of bureaucracy, a man who was neither too honest, nor too impatient, nor too desirous of getting things done or getting things changed, nor too sensitive or too conscientious and who was backed by good connections, was fairly sure to have a successful career.

Now Chinya was normally intelligent, normally educated, normally tame and conservative, but he was of the quiet and cautious type and he had the great virtue of timidity which would ensure that he would not get into trouble, while Sunya was too frank and open and headlong. Chinya was by temperament inclined to draw back and his severe father had beaten all courage out of him, while Sunya had been left untamed and unshaped because he was the youngest boy. Mrs. New's final judgment was that with her own official backing, Chinya would be a safe prospect for a good official career, while Sunya would be unpredictable and might have those original ideas which the orthodox gentry so dreaded. So her heart warmed toward the quiet and cautious Chinya.

Mrs. New was not a cynic, but only an ambitious, practical, and able woman, profiting from her real knowledge. Had she not only trained her husband but also pushed him forward and got him job after job?

153

Was he not a harmless, stingless common fellow? Had she not amassed a fortune for him? Was she not because of this the talk of Peking? Would her husband dare to pretend before her that his being Finance Minister was not entirely and absolutely due to her connection with Madame Wang, who was her first cousin and wife of one of the Grand Councilors? Her husband's name "New" meant "ox" and her own family name was "Ma" or "horse," and there were ballads current at the Peking tea houses linking their names and satirizing the Finance Minister for his rapacity. One of them in four-word lines was as follows:

> Huang niu pien t'i,
> Pai ma to to
> Niu ma ch'i o,
> Pohsing peng huo.

> The yellow ox has cloven hoofs,
> The white horse goes trot-trot.
> Ox and horse yoked are together,
> Woe to the people's lot!

Mrs. New had a nickname *"Ma Tsupo,"* this being the name of a Zen-Buddhist saint and meaning all-powerful "Grandma Horse." As the connotation was slightly complimentary, people came to speak of her as *"Ma Tsupo"* sometimes in her presence, and she secretly rather liked it. Mr. New was pleasantly called by his friends, "New the God of Wealth." In this connection there was another ballad which was not so complimentary, about the ox eating cash from the "money tree" which filled its big belly.

> Hao niu pu ta hou yuanti;
> Hao ma pu ch'ih mench'ien ts'ao.
> Yaoch'ienshu hsia
> Ch'ih ko tup'i pao.

> Good ox won't trample its own back yard,
> Good horse won't graze before its own front door.
> But under the golden money tree,
> They lick the gold up from the floor.

The "money tree" was a tree whose branches consisted of strings of cash, and whose fruits were round pieces of gold, hanging down like strings of elm-seeds. All one has to do is to shake the money tree, and the gold rains down on the ground to be picked up.

. ∴.

At about this time, the ladies heard that His Excellency New had arrived for the wedding dinner. He came with his usual pomp, bringing four sedan-chair carriers and eight guards, all of whom had to be fed and tipped. Mr. Tseng received him in the front hall where Mulan's father and Tsiang, the Imperial Physician, were. They bowed in the official fashion, with "His Excellency" this and "His Excellency" that, and Mulan's father endured it.

Now Mr. New had not at first understood his own rise to power. He was made by his wife before he knew it. His face was a lump of flesh, and not very good flesh at that, but since his rise the Peking astrologers had held it up as an example of a "face of luck." It was true, according to the philosophy of fortune telling, that fatness meant good temper and therefore meant luck as a general principle. But in this case, it was not simply a face of jovial good temper; it was not even an intelligently sensuous face, but showed the stamp of mediocrity and the mark of greed.

He was of an old Chinese banking family owning money shops in Peking and Tientsin. In the middle of the century the Chinese system of imperial examinations and civil service had begun to collapse, and academic degrees and titles could be bought at a definite price, especially on occasions of floods and famines when the government wanted to raise money. Thus Mr. New had bought a *chujen* degree and through further "contributions" to a powerful eunuch, was made Chief Quartermaster of the Ministry of War in charge of purchases of food and material for the army. The investment proved a very good one and paid him high returns, and with Mrs. New's relationship with her cousin who was the wife of a Grand Councilor, his record thereafter was one of smooth sailing in the sea of officialdom.

Mr. New therefore acquired self-confidence and tended to assume airs before everybody except his wife, who was one year older than he. He convinced himself that he was not stupid and mediocre, and he did this by lecturing others, especially inferior officials, who smiled and joked about him behind his back, but were extremely courteous, even obsequious, in his presence, because they knew he liked it. This in turn increased his confidence in himself. He had instituted a taboo in his household, so that the servants who always talked against their master behind his back, never spoke in his presence the word *"niu"* for "ox" or "cow." There were alleys in Peking which had queer names; there were an Ox-Tail Alley and an Ox-Hair Court and one of the sycophant secretaries in his household had started the fashion of calling the Ox-Hair Court "Minister's Court," or "His Excellency's Court" and His Excellency had approved. But this was a dangerous precedent, and one of the servants in the New Family jokingly suggested that Ox-Tail Alley should also be called His Excellency's-Tail Alley, which would be ridiculous, and cow's milk should be called "His Excellency's milk," which would be worse.

As for the rest, Mr. New was a generally respected minister now, so far as appearances went. Left alone, he was not a bad fellow. Only the curious pried into his origins. While he was running the Finance Ministry, Mrs. New ran his money shops, which had grown tremendously and were in fact a legal channel for accepting deposits as bribes. And no one publicly inveighed against official corruption more complacently than Mr. New himself. Mr. New had also acquired some polished literary phrases, a very necessary accomplishment for official intercourse. But once in a while he would make a slip. There is a certain phrase of eulogy, "a stork standing among a group of hens," meaning a person distinguished in talent and beauty among his fellows. It is a fine-sounding phrase, and once Mr. New, while making a public speech, used it mistakenly for a phrase of modesty about himself, beginning thus, "I have the honor of being in your midst, like a stork standing in a group of hens. . . ." The few who perceived the error refrained from laughing out loud, and Mr. New was not conscious of it. But whispers went round after the speech, and it became a standing joke in Peking officialdom.

Mr. New, like Mr. Tseng, was from Shantung and knew Yuan Shihkai. It was he who had introduced his fellow-provincial to Yuan, who was then rising rapidly to become probably the most important Chinese official in the Manchu Government, holding real military power with his "new army." Through this connection Mr. Tseng was appointed Vice-Director of the Government Telegraphs, and thus there was a deep tie of obligations between the two families.

. .

So that night the party sat down to the wedding dinner.

156

Three tables were set in the banquet hall in the third court, which was decorated with the scrolls of red silk presented by the Yaos, the News, and the Imperial Physician. Mulan's maternal uncle, Mr. Feng, joined them just before the dinner hour. Besides the men and women, who mingled on such occasions, there were the boys and girls of the three families. Chinya and the elder New boy sat at the men's table, while Sunya and the younger New boy sat at a separate table with the four girls. At another table sat the women with the small children. Mrs. Sun, as the bride's mother and a close relative, was given the seat of honor. Coral, Mulan's adopted sister, had not come, and Mrs. Yao said that she was not well and someone had to stay at home, since they could not leave the entire house to the servants.

Since this was a feast, although informal, wine was served. While the men talked and drank, Mrs. Tseng profoundly apologized to the ladies for the absence of the bride and her inability to "present wine" to the guests, but she invited them to "see the bride" after the dinner. The physician's wife and Mrs. New, who did not know the bride, were eager to see her. Toasts were drunk to the health of the bride and groom by Mrs. New, and she congratulated Mrs. Tseng and commented on the beauty and manners of the bride. Mrs. Tseng joined in the praise, saying, "This daughter-in-law of mine is loved by all her superiors and inferiors. From childhood, she has been an intelligent and well-behaved girl. I don't mind saying it among ourselves, Mrs. New, although she is my own niece. You see her today all dressed up as a bride and you think she is a beauty dropped down from heaven, but after a while you will find out she is complete in the four virtues of women. I have to thank her parents for bringing her up so well. I only hope Ping-erh has the luck to enjoy it."

There was a moment's silence, for no one wanted to mention illness on that day.

Mannia's mother was touched at the sight of this happiness, and she missed her husband and thought how happy it would make him to see their daughter married into such a good home. Also she had not been able to see her daughter since the ceremony, and could not until the next day, both because she was the bride's mother and because she was a widow, who normally could not enter a bridal chamber. Now at Mrs. Tseng's mention of the bringing up of Mannia by herself and her dead husband, she felt a twitch at her heart and tears welled forth from the corners of her eyes.

Mrs. Tseng and the other ladies instinctively knew why she shed tears, and Cassia said hastily to divert her attention, "I drink a toast to you and guarantee that next year you will be a grandmother, and your grandchild will become a high official, and you will be a grand lady decorated by the Imperial Court," and everybody agreed and laughed.

"I am a useless woman," said Mannia's mother, "and ignorant of the customs of Peking. Even at this wedding, I am not able to do a thing. Everything is done for us, mother and child, by the bridegroom's parents who have been so kind to us. All I do is to leave this piece of my flesh, and hope she will be a dutiful daughter-in-law and not abuse the love of the elders of the family." She wiped her eyes with her fingers.

After dinner, Mannia's mother retired to her court while the party went over to see the bride. Of the men, only Mr. Feng and the Imperial Physician went. The bride had been prepared for this. With the help of the bride's companion and Snow Blossom, she had changed her dress, but was still wearing the bridal headdress. As they were anxious not to disturb the bridegroom, Mannia was to be seen by them in the rear room, which was very small and crowded, and the company being all close friends and relatives, no one tried to joke or make embarrassing remarks to the bride with the usual object of inducing her to smile.

The bride stood still before her bed to be looked at, with the strings of pearls and beads hanging down from her hair, and she was indeed beautiful. Mulan and Mochow went to her side ready to protect her, although she needed no protection.

The doctor went into the front room to see Pingya, and when he returned, he was asked to sit down, but he said, "There is no need. I shall soon be going." He was a soft-voiced old man, with a flowing white beard, and he was now holding in his mouth a pipe two feet long.

"This is the Imperial Physician," said Mulan to Mannia, and then she said to the company, "They two are both the bridegroom's doctors. One cures the body and the other cures the heart."

Mannia blushed when she heard the name of the doctor and remembered the desperate interview she had had with him two days ago, though the others did not know of this.

The company soon went away, leaving in the room only the bride's companion and her two maids, who helped the bride to undress.

When all was ready, the bride's companion said some auspicious words and urged the bride to retire into the bridegroom's room and closed the door behind her.

Mannia was left alone with Pingya. But she found him sleeping, and she was afraid to waken him from the rest that he so needed. She kept silent as she saw that everything was made ready for him for the night. Then she pulled the curtains together about his bed and went into the next room which was her own.

There she sat alone beneath the red candle lights, thinking for a long, long while, of all that had gone before and all that was to come.

CHAPTER XI

WHEN Mulan and her family returned home that night about ten o'clock, her father was angry. He had discovered only at the wedding dinner that his son Tijen had unceremoniously slipped away and absented himself from this important family occasion. On their way back, Mrs. Yao had inadvertently remarked that Silverscreen also had come back, and then had quickly diverted the talk to some other topic. The first thing Mulan's father asked Coral was, "Where is that seed of sin of mine?"

"Don't ask me," answered Coral, shortly. This was a strange answer from Coral, who was seldom in a bad mood and almost never rude.

"What do you mean?" asked Mr. Yao.

"My surname is Hsieh," said Coral, "and I cannot interfere with affairs of this family."

This was unheard of. Coral had been brought up in the Yao family like their own children and they never thought of her as other than their own kin and she was called regularly "Eldest Daughter." Moreover, she was a simple, happy woman with a simple view of life, and it was unlike her to say such a thing.

"What is the matter?" Mulan asked. "Who has offended you?"

"Didn't you yourself offer to stay at home because you said you were unwell?" asked the mother.

"Nobody has offended me," said Coral, trying to smile, and regretting the remark she had made, particularly in the presence of the father.

Mochow nudged Mulan and whispered that Coral's eyes were red. "Somebody has offended you," said Mochow. "It must be Elder Brother."

She felt certain that something had happened, that Tijen had done something wrong.

"Where is that rake of mine?" demanded Mulan's father, again.

"He is sleeping in his room," said Coral.

Mr. Yao walked away with his heavy "tiger steps." Everybody was holding in her palm a handful of perspiration. Brocade, the maid, let an audible giggle escape into the silence, and all the maids, Bluehaze, Brocade, and Frankincense, who were waiting to assist the young ladies and the mother to retire, were told to go to bed. They went, all excited and hoping that there might be some drama soon to see in the household.

When the maids were gone Coral told what had happened. She was having her dinner alone, when the servant said that the young master had returned unwell and was having his food in his own room. She added that Silverscreen also had returned and come in by the western side door.

"You mustn't tell Father about it," said Coral. "But I felt that something was wrong and thought it my duty to see him if he was unwell. So I went over to the eastern side and found him perfectly well, eating his food with Silverscreen serving him. Silverscreen was pinching his ears when I went in, and both were laughing. They thought I didn't know they had returned and they were greatly embarrassed. 'I didn't like the wedding crowd and I came back—and Silverscreen had a headache,' Tijen stammered. I didn't say anything and merely asked them how the wedding was, but I did not leave and sat talking with him, and he gradually got more and more nervous and annoyed. He asked me why I didn't want to retire, and I said I had to wait until you returned to hear all the news and that I was not thinking of sleep. Then he paced about the room, and suddenly a piece of a red embroidery fell from his clothing. I didn't know what it was, and he looked embarrassed and stooped to pick it up and just then Silverscreen disappeared. All of a sudden, he began to lecture me. 'I know your good intentions,' he said. 'But I'll do what I please. I don't want you to interfere with my affairs.' I said I didn't know what I was interfering with. Then he said, 'I call you sister only by courtesy. My surname is Yao and your surname is Hsieh, and this home is my home. You don't have to interfere with my affairs.' I was so taken by surprise and so angry I couldn't reply. I could only come away."

"I shall tell him to apologize to you," said Mulan's mother.

"Don't make a small thing into a big thing," said Coral. "You have been kind to me and I will serve you till your old age. But when you

161

become ancient ones and Mulan and Mochow are married, this will not be my home and I will look after myself."

"Mother," said Mulan, "you cannot allow our brother to bully her like this, and indulging him is not for his own good. Even if we are girls and sooner or later must leave this family, still it is our own home, and I will not allow a Siamese fighting fish to upset a glass bowl of goldfish! If this goes on, what will be the end of this Yao family? I don't believe that only girls ought to be good and boys can be bad. Men and women are equal."

"Mulan!" Her mother cut her short, for this was heresy—learned from modern essays.

"What I know is," said Coral, "Silverscreen is twenty and Tijen is seventeen. This can't go on forever. If in one case out of ten thousand something should happen, it would not be good for the name of the family."

But Mulan only heard her mother say this for the thousandth time, "I hope he will gradually change."

· ·

Silverscreen had come to the household at the age of eleven, being brought from Hangchow by Mulan's uncle. Being three years Tijen's senior, she was assigned to look after the boy and had done so ever since. She was clever, able, and pretty, but there was in her a touch of Ningpo vulgarity and Ningpo audacity. When quarreling with the other maids, she still had the Ningpo habit of pointing to her own nose whenever she said "I."

Bluehaze was a Peking maid with excellent Peking speech and manners and had been sold into the family for eight years' service after Silverscreen came. Brocade and Frankincense were also from the north. Thus Silverscreen was the only southern girl serving in the Yao family, and the northern maids were apt to join together against her. The others had learned to understand the southern dialect, because Mrs. Yao still spoke with a strong Yuyao accent. When Silverscreen talked to the mistress in her dialect, the other maids did not like it. But on the whole she was well-behaved in point of manners and did her own job well, and was fully capable of standing by herself against any northern combination. The Yao children all spoke Pekinese, but Tijen had associated so much with Silverscreen that he contracted from her

162

the Ningpo idiom "ala" for "I," reinforced in time of argument by pointing to the tip of his nose.

When Coral had left Tijen's room he was hoping that Silverscreen would return of her own accord. He was afraid to attract attention by calling her. But she had been frightened away and she was too sensible to come back now. After waiting for a quarter of an hour in vain, Tijen lost his patience. He was used to having his own way. Instead of calling for Silverscreen, he smashed a cup on the floor. An old woman servant, who knew all that was happening, came at the noise and asked him what he wanted. Seeing that it was not Silverscreen, he shouted to the woman to get out, and worked himself up into a frenzy and lay panting on a sofa.

When his father appeared unannounced at his door, Tijen felt as if he were seeing an apparition and his father's eyes had a sharp, direct gaze. In that face there was no smile. Although he was not caught doing anything wrong, he felt the full extent of his guilt under that fiery gaze. He was not studying and he was not sleeping, and Mr. Yao saw that his hair was disheveled and his face gaunt and wild. He came steadily toward his son, demanded to know why he had left the party, and before the boy could reply, gave him a hard slap on the cheek. It was such a powerful boxer's blow that Tijen staggered and collapsed on the sofa. Without a further word, his father turned and walked out.

Tijen suffered both a strained neck and spiritual torment for days afterward, not knowing exactly what the punishment was for, nor if Coral had told the full story. His sisters did not speak to him, his mother was stern and cold toward him, and even Silverscreen, afraid, kept aloof from him.

. ˙.

Thus Mulan did not go to see Mannia until the third day, when the Tsengs' grandmother arrived with Li Yima. A gift from the grandmother was accompanied with a request to see Mulan and she and her sister went to pay their respects. To their surprise, they found Mannia already doing away with all formalities as a bride and attending to Pingya like a wife, with the assistance of Little Joy and Snow Blossom. Pingya seemed to be improving, and Mannia was radiantly beautiful and happy for exactly a week, the happiest week in her life.

Now, the grandmother had brought from Shantung some country-style *tsungtse*. These were solid triangles made of glutinous rice stuffed

163

with ham and pork or black sugar and bean flour, and wrapped in bamboo leaves and steamed. She had these made specially, although the Dragon-Boat Festival was long past, because she knew that her grandchildren and indeed the whole family loved them. Pingya had been fond of the village *tsungtse* ever since his childhood, and at supper of the seventh day after the wedding he wanted them so much that Mannia could not refuse him. She sent Snow Blossom to ask advice from Mrs. Tseng, who said to give him a little only. Mannia gave him half of the sweet pyramid, the size of a man's fist, and kept the other half for herself, but when he had finished, he snatched the other half from her and they struggled a little and then she let him have it. She was pleased that he was so strong as to be able to fight for his food; she begged him, "Pingko, better eat a little less," but he would not listen.

At midnight, he began to complain of pain in his stomach, and the pains grew and Mannia sat beside him all night, thoroughly frightened. By daybreak he was very ill. When she saw the gray light of the dawn coming through the window, she sent Snow Blossom to go and tell his mother. For half an hour after the mother's arrival, Pingya remained conscious and then suddenly he began to sink. The Imperial Physician came and found that his pulse was very feeble. Still Mannia kept up her courage. She placed her mouth against Pingya's nose to blow breath into it and when she saw that he was trying to cough up something which caught in his throat and blocked his breath, she bent over and literally sucked the lump of mucus out of his mouth. If the gods had hearts, they could not have seen such a sight and not have saved him. But the gods were blind or deaf, or on a holiday far away.

Exactly at midday, Pingya died.

Mannia clung to his body, calling, "Pingko, come back," and put her lips to his nostrils again and again to blow her breath into him. Even Pingya's father and mother in their first grief saw that the hopeless, pathetic struggle of the bride was more tragic than the death of the bridegroom.

After a time her grandmother came and with her mother forcibly dragged Mannia from the deathbed and laid her on a bed in the western room, and the grandmother sat over her, and Mulan and Mochow came in with their mother and they all saw now how young and small a girl she still was. But none of them could help her.

"Can it still be true," Mulan thought, "that if you yourself are right, nothing that happens to you can ever be wrong?"

. .

Li Yima had helped to make the *tsungtse*. That night Li Yima added insult to injury by saying in Cassia's hearing that Mannia had brought Pingya bad luck, that it was the bad luck of the Sun family that caused this death to the Tseng family, implying that Pingya died because he had become the son-in-law of a family which was destined to die out. Cassia bluntly charged Li Yima with putting a curse upon the grandmother's family to make it die out. This became known to the grandmother, who was very angry, and from then on Li Yima lost the grandmother's protection and became degraded in the family.

Mulan stayed away from the Tseng house until the laying of the body in the coffin should be over. She heard that Mannia would neither eat nor drink and that she was ill in bed desperate with grief. On the third day, Cassia came to ask permission for Mulan to go over and try to comfort Mannia, since nobody else could.

"Last night," said Cassia, "her mother and I spent the whole night with her, but she would not speak, and when we asked a question she would not answer. Her mother and I talked about it and have come to the conclusion that we must borrow Mulan's company for a few days. The other things we will all attend to, and all we want is for Mulan to keep her company."

Mulan's mother consented and she went with Cassia in her carriage, and Cassia whispered to her that there was another reason for her to come, for vigilant guard should be kept lest Mannia in her despair should seek a "short-sighted way" out, by which she meant suicide. Such martyrdom might be worthy of a poem or perhaps a stone monument, beautiful to be told as a story or recorded in the annals of the district history, but not for the Tsengs, who loved Mannia so much.

This was the first time Mulan had ever had anything directly to do with a funeral and she was afraid of the proximity of a coffin, but when she found that Mannia was in a separate court, she thought she would not mind remaining even at night.

Mannia had been carried to the court where Mulan had seen her on the day of her arrival. How much had passed in these ten or twelve days! Mulan had the feeling that Mannia was the victim of an unknown force, cheated by Some One or Some Thing—she did not know what. Was the Tao a Master of Irony? Mulan wondered.

She found Mannia asleep, with her mother watching over her, and seeing that the mother was tired, she told her to go and take a rest. As she sat watching over the bereaved young bride, an inspiration came to Mulan. Mannia's dream during her first afternoon in that very room became suddenly as clear as daylight to Mulan. The porcelain Goddess of Mercy still stood there, smiling her kind, unfathomable smile. The Goddess was loved because she was the Spirit of Great Kindness and Great Mercy, Saving the Afflicted and Saving the Distressed. It became clear to Mulan that the dark corridor lined with coffins and the coffin panel bridging the ditch over which Mannia had to pass in her dream represented the funeral and mourning for Pingya. But beyond that bridge there was the Palace of Eternal Light, where Mannia would live in peace. As there was Death, so there was Resurrection. Could she bring Mannia to see that?

Mulan took up the Goddess's image, and carried it in her two hands to a table in front of the bed, so that Mannia would see it when she opened her eyes. Mannia had dreamed that she, Mulan, was the girl in black who brought her charcoal in a snowstorm.

She called Little Joy softly and told her to borrow a black dress from Snow Blossom or Phoenix and when it was brought she put it on and sat beside Mannia on the bed.

When Mannia stirred, Mulan said, "*Chiehchieh,* I have brought you charcoal."

Mannia opened her eyes and saw the Goddess of Mercy and the girl in black whom she had seen in her dream.

"Is it you, *Meimei!*" she asked, faintly.

"It is I," said Mulan. "I have come to bring your charcoal in the snowstorm."

"Where am I?" asked Mannia. "Is there snow?" She looked around at the room. "Why am I here?"

"You are in the Tseng Family Temple," said Mulan. "It is snowing outside. You have been dreaming that you were married and a bride, and that your husband Pingya died and when he died you were very miserable. But you see behind this temple there is a corridor and behind the corridor there is a bridge, and behind the bridge of coffin panel, there is a palace. Out there Pingya is waiting for you. Do you remember?"

"*Meimei,* you are deceiving me," said Mannia. "There is no snow outside."

Just then by chance there was a sudden summer shower and the heavy raindrops made a loud patter on the brick pavement of the yard and the water from the roof ran down the lead pipes, with a musical intonation.

Little Joy's voice calling that the washing must be taken in, brought Mannia back to reality.

"No, Pingko is dead!" she said dully.

"I have deceived you and yet I have not," said Mulan. "It is not snowing, but see the beautiful shower."

But over and beyond the sounds of the rain Mannia heard in the distance drums and bells.

"What is that? It is just like the music in the air that I heard a while ago."

"The monks are saying the mass in the other courtyard," said Mulan.

"Pingko is dead! I know it!" Mannia repeated.

Thus Mulan so whimsically mixed dream and reality at Mannia's waking moment that even death lost part of its sting, touched as it was with a sense of dreamlike unreality.

In place of bitterness and complaint against fate, the vision gave Mannia an understanding of the pattern devised by the gods that she was destined to live through, and this acceptance of fate became her salvation. She believed in fate, in the divine dispensation of all things, and in the Goddess of Mercy. Now she half believed that she herself was one of the fairy girl attendants in the Palace of the Goddess of Mercy and that her punishment was for something she must have committed with Pingya in a previous life.

Meanwhile everyone was so kind to her. She was to remain a daughter-in-law of the Tseng house, the house of her husband. For so both men and ghosts wish to live—with their families. Mannia's spirit found a haven in the Tseng home, in this world and the next.

And so on the afternoon of the third day she found voice to wail before the coffin as she should according to custom. When Cassia and Snow Blossom heard her wailing so, they went and told Mrs. Tseng that the worst was now over. And they gave the credit all to Mulan, who by her whim had done something cleverer than she knew.

Once more Mannia was clad in white from the knot on her hair to the shoes on her feet. She had loved the white of mourning ever since her father's funeral, and no color suited her better. In it she had a kind of ghostly beauty. Mourning is sometimes a purely social convention, sometimes an expression of rebellion against the gods, celebrated with defiant pomp and lavishness. Sometimes it is a natural act of love for the deceased, and then it is simple and sincere, and the mourner comes to love the ceremonies as devout Buddhist monks come to love the acts of prayer and singing at divine service. This was not Mannia's first mourning, for she had mourned for her father and her brother, but her mourning for Pingya was different. It was deeply personal and full of a spiritual meaning for her, as she wailed every day before her husband's coffin and lighted the candles on the altar. To Mulan and to the Tseng family, the regularity and devotion of her services was inexpressibly beautiful and dignified.

Mr. Tseng wanted to buy a lot in the South City for their family cemetery, because he thought his family would settle at Peking for good. But the grandmother objected because her husband's grave was in the ancestral burial ground at Tai-an where she herself wanted to be buried. Taking Pingya's remains back to Shantung was out of the question for the present, for Mannia could not stand the voyage. The coffin was therefore removed to the family temple just in front of Pingya's court where it was to lie until spring.

So it was decided that Mannia should stay permanently with her mother in the court where Pingya died, and Snow Blossom and Little Joy were to serve them. Her mother slept in the same room with her, for she was timid after dark, and the white porcelain image of the Goddess of Mercy was put on her bedroom table. Mannia began to incline more and more toward Buddhism. Though she could have everything she wanted, she preferred an austerely simple arrangement of her room. She never touched her jewels again, and kept only the silver candle stands and the beautiful foreign oil lamp that had shone upon her wedding night.

Soon she started a long vegetarian fast for the benefit of her husband's soul, and began to embroider portraits of buddhas and bodhisattvas. It was as if she had taken the vows of a nun while living in a rich private mansion. The court was pure and quiet, secluded from the noise of the world, and she had her pomegranate trees with bright red blossoms, her fish pond, and the stone benches and potted flowers in her courtyard.

What broke the monastic effect of the courtyard that winter was the coming of a baby.

Mr. Tseng was concerned about maintaining the lineage of his eldest son, and his wife secretly asked Mannia's mother to find out whether a child might be expected. In the first month Mannia's period did not come and when she told her mother about it, her mother told Mrs. Tseng, who wanted to believe that her daughter-in-law "had happiness" in her body. But Mannia said to her mother that it was impossible and to Mulan she swore that she was a virgin, and Mulan told her mother, who told Mrs. Tseng, and so the family knew that their hope was vain.

Mrs. Tseng thought that entirely apart from the demands of the family system for a son for Pingya, the nights would be long for the young widow, especially this first winter, and that an adopted baby would occupy Mannia's mind and keep her from brooding. Mr. Tseng therefore wrote to their own clan in Shantung and found there was a little year-old boy whose mother was willing to let him come to Mannia. He was brought to Peking and Mannia loved him and when he was in her hands she felt that she was a mother and was founding a family line for Pingya.

The boy was named Asuan.

CHAPTER XII

AFTER Mannia entered the Tseng family Mulan's visits became much more frequent so that she ceased altogether to be considered a guest in the house. She often stayed for dinner and sometimes for the night, with her mother's permission. There had been as yet no formal talk on the part of the parents about her engagement to either of the Tseng boys because their parents still wished to see her often, which could not be if she were definitely engaged, and she was yet young. But they tacitly assumed that her parents would not engage her to any other young man without speaking to them first. So if Mannia already had both her feet inside the Tseng threshold, Mulan might be considered to have one foot in. The Tsengs could always catch her hind foot if she tried to run away.

Mulan's parents did not know yet exactly what to do with her, especially her father. A Taoist was naturally more liberal-minded than a Confucianist. A Confucianist was always quite sure that he was right, while a Taoist was equally sure that everybody else was right and he himself wrong. So the nonconformist Mr. Yao was liberal toward Western ideas, and even talked about "free marriage" for his daughters—meaning marriage by the boy's or girl's own choice—which fitted very well with the Taoist doctrine of noninterference with nature. He thought the Western idea of trusting a young man's or young girl's marriage to the blind impulse of unadvised youth wonderfully subtle and profound, like Taoism itself. He believed that marriage affairs were destined by heaven and he had not yet "interfered" with even his eldest son's engagement.

Meanwhile Mulan called Mr. and Mrs. Tseng "Father" and "Mother" and called the Tseng boys "Elder Brothers," and Sunya, who was one year her senior was her "Third Brother."

It was now deep winter. Winter in Peking is insurpassable, unless indeed it is surpassed by the other seasons in that blessed city. For

Peking is a city clearly marked by the seasons, each perfect in its own way and each different from the others. In that city, man lives in civilization and yet in nature, where the maximum comforts of the city and the beauties of rural life are perfectly blended and preserved, where, as in the ideal city, man finds both stimulation for his mind and repose for his soul. What great spirit organized this pattern of life so that here at last the ideal of human living should be realized? True, Peking is naturally beautiful, with its lakes and parks inside the city and its girdle of the transparent blue Jade River and its skirt of the purple Western Hills outside. The sky also helps: if the sky were not such a clear deep blue, the water of the Jade Spring could not be such a transparent jade green, nor the slopes of the Western Hills such rich lavender and purple. True, also, the city was planned by a master architect as no other city was ever planned on this earth, with a breadth of human spirit, an understanding of sublimity and grandeur and the amenities of domestic living, paralleled nowhere else. But Peking as a human creation was not the work of any one, rather the joint product of generations of men who had the instinct for beautiful living. Climate, topography, history, folk customs, architecture, and the arts combined to make it the city that it is. The human element in the life of Peking is the great thing. The unmistakable poise and leisurely accent of the speech of a Pekinese boy, girl, man, or woman is sufficient evidence of this human culture and this geniality of life. An accent is but the spiritual voice of a whole people.

Mannia, secluded in her mourning and never venturing outside her courtyard during the half year after Pingya's death, felt rather than saw the Peking atmosphere. She felt the charm of Peking winter, its dry, crisp, cold air and its gloriously clear blue sky, and the provisions for winter comforts inside the house, so different from the dreary winter in Tai-an. When a snowstorm was raging outside, she could keep the potted begonias blooming in her rooms, for the thick padded door-screen, the papered windows, the heavy carpets, and the stove kept the rooms warm and comfortable, and one could work well deep into the night. She had really no use for a sable coat of Pingya's which Mrs. Tseng told her to turn into her own. For the most part, she was making the eight pairs of embroidered shoes which she as a bride should have presented to her mother-in-law on the morning after the wedding, during the formal reception, but which she had not been able to make because of Pingya's illness. These presents to the mother-in-law had to be the bride's own handiwork, being her chance to show off her needlework, as well as a sign of dutifulness, and they could not be slipshod work. Women were happy and proud to wear shoes made by their daughters-in-law since it meant respect for their position and that they had good thrifty daughters-in-law.

But Mulan was a child of Peking. She had grown up there and had drunk in all the richness of life of the city which enveloped its inhabitants like a great mother soft toward all her children's requests, fulfilling all their whims and desires, or like a huge thousand-year-old tree in which the insects making their home in one branch did not know what the insects in the other branch were doing. She had learned from Peking its tolerance, geniality, and urbanity, as we all in our formative years catch something of the city and country we live in. She had grown up with the yellow-roofed palaces and the purple and green-roofed temples, the broad boulevards and the long, crooked alleys, the busy thoroughfares and the quiet districts that were almost rural in their effect; the common man's homes with their inevitable pome-granate trees and jars of goldfish, no less than the rich man's mansions and gardens; the open-air tea houses where men loll on rattan arm-chairs under cypress trees, spending twenty cents for a whole after-noon in summer; the enclosed teashops where in winter men eat steaming-hot mutton fried with onion and drink *pehkan* and where the great rub shoulders with the humble; the wonderful theaters, the beautiful restaurants, the bazaars, the lantern streets and the curio streets; the temple fairs which register the days of the month; the system of poor man's shop credits and poor man's pleasures, the open-air jugglers, magicians, and acrobats of Shihshahai and the cheap operas of Tienchiao; the beauty and variety of the pedlars' street-cries, the tuning forks of itinerant barbers, the drums of second-hand goods dealers working from house to house, the brass bowls of the sellers of iced dark plum drinks, each and every one clanging in the most per-fect rhythm; the pomp of wedding and funeral processions half-a-mile long and official sedan chairs and retinues; the Manchu women con-trasting with the Chinese camel caravans from the Mongolian desert and the Lama priests and Buddhist monks; the public entertainers, sword swallowers and beggars, each pursuing his profession with freedom and an unwritten code of honor sanctioned by century-old custom; the rich humanity of beggars and "beggar kings," thieves and thieves' protectors, mandarins and retired scholars, saints and prostitutes, chaste sing-song artists and profligate widows, monks' kept mistresses and eunuchs' sons, amateur singers and "opera maniacs"; and the hearty and humorous common people.

Mulan's imagination had been keenly stimulated by her childhood in this city. She had learned the famous Peking nursery rhymes with their witty commentary on life. She had, as a child, trailed on the ground beautiful rabbit lanterns on wheels and watched with fascination the fireworks, shadow plays, and Punch-and-Judy shows. She had listened to blind minstrel singers telling of ancient heroes and lovers, and "big-drum" storytellers by whom the beauty of the Pekinese language was brought to perfection of sound and rhythm and artistry. From these monologue declamations she had first realized the beauty of language, and from every day conversations she had unconsciously learned that quiet, unperturbed, and soothing style of Pekinese conversation. She had learned through the annual festivals the meaning of spring, summer, autumn, and winter, a system of festivals which regulates life like a calendar from the beginning to the end of the year, and enables man to live in close touch with the year's rhythm and with nature. She had absorbed the imperial glamour of the Forbidden City and ancient institutions of learning, the religious glamour of Buddhist, Taoist, Tibetan, and Mohammedan temples and their rites and ceremonies and the Confucian Temple of Heaven and Altar of Heaven; the social and domestic glamour of rich homes and parties and exchange of presents; and the historic glamour of ancient pagodas, bridges, towers, archways, queens' tombs, and poets' residences, where every brick was fraught with legend, history, and mystery.

She also early began to learn the rich Peking folklore, with its gods and superstitions, and its beauty. Two legends especially she loved and believed in and later told to Mannia. One was that of the big copper bell at the Bell Tower north of the Palaces. The master of the foundry had failed in several attempts at casting the copper bell and was threatened with punishment by the Emperor. To save her father's life, the daughter leaped into the pot of molten copper, when no one was watching, and then the bell was cast without a crack. Hence on windy or rainy nights one could hear in the bell's notes a plaintive whine which was the song of the soul of the bell caster's daughter, and now she was worshiped in the Bell Mistress's Temple near by, and known as the "Holy Mother of the Bell." The other legend was connected with the Kaoliang Bridge outside the West City which was named after a eunuch. When the great Emperor Yunglo had rebuilt Peking, there was a great drought in the year 1409 and a shortage of water supply in the city. The Emperor dreamed one night that outside the West Gate he met a white-haired old couple, the husband pushing and the wife pulling a wheelbarrow carrying an oil hamper. The Emperor asked what was in the hamper and the old man replied that it contained water for the city of Peking. The next day he consulted his general about this dream, and sent his eunuch Kao Liang to go forth outside the West Gate, and ordered him that when he met an old couple answering to the description, he should poke through the oil hamper and hastily turn his horse round toward the city, but he must not look back. Kao went forth as he was told and indeed met an old couple pushing a wheelbarrow and he poked at the hamper, and hastily turned back on his horse. Behind him he heard the rush and roar of an oncoming flood of water, but when he got to the West Gate, he could not help turning back to look and immediately he was caught by the flood and drowned. The Emperor therefore built this many-arched stone bridge in memory of him. Today the bridge still stands across the Jade River where the Empress Dowager used to get into her boat to go to the Summer Palace. Willow-covered embankments surrounding farmers' fields, with peasant women kneeling and washing garments in the water and the common people loitering and fishing on the banks and paddling in the river, give that suburb a peculiar rural beauty suggestive of the South. It was one of Mulan's favorite outing places in summer.

Mannia, as I say, saw little of Peking in that first half-year of her widowhood. But she had that sense of hearing which women in their seclusion developed. The sounds were strange and beautiful. Early in the morning she heard from her courtyard the wonderful street cries of the Peking hawkers. She heard the evening drums from the Drum Tower and the morning bells from the Bell Tower, for although they were about a mile from the Tseng home, their pealing notes could be heard over half the city. The drums marked the watches for the night, and Snow Blossom told her their meaning so that when she lay awake at night and heard the drums, she knew that at the fourth watch the poor court officials and ministers had gathered at the Tunghwa Gate of the Forbidden City, and that at the fifth watch, at daydawn, they were going in for the imperial audience.

Many of the things Mannia experienced were not entirely new to her, but everything was done better or was prettier than in her home town in Shantung. Before she started on her vegetarian period she learned that Peking sausages and ducks were better than Shantung sausages and ducks; the Peking dumplings that she ate at Winter Solstice were daintier than the Shantung *tangtuan;* and Peking had such a variety of pastries and sweets, and all sorts of "small foods," the names of which do not matter because one must eat them in order not to be deceived by their namesakes in other parts of the country. She insisted on the excellence of Shantung cabbage, but she found Peking had just as good cabbage which became the more delicious as the season grew colder. Now she still took the dumplings, and she took the *lapacho*, a gruel eaten on the eighth day of December, consisting of glutinous millet, rice, glutinous rice, red dates, small red beans, water chestnuts, almonds, peanuts, hazelnuts, pine seeds, melon seeds, cooked together with white or brown sugar. It was such a different *lapacho* that she dared not think of mentioning Shantung *lapacho* in the same breath.

Concerning this *lapacho* there is a tale about Mulan and Sunya.

. ˙.

On the twentieth of December the Tseng family were invited to a feast at the home of the Imperial Physician, and the Yao women and girls were also invited. It was the day of the "Sealing Up of the Seals," when officials were supposed to close up their offices for the New Year holidays. While at table, Cassia spoke in everybody's hearing about the embroidery of Mulan and Mochow and said that she had never seen finer work or better designs and matching of colors. Usually the designs on women's shoes followed conventional patterns, but Mulan had introduced the "posture of branches" of paintings into the design of a flower branch on the shoes which the sisters were making for New Year presents to their mother. Mochow also made a colored design of a duck which seemed to stand bodily out of the satin background.

"Seeing is believing," said Cassia to Mrs. Tseng. "We must stop on our way home for you to see those shoes."

"Don't listen to her," said Mochow modestly. "But you have not been to our place for a long time, Auntie Tseng. Come with us after dinner."

Mrs. Tseng wanted to see the shoes, for she admired the Yao sisters very much. So they came to the Yao home and saw what the sisters had done and the duck did seem actually to stand out of the black satin background because of the skillful use of different shades of color.

"It would be a pity to wear these," remarked Mrs. Tseng. "They ought to be presented to the Palace." And she said to Mrs. Yao, "What sort of a belly have you that you gave birth to such daughters? This reminds me that the *lapacho* which Mulan cooked and sent us the other day was extraordinary and grandmother loved it so that she ate two bowls of it. The nuts seemed to melt in the mouth. Old people have no teeth and they like what is soft."

Mulan was pleased and said, "I will come and cook some for her if she likes it so."

What a blessing to marry a daughter-in-law who knows how to cook, thought Mrs. Tseng in her heart.

And so Mulan went with them when they returned to their home. She found Mannia playing with the one-year-old baby. It was a bright afternoon and a few pots of chrysanthemums, ready to wither and standing in the room in the white winter daylight, gave the place a cold, quiet splendor. The baby was lying on the bed in Mannia's mother's room and on the bed were several of the satin shoetops on which Mannia had been working.

"Have you finished those?" Mulan asked.

"I have made only six pairs," said Mannia, "and I have still two more to make, and the year is drawing to a close. I have to work at night, but sometimes the baby makes it impossible for me to take more than a few stitches at a time."

Mulan saw on the wall the "chart of disappearing cold," composed of nine rows of nine circles each, which was a way of counting the days from the winter solstice to the appearance of spring. By the time the eight-one circles were filled in the cold season would be over and the spring weather would set in. Mulan went to the wall and drew two shoes across the remaining ten days before the New Year.

She bent her fingers to count and said, "You have only ten days left. How are you going to do it?"

"I could do it easily if it were not for the baby," said Mannia.

Mulan whispered, "Let me take this pair back and do them for you."

Now Mannia was inordinately proud of her needlework, and would never have thought of having anybody do it for her, and she had had no chance to see how skillful Mulan and her sister were.

"If the needle stitches are different they will be detected at once," said Mannia. In embroidery the stitches had to be perfectly even and smooth and as close together as possible. The slightest bend in the border of flowers would be a mark of careless work, and it taxed a girl's eye to the utmost to make each stitch come within a hundredth of an inch.

Mulan picked up the embroidered patterns lying on the bed and scrutinized them. "I can do it, I think," she said, smilingly and proudly. "I dare not say I can equal you, but certainly I will not disgrace you."

Phoenix now came to the door and said that *Taitai* said she was not serious about asking Mulan to cook *lapacho*, but that the grandmother would be highly pleased to have peanut soup as Mulan cooked it.

"We all loved your *lapacho*," said Mannia. "How did you do it?"

"There is no fairy magic about it," said Mulan. "I only learned from the medical books to put an ingredient in to make the nuts soften quickly. If *Taitai* approves I should like to cook some now."

Phoenix went to report to Mrs. Tseng and came back to say that *Taitai* had sent her to help.

"Where is Snow Blossom?" asked Mulan.

"She is unwell with a little cold, in the other room," replied Mannia.

"The stove here is not big enough," said Phoenix, "and we shall have to get one from the kitchen." She asked a servant to bring a big stove and set about helping Mulan to make the preparations. Snow Blossom heard what they were doing, and she got up to help, but Mannia and her mother would not let her do so.

"This is my duty," said Snow Blossom, "and I dare not bother Phoenix with it."

"But she is sent by *Taitai*," said Mannia.

Now Phoenix was a proud girl and served those she wished to serve. She was unemotional, straightforward, and would not go out of her way to please people, as Snow Blossom would. Snow Blossom was "round" while Phoenix was "square" in her ways. She had not been very courteous to Mannia and her mother, which made them feel uncomfortable.

So Snow Blossom made an effort to get up and help. While Phoenix was away, she said, "It is only a slight cold, and I lay the whole day yesterday and am feeling quite well now. I don't want people to think that I am shirking my duty."

"Who would think so?" countered Mannia.

"I know you wouldn't but there are others," Snow Blossom answered.

177

"You should not go about yet," said Mulan. "But if you insist, we will send the peanuts to your room and you can work on them until the fire is ready."

So a stove was set in the central room and Little Joy attended to the fire. The people in the kitchen were excited over the news that the daughter of the Yao family was going to cook something for the grandmother.

Phoenix seemed to work very willingly, and Mannia said to Mulan privately, "It is strange that you can direct her to do things. Mother and I are afraid to ask her to do anything."

"People are different," said Mulan. "It depends upon how you use them. I think that Phoenix will be a wonderful help here one day."

It was marvelous indeed that in about an hour the soup was ready so that the peanuts almost melted in the mouth. The soup was viscid and soothing for the throat, peanut soup and the almond soup being not only nourishing, but also good against coughs and hoarseness. Phoenix and Little Joy dashed about distributing bowls to the different courtyards, and the grandmother was so pleased that she jokingly said she would keep Mulan as her serving maid just to cook it daily for her.

Now the boys had gone to a temple fair to buy New Year things. Mulan had asked Sunya to buy a kaleidoscope for her little brother Afei. This was a new toy that she had seen at the Tsiangs' home and she was fascinated by it. The changing colored symmetrical designs were wonderful to her. When the brothers returned, Sunya therefore came straight to Mannia's court. He had bought two kaleidoscopes and Mulan was delighted, but when she asked the price he would not tell her.

"You don't have to pay him and he won't take it, I think," said Mannia. "You had better pay him with a bowl of the peanut soup."

There was really only one bowl left, which Mulan and Mannia were going to share, but Mulan took the bowl and gave it to Sunya.

He had come in from the cold outside, and so found it doubly good. "Where does it come from?" he asked. "I have never tasted anything like it in our house. Is it a present from some family?"

Mulan smiled in silence.

"What would you give me," asked Mannia, "if I arranged so that you could have it everyday?"

"I would kowtow to you," said Sunya.

"Good! This is nothing difficult. The person who cooked it is standing right before your eyes," said Mannia, pointing to Mulan. "You ask her whether she is willing to bear the surname Tseng, and if she will, you will enjoy even better luck than this peanut soup."

But Mulan had suddenly disappeared. From the other room came her reply, "People are never satisfied with what they have. This is strictly a cash bargain and no credit: a ten-thousand flower mirror in exchange for a bowl of peanut soup. You enjoy your 'mouth-luck' and I enjoy my 'eye-luck.' If you are thinking of having another bowl of peanut soup, it depends upon whether I want another ten-thousand flower mirror."

When Sunya went to his mother's room and found that Chinya had already eaten his bowl and his mother gave him the bowl reserved for him, Sunya ate it without daring to reveal that he had had some already. When his mother asked him if it was good, he answered "Not bad," without enthusiasm.

"Not bad!" said Phoenix, who was there and overheard. "At the other court he said he would like to have it every day!"

"So you have had some already!" said the mother surprised, and Sunya felt very embarrassed. He did not know why he should feel embarrassed, but he was.

. . .

When Mulan went to say good-by to the grandmother, Mannia went over with her, and she found Mrs. Tseng and Cassia keeping the grandmother company.

"My child," said the grandmother, "how clever you are! I have lived to such a grand age without tasting peanut soup that was so good."

"That is nothing; it is my filial piety and respect to your old person," replied Mulan. "If your old person likes it, I'll teach Damask to make it, and you can have it every day." Damask was the personal maid of the grandmother.

"A family like ours has everything," said the grandmother, "and we ought not to indulge in too many good things. If we learn to value grain and eatables and not waste them, it will lessen our sins. I am only afraid that even the eatables our maidservants throw away would make a poor man's good meal. Only this peanut soup is cheap poor man's food and it comes from the soil, and my old person likes it because it requires no chewing. How did you do it?"

179

"It is not a fairy formula," replied Mulan. "You just add some soda to it. I learned it in the books."

"What a feat for her," said Mrs. Tseng. "Books are open to everybody, yet our boys have not learned from them. Our Sunya really can't compare with her in books or in general understanding of grown-up manners. Grandmother, you have not seen the embroidery the sisters are doing."

While Mrs. Tseng was telling what they had seen that afternoon, Mulan turned aside and went outside to give Damask instructions about cooking the peanut soup. She had brought the pair of shoes from Mannia's room to be embroidered, wrapped in a silk handkerchief, and she was afraid they might be discovered.

Mrs. Tseng then told the story of the peanut soup and how Phoenix had revealed that Mulan had given Sunya a bowl and how he had been embarrassed. This delighted and amazed Cassia and Mannia and the grandmother, and when Mulan re-entered the room, she found them all laughing.

"What is it?" she asked.

"Sunya ate one bowl in our room and then went and ate another bowl in *Taitai's* room," said Mannia.

Mulan at once understood and blushed as she rarely did.

"It is very good that the young people get on so well with each other and I am pleased," said the grandmother, trying to save Mulan from her embarrassment.

"It was not a gift, but a cash bargain," Mulan said quickly. "He bought a kaleidoscope for my younger brother Afei, and the soup was the payment."

And Mulan carried home the kaleidoscope and the silk package with the shoes to be embroidered, feeling somehow that the episode had greatly amused her, but not quite knowing why.

CHAPTER XIII

Two years later, when Mulan was sixteen, she went through the most exciting emotional experience she had yet known. She went to school, she got engaged by her parents, and then discovered she was in love.

The person who was connected with all these happenings and who had great influence upon her life during this period was one Mr. Fu from Szechuen. This Mr. Fu later became the Minister of Education under the Republic, and was responsible for officially adopting the alphabetical writing which has ever since been taught in schools along with the regular characters.

Mr. Fu was a small, thin man with a small mustache, and an opium smoker, but what a brilliant, imaginative scholar he was! His two great hobbies were visiting famous mountains and collecting and editing old books. He had a modern educated wife, and when they were in Peking, hardly a year passed without the couple's leaving the capital for visits to some historic mountain. They had actually spent a period living in the mountains as recluse scholars, and when he traveled he had for his baggage only a roll of bedding, with a few socks and robes inside, and a trunk of books in early editions, with the dirty socks put in the same trunk with the books. At a later period, when he was lecturing at the university on Chinese bibliography and ancient editions, on which he was an acknowledged authority, he insisted on giving his lectures lying down on a comfortable sofa. The students looked upon that thin, short, and well-smoked man with prodigious respect.

This scholar combined his learning with extreme intelligence, and his passion for ancient scholarship was equalled by his zeal for popular education, in particular girls' education, in which he and his wife were pioneers. Even in his twenties, he was regarded in his home province in western China as a brilliant young man of great promise, and at twenty-six, he passed the imperial examinations and came out with the high degree of *Hanlin,* and in another examination was awarded the post of an Editor of the Hanlin Academy as number one of the first grade. He was on his way to Peking with his family when the Boxer Trouble broke out, and he became secretary to the Viceroy Yuan in 1903. As Mr. Tseng also was serving under the Viceroy, Mulan's father had made the acquaintance of Mr. Fu. The breadth of Mr. Fu's views attracted Mulan's father and they became friends in a sense that Mr. Tseng and Mr. Fu never did. Mr. Fu had been requested to go down south to organize and train new troops, and when he returned to Peking he was made Associate Director of Educational Affairs of Chihli. In 1906 he organized the normal school for girls at Tientsin, with his wife as the principal.

Through Mr. Fu's friendship with her father, Mulan was sent to this first government girls' school and so was among the first to share in the benefits of the movement for girls' education. Again through Mr. Fu, Mulan's family came to know Lifu, a Szechuen boy of whom Mr. Fu had always spoken highly. He and his wife often visited Mr. Yao's home, and Mrs. Fu took an active interest in securing the Yao sisters as pupils for her school.

Mr. and Mrs. Fu were spending the spring recess in Peking. Mulan's family was going to spend three or four days at their summer house in the suburb near the Western Hills, because from April 1 to April 15 there was a festival at the Temple of Lake-Blue Clouds. As Mr. and Mrs. Fu were both extremely fond of the hills, Mulan's father had invited them to join the party and stay at their country house.

Mulan had asked Mrs. Tseng to allow Mannia to come. The Tsengs were less romantic and they did not have a country house, and Mrs. Tseng said that she had visited the Temple only once and that was twelve years ago when the boys were still small. Now, although Mannia had been in Peking for a year and a half, she had not been out of the house more than a dozen times and then chiefly for shopping occasions in the South City district, and for a few visits to places like the Confucian Temple, where she had seen inscribed on stone tablets the names of all the successful candidates in the imperial examinations of the previous centuries. Mr. Tseng permitted this because of his Confucianism and because he thought women who appreciated such things were more likely to bring up their children to be scholars and candidates. She had not even gone with her mother to see the lilacs at Fayuan Temple in spring, as flowers were considered too disturbing for a young woman's heart, nor had she gone to see the great and beautiful Lama Temple, because it was possible that she might see the obscene images concealed behind dark curtains, and revealed on paying a tip to the monks. Still, as Mrs. Tseng said, visits must be allowed as a general principle because a visit to a temple was a pious thing to do.

Mannia was becoming more and more like a Buddhist, and was gradually gaining the confidence of her parents, who nevertheless intended to protect her against all the distractions of this world.

"She will stay in my room and sleep in the same bed with me and I will be responsible for her," said Mulan. "She has never had a chance even to see the hills."

"Lan-erh, you are full of spirit indeed!" said Mrs. Tseng, who had come to call Mulan by this familiar name. "I have seldom seen the hills and yet I have lived to this respectable age. But I think it is not a bad idea for her to go with you and relax her mind a little. I will ask your adopted father about it."

On the twelfth of April, therefore, Mulan's family and Mannia and Mr. and Mrs. Fu were at the country house near the Western Hills beyond the Jade Spring Hill. Mr. Yao's idea of true rural life was that it could be enjoyed more without the maids, and although they took along a cook, the daughters often prepared the meals themselves.

To Mannia, unused to the imperial glamour of Peking, the trip was an intense delight. Everything fascinated her—the tall Gate Tower and the thick wall gate of Hsichihmen, looking like a tunnel forty or fifty feet long, the donkey drivers and small shops outside the gate, the common people sipping tea in open tea houses, the broad, pleasant, stone-paved imperial road to the Summer Palace, with the great willow trees on both sides already putting out slender green leaves, the beautiful countryside with the purple slopes of the Western Hills in the distance under the clear, blue sky, the glimpses of the ruins of the Old Summer Palace over the walls, then the Summer Palace itself with its golden roofs and pavilions.

It was the rural neighborhood of the Jade Spring Hill which she found most delightful, with farmers' houses all around and white ducks swimming in the canals, and the Western Hills that embraced the city of Peking like the arms of a mother around her child. It was here that Mulan's house stood. In front one saw the white Marble Pagoda near the Jade Spring and the Longevity Hill of the Summer

Palace, hidden in green foliage, while the hills behind were dotted with temples.

They arrived in time for lunch, and in the afternoon they visited the Temple of Lake-Blue Clouds. They climbed the four flights of stone steps up the Marble Stupa and finding it rather crowded with visitors and the time still early they went on to the Temple of the Sleeping Buddha, where they saw a copper Buddha more than twenty feet long, in a reclining position, and beside it the many votive shoes offered by emperors and princes, some several feet long, made of embroidered yellow satin. Mr. Yao advised them not to tire themselves out as they were planning to go on a longer trip the following day to visit one of the "Eight Big Places," that is, a group of eight temples near one another.

So the next day they went to Pimoya, or the Cliff of the Occult Demon, the most picturesque and austerely beautiful part of the Hills. This cliff was hidden at the top of the hill behind a group of temple buildings, which were again hidden among trees in a snug corner of a crag. The older ladies and Mannia went on donkeys, but Mulan and Mochow preferred to walk with the men and boys, and the girls' voices mingled with the golden laughter of the donkey boys on that clear spring day.

The ladies had all got down from their donkeys at the Temple Gate and when they reached the cliff, they were rather out of breath. Mannia, in white, still looked like a young girl except that her hair was done up, while Mulan and Mochow wore braids. Mulan had a way, when she was walking or standing, of holding the tip of her braid, and bringing it in front, whisking it around her forefinger in circles in fun.

Now the Cliff of the Occult Demon was really in the shape of a natural cave about fifty feet deep, formed by a single overhanging rock jutting out at an angle as its roof; and people standing under it had a feeling that if the cliff should fall down, they would be crushed into sausage. Before the cliff there was said to be a deep pond, now covered up by a huge stone, for fear people might fall into it. Mulan's father explained the legend about the two dragons concealed in the pond. A Taoist saint of the sixth century had taken two boys as his pupils or acolytes; and once there was a great drought, and the two boys jumped into the pond and were transformed into green dragons and caused rain to fall. Hence there was a pavilion here in honor of the Dragon Kings.

The men of the party went on ahead. When Mulan reached the entrance to the cave, she saw a middle-aged woman, in ordinary black dress, sitting there with a girl of about ten, and they heard a boy's voice and saw a rather thin boy, of about sixteen, dash from a stone house near by and stand talking and gesticulating to the mother and child. He had bright eyes and a straight nose and sensitive features. He was wearing a pale-blue cotton gown, and the bright pale-blue matched well with his white young face and agile body. "Mother," the boy was saying, "this is the Chapel of the Saint Lu Shih and his two boys who became dragons." Something in his voice and face arrested the sisters' attention and with Mannia they stood at a distance watching him talk to his mother and young sister.

"That was a nice story. But whoever saw the dragons?" said his mother.

"Emperor Chienlung did," said the boy, still smiling and gesticulating. "He came one day to this place, and saw the shape of two little green sea-animals in the pond and the monk pointed them out to the Emperor and said they were dragons and the Emperor laughed and said, 'Why, they are only little one-foot fish.' Upon that, the dragons became bigger and bigger and shot up from the pond into the air and went up on top of the hills and were lost in the clouds."

"You are fooling me," said his mother.

"No. The dragons were so big you couldn't see their heads or tails, but the Emperor saw a huge dragon's claw as big as a mountain stretching down from the clouds and its scales were green and sparkling, and the Emperor saw it and was frightened and went home with a stomach-ache."

The boy's mother was laughing loudly and one could see that she was a happy woman. He was apparently the kind of son who made a lonely woman's life full and happy, compelling her by continuous surprises to wonder at herself for giving birth to such a boy.

The girls, amused at the story and the boy's lively manner of telling it, laughed a little too, behind their handkerchiefs. Mochow said that she thought she had seen the boy somewhere, and Mulan thought so too, but could not recall where it was. She liked his excited face and manner. She could not be sure whether it was an actual legend or one he had made up on the spot to please his mother.

Just then Mr. Fu came strolling back and seeing the boy exclaimed, "Why, if it isn't Lifu!" and went to greet them. The boy's mother was extremely polite toward Mr. Fu, although he seemed to know them well. Turning, he called, "Come and meet Mrs. Kung and her children." And Mr. Fu introduced them, saying, "This is Mrs. Kung. This is Lifu and this is his sister. They are our Szechuen fellow-provincials." The mother was all smiles. As she came closer, Mulan saw that there was something about the boy's forehead and eyes which made him look distinguished in spite of his common attire.

"*Liaoputeh!*" said Mr. Fu, in enthusiastic praise, "You see our Szechuen produces men. Born of the Spirit of the Omei Mountains, I should say!" Mulan looked at the boy with even greater interest, for she knew that any one praised by Mr. Fu must be worth something.

Lifu was embarrassed, and his mother said, "We are common people but Vice-Director Fu has been unusually kind to us, mother and children."

The boy made to Mr. Yao the low bow peculiar to the ancient customs of Szechuen, and turned to Mrs. Yao and made another deep bow. Of course he ignored the girls, as was good form.

"Are you related to Confucius?" asked Mr. Yao because their family name was Kung.

"No, we have not the honor," replied Lifu. "If all people by the name of Kung were descendants of Confucius, then Confucius would be disgraced."

Mulan could not help smiling at the appropriate remark. Lifu spoke very fast and seemed eloquent and at ease in company. Mulan's father also laughed, and even Tijen for once felt attracted toward a person of his age who dared to say what he thought.

"But at least Mrs. Kung comes from the family of Yang Chisheng, and that is something, and he lived only three centuries ago," said Mr. Fu. "I think the boy has something of Yang Chisheng in him."

Mulan had heard her father speak of Yang Chisheng, because outside the Chienmen Gate in Peking there is an old house supposed to be where Yang had lived. Yang was a scholar and official under an extremely corrupt government at the end of the Ming Dynasty, who knowingly risked his life by impeaching the notoriously wicked and all-powerful premier Yen Sung, denouncing his five traitorous acts and ten great crimes. For this he was beheaded, but his prestige, honor, and courage made him remembered by posterity, and tourists still visit the pavilion where this fearless man drafted his long and suicidal memorandum to the Emperor.

"Where are you staying?" asked Mr. Yao.

"In the South City, at the Szechuen Guild," Lifu replied.

"Are you going back to the city today?" asked Mr. Fu.

"No, we are staying over, at the Temple of the Sleeping Buddha."

"Have you seen the Fragrant Hill?" asked Mr. Fu again. The Fragrant Hill, just a mile's walk from the Temple of the Sleeping Buddha, had been Emperor Chienlung's hunting park, but since hunting had been given up in the middle of the nineteenth century there was no longer any game in it.

Now although the Park was not open to the public under the Empire, it was in charge of one Mr. Ing, who was working closely with Mr. Fu on the program for women's education and who later set up a girls' school inside the Park.

"No, we could not go in," replied Lifu.

"We are visiting it tomorrow. Will you come with us?" asked Mr. Fu, and Lifu accepted enthusiastically.

It was unusual for Mr. Fu to include common persons so recently introduced in an outing party with the Yao women and girls; but apparently he accepted the Kung family as equals and close friends, for, having been a poor young man himself, he was always eager to help promising young men.

On the way back Mrs. Yao suggested to her husband that having this young man go with them might be slightly inconvenient for the young girls, and Mr. Yao answered with a short, barely audible, "Oh, well!" The girls however were excited about the sudden turn of events.

They wandered on to the Main Temple, which had escaped destruction at the hands of the allied troops during the Boxer trouble and saw the remains of some very old wall paintings depicting the Eighteen Lohans visiting the Western Hills. Coming out of the temple, they again saw Lifu and his mother coming out through the Maltese-cross door behind them, but at such a distance that they did not speak to them again. Mochow saw Lifu throw a pebble at a cypress tree and saw a raven fly out of the tree with a harsh cry. The peculiar swing of the boy's arm suddenly reminded her of the place where she had seen him first.

"Why, isn't he the very one we saw who hit the coin at Paiyunkuan," she said to Mulan.

187

Then Mochow remembered for certain. It was three months ago during the New Year Festival at Paiyunkuan, the great Taoist Monastery, a mile outside Peking, where men, women, and children of the city went for the festivities from January the first to the nineteenth. The last day was the birthday of the founder of the Northern Taoists, who was greatly respected by Genghis Khan, and whose remains were buried in the temple. There were trotting races for men and cart races for women around the temple, and great throngs of people went there to "meet the Immortal," for it was said on the eighteenth the Immortal would descend to the earth and disguise himself, and whoever met or touched him would have good luck. He might come as an official or as a street beggar, as a dog or a donkey. The excitement was in the fact that one could never be sure that a dog lying by the roadside or a beggar sleeping on an old mat was not the Immortal himself. The thing to watch for was whether a dog or a beggar or a monk or an old woman magically disappeared; and, if a beggar seen crouching in a corner five minutes ago was suddenly gone, then he was the Immortal and the visitors were glad they had given him money or had seen him. It made the people generous toward beggars and kind toward animals, and it caused a great deal of crowding and jostling between men and women, so that there was no end of fun and excitement.

Now on that day Mulan and Mochow had gone out to visit the Temple. At the entrance there was a bridge called the Bridge of Captured Winds. As this Taoist temple was called White-Cloud Temple, a rival Buddhist monk had erected a West-Wind Temple near by, implying that the west wind was going to blow away the white clouds. The Taoist founder had met this contest by erecting this bridge which was supposed to capture the winds spread by the Buddhist magic. Beneath the bridge there was a dark cave and inside the cave sat an old monk in cross-legged position. From the ceiling of the cave was suspended a big copper coin, and visitors who threw copper cash at the big coin and hit it would have good luck. The coin, however, was suspended in such a position between the angle of the bridge and the ceiling of the cave that there was little chance of hitting it, and the monks collected a great deal of cash through this pastime or superstition, whichever one chose to call it.

While the girls had stood there watching they had seen a boy hit the mark. There was applause from the spectators and when the boy walked away, pleased with himself, Mulan threw some cash and also

188

hit the coin after a few trials. There was more applause, and when the boy heard the scoring of the target and the applause, he turned round and looked at Mulan and smiled, and disappeared. "Could that boy be the Immortal?" Mochow said to Mulan.

The truth was that a moment after their meeting at the cliff Mulan had already identified him and had not said a word about it. And now when Mochow said further, "That is the boy that hit the coin at Paiyunkuan that day, do you remember?" Mulan only said "Yes, I was thinking so, too."

Lifu and his mother and sister were coming down about fifty yards behind them, and the girls could not help turning their heads once or twice to look at him, in order to make sure that he was the same boy. They saw him again pointing to heaven and earth with his right arm while leading his mother with the other arm, and they thought him very interesting.

Lifu's family caught up with them at the temple gate and went ahead, because the ladies in Mulan's party took a longer time to get up on the donkeys. As they watched the little family of three going before them, with Lifu walking beside his mother's donkey and holding his little sister's hand, Mrs. Fu told Mulan's mother about the family, while the girls pricked up their ears to listen.

Lifu's father had been a minor official at Peking. An uncle had squandered the family fortune, leaving Lifu's father rather poor, and the father had not complained but had tried to make his own living. The father had died when Lifu was nine, and the widow and children continued to live in Peking at the Szechuen Guild because the widow was a native of Peking and there were good schools. His uncle had married again, this time a modern girl, and was living in Shanghai. After the death of the father, the uncle suddenly appeared one day, in the hope of getting control of his brother's property, thinking that, since he had been a Peking official, he must have amassed a fortune. Mr. Fu had intervened and sent the uncle away empty-handed, and ever since that time Lifu's mother had been a kind of protégé of Mr. Fu and was extremely grateful to him. Struck by the brilliance of the boy, Mr. Fu had befriended him and lent him the use of his great library; and Lifu was like a baby monkey let loose in a forest, learning to climb trees and swing about from branch to branch without ever being taught.

When the party entered the valley of the Hunting Park, the sun was already setting behind the hills, and while the Summer Palace and the Marble Pagoda were still glimmering in sunlight, the park and the valley were in shade, and the cool, fragrant air from the somber pines made the day seem perfect to Mulan. Lifu and his mother were two hundred yards ahead, but still discernible in that soft afternoon light, and before they turned away in the direction of the Temple of the Sleeping Buddha, they saw Lifu waving good-by to them with an outstretched arm.

. · .

That night Mulan's parents discussed with Mr. and Mrs. Fu the idea of sending the sisters to the school at Tientsin in the autumn. While there were girls' schools in Peking, the school at Tientsin was the best, and Mrs. Fu promised to give Mulan and Mochow her personal care and attention. Besides, the sisters could come back for the week end, perhaps once a month, and the parents seemed to have been won over.

Mr. and Mrs. Fu also talked about sending Tijen to England for study. It did not matter that he knew very little English, Mr. Fu said, since he could learn it in England. Not only did Mr. Yao take to the idea, but Tijen himself responded immediately with great interest.

Mulan's mother hesitated, but Coral threw in her support. "A young man ought to go abroad and see things and broaden his mind," she said simply.

"The times have changed," said Mr. Fu. "Students returned from foreign colleges can now pass our examinations and receive the imperial degrees of *chinshih* and *hanlin* just the same. Even if you do not want him to become an official, you ought to let him have the best education that this generation can give."

"What troubles me is that he is still so young," said the mother. "Across the ocean, ten thousand *li* from home, who is going to take care of him?"

"I can take care of myself," said Tijen. "I am old enough. I will really work hard, if you will send me abroad." This was the first time Tijen had ever said that he wanted to work hard.

"Perhaps he will change entirely," said Coral. "He is now nineteen and ought to begin something serious. You look at that son of Mrs. Kung. When I saw him walking with his mother and his sister, it looked like a picture of the twenty-four filial sons. Yet hasn't he the same set of eyes, ears and nose as anybody else?"

"When a family is in poverty it produces a filial son, and when a country is in danger it produces a patriot," said Mr. Yao, quoting a proverb. This sounded like a rebuff to Tijen in his presence.

Tijen's parents promised to consider the idea. His father approved because he was liberal and rich and at a loss as to what to do with his pampered son. Tijen was enthusiastic because it meant seeing a new world and doing what the most modern and fortunate young men were doing. Returned students, walking about in foreign dress, carrying canes, and talking English, seemed to enjoy such prestige. And to be fair to him, he also meant to make something of himself.

His mother felt it to be wrong, but what reconciled her nevertheless was the fact that it solved an immediate problem. Silverscreen was now twenty-two and still in the family. She could not be married off in Peking because she was a southern girl and wanted to return to her home town, but there was no one to take her south. Last spring, when Silverscreen was about to be sent south with Tijen's uncle, Mr. Feng, something was always wrong with the date of departure, and at the last moment Silverscreen fell ill and they were compelled to give up the idea for that year. Subsequently nothing had been done about it. The situation was awkward, for a Ningpo girl of twenty-two knew a great deal. Perhaps, as Coral had already suggested to his mother, sending Tijen away from the company of Silverscreen would make him begin all over again.

When the family started for the Hunting Park the next day, therefore, everybody was in a high mood, Mulan and Mochow because they were going to school in the fall, Tijen because he thought he was going to England, and the parents because the problem of their children's education was being solved.

As the park was only a short distance, they all went on foot. It had been agreed between Mr. Fu and Mrs. Kung that they would meet at the temple next to the park after breakfast. When they arrived, they found Lifu and his mother and sister already there loitering around the stone archway outside. Lifu ran forward to greet them with a smile, but he barely nodded to the girls and to Coral and Mannia, as was in accordance with good form. Mulan and Mochow looked at him full in the face and smiled because they could not help it, for after what they had heard and seen last night, their interest in him was even more aroused.

While Tijen talked with him the girls listened, pretending to talk among themselves. Now Tijen liked Lifu after hearing his first remark about the descendants of Confucius, because he himself was usually critical of the officials and outspoken. Tijen was, in fact, a fairly brilliant boy himself, but he was somewhat of a rebel and the company of officials' children bored him. Lifu seemed to him different and he seemed to have unorthodox ideas like himself. Perhaps because he was born poor, Lifu had complete contempt for wealth, and took everybody for what he was naturally worth. When Tijen met such a person, he threw aside his own pretensions and tried to meet him as an equal. Or was it that he was in a happy mood that morning because he was going to England and wished to make good and therefore befriended one whom the elders considered a good young man?

At the foot of the Hunting Park, the abbot and a group of monks came out to receive Mr. Fu, speaking the most polished mandarin, for the monks of the Western Hills were used to receiving high officials and Manchu princes from the city. Holding a rosary in his hands, the abbot led the way. Now the park known as the Fragrant Hill lay on a steep thickly wooded slope and stretched to the hills behind. After a shaded path between tall, old trees, several long flights of stone steps rose to the main building on top, while on both sides winding roads led to various temple buildings and halls. Lifu and Tijen were walking behind the men, talking with some of the monks, while the ladies followed behind. Mulan's mother, for some reason of her own, seemed bent on cultivating the friendship of Lifu's mother so that they were walking together, while Mrs. Fu followed with the young girls and Mannia and Coral.

Before they ascended a short flight of steps, Lifu turned to help his mother. Left alone, Tijen also waited until his mother came up and went to assist her, and she was so delighted that she exclaimed, "Good son, if you were like this every day, I don't know how happy I should be!" Tijen felt very pleased with himself and said, "Mother, at home you have all the maids to serve you, and there is no need of me. At least I have a filial son's heart."

"Don't boast," said his mother. "You saw how Mrs. Kung's son was helping his mother and felt awkward not to help your own mother. It will do you good to make friends with him and learn something serious from him. Lifu, will you be willing to be friends with my boy?"

"Mrs. Yao, you are joking," replied Lifu. "If you don't think me unworthy, it will be an honor to me."

When Coral and Mulan and Mochow saw Tijen helping their mother up the steps, they nudged and looked at each other in amazement. The mothers exchanged inquiries about their boys' ages, and Mulan's mother learned that Lifu was sixteen, three years younger than Tijen. Something sank into Mulan's soul when she heard from Mrs. Kung that since her husband's death, they had been living on their rents and were now planning to sell some houses in Szechuen to enable Lifu to go to college, and that they were staking everything upon Lifu's education. Mulan knew that there were poor people, but she did not know among her acquaintances people who sold their little property in order to put a son through college. She liked the idea.

Now a monk suggested that they take the footpath at the side which would be less tiring, and the ladies went off on the left. They were shown into an enclosure and on entering the yard, they saw a hall facing a cliff capped by tall green trees, with water running down the face of the cliff and collecting in a clear pool beneath, while in front of the hall was a paved yard with stone benches and tables. It was such a beautiful and quiet enclosure that Mulan involuntarily gasped, and then she heard Lifu exclaim, "Oh, what a place for a library to study in!"

Tijen took out his camera and said, "I must take a picture here." The camera was one of the things that Tijen was serious about, and he had learned not only to take pictures, but also to develop them himself, for which his father gave him all the money he wanted, considering it one of the things that would keep him out of mischief.

The ladies were therefore asked to stand together in a group. It was a peculiarity of Mulan's that when she saw something very beautiful, one, but only one, tear would gather in each of her eyes, so that now when Coral saw Mulan wiping her eyes, she teased her and said, "Why do you weep?" and Mannia said, *"Meimei,* what is the matter with your eyes?" so that Mulan became the center of attention, but she merely smiled and said, "Nothing." Lifu and his mother watched from a little distance and Mulan's mother asked them to come and stand together for the picture.

"Come along! We are all like one family with Mrs. Fu," said Coral.

Finally Mrs. Fu had to drag Lifu's mother until she came. It happened that Mulan and Mochow were standing at the end and Lifu's place was next, but he stood at least a foot away from them.

It turned out to be one of the best pictures of Mulan because she was so excited and confused, with her head inclined and her hand half raised, as if about to wipe her eyes again. She looked beautifully miserable.

Lifu was so naturally uncomfortable in the company of young ladies of his own age that he kept close to Tijen. Mulan, Coral, and Mannia kept together because Mulan felt responsible for inviting Mannia and wanted her to enjoy herself, while Mochow walked with her mother and Mrs. Kung and, being a quieter girl, she kept silent while the two ladies were talking and Mrs. Kung liked her for it. The result was that Lifu and the girls never exchanged a word the whole morning until the lunch hour.

Before they left the temple to wander among the various yards and buildings in the park, the monks had asked whether they should serve a vegetable or meat dinner. Mulan's mother said that she and Mannia would have a vegetarian dinner, though the men would not be satisfied except with meat courses; but Mr. Fu said that of course they should all have a vegetarian dinner at this place, for not until one had tasted a vegetarian dinner prepared by the monks could one talk of vegetarian food at all. The monks of the Western Hills served such vegetarian dinners as might satisfy a prince. They had dishes called "ham," "chicken," and "fish rolls," all made of bean curd to resemble the meat dishes in appearance and taste, and green vegetables cooked with liberal use of oil, and a great variety of the most dainty rolls and pastries.

When they came back to the temple at the top, they found two tables laid ready in the hall, with silver spoons and ivory chopsticks. Mr. and Mrs. Fu assumed that they would be the hosts for the day and therefore sat at different tables, Mrs. Fu with the ladies and Mr. Fu with the men. But as there were more ladies than men, the plan was upset by Mr. Yao's preferring to sit with his daughters and abruptly taking his wife and Mrs. Kung to the table with the boys. There was confusion because there were still too many at the girls' table and Lifu's mother insisted on asking Mochow to their table, while the two little children, Lifu's sister and Mulan's young brother, finally sat with the young ladies. The result was that at one table Mulan and

Coral were looking after the children, and at the other Mochow and Lifu were looking after their mothers. The abbot sat at a distance and saw that everything was in order before wishing them good appetite and retiring.

Now at table the conversation turned upon the inscriptions of the Emperor Chienlung's handwriting which were found everywhere among the temples in the Western Hills. There was one right in front of the temple.

"The Emperor must have been quite proud of his own handwriting," Mr. Yao remarked.

Mulan was just thinking that it was below an emperor's dignity to leave his writing everywhere he visited, when she heard Lifu say at the other table, "Things are precious only when they are rare. Isn't it too cheap for an emperor to leave his writing about everywhere?" So they evidently had the same thoughts. But Mochow thought these remarks unfair to the Emperor, although she kept quiet.

"Do you like Chienlung's handwriting?" Lifu asked Mr. Fu.

"Oh," said Mr. Fu, "it is correct and strong, but you cannot say that it is brilliant or extraordinary."

"Nor have I ever seen a single good poem inscribed by him," said Lifu. "It is the usual court poetry—always in praise of peace and prosperity and the phoenix and the purple air—just what you expect him to say."

Suddenly Mochow asked, "Is it bad poetry because he says what you expect him to say?" It was a direct challenge to Lifu, although she merely said what came to her mind on an impulse.

Lifu looked at her surprised. He had to make a direct reply. "If you say what you are expected to say, of course it is bad poetry," he said.

Now Mochow also felt forced to say more in reply. "But that depends. Poets and recluses are not of the ordinary run of men and therefore do not say the ordinary run of things. But Chienlung was an Emperor. He had to say what was expected of him to say, because he had to do what was expected of him to do. What is bad poetry for a recluse is good poetry for an emperor who had to rule the country and feel the common thoughts of the common men and women he ruled. An emperor has to be commonplace."

Mochow stopped, thinking she had allowed herself to say more than was good form, and she did not mean to begin an argument.

"According to you," said Mr. Fu, "even his handwriting is also good handwriting because it is of the normal and well-proportioned and not the eccentric and brilliant type."

"Well, it is round and full," said Mochow. Then she thought of the "Eight Eccentrics of Yangchow," who were great impressionist poets and painters in Chienlung's time and she went on, "It would not do for an emperor to be eccentric. If the Eight Eccentrics of Yangchow were to become emperors, wouldn't it be disastrous for the world?"

"Mochow, how dare you argue with Uncle Fu?" said her mother, who did not understand what it was all about but who knew that it was bad form for her fourteen-year old girl to be arguing with a famous scholar.

"Let her say what she thinks. I like to hear it," said Mr. Fu. Gossip at the other table had completely stopped and all were prepared to listen to what Mochow had to say.

"I was only trying to say a good word for the Emperor," said Mochow. "Even ordinary tourists often scribble their signatures and poems on pavilions and cliffs and temple walls, so why should not the emperor of a nation be permitted to do the same? He rebuilt so many of the temples here, and his courtiers would have asked him to leave inscriptions for posterity to remember him by even if he did not want to. After all, he was a peacetime Emperor and a patron of arts and literature, and his poems were just the kind to decorate an era of peace and prosperity. Court poetry had to be like that. You can't say his handwriting is exotic, but an Emperor's has got to be square and orthodox. It is round and full, and squarely built, and conceals strength behind its soft, round contours, as an Emperor's character ought to be."

"People are born different," said Mulan's father with a contented smile. "Mrs. Fu, you see my third daughter's handwriting is like that, round and full, and neatly formed one by one. Mulan's writing looks like a man's."

"These things cannot be helped," said Mrs. Fu. "The handwriting is an index of character. You can't form regular characters if you have an irregular mind."

This statement, while truly Mrs. Fu's own opinion, was also a reflection of her husband's, who went further and believed that you could tell a man's fortune by looking at his handwriting. Along with his progressive ideas Mr. Fu, like many old scholars, who always had a touch of mysticism in them, also sincerely believed in astrology and fortune telling. Nobody could argue Mr. Fu out of this belief.

"You can tell from his writing whether a man is going to be long-lived or short-lived," said Mr. Fu.

"That is what I say," said Mochow. "Chienlung lived to eighty-nine and had the longest reign of any emperor in history."

"I don't believe it," said Lifu.

"You are too young," said Mr. Fu.

"I don't know why I can never learn to write good characters," said Lifu.

"You have too much of the spirit of eccentricity," said Mr. Fu. "This is not bad in itself, but it needs discipline. The highest type of character is of course that which contains a grain of eccentricity or freedom of spirit but manages to come back to normal balance. What you need is somebody to hold you back."

Mr. Fu went on to expound his all-embracing Dualism. All life was the result of two forces—centrality and eccentricity. Without eccentricity, there would be no progress, and without centrality there would be no stability. Man's life results from the harmonious complementing of these two opposite principles, like the inter-breeding of the *yin* and *yang* which produces the four seasons of the year.

Suddenly they heard Mulan and Coral laughing out loud. Everybody turned and looked and someone asked, "What are you laughing at?"

"Nothing," said Mulan, and laughed louder than ever.

"They are laughing at me," explained Mannia. "Mulan was saying that my writing looked like a little mouse, and that was why I was timid like a mouse."

"I was merely joking," explained Mulan. "According to Uncle Fu, whoever writes characters like a cat can eat the mouse up."

"That depends," said Mr. Fu. "Did you ever hear of a rat biting a cat?" Thereupon Mr. Fu told the story of the rat who grew so big and fat in time of famine that it fought off a cat and forced the cat to run away.

"What is your writing like?" Mrs. Fu asked Mulan.

"My writing doesn't resemble anything—well, perhaps it resembles a snake," answered Mulan.

"A snake also can eat up a mouse," remarked Mochow from the other table.

"Sister, do you think I'll eat you up?" Mulan asked Mannia.

"Perhaps, when you are very hungry," Mannia answered.

"If that's the case, shouldn't I be eaten up by everybody?" said Coral, "for my writing is like chestnuts, neither round nor square, and you can never place it in a straight line."

"What is your sister's like?" asked Mrs. Fu.

Mulan paused a little. "Hers is like a partridge in spring, round-bodied and smooth-feathered."

At this moment, the monk in charge of guests appeared and heard the word "partridges," and profoundly apologized for the poor food, saying, "I am awfully sorry we are not able to serve partridges."

The whole company laughed and had to explain that they were talking about handwriting. Mr. Fu took out a ten-dollar bill and gave it to the monk, thanking him for the delicious dinner.

. .

Mulan so far had not exchanged a word with Lifu. After dinner they rested a little because Mannia was already complaining she had had enough climbing and walking for the day. About three o'clock, Mr. and Mrs. Fu suggested going to the hills beyond but the ladies declined, and Mrs. Fu had to stay with them, saying that she had been up herself, and Mochow, being plumper and quieter, also said she would stay with her mother because she never liked climbing. Tijen avoided going because his father was going, and Lifu's sister was too small. As a result, only five went up: Mr. Fu, Mr. Yao, Lifu, Mulan, and her little brother Afei. Mulan loved climbing high hills and looking at the splendid views.

It was less than a mile to the Half-Way Pavilion, but the way was mostly upwards. Mr. Fu, like all thin men, was a good climber, and Mulan's father, even at his age, went up with easy steps as though he were running on level ground. He could still walk a hundred *li* a day if he had to. Lifu felt he was thrown into Mulan's company and could not ignore her entirely while the elders were walking ahead. He became very nervous, cracking his knuckles and opening and closing his fingers again and again, because he had grown up among books and had not known pretty girls before, and so he talked to the child. Mischievous ideas were playing about in Mulan's head.

She made a ridiculous start by saying to Afei, "You ask Mr. Kung if he was at the Paiyunkuan Festival last New Year." And Lifu answered by saying to Afei, "You tell your sister that I was there and saw her throwing the lucky coin at the Bridge of Captured Winds."

This way of talking was so amusing that they both laughed aloud and looked at each other, and there the conversation between the two started.

There was a tall white pine fifteen yards ahead of them, standing erect and alone on a knoll, its silver bark lovely against the green slopes.

"Mr. Kung," said Mulan, "can you hit that white pine?"

"I will try if you will," he said.

He picked up a round stone the size of an egg and threw it and the pebble hit the trunk with a dull thud.

"Good!" shouted little Afei.

Mulan was abashed, being about to make a most unwomanly gesture, but she threw a stone and missed the tree by a foot. Lifu encouraged her. She missed it a second time, and he showed her the way of holding a stone between her fingers and the two ways of throwing, one overhand, from above the shoulders, and the other underhand, from below.

"And the way you stand is wrong," said Lifu when she was about to try again. Mulan knew it, but she refused to place her legs apart. With her feet close together she tried the new overhand throw and hit the tree and tottered and almost fell over. Lifu gave a shout of applause, and Afei a shout of admiration, and Mulan herself a shout of triumph.

So she was very happy. Unconsciously, she started to whistle. Lifu was surprised.

"Why, can you whistle?"

Mulan looked at him with a full smile and continued. It was the tune of a song of the twelve months of the year, a popular folk song, and Lifu joined her, as they went up. Old Yao turned to look and saw that his daughter was very happy; he said something to Mr. Fu and Mr. Fu turned back to look, too.

As they went up and up a new view opened before them. Below lay deep ravines and steep green slopes, and in the distance the farther hills. Up there, among the hills and clouds, Mulan was in her natural element. The spring air was exhilarating and the birds seemed to feel, as Mulan did, a sudden release of energy and were flitting across the valley, their cries and chirps filling the sky.

At the Half-Way Pavilion, the party rested. Mulan asked what were the queer-looking structures with crenelated walls which they had seen in the distance, and her father explained that Emperor Chienlung had built them to resemble Tibetan buildings and terraces so that his soldiers could practice scaling Tibetan fortresses, and some were ruins of monuments commemorating his victory in Tibet, and one had been a terrace from which the Emperor used to watch the archery contests of his troops. Most of the buildings had long since crumbled, and Mulan thought of the phrase, "for one general to achieve fame, ten thousand skeletons must lie exposed" and remained silent. Peking was near enough the Mongolian plains and there were enough Tibetan priests in the city to give one a sense of empire; and the Temple of Lake-Blue Clouds, the Temple of the Sleeping Buddha, and many other places bore traces of Genghis Khan and the Mongol rulers.

"Hm!" spluttered Mr. Yao. "Have you read the Ode on an Ancient Battlefield, Lifu?"

"Yes, it all comes to this— *'And where are they now?'* " answered Lifu. "I should like to go and see Tibet some day," he said almost to himself.

Mr. Fu began to sing an air from the opera *Lilingpei* and intoned the words of the dying general with great abandon and emotion, and Mulan softly followed, to the great amazement of Lifu. Mulan had a most unusually soft voice. The passage was one of the most difficult airs, and Lifu himself had never learned to sing. It was a sad tune, and Mulan was feeling now that life was sad and beautiful.

But if Mulan surprised Lifu by throwing stones and whistling and singing operatic airs, Lifu surprised her by a remark on their way back to the temple. Mulan had said it was a pity the others had not come along and seen what they had seen, and he asked, "What do you think is the most beautiful sight you have seen today?"

"At the Half-Way Pavilion," she answered. "And what do you think the most beautiful you have seen?"

"The ruins," he answered.

. ·.

Now Mrs. Yao hoped that Lifu would become a friend of Tijen and invited the Kung family to dine with them that night, so that the party returned together. Everybody was hungry and they had an early supper. Mr. Yao and Mr. Fu were both good drinkers, and as the saying goes, "When one meets an old friend, his wine intestines widen." After dinner, they sat in the open and discussed the plans for the children while watching the moon rise over the Summer Palace.

"Send Tijen to England," said Mr. Fu. "You have plenty of money. The new learning is the thing. This is a new world and one has to know the world events beyond the ocean. It will not do to learn the Four Books and Five Classics by rote any more." Within that small frame of his, Mr. Fu's spirit expanded under the influence of the wine and the moonlight, and he talked of his visions of the future and the world beyond.

The mother still could not quite make up her mind. Tijen's going abroad and the girls to school at Tientsin would mean such an upset in the family, and her instinct was against upsets. But Mochow said:

"Brother, you ought to go. A man ought to travel and see the world, and not stay in one place."

"Yes," said Mr. Fu. "Get him away from your rich comforts and you will make a man of him. Abroad, he will have to take care of himself and will not be surrounded with maids to prepare his baths and attend to his washing and pour him tea. If he wants tea he will have to make it himself. It will be good for his body." Such an argument was conclusive for Mr. Yao.

They were planning to return the next day, but Mr. Yao said, "Tomorrow will be the fifteenth and the moon will be still better." But the mother was anxious about leaving the house alone with the maids, and Mannia was also worrying about the baby, although he was in her mother's care. As a result, the ladies left the next day, while Mr. Yao remained with Mr. and Mrs. Fu for another two days.

CHAPTER XIV

$\mathcal{M}$ULAN went home with Mannia before going to her own house. Mannia's parents were pleased to see her but it somewhat frightened Mr. Tseng that she looked so fresh and young and he had misgivings whether he should let a young widowed daughter-in-law be seen so much in public. For Mannia had continued to grow up after she became a widow at eighteen, and was now tall and more beautiful than before. Mulan also frightened him a little because she seemed to have grown, too, with that subtle transformation that nature brings to a girl of her age. Her face and cheeks were a little rounder, her eyebrows and eyelashes darker, and her eyes were a little brighter, while the journey outdoors had heightened the natural glow of her complexion. He wondered whether he would have the luck to have such a daughter-in-law, and also what would be the fate of a woman too distinguished in beauty and talent.

Mannia announced the news that the sisters were going away to school.

"It isn't certain," said Mulan. "My parents are only talking about it."

"Still going to school at this age?" said Mr. Tseng. "Taking girls from their homes and letting them stay away at schools is getting worse. And why go so far as Tientsin?"

Cassia said, "They are not of our family and how can we assume the right to interfere?"

Mr. Tseng only smiled and Mrs. Tseng said "Mulan is just like my own daughter."

"We had better be careful," said Mannia. "If you let the pigeon fly away you don't know whether she will come back."

"What are you saying?" said Mulan. "I am going away only to study, and every month I will come back to pay you my respects."

When Mulan went home and was in her own room changing her dress, Brocade the maid came in and told her, "When you were away the house seemed so big and empty. Frankincense went home to see her people, and Silverscreen and I felt very lonely. The day before yesterday we went together to see Bluehaze's baby." Bluehaze had been married off to Lotung's son, who was working in a Wang household.

"And how is Bluehaze?" asked Mulan.

"She is very well," said Brocade, "and her baby is very pretty. It was the baby's 'full month' and *Taitai* had not thought of it, and we decided on your behalf to make the baby a present of a pair of tiger-head shoes and two dollars. We three also put together some money and bought the baby a little bracelet. Bluehaze said to thank you first, and in a few days she will be coming with the baby to pay her respects."

"It was good of you to think of it," said Mulan. "Was Silverscreen all right?"

"It is difficult for her," said Brocade. "With everybody else away, we two talked much together, and I began to think that she is not entirely to blame. We maidservants are not like you daughters of the household. We serve our master or mistress for five or ten years, but each has got to think where she will be in the end. As for me, I wish to serve you all my life, if I may . . ."

"Of course, Brocade. We grew up as children together, almost like sisters, and it would be hard for us to part."

"But for Silverscreen, it is different," Brocade went on. "She came first to the house, and she had the privilege of serving the eldest young master. But she is already over twenty and older than he, and she is in a position both too high and too low. She cannot wait until he is married, and she is too used to the comforts of this family to go home and marry a country lad, and she is unwilling to leave Peking. Bluehaze is married, and Frankincense has her parents here in the city and although I have lost my parents, I know that if I stay with you, I cannot make a mistake. But what can she do?"

"What you say is quite true," said Mulan. "Even bamboo shoots in the earth push upward. Who does not want to be exalted among his fellows? But if she does not want to go south, can't we pick a husband for her and marry her off in Peking?"

"It all depends on the heart," said Brocade. Mulan looked steadily at Brocade as she continued. "There is nothing in this world that you cannot provide for, except the heart. If her heart is set another way, everything is easy; but if her heart is set this way, then it is a problem indeed. The young master is handsome and kind to her, and, when he is in high spirits, he can talk so well. When he is displeased, of course, he has a temper but that is to be expected in men. And, even if she were willing to go away, he might not agree. She said . . ."

At this moment, Frankinscense came in to say that Silverscreen had a stomach-ache and Tijen had sent her to get medicine. Silverscreen had been subject to these pains in the past year and nobody was surprised. But late in the afternoon, Silverscreen became apparently much worse than usual. Tijen came to his mother's room, looking very pale, and said perhaps they ought to send for a doctor. Coral said, "Wait and see. It is nothing new. Give her a laxative and Spirit-Calming Powder, and tell her not to take food, but give her some last year's lotus soup."

"It must be that you have told her you are going away to England," said Mochow.

"I told her I was going," said Tijen, "and she said she was glad I could go abroad and see the world beyond the ocean."

"I still say the same thing," said Mochow.

"You do her an injustice," said her brother. "Her lips are all pale. Can such pain be affected?"

"I don't say her pain is affected. But I say that if you tell her you are not going away, the pain will disappear."

"Have you really decided to go?" asked Coral.

"Certainly," said Tijen. "None of you really understand me. You blame me for not working hard and for saying silly things about studies. But that is what I believe. All 'studies are for official glory,' it is said. Tell me why I should seek official glory and why I should study hard. Place yourself in my position. Does our family need me to earn money or to become an official? You all praise Lifu, but his mother is looking to him for support. Still I want to be a man as much as others, and I have to know the world, and taking studies abroad is different."

His mother was very pleased with this speech. Tijen had an unusually fair complexion and a straight nose like Mulan's and thick, dark eyebrows like his father. These and a little mustache peeping out from the sides of his upper lip gave him a manly appearance, and just now, he was having one of his outbursts of eloquence, and seemed noble and determined and sincere.

"If you have truly made up your mind to work upward and be a man, all is well," said his mother. "Yesterday, when you fulfilled your filial piety to me, I gained much face in the presence of Mrs. Kung. I don't want you to earn money or become official; all I want is that you be a man like others. But you must correct your temper and must not smash things whenever you are displeased."

"That is because we have things to smash, mother, and we can pay for new ones. If rich people who can afford to break things don't smash them and buy new ones, how are the artisans ever going to make their living? Money, money, money! Why was I born into this rich family? Mencius said, 'Therefore when Heaven intends to call a man to a great mission, He always first hardens his ambition, belabors his muscles and bones, starves his body, denies him the necessities of life, and frustrates what he sets out to do, so that his ambition may be kindled and his character be strengthened and he may learn to do what he could not do before.' But I have neither labored nor starved. Heaven must have a small opinion of me!"

Mochow and Coral laughed, but their mother did not understand all this literary effusion.

"I never heard Mencius so interpreted," said Mochow. "Do you really understand Mencius?"

"Of course I do."

"Mencius also said that sages and ourselves belong to the same species and all men are created equal, that the only difference between men and beasts is the little spark that is the human sense of right and wrong. If it is right to smash things it is also right to pour grain down the gutter. You misread Mencius and then blame Heaven for your own faults."

So Tijen was effectively stopped. "You are also like your Second Sister," he said. "You have grown big enough to lecture me."

. ˙ .

Now Tijen was very tender towards all girls except his own sisters. Silverscreen was sleeping in her room in the same yard. When he came back to her room, he found her lying with her face covered by a sheet. He gently lifted the sheet and asked how she was feeling, but Silverscreen abruptly turned her face away.

"You were gone a long time," she said, and Tijen saw she was wiping her eyes. "I had a violent pain a moment ago, but now it is better."

"You must not have a sad heart," said Tijen. "If you give your stomach a little rest tonight, probably you will be well tomorrow. You are to have only lotus soup and we shall not call the doctor at least until tomorrow."

Tijen pulled away Silverscreen's hand which was still covering her face, and said, "I was arguing with Third Sister about Mencius. They all seem to be against me. Only you understand me; only we two understand each other in heaven and earth."

Silverscreen smiled. "When you are away, there will be others who will understand you better, and then will you think of a bondmaid of your childhood?" She spoke like a full-grown woman to an innocent boy, and her voice had a softness which enchanted him. Her speech was direct and had none of the yielding, hesitating tone of a refined girl, and her voice as well as her features bespoke the peculiar Ningpo vitality. It is said that when a Ningpo girl wants to get a Shanghai boy, the boy is doomed, and Tijen, in spite of all his eloquence and good physique, was at heart like an effeminate Shanghai boy. As he justly complained, he had neither labored nor starved, and he was only a softshell clam. The remark of Silverscreen annoyed him a little, for he was sincere toward her and he replied:

"You don't believe me? If I ever forget you one day, or if I don't mean what I say, may a malignant boil grow on my lip and may I die of a convulsion and after death be changed into a donkey to be ridden by you in the next incarnation!"

"Why swear like that on a clear, bright day?" laughed Silverscreen.

"But you force me to! This is my chance to be a man and I must go. You care for my dog for me, and if I am unfaithful to you, when I return, I will be less than this dog, and you can kick me and beat me all you like, and I will sleep under your bed."

Tijen loved all foreign things—foreign cameras, watches, fountain pens, even atrocious foreign pictures, and he kept a foreign pointer that he took with him wherever he went, although Silverscreen always fed it. Tijen did not know how to treat a dog and in his fits of temper had kicked and abused it, to the dog's great bewilderment, so that it was more faithful to Silverscreen than to its master. Now, pointing to the dog, he said, "Can a man be less faithful than a dog?"

"In cleverness man is higher than a dog; in faithfulness a dog is higher than a man," replied Silverscreen. "It is not that I don't believe you. When you have a chance to go abroad, you ought to go. I have no right to interfere with your future. But who knows when you will come back, and I am of age already. Even if I want to wait for you, things may happen that I cannot help. If I don't marry and grow into a yellow-faced old maid, people will laugh at me and say, 'What are you waiting for?' How am I going to answer? And if I let others do with me as they like, will not my body belong to someone else when you come back? In this life, it is best not to be born a girl; a girl has no control over her own future."

Silverscreen sighed and gave an expression of pain, and perspiration gathered on her forehead, and Tijen wiped it for her.

"It is all right," she said. "You are so kind to me and I am grateful. But we have been talking nonsense. You are born a master and I a slave. Each has his own star and what is determined at birth cannot be changed. I am not sold to your family for life and one day surely my family will come to claim me back and I will marry a country boy and go back and be a farmer's wife. I have been well-fed and well-clothed in your home, and that is already good luck enough for me, so let us not talk of the future."

The dog gave a short bark, smelling the food coming. A servant lifted the screen bringing a bowl of lotus soup on a tray and said to Tijen, "The dinner is served. *Taitai* is waiting for you to go down."

"Tell them to go ahead. Why should I be eating at this moment?" Tijen was taking great liberties now because his father was not at home.

"I will feed you," said Tijen when the woman servant was gone, and Silverscreen let him. The soup was not sweet enough, and Tijen started to go to the kitchen to bring sugar, but she said, "Don't! Beware of gossip," and he turned back.

Then she said, "You had better go to your supper. I am all right, and you must keep up appearances." And Tijen left as he was told and came back after dinner.

The next morning Tijen announced to his mother and sisters that he was not going to England after all. Silverscreen was better than England.

. ˙ .

But when his father returned, Tijen had not the courage to say to him that he was not going.

"You had better cut off your queue," said Mr. Fu one day, "and have some foreign suits made."

Cutting off one's queue was to be ultra-modern in those days. It was slightly dangerous, for it might be taken as the sign of a "revolutionist" who was plotting the overthrow of the Manchu Empire. Revolutionists often cut off their queue, because the queue was a symbol of subjection to the Manchus. But it was allowed and thought natural in students who went abroad.

This appealed so much to Tijen that he said nothing more about not going to England, and during the following months his sisters were interested and amused by his foreign haircut and foreign suit and the neckties and studs and buttons that went with it. Tijen felt so smart and modern and was so pleased with himself that he behaved like a new being. Silverscreen who had to attend to his garments and laundry was constantly getting them mixed up, either out of excitement or out of resentment. The foreign shirts were so ridiculously long and the sleeves were cut in such a queer way that they twisted all along and it was difficult to tell which was the outer side of the cuffs and she often put his cuff links wrong side out. She lost all hope of learning how to press his coats and how to fold them in trunks.

"How is it that foreign dress has so impossibly many pockets and buttons?" she said one day. "Yesterday I counted, and there were fifty-three buttons, all told, inside and out, on his body."

But Tijen was happy and learned to walk with his hands in his trouser pockets and to wear bright ties and a watchfob in his vest and to rest his hand in his coat lapel and swing a stick, as he had seen the smart returned students and foreigners doing.

And Mochow helped Silverscreen because wearing foreign dress was such a distinguishing thing for a young man at that time that she took pride in seeing her brother so well attired, and she learned to press his coats for him.

Lifu, who now often came to see them, looked old-fashioned and slightly shabby beside Tijen. He did not care particularly about visiting the Yaos, but the mothers had become very friendly with each other and everybody tried to make him welcome. Gradually he lost his uneasiness in the rich home although he never felt himself in his natural element, and there was a distinct barrier between him and Tijen, due to wealth, whose ease he admired. He tried to be polite and sociable but he did not allow himself to joke in the presence of the sisters and always kept himself at a discreet distance. Once, with great shyness, he repeated at the insistence of the sisters the first page of the *Thousand-Character Text,* word by word backwards, because they had heard from Mr. Fu that he could do it. Often he was silent for some moments, but when he was speaking of what he thought or believed, he talked with such incisiveness that showed him as a master of what he knew. Once he said to Mulan, "It is a pleasure just to know a thing is so, when it is so."

Social intercourse between boys and girls was gradually becoming more and more permissible in those days; but the sisters, brought up in the old tradition, were always reserved and dignified in the presence of male visitors. Behind Lifu's back, however, they could not help discussing him.

His argumentative and serious mind particularly attracted Mulan. Her brother by contrast had a fine appearance, eloquence, fitful generosity and amiability, some cleverness in ideas, but never serious-mindedness. It really was not his fault, but the contrast was entirely in Lifu's favor except as to his dress.

Tijen had bought a beautiful pair of shoes made in England, which cost thirty-five dollars. Lifu also had a pair of foreign-style leather shoes but locally made, which he had to buy for physical drill at school. But he never acquired the habit of polishing foreign shoes and the leather had worn down to a dry, scratchy gray. Mochow remarked one day when he had gone:

"Have you seen his shoes—how dirty they are? I really felt I wanted to take them from his feet and let Silverscreen give them a polish."

"Polished or not, what difference does it make?" Mulan said.

"Appearances count," said Mochow.

"Appearances don't count," replied her sister.

And so a few days afterward, when Lifu walked in again with his unpolished shoes, the sisters could not help giggling and looking at each other. Mulan eyed Mochow as if to challenge her and Mochow summoned up courage to say, "Lifu, may I ask you a question?"

"What?" said Lifu.

"Your *hsieh*"—which was the word for shoes.

Mulan began to laugh, and Mochow could not finish her sentence and Lifu wondered what there was to laugh about. Mulan saved the situation by saying, "We were going to test you. Uncle Fu said you could say from memory the words of any rhyme in the rhyme book. Tell us what are the words in the ninth rhyme, *Hsieh?*"

Mochow was amazed at Mulan's quick wit, changing the *hsieh* meaning "shoes" into the *hsieh* meaning "crab" which was the name of the ninth rhyme in the book.

Lifu rattled off, "*Hsieh* (crab), *chieh* (explain), *mai* (bug), *chuei* (extinct animal), *nai* (milk), *wei* (dwarf), *kuai* (kidnap), *p'ai* (swing), *pa* (finish), *hai* (frightened) . . . Let me see. There is *k'ai* (model) and *ai* (to lean) and *ai* (silly)."

"Splendid!" exclaimed Mulan. "I don't blame Uncle Fu for saying such nice things about you."

"This is really foolishness," said Lifu. "It is merely a trick to fool people who cannot write poetry. It is meaningless to set a rhyme for a person to write a poem in, and it often kills good lines that the person might otherwise write, if he could choose his own rhyme. Besides, those rhyme books are at least seven hundred years old, and there is no reason why modern people should not have their own rhyme book to suit the modern pronunciation. There was no rhyme book in Confucius' times and yet there was much good poetry in the *Book of Songs.*"

By this time, both sisters had forgotten about his shoes, shabby though they were.

"I agree with you," said Mulan. "Pronunciations must have changed. For instance, *Hsieh* must have been pronunced *hsiai* or *hiai;* otherwise how could it rhyme with *mai, nai* in the rhyme book?"

"That's it," said Lifu. "We still sometimes say *panghsieh* and some times say *panghai* for crabs in the different dialects, and sometimes say *hsiehtse* and sometimes say *haitse* for shoes."

"Quite true," said Mochow, smiling. "We say 'polish *hsiehtse*' in Peking and Silverscreen, who is from Hangchow, says 'polish *haitse.*' The other day she said she wanted to 'polish shoes' and I thought she was going to polish a baby."

"If you don't believe me, I'll call her," said Mulan.

Now Lifu began to look down at his shoes and Mochow was aghast.

Silverscreen came in, and Mulan said, "Silverscreen, will you shine the baby for Mr. Kung?"

Then they all laughed, and Silverscreen actually brought in a box of shoe polish and made Lifu's only pair of leather shoes shine like new, and he was amazed and Mochow was satisfied.

Of this episode, Lifu knew only half. It was years later that Mochow told him the other half.

.·.

One day in June, Mrs. Tseng was playing chess with Mannia while Cassia was looking on. Mannia had just gone through the second anniversary of her husband's death and looked somewhat tired. Asuan, her child, now able to run about, was playing by her side.

Mrs. Tseng said, "Why is it that we do not see Mulan these days?"

"Who knows what she has been doing?" said Mannia. "She hasn't been here since she came to see Mr. Fang at the end of last month." Mr. Fang, the old teacher in Shantung, had come to Peking to live with the Tsengs for the rest of his life, because his wife had died and he was childless and alone. Mr. Tseng gave him nominally a job keeping accounts, but he was too old to be of any real help. To the children, once their teacher, he was their teacher for life, as was the old custom, and he had to be treated with the respect due a teacher.

"Probably she is busy with preparations for her brother's departure," added Mannia.

"When is he going?"

"I am told that it is at the end of this month."

"How is it that one has to go abroad to study foreign books and how can his mother let him go? I wouldn't let our little Sunya go so far."

"The other day when Brocade brought the presents for Mr. Fang from Mulan, I took her to my room and inquired, but she would not say anything. But the next day when Mulan herself came to pay Mr. Fang her respects she herself told me it had something to do with their maid Silverscreen. His mother has been persuaded that if he could be taken out of Silverscreen's company and sent abroad, he might be a changed man."

"But why send a boy beyond the ocean just to get him away from a maid?" asked Cassia.

"Who knows?" said Mannia, turning her eyes back to the chess board. She had been so absorbed in what she was saying that she did not see that her "cannon" was about to be eaten up by Mrs. Tseng's "soldier" which had already crossed into the enemy territory. Mrs. Tseng was so much better at chess that she could give Mannia the handicap of one "horse."

"I think you'd better give up," said Cassia. "When *Taitai's* soldier comes across, it is as good as a chariot and she can drive right up to the palace."

"Get your cannon out of the way," said Mrs. Tseng. "I see you are not looking well these days, and it is so hot. You might go and visit Mulan and move about a little. It will do you good."

But Cassia said, "I think it is a better idea for us to give Mulan and her brother a dinner. It will serve several purposes, as a farewell party for Tijen, and to welcome Mr. Fang, and to return the invitations Mannia has had from Mulan. It does not do to eat others' food without giving return. So we can pierce three hawks with one arrow. Let it be a young people's party, and Mannia and the brothers be the hosts."

"Do you really mean it?" said Mannia, all excited. She had never given a party of her own. "I had the idea, but dared not mention it. I will pay for the whole dinner myself. I can never use up my monthly ten dollars and what do I need to save for?"

"You are right; money is good only for making sentiments, for the needs of human intercourse," said Cassia. "Still it is better that the dinner go in the names of all three of you as hosts. You must let the brothers also have a chance to welcome Mr. Fang and it is better to do it altogether than to have three separate dinners, and, secondly, it is more appropriate for the boys than for you to give the farewell dinner to Tijen."

"And what about Ailien?" asked Mrs. Tseng.

"We'll do it like this," said Cassia. "Divide it into three, and I will pay for Ailien's share, and *Taitai* will pay for the brothers, and Mannia, you will pay your share."

"Why must it be like that?" said Mannia. "The dinner will be in all our names, but I want to pay for the whole, and I can well take out twenty-four dollars which will be enough. We will give it in my courtyard; it is very cool out there. Mother, please give me this face."

"If she insists, let it be as she wishes," said Mrs. Tseng.

"Whom shall we ask?" said Mannia.

"As you please," said Mrs. Tseng. "The sisters of the Yao family and their elder brother and Afei, if you like. On our side, just you and the children. Their school will close next week."

"Shall we include the News?"

"I don't think so," said Cassia. "And I don't think Suyun would come now even if we invited her." For Suyun was about to be engaged to Chinya. The past six months was a good half-year for her father, Finance Minister New. The weather was good and there had been large crops and prosperous trade, so that the government revenues were high and there was a lot of "grease" for the palms all the way up to the Finance Minister himself. The Minister had said to his wife and sons, "If Heaven follows man's wishes and the next crop is just as good, and the country at peace, I shall go back this winter to offer my thanksgiving at the ancestors' temple. All this comes from the august virtues of the Emperor and the occult blessings of our ancestors. When we drink water we must think of its spring. You must remember that." Mr. New was so happy that at the Dragon-Boat Festival in May he had decided to celebrate his good fortune by the wedding of his eldest son to a Miss Chen, and spurred by his wife, he went on to the engagement of his daughter Suyun to Chinya. The horoscopes of the girl and boy had now been exchanged and the formal engagement was about to take place.

"This reminds me of Mulan," said Mannia. "We had better hurry or she will be stolen away by somebody else. Such a fairylike girl is sure to get engaged very early, and whoever has the faster leg will get her. I heard the other day that the family of the Imperial Tutor Lin of Foochow was going to 'sue for marriage' from the Yaos. We must not delay from year to year."

"What she says is right," said Cassia.

"I have been thinking, too," said Mrs. Tseng. "I really don't know why I have been letting it drag on. I always think of Mulan as mine."

"But we must hurry," said Mannia. "She is going away to school."

"Why are you so anxious?" said Cassia. "Is Sunya going to marry her or are you?"

"I *am* anxious," Mannia replied, "and since Chinya is getting engaged, why not think of Sunya also? You will get an intelligent and obedient daughter-in-law, and I shall get a good companion in the house. Besides, this marriage is predestined. If she had not got lost, we would never have come to know her. Where else are you going to find another like her?"

"I don't blame you," said Mrs. Tseng. "Let anyone see her and his mouth will water. But I will have to ask Little Number Three himself."

"There is no need to ask," said Cassia. "If the match can be made, our flat-nosed Little Number Three ought to consider himself very lucky."

"Don't you worry," said Mannia. "I see Sunya's face turn red and bashful whenever she is mentioned. The other day when she was here and was talking with Chinya and me and the teacher, Sunya heard that she had come and rushed in and stared at her so that she was embarrassed. Then he said slowly, 'Lanmei, are you going to England to study? Why listen to Mr. Fu?' She looked at him in surprise and said, 'What is that?' 'They say you are going to England,' he said, looking so frightened. 'You have been misinformed. It's my brother,' she said calmly. Sunya looked so relieved that he jumped up and said, 'Is it true? Is it true that you are not going?' 'Of course it is,' said Lanmei. 'What should I go abroad to become a foreign lady for?' 'That's what I came to ask you,' he said; 'I was frightened. You are not deceiving me?' 'Why should I deceive you, you silly,' she said smiling. 'Suppose I were really going to England to become a foreign lady, what would you do?' 'If you should go, I would go with you,' said Sunya, and his face became red and white by turns and he turned to me saying, 'Didn't you tell us that she was going to England and that it was Mr. Fu's idea?' I told him he was mistaken. Old Mr. Fang was so taken by surprise that he watched them both and didn't say a word."

"How did Mulan look? Did she show anything?" asked Cassia.

"She was blushing and embarrassed, and I think that may be why she is keeping away from us now."

The dinner was given two days later, and Mulan came with her sister and brothers. They talked of Tijen's voyage and of England and foreign battleships. Tijen was sharing the seat of honor with old Mr. Fang and he was in high spirits and entertaining, and everybody looked at his foreign dress with great curiosity. Mr. Fang was also very happy and got very drunk before the dinner was over. Mannia noticed that Mulan did not act quite naturally toward Sunya, but Sunya was the liveliest and happiest of all.

.·.

So everything was progressing smoothly for everybody except Silver-screen, who was becoming silent and resigned. Mr. Fu came back from Tientsin in the last week of June to give advice and help arrange for Tijen's voyage and he promised to go with Tijen to Tientsin and see him off on the boat. Tijen's father had softened toward him and took him on several trips to the city and began to talk to him and to give him low-voiced advice. His mother, who was often crying, prepared special food for him every day. The house was quite in a turmoil. The mother felt a sense of disaster, but she had made up her mind that the problem of Silverscreen should be settled once and for all, and she wondered what her son could see in this Ningpo girl and hated her for causing all this confusion and making her accept the unwilling sacrifice.

A few days before the date of departure, Tijen's mother thought of the queue that he had cut off and asked him for it, saying that she wanted it for padding her own coiffure, and he told her that he had given it to Silverscreen already. This troubled his mother very much.

"My son," she said, "you are going away and I don't know when you will be coming back. You are now grown up and should be thinking of serious things. Silverscreen has served you for all these years, and I don't mind your wanting to be fair to her, but she is a bondmaid and soon she must be married off."

"She is a bondmaid, but isn't she a human being also?" said Tijen rather hotly. "I don't know when I shall return, but I have asked her to wait for me. If I don't come back in three years, you can marry her off. I have also given my dog to her, and while I am away, the dog belongs to her."

The mother was horrified.

"My son, you are going to study now. Why are your thoughts still centered upon girls?"

"You will promise that you will keep her here while I am away," said Tijen.

And his mother promised not to send Silverscreen away, if her family did not come to claim her.

Tijen happily went back to Silverscreen to tell her the news.

"You wait for me," said Tijen to her. "I am the eldest son of the family, and if you stay with me, you need not worry and the Yao fortune will be enough to keep you in plenty and comfort all your life."

This was more than Silverscreen had hoped for. She was neither well nor exactly unwell these days. She helped in all things concerning Tijen's packing, but she was somehow exempted from the other household duties and did not go about much. Of all the maids in the house, she was now the eldest and she paid the most attention to her dress.

She was trying the keys for the trunks in Tijen's room. When she heard Tijen's words, she turned a key, and the lock clicked and it seemed that a decision had been made. Slowly she rose and walked to a mirror and looked at herself and smoothed her hair.

"Are you talking seriously or are you making fun of me?" she said with an artful smile. Although a bondmaid, she had learned the gestures and glances of a girl of the family. Tijen was charmed by these movements of a girl's fingers smoothing her hair, turning her palm downward or inward in drooping gestures and showing her painted fingernails to the best advantage.

"In this world the most undependable thing is man's heart," said Silverscreen. "Everything depends upon you and if you are sincere, I can take care of myself while you are gone."

Tijen had come close behind her, and she turned round and pressed her outstretched forefinger at his face with a gentle force and said vehemently with her teeth together, "You *yuanchia!*" which is the term for a lover with whom one was hopelessly involved by fate, since it meant literally "predestined enemy."

"Will you promise to wait for me?" asked Tijen again.

"That is easy," she said. "If your heart does not change, they cannot drive me away from this house. And if the worst comes, there is still death."

"Hush, you must not die," he said. "You must live and enjoy life together with me when I come back."

"Death is nothing extraordinary. Everybody must die sooner or later," said Silverscreen. "Who can foretell things in this world? The only difference is whether one dies in a worthy manner or not. If one dies and there is someone to shed a tear over one's grave, that is what I call a worthy death. But if one dies without a single person's sympathy, that is what I call a death not worth dying."

"Stop such talk!" he said, quite frightened. "My mother has promised me and you need not worry. What I hate most is to hear a pretty young girl talk of death!"

"Even as there is reunion, so there must be parting, and even as there is living, so there must be death," said Silverscreen, quoting the proverb. "You don't like to hear girls talk of death, but you have never been a girl yourself. A girl's life is even cheaper than a man's and there is nothing difficult about death."

Tijen suddenly became very sad. "If that is the case, let us all die, and there will be neither parting nor reunion, only peace and not all this trouble and confusion."

Now Silverscreen had talked of death only because it was a common mode of speech among servant girls. The truth was that there was a born tenacity in her not only to live, but also to beat all life's mishaps. When she saw from the corner of her eye that he was taking her seriously and had become very sad, she came close to him and, sitting by his side, said, "I won't die if you are true to me—I won't die under any circumstances. But you must not stay away too long. It is hard to tell how things will change in a few years."

Tijen, lying back in his chair, seemed not to hear her. "Perhaps what you say is right. 'Even as there is reunion, so there must be parting, and even as there is living, so there must be death.' But since there is death and parting, why have reunions and life? Isn't it just being busy in vain?"

"I won't die—I won't die. Is that enough?" said Silverscreen.

"Who knows about you girls?" said Tijen. "I have often wondered why there must be girls in this world." Silverscreen looked at him puzzled; he was apparently in one of his moods for saying queer things. "The difference between boys and girls is only that there is one piece of flesh more or less on the body, but imagine all the trouble! Now take yourself and Brocade and Frankincense and Bluehaze. You are all as clever and intelligent as I am, and more beautiful, and you are better characters. Now I am your master, but after a few years you will all be married off, and who can interfere with whom? I really don't understand this life. Sometimes I say to myself, suppose the girls were born the masters and I and Afei and my sisters were born the servants. Life still would not be much changed and probably I would take it just as naturally, and I really can't tell who would have the advantage over whom. You try to think: my father has all this property and all this money. There are dozens of men working for us, probably sixty or seventy in all the shops—every day opening shop, closing shop, being polite to customers, selling things, keeping accounts, chasing after debtors—and hundreds more—mostly men running about to gather herbs and teas in all parts of the country and putting them in junks and loading and unloading them or carrying them on their shoulder; and we sit here eating what we like and going about as we like. They are all working for this Yao family; but you look at this Yao family. However you reckon it, there are more women than men in it—my mother, Coral, Mulan, Mochow, and all of you and the servants. Isn't it true, then, that hundreds of men, with my uncle at the top, are foolishly earning the money for you women to spend it? Are we slaving for you or are you slaving for us? That is why I don't want to work and am only spending money. That is probably also why my father doesn't want to work. And now I am going to England. We are buying trunks and clothes and booking passage and I shall be staying in hotels. What else am I really going to do except to spend money? Sometimes I think it would be nobler for me to take your place and do a little work and earn my simple meal. Honestly, suppose I were your maid and you were my master, and I had to do the packing for you, and you had to do the traveling—would you change places with me?"

Silverscreen hesitated. "Packing is a woman's job and traveling is a man's job," she said. "How can men and women change places?" She did not know just what he meant but she could not help being amused, as she often was, for he could be a very entertaining talker. But when he was gone again, she thought to herself how wonderful it was that she, a poor, helpless girl from the south, had been lucky enough to grow up in this rich home, and how wonderful it would be if indeed, as he had said, she were the young mistress of the house, or at least, if his promise came true and she should share with him forever the security of the Yao fortune.

· ·

Now all arrangements had been made, and on the last day Mrs. Yao realized that her son was really going, perhaps for years. The father had become even more kind to him, although he had not said many words. Afei constantly hung about his elder brother and Tijen again felt himself the lucky and important boy of the family and behaved like a big brother to Afei and to his sisters.

That night at supper, the mother shed tears, but the father comforted her and said again, "Going abroad to study is a good thing."

"It is only hard for the heart," she said, amidst her tears. "I was thinking that he has never left his home since childhood and he is still so young."

After supper, the family sat together in the mother's room, the father smoking his water pipe.

"Tijen," the father began very softly, "I don't mind spending ten or fifteen thousand dollars on your trip abroad; money is made for man's use anyway. But I want you to decide to be a man. You are the eldest son; if you follow the right course, this family profits; and if you go wrong, the family suffers. Take degrees if you want, but the important thing is to learn to be a man.

> The affairs of the world, well understood, are all scholarship;
> Human relationships, maturely known, are already literature.

Travel about if you like and see Europe, and open your eyes. But you must correct your lump of silly spirit and must not waste your intelligence on trivial things. Think what Mrs. Kung's son could do with your opportunity if he had it."

"And there is another thing," said the mother. "Don't get mixed up with foreign girls. I will not recognize a foreign daughter-in-law. We are Chinese and our manners are different from theirs. Also, everywhere you go, be sure to write us letters."

Mulan, seeing that her mother was about to shed tears again, said gaily, "And in your letters tell us if there's really a country called the Kingdom of Grape Teeth," which is the Chinese meaning of the name Portugal. "I heard that the Empress Dowager did not believe there was a country by such a funny name, and when the Portugese Minister was about to be presented to her the first time, she said that people must have been fooling her. 'How can there be a country called Grape Teeth?' she said. 'If so, there must be also a Kingdom of Bean Teeth and a Kingdom of Bamboo Teeth.' "

Even Mulan's mother laughed. "I promise," said Tijen, "that I will take a train from London to Portugal and write you a letter from the Kingdom of Grape Teeth."

It was an evening of perfect peace and harmony between father, mother, and son, and between brothers and sisters. Seldom again in that household was it possible to find such peace and harmony and innocent hope.

CHAPTER XV

THE next morning the whole family saw Tijen off at the railway station, except the mother, who was weeping at home, and Coral, who stayed with her. It was an exciting event, for there had never before been a parting in the family. Lifu also came and met them at the station and went into the train with the sisters to have a last chat with Tijen. Sunya and Chinya came rushing into the station at the last minute, when the rest had already come down from the train, and had time only to exchange a few words with Tijen and to hand him a package of presents through the window. Tijen at the window with his white collar and scarlet tie below his white face and high, straight nose appeared really like a "foreign devil." Mr. Yao stood on the platform silently watching the train pull out of the station. When it had at last disappeared, the Tseng boys turned and saw the strange boy, dressed in a sky-blue "bamboo cloth" cotton gown, standing near Mulan. Waiting to be introduced, Lifu looked at these boys dressed in gowns of lake-water silk gauze, topped by black satin vests with coral buttons, their queues smoothly made in loose plaits, and wearing brand-new double-nosed black satin shoes and white socks. The Yao sisters, too, had come in their best, wearing heavy cream crepe jackets with extremely narrow sleeves and thick damask trousers of duck's-egg green, for the narrow sleeves had now suddenly come into fashion in place of the broad, flowing sleeves of earlier days. The plain cream jackets were set off by bright green-jade buttons which looked cool on this summer morning. Mulan wore tiny, pear-shaped ruby earrings, and Mochow wore earrings of aquamarine, and each had small tresses coming down from the temples about an inch in front of the ears. Lifu felt out of place in that company of brightly-dressed youth and beauty. Both girls were blowing their noses hard, and Mulan said to the Tseng boys, smiling through her tears, "Thank you for coming." "We are sorry we were

220

late," said Sunya, and he looked at Lifu, and Mulan said, "Oh, this is Mr. Kung, a friend of Mr. Fu." They bowed to each other, and Mochow noticed that Lifu's foreign shoes were again threatening to become gray, although blacker than they had been before.

The party came out of the station, and their carriage was driven up to the curb. Mr. Yao offered to take Lifu in their carriage to his home, but Lifu said that as his home was very near he would walk. "Come and see us often when you have nothing to do in the vacation, even though Tijen is away," said Mr. Yao, and Lifu promised. He then stood by to see them get into the carriage and bowed to them and saw their carriage roll off before he started to walk home.

Mr. Yao was very silent. He took Afei's hand and held it. He was thinking that perhaps he had been too severe with Tijen and had kept him too much at a distance, and he determined not to let this happen again with Afei. He would become as affectionate and familiar with the little boy as he was with his daughters.

In the carriage Mulan said, "I have a strange feeling, as if a great weight had been lifted from our family."

"Do you think he will change henceforth?" asked the father, perhaps remembering his own youth and sensing that the young blood in his son's veins had not yet run its full course.

"He is being given such a great chance," said Mochow. "Perhaps seeing the world and coming under the best professors in one of the best universities of the world will change him."

But her father said, "You are young, and so you speak like this. Our family has money and so we spend it. Yet going abroad or not going abroad has nothing to do with one's studies. Scholarship or acting like a man can be learned anywhere. You saw what good manners Lifu showed in bidding us good-by. In the presence of grown-ups, he knows how to hold his own and yet to be at ease and keep people's respect. Does one have to go abroad to learn these things?" And Mochow and Mulan said no more after these words from their father.

To Lifu the matter had a different aspect as he walked home. He did not know whether he was jealous, or was momentarily excited at the sight of another young man going abroad for studies. He had heard about Cambridge and Oxford, names that kindled his desire for knowledge. He was not sure whether Tijen appreciated what a chance to study at Cambridge or Oxford meant or whether he was going there at all. That vision of an education abroad was to Lifu an ideal, to be attained perhaps some day far off.

He also felt that the society of the Yaos and the Tsengs was above him and that he could not stand their way of living. His friendship with Tijen had not grown, for Tijen shared with him only the ability to criticize the rich and the powerful, or, as they said at school, to write essays "reversing historical verdicts"; beyond that they had nothing in common. There was in Tijen nothing positive, nothing serious, and he regarded the Tseng boys as in the same class, and thought that these families belonged in a world by themselves. At their first meeting at the Western Hills he had been surprised that the Yao sisters could cook their own meals and only for that reason had a better opinion of them. Traditionally he had a dread of the daughters of rich families. It was true that these girls were both good-mannered and well-educated, but he had no sense of feminine charm. The other day he had condescended out of politeness to let his shoes be polished; but he thought polishing shoes was a thing totally irrelevant, and that having one's shoes polished by a kneeling maid was a degenerate form of living. Yet he liked and appreciated things of good quality, such as he saw in Mulan's home, for he was that true aristocrat—an aristocrat of the senses.

He and his mother and sister were occupying a house of three rooms in the Szechuen Guild House, where they lived since he was born. There was an empty lot before the gate with a dirty creek flowing by, and he had played under the big persimmon tree as a child. Even when his father was a minor official, they had lived in these rooms, because they did not have to pay rent, although his parents had saved enough money to buy a house in the Southern City, but this they rented out to add to their income. Mr. Fu's influence had something to do with their ability to occupy the rooms long after his father died. While the gatekeeper claimed he had seen Lifu grow up, Lifu realized he had seen the gatekeeper grow into a grandfather. The very doorposts and door passage and the pair of stone lions outside the gate were as familiar to him as the old top which still lay in his desk drawer. He had seen the door grow lower and the passage grow narrower and shorter as he grew up, and he had himself helped to make the old stone lions so smooth on the surface. There was a stone ball inside each of the lions' mouths, cut from the same stone but rolling freely within, and he had tried many times to get the ball out of the lion's mouth, until he grew bigger and wiser and gave up.

The house had a green gate with a red disc in the center, and inside the gate a passage led by a left turn to a brick-paved courtyard. Their own suite of rooms, reached from the yard by a narrow door to the right, consisted of the traditional "two open and one dark," that is, one parlor-study-dining-room occupying two-thirds, while a bedroom occupied the other third. He was still sharing the bedroom with his mother, his little sister sleeping in the same bed with his mother, while he slept in a bamboo bed near the window facing the courtyard. Two rooms on the eastern side of the court served as kitchen and general storeroom, and a servant slept there.

The court was paved with ancient bricks, some of them broken, and in the middle was a boy's amateur sundial. The support consisted of a broken stone slab two feet high that Lifu had picked up and persuaded the gatekeeper to help him carry in and stand on its end in the yard. On top of this stone support, Lifu had placed a whole gray brick, one foot square, and on top of the brick a ten-cent sundial consisting of a wooden box with hour markings, a red string to cast the sun's shadow and a small disc in the center containing a compass. As the top of the slab was uneven, he had placed broken bricks below it to keep it level, and the effect of the three-inch wooden dial on this huge support in the middle of the court was comic. It must be confessed that at times he had removed the sundial box and used the same place to set a trap for sparrows.

But he had also done bigger things. He had once put a pole beside the sundial and stretched a string straight from the pole to the southern end of the yard in a line strictly parallel to the red string on the small sundial, and had then started hour markings on the pavement by checking with the shadow on the little model. His mother had permitted him this amusement, as she had permitted him so many other things in her indulgence, especially as the sundial was traditionally associated with the idea of "valuing inches of the sun's shadow" for a hard-working pupil. But a string across the middle of the courtyard was a nuisance and both his mother and the servant had several times tripped over it, so that he had to abandon the experiment. However, the hour markings in words of the duodecimal cycle of twenty-four hours could still be seen on the face of the bricks in the yard, to the surprise of occasional visitors, and Lifu had learned from the experiment a definite sense of the shifting of the sun's angle in winter and summer.

The parlor was typical of middle-class households, with his father's portrait in the middle of the eastern wall flanked by a pair of scrolls written by a late Premier Weng, which were among their few valuable heirlooms. The scroll was inscribed to his father, who had solicited it through a friend. The floor was covered with a matting and the ceilings and windows were covered with white paper, giving the rooms a fairly neat appearance. An ordinary redwood square table stood against the wall and was used by the family of three for a dining table. Lifu's small desk stood at the window on the eastern end. Some wooden chairs, a rattan settee with cushions, an old rattan desk chair, brown and smooth, and a semicircular table against the eastern wall below his father's portrait completed the furniture. In the open shelves was the collection of books, largely the legacy of Lifu's father, including one especially valuable edition of the history, *Tsechih Tungchien,* and some standard collections of poetry and essays, and there was no more extraordinary evidence of classical scholarship than the regular edition of the *Thirteen Classics.* For his father had got along comfortably, as most officials did, without knowing more beneath the surface of classic commentaries and philological scholarship than was necessary for passing the imperial examinations. There were some reference books, and Lifu had added to the collection his modern textbooks and a bound volume of Liang Chichao's *"Essays of the Drink-Ice Studio,"* which he had thoroughly devoured, and which represented to the China of that decade all the new thought and new knowledge of the West.

There was no question that Lifu was the master and lord of this little court. His mother was continuously puzzled and surprised by him, as many fond mothers have been by their own offspring.

The puzzle was that Lifu happened to be dropped in her lap and born right. His mother simply gave him love, but no education. When she heard Mr. Fu say extraordinary things about her son, she just smiled and did not know what to reply. Just as Mrs. Tseng had complimented Mulan's mother by saying, "What a good belly you've got!" so Mulan's mother had complimented Lifu's mother. But the prouder she was of her son, the more modest she became about herself. They had raised a brood of chickens in the courtyard that spring, and the mother had said to her son and daughter one evening, when they were happy together under the lamplight: "Look at that black, heart-spotted old hen. How did she give birth to the pretty little chickens, with such tiny, red beaks and such black round eyes and such fine coats of down! Sometimes I have thought I was that black old hen." Lifu remembered that his mother had often told him that when he was born there was a little bit of dry skin in the middle of his upper lip, which was very pointed. And so the analogy of the chicken's little beak came back to him again.

"Thirty-five dollars for a pair of shoes!" Lifu had exclaimed when he had returned from the station and was talking of those he had met. "That would be enough for my school tuition for two years!"

"When you go to college this fall, it will cost much more; seventy or eighty dollars for a term," said his mother. "That reminds me that you ought to go and collect the rent. It's the end of the month."

And Lifu ran to collect the rent for his tuition.

. . .

Late in July, Mulan's uncle, Mr. Feng, returned with his wife and a seven-year old daughter, Redjade, from Hangchow, where he had been for the past year. Redjade was a most unusual child. It took a long time for the sisters to befriend her and get her to talk freely or to accept food or gifts from them, and when she did accept, she would say "thank you" like a stranger. Days passed before she began to feel at home and play freely with Afei. Coral thought that perhaps the child was afraid of her Peking cousins, but it was unnatural for a child to be so reticent. In an amazingly short time, however, she learned to talk with the Peking accent and to imitate the speech of her cousins. She was so intelligent that she had picked up a few written characters when she was only five, and Mulan and Mochow soon began to teach her more characters. After a few weeks' stay, she began to be very talk-ative, and, when the sisters asked her why she was so silent at first, she replied that she was afraid of speaking the Hangchow accent and being laughed at.

Mr. Feng's return put an idea into Mrs. Yao's mind. She was determined to get rid of Silverscreen while Tijen was away. She would be fair to Silverscreen; she would marry her off properly and find as good a match for her as she could. But she would not tolerate her tyrannical hold over her son. No woman can understand the fascination of another woman for a man. She regarded Tijen's infatuation for Silverscreen as merely a youthful episode, brought about by daily contact at the adolescent age, and believed that once she was out of the way her son would forget about her. She had not yet chosen a daughter-in-law for her son, and she was not going to have a concubine thrust upon him before he had a wife. She had been forced to go to the length of sending Tijen abroad to take him out of Silverscreen's company and she hated her for forcing the sacrifice upon her. She had thought of a plan of her own and had not told her daughters about it, but when her brother came she confided it to him. He was to be the accomplice and to say that he had seen Silverscreen's aunt at Hangchow, who had told him to marry her off, since she was now of age, and to find a good husband for her in Peking.

So one day Mrs. Yao called Silverscreen into her room to have a talk with her. Silverscreen felt that something was wrong. Since Tijen's talk with her about his mother's promise to keep her until he returned, she had shown an unusual interest and desire to please everybody again, including the mother, but she knew that the mother disliked her, for she spoke few words with her.

Silverscreen came in, and standing near the door, said, "*Taitai,* you sent for me?"

"Yes, come here. I want to talk to you," said Tijen's mother, and Silverscreen came nearer to her. "You have been in our home now for some ten years," the mother began, "and you are already grown. According to custom we have to think of your future, and this has been on my mind for a long time. Last year we tried to send you home to the south, but you were ill and could not go. I think, although you are a southerner, you do not have to insist on returning south. What do you think?" Mrs. Yao paused to watch Silverscreen's expression and saw that her eyes were cast down, and her body was trembling, as Silverscreen said, "*Taitai,* tell me what you have to say."

So she went on. "I have thought of a way for you. As the ancients say, 'A boy grown big should marry and a girl grown big should wed.' You have been serving my son very loyally and we want to find a good man who can work for his living for you, and you will have your own home and not be a bondmaid any more—like Bluehaze, who now has a husband and a child of her own."

Silverscreen still refused to speak, and Mrs. Yao continued, "Last week Second Uncle returned from the south and said he had seen your aunt. Your aunt's idea is that since it is difficult to find a man to take you down south and since you are already of this age, we should find a man for you in the capital. I will provide you with a complete trousseau."

Then Silverscreen spoke: "*Taitai*, I know your good intentions and appreciate them. Since I came to your home over ten years ago, I have received your kindness and I hope that I have not committed any great mistakes. If you will allow me, I am not in a hurry to leave you. Bluehaze was married only last year, and I am not yet of her age. Although the young master has gone abroad and I have less to do, there are enough in this house to be helped, and, although my contract was for ten years, I am willing to serve you a few years more. It will not cost you much—only a bowl of rice now and then, and I do not have to have new dresses. When the time comes you can just send me away and I will go and you need not give me a trousseau."

"It is not that I want you to leave. Your aunt said that you should."

"If that is her idea, why did she not write me? She could have asked some one to write a letter for her. This is not a small matter."

"But she told Second Uncle, and that should be enough. Don't you believe his words?"

"It is not that I don't believe Second Master. But this is a great step in my life, and for my own protection I must have a written word from my family. We girls of poor fate have to take what others like to give us. If *Taitai* does not want me, I have no other way but to leave, but I must have a written word."

Silverscreen was now in tears. Mrs. Yao felt she was defeated, but she said, "If you insist on a written word, that can be done also. But I have made up my mind already. When I have news, I will tell you," she ended severely.

Silverscreen wiped her tears and went away, frightened, confused, and bitter. She felt she had been cheated, and that she had right on her side, and that the mistress was deceiving her son, for he had asked her to wait and had made her a promise. But this was something that she could not have told in her own defense, even to save the situation. In her own room she fell upon her bed and cried wildly, "This is the way his mother turns me out as soon as he turns his back!"

Silverscreen's continued weeping was heard through the house and created confusion and excitement. But the mistress was heard to say aloud, "It is nothing bad we're doing to her. A girl must marry when she is grown. We cannot feed her for life. A little bondmaid like her must not be too ambitious." And every man and maid in the house knew what the mistress meant.

Now Coral and Mulan and Mochow heard of it, but when their mother was angry, they dared not say a word. At first, Mr. Yao thought that his wife was giving an ordinary lesson to one of the maids, but when he learned that it was more serious, he came over to the mother's room and asked what it was about. The sisters were all gathered in the room but the maids had run away, not daring to listen. The uncle was away at the shop, and, when the father asked about the affair, the mother told him that her brother had brought back word from Silverscreen's aunt to marry her off in Peking. "Is this true?" said Mulan's father. "He has not told me about it."

"You are a man, and this is a domestic affair, that is why he hasn't told you," replied the mother.

"What does Silverscreen say about it?" asked Mulan's father.

"She says she wants a written word from her aunt before she will leave. She—wanting a written word when I have told her what she is to do! I never heard of such insolence!"

"But it is not difficult," said Mochow. "And a letter from her family would be our protection. They have not sold her outright to us, and we do not have the right to do with her as we please. Unless we get the contract back, they can demand the girl from us."

"What of those bondmaids that die of illness, or run away? If she had a home or a relative in this city, I would tell her to pack up and leave this very minute."

The affair was left undecided. When the father went away, the mother told Mulan in a low voice to ask Lota to tell the uncle that *Taitai* wanted to see him as soon as he came back. Mulan felt there was something clandestine about the whole matter, but she did not say anything. She felt that her mother was perhaps taking a step that had to be taken sooner or later, but that she need not have done it so soon.

After half an hour, Brocade came in and Mulan asked how Silverscreen was. "She is still crying. She says that she lost her parents when she was quite young and her uncle sold her for two hundred and forty dollars to pay a gambling debt, and that the term was ten years, which expired last year, and she was then willing to go back, but the young master would not let her. She says he has told her to wait and has made *Taitai* promise to keep her at least for three years, but of course she could not say so to people. So I told her, 'You gain nothing by being stubborn. The young master is gone, and there is no one to defend you.' And she said, 'If *Taitai* insists on my going, I will go, but I must have a written word from my family.' You wait and see. She is a stubborn girl and there is a second act to watch yet."

"Really!" said Mulan. "She is talking *Shaohsing* mandarin. But you must not say a word about this to *Taitai*. It is nothing beautiful to be aired about. Such a matter ought to have been settled before my brother left. If it is true that my brother has promised her, this is somewhat hard on her."

"May I make bold to say something?" asked Brocade. "He was very kind to her and a human being cannot be blind to sentiment. You saw how his dog looked that morning when he was leaving. That animal must have felt that its master was going far away. Why then wonder at a human being? It is disgraceful to admit it, but this boy and girl affair was inevitable. If I were to be ordered to leave you now, I would feel very bad too," Brocade added.

"Ah, but you and I are different," said Mulan.

"But you must think," Brocade insisted, "almost from childhood, she took care of the young master, attending to his toilet in the morning, making his queue, fetching and finding things for him, until he got so used to her that nobody else was able to attend to him, or to find or remember where his things were. After he left, she had nothing to do and suddenly she seemed lost and absent-minded. It is perfectly natural and one cannot blame it on her. And now again suddenly she is to be sent away; can we wonder that she is feeling very badly about it?"

Now the uncle had come back and was closeted with the mother for over half an hour. At dinner Silverscreen appeared as usual to serve them, with the other maids, but she looked none too pleasant and for the most part stood idle. When Frankincense, who had taken the place of Bluehaze, was about to refill the rice bowl for Mrs. Yao, the latter said, "Don't do it. I want Silverscreen to fill it." Silverscreen came and refilled the bowl and when she was about to hand it back to the mistress, a tear dropped into the rice just as she was setting it on the table, and she quickly took it up again.

"Cheap *tsangfu!* Are you unwilling to serve me?" shouted the mistress, who had not seen the tear drop. *"Tsangfu"* actually meant "a whore" but was not an uncommon word of abuse among low-class women. "Go away!" and she pushed Silverscreen hard. "I have fed you until you are so big, and you have not a bit of gratitude. You have turned this house upside down, and broke up the family peace. On account of you, the young master has to be sent abroad, and you have caused us, mother and son, to part. You have insane ideas! A poxy toad thinking of eating swan's flesh!"

Stung by shame, Silverscreen wept aloud, covering her face with her arm and answering, "I have not eaten up the young master, have I?"

The angry mistress rose from her seat to rush toward Silverscreen, but the uncle checked her, and Brocade quickly tried to stop Silverscreen from going further.

"Little bondmaid, you are being rude in the presence of the master and mistress," said Mr. Feng.

Mr. Yao sat and watched and said not a word.

Silverscreen turned. Her face was injured and defiant, for she could stop her crying as quickly as she had started it.

"Master, Mistress, Second Master," she said, "you will excuse me. I have been in your house these many years, and if I have made any mistakes I am ready to take punishment. Young Master has gone abroad to study, but what has that got to do with me and why blame it on me? It was my duty to serve and please him, and if he treated a bondmaid kindly, that is your son's business. Tell me what sin I have committed and how I have turned the house upside down, and punish me as you like."

"Listen to her glib tongue!" said the mistress.

"Silverscreen," said Coral the pacifier, "if you have things to say, say them properly. You should not be rude."

"If you want me to go, I'll go," said Silverscreen. "If you want me to die, I will die before your eyes."

The threat of death or suicide was the commonest weapon for a servant to hold over the head of her mistress. "Who wants you to die?" said the uncle. "Your family's contract with us was for ten years. Last year I was ready to take you back and you would not or could not go. This time your aunt told me to make arrangements for you and we are following your aunt's instructions. If you want a written word from your aunt or uncle, that can be done also. I will write to her. Meanwhile there is nothing to argue about. What do you think?"

"If the master does not think me rude, I will say this," replied the maid. "My term has ended. Either you must find some one to send

230

me back, or if I am to be given to people here, I have to have my aunt's written word. I know that my aunt does not care whether I'm dead or alive, but marriage is a big affair in life. I am not in the class of young ladies with parents to look after me, and I must look after myself and marry with my own consent. I will not be married off to Mongolia or Kansu."

"Then everything is settled," said Mr. Yao at last. "We will find a good match for you here in Peking and I don't think you can be bullied by anybody."

So the affair was left there for the present. But Mrs. Yao became more and more abusive, so that it was clear to Silverscreen that she had no choice but to leave sooner or later. Whenever she spoke of her, Mrs. Yao would refer to her as "that shameless little whore." But Silverscreen somehow managed to have herself reported to the mistress as saying, "Even a dog kept for ten years need not be beaten away from the house. Men and women are worse than dogs."

CHAPTER XVI

THAT summer there was a pouring rain for ten days, which was quite unusual, for in Peking the summer rains usually come only in brief torrential showers, leaving the city cool and pleasant as soon as they are over. The rains prevented visits, and the sisters stayed at home, amusing themselves with Redjade and making her tell them stories about Hangchow. The news that the Yaos were trying to find a match for Silverscreen soon reached Bluehaze, and one day she paid a visit to the house, to act as the intercessor for Silverscreen, and she promised to help find a match for her.

To the amazement of the family, they now received a letter from Tijen that he had not caught the boat at Hong Kong and was staying at a hotel there. This worried his mother very much, and it was proof that he could not yet look after himself, and his father was infuriated. The letter was not clear. Apparently his baggage had been sent on board the ship, for the letter said that he had telegraphed the company at Singapore to send his baggage back. This was puzzling, for it would have been logical for him to take the next ship and claim his baggage at Singapore.

What had happened was that on board the boat from Tientsin, he had made the acquaintance of a returned student from England who told him about the hazing at English public schools and the fights and hardships and about fags who had to serve dinners and shine shoes for the senior students. The teller colored his stories a little for effect, and it sounded like a dismal life. For Tijen had forgotten all about the passage he had quoted from Mencius about Heaven "belaboring a man's muscles and bones and starving his body" before "calling him to do great things." He could not make up his mind, and at the last minute, after having sent his baggage down to the boat, he decided not to go.

At Hong Kong he had plenty of money to spend and the chance

to spend it with a freedom unknown to him before. Being gregarious by nature and obviously well provided with money, he made many friends at the hotel, who took him to carousing parties. The more he saw of Hong Kong life, the better he liked it. As he did not know his own intentions, he could not make them clear in his letter.

The next mail that came three days later brought word to his family that he liked Hong Kong and wanted to perfect his English there before going abroad. He intended to enter a Hong Kong college for English studies. His father was still more infuriated.

This time a letter came for Mulan also, saying that he was sending a set of Cantonese ivory buttons for each of his sisters and a silver powder case for Silverscreen, which he asked Mulan to give to her. There was nothing for the parents. The sisters thought of saying nothing to Silverscreen and passing the powder case to the mother, but feared that since he was remaining at Hong Kong he would soon find out.

Tijen's mother was more than mortified. As the situation in the house stood now, the gift to the maid looked almost like a direct and intentional rebuff to what the mother was planning to do. She was afraid lest her son should come back, and she decided to hurry Silverscreen's marriage.

But Silverscreen was overjoyed and decided to dally. One afternoon she asked leave to go out in a pouring rain and visit Bluehaze, saying that she had promised to return her call. But Mulan suspected that she had gone out to ask some one to send a letter to Tijen.

The rains were not over until the beginning of August. All this time neither Lifu nor his mother had paid a single visit to the Yaos since Tijen's departure. The family were too much occupied with Silverscreen's affair to think of other things. Tijen sent picture postcards from Hong Kong to the Tseng boys and also one to Lifu in their care. This reminded Mrs. Yao of Lifu, and she said, "Why haven't Mrs. Kung and Lifu visited us for such a long time?" So when the rains stopped, she sent a servant to take some presents to Mrs. Kung and to ask them to come and see them. The servant came back and reported that a tree branch had crashed down on the roof of Mrs. Kung's house in the Szechuen Guild and made a big hole in it and that the family were living in the kitchen, with their furniture and trunks stacked in the passageways.

The next day, Lifu came to thank them for the presents. He was

233

prompted to come partly by the news which the servant had told them about Tijen's having given up going to England. To him, it was unbelievable. On being asked how their house was, Lifu said that the accident had happened at night when there was a storm and that the house became impossible to live in. The courtyard also, he said, was flooded, and other houses in the Southern City had fallen down, too.

"Why didn't you move to some other place?" Mr. Yao asked.

"All the other rooms in the Guild are occupied, and how could we move during those days of rain?"

"We did not know, or we would have asked you and your mother to come and stay with us. Will you not come now? Tijen's room is empty, and the three of you, mother and children, can stay in the same room."

"Thank you," said Lifu. "The rain has stopped and we are going to get masons to repair the house now."

"But the repairs will take some days, and you and your mother cannot be staying in the kitchen while the repairs are going on," said Mrs. Yao. "Ask your mother to come here and you can go back when your house is ready."

Lifu hated the idea. He thought he would not be comfortable living in the rich man's house, and he said he must stay and watch the repairs while they were going on. But Mr. Yao, who was seriously interested in the boy, said, "You cannot decide. I will go and talk to your mother."

"I will tell her, then, Uncle Yao. You must not disturb yourself on our account."

"Oh, I have not been out and I want a ride," said Mr. Yao.

So then he went off in a carriage with Lifu and persuaded the mother to get ready and come as soon as they could. The mother was equally unwilling, but Mr. Yao was very kind, and they decided to yield when he said, "If you don't come, we shall be ashamed before Mr. Fu." For that reason they accepted. They put together their more valuable things to take with them, and left the rest in charge of the old gatekeeper, who the previous day had learned of the standing of the Yao family from the servant, and who now received a handsome tip from Mr. Yao. Lifu's family therefore rose in importance in the eyes of the old gatekeeper and of the other families at the Guild.

So the next day, taking advantage of the weather, Lifu's mother and the servant were busy washing their clothing, which had accumulated for some time, in order to make a presentable appearance as guests. As the day was still cloudy, Mrs. Kung spent much time drying the laundry over a fire, while her son was getting other things ready and making arrangements for the repairs. The estimate rather frightened the mother and son, for a new beam had to be put in, and it would take a master mason and an apprentice seven or eight days, and the whole thing might well cost as much as twenty dollars, which would cut into Lifu's tuition. But the mother said they would save something on food by staying with the Yaos and if necessary, they could borrow half a month's rent from their tenant, who had always been very prompt with her monthly payments.

"Perhaps Mr. Fu can ask the college authorities to let us delay paying the tuition a few days," suggested the son.

"I shouldn't do that," said his mother. "If he hears of it, he will probably insist on lending us the money. Even though he has been so kind to us, I am glad we have never yet borrowed a copper from him. Your father and I were determined to get along without borrowing and we always did. How you are going to repay Mr. Fu for his kindness depends upon you when you are grown up."

"Mother, may I ask you a great favor?" said Lifu.

"What is it, my son?"

"I want ten cents to buy a box of shoe polish. You know I don't care for such things, but my shoes are so conspicuous when I am with the children of the Yao and the Tseng families."

"That is why I always say foreign things are expensive," said his mother. "I would never approve of buying foreign shoes if they were not required by school for drill. Ten cents would last two months for my needle and threads."

But she consented and Lifu went off to buy his first box of shoe polish and came back and blacked his shoes very bright.

The following morning, the Kungs appeared and the Yao family were gathered in the hall to meet them. Lifu's sister had never been to the Yao home before. Mochow asked what her name was, and her mother said, "Her name consists of only one word, Huan, and we call her Huan-erh."

"She is quite like you," Mochow said and Mrs. Kung replied, "Yes, she's more like me, while Lifu is more like his father."

Now Tijen's room on the east had been made ready for them, and

Mrs. Yao showed them to it. It was elegantly furnished with a shining foreign brass bed, which was considered a highly fashionable thing to have. Lifu discovered in the "cracked-ice" latticed cabinet a number of things that Tijen had left behind, including many silk gowns and a number of Chinese and foreign shoes. The room was somewhat dark and looked out at the back on the court where the family's living rooms were. Lifu felt it comfortable and cozy.

As soon as the guests had gone into their room, Mochow and Mulan nudged each other, and each wanted to tell the other the great news. "Did you see his shoes, shined so bright?" exclaimed Mochow. "Didn't I see them?" said Mulan. "I saw them the minute he walked in. And I know he must have slept on his blue gown under his pillow last night. You can still see the folded lines."

It had been Mr. Yao's idea since the return of the uncle's family, that they should all dine together to have the sense of "being lively" with many people around. Lifu and his family therefore appeared for lunch in the same dining room, and when all were seated Mr. Yao counted twelve persons sitting at the round table, and there was an air of noisy liveliness and Mr. Yao was very happy. Mrs. Kung was a courteous woman and had to be helped to the dishes in the center of the table. Lifu was an extremely fast eater, and wanted to refill his own rice, but he was slightly embarrassed to have his bowl refilled by Frankincense, who served it on a tray of beautiful lacquer with fine gold tracings. The sisters ate more or less silently and watched and were unaccountably amused. Even the usually quiet and dignified Mochow showed a tendency to smile whenever Lifu said anything.

They were talking about the Tsengs and Chinya's engagement to Miss New. "Is she of the family of New the God of Wealth?" asked Lifu interestedly.

"Do you know them?" asked Mrs. Yao.

"No, but I know the second son, Tungyu. He was in the same school with me, but I haven't seen him for a long time."

"Why?" some one asked.

"Mother, may I tell?" asked Lifu.

"You had better not," said his mother.

Mulan's curiosity was excited and she said, "Never mind, it is in the family. We won't tell it."

"He took a pistol to school to threaten the teacher, and was dismissed," said Lifu.

"A pistol to threaten a teacher! How?" asked Mulan.

"He stayed in each grade for several years. He was quite intelligent but would not study. The last time he knew he couldn't pass the grade, which would mean again being kept for another year, and so he took a pistol and went to the teacher's room to demand that the teacher pass him. The teacher yielded and then threatened to resign. I don't know what happened afterward, and he didn't come again."

"How did such a young boy come to have a pistol?" asked Mrs. Yao.

"He always went to school with two servants, one carrying his books and one bodyguard armed with a pistol to protect him. At first he had only one servant, but he said his father needed to say just one word and the principal would lose his rice bowl, and he abused every teacher and pupil. Once he abused the sister of Pingkuei, our classmate, and Pingkuei got together a few of the bigger boys and watched for a chance and waylaid him in the dark and beat him. So the bodyguard accompanied him afterwards."

"Was the principal dismissed?"

"No, they beat him outside the school, and it was dark and he could not tell who it was."

"Why, this is quite unbelievable!" said Mrs. Yao. "The last time I met Mrs. New, I think she told me her second son was now an official in his father's office, and she was quite proud of him."

"Yes," said Mulan. "Do you remember what she said? 'You look at him, so young, not quite twenty, and yet an official of the capital, and everybody so polite to him. Soldiers salute him and stand at attention until he is a long way past, and even elderly officials mix and talk with him quite freely.' She was so self-satisfied that nobody contradicted her."

"That is why China lost the war with Japan," said Lifu.

His mother apologized. "You must pardon him for talking so freely in the presence of elders."

"Why?" said Mr. Yao. "It is better this way, just like one family. I don't insist on strict rules in my family."

After lunch, Afei begged his father to take him to see the "flood." He had heard that the northern section of the city was quite flooded, because the lake had swollen. The father asked his daughters and Lifu if they would come too. Lifu said he liked nothing more than seeing water and would take his little sister. But Mochow said that "big water" was just water all the same, and that she was going to

237

stay and iron some clothing. The result was that Mr. Yao went with Mulan, Lifu, and the three young children, including Redjade. The party was too big for the carriage, and they went in four rickshaws, Redjade sitting with Afei, while Lifu rode in the rickshaw with his sister.

When the party was gone, the mothers and Mochow sat talking, and after a while Mochow, left alone with Lifu's mother, mentioned the ironing she was going to do.

"How is it that you are doing the ironing with so many maids and servants around?" asked Mrs. Kung.

"We sisters always iron our own clothing, whenever we can," Mochow explained, "and sometimes we iron our parents' special things. This is a girl's regular job."

"The more I see of you sisters, the more I marvel—you can cook and sew and wash and iron, and at the same time read books as well as the boys."

"Girls learn to read books when they can," said Mochow. "But cooking and needlework are a woman's job. Otherwise how could she run a home?"

"It's your mother's excellent training. In other homes as rich as yours, the daughters wouldn't do these things."

"Auntie Kung," Mochow said, "have you anything to iron? Give it to me and I'll iron it for you."

"Thank you, I don't iron my things. Only silk dresses and silk skirts for special occasions are ironed."

But Mochow was so sweet and insistent that Mrs. Kung went and got a black silk dress which she had brought along as her best, and Lifu's best silk gown. The difference between Lifu's clothes and those of the Yao and Tseng boys was that Lifu's were never ironed, but only pressed smooth at the time of folding. Ironing was a luxury for homes that could afford maids and servants. Mochow soon discovered that she was ironing a boy's gown, for the sleeves were so narrow. She pressed it very hard and smooth, and she took needle and thread and mended a buttonhole that was slightly loose, and returned the garments to Lifu's mother. Mochow did not tell Mulan about this when she came back.

.·.

The lake where Mr. Yao had taken the young people to see the

238

flood was north of the Imperial Palaces. It was only a quarter of an hour from their home. Going north from their house, they turned left at the street of Iron Lions and then along the northern wall of the Forbidden City until they saw the lake on their right. Actually the water of this small lake was connected with the "Three Seas," as they were called, inside the Palaces, but the willow embankments and the lotus flowers had made it into a place of popular amusement. On summer afternoons there were large crowds and storytellers, sword fencers, musical entertainers, and sellers of cold drinks, but in the mornings there were fewer people and the place had a rural beauty all its own.

This afternoon it was almost completely deserted, because of the flood. The muddy water had risen nearly to the level of the embankment leading north to where the restaurants and temples were. A few women were sitting in round tubs floating on the water, trying to pick lotus pods that had not drifted away or been destroyed by the flood. From the road on the south, Mulan could see the purple Western Hills in the distance, while the restaurants on the northern side nestled in the green shade of willow trees newly bathed by the rain. A boat tied to the bank gave an appearance of strange calm and beauty. In order to cross over, the party had to go by the embankment and the rickshaw pullers had to splash through mud and water on the way.

They got down from the rickshaws after reaching the northern side and walked on foot to a restaurant. The waiters knew Mr. Yao and welcomed them. "We just want a room upstairs with a veranda facing the lake to see the view. The children want to see the big water."

"Well, *Laoyeh!*" said the waiter. "What elegance of spirit! We have not seen a single customer these days, and you are the first."

They were shown upstairs and took seats on the balcony. Mr. Yao ordered some fine Lungching tea, melon seeds, and fresh lotus pods. The day was clear, and looking across the water they saw the tall square Drum Tower in the near distance and the curiously shaped Tibetan dagoba, rising into the sky from the Peihai Lake in the Imperial Palace.

Mulan was sitting on a low chair, picking lotus seeds from a pod in her hand, and looking at the lake through the red balustrades. Redjade, having been brought up in Hangchow, was quite familiar with such things and was working away at the seeds with her nimble fingers, sitting at a high table with Afei and Huan-erh. Mr. Yao lounged in a low rattan chair. Lifu was sitting close to Mulan on the balcony and watching her pick the seeds. He had eaten sugared lotus seeds, but he had never eaten them fresh from the pod, and was staring with great interest.

"Do you eat them raw like that?" he asked rather foolishly.

"Of course," said Mulan, and she took one she had just plucked out and gave it to him. Lifu tasted it and said, "It is good, but different from the sugared ones. It is so mild you almost don't taste anything."

"That is just it," said Mulan. "We eat it just for its pure *mildness* and its slight fragrance. That is why a busy man cannot enjoy it. You must not think of anything when you eat it."

Mulan showed him how to pick a seed, and after eating it, Lifu exclaimed with delight.

"If you shout, you will lose the flavor again," said Mulan. "You must chew them slowly, one by one. After a while, take a sip of good tea and you will find a pure fragrance remaining in your cheeks and palate for a long time."

And so, drinking tea and chewing lotus seeds and watching the lotus-picking women passing by in their round tubs, they talked of sundry things and about their respective plans to go to college and school. Finally their talk turned to Tijen.

"It is unbelievable," said Lifu, "that he had a chance to go to England and study and wouldn't go."

"Mulan, Lifu," said Mr. Yao, "you young people write to him and try to persuade him. I have nothing to say to him."

"We have tried to persuade him," replied Mulan. "Two nights before he left, sister and I talked to him, and sister talked until she almost cried."

"What did he say?" asked her father.

"Why, he said he had the same heart and the same ambition as anybody and told us not to worry, and swore that when he was in England, he would bury his head in his books for twelve hours a day and get the highest marks just to show us. You know how he is. He can promise anything and talk your head giddy when he wants you to do anything. But Father, you must talk to him also, when he comes back—or is he going to stay in Hong Kong?"

"I have written a letter to a friend to find out what he is doing," said her father. "He has about twelve hundred dollars with him, besides the draft on London, and when his money is used up, which

I know won't be long, and when he writes for more, I must decide. But how can I talk to him? I get angry every time I see his face. Suppose he really comes back, do you think you would want to talk to him again? Can he still be called a man?" The thought of Tijen had made the father angry, and Mulan saw his big eyes, his gray hair, and the swollen veins on his high forehead and thought he looked very sad also. . . . "Perhaps it really does not matter," continued the father. "It's just as well that he hasn't gone to England. It will save me some money. Probably all he would learn from England would be playing with cameras. Seed of sin! But if rich men's sons were all good, the rich would always be rich and the poor always poor. Heaven's Way goes round!"

His momentary anger passed and he turned and began to play with Afei as if nothing had happened. He must have been thinking of the future of his younger son, and of his daughters. Lifu kept very quiet all this time, but his presence offered a silent contrast to Mulan's absent brother, and Mulan felt how happy the family would be if her brother had been like Lifu, and how proud she would be.

Mulan was puzzled, for here was a boy left without a father, and he was poor, yet he was as well-bred as any rich man's son. There was something naturally refined and aristocratic about Lifu in spite of his uncouth dress. She wondered whether their both hitting the copper coin at their first chance meeting at the monastery had any prophetic meaning. She could not forget what he had said about the ruins.

"You love ruins, don't you?" she said.

Lifu remembered what he had said at the Western Hills. "Yes," he said, "but it is not the stones and bricks themselves; it is because they are so old."

"Some day we can go and see the ruins at the Old Summer Palace together. Shall we?" asked Mulan.

"Yes, I would like to go, if we can get in," said Lifu.

Just then they heard shouting and commotion below them. They rushed downstairs and learned that a girl picking lotus had been drowned in the lake. Her tub had capsized and people had heard her scream for help and seen her come up once or twice and then disappear. Her family rushed to the rescue but it was too late. Those standing around the drowned girl's weeping mother said that there were many "water ghosts" in the lake, for many women had been drowned in it. Redjade, who was an extremely sensitive child, turned pale. The incident made a deep impression upon her, and for days afterward she kept asking what happened to that girl when she was drowned, until her mother forbade her to mention it again.

The party went back, much excited and saddened after the incident.

. . .

When Lifu returned he told his mother what they had seen, and his mother said to him, "You had better change. Here is your new gown, all pressed for you. In this house, you must dress like the others."

"When did you press it?" said Lifu. "Am I going to look like the dandies?"

"Put it on, put it on!" said his mother. "It was pressed for you by their third daughter."

Lifu changed into the new gown and felt that he was being corrupted, but the gown and the bright shoes worked a change in his appearance. At dinner, Mochow had the satisfaction of seeing Lifu wearing the silk gown smoothly pressed by her hands but she kept this satisfaction to herself.

They had bought a big eel which had come out of its mountain pond with the flood, and everybody enjoyed the unusual delicacy. After dinner, they sat in the parlor. Usually the family would retire to the mother's room for a chat, but with so many people there, Mr. Yao ordered the parlor, which was usually closed except for receptions, to be opened and tea to be served there. It was large and lofty, the size of two rooms, fitted out in the old, simple, grand style. A "palace lantern" three feet high was suspended from the ceiling and cast its light over the heavy blue dragon-and-cloud carpet and the window curtains of light cabbage green. At the western end stood a large black cedar couch with hard blue satin cushions and a cedar service table before it and two footstools at the sides. Everything was big and simple and severe. A high mahogany table, made in solid straight lines, stood against the north wall, with only three curios on it. One, in the center, was an old gold inlaid cloisonné tripod. There was a rare marble panel, two feet square, with natural markings suggesting a landscape in mist and rain, containing half concealed hilltops and groves and two unbelievably realistic fishing junks. Another marble panel had natural markings resembling a large duck; the duck's head and beak and neck were almost perfect, while light tracings suggested the outline of the body and a splash of brown impurities suggested the webbed feet.

On the wall above the couch was a landscape painting by Mi Hsiang-yang, fifteen feet high, so old that the silk and ink merged and suggested a marble effect, but Mi's ink was still rich and luminous, and black like varnish, and his strokes were powerful and strong. A number of hardwood erect chairs, and a few Cantonese hardwood easy chairs, were placed around the room. The total impression was one of grandeur and simplicity in mahogany and marble.

That night the unusual happened, for Mochow was gay and Mulan was quiet and pensive. The ladies were talking together, while the father sat in one of the hardwood easy chairs, smoking a cigar and talking with his brother-in-law. Mulan sat alone, inclined in one of the low chairs, and did not seem to listen.

"What is the matter with you?" said Coral.

"I just don't feel like talking tonight. Perhaps it is the eel. It was so rich and oily."

Actually Mulan was puzzled by thoughts that occupied her mind. She had been thinking of the drowned girl and how they had eaten lotus seeds that might possibly have been picked by the hands of the drowned girl. And her mind turned upon Lifu and Tijen who constantly changed places in her mind, to such an extent that she even mixed up Lifu with Silverscreen. "I must be crazy," she thought, "it must be the eel." But she was worried. Her mother had told her that Bluehaze had come and suggested a match for Silverscreen with a wheat merchant and she knew that her mother was determined to hasten the match. Moreover, her mother had forbidden her to breathe a word of it or let Tijen know. On the other hand, she had learned from her father that afternoon that Tijen might soon return. If he should return and find Silverscreen married off so quickly in his absence, there would be a storm in the family.

. ·.

Lifu often went back to his house in the morning or afternoon to see the progress of the repairs. In the evenings the family usually gathered in the parlor, talking till quite late, with Afei and Redjade sometimes the center of attention, giving the company much amusement. Redjade's new-found Peking accent often surprised everybody, and she said the most unusual things. One of the things she said that surprised everybody was about tears.

"Tears come down through the nose," she said. "So the eyes and the nose must be connected. But why doesn't the smoke also come out through the eyes when one smokes?"

"How do you know that tears come through the nose?" asked Mochow, amused.

"Because I know it," replied the seven-year-old child.

Through these evening chats and the dining together, Lifu came to know all the members of the family well and gradually came to feel quite at home. When the company broke up, he would retire with his mother and sister and then read in bed until quite late. Sometimes, looking from the back window, he could see lights still shining in the girls' room and the shadows of their figures against the silk curtains. But one morning Mulan asked what he had been reading so late the night before, and he knew that he was being watched and dared not peep at the back window any more.

Some mornings he wandered into Mr. Yao's studio, looking over his library and his curios. Lifu knew nothing about curios but he was greatly impressed by Mr. Yao's great collection of seal stones. One afternoon Mulan took him to see her father's collection of bone inscriptions and he was fascinated by it. It began by Lifu's talking casually at lunch about *Shuowen,* a book on the evolution of Chinese script, which became a science in itself. Lifu had studied only the five hundred and forty primary elements of *Shuowen,* but his interest had been aroused in the principles of the composition of Chinese words and their changes, and he had come to understand the common characters better. The science of study of the bone inscriptions was only beginning, there being yet no published works on the subject. But the appearance of these earliest forms of Chinese writing, unknown before, held him fascinated, and he had enough sense to feel that a systematic study of these dirty bones would reveal many things not known even to the author of *Shuowen* himself, who lived in the second century.

"Imagine, these bones are four thousand years old!" said Mulan. "People who don't know them wouldn't pay a hundred cash a catty for them."

They went on to the collection of old and rare ink slabs, some with inscriptions by their former famous owners, and to a collection of famous old calligraphy and there they remained a long time, examining and comparing the different styles and rubbings of the calligraphy. Lifu liked the graceful, round strokes of Chao, while Mulan liked the strong, rocky, square-shouldered, sharp-cornered, and rigid forms of

244

Wei inscriptions. Lifu explained innocently that men liked what was graceful and women liked what was strong, "like boys liking girls and girls liking boys," and Mulan blushed.

Lifu never thought of love, and he seemed proof against feminine charm. Yet he liked Mulan because she understood these things and had so much intelligence and spirit. He had found in her a very good companion for conversation, and he felt that she was exquisitely beautiful, even as Chao calligraphy was exquisitely beautiful. That was all. In these matters of feeling, however, Mulan, although of the same age as Lifu, was two years more mature, as girls always are.

One morning, remembering that Mr. Yao had suggested their writing to Tijen to exhort him to reform, Lifu was beginning a letter in the parlor, which was now regularly open. Mulan saw him, and asked what he was writing, and he told her. It was a good test of his pen, and Mulan said that she and her sister were going to write to Tijen also. Mulan therefore sent Brocade to call Mochow, who came in her white jacket, with her hair very smooth and bright, and she said with a smile, "What are you two up to now?" Playing with her braid in her hand, Mulan said, "Brother Lifu was going to write to Brother, and I thought we might all write to him." "Brother" was a common form of courteous address among friends, and Mulan now used it in speaking to Lifu.

"That's right," said Mochow. "We should have written already. But Mother has asked me, when we write to Tijen, not to mention our plan to marry Silverscreen, and to ask him not to return too soon."

Mochow glanced toward Lifu, and Mulan said, "Never mind; Brother Lifu knows all about Silverscreen's coming marriage. Only she herself doesn't know."

"It is hard to write letters of exhortation, especially in my position," said Lifu. "What shall I say?"

"I have an idea," said Mulan. "What I hate most is the writing of letters in the style of the *Correspondence of Autumn-Water Studio*. Let's try to write the Ming style of letters, or the Chin style of short notes! Do away with all formulas of courtesy and plunge straight into the meat abruptly, making it short and pithy. Nobody is allowed to exceed a hundred words. This is effective and it saves time over the conventional forms, which cannot be much improved anyway."

"That's a good idea," said Mochow. "Should there be a time limit?"

245

"How about burning one stick of incense as the time limit?" suggested Lifu.

They all agreed, and so ink slabs and brushes and "flower letter-papers" were brought in, and an incense stick was lighted. Lifu and Mochow sat over a table, while Mulan walked about, scratching her head, and now and then peeping out of the curtained window.

"Will you sit down?" said Mochow. "You make me nervous." But Mulan merely smiled, slowly running her fingers through the end of her braid.

Lifu finished first; Mochow was about to finish her letter, and the stick of incense was already burning low. Mochow gave Mulan warning and Mulan came to her seat and said, "Gracious! I haven't even ground my ink yet."

"Use mine," said Mochow, and Mulan began to write rapidly and in a short time, her letter was finished. They read Lifu's first:

> Lifu bends his head (*greeting*). Brother, you are sailing with the long wind over the ten thousand miles of waves. How happy you are! How envious I am! Your younger brother is tied like a pony to a stable post. The summer rain has demolished our house, and my mother and I are staying in your home temporarily. If after the costs of repair, we are able to collect enough money for the college tuition, I shall be indeed lucky. I wish Brother the greatest future. Perhaps my stupid self will forever wag its tail in the mud only.

Mochow said, "Good! You are attacking him from the reverse side. And you haven't wasted a single word."

Next they read Mochow's letter:

> Sister Mochow bows to you. From your letter I learned that you were delayed at Hong Kong—is it possible that this was what Mencius meant by "frustrating what one sets out to do"? If so, Heaven must be changing his opinion of you and calling you perhaps to a great mission. But "frustration" is from Heaven, while strengthening one's ambition depends upon the man himself. Mother is worrying about you and is getting thinner. Take good care of yourself in a hot country like the South.

"Well put and dignified," said Lifu. Next they came to Mulan's letter:

> Sister Mulan bows to you. What about your promise to send us a note from the Kingdom of Grape-Teeth? Or is Grape-Teeth

going to be changed into Mushroom-Teeth [a pun upon *Hong Kong,* meaning *Fragrant Harbor*]? But whether Grape-Teeth or Mushroom-Teeth, or even Bean-Teeth, you must not change teeth too often [a pun upon the name of a famous ancient cook]. Your sister thanks you for those ivory buttons. But why no presents for Mother? For days it has rained and the weather has suddenly become cool. If you could be sharing the brushes and ink slabs with us, how happy we would be!

"How charming!" said Lifu, and they were all laughing.

Just then Frankincense came in, with a big bunch of cassia flowers in her hand, to announce that Mannia had come. As a familiar guest, Mannia had followed the maid in and was already standing at the door.

"Mulan!" cried Mannia. "What are you doing, enjoying yourself so?"

Mulan, overjoyed, rushed to her. "You haven't been to see us for a long time."

"And you wouldn't come to see me. I've brought you some cassia flowers from our garden. Most of them were destroyed by the rain, and even these have lost their fragrance."

"You have already met Kung *Shaoyeh,*" said Mulan to Mannia. "He is staying here because their house fell during the rain."

"Of course," replied Mannia. "I know even that you went together to see the flood."

"How do you know?" asked Mulan.

"I have been told."

Lifu, standing, made a deep bow.

Mulan remembered then that when they were coming back from the lake and looking at the mother of the drowned girl with the crowd about her, the gatekeeper of the Tsengs had been there and stopped and talked with them. When he had reported that he had met Miss Yao and that there was a boy with her, Mannia had decided to come and see Lifu. She knew it must be he, because her brothers had told her about meeting Lifu when seeing Tijen off at the station.

They talked of Tijen and other things of the household, and Mannia went home with a very favorable impression of Lifu, and decided to act quickly.

When Mannia left, Mochow said smilingly to Mulan, "Your good sister came to spy upon you. She certainly did not come to present you cassia flowers."

247

"What is there to spy upon?" replied Mulan.

And Lifu looked as if he did not understand.

. .

One day Lifu returned from his house to report a piece of good news. "Would you believe it, Mother? The Szechuen Guild is going to pay for the repairs. It is true! Old Wang, the gatekeeper, himself told me. He was very courteous and showed me the letter from the Guild Directors."

The mother and son puzzled over it, and decided that it must have been Mr. Fu again. But how had he come to know about it, since they had not written him at Tientsin? He appeared a few days later, for he often traveled between the two cities, and came to see Mr. Yao as he always did. He was very glad to see Lifu and his mother so well taken care of. Mrs. Kung mentioned the matter of the Szechuen Guild, and said: "I presume it is you trying to help us, mother and son, again. I don't know how to thank you."

"If you want to thank anybody, thank Uncle Yao. I had nothing to do with it, except writing a letter." Mr. Fu then revealed that he knew all about their staying at this house, for Mr. Yao had written at once to inform him about it. Moreover, Mr. Yao said he would secretly give a donation of two hundred dollars to the Szechuen Guild to pay for the repairs, but that his name was to be kept out of it.

"What are we to do, after receiving so many kindnesses from Uncle Yao?" asked the mother.

"You can thank him, if you like. I don't think he minds my telling you the secret."

When Lifu and his mother went to thank Mr. Yao, he said, "Oh, it is not on account of you. I have been wanting to do something for the Szechuen Guild for a long time. Do you know that I owe Szechuen a debt? Half of the medicinal herbs in my shops come from your province."

This was a great relief to Lifu and his mother. It gradually became known, and Mrs. Kung and her son rose in the respect of the gate-keeper and the people at the Guild House, because they were the protégés of two influential patrons of the Guild.

Mid-Autumn—the fifteenth of August—was one of the great festivals of the year, and Mr. Fu was invited to come for dinner with the Yao family. It was also the last evening of Lifu's stay at Mulan's home. Mr. Yao ordered a big hamper of the best crabs, in accordance with the custom of eating crabs at Mid-Autumn.

He suggested having the dinner in the stone court in order the better to see the moon, but Coral said that the weather had turned cold and was still damp, and since the crab was "cold" in effect, they had better have it inside, and they could still draw the curtains apart if they wanted the moon. And so warm wine was served, and before each person was a dish of vinegar mixed with soya-bean sauce and ginger, which was necessary for counteracting the "cold" effect of the crabs.

There was nothing all members of the family were more agreed upon and enthusiastic about than a crab dinner, and there was always excitement about it. True, the crab was a gourmet's joy, with its unique fragrance and shape and color. At Mid-Autumn it was always excellent, and the plentiful rain this summer had not affected it in the least. But the excitement was also largely because it was a change from the ordinary dinner served by servants, and everybody had to work actively for it. It was not the eating so much as the effort to get at the food, which made every little morsel all the more appreciated. Some ate quickly and some ate slowly. Some liked the roe of the females and some liked the meat of the males, and others preferred to work at the legs. It was like playing cards—a test of one's temper. Some chewed the meat clean, while others gobbled whole mouthfuls without discrimination. By the end of the dinner, all was usually in confusion, with crab shells and legs piled high in the center of the table.

When they were all seated, a big green plate, two feet in diameter, containing the beautiful red crabs, was brought in. A shout of "Ah's" went up from the whole table. Both Mr. Fu and Mr. Yao rolled up their sleeves. Mr. Fu asked Lifu to roll up his sleeves, and Lifu said, "We are doing better than Confucius. He had a short sleeve only for the right hand."

"That was because he was only writing," said Mochow. "If he had been eating crabs, he would have had both sleeves short, too."

Everybody laughed, and Mr. Fu said, "That proves Confucius never ate crabs."

"I can prove that he did," said Mulan.

"How would you prove it?"

249

"You remember that Confucius always ate ginger. That puts him under the strong suspicion of eating crabs."

"You are talking delightful nonsense," said Lifu.

"Wait a minute. I haven't finished yet. The *Thousand-Character Text* begins with the sentence, 'Heaven Earth Black Yellow.' 'Black Yellow' means the color of the crab roe and membrane. That proves there was 'Black Yellow,' since there were Heaven and Earth. How would such a clever man as Confucius not know how to eat crabs?"

This threw the whole company into louder laughter; and Coral, unable to restrain herself, accidentally smeared her face with the "yellow" of the crab.

"Then why didn't the *Analects* record it?" asked Mochow.

"Oh, the disciples could not record everything, or some of the records didn't survive the 'burning of books.' One has to use one's imagination in reading the ancient books," said Mulan, picking at a crab's leg. "I can imagine Mrs. Confucius having to make a special dress for eating crabs, since he had a special house jacket with one sleeve shorter than the other. How trying a husband! How hard it must have been to be a sage's wife."

"Seriously, I want to test you," said Mr. Fu. "Where is your authority for 'black yellow' as referring to crab?"

Mulan replied at once, "Doesn't the poem about the crab in *Red Chamber Dream* say:

The roads and ways before its eyes are neither straight nor across;
The spring and autumn in its shells are black and yellow in vain."

"Oh, you must eat, Mulan. You are talking too much," said her mother.

Everybody could see that Mulan was a little flushed and talking more than usual.

"It is early yet," she said. "It takes me the same time to eat three crabs as for my sister to eat one."

"You are not eating crabs. You eat crabs as if you were eating cabbage or bean curd," said Mochow.

Mochow, who had not finished even one crab, was an expert. She chewed every part so clean that she left on her plate only thin, white pieces like glass or transparent shells.

Now a maid brought in a steaming hot new dish and cleared away the shells. "Wait a minute," said Mochow. "The legs will keep me chewing for another quarter of an hour."

"Don't try to save the legs. Let the maids and servants have them," said Mr. Yao.

"Oh, I saved out two for each of them," said Coral.

Now Mulan fell to eating seriously.

She drank a cup of wine, then another, and became talkative again. When she asked for a third cup, Mr. Yao remarked, "What high spirits you are in tonight! You had better stop."

"I am all right," replied Mulan. And she drank the third cup. She had a certain capacity for wine, but she was getting into the hilarious state of semi-intoxication, saying light, silly, and sometimes brilliant things. "The crab is a unique creature; the crab is a unique creature," she said.

Lifu and Mulan raised their cups and drank to each other. Happiness is so akin to sorrow and pleasure to pain that no one could say whether that night she was happy or miserable.

Soon the party left their seats to wash their hands with wild chrysanthemum leaves and water, while the table was cleared and laid again for a simple meal of rice congee and salt eggs and pickled vegetable roots.

When the dinner was nearly over, Mr. Fu said, "It is a pity that schools nowadays don't teach old poetry. Otherwise eating crabs and writing poems on the occasion would be a great pastime."

"I have a suggestion," said Coral. "Let's play 'Break the Cassia and Pass the Cup.' We have the cassia flowers Mannia brought the other day." The game consisted in passing a twig of cassia flowers round the table, while some one beat a small drum, and any one found with the twig in his hand when the drum stopped had to take a drink and tell a joke or a story.

The game was played with Afei beating the drum. It stopped first at Mr. Fu, and he had to tell a story. He began: "Once upon a time there was a school teacher who couldn't find any pupils to come to him, and so he decided to become a physician. He read a few medical books and began to practice. Unfortunately he killed his first patient. The patient's family wanted to sue him in court for manslaughter, but the affair was settled by the physician's undertaking to provide the cost of the burial. As he was too poor to engage under- takers, he started out with his wife and son to carry the corpse themselves to the burial ground. The dead man, however, weighed two hundred pounds and on the way the wife demanded a rest. Before she got up again to carry the corpse, she sighed and said to her husband, 'My good man, next time you go out to cure a patient, you should pick a thin one!'"

The company laughed, and the game continued. The drum stopped again when the twig was in Mulan's hand. She had eaten a lot of oranges, and was still feeling brilliant. And she began: "Once upon a time, there was a big army of crabs which the Dragon King had appointed to guard the approach to the sea. The Crab General drilled them every day on the beach, and people could see thousands of little crabs executing maneuvers on the sand. A Snake Spirit raised a rebellion in the sea, when the Crab General happened to be ill, and the Dragon King appointed Fairy Mother-of-Pearl to take command. She went up to the surface of the water and standing upon a rock in the sea facing the shore, she commanded the crabs to fall in line. The crab soldiers all came out of their underground caves and stood in line, eyes to the right. The line was so perfect that the Fairy was amazed. Fairy Mother-of-Pearl then gave the command 'Forward march!' Instead of advancing straight into the sea, they went sideways to the right along the beach. The Fairy Mother-of-Pearl then commanded 'To the rear march!' and the platoons began to move sideways to the left. The Fairy was helpless, for she could not make them come forward into the water and asked the Crab Lieutenant what to do. The latter asked permission to give the command, and he said, 'Battalion to the left, march!' and lo and behold! the crab army marched straight forward into the water. So Fairy Mother-of-Pearl was greatly puzzled and asked the Crab Lieutenant for an explanation. The Crab Lieutenant replied, 'Your Highness, they are all returned students from England!'"

Everybody at once understood and laughed, for English writing was known as "crab-walk writing" because it went horizontally across the page.

Next the twig was found in Coral's hand. "I have no story," said Coral.

"No excuse for any one," cried the company. "Anything to make us laugh will do."

"What about a tongue-twisting rhyme?" suggested Coral. The company assented. And Coral began to say a tongue-twisting, jaw-breaking rhyme consisting of confusingly similar syllables, something like this:

> A big dark dog met a bad black duck.
> Now did the big dark dog bark at the bad black duck?
> Or did the bad black duck peck at the big, dark dog?

All of them, from Redjade and Huan-erh to the mother and even Mrs. Feng, tried to say the rhyme as fast as possible. Only little Afei and Redjade got through the rhyme safely, while Mulan's mother ended up in syllables like "big bark darg" and "blad black dark."

"You see," said Coral, "it's they, the two children, who got it."

Mr. Yao was walking about, and stopping before the window he said, "Look! there is a double halo around the moon."

"We all forgot about the moon," said Coral. They all looked and saw that there was a brilliant mass of white clouds around the moon, while near the center there were two concentric rings of halo.

"That forebodes evil for the country," said Mr. Fu. "Strange phenomena have always appeared at the ends of dynasties. This is a time of unrest and we do not know what is going to happen."

"The unrest comes from the human heart," said Mr. Yao. Quoting a popular poem that an unknown poet had scribbled on a pavilion wall on top of a mountain pass, Mr. Yao said,

> "Heaven peaceful, earth peaceful,
> Human heart not peaceful.
> Human heart being peaceful,
> All under Heaven peaceful."

The party remained talking for some time and then retired to bed.

CHAPTER XVII

CURIOUSLY, getting half-tipsy and slightly misbehaving herself that evening gave Mulan a sense of individuality that she had never felt before. She had been talkative, brilliant, and happy. When she went to bed she felt a liberation of herself—due, no doubt, to the wine. For the first time she was aware, as she lay in bed, that she was living in a world by herself, that there was even such a world all her own. It was difficult for her to account for such a feeling, but behind or within that new world, she was vaguely aware also of Lifu.

Early one morning, soon after Lifu's family returned to their own house, Mrs. Tseng and Mannia appeared at the Yao home. Mochow happened to be alone in the parlor arranging flowers in vases, and she sat talking with them about family affairs. Little Joy had come with them, and Mochow remarked that she had changed and grown more refined since her arrival in the capital a couple of years ago, although she remained the simple-hearted peasant girl.

Mochow felt that there was some reason for Mrs. Tseng's visit at this morning hour. Mulan, with a bunch of flowers in her hand, came gracefully into the room from the garden.

"What wind blew you here—so early in the day?" she asked delighted to find them there.

Frankincense appeared to say that Mrs. Yao was ready and would soon be coming out, and Mannia said to Mulan with a smile, *"Meimei,* you can go away. Today we are not come to see you, but to see your mother."

Mulan taken by surprise, saw at once not only Mannia's smile, but also the smile on Mrs. Tseng's lips. "What is it? Are you driving me away? What about her?" she said, pointing to Mochow.

"Yes, you had better both go away. This has nothing to do with you," replied Mannia.

"All right," said Mochow. "We will go in." She said good-by to them and drew Mulan away.

Mulan muttered as soon as they had left the room, "What trick are they up to?"

"I'll wager with you that it's your 'happy affair,'" said Mochow. "Your mother-in-law has come to claim you."

At the mention of her engagement Mulan felt a strange elation, although she really did not know what to think. Mochow laughed and was excited as she seldom was.

"What is there so funny that you are laughing so?" said Mulan.

"If you don't laugh now, when are you going to laugh?" replied Mochow.

But Mulan was all confused. She felt as if her destiny was being decided one way or another, and that she was plunging into something fateful and eternal when she had not yet made up her mind. "Maybe it is *your* happy affair," said Mulan.

"No, no, they don't want me," said Mochow happily. "You will see, I am going to have a new brother-in-law. This match—there is no question. It is all fixed."

"Is it?" said Mulan. She seemed deep in her thinking and Mochow suddenly became grave when she saw her sister act so.

"Isn't it a good match?" she said earnestly. "You will be well married into a rich official's home. And Sunya is good in appearance and good in temper. What more do you want?"

"*Meimei,* don't speak so. If you think he is good in appearance and good in temper, you marry him," said Mulan quizzically.

Well married? By all social standards Mulan would certainly be considered well married into the Tseng home. Yet this proposal was coming at a time when she was just beginning to feel free, when she had first felt a kind of intoxicating, delicious happiness she had not known before, a happiness that she found in Lifu's presence. This had so engrossed her thoughts that in the last few days since Lifu's family moved out, she had still lived in that world of happiness all her own and had almost forgotten about Silverscreen's affair. She forgot, too, that she was tied to the Tseng family by a number of old ties, that tacitly at least, the families considered her engaged to Sunya. Yes, Sunya was beyond question a good match, but her heart troubled her.

For the first time, she felt jealous of her sister. Nothing had yet even been suggested about Lifu, yet she had a premonition that Mochow was going to be engaged to him sooner or later. If she could only change places with her! She looked sidelong at her sister and said, "Didn't I always tell you you would be luckier than I?"

"How luckier than you, sister?"

"Nothing," said Mulan.

Mochow could see that her sister was acting strangely, but she did not press the question further.

Mulan believed, too, that one's matrimonial destiny was decreed by fate. So, when her mother had consulted her father and got his approval and came that evening before supper to speak to Mulan alone in her room, Mulan merely smiled and her mother took it for consent.

She could not sleep that night. The die was cast, and it had to be so. She began to think of Sunya—that boy who had smiled such a broad smile at her when she first saw him in the boat on the Grand Canal. How Fate had indeed thrown them together! How everything had happened and developed so that there was no escape! She thought of how Sunya had looked, and how easy it would be for her to get along with him. For of him she had no fear. Then she thought of how kind his mother had been, and then of Mannia. For a moment she hated Mannia for interfering in her life like this. But her thoughts always went back to Lifu, to his studies and to his "ruins." How happy she had been only four or five nights ago when she and Lifu drank a toast to each other! How would he take the news of her engagement? Had he ever suspected that she cared for him? When she thought of this, she felt her cheeks burning hot as if the effect of the wine were still upon her.

When the sisters retired, Mochow had wanted to congratulate her again and to start conversation about the engagement but Mulan had merely smiled, and said, "If it is settled, then it is settled," and Mochow had looked disappointed and said no more. Now in the half-darkness of the night Mulan could see her sister sleeping peacefully in the other bed and thought her indeed a lucky girl.

For the next few days, she tried not to think of Lifu but occupied her mind with thoughts of her new situation and of the Tseng family. In that family she had no reason to be afraid of anybody but Mr. Tseng. As the youngest daughter-in-law, her responsibility would be light. Yet there would be Suyun, Chinya's bride-to-be, and she wondered what kind of life she would have with her as co-daughter-in-law, usually a trying relationship.

The horoscopes of Mulan and Sunya must be exchanged before the formal engagement. Mr. Fu had come to Peking again, and when Mulan's mother asked his opinion as an amateur philosophic fortune-teller, he said that Mulan was "gold" and Sunya was "water" and that "gold would sparkle in water." The match was propitious. Quoting a poem, Mr. Fu said:

> "Rocks containing jade make the mountain lustrous;
> Water concealing pearls makes the river enticing."

This was said in everybody's hearing, including Mulan's and they congratulated her.

Now human beings are of the five types represented by the Five Elements: Gold, Wood, Water, Fire, Earth. Marriage is a science of matching types. There are types that beautifully complement each other, and types that, if not mutually destructive, would hasten one another toward common destruction. "Inbreeding" between a boy and a girl of the same type should be discouraged because it would only emphasize or augment the original tendency in the husband or the wife. This is clear enough: marrying an indolent ("water") wife to an indolent husband would only make matters worse, and marrying a quick-tempered ("fire") husband to a quick-tempered wife would just burn up the couple. A person with fine texture and fine features and quick intelligence is Gold or Metal. A person with prominent bones and joints and inclined to be lanky is Wood. A person fleshy, indolent, phlegmatic, with lines flowing downward is Water. A person hot-headed, quick-tempered, shifty-eyed, volatile, with the forehead sloping upward, is Fire. And a person steady, calm, with round, full lines and surfaces is Earth. Within each type, there are sub-types or varieties, both good and bad, even as we have wood that is fine-grained or loose-grained, smooth-grained or knotty-grained. For instance, Gold will cut into, or "overcome," Wood; yet a prominent-jointed, cross-grained, broad-faced, and knotty-fingered Wood might blunt the edge of a soft Metal, or to put it more simply, a coarse, brutal husband would make a high-strung, fine-featured wife suffer.

"And what is Mochow?" Mrs. Yao asked Mr. Fu when she found him alone that afternoon, after she had thought over what he had said.

"Mochow is Earth," said Mr. Fu. "Steady, calm, round, and full. These are most valuable and lucky qualities. She has the 'physiognomy of luck.' She will be a great blessing to her husband, but she would be a bad match for Sunya. While Earth would mix with Water, yet the result would be soft and muddy and nothing great would come of such a match."

"I don't mean that," said Mrs. Yao.

"Then what do you mean?" he asked.

Mrs. Yao whispered something in his ear, and he laughed and his eyes twinkled and Mrs. Yao waited half a minute for his reply.

"Excellent! Excellent!" he said.

"Tell me. Don't just exclaim 'excellent!'"

"Well," whispered Mr. Fu, "Lifu is Wood, and very good wood at that. Earth nourishes Wood, and Wood prospers. He is as hard as red sandalwood, and you can't crack it. But he needs softening. He goes with Mochow's Earth even better than with Mulan's Gold, but if he should marry a volatile, quick-tempered wife, it would burn him up."

Neither girl knew of this conversation, but Mrs. Yao told her husband that night what Mr. Fu had said, and Mr. Yao said, "Of course. One Lifu is worth three Sunya's and ten Tijen's."

"What do you say of our Tijen?" said Mrs. Yao.

"He is like a loose-grained tree with a rotten trunk. The core or heart is all eaten up already. What can you do with it? It is not even good for fuel."

"I don't believe our son is worse than others," said the mother, "and when you hear him talking, he seems so sensible and he means so well."

"That is just it," said her husband. "When you knock on a hollow trunk, it makes a good noise."

And the mother had a picture in her mind of a little fire, which was Silverscreen, consuming the dry and quickly burning fuel that was Tijen. She told her husband that her brother had written to Silverscreen's aunt promising to pay her fifty dollars if she would write the letter demanded by Silverscreen. But she did not tell him that she had asked her brother to forge a letter for the purpose, in anticipation of the real letter, in order to hasten the marrying off of Silverscreen before her son's possible return.

. : .

Shortly before Mulan and Mochow were to go away to school at Tientsin, Silverscreen disappeared. On the morning of the previous day, Mr. Feng had shown her what purported to be her aunt's letter, asking Mrs. Yao to find a good match and marry her off in Peking.

Now Silverscreen had known of the mistress's intentions to marry her off quickly and she had been sparring for time. She had secretly had a letter of her own written and sent to Tijen at Hong Kong, but there was no way of receiving his reply. Her letters could be intercepted at home, and she had no one to trust.

When she was shown the letter, supposedly from her aunt, she was dumbfounded. She silently calculated the days, and did not quite believe that a letter from Hangchow could come so soon. Still there was the letter, there was no question of signature because her aunt could not write or sign her name, and her demand for a written word had been fulfilled.

So in the night, after everybody had gone to bed, she took cover in the dark and slipped out to the vegetable garden and disappeared through the back door. Thus she escaped, taking with her Tijen's dog and a package of her clothing and two jade rings which Tijen had given her. He had told her that one of the jade rings was worth three or four hundred dollars. It was not until breakfast time that Brocade reported that Silverscreen was not in her room and her bed had not been slept in. Only at ten o'clock did they discover the dog's footprints clearly leading through the garden to the back door, which stood open.

Silverscreen had lived in Peking for years and had a fair knowledge of directions and of the different sections of the city. She hired a rickshaw and went to the southwestern sections inside Shunchihmen Gate, which she had chosen as being safely distant from the Yaos' home and yet crowded enough for her not to be too conspicuous, and she took a room for the night, in a small hotel in the South City near by. The dog was a great nuisance because he might lead to her discovery. In the morning she gave the dog a piece of meat and tied him to an iron bedpost in her room, and went out to a jeweler's shop to sell one of her rings. She was well-dressed and the first jeweler offered, to her surprise, one hundred fifty dollars for the ring. Having an idea of the real value of the ring, she went to the next jeweler and demanded two hundred dollars and sold it. With that money in hand, she was sure of half a year's support. She would be careful with her money and she still had another ring and so she could wait a year without work for Tijen's return. She began to swear revenge in her heart. She swore that if Tijen did come back, she would do all in her power to keep him from his mother; she was a woman and knew Tijen's weakness.

Posing as a woman from Shanghai, she set out to look for a room. The rooms in the cheaper houses were rented out separately, and sometimes several families lived in the same courtyard, but Silverscreen avoided such houses as being too open to any strange people. Finally she chose one in an out-of-the-way alley with only a yard, belonging to a couple without children. The owner was a Kiangsu merchant who had fallen upon bad days, and his wife was a former singsong artist. They had a big room on the east to let. The furniture was shabby, consisting of a wooden bed, a wash stand, and a mahjong table now used as a common table, on which stood an old kettle and a teapot with cups. The rent asked was four dollars, but Silverscreen beat it down to three dollars and sixty coppers. Finding that the girl spoke Shanghai dialect, the woman was very cordial and made her welcome. Mrs. Hua was still young and must have been a beauty but now she had a mouthful of black teeth, and Silverscreen saw an opium set on her bed. She learned later that the man had eloped with this sing-song artist, and had come north with a thousand dollars in his pocket, after paying six hundred dollars to the artist's "mother." Then he was disowned by his parents, and forced to keep a fruit and candy shop at a bazaar at West-Four Pailou, and for some years the wife had tried to help out by singing at one of the better tea houses. But with their opium habit, they had found it hard to make ends meet, and now the wife had given up singing. The house was far from being orderly, but they still could afford an old woman servant who cooked and washed for them.

Having made the arrangement, Silverscreen returned to her hotel, paid the bill and led her dog to the new house. She explained to Mrs. Hua that her husband was traveling in the south and would not be back for some time, and the woman did not ask questions.

Silverscreen soon found out that during the daytime when the husband was away, there were men visitors coming to see the woman. Whether they came for a smoke or something else she did not know and dared not ask. Once she noticed that the husband returned at sunset, and when the woman servant told him that there was a "guest," he turned away again.

After some days Mrs. Hua asked why the dog was kept tied all the time. By this time Silverscreen knew the woman's past history and so she confided her own story, and the similarity of their positions made the woman sympathize with her. As Silverscreen found it convenient to tell her the truth, so the woman also found it convenient to let her guess what she was about. She had asked Silverscreen to lie on the couch with her and smoke a pipe, but Silverscreen had refused. Once in that position, a man visitor appeared, and Silverscreen started to go away, but the woman asked her to stay for a while.

Step by step, Silverscreen learned the seductive arts of woman, and what was most important, that woman's philosophy. "There is no justice in life," she said one day. "Look at me, sold by my parents in my childhood. Get what you can out of life and don't lose hold of your man once you get him. Your mistress has really no conscience. It would not cost her more than a bowl of rice to keep you. As you say, even a dog kept for ten years would not be beaten from the house like that. But listen to me, keep your boy when he comes back. I know men and I know how."

"If you keep the secret for me," said Silverscreen, "he will reward you properly when he comes."

One day Silverscreen was convinced and decided to learn to smoke opium. The woman had explained to her the charm of the lantern, and how its small soft light and the smoke at once made any room look familiar and made a man feel thoroughly comfortable and relaxed. She explained how a woman looked so much more charming when she was reclining on the couch chatting with a man, or sat preparing the pipe for him, with the light of the lantern shining up into her face. But Silverscreen smoked only to learn how to play with it as an accomplishment, and guarded cautiously against forming the habit herself.

As a matter of fact, Silverscreen came to realize that Mrs. Hua was quite accomplished, charming, and a good talker. With the woman's assistance she sent a long letter to Tijen about what had happened, where she was, how his mother had broken her promise and the names she had called her, and how she herself was faithfully living up to her own promise and waiting for his return.

.·.

When Silverscreen disappeared from the Yao household, the other bondmaids disclaimed all knowledge of it. Lotung was sent to find out whether his daughter-in-law Bluehaze knew anything about it, and she came immediately to express her own surprise. Mrs. Yao consulted her brother, who thought it was awkward but not important, so far as the maid's aunt was concerned; and Mrs. Yao in her matter-of-fact way was glad to be rid of the girl in any case. Since she had run away herself, there was so much less responsibility on the family. She merely remarked that the foolish maid did not appreciate their help and was merely getting into trouble for herself. "A bondmaid is a bondmaid," she said. Mr. Yao, however, did not think the matter would end there. All wondered how the maid was going to support herself, and were amazed that at least she had not stolen jewels and curios from the family, as she might easily have done, and they gave her credit for that. They thought that the dog's being with her might sooner or later lead to her discovery, but no energetic effort was made to trace her. Mulan alone thought that it was romantic of Silverscreen to have taken Tijen's dog with her. That sounded like faithfulness.

On top of all this confusion, there was the formal engagement of Mulan to Sunya and the distribution of presents to friends and relatives which served as the announcement of the engagement. Lifu's mother, of course, received a share of the presents, and the mother and son both came to express their thanks for Mrs. Yao's presents and to pay a call, as was dictated by courtesy, and also to see the sisters before they went to school.

Not until it was announced that he and his mother had come did Mulan realize how deeply she cared for Lifu. After talking with her mother, the mother and son came to congratulate Mulan.

"Lanmei, congratulations," said Lifu after his mother, and he smiled.

"Thank you, Brother Lifu," said Mulan also smiling, but the smile almost choked her.

Her gaze at Lifu was direct and full, and her voice faltered when she said "Brother Lifu." It was such a brave look that he felt it like an invisible shot, carrying a message beyond words, something whole-hearted and soft and tender. Never had a beautiful girl smiled such a full smile at him.

Then Mulan became lively and unaccountably happy in Lifu's presence. The wine of love once more emancipated her, and she was gay, hospitable, and more talkative than usual.

Now well-bred girls in those days would never admit that they were in love, or permit anybody to say so, for it was nothing short of a blot upon a girl's character. Yet when Lifu left, she strangely felt that another happy half-day was over and hungered for more to come.

She carried with her to school a heart torn between guilty thoughts of Lifu on rainy and cloudy days, and more proper thoughts of Sunya on bright and sunny days. She had wanted to take along also the photograph taken by her brother in the Hunting Park, with Lifu in it and herself in that snapshot gesture of a half-raised hand and a miserably smiling expression, but she had not the courage to do so.

. · .

Tijen in Hong Kong had received Silverscreen's letters. He was furious at his mother and sent a hundred dollars, which convinced the landlady that Silverscreen's story was true and increased her respect for her. In his letter he asked her to wait for him but to keep her where-abouts entirely secret from the family. His first impulse was to take the next boat back and settle accounts with his mother, but on second thought he was afraid of what he had done. At least his father had as much right to be angry with him as he had the right to be angry with his mother. So he stayed and registered in a school. Bad as he had been at home, he had yet never frequented the sing-song houses in Peking, but now in Hong Kong he debauched himself as long as his money lasted. But while enjoying himself with women, he did not mean to give up Silverscreen and he knew that soon he would have to come back.

In the meantime, his father had received a report about what Tijen was doing and was biding his time, knowing that soon Tijen's money would be used up. He had also written directly to the ship company to claim the refund of fare lest it should fall into his son's hands.

The uncle had now received a letter from Hangchow. It was signed by Silverscreen's uncle instead of her aunt and it bore his seal. The instructions were as asked for, but the manager of the tea firm had sent a separate letter to explain that Silverscreen's uncle had demanded one hundred dollars instead of fifty, which had accordingly been paid. Since Silverscreen was now gone, the uncle did not worry about it, but merely kept the letter. Nor did he bother to let Silverscreen's family know that the maid had run away. And Tijen wrote letters home, pretending not to know anything about Silverscreen's disappearance from the family, until his mother should think fit to inform him of it.

CHAPTER XVIII

TIJEN's money was gone sooner than he had thought—how, he could not understand, although he remembered that he had lent several hundred dollars to two friends, who later disappeared.

Toward the end of November, his father received a letter asking for money, and replied peremptorily telling his son to return or he would cut him off entirely.

So one day during the winter solstice recess when Mulan and Mochow had returned to their home, Tijen arrived. His appearance was greatly changed. He looked gaunt and pale, his eyes were sunken, his cheekbones stuck out, his hair was long, and he had grown a wisp of a mustache and wore a pair of dark spectacles. Moreover, he had arrived home with exactly thirteen cents in his pocket.

The mother was both shocked and happy. "My poor child, how you must have suffered! There was no one to take care of you in a strange city. I never believed in sending you away at this age." She immediately ordered chicken noodle for him. As the noodle was being placed on the table, Coral said to Tijen, "Now you must eat. In this soup there are at least three or four chickens. Three days ago Mother asked people to kill a chicken, but you didn't come, and every day we killed one more chicken, and we have stewed them all down to this bit of soup. If your eyes do not brighten after tasting it, the chickens have died an unjust death."

While Tijen was having his soup, surrounded by all the women of the family and the maids and servants, his father swept into the room. Tijen immediately stood up. Mulan saw that her father's eyes were distended and she thought he might strike Tijen on the head then and there; but the father merely grunted and walked out again, and kept away from him the whole day. He did not even appear for lunch, probably to give the mother and daughters and son a period of peace.

264

After lunch, when Brocade gave Tijen a hot towel, he casually asked her, "Where is Silverscreen? How did she disappear?"

"We don't know, young master. One night she disappeared and so just disappeared," replied Brocade in a ringing voice, biting her lip and looking wistfully at him and at the mistress.

"Your dog disappeared with her," said Afei.

"So after all the dog was more faithful," said Tijen impulsively and more brusquely than he had intended.

"Are you praising the dog or are you condemning human beings?" asked Mochow.

"Sister, you are still like that," said Tijen. "I was only asking. But since there was the dog, wasn't it easy to find her? Did you try to find her? Even if you didn't care for Silverscreen, you might have cared to find my dog. The moment my back was turned, they were turned out of the house."

"My son," said the mother, "you misunderstand. Nobody drove the maid away. She ran away herself."

"She must have had a reason for running away," he insisted.

"Well," said his mother, "your uncle returned at the end of July shortly after you departed, and he brought word from Silverscreen's aunt that she was to be married off in Peking. . . ."

"Did you try to marry her off?" asked the son. "You promised me."

"It was the girl's family. You don't understand. You were going away for years, and their girl was of the age to marry and her term had expired. How could we prevent them from wanting to marry her off? There was her aunt's letter."

"Her uncle's," corrected Mrs. Feng, who usually did not speak much and was extremely obedient to her sister-in-law because her husband's position was entirely dependent upon the latter. Now Mrs. Yao looked at her and said, "She is right. Her aunt told your uncle before he left, but Silverscreen demanded a written word and her uncle then sent the letter."

"No, Mother, it was her aunt's letter, not her uncle's," said Afei, who had heard of the forged letter but not of the uncle's letter that came later. Brocade suppressed a smile and the sisters who also did not know of the uncle's letter, looked at each other in surprise. Tijen noticed the confusion.

"You, little child, what do you know about it?" said the mother, scolding Afei. "The uncle's letter is still here, if you don't believe. Have you got it?" she asked Mrs. Feng.

"No. He keeps it at the shop," said Mrs. Feng.

"I'll ask him to show it to you," said the mother. "But bygones are bygones. We do not know where she is now. Don't waste your thoughts on such things."

"I don't think you would care even if she died," said Tijen, angrier than before.

"My son, you are crazy," said the mother. "She ran away and even if she starved to death, it was her fault. We tried to arrange a good match for her. Bluehaze suggested a very good merchant. Your mother didn't do wrong."

Tijen flew into a rage. "You drove her away. I know it. You tried to *marry* her off. You promised me not to, and you broke your promise. Didn't you? Didn't you?"

His mother began to weep and said, "It is difficult to be a mother." He was really unashamed, but his sisters were ashamed for him and came to their mother and tried to comfort her. Frankincense brought a hot towel to the mistress, while Mulan said,

"Brother, I think this is enough. You were going away to England and then you wouldn't go. You were to be gone for years, and how could you at the same time expect to hold up other people's affairs? Mother was doing nothing wrong to marry her off when her term had expired. And now on the very day of your arrival, you have made Mother cry. Is there ever going to be peace in this family?"

"Good! You are all good, and I am the only bad son in the family," cried Tijen. "If you don't want me to ask questions, I'll get out and let you all have peace."

The mother said through her tears, "Just on account of a bondmaid, there has been no peace in this house. I don't understand what you see in her. When you are grown up, my son, a family like ours can find ten better bondmaids for you, if you like. Now you are tired, go and take a rest."

Mulan was angry because her mother was so soft toward her brother.

.·.

Now at supper, the father sat down at the table with an expression that frightened everybody, most of all Mrs. Feng and her daughter, Redjade, who had never seen such a look on his face. The old man, though short in stature, had a big head and powerful, penetrating eyes, and the hair on his temples was now a beautiful gray, and when he was angered, he looked very impressive. Tijen ate his rice quietly, knowing that the time of reckoning was near. He looked ridiculous, in that Chinese home, with his foreign dress and little mustache and dark spectacles, as if he were an imported monstrosity—no longer a son, no longer a Chinese. The sisters also sat and ate quietly and there were moments of tense silence. Coral tried to lead the conversation by asking Tijen why he had arrived a couple of days later than they expected, and he answered in an abnormally hoarse manly voice that the voyage was rough. Upon hearing Tijen's voice, the father glowered.

"What did you come back for?" he growled.

"You asked me to, Father," replied the son.

"Don't let off your wind! Did you think I would provide you funds to go whoring in the South? The *niehchang!*" In the past months Mr. Yao had changed his reference to his son from *niehchung* (seed of sin) to *niehchang,* or a predetermined disaster in one's life brought about by some previous sin. It meant the wages of sin, the stumbling block to a peaceful life, the inescapable snare set by the devil; hence its variation, *mochang,* which meant literally "devil's stumbling block."

"He just came back," said the mother. "You ought to leave him a little face, at least before the servants."

"What? Face?" shouted the father aloud. "Has he still got face? Can he still be called a man? What did you go abroad to learn but such monstrosities? Take off your spectacles. . . . Give them to me!"

The father crunched the pair of spectacles in his powerful right hand, until they were only a mass of twisted wires and broken glass. His hand was pricked by the broken glass and bled, but he refused to have anybody do anything to it. With the bleeding hand he pushed his bowl and plate aside, and he pushed his chair back and rose and paced the floor, and no one dared to touch the food. His face and beard became smeared with blood and he looked fearsome. Afei began to cry, *"Brother!"* and Mr. Yao said, "Be silent! That is not your *brother;* that is the devil's stumbling block! Let him be a warning to you! If you grow up to be like him, the Yao family is finished!" Mulan, who sat next to little Afei, hushed him, while Mrs. Feng held Redjade's hand in fear and stared her into immobility.

Turning sharply, the old man addressed his elder son: "I am not going to flog you. And I won't ask you for accounts—how you spent a thousand two hundred dollars in three months. But I am through with you. You had better make up your own plans as to what you are going to do."

Now Tijen had risen and stood at attention, and Mr. Feng also had left his seat. In a repentant voice, Tijen said, "Father, I was wrong. But now I am going to study."

"Study?" sneered his father. "You had your chance and now you are not going to have it. Do you know what you need? Starvation is the best thing for you. If you know what hunger means, you will appreciate more where you are." Mochow could not help remembering the quotation from Mencius and looked at her brother. With his gaunt face he really looked as if he had not been well-fed.

"Shut him up in my study and let no one give him food for a day."

Tijen felt both rebellious and frightened. It was Mr. Feng who spoke up, in his best business tone. "Brother, let me say something. My nephew of course is wrong. Isn't that so? But the rice is already cooked and there is no use going over the old accounts now. Isn't that so? Of course going to England is out of the question. But going to college here is also unnecessary. He will be twenty this New Year and ought to learn business, don't you think? If you agree, have him come to the shop and get acquainted with the business and help in writing letters."

Coral also stood up and said, "Father, the rice is getting cold. You ought to eat something. These things can be discussed slowly."

"I am not hungry and what should I eat for?" replied Mr. Yao. "Shut him up tomorrow." With that he walked out of the room.

The children now began to eat, but the women finished hurriedly what was in their bowls. It was a dismal dinner.

"Now you ought to reform, Brother," said Mochow. "It is getting beyond all bounds of decency. At least you ought to keep up an appearance to please our parents. Our parents are old and you ought to feel guilty to cause them worry. After all, you are the son and the home is yours. A man living in this world must have face among his fellowmen. If you follow Uncle's advice and settle down to learn business, we sisters can also have something to be proud of. Otherwise, how is this going to end?"

"You are always saying that," Tijen muttered.

"If you keep on doing the same thing," said Mulan, "of course we keep on saying the same thing."

Now Coral asked Brocade to warm up some rice and soup and some

268

other dishes to serve to the father. When it was ready, Coral proposed that, as a first sign of reform and a natural act of filial piety, Tijen should personally carry the tray of food in to his father. But Tijen sullenly refused. In the end, Mulan went with Afei, knowing that the child was sure to soften the father's anger. The sister and brother went and peeped in from the back window and saw their father puffing at his water pipe and reading a newspaper. Mulan made Afei take the tray and went in with him.

The old man looked up in surprise, and when he saw his daughter and his little son, his heart was touched.

"Will you be a filial son?" asked the father.

"Yes, I will," answered little Afei.

"Then don't be like your brother. Do what he doesn't do, and don't do what he does."

"I will take care of him, Father," said Mulan.

She saw that there was a slight clot of blood on his beard, and she made Afei go and bring a hot towel and wash it off.

"Are you really going to shut Brother up tomorrow?" asked Mulan.

"Yes. It will do him no harm and may teach him a lesson. He ought to know what hunger means."

The next day Tijen was locked in his father's study, and the father carried the key with him. But in the afternoon when the father was away, the mother came to speak to her son through the partition, and managed to have a panel taken down and to slip in some steamed and stuffed buns for him, and hurried away, asking him to leave no traces of the food.

．∴．

Mr. Feng was a typical business man. His position in the family was unique and secure, since he was the brother of Mrs. Yao and was practically the manager of the big business owned by the Yaos. He was somewhat bony and square-faced like his sister, always wore a "melon cap" with a red button on top, and carried a one-foot pipe with a jade mouthpiece. He had the merchant's typical manner of talking, which was interspersed with many silent "hah's" and "haw's" and ran the gamut from silent whispers to vociferous shouting as circumstances required. He had acquired all the nuances of raising his voice in an emphatic tone of determination and repudiation when bargaining for a purchase, and softening it to a heartfelt cordiality when closing the bargain, knowing how to appear to stand his ground when he was prepared to yield, and yielding abruptly with a gesture of friendship at the last moment as if he was conferring a favor. He knew how to condemn or deprecate what he desired to buy and to extol to perfection what he wanted to sell. All those hot arguments, those red-faced, loud-voiced repetitions, did not mean anything except that he didn't like the price you quoted, and a stepping down on his part was always conveyed by a whisper in your ear, as if it was the greatest diplomatic secret and you were his most intimate confidant.

He had run the big business efficiently and well, and enjoyed the confidence of his sister and brother-in-law as no manager who was not a member of the family possibly could. Mr. Yao, being an extremely intelligent man, kept the essentials of the business reports clearly in mind, was consulted on and made the most important decisions, but left to Mr. Feng all the minor details of which he did not want to hear anything. Mr. Feng drew a ridiculous salary of sixty dollars a month but received an annual bonus running into thousands as was the general practice even with most of the other employees. By this time, he had acquired a fortune of his own running into several tens of thousands.

His proposal that Tijen go into the business was a sound one, not because the business needed him, but because he needed an occupation. It was sound also because the uncle could talk with Tijen and influence him in a way that the father, who would not talk to his son, could not. But the uncle also knew that Tijen was not likely to take the business very seriously.

The following day, therefore, Mr. Feng came to the study where Tijen was still confined, telling him that he had his father's permission to take him to the shop. It was to be nothing difficult; he had only to watch how the employees were running the business, and this morning it was more an excuse for getting him out of the confinement. It was understood that he was to stay for lunch at the shop as Mr. Feng always did. At the shop, Mr. Feng showed him the letter from Silverscreen's uncle, with the signature and seal, which he had kept locked in his office desk.

After lunch, Tijen made the excuse that he wanted to call on a friend he had met on the voyage and went to see Silverscreen. He had her address, and, as he came near and looked for the house number, his heart palpitated with excitement. It was a small mud house with an old unpainted door. An old woman came to answer the door, and at that moment he heard his dog barking inside excitedly, and knew he had come to the right house.

"Aren't you Yao *Shaoyeh?*" asked the woman.

He thought it strange when he went in, that Silverscreen did not come rushing out to welcome him. The dog jumped at him and ran around and jumped upon him again, placing its forepaws on his shoulders and standing on its hind legs. Tijen, eager to see its mistress, pulled its paws down, and the dog with almost human intelligence led him to Silverscreen's room on the east. But the door was shut and the dog sat on the doorstep and barked. The woman servant led Tijen up to the main room, where a thin woman about thirty stood at the hall door. Tijen thought at once that she had very beautiful eyes and well-plucked eyebrows.

"Come in," said the woman, greeting him with a smile that was spoiled by her black teeth. He went into the barely furnished hall, and still there was no Silverscreen.

"My name is Yao," he said.

"Of course I know. Your young mistress has been waiting for you for days." She told the woman servant to ask Silverscreen to come out. The woman replied that Silverscreen was not well and that her door was locked from the inside and she would not open it. Tijen wanted to rush over, but the landlady said, smiling. "It must be that she is angry. You don't know how anxiously she has been waiting for you the past three or four days. She could not even eat her meals, and she went and stood watching at the door. She even let the dog out to see if he could find you."

"That is strange," said Tijen, and he went to Silverscreen's door and knocked, calling, "Silverscreen, what is the matter? I am back now."

No reply came from within. Mrs. Hua also called, "Silverscreen, open the door. Your young master is come. How can you refuse to see him?"

Silverscreen's voice came from within. "What is the purpose of seeing me? You go back to your home and forget about me. Whether I am dead or alive has nothing to do with you."

Now Silverscreen's letter from Tijen had told her that he would arrive about four days ago. He had arrived late because he had stopped at Tientsin to have one last wild night of freedom and to spend his last dollar. Silverscreen had kept herself rouged and powdered in antic-

271

ipation of his coming at any moment. As the days passed, and she waited and waited, she became angry, thinking that he was neglecting her. Mrs. Hua then taught her that when he did come, she was to pretend to refuse to see him, while Mrs. Hua herself would tell him how she had been thinking of him, how true she was to him, in order to soften him, and she would see to it that he did not leave without seeing her. So when Silverscreen heard the dog barking, she had bolted the door and taken off her jacket and jumped into bed, and then jumped up again to make up her face.

Tijen looked at Mrs. Hua and scowled, but she was only smiling. "This is your lovers' quarrel. You had better apologize to her, for she waited for you for four days and you didn't come to see her."

"That is truly unjust," said Tijen. "Silverscreen," he called again. "You must listen to me. I arrived only day before yesterday, and I could not get away because I was locked up by my father. I will explain everything." When she heard this, Silverscreen's heart softened, and she rose to pull the latch and let him in. He heard her giggle and then saw the door open and rushed in and took her in his arms, and the dog rushed in with him.

"It is all right now, it is all right now," said Mrs. Hua and walked away.

Tijen, who had read the *Red Chamber Dream*, literally licked the rouge from Silverscreen's lips like Paoyu.

"Slowly, slowly, now," said Silverscreen, pushing him back, laughing. She called to the servant to make tea and led him further into the room.

Tijen saw a transformed Silverscreen. She was wearing a white underjacket and a red satin vest with a close line of silk buttons, and beneath she wore green silk trousers and embroidered satin shoes. Her hands were white and soft and she wore a pair of jade earrings and her eyebrows were carefully plucked, like the landlady's. And there was a lock of hair an inch long before each of her ears, evenly clipped.

"Close the door. It is cold," she said.

Tijen saw her bedding lying half unfolded and asked, "Were you sleeping?"

"Yes, and I was ill. I almost died of waiting for you."

She started to put on her jacket, but Tijen saw that the room was not well heated by the small stove and said, "You had better jump into bed again or you will catch cold."

So she sat in the bed and covered herself with the bedding, leaving however, her white arms and her close-fitting red vest well exposed, while he sat on the edge of the bed and admired her while he told her what had happened at home.

The old woman brought tea, and Silverscreen told her to add some coal balls to the stove, and when the servant had left, Silverscreen told him to go and bolt the door.

"Is it all right here?" he asked.

"It is perfectly all right. Nobody can interfere with us here." Tijen was happy and proud and felt that he had a mistress of his own. "We are free here, not as we were in my home."

"What do you think of me now?" she asked.

"You are marvelous," he said.

Pointing to the dog crouching by her bedside, she said, "I have kept him and fed him exactly as when you were at home, and I have kept your queue. I have played my part, haven't I? If I had not taken the risk and run away I should be married to someone by now."

And Tijen said, "And I, too, will keep my word. If I had not turned back on the way to England, I should have lost you."

"I thank you," she said and drew him close to her and kissed him. He lay on her breast and she fondled his cheek and said, "Why are you so good and your mother so cruel? I seemed less than a dog in your house. After you were gone, every time she opened her mouth she called me 'little whore.' I saw that it was hopeless but I could not tell her to her face that she had broken her promise to you. I don't know how many nights I cried myself to sleep, for I thought it would be too late when you should return. Bluehaze was arranging a match to bundle me off like a can of garbage, and they thought I didn't know. The whole family kept the secret from me. I tried to play for time and demanded a letter from my aunt, for I didn't believe them. Then my aunt's letter came, and I thought I had to run away, or I would fall into their trap and be married off blindfolded. I don't even believe that my aunt's letter was genuine, because I reckoned that it could not have come so soon."

"What?" asked Tijen, sharply. "Was it your aunt's letter or your uncle's?"

"They showed me a letter which they said came from my aunt. I couldn't read. So what could I do except to pretend to believe them? I have kept it. Open that package and I will show you."

Tijen brought the package which lay at the end of the bed, and Silverscreen took out the aunt's letter.

"The rascals!" said Tijen, dumbfounded. "I never thought my mother would do such a thing! Why, I saw this morning your uncle's letter with my own eyes." Silverscreen had never known of the uncle's letter, and it was her turn to be surprised.

"Well, that's what your good mother did to plot against me," said Silverscreen. "That is what they were doing behind your back. I guessed it, but what could a bondmaid do except pretend to be dumb and deaf and let people do as they liked?"

"I must ask my uncle about this."

"No, you must not. They would know that I am here. It is all over now and I am free. So long as I have you, what do I care?"

"Only it makes me angry every time I think of what they did to you."

She continued to fondle and kiss him.

Thus they sat for a great part of the afternoon, until the short winter day was drawing to a close. Silverscreen asked him to stay for supper, but he said he could not because it was his first day in the shop and he had to go back there first before returning home with his uncle.

Nevertheless, with great forethought, Mrs. Hua the landlady had prepared four dishes of white-cut chicken, dry sugared, smoked fish in the Shanghai style, cold-cut steamed abalone, and boiled chicken gizzard in plain soya-bean sauce in the Ningpo style, which Silverscreen knew that Tijen loved. He was urged to stay at least for a drink. Hot wine was served, and the three sat down to celebrate his homecoming, and Tijen began to like Mrs. Hua and to pay her compliments. He took out twenty-five dollars and gave them to Silverscreen, telling her to buy herself a new quilt and bedspread and a few other new things for the room. He also wanted to give five dollars to the servant, but Silverscreen said, "You must not waste money like that. Give her a dollar and she will be very pleased. This is like building a home now and we must economize." She called the old woman in, and, taking a dollar bill in her hand, she said proudly. "Here is a dollar for you from Yao *Shaoyeh*. Quickly thank him and attend upon him well next time he comes." The old woman took the bill and made a half curtsy, and said, beaming with smiles, "Do not worry. Although my old eyes are dim, I can still recognize a gentleman's son from a poor stuffed bag in the streets. When the young mistress talked about you, I thought how you must look, and now I have seen you, and indeed what she said is true. I don't know what merit she must have acquired in her previous life to know a person like you."

When Tijen left, he found it hard to prevent the dog from following him. Silverscreen saw him to the door, and whispered in his ear that the next time he came, he should bring a present for the landlady. He went away exalted and happy, feeling that he had found a new life and proud that he had so enchanting a secret.

CHAPTER XIX

ꜰᴛᴇʀ the short Winter Solstice recess Mulan and her sister left to go to school again and did not return until the New Year, which came about a month later in February as it is reckoned in the West. They told none of their fellow students what they had gone through at home during the short holidays, but it was evident that to every girl the significant and interesting things happened outside and not at school.

Upon their return for the long New Year holidays, they brought a classmate Sutan, a new friend, whose home was in Shanghai. She was a deathly pale girl, emotional, excitable, and good in the Chinese subjects in spite of her Christian surroundings, for her mother, Mrs. Chien, was a Christian. Mulan learned that she was a kind of a rebel in the family, entirely different from her brother and sister, and had decided to enter a government school in spite of her mother. She had extraordinarily beautiful handwriting, and had read many of the old novels, She was witty, she could sing operatic airs like Mulan, and she would jiggle her knees like men when sitting. At school the girls lacked a stringed instrument, but when they hummed the airs in their school bedroom, Sutan would tap her fingers on her knee to keep time and hum the instrumental parts which came between the vocal parts. Under her influence Mulan read a number of old novels, so that her eyes suffered from reading the bad print. In later years, Mulan became slightly shortsighted, but she always refused to wear spectacles. It was so slight that nobody would suspect it unless she told it herself, but it gave her eyes a queer, dreamy expression when she was looking into the distance. Sutan also gave her some ideas of the Christian religion and Christian practices, both favorable and unfavorable, and the Christian influence showed itself in Sutan's belief in "free marriage," or marriage by the girl's or boy's own choice. She approved of everything Chinese except the ideas of womanhood and marriage. This seemed like a contradiction; but it was not, because it was clear that Sutan was the type to have love affairs, whether in ancient or modern China. Among the ideas of the West she approved of those she liked or believed in herself.

When New Year came and Mulan found that Sutan would be compelled to stay at school because her home was in the south, she invited her to come and stay at her home in Peking during the holidays.

The sisters were glad to find that Tijen was getting settled and their father was no longer angry. Every day Tijen went to the shop with his uncle, and, being satisfied with the appearance of having an occupation and with his freedom to see Silverscreen, he did not raise the question of the forged letter. His uncle did not stop him from going off in the afternoon to "see his friends," and if he came home late or was out in the evenings, either being invited to dinner or going to the theater, as he told his mother, that was a grown-up's freedom. Even his uncle had not yet suspected that he was keeping up the relationship with the bondmaid. He would ask for money, a few tens of dollars at a time, but his uncle thought this nothing surprising.

For Tijen was far from being a fool. Silverscreen had begun to ask for money, putting forward the very sound reason that unless she saved up something for her protection, she would be left completely destitute if his father found out or something else went wrong. But Tijen knew that New Year was the time for closing accounts, and he did not want to frighten his uncle or to have his expenses come to the knowledge of his father. He thought it best to wait until the New Year was over before starting any trouble. So at least during the New Year's holidays, there was peace and happiness in the home.

Tijen's happiness was complete. If there had been no Silverscreen, he would certainly have found other women in the district outside Chienmen; if Silverscreen had remained at his home, he could not have indulged himself with such complete freedom. Now here he found not only a free Silverscreen in a separate establishment, but he also found that during his absence she had completely changed into a well-dressed, mature woman, versed in the arts of entertaining men. Both Mrs. Hua and Silverscreen soon saw how happy and relaxed he was in their place, and they did their best to keep him satisfied. His twenty-five dollars was at once spent to beautify the interior; and, when Tijen remarked that a picture on the wall was awful, it was taken down the next day and a foreign painting of naked women,

277

in a redwood frame, was put up. There were new mirrors, new basins, and new chairs, and when he came he was treated as the master of the place. No one scolded him and no one contradicted him there, and he was always being surprised by some food that Silverscreen knew he especially liked. The landlady was talking of giving the main bedroom to Silverscreen and moving out herself to the eastern room. Tijen promised to furnish the little place exquisitely, but told them he had to delay his plans until after the New Year. Meanwhile, he spread out his visits so artfully that he was not away from home more than one evening a week, for which he could easily give excuses to his family.

· ·.

Both sisters had secretly regretted that they had not seen Lifu during their last vacation at the Winter Solstice. It was merely an accident. Lifu and his little sister had often come to the Yao house. Mr. Yao found the home lonely with the daughters away and when Lifu came, he often talked with him and encouraged him to come again. A kind of friendship sprung up between the old man and the young boy, and Lifu, used to the conversation of Mr. Fu, found it easy to follow the discussions on current politics and literature with Mr. Yao. Strange to say, the man was more progressive than the boy. Recently he had put up a showerbath in his room and added the morning shower to his midnight breathing exercises and the rest of his physical regime. Sometimes he would go to the Peking Hotel to eat foreign food. He believed in an alphabetical writing for Chinese at a time when very few people even thought of it. His criticism of literature was severe. Lifu was getting into that stage when he began to love the balanced decorative style of the Six Dynasties, but Mr. Yao told him with a suggestion of contempt that it was merely decorative, dead, and useless, a jumble of sounds and phrases. "Read Fang Pao, Liu Takuei, and the Tungcheng School," the old man said. "And read the philosophers." Mr. Yao's favorite philosopher was the brilliant Taoist Chuangtse, and it must be credited to his influence that Lifu's mind first developed after reading Chuangtse, which made him later iconoclastic in thought, especially in respect to the past. Sometimes at first, Chuangtse and Taoism proved too difficult and profound for his young mind; he merely felt the brilliance of Chuangtse's style and the quaintness of his imagery,

278

and was charmed by his humor and his devastating skepticism, which seemed to turn the world upside down.

But Mr. Yao's influence was also constructive. The old man's eyes shone when he spoke of the West and the vast learning behind it. Mr. Yao could not read a single English word, yet he observed many Western things. His enthusiasm for science was limitless. He spoke of the sciences of "Sound, Light, Change (chemistry), and Electricity" and warned Lifu even against History. "Study the things themselves and not what people say about the things," he said.

Taoism and science were the two great enthusiasms of Mr. Yao, and were somehow completely harmonized in his mind. Perhaps this was natural, because Taoism showed an interest in nature, whereas Confucianism was interested only in human relationships, in literature and history. The great Taoist Chuangtse felt the fascination of nature, its endless procession of the seasons, its laws of growth and decay, the diversity of its creatures and the mystery of the infinite and the infinitesimal. Its cosmos was a cosmos of change and flux and interaction between conflicting forces, obeying the silent laws of an impersonal, nameless, speechless god which should not have been named at all, but which the Taoists were forced to call by the name of "Tao," while insisting that it was unnamed and unnamable. Mr. Yao's idea was that with Western science now opening up the mysteries of nature, Lifu, as a young man, should not miss the opportunity of delving into the new discoveries.

"For us, a sound was just a sound and a ray of light was but light," he told Lifu. "Now those foreign devils have made a science of it and have produced gramophones and cameras and telephones. I have heard there are moving pictures but I have not seen one yet. Learn the new things of the new world and forget about history."

This was much farther than his friend, the old scholar Mr. Fu, was willing to go. Lifu admired the spirit of youth in old Yao and was more impressed than if a young student returned from England or America had told him these things.

But Lifu was interested in literature. Here Mr. Yao influenced him by lending him the translations of Western novels that Lin Chinnan was making. Lin's translation of Conan Doyle fascinated Lifu and gave him his first genuine enthusiasm for the West. Lin was an old Foochow scholar and could not read English, but he did his work by having a student returned from England orally translate the sentences for him. His most marvelous feat was that he did what no writer had done before in using the classical language to write long novels, in a style that was consistently readable and did full justice to the varied content that a novel required, and this was the reason for his popularity.

In a copy of Lin's translation of *Ivanhoe*, Lifu found the pencil markings of Mulan and some marginal comments about Rebecca and Rowena that were extremely amusing. It seemed that Mulan's sympathies were naturally with Rebecca, and where Ivanhoe was blind to Rebecca's love for him she would write *"hutu!* or *"hutu! hutu!"* (muddle-headed! muddle-headed!). In the passage where Rebecca was reporting the battle around the castle and the wounded Ivanhoe was interested only in the battle and entirely unconscious of Rebecca's concern for him, Mulan wrote, "Even the wisest in the world is sometimes the most muddle-headed." These markings were apparently made some time ago—Lifu wished he could know when.

. . .

It was the twenty-eighth of December. Mr. Yao had invited Lifu and his mother and sister to come for dinner. It was also the birthday of the grandmother of the Tseng family. Every year there was a home dinner in honor of the grandmother and Mulan usually went. This year, however, it was different, for Mulan was already engaged to marry into the Tseng home and wanted to avoid going there. In the morning, therefore, she asked Brocade to take a basket of dates and Fukien oranges as her birthday presents to the grandmother, and instructed her to say, in case they asked, that she could not come for dinner.

As Brocade was getting ready, Mulan heard Tijen calling in his room for Laima, a middle-aged woman servant who had been assigned to attend to him and his things since his return. Being used to the smooth service of Silverscreen, Tijen now missed her at home and found the woman stupid and unsatisfactory. Whereas a well-trained maid's service was a pleasure, the woman's service was very prosaic. He would not talk with the coarse, middle-aged woman as he used to talk with Silverscreen. He found much fault with her, perhaps because she really did not know where his things were and did not anticipate his wishes as well as Silverscreen had, or perhaps because he disliked her. But with the return of the sisters and with their guest Sutan, there was a shortage of service, and it was near New Year's Eve and every servant was very busy. Laima was helping in the kitchen making New Year puddings, and she thought the young master could take care of himself. As a result, that morning, Tijen was unattended.

When Mulan heard her brother calling she told Brocade to go to him. When Brocade came to his room, she saw him standing in his shirt, shorts, and slippers. She stood at the door and told him that Laima was busy and asked if there was anything he wanted.

"I don't know where she has put away my collar buttons," said the young master. "Can you look for them for me?"

Brocade, who avoided Tijen as much as possible, did not know what to do, for she did not like to go in and she could not simply turn away. "I don't know where they are," she replied.

"Look in the drawers of that cabinet and see if they are there."

Brocade went in to look in the cabinet and could not find them. She went out and soon came back to report that Laima had not touched them and did not know where they were. Tijen, putting on his socks, said to Brocade, "You look for them. They must be in the room." She began to look everywhere. Then she heard Tijen grumbling that there was a hole in his sock and cursing the "silly servant" for putting his socks away unmended. Brocade was now looking on the floor to see if the buttons had dropped. Tijen noticed then that she was dressed in a bright blue jacket with colored trimmings and that she had a mass of jet-black hair in a thick braid. She was more slender than Silverscreen and now he watched her in that intimate crouching posture, which gave him pleasure. When she stood up again, he saw that her face was flushed with the effort and he said, "Never mind. I will wear a Chinese robe today."

"It is because you want to wear foreign dress that you have all this trouble with buttons," said Brocade.

"If Silverscreen were here there would be no trouble," he said. "Why did they ask such a stupid-headed old woman to take care of me? If you came to serve me, perhaps you would be even better than Silverscreen."

"Don't talk nonsense. I am not Silverscreen," replied Brocade curtly.

"Why do you all combine against me? Even when my sisters were away, you would not come to serve me, neither you nor Frankincense."

"Why ask me?" replied Brocade, not caring to discuss the topic.

"Shall I look for the buttons or not? Your sister has asked me to go out and I am busy."

"I will wear Chinese garments. Get me the things in the cabinet."

Brocade took out a Chinese gown and silk underjacket and trousers for him, and he once more felt the pleasure of having a pretty, understanding maid busy serving him in his chamber. Brocade placed the garments on his bed silently and was ready to go. Tijen held out his hands and said, "Good *meimei*, I'll ask for you, if you will come and serve me." Now *"meimei,"* meaning "little sister," was also a term used among sweethearts, and Brocade drew back her hand and said: "Be dignified. Who is your *meimei?*"

He saw she was angry and said smilingly, "I was only joking. What is the harm?"

Brocade spoke with anger and contempt: "We are slave girls and have no right to joke with you, and you as a young master ought to have a young master's dignity. And don't think that because a girl's body is sold to your family for service, therefore it becomes common ware for masters to trample upon. I have neither Silverscreen's ambition nor Silverscreen's ability. And where did she end?" With that she walked out of the room.

Tijen was enraged to be snubbed by a maid, but he could do nothing about it. He put on his gown and prepared to leave hurriedly for the shop, for they were closing accounts for the New Year and his father would be there.

When Mulan asked what kept her so long, Brocade answered, "He lost his buttons and asked me to look for them, and he talked a lot of foolishness. Did he ever say anything that was not foolishness?"

"What did he say?" asked Mulan.

"He wanted me to be a second Silverscreen, and I told him to get the silly idea out of his head."

"Good for you!" said Mulan.

Brocade went off to take the presents and came back to say that Mrs. Tseng insisted that Mulan should go to the dinner. "What will that be like? I haven't the face to go," said Mulan. Toward five in the afternoon, Snow Blossom came to urge Mulan, saying that the grandmother was thinking of her. Mulan was still more troubled, for although she had not seen Sunya for half a year, it would be embarrassing to sit at dinner with him, and it was equally true that she had not seen Lifu for several months. She consulted her mother, and they decided that she should go and pay her respects to the grandmother but should not stay for dinner. She put on a silver-fox jacket with a bright blue satin top, and went with Snow Blossom. There she saw Sunya in the grandmother's room. They smiled at each other and exchanged a few formal questions, but Sunya was as shy as Mulan. Mannia rushed into the room, and said laughing, "This time you have to call me sister-in-law! When you cook *lapacho* for Sunya, all of us will get the benefit of it." Sunya was so embarrassed that he excused himself and left the room. They all knew that it was awkward for Mulan and did not insist upon her staying for dinner.

Mulan knew that she wanted dinner at home as much because she wanted to see Lifu as because she could not very well stay and sit at the same table with Sunya. When she came back and heard Lifu's voice, she knew that Sunya had a fuller and more pleasant voice, and yet Lifu's voice gave her a pleasure that she could not suppress in herself. Both called her "Lanmei," and Sunya spoke with a perfect Peking accent, but in Lifu's pronunciation she could detect the slight Szechuen accent, caught from his father and the Szechuen families at the Guild, and she thought she liked that Szechuen accent, too.

Late in the afternoon, her father sent word that he was busy and would stay with Mr. Feng for supper at the shop. Then Tijen, learning that his father would not be home for supper, sent the rickshaw boy to say that he also would be late and took the opportunity to go and see Silverscreen. The dinner therefore became more like a young people's party, with Lifu and Sutan as the guests.

Tijen came in quite late, when they had finished their dinner and were planning to play mahjong. Now Mochow was good at mahjong, but Mulan was bad because she was too excitable. So many wanted to play that they decided to have two tables. It was found then that Lifu could not play. Mulan said she did not care much for it, either, and would keep company with Lifu as a guest. Finally, Mrs. Yao, Mrs. Feng, Mrs. Kung, and Brocade sat at one table, while at another sat Coral, Mochow, Tijen, and Sutan. The maids were often asked by the mistresses to play with them, in order to make up a table, and Brocade, at first asked to play at the young people's table, said, without giving any reason, that she wanted to play at the other table and asked Coral to change places with her. Tijen eyed her silently.

While the others were playing mahjong, Mulan sat in the same room talking with Lifu and pretending to be playing with her younger brother Afei. She had nothing to keep her hands busy and asked Afei to come and let her rebraid his queue. Frankincense brought in a comb, and Coral turned and said, "Why braid his queue at this time of the night?"

"You mind your own business," said Mulan playfully. She parted Afei's hair in the middle and made a braid on each side, like Redjade's. Lifu saw what she was doing, but Mulan made eyes at him to keep quiet. Frankincense too saw what was going on, but she kept quiet; and Redjade, who stood watching, wanted to ask her mother to see, but Mulan hushed her. It was Mochow who first looked at them and said, "Everybody look! Second Sister is making Afei up as a girl." Mulan, a little annoyed, hurriedly tied the knots and made Afei stand side by side with Redjade, and sent them up to her mother, holding one another's hands, saying, "See! They look like a pair of fairy girls in attendance upon the Western Queen Mother of Heaven!" Everybody turned and looked and laughed.

"My Mulan is always thinking up these things," her mother said to Lifu's mother.

"I wasn't *thinking* at all," replied Mulan. "You people were playing and my hands were idle. I wanted to braid his queue for him freshly. How did I know that it would turn out to be two queues?"

"It is an excellent idea, too," said Lifu's mother. "They really look like twins, hand in hand together!"

Now Afei took Redjade's arm and said, "Let's play foreigners, husband and wife. They walk hand in hand." But Redjade was a sensitive girl and she immediately withdrew her arm and ran to her mother, and turned round and complained, "Afei takes advantage of people."

Mrs. Feng quickly said, "He is only playing and not taking advantage of you. And you must not call him Afei. Call him Second Brother. You are growing older now and you must learn the rules. Now go away and don't disturb us."

"By the time they grow up, Chinese husbands and wives will be walking hand in hand like foreigners," said Sutan. "They certainly will be having free marriage."

Now when Afei was refused by Redjade, he went to Lifu's little sister who had been standing quietly by her mother, watching the game. He pulled at her and said, "Let's play foreigners. Give me your arm." Huan-erh was naturally shy, but her politeness as a guest prevented her from turning away from Afei, and besides she wanted to play with

Afei and this was her first chance. So she let herself be led across the room and around with Afei proudly swinging a duster for his "foreign cane." The mothers looked and laughed, when suddenly they heard a whimper and found Redjade sobbing by her mother's side.

"People asked you first to play and you refused," said Redjade's mother, "and now what are you crying for?"

Redjade, who was only seven, would not be comforted. When Afei's mother saw the state of affairs, she called to Afei and said, "You must also play with your little cousin-sister." Before Afei realized what it was all about, Huan-erh had left him, and slipped away to her mother. He came up to Redjade to beg her to "play foreigners" with him, but she said angrily, "You play your play and I cry my cry. What business is it of yours?" and abruptly tore herself away from him and stamped her feet and fell to crying again on her mother's knee.

"You don't know this child of mine," apologized her mother. "She has a small body but a big temper."

Afei stood, not knowing what to do. Coral said, "Afei, you had better apologize to your cousin-sister." Afei went to Redjade and asked for a thousand pardons, but she still said, "Leave me alone." Finally he said, "*Meimei,* I will play with you for my whole life, and won't play with anybody else. Is that enough?" Redjade was then satisfied and she stood up smiling through her tears. Brushing a forefinger across her cheek, she said to Afei, "You ought to be ashamed! You are a boy and you dress your hair like a girl's." He began to pull his braids apart by sliding the knots down and Redjade began to laugh.

As the game went on, Mulan asked Lifu what he had been reading, and he mentioned the translation of *Ivanhoe.*

"Your father lent it to me," he said, and added, "Aren't those pencil notes yours?"

Mulan thought for a moment, recollected, and felt embarrassed. But she tried to turn the discussion to the work of Lin Chinnan in general. Since Lin was her favorite author and Lifu also was enthusiastic, they struck up a lively discussion.

"Why do your sympathies seem to be with Rebecca?" asked Lifu. "I like Rowena better."

"That is very natural. The reader's sympathy is usually with the deserving but unsuccessful one at marriage. Most readers sympathize with Taiyu in *Red Chamber Dream* for the same reason."

At the word "marriage" Coral pricked up her ears and said, "What are you two talking about with so much interest? Talk louder and let us hear it."

"I know," said Mochow. "Second Sister is talking about *Red Chamber Dream,* and her sympathies are with Taiyu."

"Oh," said Tijen. "I know. Second Sister likes Taiyu and Third Sister likes Paotsa."

"Whom do you like?" asked Sutan.

"I like Paoyu," replied Tijen.

"You ought to be ashamed of yourself—that effeminate young man!" said Mochow. To Sutan, she said, "Whom do you like best?"

"I like the cousin Hsiangyun," said Sutan; "she is so boyish and romantic."

"Bravo!" exclaimed Tijen.

"Whom do you like best?" Mulan asked Lifu in her low, gentle voice. Lifu paused a moment, and said, "I don't know. Taiyu weeps too much, and Paotsa is too capable. Perhaps I like Tanchun best because she is a combination of both, with the talent of Taiyu and the character of Paotsa. But I don't like the way she treats her mother."

Mulan listened silently and then said slowly, "Alas! No one is perfect in this world."

Calling to Coral, Mulan said, "Big Sister, I know whom you like best. Li Huan. Am I right?"

"In that novel everybody likes himself," replied Coral. "If we talk on like this, we shan't be able to play mahjong at all."

When they had finished one round of the game, which Sutan had won, Tijen said that he had had a busy day and had a headache, and Mochow suggested that they stop and join the conversation. So the young people broke up, and Coral, who still wanted to play, went over to the ladies' table, where Brocade soon surrendered her place to her.

Tijen began to complain it was too hot and asked the maid for a hot towel and began to take off his fur-lined gown. He was wearing a brown silk jacket and trousers. His mother saw him in his jacket and said, "Of course you are feeling too hot. You didn't change when you returned. But you will catch cold. Frankincense, go and bring a lined gown for the young master."

Tijen was sprawling in his chair with his legs wide apart. When Frankincense brought his gown, he stood up and put it on, but left both the collar button and the bottom skirt button open. He never buttoned his collars, so that when he was wearing three or four jackets and gowns, one on top of another, one could see a whole series of unbuttoned collars open at the neck. It was perhaps a sign of his intolerance of restraint. Mochow, to whom disorderliness was always painful, said to him:

"Brother, when you wear a gown, at least wear it like a gentleman. You button it neither at the top, nor at the bottom. Look at Brother Lifu. Doesn't one look neater when his collar is buttoned?"

"What do you mean by not dressing like a gentleman?" replied Tijen. "Father's collars are not buttoned. One's head is not free otherwise."

"What about the bottom button, then? What is your theory about that?"

"I can walk better with it open. Besides, when Silverscreen was here, didn't I always have my gown buttoned very neatly?" His mother looked up sharply at the mention of Silverscreen's name.

"I admire you for the impudence to say it," said Mochow. "Even your gown has to be buttoned by a maid! I think if you had taken Silverscreen along to England to button your coat for you, you would not have come back."

"Perhaps not," said Tijen.

Mochow was annoyed by his insolence and she went on, "Even when you wear foreign dress, your last waistcoat button is always left open. Does that, too, help you to walk better?"

Tijen began to laugh knowingly and exasperatingly.

"*Meimei,*" he said proudly, "don't talk about what you don't know. There is 'scholarship' even in wearing foreign dress. To leave the last waistcoat button open is exactly the thing to do. They call that the Cambridge style. People would laugh at you if you buttoned up the last waistcoat button."

He was triumphant, and Mochow was temporarily defeated. But she soon renewed the attack and said, "Oh, I see, you haven't been to Cambridge, but you have already mastered Cambridge 'scholarship'! I didn't know that Cambridge scholarship consisted only in not buttoning the last button of one's waistcoat."

Tijen felt the sting of his sister's words. Mulan tried to soften it a little for him, and said, "I don't really believe that every gentleman in England leaves his last waistcoat button open. Perhaps it has to do also with the condition of one's stomach."

She said this in fun, but Tijen replied seriously, "Perhaps, sister, you are right. Perhaps one ought to leave it open after dinner, but not before. I had better find out."

Mochow, now merciless, said, "Since you haven't been to England, where did you learn all this 'scholarship'?"

"Oh, from my tailor in the Legation Quarter," said Tijen.

Lifu was just lifting his cup to drink his tea and, unable to control himself, laughed out loud and choked, so that he had to spit the tea out all over the carpet. Mulan and Mochow also laughed. Tijen was offended but he knew how to defend himself and said, jokingly, "Don't you all remember what Father said to me on the evening of my departure? He said,

'The world's affairs, well understood, are all scholarship.
Human relationships, maturely experienced, are already literature.'

You must take a broader view, and not consider book scholarship as the only form of scholarship."

"Well, well!" said Mochow. "This is even better than your interpretation of Mencius!"

Lifu was impressed by Mochow's stinging eloquence, which reminded him of Chen Lin, the scholar in the time of the Three Kingdoms, whose philippics against his political enemy were so eloquent that it was said they cured the headache of his political chief when he read them. So Lifu said, "Tijen's headache ought to be cured now."

"What do you mean?" asked Mulan.

"Your sister is a little like Chen Lin."

Mochow felt highly complimented, and said, "No, his headache ought to be worse." But all this was lost on their brother.

Mochow saw that Lifu's gown was wet with the spilled tea and got a dry towel to give him, and he took it and thanked her. She would have liked to wipe his gown for him, but dared not.

At this time, their father and uncle returned. Seeing everybody in good humor and Lifu wiping his gown, the father asked what they were doing.

"We were talking about scholarship, and Brother Lifu laughed so that he got choked," said Mulan.

"Is scholarship as interesting as all that?" remarked the father, and he was much pleased.

The party broke up soon, after Sutan had entertained them with an imitation of a Christian pastor's speech which set everybody laughing.

CHAPTER XX

*D*URING the New Year there were exchanges of visits among both young and old. The occasion was now embarrassing for Mulan, and she and her family did not stay long at the Tsengs, but Mrs. Tseng and Mannia and Cassia came to have long talks with Mulan and her family. The Tseng brothers had to come and pay their respects to Mr. and Mrs. Yao, and Mulan hid herself and refused to come out to see them, and so was teased by her sisters.

When the vacation was over, Mulan went back to school with a heavy heart. Their mother had complained that when the sisters were away the house was lonely, and that Afei had nobody to play with except Redjade. But their father was against any change of school, and insisted that they go on with it, especially because Mrs. Fu was most kind and had been personally looking after them. The result was that Mulan and her sister continued to study in that school until the summer of 1908, when Mochow became ill and was forced to stay at home, and Mulan stayed with her. By that time, the Tsengs were talking of Sunya's marriage, and Mulan broke off her studies and began to make preparations for the wedding.

While at school, the sisters came home often during holidays and in the vacations. But it was at school that Mulan discovered what separation meant. Lifu had never openly made love to either of the sisters, nor did they enjoy the freedom of going about that modern girls now enjoy. They never corresponded with Lifu, and of course Mulan never wrote to Sunya, or received letters from him. The ancient system had not yet broken down, and Mulan never doubted that she was going to wed Sunya, and she had come to accept her lot with composure. But when spring came she was seized with a strong and sad longing to see Lifu, to talk with him and hear his voice again. In the company of flowers in the morning or of the moon at night, reading before the window or walking in the school garden at dusk, she could not brush from her mind the image of Lifu's face, and Sutan and Mochow often saw her sitting alone on a rock beneath the flowers, holding a book in her hand and staring into space. All these thoughts she could not tell her sister, and, because of her sister, she could not tell Sutan. Sutan, being somewhat out of her family's control, sometimes sang little love lyrics of sad longing, of the lower type sung by sing-song girls. The sentiments were often very real and deep, but the wording was popular if forceful, and sometimes verged on the sensuous. Mochow would not countenance the singing of such love ditties in their room, and even Mulan disapproved because of the associations. But Mulan began to love the lyrics of the Sung period, known as *tse,* which had lines of irregular length and were entirely of musical origin, being texts written for set tunes and limited by the rigorous requirements of musical tones as determined by the tune. Being too young, she did not like the poems of Su Tungpo as much of those of Hsin Chiahsien and Chiang Paishih, and she used to con over the little volume of the great Sung poetess Li Ching-chao. The syllables in that poem which began with the famous seven doublets (*Hsinhsin, momo, lengleng, tsingtsing, tsitsi, tsantsan, tsitsi*), with the rhyme set in the "entering tone" ending in "stop" consonants, seemed to drop upon her heart like the rain on the colanut leaves:

> So dim, so dark,
> So dense, so dull,
> So damp, so dank, so dead!
> The weather, now warm, now cold,
> Makes it harder than ever to forget.
> How can thin wine and bread
> Serve as protection
> Against the piercing wind of sunset?
> Wild geese pass overhead—
> That they are familiar
> Makes it more lamentable yet!
> The ground is strewn with staid
> And withered petals;
> For whom now should they be in vases set?
> By the window shut,
> Guarding it alone,
> To see the sky has turned so black!
> And on the colanut
> To hear the drizzle drone

At dusk: Pit-a-pat, pit-a-pat!
Is this a mood and moment
Only to be called "sad"?

In the summer the sisters found at home an outward calm was preserved. There would be nights when Tijen returned very late, and
their mother would sit up until his return. He always said that he
was invited out to dinner or the theater, and he did seem to have many
friends who were willing to help him give this impression. When he
came home at two o'clock in the morning, he was annoyed to find
his mother sitting alone in her room with the light burning waiting
for him, for she did not trust him to serving maids any more. She
would come out of her room and, holding a lamp, walk across the
dark corridor and courtyard in that dreary hour when everybody else
was asleep, to see that her son was safely home. She hoped that by such
sincerity and devotion she would be able to touch his heart and keep
him on the right path. He was both touched and annoyed, and
begged her not to sit up for him.

"Please don't wait for me," he pleaded. "Suppose you should fall
down in that dark courtyard at night."

But she would not listen to him. When Silverscreen knew that his
mother was waiting for him, she took a secret delight in detaining
him as long as possible, and she thought that this was a form of
penance which she was able to impose upon her former mistress.

When he did not come home very late, he would find his sister
waiting also. Mochow came to be a more constant companion of her
mother on these nightly vigils. She could keep awake if necessary,
while Mulan's eyes would tire and she would go to bed first. And the
next morning when the mother slept late, Mochow would get up at
the usual hour.

The mother believed that Tijen was gambling though she kept it
a secret. The father's attitude was difficult to explain. He apparently
did not care, or he was thinking of his own youth, or he was
fatalistic. He thought that his son was indulging in the usual youthful
follies, but since he had given up schooling and was going into
business, such entertainments were part of a business man's life. But he
did not know, as the mother knew, that Tijen had taken thousands
of dollars from the business. Soon after the *Chingming* Festival, Tijen
had come to his uncle for two thousand dollars to pay a gambling
debt. The uncle noticed that his withdrawals were becoming more

and more frequent, and did not dare take the responsibility. Tijen asked him not to let his father know, and the uncle said it would be all right if his sister, Tijen's mother, knew about it. Tijen got the money, and his mother and uncle plotted to guard the secret from his father. Having cleared his own responsibility, the uncle did not care and he wanted to please Tijen as the heir of the family, nor did he bother about his frequent absence from the shop. But once the way was open, Tijen began to draw more and more, a few hundred dollars at a time.

The thousands of dollars he had taken were invested by Silverscreen in jewels and clothes, so that she appeared as well-dressed as any rich man's mistress. She was now occupying the main rooms of the house, the landlady having moved to the room on the east. Tijen was also generous to the landlady who had become a sworn sister to Silverscreen. The landlady's husband, seeing that they were now better off, did not want to go to the fruit and candy shop any more; but his wife persuaded him to keep at his job, saying that it was more dependable and a job was good for him. The landlady, however, did cease to receive men visitors, and devoted her charms to young Tijen, who found her gifted and versatile, a good singer and a teller of amusing stories.

Silverscreen had told Mrs. Hua that Tijen would object if he found out that there were men visitors at the house and asked her to give that up. The landlady jokingly replied by asking what she was to get in return, and how was Silverscreen going to reward her for helping her in this affair.

"I can easily ask him to give you something every month, or I can give it to you," said Silverscreen.

"I will not take the money for doing nothing," replied Mrs. Hua. "I was doing those things partly for money and partly for pleasure. It is no kind of life to sit in the room all day and see only that good man of mine at night. I'll tell you what we will do." She whispered something in Silverscreen's ear. "I know this will please him the more. I know men. What if he gets tired of you and goes to some other woman? You and I are sworn sisters, and it is better than sharing him with some unknown woman."

To Silverscreen, whose one ambition was to tighten her hold upon Tijen and keep him from his mother, it seemed like an extra weapon in her hand; and on the whole, she thought it a fair price for making the landlady give up her visitors. Also Silverscreen was conscious of her own youth. So one day when Tijen whispered to Silverscreen in a half-serious and half-joking manner, he found to his surprise and delight that she was ready and willing, and he praised her generosity and believed that she would do anything to please him.

And so the two women watched over him and always made him welcome, and when he was absent for over a week, they would charge him with being unfaithful with other women, and he would always swear that he was true and faithful to them.

. .

One day to the great surprise of the whole family Tijen's dog appeared at his home. Tijen was away at the shop when it came to the gate and was recognized by Lota, who came in all excited to report to his mistress.

Two nights before, on leaving Silverscreen's house, Tijen had jumped into a rickshaw and the dog had followed him unnoticed. Halfway, Tijen saw her and got down to send her back. But when he got into the rickshaw again, he saw that the dog was still following him, her leash trailing in the street. It was late in the evening and Tijen could not take the dog back. Finally, in desperation, he gave up the rickshaw and went into a teashop and came out through the back door. The next afternoon he went to Silverscreen's house to ask if the dog had found her way back, but she was apparently lost. Now she turned up at her master's home, looking very hungry.

The arrival of the dog, after an absence of nearly a year, aroused much speculation in the family. The question of Silverscreen was raised again. Where was she? Was she in Peking? What had happened to her? The dog went to her old room and sniffed about. Apparently finding the smell and atmosphere of the room wrong, she crouched down and lay perfectly still on the floor, looking at people only from the corners of her eyes, as if thinking of the good old times and wondering at the change. When the family gathered to look at her, she got up and sniffed at the mistress and the sisters and Afei, and went back to lie down again, seemingly disappointed. Laima was asked to give her some left-overs from the kitchen, and she sniffed at the food for some time before eating it, as if she were suspicious.

"Perhaps something happened to Silverscreen, and the dog has been wandering around," said Coral.

Mrs. Yao was silently staring at the dog, as if she were a bringer of ill omen. "That little whore must be still somewhere near," she said at last.

"It is difficult to say," said Mulan, to allay her mother's fears, though suspicion was rising in her own mind. "She must have lost her mistress. Perhaps Silverscreen left the city and could not take her and so abandoned her."

When Tijen returned, the family waited to see how he took the news. But he had already been informed by Lota at the gate, and when he came in and saw the dog he affected to be surprised. The dog jumped up and wagged her tail and jumped about to express her joy.

"This proves that Silverscreen is still somewhere in Peking," said Tijen. "Why didn't you try to find her? She may have starved to death!"

"If that is the case," said his mother harshly, "it was her own fault. It is a dog's nature to run about in spring after other dogs. A bitch is a bitch. You are lucky she is dumb and does not understand human language, else I would like to ask her a few questions."

But this marked the downfall of the dog. The stupid Laima was at first put in charge of her, but soon she became nobody's concern and slunk about in the kitchen eating what she could find. Tijen was away in the daytime and had neither the time nor the inclination to look after her. Sometimes she would wander in the streets for a half-day and return before anyone missed her. Being a pointer, she would raid the chicken yard and create havoc in the vegetable garden by chasing the chickens and ducks, and then she would be kicked by the women servants or beaten with a stick. When summer came round, she was soon pregnant and delivered a brood of four cross-breed puppies, looking more like their mother than like their unknown Chinese father. Tijen took one of the puppies, saying he would give it to a friend, and brought it to Silverscreen's house.

"Why do you bring this 'seed of sin' here?" asked Silverscreen.

"Don't you know," replied Tijen, "that foreign ladies like to play with puppies, and would be glad to pay a high price for it? You keep it for me."

Seeing that Tijen wanted it, she kept the puppy and was glad to be rid of its mother.

One night Tijen came home about midnight thoroughly drunk. It was the first time this had happened. He banged at the door and was shouting before Lotung got up to open it. Lotung tried to assist him, but was brushed aside and Tijen went staggering along the eastern corridor, mumbling to himself, while Lotung held the light. The dog was sleeping with her brood in the corridor.

"Be careful, there is the dog," said Lotung.

"Ha! Ha!" said Tijen. "My father called me seed of sin, but here is really seed of sin." He reached down to play with one of the puppies, but lost his balance and fell flat on the floor. The puppies yelped and the mother barked sharply. But Tijen lay on the floor comfortably, refusing to get up, and caught one of the puppies and held it in his hand and laughed when the mother dog barked again. Tijen struck the puppy, shouting "Seed of sin! Seed of sin!" The dog bit at Tijen's sleeve to make him release the puppy. Tijen flung the puppy hard against the wall, and turned round to fight off the maddened mother; when Tijen struck at her hard to free himself, she bit his hand and then ran to the injured puppy. All this happened too fast for Lotung to help, and Tijen turned smarting with the pain, and scolded the servant by asking him whose rice he was eating. The other puppies were leaping about, yelping to add to the confusion, and both Tijen's parents rushed into the corridor from different directions.

"My son! my son! What has happened?" cried the mother and then she stumbled upon something in the dark and fell to the floor near the corner of the corridor. Lota had hastened to put on his jacket, and came out into the dark courtyard, barely lighted by the flickering oil lamp which Lotung had hurriedly set on the floor while he attended to the young master. In that moment the lamp was upset. In the darkness, a moan told the father that the mother had been hurt. With surprising quickness, the old man found her still sprawling on the floor crying "Bitter fate!"

"Light, Lota!" shouted the master, while he guarded his wife in the darkness against the infuriated dog. Lota had rushed back to bring a lantern and with him appeared Mulan and Mochow in their thin pajamas, with their hair undone. They saw Tijen sitting on the floor looking very silly, and then saw their father assisting their mother slowly to her feet.

They rushed to their mother.

"Look out for the dog!" shouted the father.

Turning the mother over to his daughters, Mr. Yao advanced

toward the dog, which was still growling wrathfully, ready to attack again any one who touched her puppies. One after another of the maids and women servants ran out, so that the whole household was awake. Lota brought a stick, and the dog, frightened, ran away, followed by her puppies, the injured one limping and yelping behind.

"My son, my son!" said the mother. "I knew there would be this day. Where did it bite you?"

Tijen, now upon his feet, realized that his father was there and though he now felt sobered, he thought it best to pretend to be drunk. "I'm all right, I'm all right," he said, with a twirl in his tongue, and leaning upon Lotung, he staggered away. The father assisted the mother in and said to his daughters, "You had better run in quickly. You will catch cold in the open at this time of the night."

The procession went in by the dim light of lanterns, with a hubbub broken by moments of tense silence. The father was grim and silent. Tijen was laid upon his bed, still pretending to be drunk. Tijen's hand was bleeding, and the mother's arm was hurt and her face was deathly pale. She was escorted to her room and put to bed. The father felt her wrist and found that the bones of the wrist had been dislocated. This was a boxer's job, and with his powerful hands he pressed the bones back into position. The pain was excruciating and she shrieked at every touch; and, when the operation was over, she lay exhausted, moaning feebly.

The maids and daughters were busy with bandages and basins for the mother and preparing a hot medicinal wine to strengthen her heart. Mr. and Mrs. Feng, informed that the *Taitai* was hurt, got up quickly and came over, and the whole family, except the children, sat up to keep Mrs. Yao company until she dozed into sleep. The lamplight was turned low and they sat in the mother's room, talking in whispers. The sky was already gray when she fell asleep and all retired to bed in the summer dawn.

The next day Tijen did not get up till noon and did not go to the shop. Coral was in his room when he awoke with an aching head.

"What happened last night?" he asked.

"Look at your hand. And Mother's wrist was dislocated."

"Is it serious?"

"I don't know. She was still asleep, when the doctor came, and we didn't like to wake her up. I think he is in her room now."

Tijen was silent. He felt a genuine remorse, and he was afraid

296

of facing his father. "How is Father?" he asked finally. "Has he said anything about me?"

"No, but you know what you ought to get. If Mother should be permanently injured, how would your conscience be?"

"What shall I do?" Tijen asked her.

"The best thing for you to do is to go in and ask for pardon."

Coral helped him to dress, and when he still hesitated to go in and face his father, she told him that he had to take the consequences of what he had done, and almost dragged him to his mother's room.

Mr. Yao was ruminating on what to do with his son—the insoluble problem of what to do with a young man gone wrong. Flogging, he knew, was useless. He had not flogged his son for years, and he was now too old to be disciplined by force and too independent to listen to exhortation, and at the same time too young to know that he was a fool. So it was with controlled anger that he saw his son come in sheepishly with Coral pushing him from behind.

Tijen, standing before his father, said "Father, I was drunk last night. I was wrong."

"Do you still consider me your father?" replied the old man, fuming in his anger, and Tijen stood perfectly still and silent.

"Kneel down before your mother and apologize. You nearly took your mother's old life, you unfilial son!"

Tijen knelt down beside the mother's bed, and begged her pardon. She broke into tears and said, "If you still consider me your mother, you ought to reform. Get up, my son."

Tijen started to rise, but the father forbade him.

"You devil's stumbling block! Family-ruining seed! Disgrace to our ancestors! The difference between men and beasts is a sense of shame and the desire to have face. Since you don't want to have face among your fellow-men, I don't know what to do with you. The Yao family is finished now. When the daughters are married off, I shall sell the whole business and give it to schools and temples and go and be a monk in the mountains. When you go out to pull rickshaws, then you will appreciate what you have now."

"You are not serious," said the doctor, trying to pacify him. "Don't talk of becoming a monk, with such a fortune as yours. A young man sometimes makes mistakes." His voice, muffled by his long beard, was soft and soothing.

"I am serious," said Mr. Yao. "I had rather give this family fortune

297

to any cause than see it squandered by this seed of sin. Let him kneel there for two hours, and let no one interfere."

So Tijen knelt in his mother's room for two hours, until his knees were stiff and numb, while his head was reeling and wracked with pain, and his sisters and the maids came to look at him; but nobody dared interfere.

In the family at least, Tijen was disgraced. Mulan gave Afei a long talk about drinking and gambling, with his elder brother as the object lesson. At dinner table that evening, when Frankincense was about to refill his bowl with rice, the father said, "Let him fill it himself. He is not a man." Angry with shame and sullen at the public disgrace, Tijen stood up to refill his own rice. He hated his father for making him lose face before the maids.

His mother lay in bed for three or four days before she was able to get up and it was weeks before she was able to hold her rice bowl again. Even then, there remained a lump on her wrist, so that the family had something else to remember Tijen by. After this incident, Tijen refrained for some time from coming home late, and when he did, his mother did not sit up to wait for him.

. . .

The following summer Mochow fell sick. The sisters stopped going to school for several reasons, first, because of Mochow's illness; second, because Mr. Fu had been asked by the Viceroy to open a girls' college in Peking and he had gone south to solicit funds and recruit students; and third, because the Tseng family were planning for the wedding of Sunya and Mulan. Chinya had been married in the spring, while the sisters were still at school, and early in the summer, Mannia had come to visit Mulan and told her that Mrs. Tseng was dissatisfied with Chinya's bride, and that being the child of New, the God of Wealth, she had such an air of rich man's daughter that nothing was good enough for her.

"As far as Suyun is concerned, I don't even exist," said Mannia. "I am still called the eldest daughter-in-law, but in her eyes I am cheaper than dust. Barely had the honeymoon passed before she began to complain of Chinya, although he treated her like a princess. Never was a thing brought up but she would mention how it was done in the New family. Mother put up with as much as she could stand, but the other day when Suyun was again comparing the fish we had

298

for dinner with the fish at her home Mother said to her, 'Remember, now your name is Tseng.' Upon that, she left the table and walked out of the room, and returned to her home and stayed away for three days, and Mother had to ask her to come back. I dare not open my mouth in her presence. When she sees my mother, she won't even look at her. This kind of marriage will only bring trouble between the two families. She has brought two maids from her house, and nobody else is allowed to go into her bedroom or touch her things. Even if I am born of a poor family, I have seen the daughters of rich families, like you sisters. How can it be that she has no knowledge at all of manners just because her father is a minister and her family is rich? When the whole family is sitting together and talking, she alone keeps quiet as if she were bored. Her powder is at least three inches thick; and, when she opens her lips to speak, it seems as if the corners are gummed together and only the center of her mouth moves."

Mannia tried to imitate Suyun's lips, affecting a small coquettish mouth, protruding the lower lip as if to make a contemptuous gesture. But Mannia's face was beautiful and Mulan laughed and said, "If she did it as prettily as you do, it would be very charming. I don't see why a person can't talk naturally if she must talk."

"I am stupid," said Mannia. "But, *Meimei*, you are equal to her in every respect and cleverer than she by far. As for money, your family, too, has millions. I am waiting to see what will happen when you come. You can talk better than she, and if we stand together we shall have no fear of her."

"We have money, it is true," said Mulan. "But you don't know all about my family. There is one thing in which we lose face in comparison with others. That is my elder brother."

"You have told me about him. He is irresponsible and quick-tempered, but he is not so bad after all," said Mannia.

"I can't tell you everything now," said Mulan. "But I will tell you that I suspect that he is keeping a mistress outside and that it is Silverscreen. And I think he smokes opium. This is an absolute secret and you must not tell anybody. I do not even discuss it with my own mother."

"But this cannot be called unique," Mannia insisted. "Suyun is no better off. Her two brothers are the worst rascals in town, profligate and running after girls. If that kind of a family keeps its prosperity for long, Father Heaven has no eyes. I am opening my eyes wide to wait and see how they end up."

"My father has always told me," said Mulan, "that he has seen with his own eyes how some poor families rise up and some rich families go down. He always says that if it were not so, the rich would always be rich and the poor always poor. He tells me that the most important thing is not to depend upon money; one should enjoy one's wealth and yet be prepared any time to go without it."

"With such a father," Mannia said, "I don't wonder that you sisters are so well brought up, without the slightest rich man's smell. But the whole capital hates that rapacious God of Wealth."

. . .

At this period Mulan's father often talked about taking a trip abroad. When in a good mood, he told his daughters he would like to see the South Seas, by which he meant the Malay Straits and the Dutch East Indies. When in a bad mood, he said he was determined to spend his fortune before his son could squander it for him. Mr. Yao played with the idea so much that at times it looked like an old man's last dream of gratification in this earthly life, and at times it seemed like a threat to dissolve the family fortune and perhaps to disappear altogether himself from the family, as devout Taoists sometimes do.

But there were two things he wanted to do before he went abroad. First, to fix a date for Mulan's wedding, and second, to engage Mochow to Lifu. The Tsengs had informally sounded his opinion on the wedding, proposing to have it in the spring; but Mr. Yao had been unable to make a definite decision because of this idea of going traveling. Of course, he wanted to be at the wedding because his presence was important and because he loved Mulan; but he did not want to have to hurry back. At last he promised the groom's family that they could have the wedding in the autumn of the following year.

As for Mochow's engagement, he had to wait till Mr. and Mrs. Fu came back from the south, for they would be the logical persons to approach Mrs. Kung as the go-between. Lifu had not yet been graduated, but wise parents were always early on the watch for ideal sons-in-law for their daughters. Mr. Yao academically believed in "free marriage," but when it came to his own daughters, he could not be quite a Taoist, leaving everything to "nature" and nature's blind chances. Besides, "Chance" in Taoism, while determined by invisible causes, was indicated by the sequence of events. Mochow's marital chance was indicated clearly enough; Lifu was ideal, and not to seize the chance when it came along was to go against Tao.

Mr. Yao realized that he was ahead of his times, that it would be unfair to let his daughters stand alone, trying to catch husbands, while the other girls of their generation had their parents' planning, forethought, and help in finding the best young men of their age. Time was important, for the best young men were usually spoken for ahead. In other words, "free marriage" was to him a Utopian idea to toy with. Why, a modest girl would rather die unmarried than use her charms to hunt and capture a husband for herself! How cheap and undignified it appeared then, and how cheap and undignified it actually became as he saw it later!

In the present generation after Mulan, some of the best girls remain unmarried because times have changed. The best girls are too decent to go out hunting husbands for themselves, and their parents have lost the power to arrange matches with parents of desirable young men.

Mochow's engagement was precipitated by Mr. Fu's sudden return and by the events of October, 1908. While at West Lake, Mr. Fu suddenly received the news of his promotion to be Educational Commissioner of Chihli Province, and he hurried back to Peking, arriving on the sixteenth. Both Mr. and Mrs. Fu were more than willing to arrange the match, and Mrs. Fu went to Mrs. Kung that very evening.

The match was promptly made. "Family cards" were first exchanged, bearing the names of the three generations of the bride's and groom's ancestors and their own names; and then followed the exchange of the boy's and girl's birth, date, and hour, or exchange of horoscopes.

Mr. Fu arranged the match and, after an audience with the Emperor and the Empress Dowager, departed for Tientsin to assume his new office. He always prided himself on being received in Their Majesties' last audience. For on the twenty-first, the news came of the death of the Emperor and the Empress Dowager within three days of each other.

In the midst of this confusion the formal engagement of Mochow and Lifu was celebrated by an exchange of gifts, the groom presenting the bride with a pair of gold bracelets, and the bride presenting the groom with hats, suits of silk clothing, a jade-handled writing brush, and an ancient ink slab. As a modern innovation, there was also an exchange of photographs. The bracelets were Mrs. Kung's own, for she had long ago reserved them for her future daughter-in-law. The ceremony was simple, and Lifu's mother did not make pretensions of being the equal of the bride's family in wealth. No dinners were given because of the national mourning. When neighbors living at the Szechuen Guild came to congratulate Lifu's mother she replied, "As regards family status, we dare not compare with the Yao family. We wouldn't have dared to marry such a rich man's girl for a daughter-in-law, if we did not know that Miss Yao was such a steady, thrifty, and well-bred girl, entirely different from other rich men's daughters. I really don't understand how my son came to have such luck. It was all Uncle Fu's work."

As for Mochow, her father had said to her, "We have decided on this match for you, and we presume you have no objection."

"If I had objection, I would have told you," replied Mochow. It was somewhat awkward for a girl to have to say this, but Mochow was not soft and bashful. She was practical and when things were proper to say she would say them.

Mr. Yao said kindly, "You two daughters are being married off differently, but in our minds we are perfectly fair to you both. The Tseng family has money, but the Kung family is poor. Do you mind?"

"No, Father," replied Mochow. "Money does not matter."

"Are you sure?" asked the father.

"I am sure," Mochow smiled.

"Well, I knew you would feel so. A good thing, a good thing, I tell you. Lifu is dependable for life. And he is the only son, and he is filial toward his mother. It will be a happy, small family."

Mochow was now only sixteen, but she was mentally mature and naturally steady of character. If she was inwardly happy, she did not show more than an irrepressible quiet smile on her lips. But Mulan was so happy and excited that when she congratulated her sister, there were tears in her eyes.

· ·

The country was plunged into national mourning, and all celebrations and festivities were forbidden for three months. The ignorant old woman who ruled for the entire last half of the nineteenth century did more than any other single person to hold back China's progress. Without her the progressive Emperor Kuanghsu would certainly have gone on with his reforms. To the end, the Emperor, like an eagle

302

deprived of its wings, remained submissive to his aunt. Ignorance added to a strong character was a double curse; stupidity joining hands with stubbornness was twice stupid. She had practically dethroned and imprisoned the Emperor at the Yingtai Terrace inside the "South Sea" Lake in the Palace. One cold winter, a eunuch who took pity on the Emperor and had the windows repapered to keep out the wind was summarily dismissed by the Empress. She knew that there would be terrible revenge upon her memory and her soul, should the Emperor outlive her. So when her strength was giving out from prolonged dysentery and she knew that her days were ended, she had him poisoned just two days before she herself died. The Emperor, however, had not forgotten the treachery of Yuan Shihkai, who had betrayed him on the eve of the planned *coup d' état,* with such tragic consequences for himself. On his deathbed, he bit his finger and wrote in blood his last will that Yuan was to be dismissed from office forever.

Revolution was in the air. The Chinese people were dissatisfied with the foreign Manchu rule, with its weakness, ignorance, and incompetence, and its procrastination over the promised constitution. A baby Emperor, three years old (who is today the puppet Emperor of "Manchukuo") was put on the throne; and his father became Prince Regent, ruling on his son's behalf. If ordinary businessmen did not know the political trend, all the more intelligent people knew that the force of revolution could not be suppressed for long. Mr. Yao was one of these farsighted persons. And the death of the old Empress and Emperor coincided with his decision to go to Hong Kong, Singapore, and Java. He had now thoroughly convinced himself that too much wealth was bad for his sons, and he wanted to aid the cause of the revolution. This he could tell to nobody, not even to his wife or daughters, or to his brother-in-law or to Mr. Fu, for—it amounted to treason against the Empire.

Mr. Yao left in November for the south. Against his wife's wish, he took Afei with him on the trip, for as he grew older it was noticeable that he became more fond of his younger son. He was taking no risks with him and was assuming personal care of him. The sisters learned after their father's departure that he had taken fifty thousand dollars with him and had told the uncle that he might ask for more. Their mother had asked him what he was going to do with so much money, but he had flatly refused to tell her. The sisters guessed that it had something to do with his dissatisfaction with Tijen and his threat to break up the family fortune. But the business and property were worth nearly a million, and unless he sold out everything and dumped the money into the sea, the fortune could not be broken up easily. He promised to be back in the following spring or summer, in time for Mulan's wedding.

Tijen felt that his father had taken money that belonged to him and Afei and was purposely squandering it, and he told Silverscreen so. At New Year's Eve, he went to his uncle and demanded fifteen thousand dollars to pay his gambling debts. The issue was brought to the mother, but Tijen insisted that he had lost at the gambling table and had to pay before the New Year. He promised never to gamble again and this time he meant it, he said.

"This is a very great sum, and your father will have to know when he comes back," said his mother.

"Mother, save me this time, and I promise not to do it again," he insisted. "When Father comes back and learns it, it will be all over. Can he make me spit the money out from my belly? I will face him myself and let him beat me if he wants to. But he also is helping to squander our money."

Tijen was staying out late at nights again, for the father's absence was a great chance for him and he feared no one at home. His uncle did not interfere so long as his mother did not.

Then he began not to return home at all at night. The first time this occurred, his mother asked for an explanation, and he angrily said that he was grown-up and was not to be shut up by anybody. The periods of his absence gradually lengthened and sometimes he would not come home for three or four days.

Those were sad and dreary days for the mother. She longed for the pleasure of sitting up past midnight to wait for him again, knowing that he would come, but now he seemed to be quite out of her reach.

One day in the following spring, after an absence of five nights, she asked again for an explanation. He said, "Mother, I can't explain. You had better not know. It is useless. I am doing what is right, and you must believe me."

"Is it Silverscreen or is it not?" Mochow blurted out point blank in indignation.

Tijen hesitated, and then throwing all pretense overboard, he said firmly, "Well, it is. I knew Mother wouldn't like it and I was sparing her the pain."

At this the mother became hysterical. Words of abuse flowed from her lips, as if she were any ordinary injured woman. "Where is that little whore? Where is that she-fox? I shall match this old life of mine against hers! She is a vampire sent by the King of Hell with a pitchfork to hook my soul away from my body!"

The secret was out, and Frankincense, who was in the room, rushed to tell Brocade, and came back immediately, followed by Brocade, regretting the loss of every second. They stood at the door and heard Tijen make a still more astounding announcement.

"Mother, you have to listen to reason," he said. "You are a grand-mother without knowing it. Someone has borne you a grandson and you still call her a whore. Well, whore or no whore, she is the mother of my child, and I am standing by her."

"When? Where?" cried Tijen's sisters.

"Last month. And it is a boy. That was why I had to stay away. I did not want to cause trouble, and so I could not explain. Since mother broke her promise to me and drove her out, I have been taking care of her, if that's what you want to know. Now the rice is cooked and I can't abandon her. The most important thing in a man is his conscience."

His mother was now aghast and speechless. The news of the grand-son threw her into worse confusion and promised greater complications than her matter-of-fact head could grasp at the moment. She had only one clear feeling now, that she, the mother, was defeated and Silverscreen, the maid, had won.

Silverscreen had hoped for this. The birth of a grandson would complete her triumph and establish her in an unshakable position. And a boy it turned out to be! Oh, joy of mother and triumph of woman! After the birth, she had wanted the news to come out and to see how the mother would take it, but she had advised Tijen to wait until his father's return, as she felt he would be more reasonable and would accept the situation better than the mother, and perhaps install her again in the status of semi-maid and semi-mistress. How triumphant she would be, if she walked into the house again, her blood joined with the blood of the Yao family! But now Tijen had blurted it out.

His mother swore she did not want to see the face of that maid ever again. But she wanted the grandson, blood of her blood. Mulan and Mochow tried to calm her, but her hatred against Silverscreen seemed deep as the sea and as old as woman. There was little chance of her taking the maid again into her household on account of the baby. She consulted her brother and he advised her to leave the matter as it was and wait till the father's return.

Mulan wormed Silverscreen's address out of Tijen by promising to help to bring their mother around. So one day, the three sisters set out on one of the most exciting adventures of their life, to see Silverscreen and the baby.

Silverscreen had been warned by Tijen. When they came she was courteous and dignified, and she still addressed them as the "Eldest," "Second," and "Third *Hsiaochieh.*" The landlady, knowing the standing of the family, was awed by the presence of the three pretty and rich young ladies in her house. Tijen was not there, and Silverscreen served them tea herself in the old manner. Mulan looked about and saw that the rooms, although small, were very neatly and exquisitely furnished with the exception of the terrible picture of a naked foreign woman, and she knew where the money for all this had come from. One thing she did not like was that Silverscreen the maid was now dressed all in silk from head to foot and wore a pair of beautiful jade bracelets on her arms as if she were a real lady.

"*Hsiaochieh,* I beg your pardon," said Silverscreen. "There was a misunderstanding. Your mother thought I was a fox-spirit, but you treated me very well and your brother has a good heart. That is why I am still living today." Satisfaction and triumph were noticeable in her words.

"Let bygones be bygones," said Mochow. "We are not come to settle old accounts, but to see the baby. Where is he?"

"Come inside," said Silverscreen, and she led them into her bedroom, where a plump baby lay in a white-enameled foreign cradle. Silverscreen took him up and held him proudly in her arms to show him to the excited visitors. The baby had a pointed nose just like their brother.

"Lend the baby to us," said Mulan. "We will show him to *Taitai* and bring him back to you. She will be pleased when she has seen the baby."

Silverscreen stoutly refused, but when the sisters had departed, she regretted what she had done and began to have fears lest the baby's family should come and forcibly take the baby away. She told Tijen this and suggested moving away to another hiding place.

"If they kidnap the baby, can't I kidnap it back again?" said Tijen.

"In that case, even I will go to the house," said Silverscreen. "They can of course prevent me from getting in, but I can die before your family door."

Nevertheless, Tijen was persuaded to move into another house outside Chienmen. And Silverscreen the mother stood guard day and night over the baby and never let him out of her sight.

What her maternal instinct feared came true. One day, Lotung came with several women servants to her new house, and demanded in the name of the *Taitai* that she give up the baby.

Tijen was not in the house, and Mrs. Hua, who had moved into the new house with them in their nondescript relationship, happened to be away. Silverscreen was sitting by the baby's white foreign cradle with the pointer lying by her side. The dog was now fully grown and was called "Golo," which was Silverscreen's idea of the word "Girl."

Silverscreen's face turned pale, and the dog growled hostilely at the group of strangers. Hushing the dog, she stood over the cradle, facing them with her hands sheltering the baby, and demanded, "What do you mean?

"*Taitai's* orders," replied Lotung. "This is a Yao family child, and *Taitai* demands her grandson."

"How?" she said. "The baby is mine. Young Master has said nothing about it. If the grandson is to be returned to the Yao family, there must be an arrangement."

"That I don't know," replied Lotung. "Orders are orders."

"Don't you dare touch my child, or you'll have my life to reckon with. Isn't the child's father still living?"

"I am here only to carry out the *Taitai's* orders," said Lotung firmly.

"You will not take him," shouted the mother desperately. "Did she give birth to it, or did I?"

Lotung came forward menacingly and held Silverscreen, while commanding the women servants, "Take him away."

Silverscreen began to fight and shriek with all her mother's milk-energy. At once the dog jumped upon Lotung, while a woman snatched the child from its cradle. Lotung released Silverscreen and turned to fight off the dog. The woman was running out with the child.

"Golo!" screamed Silverscreen. "Go! Bite! That woman!"

Golo dashed in pursuit and bit at the woman's shoulder from behind. She screamed in fright and tottered, letting the child slip, so that it almost fell to the floor. The mother gave a shriek of terror. Another woman caught the child as it fell and ran out of the door with the dog after her. Fearing now that the baby would be injured, Silverscreen shouted, "Golo! Come back!" The dog turned and looked at her as if puzzled, and Silverscreen tried to dash out herself to stop the woman, but Lotung held her. Silverscreen bit his arm and pulled his hair to set herself free.

When the baby was gone, Lotung let go his hold on Silverscreen and ran out after the others. In desperation the mother saw her baby carried away. She let forth a primitive mother's wail mingled with a string of Ningpo curses. "Chopped by a thousand knives! F— your elder sister, younger sister, paternal aunt, maternal aunt, and all your three generations of bitches! Thief's bones! I will have my baby back yet, and you son of a bitch will die of apoplexy and roll down to the eighteenth hell and stay there for ten thousand generations."

When they were all gone, she broke into a flood of tears. Mrs. Hua returned ten minutes later to discover her lying on the bed weeping and still cursing on with her inexhaustible flow of expletives.

.·.

When Tijen came and learned of the kidnaping, he was furious. He talked as if he could murder his mother, but there was a great difference between Tijen's actions and his words.

"What are you going to do?" Silverscreen demanded.

"Do? I will kidnap the child back, even if I have to murder somebody."

"Slowly, slowly. The proverb says, 'An urgent thing must be done slowly,'" said Mrs. Hua. "This is a big and complicated business. You go and speak to your mother first. Persuade her to let Silverscreen come into the family. That is my advice, but don't you two forget about me."

"I need your help now, and I shall never forget you," said Silverscreen. "If I should die, would you take care of the child for me?"

"Don't talk nonsense," said Tijen. "I have an idea. Mrs. Hua, you come with me and speak to my mother as woman to woman. Anyway, I need you—I should not know how to carry the baby back."

So Mrs. Hua went with Tijen to his house, and he took her into his mother's room.

"Who are you?" Mrs. Yao angrily demanded of Mrs. Hua, without speaking to Tijen.

"I am Silverscreen's friend," said Mrs. Hua. She had lost heart the moment she came into the mansion and saw the style in which the family lived, and now she went on to speak half-timidly of the baby.

"Mrs. Yao," said Mrs. Hua. "I am only a bystander, and have no right to interfere. But the proverb says, 'The bystander sees more clearly than the man in charge.' Of course, the child belongs to the Yao family, and should come here. But the mother-child relationship is of God's own making. Since the baby is to come back, some arrangement must be made for the mother to see him. Even the Emperor dare not separate a common mother and child. You are a mother yourself, and should think for your daughter-in-law."

"That shameless whore my daughter-in-law?" replied Mrs. Yao. "Whenever did I send a red sedan chair to welcome her into my house?"

Mrs. Yao would listen to no persuasion. She would not give the baby back, and she would not let Silverscreen come into her house.

"Well, since you won't compromise," said Tijen, "I must take the baby back."

He went into the next room where Coral was taking care of the baby and demanded him. Coral tried to hold the child, but Tijen thrust her away with a strong arm and seized the crying child from his bed.

"Take care, you'll kill him!" cried Coral.

"If I kill him, he is my child and not yours," he said.

He carried the baby out and gave him into Mrs. Hua's unwilling arms, and commanded her to follow him; but the women servants were ordered by the mistress to hold her back. At this, Tijen turned and fought the women servants and snatched the child again, while Mrs. Hua in the confusion, fled out of the house alone.

Lotung, running in, met Tijen in the courtyard face to face, and Mrs. Yao shouted to Lotung in her home dialect to stop him. With the delicate load in his arms, Tijen was blocked.

"Stop him! Get the baby!" the mistress shouted. The women servants rushed out again. Lotung, glad of the chance to use his muscles, fell back and blocked the door to the second hall through which Tijen must pass. The women servants swarmed around him and pulled at his coat. With his hands occupied, he gave up in desperation and rage and finally handed the baby to Coral, and went out, slapping Lotung in the face as he passed him.

Seeing Tijen and Mrs. Hua come back without her child, Silverscreen was dismayed and fell to crying, hardly listening to Tijen's explanation. The next day, after Tijen had gone to the shop, Silverscreen herself went to Tijen's home. When she was denied entrance she began to create a scene outside the gate. She tore her hair, screamed and shouted, wept, and cursed.

"Heaven's justice and human conscience!" she cried to the crowd which collected to listen to her harangue. "They snatch my child away and deny me entrance, trying to separate us, mother and child! Neighbors and street people, I appeal to you!"

This was very embarrassing for the family. "Separating mother and child" was a grave charge that could have won a case even if brought before the Emperor and a sin that cut at the foundations of Confucianism. Although legally Tijen's son belonged to his father's family, yet according to law they were also responsible for the mother. The onlookers exchanged questions and sympathized with the crying woman. Lota came out and tried to calm her and finally asked her to go inside and talk it over. But Silverscreen now refused.

"Give back my child! Give back my child!" she cried as if she were mad. "If not, I will die here before your eyes."

She saw the stone tablet sunken in the ground and went over and knocked her head hard against it again and again. When Lota pulled her away a little stream of blood was running down her forehead. Then Lota and Lotung dragged her inside by force, and she kicked and shouted that they were going to shut her up.

The gate was now closed and the crowd, denied the spectacle, and hearing only her raving inside, began to disperse. Silverscreen was seated in the gatekeeper's room, shrieking and sobbing alternately until Mulan and Mochow urged their mother to talk with Silverscreen and said, "If she really commits suicide, it is not a pretty thing to be talked about. She has a temper, you know."

Their mother was adamant. "The grandson is ours and not hers," she said.

"Then let her stay," said Coral, who was softening toward Silverscreen because of the child.

"Do you expect me to tolerate that vixen again in my house, after she has taken my son away from me?" Mrs. Yao demanded.

It was Brocade and Frankincense who went out at last and spoke to their old companion and comforted her.

"You can listen to me," said Brocade, "because I am of the same rank as you. Is this the place where you can win by being stubborn? And do not take a short view. If you die, what do you gain by it? Can your family come up from Hangchow and sue this kind of a family? I should advise you to go back and consider it slowly. It is not a thing that can be decided at once."

Silverscreen realized she was defeated. The child, which was to have been her strength, had now become the source of her weakness.

When she was completely exhausted, Brocade escorted her home, dazed and half out of her mind. When Tijen came he found her lying in bed and moaning, "My son! My son!"

She refused to get up even when he begged her to do so for his sake. Nor would she eat whatever food Mrs. Hua brought to tempt her. She lay all day without washing and without combing her hair, and so in despair Tijen was compelled to leave her.

He was grieved for her and yet resentful, too, that he was put to such trouble and confusion. It seemed to him now that perhaps no woman was worth quite so much trouble as this.

Three days later he came again. Mrs. Hua told him Silverscreen was just the same. In some impatience he pushed the closed door of her room. It opened with difficulty and he had to use a little strength. When he got in he looked behind and saw Silverscreen. She had hanged herself.

Was Silverscreen a good woman? Yes, but was there ever a bad woman? A slight change of circumstance and standing, and she would have held for life a position exactly similar to that of Mulan's mother— mistress of a huge fortune, an able housewife, and a devoted mother, perfect in her children's eyes.

. ˙ .

The news of Silverscreen's suicide was brought to Mrs. Yao by Tijen himself.

311

"You killed her! You killed her!" shouted Tijen in his rage. "And you will pay for this. Her curse is upon you and upon this house. Her ghost will strike you one day, and follow you and harass you to the end of your days!"

His mother's face turned pale, and she said, "My son! My son! For the sake of a maid, you have cursed your own mother!"

"It is she who cursed you and this house. And, mother, you deserve it!"

Mrs. Yao held up her hands in terror to stop him.

Tijen did not speak to his mother for a month. Though she pleaded, he would not listen to her. He could not forgive her now that Silverscreen was dead. His mother seemed to have aged suddenly, but he would not allow himself to heed it from this time on. He came back only now and then to get some of his things.

Mr. and Mrs. Hua helped him with Silverscreen's funeral, at which Frankincense and Brocade were allowed to be present, and they buried her in the outer city. Mr. Feng also offered to help, but Tijen did not want any member of his family to be present at the funeral. He had now rebelled against his whole family and was further out of his mother's reach than ever.

About a month after this, Mr. Hua died of pneumonia. Tijen found in Mrs. Hua a person who thought kindly of his dead mistress, and he stayed at her house. She was understanding, sincere, and alternately amusing and comforting to him, and he listened to her as he did to nobody else. He began to take opium in her company, and found such moments beautiful and calm, in contrast to the jarring world outside. Because of the difference in their ages, Mrs. Hua was a mother-mistress-landlady to him, all in one. When he went as he often did to seek pleasure and comfort among the women in the red-light district outside Chienmen, Mrs. Hua did not stop him, but on the contrary gave him experienced advice, so that he was saved from becoming involved in worse predicaments. Thus she kept a strong hold upon him and he retained always a sense of loyalty toward her.

At last he went home, but still in anger. He went to his mother and shouted to her, "You have killed the mother of my baby. Now I don't care. If my father wants to disown me, let him disown me! I don't care if the whole Yao family goes to ruin, do you hear?"

His mother did not answer him any more. She only looked at him pitifully and in silence. During these few months her hair had turned white. At night, she would shriek in her dreams and she became afraid of the dark, saying that the ghost of Silverscreen was following her.

Silverscreen's child was called Poya and was put in the charge of Coral. Curiously Mrs. Yao now developed a superstitious dread of Poya, although he was her "eldest" and only grandson. Coral now had to bring Poya up away from the presence and sight of Mrs. Yao.

When the father returned with Afei he found his home wrecked, his wife years older, and everybody sad and sober. When he was told of the fifteen thousand dollars Tijen had taken at New Year's Eve, he merely said, "Very well!" But those two words sounded terrifying to the daughters.

But when he heard of Silverscreen's death, he blamed the mother for not taking her in. "After all," he said, "she is the mother of our grandson." And he went himself to see Silverscreen's grave and ordered some alterations, and said that a tablet should be put up in their family niche, on which were inscribed the words: "The seat of the spirit of Chang Silverscreen of Ningpo." So Silverscreen after her death was installed in the Yao family of spirits. The mother was mortified, but accepted it as a propitiatory gesture toward Silverscreen's spirit.

It was in such circumstances that Mulan was preparing for her wedding. She had been collecting pearls and jade for her wedding jewels, and hearing of it jewelers came to the house with packages of the most astonishing necklaces and bracelets and rings and jade pendants, and she chose carefully what she wanted. But the home atmosphere was so changed with Tijen's hostility toward his mother and the mother's abnormal fears at night that sometimes Mulan wished for her own selfish reasons she were to be married off at once and gone to live in a more peaceful home, the home of the Tsengs.

One evening, after supper, the father said to the family, in a very sad and serious tone, "Good and bad luck are predetermined. I am waiting only for Afei to grow up. After Mulan and Mochow are married and Afei is grown up, I shall go my way, and you will go your way."

The sisters were struck with a deep terror. They could not believe that one day the father would separate himself from them all. And they hated Tijen deeply for bringing the shadow of a tragedy to their family.

"Father, even if we don't count, you must be fair to Afei," Mulan said with tears in her eyes. "And there is now the grandson to live for. Sometimes a bad bamboo tree grows good bamboo shoots."

But the father only repeated to Mulan a poem written by Yu Chuyuan, in his happy old age. It was called "Farewell to My Family."

> What is family then but a phrase?
> Casual travelers met on their ways.
> The Punch-and-Judy show is done,
> Take the stage down, the props and stays.

CHAPTER XXI

*P*ERHAPS the fortune tellers are wrong. Perhaps—and this may be nearer the truth—fortune telling is an art and not a science, even as the practice of medicine is an art and not a science. If a doctor's pronouncement were the dictum of Science the Absolute, there would be no advantage in having old, experienced doctors, and there would be no need for consultations in emergency cases, for one doctor to ask another doctor, "What do you think?" To us lay-men, however, who need faith in something absolute, professional men have to give an appearance of certainty and possession of the Truth. Thus the analysis of faces is like the diagnosis of symptoms. There are no hard and fast distinctions among faces of the Gold, Wood, Water, Fire, and Earth types. The sub-types merge into one another. It is a question of the predominance of a certain type, and the combinations of types are infinite in their differences and nuances. It is the experienced physiognomist who sees the nuances. As regards Mulan and her sister, all that was clear and certain was that Mulan had longer eyes than Mochow's, eyes of passionate intelligence, that she was thinner and sharper in her features, more volatile and more spirited than Mochow, while Mochow, being of the spirit of the Earth, had round eyes and round, fleshy features, and was more steady and practical than Mulan. The comparatively white softness of Mochow's skin was a point in her favor, indicating fineness of texture and an easy, comfortable life. East and West, from ancient to modern times, the ideal woman has always been conceived to be one white of skin, supple in flesh, and soft and round in her contours.

One could be quite prepared to believe that Mochow would have made just as successful a match with Sunya, and Mulan with Lifu. Whatever the "elements" of all four, they were all fairly good sub-types. Mochow, with her practical wisdom, would be naturally happy in a great, rich household like that of the Tsengs, taking great interest in all the details and getting along alike with the superiors and the inferiors. On the other hand, Mulan would have changed Lifu's family life, making him take more journeys of pleasure and would lead him on perhaps a more poetic, if less orderly course. She would have found sipping wine with Lifu in the moonlight on a Soochow canal boat an irresistible pleasure. She was not the careful, saving sort, and Lifu might have been poorer; but she would have contrived inexpensive and novel delights for him. With Lifu's impetuous genius, however, she might have been less successful in keeping him out of harm's way. Or she might have been like the wife of Yang Chisheng, an ancestor of Lifu's mother, who begged to die in her husband's place when he was in prison.

If there had been then a system of marriage by the boy's and girl's own choice, Mulan might have married Lifu, and Mochow might have married Sunya. Mulan would have announced that she was in love, that is, in a condition inexplicable, mysterious, and out of her control, which should supersede and override every other consideration, and as happens nowadays, would have broken the engagement with the Tseng family. But the old system was still intact, and Mulan did not so much as confess even to herself the guilty feeling of love for Lifu, and she never doubted she would like Sunya. Her love for Lifu remained an innermost secret of her heart.

As it was, Mochow did the work of pulling Lifu back and restraining him, while Mulan did the pushing of Sunya and spurring him forward. But since it is more natural for a woman to pull her husband than to push him, perhaps Mochow was the happier woman. For Mulan to push the impetuous Lifu might have been disastrous after all.

Mulan was married at nineteen (or twenty by Chinese reckoning). In the summer of 1909, the ceremony of "requesting the date" of the wedding was formally gone through by the Tseng family sending the "dragon-and-phoenix card," the dragon representing the male and the phoenix the female. It was accompanied by "dragon-and-phoenix cakes," silks, tea leaves, fruits, a pair of living geese, and four jars of wine. Mulan's family indicated approval by a return card accompanied by twelve kinds of pastry. According to the ancient classical tradition, which included the ceremony of the bridegroom's personally going to welcome the bride at her home, the advantage seemed to be entirely on the bride's side, since her family appeared to be conveying a favor on the groom's family by giving the person of their daughter.

By consent of the two families, Mulan's wedding was to be one of the grandest Peking had seen: first, because both sides had plenty of money; second, because Mr. Yao was very fond of his daughter and the Tsengs were very proud of the bride; third, because Chinya's wedding had been celebrated with great pomp, and in fairness to Sunya and for appearance's sake, the Tsengs wished to keep up the standard; and fourth, because Mulan's father had begun to take a very light view of his wealth. There was no better way of squandering his money than for the wedding of his favorite daughter—to see happiness while it lasted. Wealth was to him like a fireworks display tracing lines of fire in the dark sky—with plenty of splutter and brilliance, and ending in smoke, ashes, and the charred ends on the ground.

Mr. Yao indeed went to the trouble months ahead of ordering special fireworks from Fukien, which, what with transportation charges and bringing a pyrotechnist also all the way, cost him nearly a thousand dollars. Afei had seen such fireworks when he was in the south with his father, and he had told his sisters and Redjade how wonderful they were.

Hundreds of guests were invited, including the highest officials and Manchu princes and princesses. Yuan Shihkai had been dismissed from office and was living a retired life back in his home in Honan, but his red silk scroll was prominently displayed along with those of New the Minister, Wang the Grand Councilor, and the Manchu princes. The names of the senders of such red wedding scrolls, displayed in hall after hall in the Tseng mansion, read like a list of the Court Register—names like Grand Minister of the Supreme Military Council, Chief of the Imperial Guards, Chief of the Metropolitan Gendarmerie, Viceroy of Chihli, Viceroy of Shantung, and the Manchu Barons.

The whole Tseng mansion had been done over for the occasion. Grandmother Tseng was feeling well this summer, and she had wanted this to be a gay affair. As the wedding was in the beginning of October, when the air was keen and cool, the wooden panels of the first hall were taken down, turning it into a terrace connecting with the stone courts in front and behind. Mattings, supported by scaffoldings forty feet high, were erected over the courtyards and on the sides, so that the effect as one entered, after passing behind the green and gold-sprinkled four-panel wooden screen, was like going into a huge hall eighty feet deep, with red candles three feet high and red silk scrolls four or five feet wide and fifteen feet high lining the walls all around so close together that on some of them only the names of senders of the gifts were exposed to view. Characters a foot high in gold-foil paper or gold-lined black velvet, reflected by the candles, gave the great hall the total effect of a mass of red and gold. Stone steps led up to the inner main hall, where the wedding ceremony was to be performed. The center was wide open, showing the red scroll of Baron Tao in the center, flanked by that of Privy Councillor Na on the right and that of Grand Councilor Wang on the left. To the right and left of these three, and next to them, were a scroll from the Minister New in the capacity of parent of the daughter-in-law Suyun, and one from an obscure brother of Mrs. Tseng in the capacity of maternal uncle, who was extremely important at the wedding as representing the mother's family.

Gardeners, carpenters, and painters had been at work making the whole place look like new. The winding corridors on the west leading into the maze of living courtyards were repainted, walls were whitewashed, and windows and ceilings were repapered. The grandmother had moved back to the main court at the rear, where it was easier for the family to pay her their daily visits. Her court southeast of the room where Mannia had first stayed was now occupied by Suyun, being separated by a narrow covered alley and a small garden. On the west a rockery surrounded by creepers separated Suyun's court from the small court, where the old teacher Fang had lived; and beyond was an old hall designed for summer use because it was near to the vacant stretch of trees and débris in front of the family temple. This hall had been converted the year before into pleasant living rooms, and in the summer Mr. Tseng stayed here with Cassia. It was the furthest southwestern court in the mansion, looking out through a moon door upon the vacant space; and, when they planned the wedding of Sunya, Mr. Tseng gave it up in favor of his son, because Mrs. Tseng remembered how fond Mulan was of open views. In the vacant stretch, part of the ground had been cleared and a temporary wooden stage set up for theatrical performances which were to last three days and three nights. An open path toward the north led to a door opening directly into Mannia's court in the rear, while another path from the south door of the courtyard led through a small hexagonal pavilion directly to the main gate. Behind was the Calm-Heart

Studio, where Mannia and her mother had first stayed on their arrival from Shantung.

As the wedding drew near, the work of preparation was enormous. A number of Mr. Tseng's minor associates at the office had been borrowed for the occasion, and these, together with a few relatives from Shantung and officers of the Shantung Guild, came and stayed in the house for a week before the wedding, dividing among themselves the work of sending wedding cards and receiving and recording wedding presents, tipping servants who brought gifts, engaging theatrical troupes and musicians, planning the procession and renting the paraphernalia for it from professional firms, arranging sedan chairs and dinners and borrowing furniture from the Guild. Four servants were assigned to look after the candles and lights and hangings throughout the house; four to look after the cleaning and arrangement of furniture and sweeping the floors; two to be responsible for the table silver and ivory chopsticks; and eight, with the assistance of the group looking after the furniture, were just to prepare and serve tea to visitors. The work was strictly divided between that for the men guests in front, and the women guests behind, with the main hall as the dividing line. The women guests who overflowed from the third hall were to be accommodated in the One-Insight Hall, west of the third hall and east of the Calm-Heart Studio.

When the arrangements were begun, the grandmother had said that things were to be done just as at the wedding of Chinya last year; but, since she was in good health this year and in a good mood and was very fond of Sunya and Mulan, she approved of everything proposed, such as the theatrical performances, which had not been given at Chinya's wedding. The family was glad to see the grandmother in such high spirits, and anxious to please her, and consequently the preparations went far beyond the first plans.

The morning of the sixth, the day before the wedding, Mrs. Tseng, Cassia, Mannia and her mother, and Suyun and Chinya were all gathered in the grandmother's room. Mrs. Tseng was asking Chinya if the arrangements were complete. Chinya, who as the eldest son was directing the men's part of the arrangements outside, said, "The drums and music have all been ordered. What we are to do today is to borrow furniture from the Guild. Red scrolls will still come from time to time and will have to be hung up. The dinners and lights and candles are all in charge of special persons, and we don't have to worry about them. Only the kitchen on the east has not yet been completed, and we have to see before the day is over that the stoves and chimneys are all in order and ready for tomorrow. There is only one trouble. Another important wedding is going on tomorrow, and the beautiful wedding sedan with painted glass that Suyun came in last year has been rented. There is not a second one in the whole of Peking. But I have thought of a way. Last March, at the wedding of Prince Tao's third son, the bride rode in a horse carriage. Customs are changing and we may just as well do the same."

"That is a good idea," said the grandmother. "You go and borrow the carriage from Baroness Tao. A carriage with four fine horses, decorated with silk and gold and red velvet flowers on their heads, will be very impressive."

"I don't believe that you really can't find a single wedding sedan in the whole capital," said Suyun to her husband. "Why need it be the same sedan that I came in?"

"I think the horse carriage is a good idea. It is novel and splendid." said Ailien.

"With your permission, I may say something in the presence of the grandmother and *Taitai*," said the maid Snow Blossom. "I think since this wedding is so grandly planned we should not use any old wedding sedan. All this wedding is for is to welcome the bride, and when we are marrying such a fairylike beauty as Mulan, to put her in a common wedding sedan would be both out of harmony with the occasion and unworthy of the bride."

Suyun looked at the maid and said no more.

"Let it be done," said Mrs. Tseng. "You send someone to borrow the Baroness's carriage and tell them not to fail on any account to come tomorrow in time for the wedding."

"Well, go then, since everybody is of the same opinion," said Suyun, eyeing Chinya. When he went out, she said to the others, "It seems everything outside depends upon him. He has lost several pounds in the past week."

"To run about for the wedding of one's own younger brother is one's natural duty," said the grandmother. "We ought not really to be so extravagant, but thanks to Buddha, everything is peaceful, and little Number Three is my last grandson, and Mulan is such a charming girl. After seeing their wedding, I shall die content. I don't know how she looks now. She hasn't been to see us for over a year. But it is natural for a girl to be shy."

"Grandmother, you will be surprised," said Mannia. "The older she grows, the more beautiful she is. She is quite tall now."

"This afternoon there will be the parade of the bride's trousseau," said Mrs. Tseng. "I hear there will be seventy-two cases on parade."

"So Little Joy was told by Brocade," said Mannia.

"I cannot wait to see it. It will be dazzling to look at," said Ailien.

"That also is to be expected," said Cassia. "Since both families have agreed to make a lively wedding, the bride's family of course want to do their best. Mulan is their favorite and they have so much money."

At the mention of money, Suyun felt offended. She had had a parade of forty-eight cases of her trousseau, which was considered splendid, and she was mortified to hear that Mulan was going to have seventy-two. She considered herself the richest daughter-in-law, which was true, and she knew that Mulan's family had money, but she never dreamed that Mulan would have a finer trousseau than hers, as if purposely to put Suyun at a disadvantage by comparison.

"We are lucky," she said. "Maybe we are marrying not only Miss Yao, but also half of the Yao fortune."

Mrs. Tseng was a little angry, and she said, "Really, the number of cases does not matter. We are marrying her and not her goods, and besides, we have no right to say anything until we see the things."

And Suyun went back to her room chagrined.

In the afternoon, Mulan's trousseau began to arrive at about three o'clock, accompanied by eight men attendants, besides the eight attendants sent by the groom's side to welcome it. The trousseau came in seventy-two open exhibit cases in the order of gold, silver, jade, jewelry, bedroom outfits, library outfits, antiques, silks, furs, trunks, and quilts.

The parade had attracted great crowds, blocking the traffic around East-Four Pailou for five minutes, and women who did not see it greatly regretted missing one of the best trousseau parades of Peking. Standing in the front row near the Pailou was a woman who took special interest. It was Mrs. Hua. She had been told the hour of the parade by Tijen, who had told her that his father was marrying Mulan off with fifty thousand dollars' worth of trousseau, besides the antiques, some of which were priceless. Mrs. Hua stood watching case after case

321

pass, each carried by two coolies, and the more valuable jewelry and gold and jade covered in glass cases. These were some of the things Mrs. Hua saw pass before her: 1 gold *juyi* (which was a ceremonial object merely for display), 1 silver *juyi,* 4 jade *juyi,* 1 pair of solid old gold bracelets of dragon design, 1 pair of gold-fibered bracelets of lobster-feelers design, 1 gold lock pendant, 1 gold neck ring, 1 pair of gold curtain hooks, 10 gold ingots; 2 sets of table silver, 1 pair of large silver vases, 1 pair of small silver vases, 1 set of silver-inlaid lacquer trays, 1 pair of silver candlesticks, 1 small Siamese silver Buddha, 50 silver ingots; 1 set of jade animals, 1 set of amethyst, 1 set of amber and carnelian (Mulan's private collection), 1 set of jade brooches, earrings, and finger rings, 1 large jade hair ornament, 2 large jade phoenixes for hair decoration, 1 large jade box, 1 small agate box, 1 old brown jade pot for writing brushes, 2 pairs of emerald bracelets, 1 pair of jade-inlaid bracelets, 2 jade pendants, 1 pure white jade Goddess of Mercy, a foot high, 1 pair of white-jade seals, 1 pair of red-jade seals, 1 jade-handled walking stick, 1 jade-handled mosquito-swat of horsehair, 2 pipes with jade mouth-pieces, 1 large old jade bowl, and 6 pots of jade flowers with crystal petals; 2 long pearl necklaces, 1 set of pearl brooches, hairpins, earrings, and finger rings, 1 pearl-studded bracelet, and 1 pearl-studded neckpiece. Then came cases containing old bronze mirrors and new foreign mirrors, Foochow lacquer toilet cases, white copper hand warmers, water tobacco pipes, clocks, bedroom furniture, Yangchow wooden bathtubs, and the usual commodes. Then followed the stationery and antiques, such as sandalwood curio cabinets, stands, and stools, old ink slabs, old ink cakes, scrolls of old paintings, Chenghua and Fukien white porcelain, 1 Han tripod, 1 copper tile from the roof of a third-century copper pavilion, and 1 glass case of bone inscriptions. A case of carved ivory followed, after which came 10 cases of silk, gauze, crepe, and satin, 6 cases of furs, 20 red lacquer trunks of clothing, and 16 cases of silk bedding, which were partly for the bride's own use and partly for distribution to the bridegroom's relatives as the bride's presents.

When all the cases had arrived, the bridegroom's family were impressed beyond their expectations. "Mulan is the luckiest girl I have ever seen," said Mannia. "She has the beauty and the things, or the things and the beauty. Such things for a bride without her beauty would be a grave injustice."

But Mrs. Hua, standing there in the front row at a street corner, staring at the display and especially the gold ingots and the jade, had thought her eyes would fall out trying to follow the steadily moving spectacle. When she went back, she made up her mind to give a sound talk to Tijen, advising him to keep on good terms with his father and not risk being disowned by too free behavior. And so two days later when Tijen came, she said to him:

"Had I known how rich your family really were, I would not have dared to go into your house that day. And you are born the eldest heir! Don't risk losing your home and your family, my boy. You will be a fool if you do. Try to please your parents, and leave me alone. I don't mind, so long as you don't forget about me entirely."

"Huh!" said Tijen. "Do you know why my father is giving away all those jewels and things to my sister? He is competing with me in throwing his money away. He took a hundred thousand dollars on his trip to the South Seas—Heaven knows what for—and this wedding has cost another fifty thousand. If he keeps on like this, in a few years we will have nothing. You didn't see the diamond brooch Mulan wore on her wedding dress. That alone cost five thousand dollars."

"Why is it that your younger sister is married before you?" asked Mrs. Hua.

"I don't know. It just happened so. Mulan's match was arranged three years ago when I was leaving for England. And then things just happened!"

In her own mind Mrs. Hua began to make her own plans for Tijen.

• •

But to go back to Mulan's wedding. The trousseau, the procession, the dinners, the theatricals, the music, all were but the setting for the jewel that was the bride. If pomp and circumstance meant earthly happiness, the consummation of an earthly dream, Mulan had it. Yet she shed tears on her wedding morning, as brides so often do, tears that come from the most unsuspected corners of her heart. She took Afei into her room, and with tears gave him as a parting present a round jade paperweight that she had kept on her desk. Later Afei always placed it on his desk and he never parted with it.

"Your sister is going into another home now," she said to Afei. "Third Sister still remains at home. You must listen to her and obey our parents. You are eleven years old now. Determine to grow up into a good man, a famous man, not like your eldest brother. You should be proud of the Yao family and act so that we sisters shall be proud of you. When Lifu comes, be with him as much as you can, and make friends with him. Eldest Brother is hopeless now, and the hope of the Yao family is entirely in you. We sisters are girls and do not count. You never knew what we lived through while you and Father were away in the South." When she finished, tears were already rolling over the brims of her eyelids.

There was such love in his sister's eyes that Afei remembered every word of what she said and thought much upon it, and these simple words kept Afei straight throughout his growing years. Later, he could never speak of this incident without profound emotion; and it was this sister's love, even more than his mother's, that meant most to him all his life.

In the old China, one's motive for being good lay in the desire to live worthily of one's family and preserve its name and fortune. Only so can we explain the strong moral tradition, the emphasis on conduct, and the platitudes and interminable moralizing that permeated literature and history from the classics down, and followed a person even to his coffin.

But it was also because Mulan ardently wished she had been a boy that she injected into her younger brother the pride of family and all the passionate hopes and longings that were part of herself and unrealized. How many girls in those days had dreams that were never fulfilled and ambitions that were never satisfied, hopes that were thwarted on the threshold of marriage, and later lay dormant in the breast and were expressed in the form of hopes for their sons! How many wanted to go on with their studies and could not! How many wanted to go to college and could not! How many wanted to marry the type of young man that they cared for and could not! The vague ideals that adolescence shaped in their girls' minds were like flower buds plucked before their time or broken off by the wind. These were the lovely unsung women, the silent heroines, who married husbands either worthy or unworthy of them, and whose record was left for posterity only in a simple tombstone standing before an earthen mound among wild berries and thistles on some village hill.

Mulan was more luckily married than many or most of these. She had never really made love to Lifu, and she went into her marriage with a clear conscience. Sunya loved her, she knew, and there was no question that she would love her husband after she married him. Such love would have no insomnia in it; it was the natural condition of

324

two normal young people of opposite sex paying each other the unique compliment of giving their lives to each other as companions for the future. Under normal healthy circumstances, nature did the rest. If it is true that it is hard for a wife to remain on the pedestal of an angel or goddess, possessing the liquid of romantic intoxication to keep her lover-husband under an eternal spell, or for the husband to do the same, it is also true that Heaven has provided for each young married couple a natural method of reconciliation, a cement of affection that patches little holes and smooths out little wrinkles in the garment of matrimony and delivers it like new again each morning, by producing in each a desire for qualities that he or she has not got, and in each an attraction for the other because of what he or she has. The charm of sex works within marriage as well as without and the clay of a humanity which must forfeit the natural charms of sex in marriage would be sorry stuff indeed.

Mulan's wedding was a solemn ceremony. The bride, center of attention, was as beautiful as the full moon, and men and women who had not seen her before, gasped at her beauty. Besides the fascination of her eyes and the musical gurgle of her low voice, she had a magical figure. As we usually say of such a woman, "Add a tenth of an inch and she is too tall; take away a tenth of an inch and she is too short; increase her girth by a tenth of an inch and she is too stout; decrease it by a tenth of an inch and she is too thin." People who liked tall women thought her tall; people who liked short women thought her short; those who liked plump women thought her full-bodied, and those who liked thin women thought her slender. Such is the magic of perfect proportions. Yet she neither dieted, nor exercised. Nature just made her so.

Times were changing, and with her new ideas, Mulan did not cast her eyes downward all the time, nor did she put on a serious countenance and avoid smiling, as brides had been supposed to do. She did not keep her lips immobile and she even talked in whispers with Cassia, who was constantly by her side; and, while bending her head in decent humility, she darted quick glances at the company whenever anything particularly interested her. Thus being a bride was less of an ordeal for her than for brides in olden times. People who saw her smile thought it a wonderful breaking away from the old standards and did not consider her a frivolous bride on that account.

All through the dinner, Mulan went about to each table with the

325

bridegroom, to drink the health of the guests. Sunya was so happy that one "only saw his teeth, but not his eyes." Now after leaving the dinner, she had to prepare hurriedly for the visit of the guests at the bridal chamber. While she was changing her dress, Cassia whispered to her that a crowd of Sunya's school friends were coming to "disturb the bridal chamber," and that the grandmother had sent her to be present at the "teasing party" to prevent the young men from misbehaving.

The custom of "teasing the bride" had for its object to make and see the bride smile, by all sorts of jokes, practical and verbal, and by submitting the bride and bridegroom to all kinds of embarrassing requirements, vociferously voted for by the teasing young men. Now the charm of a bride's smile in former times consisted in the fact that it was reserved for her husband, while the charm of a modern bride is that she has a smile for everybody. That was why the party's object was to see the bride smile. But Mulan had been to a modern school and was considered modern or "new" and she was also naturally prone to laughter.

"Suyun's own brothers are coming," said Cassia, "and they are known to be the worst bride teasers in town. But grandmother has sent Suyun, too, to tell them to behave, and they would not dare disobey, being relatives of the bridegroom's. Are you afraid?"

"No," replied Mulan. "But my shoes pinch, and I shall be dead before this day is over." Then she asked, "Where is Mannia?"

"She is out there, but she will not come in because of the custom." For Mannia, as a widow, could not come into the bridal chamber.

"Mrs. Kung and her son and daughter are also here," said Cassia.

"Lifu? Oh!" said Mulan. After a moment, she said, "Can you speak to him?"

"No, I don't know him well enough," replied Cassia.

"Then will you tell Sunya to speak to him and ask him to come in and help from the guests' side. Someone like that among the guests will be helpful. I am not afraid of teasing, but I am afraid of coarseness," said Mulan.

When the party came to her chamber, there was a classmate of Sunya's who was named Chiang. He had a fat face and he could make facial contortions and funny noises. At first he was triumphant, for every time he drew a laugh from the bride. He put out his stomach and tried to imitate Sunya's speech and walk, and told about amusing

326

things that Sunya had done at school. Even the bride's companion and Brocade, who were standing behind the bride could not help laughing. Encouraged by this, the young man went on to entertain the company with another story.

"There was once a rogue who had no money to pass the New Year," he said. "His wife asked him about money, and he said, 'Don't worry.' Just then a barber was passing the door, and he called him in to shave him. While he was being shaved he asked the barber to shave off his eyebrows; but just as one eyebrow had been shaved off, he jumped up in anger and shouted, 'What are you doing? You have shaved off my eyebrow! How am I going to see my friends during the New Year? Come, we will go to see the magistrate about this!' The barber was frightened and paid him three hundred cash to patch up the matter. The wife seeing that he had only one eyebrow, remarked, 'You have got your money for New Year's eve, but you should have asked him to shave off both eyebrows. You don't know how ridiculous you look.' 'Ah, no! Ah, no!' replied the rogue, 'we have to pass another festival yet. I am keeping the other eyebrow for the fifteenth of January.'"

The teller of the story had taken a piece of paper, wetted it with his tongue, and stuck it over one eyebrow. To everybody's surprise, Mulan not only laughed with them, but she said, "Tell us another."

"No, no," said the fellow. "I refuse. The bride has already smiled, and now she is asking me to be funny again. This is like playing a football game when the goalkeeper himself comes out and helps put the ball in. It is no game any more. I give up."

But the company insisted on his complying with the bride's wish, and so he began again:

"There was a man who was extremely absent-minded. One day he had a stomach-ache and he went to a vacant lot under a tree to relieve himself. He had placed his fan on a branch, and when he got up and saw the fan, he was delighted and said, 'Whoever left a fan in this place?' Very happy at having found a fan, he started to go away and then stepped upon his own excrement. 'Good gracious!' he exclaimed. 'Whoever was suffering from diarrhea and has dirtied such a public place?'"

Mulan burst into laughter in spite of herself, and Sunya said, "Old Chiang, I think you are best at imitating animal sounds. Do the pig's grunt for us. Imitate the Pig Spirit for us."

327

Thereupon the young man began to pretend to be drunk like the Pig Spirit in a *Hsiyuchi* episode, and went dancing round the room and grunting. This did not amuse Mulan. Lifu knew what he should do now and said, "You see you have failed to make the bride laugh this time. Do something funnier. Imitate a donkey's bray."

Chiang was now monopolizing the show, and he put his two hands to his head like donkey's ears and went up to the bride and bridegroom and brayed like a donkey. Still Mulan did not laugh. And Lifu looked at her and said, "Bride, you should laugh. Doesn't this donkey bray very well?"

Quickly she realized that Lifu was helping her and she picked up the cue from him, and smiled and said, "Mr. Chiang, you are wonderful, and I thank you for all the trouble you have taken to entertain the party tonight."

At this sudden turn the company was taken by surprise. What the bride said seemed to turn the tables upon the joker, and he walked away, shaking his head, feeling that he had made a fool of himself to entertain the bride, and now she had thanked him for it! This was an anticlimax, and no one tried to be funny any more. As Tungyu went away to see the theatrical performance outside, he said to his brother, "Never since we were born have we seen a bride teaser teased by the bride. This is really a modern girl!"

The guests dispersed, but still the bride and bridegroom had to wait for any possible guests who might want to come and see the bride. When Sunya's classmates had gone, he thanked Lifu for his help, and Mulan also said, "Thank you, Brother Lifu," and they laughed together at the discomfiture of the joker.

Lifu excused himself, saying his mother and sister were waiting to go home. Guests were now gradually leaving; but music was still heard and from the window Mulan could see the garden still brightly lighted. It was past midnight when the noise subsided and Brocade and the bride's companion assisted the bride to undress, and then asked the bride and groom to retire, locking the door behind them.

During the "joining cups" ceremony in the afternoon, Mulan had had a short talk with Sunya. Between him and her, there was not the embarrassment of the usual bride and groom left suddenly alone with each other as perfect strangers.

So now the first thing Mulan did was to take off her tight-fitting shoes, and bend down to rub her feet. Sunya watched, smiling.

328

"What are you looking at?" she demanded.

"I am looking at you, *Meimei*," he said.

He came close and offered to help her. She quickly put down her stockinged feet and said, "This has nothing to do with you. I had this awful pair of new shoes."

"*Meimei*, let me rub them for you," he pleaded.

She drew her forefinger across her face and said half blushing and half winningly, "Be ashamed!" But when he bent down to rub her feet, she kicked them for a moment and then submitted. When Sunya securely held Mulan's feet in his hands, he said, "How now? I've got you."

Her heart was beating hard. "Do you remember the first day we met in the boat on the Grand Canal?" she asked.

"Yes, and do you remember when we visited Taishan at our home in Shantung, and how we quarreled about 'your distinguished mountain' and 'my miserable mountain?'"

He rose and led her to the bed, and they continued to talk. They hardly slept before it was daybreak.

. . .

Mulan rose a happy bride. The bride's companion rushed to offer congratulations. It was to be another busy day. She had to "serve tea" to all her new relatives in the Tseng home as formal introduction to the family, beginning with the grandmother; and each elder must give her a present on the tea tray in token of the first meeting. There would be feasting that day at noon for guests who could not be accommodated on the first day; and in the evening, a dinner was to be given to the bride's entire family, known as the "meeting of relatives."

In the afternoon, Mulan seized advantage of a moment of leisure to take a nap in her bridal chamber. She needed some sleep, but hardly had she dozed off when she heard Brocade outside, whispering with a maid. Brocade tiptoed into the room, and Mulan heard her go out again and whisper that she was asleep.

"Is there anything, Brocade?" Mulan called, and Brocade came in and said, "Damask is outside and says that grandmother is in a very happy mood, with the whole family gathering around her. The bridegroom is also there. Grandmother sent me to see if you were doing anything. She would like you to come. I saw you were asleep and dared not wake you. But you have hardly slept."

"I was only dozing. How could I really sleep?" replied Mulan. "What time is it?"

"It is about four. Our family will come for dinner at five. And there is a maternal aunt who has come with her grandchild to see the bride."

"What maternal aunt?" asked Mulan.

"I haven't seen her. I hear that she is a cousin of the *Taitai* in this family, living near Peking," replied Brocade.

Mulan sat up and hurriedly began to get ready. Damask appeared now at the door, with Little Joy smiling shyly and not daring to come in.

"Come in, Damask and Little Joy," said Mulan. "Why aren't you attending upon your mistress?"

"Little Joy begged me to come with her to see the bride's watch that sings the hours," Damask explained.

"She also wants to see it herself," said Little Joy. "Is it true? Mistress Chien (Cassia) was telling us about it."

Mulan asked Brocade to show the maids the gold watch that struck the hour and the quarters on a tiny bell when it was pressed, and the maids were fascinated.

"Mistress Chien was telling Grandmother how the bride teased the bride teasers last night and everybody was greatly amused," said Little Joy.

"Is Second Mistress there?" asked Mulan.

"No," replied Little Joy. Now they were ready, but Little Joy would not let go of the watch and insisted on Mulan's taking it to show it to the grandmother.

When Mulan came to the grandmother's room, almost all of the family were there, so that the room was quite packed. The grandmother was reclining on her couch, with her maid Damask standing near her, while sitting opposite her on the same couch was an old woman between sixty and seventy, dressed in a poor woman's best, still looking very strong, like so many country women. Her grandson, a boy of ten, was dressed in a brand-new unwashed blue gown two inches too long for him. Mr. and Mrs. Tseng were sitting below the couch, with Cassia and Phoenix standing behind, while Mannia's mother was sitting on the other side, with Mannia standing behind her and Snow Blossom behind both. Mulan had been formally introduced to the family in the morning, and this was an informal family gathering. The maids standing outside had announced her coming, and there was already a great stir in the room, and the grandmother had asked Damask to assist her to sit up.

"You don't have to do that, Mother," said Mrs. Tseng.

"She is the bride," said the grandmother. "Today I pay her respect as a bride, and afterward she will pay me respect by serving me and running the household well and giving birth to boys and girls. If this family's affairs are not in the hands of my granddaughters-in-law, in whose hands will they be?"

As Mulan entered she was greeted by the laughing old grandmother. "My child, come and meet your maternal aunt from the country."

"I am sorry I am late," said Mulan, as she looked about and smiled at the entire family. She was wearing now an embroidered pink jacket with close-pleated skirt in cloud and wave design, and looking more slender than in her formal wedding dress. On her chest was a beryl pendant beautifully carved into a monkey and two longevity peaches, instead of the diamond brooch she had worn the day before. She went up to the couch and bowed first to the grandmother and then to the old aunt.

"This is your maternal aunt, my cousin-sister," said Mrs. Tseng. "You have never met her."

Brocade had followed with a tray holding a cup of tea and crystal sugar, and Mulan took it and served it to the new aunt.

"Auntie," said Mulan, making her formal address. The old woman fumbled in her jacket pocket and took out a small red paper package containing two new silver dollars and put it on the tray, saying, "Really, my niece, you look like a dough doll that people buy at the New Year."

Mulan handed the tray to Brocade and paused, not knowing exactly what to do next. The old aunt took out a pair of spectacles, and putting them on said, "My niece, don't go away. Let me look at you." Holding her hand and looking her all over, the old aunt said, "I heard Old *Taitai* say that you went to school and could read and write. It is my cousin's luck to have such a learned daughter-in-law. Come, let me look at what you are wearing on your chest. Omitabha! Is this real jade? Even the Dragon King's daughter has not such fine jewels!"

The grandmother said, "Don't worry about this granddaughter-in-law of mine having no jewels!"

Holding the bride's hand, the country aunt now began to examine

331

her rings and armlets. Touching a bracelet of deep green emerald, she exclaimed, "I am afraid you can't find a pair like this in the whole jewel street of Peking. I consider my eyes lucky to have seen such things today. Hsiaofo," she said to her grandson, "you must study hard. In future you may become an official and marry a bride as prettily dressed as your cousin-sister."

Damask whispered in the grandmother's ear, and the grandmother said, "My good granddaughter-in-law, show me your gold watch."

Mulan took it from her pocket and gave it to the grandmother, and Damask showed her how to press it and make it ring. At the sound of the chime the grandmother was delighted and turned it around and said, "Those foreigners don't know propriety, but they do make clever things."

The country aunt was aghast when her grandson pushed forward to see the watch, and she shouted to him, "Don't touch it. If you break it, you can't pay for it with a hundred piculs of millet and beans."

"Never mind, let him see it," said Mulan and offered it to him, but he dared not take it and withdrew his hands in fear.

"Let me see it," said Mrs. Tseng, and Mulan gave it to her mother-in-law, and the children rushed to see it.

"Sit down here," said Mrs. Tseng to the bride, beckoning her to a seat near her.

"How dare I sit, when Eldest Sister-in-law is standing?" said Mulan. So Mannia sat down and the grandmother said, "This is an informal party at home. Let everybody be at ease and not stick to ceremony." So Mulan also sat down. The watch was carefully passed from hand to hand, and even the other maids came to see the curiosity.

"In the twenty-sixth year of Kuanghsu," said the country aunt; "when the foreign soldiers robbed the palace, there were many people who saw strange foreign self-sounding clocks! But I have never heard of such a rare treasure as this. It must come from the palace. I wonder how many hundred years old it is." Mulan explained that her father had bought it in Singapore.

The grandmother thought of Suyun and asked why she was not there.

"I think she has a headache," Chinya explained.

"Ask her to come. The whole family is here. Say that I ask her," said the grandmother.

Suyun had been sitting in her room with a headache, which she said was brought about by the activities of the wedding day. But the truth was that she had a headache because she felt her position as the richest daughter-in-law of the house was being threatened. Her home was richer than Mulan's, but not every rich family was as extravagant with a daughter's wedding.

Now she appeared, to everybody's surprise, plainly dressed and without any jewels.

"This is my second granddaughter-in-law," said the grandmother to the country aunt. "She is the daughter of New the Minister."

Suyun was surprised to find a wrinkled old country woman in the room, and she barely acknowledged her presence and took a seat below.

"Is her father New, the God of Wealth?" asked the country aunt.

"Exactly," said the grandmother. "Do you also hear of his name in the country?"

"Do I, indeed!" the old aunt exclaimed. "There is not a person in or out of Peking who does not hear of New, the God of Wealth, and Grandmother Ma! They say they have cellars of melted gold and silver. Even their gatekeeper is worth tens of thousands of dollars and owns several pawnshops in the city and land in the country. The year before last, on the gatekeeper's mother's birthday, even high court officials had to give her presents. How is it that all the richest girls marry into our family?"

Suyun felt complimented although she did not know what to make of the reference to their gatekeeper. All eyes were turned on her but she said nothing. Mannia who was sitting next above her passed the watch to her, saying, "This is the bride's watch. We were looking at it," and she pressed the spring and the chime rang.

"Yes, it is good to play with," Suyun said looking bored, and not even lifting her hand to receive the watch; and Mannia, rebuffed, took it across the room and returned it to Mulan, who regretted that she had brought it. But the father had not examined it yet and now he began to play with it, making it ring again and again.

"This is very good," he said. "Old people who cannot sleep at night can press it and tell the time without lighting the lamp."

"If you like it, Father," said Mulan, "it shall be yours, and I will ask my father to get another from Singapore."

"I was only making a remark," said the father and passed it back, but Mulan stood up and with two hands presented it to the mother, saying, "Let this be my humble present to you Old People."

"I have already had your presents," said the mother.

"But take this as a token of gratitude to you both for saving my life when I was a child."

"Let us receive it," said Mr. Tseng to his wife. "She can have another one bought."

"Here is a father-in-law receiving a bribe in public," said the grandmother in fun. "Little Number Three, I won't allow you to bully her. This marriage of yours is a match decreed by Heaven." The company looked at Sunya and he merely smiled.

"Old Ancestor," said Cassia, "allow me to say something plainly. If this new bride of Sunya's can be bullied by her husband or anybody else, I will cut off my head to be a stool for you to sit upon. Old Ancestor, you should rather ask Mulan not to bully Little Number Three. You did not see how she made the bride teaser lose face last night."

"Tell us how you did it, my good granddaughter-in-law," said the grandmother.

"Don't believe her, Grandmother," said Mulan. "I merely thanked the young man for his trouble. Don't listen to Mistress Chien. My position here is the youngest granddaughter-in-law. Above are the parents and still higher are you, Old Grandmother, and below there are the husband and elder brother-in-law and sisters-in-law and husband's younger sisters. If I dared bully anybody, would there be anything called family order any more?"

"You hear how she talks," said Cassia.

"But what she says has reason in it," said the grandmother, greatly pleased. "True eloquence consists in being right." Turning to the father, she said, "My son, now all my grandsons are married and the family is happily united. You ought to say a few words to the young people on the principles of making a home."

So the father began with a happy smile: "Mannia, you have now been in our house for five years and I have no fault to find with you, thanks to your mother's training. Chinya and Sunya, you are both married now. Both of the daughters-in-law come of good families and are well-educated, perhaps even better educated than you are. We parents are extremely satisfied. This family is now in the hands of you young people, and we old people will soon retire. The principles of

334

making a home are all contained in the two words *jen* (forbearance) and *jang* (yielding). I was glad to see, for instance, that Mulan gave up her watch; it is not the watch, but the principle of *jang* or giving in and considering others. You daughters-in-law have been well taught at home, and I need not remind you that your first duty is to help your husbands. The better educated a girl is, the better manners she ought to show at home. Otherwise book learning is only detrimental to one's character. Serve your mother and serve your husbands. In helping your husbands, you are serving me."

The speech was well-put and restrained, but the contrast was inevitable; Suyun was morose and hard to please while Mulan had already won the hearts of the family and the servants by her cheerfulness and generosity as well as her natural charm.

Mulan's family now arrived for the "meeting of relatives," and the company went out to the parlor outside to receive them. Ailien went up to Mulan and asked, "How much does the watch cost?"

"I don't know. My father bought it for me," replied Mulan.

"If you are going to buy another one, can you ask your father to buy one for me?"

"Of course, if you really like it."

Suyun, who was standing near, said to Ailien, "If you want to buy it, you will have to buy two—one for yourself and one for your future father-in-law. Otherwise you will have to order one again from Singapore at your wedding and won't that be troublesome?"

Mulan heard Suyun make this sarcastic remark, but forbore to reply, pretending not to hear.

Mulan's family did not stay long, for it was understood that the "invitation to dinner" was a mere formality, and they were not expected to eat the food. Her parents were greatly complimented on the good manners of their daughter, and Mochow also was very much admired by all the Tseng relatives.

· ·.

The fourth day was the day for the bride and groom to visit the bride's home and for the bridegroom to be entertained by her family. They had to get up early and reach the house before sunrise, as was the custom, in connection with an old superstition about the bride not seeing the "home roof," based no doubt upon some play on words that is now forgotten. It was to be a small home party. Mulan

335

was happy to see her own home again, although she had left it only three days ago, and she was very glad to see Afei, of whom her husband Sunya had also become very fond.

That night after dinner, there was to be the promised fireworks display. Afei seemed to have made himself the sponsor and exponent of this display. He talked about it the whole day and watched the pyrotechnist set up the high pole on the west of the house near the temple ground. It was thought that the orchard at the back was too small and too full of trees which would obstruct the view, and Mulan's father wanted this to be a show for the whole neighborhood. The wedding was well known, and rumors about the special fireworks had gone about, so that at seven o'clock the alleys all round were jammed with people, and some even sat perched on the temple wall.

The series of different fireworks were arranged on horizontal bars like sailyards extending from a wooden pole about twenty feet high. The fuses were so timed and connected that once the first spark was set the scenes followed one another automatically. Before the display started, it looked like a number of packages of paper and folded bamboo frames suspended on the yards; yet these had to be so arranged and protected from sparks that they should not catch fire and burn before their time. At the top of the pole was a fairy stork, which started the show by emitting from its mouth a flame which shot high into the sky and then with an explosion broke into a cascade of falling stars of gold and purple. Then followed nine successive shooting rockets, which were called "Nine Dragons Entering the Clouds."

"This is not the best," said Afei. "There is the Rotating Monkey to come next."

True it was, for suddenly there sprang up from one of the bamboo frames the shape of a red monkey lighted from within and whizzing around by the force of its backfire, spreading from its buttocks a circle of hissing sparks, so that the faces of the women and children standing near the pole were suddenly lighted.

"That's the monkey passing urine!" cried Afei triumphantly.

Next a great green watermelon burst open, scattering sparks and making a succesion of small explosions. Redjade put her hands over her ears in fear, and Afei said, "That is nothing to be afraid of. After this comes the grapes." Afei seemed to have memorized the whole sequence. When the last cinders from the watermelon were dying out, out dropped indeed a cluster of purple and white grapes, suddenly

336

brightening the scene with a silent glow. Everybody gasped and enjoyed the beauty, watching the resinous stuff gradually burning out and dropping to the ground.

After this came the "dropping peaches" and a rotating wheel turning by its own force on the rocket principle, and then came the most beautiful scene of all. All of a sudden a seven-storied paper pagoda five feet long sprang from its frame and hung down, every story lighted from within. Two or three silent scenes followed, which spread thick clouds of colored smoke. Then came the "quick-opening lotus" and the "slow-opening lotus." Then "darting mice" were let loose in mid-air in the form of small colored flames which fell to the ground darting and wriggling in all directions and creating great excitement in the inner circle before they died away. After these came various lighted tableaus such as "Eight Fairies Holding the Longevity Peach" and "Seven Saints Subduing the Demon," with the Red Demon burning up in smoke. There were pastoral scenes and scenes of houseboats and vermilion towers with ladies sitting in them. The display ended with "Three Successive Promotions" in the form of a great rocket which gave out three successive explosions high in the air. When this was finished, the crowd went away, regretting that the end came so soon.

Redjade enjoyed the last tableaus so much that every time one burned out, she was ready to cry. "Don't burn it! Why burn it? I want to look at it forever." When the show was over, she asked disappointedly, "Is it finished?"

"It is finished," said Afei. "Of course fireworks must be finished sooner or later."

"Then I don't want to look at fireworks any more," said Redjade.

Now Afei took Redjade away, and Sunya said to Mulan, "Look at that little cousin-sister of yours. She looks so tragic. She is too sensitive." Indeed Redjade looked extremely tragic as she stood near the pole and gazed at the empty scaffold, with one or two unburnt string ends dangling in the air, in place of the towers and houseboats and gaily dressed figures that had been conjured up and made real to the child's mind by the pyrotechnist's magic, and were now completely vanished.

All the time, the pyrotechnist, who was an old man, with his queue tied around his head, had sat smoking his pipe, very pleased with his work and enjoying it as much as any child. Afei went up to speak to him and led him to see the bride. Mulan complimented the old man on his work, but found that since he was from Fukien he had difficulty in understanding her language. Afei, who had picked up some Fukien words among the Chinese in the South Seas, translated for him. Then Sunya took out two dollars and gave them to him, and he bowed low to thank the bridegroom and bride, and was delighted. Sunya asked him how he learned the art, and the old man said that his family had practiced it for a living for the last three generations.

So ended the celebration of the wedding of Mulan. But Redjade clamored for paper lanterns that would burn forever.

BOOK TWO

TRAGEDY IN THE GARDEN

Those who dream of the banquet wake to lamentation and sorrow. Those who dream of lamentation and sorrow wake to join the hunt. . . . This is a paradox. Tomorrow a sage may arise to explain it; but that tomorrow will not be until ten thousand generations have gone by. Yet you may meet him any day just around the corner.

From the essay on "Relativity" by Chuangtse.

CHAPTER XXII

*I*N THE year 1911 the Revolution broke out and the Manchu dynasty collapsed.

The Revolution was immediately successful because dissatisfaction with the Manchu rule was rife and universal. The first gun was fired on August 19 at Wuchang. Between September 1 and 10, there were outbreaks in seven provinces in rapid succession, to be followed by further uprisings in still other provinces. Each time victory was easy and immediate. Manchu viceroys in the provinces were beheaded and the Chinese governors were either arrested by their officers or went over to the Republican cause. The system of Manchu viceroys supervising or checking against Chinese governors had decayed, so that in some provinces the two positions were combined in one person, and the distinction between the two was not rigidly adhered to. The abject, conciliatory edicts issued by the Imperial House failed to satisfy the people. It issued hurriedly the long-promised and long-overdue Constitution in Nineteen Articles for which the Chinese people had fought for the last ten years; it pardoned the revolutionists; it allowed people to cut off their queues; it issued an "edict of self-condemnation." But all to no avail. That old woman, the Empress Dowager, had long since overdrawn the credit of imperial prerogatives with fantastic composure, unconscious of impending ruin, and now the baby Emperor had to pay. In fifty-four days armistice was declared between the Imperial and Republican Armies, and negotiations began for the abdication of the Emperor.

On November the sixth, Sun Yat-sen, father of the Chinese Republic, arrived in Shanghai from America by way of Europe. Four days later he was elected President of the Republic. A resolution was passed to adopt the Western calendar, which was to begin on the thirteenth of the old November as January 1 of the First Year of Republic (1912), celebrated by the formal inauguration of Sun-Yat-sen as President. Forty-two days later, the Manchu Emperor abdicated, and the Empire was at an end.

The Revolution, as all revolutions do, swept into the background a generation and a class and unhinged strong established interests. Most of all the rich and poor Manchus suffered. In order to keep up their old standard of living, Manchu princes began to sell their possessions, with the former Imperial House itself taking the lead. The wives and daughters of formerly prominent Bannermen, the descendants of the Manchu conquering army of 1644, began to take work as domestic servants. The poorer Bannermen, who had received their monthly stipends of rice and money from the Tsungjenfu, were left completely destitute. Too indolent to work, too gentle to steal, too ashamed to beg, and withal talking the most gracious and cultivated mandarin, they were a truly parasitic society of people who had been fed by the Imperial House and had not known work for the past two hundred and seventy years. The Bannermen constituted a real leisure class, suddenly fallen upon evil days. As the saying goes, when the big tree falls, the monkeys disperse. There was no racial antagonism against the Manchus as individuals, for the Manchus, being softened and weak and always polite, had fitted perfectly into the Chinese pattern. They had adopted the Chinese culture and were racially hardly distinguishable from the Chinese except by their women's dress. Now Manchu girls were all too glad to marry Chinese. The younger men took to pulling rickshaws. But their poverty was stark. Sometimes several members of a family wore the same suit by turn; while one of them was out, the others would sleep naked in bed waiting until he could come back and let them have their turns.

Here is one story of such a derelict of the Revolution. A Bannerman had spent his last copper in a tea house for a pot of tea and a sesame cake. When the cake was eaten, his appetite was not satisfied. He saw in the chinks of the tea table some sesame seeds that had fallen. Being afraid to be seen digging for the stray seeds, he pretended to mumble to himself in an angry mood, and then all of a sudden with a curse, struck the table very hard. Looking at the seeds that jumped out, he took them up and looked at them and put them in his mouth casually, saying, "I didn't think they were sesame seeds." The noise of the blow on the table had attracted the attention of a person at the next table, who saw his queer movements and knew he was too poor to pay for another cake. The man came over, and, picking up some remaining seeds and scrutinizing them in the same curious manner, said, "I didn't think they were *not* sesame seeds."

Just then the Manchu's daughter appeared and said, "Mother wants to go out and has no trousers to wear and she asks you to come home."

"What? No trousers?" shouted the Manchu in his best dignified manner. "Can't she open the big red trunk?"

"Father, you forget," said the child, "the big red trunk was pawned before the Dragon-Boat Festival."

"Then in the mother-of-pearl inlaid cabinet," said the embarrassed father.

"Father, you forget. The cabinet was pawned before last New Year."

This was what is known as "killing a landscape." Shamefaced, he walked out of the teashop with his daughter, while the other customers laughed at him.

But Manchus were not the only ones affected. The whole class of Peking mandarins went into retirement from official life. These helpless creatures had lost all their social and political bearings and found themselves confronted with a new social order and a loosening moral code which they cursed and with a younger generation which they were unable to understand. The more well-to-do had saved enough for a life of comfort. Some bought modern villas in the foreign concessions of other cities. Others, more reluctant to attract attention, went to live in common red-brick terrace houses in the alleys of the concessions, hiding their hoarded wealth, although some found it impossible to resist keeping a modern automobile because of its sheer ease and lazy comfort. Those who could afford it hired tall, husky Russians as chauffeurs or bodyguards. Some of the more practical-minded invested in business. A few were perennial seekers after political jobs, to whom taking even a short term of office was like a puff of opium for an addict, and to whom being an official and finding ways and means of feathering one's nest was the only conceivable activity natural to a "scholar." These heaven-born seekers of official power gradually dribbled back into office, corrupting the "Republican" regime from within and making it into the mockery of government that it was from 1911 to 1926.

Mulan's own home was not affected. It takes something worse than a revolution to shake a Chinese business in tea and medicine. Tea is tea and herbs are herbs, whether under a republic or a monarchy. Mulan learned later, that before the Revolution her father had sent

343

another hundred thousand dollars to the revolutionists in the South Seas. This was a strain upon his cash, but his business remained the same. When the Revolution came, he was one of the first to cut off his queue.

There was, however, a change in her husband's family. For Mr. Tseng, the stout-hearted Confucianist, the Revolution spelled the end of the world. Not that he minded the overthrow of the Manchu rule, but he was afraid of what would come after. He had never developed a friendship for Mulan's father because Mr. Yao was reformist, while he himself was a staunch supporter of all that was old in thought and social manners. Mulan found out soon after her marriage that he hated foreign books, foreign institutions, and foreign things, in spite of the gold watch, which he contemptuously regarded as the product of a lower class of mind—that of artisans. That foreigners produced good clever devices only showed they were good artisans who stood one step below the farmers and two steps below the scholars, and only one step above the businessmen. It did not establish their claim to a higher culture, to the things of the spirit. That was as far as his mind could see. And now the Revolution had come and a republic was set up. Imagine a country without a king! As the phrase "without a king and without a father" signified a state of individual lawlessness and social chaos, he believed—correctly—that the whole of Chinese civilization was being threatened. His stand against the foreign world was uncompromising and it remained so until a personal experience a few years later, when he was cured of diabetes by his son-in-law, a foreign-trained doctor who had married Ailien; he used a foreign medicine called "insulin" for the cure.

Now Mr. Tseng's first thought was a determination to retire, since he had made enough money to provide for the family comfortably for life. He saw a period of chaos coming and wanted to keep out of it. The official recall to power of his friend Yuan Shihkai four days after the Revolution broke out, did not make him change his mind.

. .

All this time the life of Sunya and Mulan as a young couple living in the shadow of a great household demanded many personal adjustments. Foremost among the young couple's duties was that of trying to please the parents, or "being a good son and a good daughter." But trying to please the parents on the part both of Sunya and

Mulan covered many things. Essentially, it was so to live as to help preserve the atmosphere of family order and harmony and, as the younger generation, to learn to relieve the parents of worries and the ordinary responsibilities of the household, both domestic and external.

Although Mulan was the youngest daughter-in-law, she had very soon gained Mrs. Tseng's confidence. Mrs. Tseng had been disappointed in Suyun, who looked out for herself and her husband well enough, but refused to take on responsibilities outside her own courtyard. Mannia, the eldest daughter-in-law, was not the type to rule over others, whether women or men servants, and she had no business ability. She was constantly afraid of offending people, even the maids, and some of the servants did not listen to her. Cassia therefore began to divide her responsibilities more and more with Mulan, such as assigning work to servants, keeping a watch over some of the older ones who tended to make others work for them, preventing gambling beyond bounds, settling quarrels among them, and also keeping a check on domestic expenses reported by the servants. The routine was easy, and Mulan generally spent the greater part of her mornings with Mrs. Tseng or with Cassia, assigning work and discussing social engagements and obligations toward other families. She had been used to this at her own home, and what differences there were, such as new relationships of the Tsengs, she soon learned and remembered. Ruling a household with twenty or thirty servants was like ruling a school or a country, the essential point being to get the routine going and to maintain justice and respect for authority and an always delicate balance of power among the inferiors with whom one had to work. Mulan rigidly kept Brocade out of general dealings with the household, which was also Brocade's wish, and chose instead Snow Blossom and Phoenix as her assistants.

Mulan's home training had prepared her for this difficult job of running a big household, and she had a realistic sense of humor which made it easier. She knew more things were wrong than she openly took notice of. For one thing, she did not want the household affairs to be better run than they had been run previously under Cassia. She was also more favorably situated than Cassia, for Cassia was always acting in the capacity of proxy for Mrs. Tseng, and made no important decisions by herself, while Mulan was a regular daughter-in-law and "young mistress" of the house. The head servant, a Manchu by the unusual name of Pien and a man over forty, began to fear Mulan

345

more than he feared Cassia, because when there were slight discrepancies in the accounts, Mulan always smiled enough to show him that she was not fooled, but did not say a word. Pien told Mr. Fang, the old teacher, and he told Mrs. Tseng one day in Mulan's presence, that the one he most feared was the Third Mistress, and Mulan said, "If he fears me, it's all right. If he does everything according to the rules, he has no need to fear me. Who is not trying to provide for his family and children? In such a big family, one has to wink at some things." Mrs. Tseng was very pleased to find an old head upon such young shoulders, and gave Mulan more and more power. Eventually, the Tseng household would have to be left in her hands.

As for Mulan and Sunya themselves, in a marriage such as theirs children are essential, not only as an obligation to the family but even more as a fulfillment of their own relations to each other. Children supply a focus of union which would otherwise be lacking between two completely different beings. Mulan and Sunya were therefore happy when within a few months it became apparent that they might expect a child. Mulan knew that her marriage was now made right and she felt tender toward Sunya, and his boyishness was tempered by periods of gravity as he thought of his child. They were happier together than she would have once believed possible.

Somehow everyone thought that her first child would be a boy. She had so longed to be a boy herself, and there were her strong qualities of fearlessness and brilliance and independence, which it seemed must find expression in a son. Mulan herself thought so.

But when the time came the child was born a girl. The family were too intelligent to be disappointed and Mulan would not allow even any feeling of disappointment in herself. But still it was true that no great celebration was made of the child's birth, such as would have been done if it had been a boy.

The child was named Aman, and she was a year old when the Revolution broke out.

• ∴ •

Mulan displeased her father-in-law for the first time by an act of childish enthusiasm. She and her husband could not conceal their joy at the downfall of Manchu regime. When the edict was issued in October allowing the voluntary cutting off of queues, she took a pair of scissors on an impulse and cut off Sunya's queue without further ado. When Mr. Tseng learned of it, he reprimanded her for her rashness.

"My father cut off his a week ago. And we are cutting off the queue by imperial decree," said Mulan. But Mr. Tseng was silent and displeased. Chinya's queue was cut off a few weeks later, but Mr. Tseng did not cut off his until the following year, when Yuan Shihkai himself had cut off his own. Yuan became President of the Republic, because Sun Yat-sen nobly but foolishly resigned in his favor. Yet it was not Sun's fault. After the Revolution, the strong man must come.

The problem now was what Chinya and Sunya were to do. Six months after his marriage, Sunya had taken a minor office with his brother in the Ministry of the Interior. With the upset of the entire government, the brothers now stayed at home. Peking was peaceful. It was a bloodless revolution as far as the Capital was concerned, and even after the abdication, the Emperor and the imperial family were allowed to remain in the golden-roofed Forbidden City, in the very heart of the Capital, retaining the title and court ceremonies and eunuchs and palace maids within the walls of the palace, living the last traces of a fast-fading imperial dream, and only thankful that their lives had been spared. Outside the Forbidden City, the man whom the Manchu House hated was reigning supreme over China. Yuan, with the generals trained under him, now held the real military power, and it was the remnants of the forces of these Peiyang warlords that were destined to rule China for the next decade.

However superficial the governmental changes were, the Revolution nevertheless ushered in a new social era. A social revolution was a change of attitude, and this decade marked a definite break with the past. Such acts as the official adoption of the Western calendar, of Western diplomatic dress, and of a Western form of government, were tantamount to open admission that the West was better than the East. Henceforth, the conservatives were always on the defensive. It was a decade of ludicrous contrasts, between the old bottle and the new wine, between social fact and socialistic theory, between a bewildered older generation and a bewildering younger generation.

Invisibly these things affected the lives of the people in our story. The change of calendar was symbolic. We shall remember that henceforth the dates in our story refer to the Western calendar and that the

347

New Year comes on January the first instead of somewhere in the middle of February according to the Eastern reckoning.

. .

The Revolution caught the family of Suyun at the lowest ebb of their fortunes, financially and politically broken and socially disgraced, with nothing to lose, but perhaps with something to gain by the re-emergence of Yuan into power.

In the previous October, a year before the Revolution, a storm of public indignation had broken over the house of New.

The crisis arose over the defiling of a convent by Tungyu and his attempt to kidnap a nun. The popular fury was so great that all the political influence which New, the God of Wealth, could muster was of no avail to protect him. If it had been an isolated case of the misconduct of one member of the family, the incident might not have developed into a disaster for them all. As it was, the convent incident was only the signal for attack by the many previous victims of the News, seeking now their vengeance.

The New brothers, Huaiyu and Tungyu, had a power-psychosis, which their mother shared and therefore encouraged. She would not tolerate criticism of her sons. Every overt act against the law, every defiance of police authority, was construed by the Mother as renewed proof that she was the All-Powerful Grandmother Horse of Peking. She had believed, and had made her whole family believe, that she controlled the finance of the country and that her position was unshakable. She was thinking in terms of a New Dynasty of Wealth. She had only one fear in this world, and that was Buddha, or to be exact, not so much the love of Buddha as the fear of Yenlo, the King of Hell. Hence she was one of the most devout of Buddhists, and her donations to Buddhist temples gave her a feeling of security and confidence that in any emergency the invisible hand of Buddha would be on her side and would protect her, her husband, and her brood. There was no doubt that she was religious.

Some of the things her sons did she knew, and some she did not know. That they and their bodyguards broke the traffic regulations of Peking, she took for granted. Otherwise where was her "face"? A man did not rise to such power without Destiny, and traffic regulations were not intended for the Men of Destiny that her sons were. But there were worse things. The situation went so far that young women were afraid to be seen in a theater balcony seat by the young News. At least once it was established that a certain person's concubine attracted the elder son's attention and after the theater was "invited" by his bodyguard to one of his private establishments for the night. The concubine returned home the next morning, but her husband dared not breathe a word of the disgrace.

This elder son was married to a weak, obedient, and stupid girl, who never dreamed of asking where her husband went. The younger son Tungyu was unmarried and had still greater freedom of action. Each had a friend who was amply rewarded for getting new women for him. There was, however, a young and pretty daughter of a rich merchant, who proved extremely recalcitrant to Tungyu's approaches, which made him all the more determined to secure her. He went to her home, and the girl's father dared not turn him out. He began to take her out, courted her openly, and professed to have fallen in love with her, and finally made a serious promise to marry her. The girl's head was turned by the prospect of being a daughter-in-law of the News. But hardly a month after this, Tungyu was tired of her and began to run after a country girl. He had forgotten all about her, and did not even give it a thought, as being not worth the bother of a New, the chosen of God. Rich or poor, a girl was but a plaything for a night, and he was the eternal conqueror.

The forsaken girl hated him and shed useless tears. Her parents dissuaded her from committing suicide by swearing revenge. Finally, one morning when she was alone, she took a pair of scissors and cut off her hair, and decided to become a nun. The girl's father was furious to see his daughter's life ruined. Prosecution was worse than useless, and he had not the proof of promise of marriage. But he would bide his time, and he had money. Grimly he set a trap for the young rake.

He hunted Peking for the most beautiful sing-song girl, until he finally found one young and pretty, barely eighteen years old, the age of his daughter, intelligent, and like all the sing-song girls, educated in all the traditional stories of romance, heroism, friendship, and gratitude. With money he bought the girl from her "mother," and kept her in his home, treating her like a princess. After the miracles of hospitality and respect were sufficiently performed, the girl asked, in old-Chinese fashion, what was expected of her that she should receive such extraordinary kindness. The father did not reply. The next day she said again, "I am overwhelmed by this kindness without any reason. You are not raising me as a concubine. What is it? Life is precious to everybody. But short of death, I will do anything you want."

The father then told her the story of his daughter and promised her a huge reward of money if she would follow his plan. If it worked out correctly, the plan would eventually make her famous, and with such a "past" behind her, she could go back into the sing-song profession and be the most sought-after queen of that world. He worked the girl to a pitch of burning hatred for the young man and deep sympathy for his daughter. There was no danger in her part of the bargain, and she was yet young. After being pledged to absolute secrecy, she consented.

The father then sent his daughter into a nunnery in a suburb where he knew the village elders, and did his best to curry the favor of the Mother Superior by promises of large donations. In his visits, he would go round to the village elders, discreetly revealing the story of his daughter. The reputation of the News being well known in the suburb, the elders listened with sympathy and silent rage.

Next the father made friends with several servants of the New household and found out where young New was accustomed to go, including the theaters and parks he frequented. In a wine shop, over cups of *huatiao,* he extracted from a servant some stories of the inner household. Then he rented for the sing-song girl a house with a servant and fictitious parents, dressed her up and sent her to the parks and theaters with the servant. After a month or so, the wild cat took the bait. A romance developed between Tungyu and the girl, who posed as a rich family's daughter; while allowing intimacies outside, she would never permit him to follow her to her home. After three weeks of secret meetings, during which Tungyu was kept constantly excited and even believed himself to be in love for the first time, the girl one day suddenly failed to appear at their appointed place. Her servant came alone to tell him a piece of bad news. Her young mistress was in distress because her parents were arranging a match for her against her will, and she was prevented from getting away, and would try to escape in a few days and come to see him personally, or at least send him news. She begged him to be true to her and have patience. After three days, the servant appeared again to tell him that her young mistress had in despair cut off her hair and decided to enter a nunnery. Now all hope was over. If he wanted to see her, he had to go to a certain temple in the suburb of Peking, after a certain day.

At home the father now prepared to send the sing-song girl into the very temple where his daughter was, and waited for his victim. His plan was merely to involve Tungyu with a nun, a contemptible sin, which in time would be exposed by the sing-song girl herself. The Mother Superior accepted her as another pretty young fool gone wrong, and the two young nuns kept the secret to themselves.

One day in September, young New arrived at the convent in his carriage and, saying that he was a relative of the new nun, asked to see her. The sing-song girl, now given the monastic name of Huineng, came out to see him. She professed to love him still and to regret what she had done, but said that there was no other way out. But when Tungyu heard this, he said, "That is easy. You just come along with me. The people here would not dare to touch me." Seeing that he intended to take her from the convent in broad daylight, which amounted to kidnaping, Huineng told him to go and come back for her in three days.

When he was gone, she rushed to the Mother Superior and said: "Save me, Mother! Save me from that young man!"

"But he is your relative!" said the Mother Superior.

"My relative! He is the son of New, the God of Wealth. I dared not refuse to see him. It was through fear of trouble with him that my mother sent me to this place. And now he has traced me here."

"Unbelievable!" exclaimed the Mother Superior.

She thought of the incident of Huikung, the merchant's daughter, only a few months since, and said, "Sister Huikung was also ruined by this young man."

"I know, I know," said Huineng. "He wanted to take me away, but I refused, and he said he was coming back in three days to get me. What are we to do?"

The Mother Superior was worried. Defiance of the News was extremely dangerous. Yet if he really came with his men to kidnap the nun, and if she suffered it to happen, the name of her temple would be dishonored, and there would be no security for the other nuns.

The story was circulated freely within the convent that something terrible was going to happen. From the nuns, it spread to the servants of the temple, and from the servants it spread to the villagers. The idea of kidnaping a nun enraged the villagers, and the village elders who knew what had already happened to Huikung came to consult with the Mother Superior. The result of the conference was that the whole village decided to give her support, for if a nun could be kidnaped in the suburb of the capital, there was no more respect for the Emperor. They decided therefore to resist the kidnaping by force.

Toward sunset on the third day, young New appeared in his carriage, accompanied by two husky fellows, but expecting no resistance. He came in with his men and demanded to see the Mother Superior. He told her who he was and called for the surrender of Huineng.

The Mother Superior refused, saying, "It is unheard of. This is sanctified ground and I refuse to have it defiled by you, no matter who you are."

Young New then ordered his men to search the convent. The nuns raised a hue and cry, and suddenly out of dark corners came village young men, armed with carrier poles, who fought off New's assistants. Completely taken by surprise, they beat a hasty retreat and went away threatening vengeance.

The next day a messenger came from young New threatening to close down the convent and punish the villagers unless the nun was handed over to him immediately. The Mother Superior, now finding herself in deeper waters than before, pleaded for time and promised a reply in two days. She had either to fight it out or to give in and she consulted the village elders.

A man over eighty, who was a kind of patriarch of the village, spoke up and said, "I have lived eighty years and have never yet seen this happen. Mother, we started this fight with you, and we will see you through it. There is still the Emperor. I will be responsible. I am not afraid of death at this age, and I will see if New, the God of Wealth, can turn this world upside down!"

Inspired by the old man, the villagers made common cause with the temple nuns. When the time came, the Mother Superior told New's messenger to tell his master to do what he liked, but that she could not let the temple be dishonored. Meanwhile she arranged for some of her nuns to be hidden in the village, while she took Huikung and Huineng to another convent, preparing for her convent to be officially closed.

The Peking government sent men to close the convent for acts of violence against peaceful gentlemen visitors. Finding that it had been deserted, the officers went to the village with a warrant to arrest the village elders as being implicated in the disturbance of public peace. The old man offered himself, but the villagers dissuaded him and sent instead two men, a scholar and an old farmer.

A few days later, the city of Peking was greeted with a surprising parade of monks and nuns and villagers going through the streets. Posters were pasted on the gates and street corners, exposing the attempt to kidnap a nun and demanding justice in the name of the temple and the village. At the head of this most unusual procession walked the old man of eighty in a white beard. Age instinctively commanded respect, and wherever the old man stopped to talk in his slow, dignified voice, he was listened to by a great and attentive crowd. That the affair had for its villain a member of the hated family of the God of Wealth won the people's sympathy, and the crowd gathered strength as it went along. When it came to the Tienanmen Square, the crowd was a thousand strong, and soon it degenerated into a mob, shouting, "Down with the God of Wealth! Down with the Ox and Horse, Breakers of the Law!" Encouraged by their success, the nuns and villagers began to wail at the palace gate, and the voices of the nuns attracted more people, so that on that day three or four thousand must have gathered at the Tienanmen, and the story spread throughout the city with lightning speed.

Such public demonstrations before the palace gate had been common in the Sung Dynasty, but were now quite rare. The Prince Regent in the palace heard the commotion outside and was at first afraid that a revolution had broken out. Learning what it was about, he sent a eunuch out to see the monks and nuns and to find out what was their complaint. A written memorandum had been prepared, and the eunuch took it in and came out again and promised on behalf of the Prince Regent that the convent would be immediately reopened, the village elders released, and the case of the young New attended to by the Court of Law.

But the temple incident and the procession only brought public indignation against the God of Wealth to a climax. Gossipers in the tea houses of Peking talked about it for months, and the city was full of undisguised denunciation of New the Minister. The News were now frightened and kept in their house.

Now there was among the imperial censors one Wei Wu, who had

353

long contemplated an impeachment of the Minister, but had been dissuaded by his fellow censors on the ground that it was worse than useless. Stirred by the public fury, Wei Wu disguised himself as a common man and went about to the different teashops to form an idea of public opinion and to gather material. Sitting in one of the popular teashops in the East City, he heard one man say, "A hundred nuns cannot be a match against one minister. 'Officials protect officials' is the rule. You mark my word. A porcelain bowl cannot knock against an iron caldron."

Another said, "If that is the case, there is no longer king's law in this country. There was another good family girl who became a nun because she had been abandoned by young New. Who does not know what these two precious brothers are doing?"

A third said, "You had better keep your mouth shut. The house of New is not so easily shaken."

"I really don't know what those imperial censors are doing," said the second man. "Their eyes must have been pasted up with mud. I am waiting to see how this affair is settled. I hear that the Minister has been on sick leave, trying to use his influence to settle it. If it is dealt with properly, even the Peking magistrate who closed down the convent should be punished."

Wei Wu drew near to the second man and said, "Ah, it is useless for us common people to say things here. It seems those censors have stuffed their ears with wax. Who dares to pull an idol's whiskers? I hear that the elder young New specializes in abducting people's concubines for his own purposes."

"Why, it is an open secret," said the man. "He keeps a house in the West City for this purpose, and he has friends who procure women for him. At home there are still more innumerable tragedies."

"What tragedies?" asked Wei Wu.

"I hear there was a maidservant in their house who was tortured to death. After the maid died, they dared not let her parents bury her for fear they would see the wounds on her body; so they buried her in their private garden."

"You are not a spirit. How do you know what happens inside such an official's home?"

"Why, even an eggshell has cracks! The best way to prevent people from knowing a thing is not to do it. Do you think in such a house-

354

hold there is any servant who is really loyal to them? Things will leak out."

Wei Wu, the Censor, went on about his detective work. He went to the convent and talked with the nuns and villagers and got the address of the father of Huikung. In the latter he found a source of important information, and he was sent to a servant of the News, who swore to the truth of the story of the maid's murder and said that he knew the spot where she was buried.

Having made sure of his information, the Censor surveyed the situation.

Since the demonstration before the palace, most of New's official friends had kept away from him. Powerful as he was, he had not many real friends at court; for, not having acquired his degree by passing the regular examinations, he had not the usual coterie of fellow-candidates and master-examiners. Yuan Shihkai was still in political eclipse and living in retirement. Grand Councilor Wang had influence that might protect him, but he was a weak character and very old. So the Censor considered the time opportune and decided upon impeachment.

Chinya was visiting his wife's home when the bombshell fell. Old New had been frightened by the public furore; but Mrs. New was still exulting in her pride and threatening dire consequences for the wretched monks and villagers, when a servant at the gate rushed in and said, "*Laoyeh! Taitai!* Bad news! A palace official and imperial guards have come in."

Mr. New hurriedly went out to receive the official. Meanwhile another servant came to Mrs. New and reported that the house had been surrounded and guards were posted at the entrance allowing nobody to pass out. Outside, the official from the palace had turned facing south as soon as he entered the hall. He bade Mr. New get ready to receive the imperial edict. Mr. New at once knelt down facing north and heard the official read the following imperial edict:

New Szetao, unmindful of Our Imperial favors, has violated the law and abused his power. He has been accused by the censors of receiving bribes, usury, and contempt of the public statutes. Moreover, he has been accused of being negligent in supervising his home and has allowed his children to abuse their power and bully the common people, deceive family girls, and attempt to kidnap a nun. Furthermore, he has been accused of the murder of a maidservant and secret burial of her corpse. New Szetao is hereby deprived of his office and all his ranks, and shall be detained together with his sons, Huaiyu and Tungyu, to await investigation. The News' house shall be guarded until the murder is solved.

After reading the edict, the official ordered the arrest of New Szetao. New was struck dumb with terror. His body was a lump of flesh from which the backbone seemed to have disappeared. The guards rolled up their sleeves and came and laid hands on him and pulled him up, and his official cap and gown were taken away.

"Where are your sons?" the official demanded.

"They are inside, awaiting your orders, sir," babbled New, his voice shaking. Nobody had thought he could be such a coward, or such a dismal figure. The official ordered the sons to be brought and they soon appeared and submitted to arrest. The father and sons were escorted out of the house to a place of detention with the palace guards.

To make a long story short, New the Minister was treated with some clemency through the intercession of Wang, the Grand Councilor. He was deprived of his rank, but was set free on account of his repentance and his old age. His property in Peking was confiscated, including his money shops, but his property elsewhere was spared him. The elder son was sentenced to three months' imprisonment for allowing his servant to torture a maid to death and refusing burial by the maid's parents and for illegal burial in his private home. The blame for the murder, which was interpreted as manslaughter in New's favor, was placed upon a manservant, who was sentenced to exile and hard labor for life. The women of the New family, luckily, for them, were spared, following the principle of clemency in dealing with Mr. New, for if the latter had been executed, the wives and unmarried daughters of such a criminal would have been "confiscated as official property" and sold at auction.

The younger son, Tungyu, was beheaded for the double crime of deceiving a family girl and abandoning her, and of attempting to kidnap a nun and defiling temple ground. He was a victim of a conspiracy, but he got only what was his due. Complete streets were emptied, and half of Peking, high and low, men and women, went to see the execution of a son of the hated New, the God of Wealth, so that on that day at least thirty thousand people were gathered at Tienchiao and a dozen children were injured or trampled to death.

The nun Huineng returned to her fictitious "parents." The nuns Huikung and Huineng had been left the option of voluntarily returning to their parents, and were urged to do so, now that the wrong on them was avenged and they needed have no fear of the young New. In the fury of the general tempest and the excitement about the exhuming of the murdered maid's corpse, no one probed too closely into Huineng's origins, and it was only after several years that the true story came to be known.

When the Revolution came, therefore, the power of the News was already gone, and they were living in social disgrace on what was left of their property in Tientsin and elsewhere. The coming into power of Yuan again in the first year of the Republic raised Mr. New's hopes of restoration to power. But even with the best of intentions, Yuan found it impossible to help him. It was some years later that through the influence of Suyun's husband, the elder brother got a minor job in a government bureau.

357

CHAPTER XXIII

No one felt a social decline more keenly or more pathetically than Suyun. She was morose and unhappy in the Tseng home, partly because of an imagined atmosphere of gossip behind her back, and partly because she was disappointed in Chinya. Hence she was living most of the time with her family in Tientsin, although Chinya had got a job in the new Republican government in Peking. Since she was bearing no great responsibility in the home, every time she asked for permission to go to Tientsin, Mrs. Tseng consented. At Tientsin, her family were beginning their new life, and she was beginning hers. In that great port, swarming with a humanity uprooted, she felt the fascination of a new kind of gold worship, the thrill of new and modern luxuries, the gaiety of dance halls, theaters, motor cars, and new fashions, the convenient obliteration of all old associations and standards and the setting up of a simple standard of social success—anyone who has money is respected, and anyone who is respected has money—with which she was in instinctive sympathy. She felt stimulated every time she came to Tientsin and remained as long as she could, and when she returned she found Peking dull and depressing by comparison. As she grew more and more used to the treaty port life, she began more and more to think of her Peking home as a prison.

When the storm broke over the News, Mrs. Tseng had forbidden her servants to discuss or mention the affair, in order to make it easier for Suyun. Mulan, too, had tried to be kind during the period when her family was in trouble, and she had urged her husband Sunya to visit Huaiyu in prison. She herself went with Mrs. Tseng to visit Suyun's home. But these visits only caused misunderstandings and were resented by Suyun. Not only did she imagine that Mulan was inwardly glowing with triumph beneath her outward kindness; but every visit of the Tsengs brought forth more unpleasant details which made it look like prying into the New family affairs. Old Mrs. New, unable or unwilling to accept her defeat, was constantly in a bad temper. She refused to believe that the News, the Men of Destiny, could be permanently disgraced and remain fallen. She still believed in herself, her son Huaiyu, and her Destiny; and she promised terrible vengeance upon the Imperial Censor and others who had turned against them. If there was one field in which she was sure of herself, it was politics.

"Let alone!" said her husband. "We can consider ourselves lucky to have got away so well, thanks to the Prince Regent's clemency in consideration of our past service."

"Huh!" replied Mrs. New. "I never thought you were so useless. If it were not for me, you would still be a Shantung money-shop owner."

Old Mr. New felt beaten and tired. Shorn of his former pretensions, he was now the same good simple man that he always had been underneath. Either tired or broken in spirit or ashamed to see people, he took to bed for six or seven days at a time, uttering groans. Mrs. New hated to see such a weak, helpless husband, and a daughter-in-law, Huaiyu's wife, who was weeping all the time. Only her daughter Suyun still had some pride. Huaiyu's wife was a weak and rather stupid woman, and with her husband in prison she felt entirely helpless. She had done well for the family by giving birth to one grandchild after another—all boys. These were named Kuochang, Kuotung, Kuoliang, Kuoyu, that is, the "Glory of State," the "Beam of State," the "Girder of State," and the "Blessing of State," names that suggested the high hopes which Mrs. New had placed in them, although the last two, who were twins, were still in their swaddling clothes.

On one of Mulan's visits, she happened to come upon a scene in which Mrs. New was scolding Huaiyu's wife, who was weeping silently with her children by her side. Her father, an educational inspector of Hupeh, had deposited fifty thousand dollars in New's money shop, and three days after the crash had come to withdraw it, since their shops were still operating in Tientsin and elsewhere. Mrs. New had refused, and there was great unpleasantness of feeling. Mrs. New was now wreaking her anger upon the defenseless daughter-in-law who did not know how to reply.

"Relatives are worse than strangers," Mrs. New thundered at her. "To throw a stone at a man after he has fallen into a well! Where is his conscience? You forget how we helped your father whenever he was in need of money. And now his own son-in-law is in prison, and he comes to press me for money. I never knew my son would have such a heartless, ungrateful father-in-law."

"This is what my father does. It has nothing to do with me," was all Huaiyu's wife could say.

Just then a servant announced that a contractor by the name of Chang wanted to see Mrs. New. She had forgotten this contractor and did not know what he wanted, but she knew that any one who came to her door these days could not be on a pleasant mission.

The man appeared, ushered in by the gatekeeper. At other times, he could not have found it so easy to get in. But times had changed, and the gatekeeper had taken it upon himself to let him in, and the contractor had promised him a share if he should succeed in getting his money. Chang was a common business man, dressed in an ordinary business suit, for now he had not even taken the trouble to put on his best to come and see the former God of Wealth.

"You muddlehead, Old Tsai," said Mrs. New to the gatekeeper. "You did not ask whether I wanted to see anybody."

"*Taitai,*" said the gatekeeper, "he said he *must* see you."

"You old dolt!" exclaimed the mistress. "So you admit a person simply because he says he *must* see me? The master is ill in bed, and there are lady guests here. You servants are all alike. Not one of you is loyal when the master is in trouble."

Mrs. Tseng and Mulan, who were visiting, retired now with Suyun and Huaiyu's wife into the next room, since there was business to discuss.

Turning to the contractor, Mrs. New demanded, "What do you want?"

"I want my money," replied Chang.

"What money? I have paid you already."

The contractor spoke in his polite but firm business manner. Showing her a piece of paper, which was the contract, he said, "*Taitai,* three years ago I contracted to build that house in Fangchia Hutung for thirty-five thousand dollars. When I built a house for His Excellency New, do you think I dared make a cent? Then you paid me twenty-seven thousand and called it paid in full. When you powerful ladies said so, what could I do? I lost seven or eight thousand dollars on that job in labor and material. You promised to give me contracts for government buildings, and I regarded that little sum as my tribute to His Excellency. After that, not only did I get not a single contract from you, but I was not even permitted to see you when I came, and Big-Ear Wang got all the jobs. I don't want government contracts any more. I want my money. Eight thousand dollars plus interest for these three years should amount to over twelve thousand dollars now. I am a business man, and cannot make tens of thousands of dollars by writing on a piece of paper like you officials."

Mrs. New refused to pay, not by arguing, but by the simple statement that she had no money, which meant that she did not intend to pay. The contractor lost his politeness and began to talk more and more loudly and even threatened legal action. Suyun was scowling inside, and it became so embarrassing that Mrs. Tseng took a hasty departure with Mulan by slipping out through another corridor. Mulan heard later from Suyun that the affair was settled by the gatekeeper's promising to advance four thousand dollars. Of this sum, the contractor actually received only three thousand.

On another visit, Mulan again came to know something which was resented by Suyun. Mulan had discovered that old Mrs. New had an illegitimate child in their house, a girl by the name of Taiyun, now eight years old. Taiyun was a very intelligent child as so many illegitimate children are, although she was not pretty as her mother had been. She had the more fleshy features and sensuous mouth of her father. But she was very active and talkative and a very devil in the house. Mrs. New's strict vigilance over her husband and forbidding him to take a concubine did not entirely prevent him from having an "affair." When she discovered it, she was furious, and compelled him to give up his mistress; and her husband, always submissive and now ashamed, obeyed like a truant schoolboy. Taiyun's mother was given three thousand dollars and sent to the south and forbidden to put her foot in Peking again under threat of dire consequences. The News were then still at the height of their power, and Taiyun's mother knew the powerful "Grandmother Horse" by reputation too well to defy her, and quietly went south, forced to give up her child. This had happened when Taiyun was only six. Now she was taught to call Mrs. New her mother, but she soon developed into a little rebel because of her surroundings.

When Yuan came back into power as President of the Republic, Mrs. New thought her chance had come, but all efforts at securing a post for her husband failed. Yuan was a great judge of men, and when he used men, he knew what was the driving motive of each—money, fame, power, or women—and he gave each his reward. But he was far from ready to blacken his new regime by using an official with such a record as Mr. New's. So Yuan merely said to his friends who spoke for Mr. New to let him "rest" for a while, which sounded very poetic. Defeated and gradually accepting the new situation, the News decided to go and live in Tientsin in the summer of 1912. Living in the foreign concession, they would make new friends, form new contacts, and be free from the atmosphere of malicious gossip.

Suyun felt this atmosphere in the Tseng home—for these things were felt, not spoken. The state of tension was increased by Suyun's attitude toward the servants. Her own maid Coldfragrance had always held aloof from the other maids, because Suyun had not encouraged her to mix and be friendly with the others. One day Coldfragrance picked a quarrel with Mrs. Tseng's maid, Phoenix, who was proud and made one, or two biting insinuations. Coldfragrance complained to her mistress; but, when Suyun came to bring the affair before Mrs. Tseng, the latter had already heard from her own maid how the altercation started and therefore refused to scold Phoenix before Suyun, who took this as another proof that she could not stand up with the others in the family.

And so Suyun often asked permission to go back to her home in Tientsin. With the grandmother on top, and the able Mrs. Tseng keeping everybody in her place in the great household, Suyun's instinct and ambition for domination were rigidly suppressed, which made her unhappy. By getting away, Suyun did not, however, cut herself off from the life of the Tseng family. Whether in ancient or in modern times, every man's life inevitably affects those of people living around him, especially those related by personal or family ties. Suyun's life influenced that of Chinya by her absences and doings at Tientsin and her new, insatiable ambitions, as much as Mulan's life influenced that of Sunya, as we shall have many occasions to hear again.

.·.

For the present, Sunya was sitting at home enjoying life, while Chinya had already secured a government job. Sunya told his father that the new government was too unsettled yet, that since there was a republic perhaps they ought not to be officials, that perhaps he could enter some other line, perhaps he wanted to study some more. As a young man of twenty-three, he was facing the usual problem of choice of professions. What he did not tell his father was that he disliked politics.

His father was himself not very enthusiastic about the republican era. It seemed that with the change of regime the whole flavor of the mandarinate had been spoiled. The new formal dress of the republican officials was ridiculous. He had submitted to the cutting of his queue as a form of indignity perpetrated upon an old man. Was he, too, if he joined the government service again, to don those ugly, fantastic pants and collars and ties and look as ridiculous as some of his old mandarin colleagues now looked? What about the foreign felt hats they were wearing with their Chinese gowns? Mr. Tseng was a cultivated esthete. To his credit, he kept his Chinese brimless silk hat to the end of his days, a hat that was in harmony with his gowns. Being used all his life to the generous, flowing lines of a Chinese gown, which gave one a leisurely, majestic gait, he conceived with horror a picture of himself wearing pants in public. It was the wearing of pants by foreign gentlemen that made them walk so fast and in so undignified a fashion like laborers and that caused them to be known as "straight-long-legs." He had seen some of the young returned students and revolutionary officials who had come up from the south, walking with canes, wearing foreign chimney hats, and talking atrocious mandarin. In his heart he despised them. He felt awkward at shaking hands—a most intimate affair, this contact of hands—when some of these young upstarts tried to shake hands with him. The very nomenclature of official titles had changed. Where were all the old associations? The literary degrees of *chuangyuan, pangyen, tanhua, hanlin, chinshih* were, of course, long gone. A cabinet minister was no longer called *langchung,* a vice-minister no longer *shihlang,* a governor no longer a *tsungtu,* and the magistrates no longer *taotai* and *fuyin.* All had been replaced by new, coarse terms containing the democratic and unromantic word "chief" —Chief of Ministry, Second Chief of Ministry, Chief of Province, Chief of District. Yes, gone were the good old days and the old mandarin! Gone were the poise, the culture, the natural dignity of the ancient scholar-officials. Gone were the red-tasseled, crystal-topped cap and the broad, belted, navy-blue official gown, the generous, square-nosed, satin, white-soled boots, the water tobacco pipe, the cadenced laughter, the graceful fingering of beards, the fine, learned literary allusions that gave charm to conversation, the polite euphemisms, the subtle circumlocutions, the smooth-running, highly rhythmic mandarin accent. In place of the cultivated mandarin had come a raw, uncultivated younger generation.

A young returned student calling himself an official of some sort came to call on him and during the conversation constantly pointed his barbaric forefinger at him. This class of officials did not even know how to talk mandarin, and in this matter the Cantonese revolutionists were the worst sinners. Even Dr. Sun Yat-sen himself pronounced the word *jen* as *"yen."* It was rumored that there was a returned student in the provisional government at Nanking, who during conferences mixed into his Chinese speech English words like "but," "so long as," and "democracy," to the discomfort of others who did not understand English. Mr. Tseng rather believed it because he had met at dinner a young man whose talk sounded to him as follows: *"Walla-walla,* what you say is not true *tkutsh frksbo; onilalala,* his *pontoyou shenshualla* is the same as yours." For a foreigner who understood only the English parts of it, it would sound as follows: "But, you see, *walla-walla-walla-walla,* but possible. On the other hand, *tati* point of view essentially *walla-walla-la-la-la."*

For this reason, Mr. Tseng and Mr. Yao had to avoid politics when they came together. The changing times liberated Mr. Yao's imagination and left Mr. Tseng untouched and unspoiled. He remained a whole mandarin, dismayed, out of touch with the times, but still proud. Mulan was certain that when the time came to lay him in his coffin, he would want to be buried in his formal mandarin cap and gown.

Since he himself was leaving the government and refused to compromise, he did not press Sunya to join the government service. He suspected, however, that Mulan had something to do with Sunya's not going into politics. Actually, Sunya was not enthusiastic about it himself. He had seen as a young man the life of the minor officials and bureaucrats in his father's office. In his eyes, this had totally deprived the officials of the glamour which people away from Peking, hearing merely the official titles, might imagine. Had his father remained in the government, he would have gone into it also, following the line of least resistance; but he certainly would have had no illusions about the glory of being an official. It was a dismal affair of fighting to get a rice bowl before getting it and fighting to keep it ever after—and that in a vitiated atmosphere of intrigue, complete cynicism, and always a little shamelessness.

One night he said to Mulan, whom he greatly adored, *"Meimei,* you know I am no good for it. I am no good for many things, but certainly no good for politics. I am no bootlicker. You should have seen how a chief of department stood at attention before father's desk and held his breath for five minutes until father looked up at him. He appeared and spoke like a mouse. People who don't know think how glorious it is to be a departmental chief, a metropolitan official. Outside he maintains a great dignity and is feared by his underlings. But I tell you this, the more severe and dignified an official is toward his inferiors, the more mouselike and cringing he is before his superiors. That is an invariable rule. That is how the fawning bootlickers get on."

Mulan interrupted. "I understand. Outside of politics a man is like a young girl of eighteen, and in politics a man is like a married daughter-in-law with babies."

Sunya smiled at Mulan's simile. "*Meimei,* that isn't always true. You keep yourself as neat as Second Sister-in-law, although she has no baby and you have."

"That depends on persons, of course," replied Mulan. "But it is true that one can't wear silk all the time when one is nursing a baby. And Brocade is such a great help. But you can't tell whether a woman is neat or not by looking at her party dress. Brocade told me that Suyun's maid told her that her mistress did not change her underwear more than once a week. Those things only a woman's husband and her maids know."

"This is just like the chief of department I was telling you about. A man wears his official dignity often as a woman wears her party dress—very good to look at when you don't look underneath. That is why I don't want to go into it. I can't cringe and fawn and flatter."

Mulan meditated. "I don't think you can flatter people," she said. "But what are you going to do?"

"What can I do?" replied Sunya. "That is really everybody's problem. There are tens of thousands of people waiting for jobs in Peking. All can't do anything, and that's why all want to be officials. You know I hated it. Every day I sat in the office and gossiped and read the papers and drank tea and signed a few papers. Be a monk for a day and strike the bell for a day—that is everybody's attitude. If father were in it, I would probably rise. Left alone, I would probably end up as a department chief, and spend my whole life kowtowing to people to keep my job. I just can't be bothered. Ambition and power and success—they are just not for me. No, *Meimei,* I am afraid you have married a man without ambition."

"Well, I suppose we shan't starve," Mulan said, and sighed. "If that is what you feel, I shall not blame you. I could see that you hated it. Then keep out of it and don't let it contaminate you. My father always said, 'Keep yourself right, and nothing that happens to you can ever be wrong.' Better change the underwear and have a single cotton gown outside, than wear silk with dirty underwear."

The phrase "cotton gown" suggested the life of the recluse. Mulan paused and suddenly said, "I will ask you a question, *Sanko.* You must answer me straight." Mulan sometimes still called her husband *"Sanko"* or "Third Brother" as a half-playful term of address, because of its sweet associations with their childhood.

"What is it?"

"Suppose one day we are poor, like the News, will you care?"

"How could that be?"

"You never can tell. I don't mean that we want to become poor. But things may happen beyond our control. Would you care?"

"Not if you and I are happy with each other. But you always have such strange ideas!" he said.

"I suppose I got them from my father," said Mulan. "When he spoke of giving up the family and becoming a monk, it always terrified me, until I got used to the idea. But it is possible. When I went out and saw the boatmen living outside the West City, I always thought I should like to be one of them. We will have one of those boats. Imagine the day when Tseng *Shaoyeh* becomes a boatman, and I, a daughter of the Yao family, become a boatwoman! My flat feet are big enough to go punting boats! I will cook and wash for you. I can cook so well!"

"You are whimsical," said Sunya. He laughed so loudly that Brocade in the outer room came in and said, "What are you laughing at?"

"I was telling him," said Mulan to her maid, "that one day we might have no money. Then he will be a boatman, and I a boatwoman. By that time, Brocade, you will be well married and have seven or eight sons and daughters. When an old friend comes, I will go up to your house and borrow a chicken and kill it for a little wine dinner. What do you think?"

"*Nainai,* you are a good joker," replied Brocade. "It is interesting to joke about being poor when you are not poor."

366

"She was saying it because she wanted me to be an official, and I said I could not," explained Sunya.

"No," said Mulan. "I was asking you whether you really meant it."

"I will tell you what I want," said Sunya. "I want 'to have a hundred thousand strings of cash tied around one's waist and ride upon a stork's back to Yangchow.'"

"*Shaoyeh* knows what is good in life," remarked Brocade.

"But there aren't such things in this world," said Mulan. "The question is whether you will have a hundred thousand strings of cash and live in Yangchow, or fly upon a stork. And if you fly upon a stork, then don't go to Yangchow. Either one or the other. Be a boatman, I say." Mulan hummed a poem she loved:

> He casts his net mid-stream his haul to take,
> She drops her line and waits her catch to make;
> When all the day's catch is 'changed again for wine,
> They paddle the empty boat home in the showers' wake.

"*Meimei*," said Sunya, "if I live long enough with you, I shall be a poet myself. I like the poem by Teng Chingyang you quoted to me the other day."

"Which one?" asked Mulan.

Sunya repeated the poem. It was this:

> We are but passing guests from who knows where?
> Say not thy home is here, thy home is there.
> It suits me—what I've got and what I've not.
> The plum-flowers bloom here, there, and everywhere.

"Do you really like that?" asked Mulan. "Then you would rather have the stork than have Yangchow. We shall then indeed be so happy visiting the famous mountains together. We can't do it now while the parents are with us. But we shall do it one day, shall we?"

Sunya was fascinated by her gaiety. "It all sounds very poetic," he said. "But who knows whether we can fulfill our wishes?"

Mulan laughed. "There is no harm dreaming and talking about it. Suppose we don't succeed, and one day you blossom forth into a cabinet minister, or an ambassador instead of a fisherman and I into a great lady! We shall then laugh at these foolish young dreams of ours."

"You *are* whimsical," said Sunya. "I shall call you Whimsy hereafter."

"Then I shall call you Fatty," replied Mulan.

. .

It was not true, as Mulan imagined, that she was denying herself the pleasures which she was reserving for a later period when she and her husband could have more freedom to travel. She meant by that only visits to famous distant mountains—to the Hua, Huang, Sung, and Omei Mountains in the other provinces and to the rich cities of the South, Soochow, Yangchow, and Hangchow. These were her remote longings, hazy and undefined. But she was living in Peking itself and she missed nothing that Peking offered of natural beauty and of amenities providing for the perfect day.

Mr. and Mrs. Tseng soon discovered that Mulan had a vice, or rather two vices, both involving going out too much for a young woman. One was her desire to go out with Sunya and eat at small restaurants, and the other was visiting the parks and suburbs. How different she was from Mannia, who was content to remain in the house and for the most part in her own quiet courtyard! Moreover, her tendency to corrupt Mannia in this respect made Mr. Tseng really angry with her.

Sunya was puzzled by the Mulan he now saw, the Mulan who changed with the seasons. Her nickname "Whimsy" clung to her. It seemed as though she intentionally made herself a reflection of the season she was living in. She was calm in winter, languorous in spring, leisurely in summer, and keen in autumn. Even her coiffure varied, for she loved to change it. In winter, on a snowy morning, she would appear in a bright blue dress, and have red berries in her vases, or a twig of wild peach or wax plum. In spring, especially toward the end of April when the willows were putting forth tiny, yellowish-green sprouts, or when lilacs were blooming at Fayuan Temple in May, she would get up late, her hair would hang loose, and sometimes she would stand in slippers tending a bed of peonies in her courtyard. In summer, she would enjoy her courtyard, which was designed for the hot season and which was by far the broadest and most open of all the courts. There were stone benches and drum-shaped porcelain stools in different places. On the western side of the court, there was a trellis with a grapevine growing around and over it, and under the trellis there was a square stone table serving as a permanent chessboard. She would play chess with Brocade or with her husband there on an early summer morning while the servants were cleaning the rooms, or late in the afternoon. Or she would lie in a low rattan easy chair, with a novel in her hand. When autumn came, in the dry crisp Peking October, Mulan could hardly stay indoors. Once she went with Sunya to the country house in the Western Hills. It was there that Sunya first saw tears roll down Mulan's face, when she was gazing at red persimmons on a distant hill, with farmers' ducks swimming in the foreground. She was ashamed of this before Sunya, and she tried to correct this old habit, but she could not.

The autumn of 1912 saw Mulan in an orgy of outings. She was now a three-year-old bride and as a married woman, she could go about with her husband with a freedom that she did not have as an unmarried girl. And besides, under the Republic, the palace parks, lakes, and buildings were one by one being thrown open to the public. They went and saw the "Three Seas" or imperial lakes in the palace on different days, including the Yingtai where Emperor Kuanghsu was imprisoned for a time. The Altar to the Gods of the Soil and Grain, on the southwestern corner of the Forbidden City, was being converted into the Central Park, with groves of century-old cypresses all around the altar. It was such a pleasure to Mulan that she frequently went out in the afternoons with Brocade and her husband to a back part of the park facing the moat, where there were fewer people. The whole family naturally went to the more important places that had previously been forbidden imperial ground, like the "South Sea" and the Throne Hall, and on these occasions, Mannia was urged by all to join them. Just walking around the stone court and terrace around the Throne Hall, a court that could have held twelve thousand people, tired Mannia thoroughly. She still retained the habit of being coy and demure and not looking around too much when in public. But while Mannia was physically exhausted, Mulan was emotionally worn out from the sight of architecture that expressed such imperial grandeur, breadth, and magnificence.

Mr. Tseng began to say he did not approve of these outings. Mulan once went with her husband on an early June morning before breakfast to smell the lotus with the dew on it in the moat west of the Coal Hill, only a short distance from her home. She also took a glass bottle to collect the dew from the lotus leaves, intending to make tea with it. Leaning on the bank, she nearly toppled over, but Sunya pulled her back in time. The ecstasy she felt on that fragrant summer morning was shared by Sunya, but, on coming home, she learned from Brocade that Mr. Tseng had heard of it from a gatekeeper and had mumbled things about the "mad young woman" going out at such a time of the day. When she heard this, Mulan hurriedly went over to see her father-in-law, dragging Sunya along and taking the bottle of dew.

"Early, Father," she said.

Mr. Tseng was reading a newspaper and did not look up. Turning to Mrs. Tseng, Mulan said, "Mother, we went out to collect the dew from the lotus leaves on the moat. We will keep this for making tea."

"I was wondering why you two went out so early," said Mrs. Tseng.

Mr. Tseng looked up. "Why did you have to go out yourself to get it? You could have sent a servant."

"We went also to see the lotus," explained Sunya.

Mulan dared not say another word.

"Aren't there pots of them in our own house? Aren't there enough for you to look at?" said the father.

"But there was a mile of them in the moat. They were so beautiful and the air itself was so fragrant," Mulan said.

"Beautiful and fragrant!" snorted the father. "You call these things poetry, don't you? But a young woman ought not to run about too much. What does it look like for a young woman to be seen out of doors in the morning and afternoon?"

Mr. Tseng knew that collecting dew for making tea was a scholar's proper pleasure and when he heard what they went out for, he found it hard to call it an offense in Mulan. He knew that Mulan was inclined to be poetic, but he was suspicious of poetry for women. Poetry was associated with romance, and romance spelled a woman's downfall. He might almost have said that poetry was not respectable for a cultivated woman. For sing-song artists, yes, but not for good family girls and women.

Mrs. Tseng was more indulgent. "The children are young and foolish," she said. "Mulan by nature loves these things. Since she went out with her husband, it was all right."

"Mulan and Sunya," said the father, "I do not mind your doing these young and foolish things, even going to the Central Park in the afternoon once in a while. But you know the Park is a place where the modern boy and girl students and young men of all sorts and description go and rove about. Remember that your sister-in-law is a widow, and it is a most improper place for her to go. I forbid you to take her unless your mother or grandmother goes too. And you yourselves must not look upon these things as your daily food. We have our own garden and you ought to be satisfied."

Yes, Mulan might perhaps be called a "frivolous" woman in those days, and in this one respect, she was a "bad" daughter-in-law.

Mr. Tseng's tone was righteous but not severe that morning, and the incident passed. Mulan cut her afternoon walks shorter and tried to protect herself by asking her mother-in-law to go with her. One Sunday afternoon, even Mr. Tseng went along, with Cassia and Mrs. Tseng and the whole family. He justified himself by accompanying the grandmother, as if he were performing an act of filial piety and were doing it to please her. Perhaps, after all, he thought it pleasant to sit drinking tea with his family under the old cypress trees and looking at the golden roofs of the palace across the moat, but he did not permit himself to express his pleasure.

Several times Mulan wanted Mannia to go and when she did not, and Mulan and Sunya went alone, she would come back and tell Mannia about it with enthusiasm, saying, "You must come next time. I will ask mother's permission."

But Mannia would say, "Better not. I am willing to stay at home. I am in a different position from you, Lanmei."

. . .

Mr. Tseng's anger came to a climax one night when Mulan and Sunya took Mannia and the little Asuan to a moving-picture theater, after dinner at a restaurant outside Chienmen. That was the first and last time Mannia ever saw a moving picture, to the end of her days, for Mr. Tseng considered such pictures immoral. They had not intended to go and had told their mother that they would be home after dinner.

Now, as far as immorality is concerned, there was as much of it in the Chinese opera as in the modern films. All the women in the house occasionally used to go and "hear" the opera, but then it was the accepted custom. A modern film was different; for it showed women, naked, or practically naked, as far as the audience could see, and it showed kissing which was never permitted on the Chinese stage, and it showed a form of rotating hugging between men and women that went by the name of "dancing." It was true that actors and actresses flirted on the Chinese stage, but they did so by furtive glances and at

371

the worst by coquettish gait and gestures. They certainly did not embrace one another and whirl round and round, permitting the audience to see the bare backs of the women. Mr. Tseng was not the only one to be outwardly horrified and secretly delighted at such a show. There was a new cinema theater near Morrison Street, and the family had once gone to see it, not knowing just what it would be like. But Mannia had happened to be ill and so had not gone.

A night club was shown, with scenes of dancing and floor shows and there was a close-up shot of a man called Valentino kissing a girl for about ten seconds.

Cassia could not help giggling, and Mrs. Tseng sat amused; but Mannia's mother blushed in the dark.

The grandmother thoroughly enjoyed herself and said, "How marvelous! How can they paint a thing like that! When that man smoked, it looked as if real smoke were coming out of his nostrils."

Mulan was fascinated at seeing what foreign women wore as underwear. Mr. Tseng thought their legs were beautiful, but decided this was something not for young boys and girls to see.

After that he took Cassia with him to the movies quite a few times. He never allowed his daughters Ailien and Lilien to go, but he had never explicitly forbidden Mannia.

In those days of the silent films, talking during the play was permissible, in the best tradition of the Chinese theater audience. Waiters served tea and threw wrung hot towels across the hall with a loud "Hey!" while other waiters caught the towels as neatly and as remarkably as if in a lighted room, so that sometimes one would see the dark shape of a wrung towel flying across the screen. Consequently talking was no annoyance to anybody, just as at a foreign dinner party where one can keep up an interminable chatter with the person beside him because everybody else is chattering. There was a tendency to raise the voice in order to be heard by the other person.

In one of the pictures, during a scene in which a society woman slipped on an evening gown to go out for dinner, an old gentleman stood up and said aloud to the audience, "Look at those foreign women! In the upper part they wear nothing on top of something, and in the lower part, they wear something on top of nothing. On top, no jacket; below, no trousers!" The audience roared, but a foreigner at the back shouted "Quiet!" in English. To his surprise, the old gentleman not only understood, but turned to him and repeated in perfect

372

English the sentence that he had spoken to the audience in Chinese. The foreigner was taken aback and laughed too at the old wit. Foreigners in Peking came to know about this old philosopher whose name was Ku, and spoke of him always with respect and admiration, which in turn encouraged him in his taunts against Western civilization. He had studied at Edinburgh and had returned and become a crank, taking great pride in his queue and his old-type Chinese dress besides using it as a sort of disguise to surprise unwitting foreigners on a train or in a restaurant whom he might hear criticizing China in a foreign tongue. It might be in English, German, or French; it did not matter, for he could always return in kind. But somehow Ku was fond of foreign movies and foreign food. One could hardly call him a *poseur;* for he was perfectly sure of his beliefs, and even if he were a *poseur,* the foreigners in Peking excused him on account of his brilliant wit. Mulan came to know him later through Paku, the poet.

That night at the restaurant, Mulan, Sunya, and Mannia had a delicious dinner of carp's head, followed by a dish of tender and fragrant beans which had just appeared on the market. Sunya, as usual, was very happy after a good meal and a few cups of wine, for as Mulan had found, he was a sensualist. His pores glowed with happiness and his face was warm and tense. At such times, he would clear his throat constantly, and expectorate more than usual.

"Shall we go to see a movie?" he suggested.

"I don't think I should," said Mannia.

"Father might object," said Mulan.

"I will be responsible," said Sunya. "You should not miss a thing like that. It is truly marvelous."

"What is it like? I can't imagine," said Mannia.

"It is all on a screen, like a picture. But everything in it moves and is living. Come along!" said Sunya.

So they went. It was a harmless show, and there was a clown called Charlie Chaplin who was very funny with his cane and his pants and his feet. Mannia had never laughed so much in her life.

But Mr. and Mrs. Tseng were expecting them early and were worried; and, when they came in about half-past eleven, the mother exclaimed, "Where have you been?"

"Oh, we have been to a theater," said Sunya.

"We went to see a movie," said Mannia innocently.

"What!" shouted the father. "This is all your doing, Mulan! What did I tell you the other day! Is a movie the kind of a thing for a widow to see?"

"It was I who suggested it and took sister-in-law there," explained Sunya.

"That is enough," said the father. "Mannia, I don't blame you, if you realize now that you were wrong. But I forbid you to go again. As for you, Mulan, you took her there knowing what it was like. She is not like you; she is a widow. Don't you try to turn her head by dragging her out again. There are places and places."

"I am sorry, Father," said Mulan, ready to cry, but she found no tears. Her father-in-law had never spoken so harshly to her before.

"It was my fault," said Sunya again. "It was a comic film and we thought it was all right. It was a Charlie Chaplin picture."

The father's fears were allayed. He himself had enjoyed seeing a Charlie Chaplin picture, and somehow his anger melted at the thought of that funny man, but he refused to smile and merely said, "Oh!"

Mulan and Sunya went back to their room and Mulan said, "It was my fault. I should have known. But I wanted her to see it at least once."

"No, I was responsible," said Sunya. "But Father would not believe me. But we must make him see that times have changed, and we can't shut her up like this. What is all this idea of protecting her?"

"You can say that to Father," said Mulan, "but I cannot."

To Mulan's mortification, Mannia came the next morning and blamed her for taking her to the theater.

"What harm did it do you?" asked Mulan.

"None," replied Mannia. "I am glad I have seen it once. But we must obey and I really don't mind. If you don't think about it and don't see it, you pass your days just as easily. My mother says there are things in motion pictures that are not very nice, and she agrees with Father."

CHAPTER XXIV

ONE place in Peking that Mulan had not visited was the ruins of the Old Summer Palace. It was a conscious omission.

That autumn when she and her husband had stayed in the Western Hills for a few days, he had suggested seeing it on their way back, and she had thought of it, too. Passing its mile-long wall on the road to the New Summer Palace, she had seen the tops of mounds and glimpses of ruins above the wall, and a break in the wall permitted her to see fields and swamps now overgrown with tall grass and reeds forming a scene of rural desolation.

Mulan's mind had invested the place with the sentiment of past imperial glory. It would not be right for her to see such a place except in the company of Lifu, for here were ruins such as Lifu loved. Years ago, watching the flood at Shihshahai, Mulan had casually promised Lifu that they would see the Old Summer Palace together. This unfulfilled promise between them now had a secret and sacred character. The memory of it lingered in her mind like an unfinished melody. Sunya would enjoy the ruins, but to see them without Lifu would be, she felt, a violation of her aesthetic conscience. So she, Mulan, had said to Sunya, "Let us ask Mochow and Lifu to see it one day together. It will be more fun."

"Father might object," said Sunya.

"*My* father won't object. Lifu comes to our home often, and my father makes Sister see him and eat luncheon at table with him. It is so different from our days before marriage."

"Why, then, we will ask them," said Sunya.

"Lifu loves ruins, you know," Mulan said. "I once promised him to see the Old Summer Palace with him . . . Are you jealous?"

"No, why should I be?" replied the easy-going Sunya.

So they decided to go home without seeing the Old Summer Palace that time.

375

As a matter of fact, Lifu had often come to see them, and he and Sunya had grown to be friends because of Sunya's frank admiration of Lifu's talents and ability.

"Between you two sisters, your *meimei* is the lucky one," Sunya said to Mulan. "You know I am no good. What can I do in this world? Whimsy, the only thing good about me is my 'wife-constellation.' "

"My 'husband-constellation' is not bad either, Fatty," said Mulan, touched by his self-deprecation.

"It is strange," said Sunya. "The power you women have over men. Look at Mrs. Hua's influence over your brother!"

"It is amazing," Mulan agreed. "I should like to know that woman better."

What had happened was that, under the direct influence of Mrs. Hua, her brother had reformed, according to his own story. He had given up opium and he went to the shop every day and came home regularly every night.

Mrs. Hua was by this time the owner of a curio shop and a respectable woman. After Mulan's wedding, or rather after seeing Mulan's trousseau parade, Mrs. Hua had changed her mind about Tijen. Silverscreen's death had touched her deeply and an attachment grew out of the common sorrow between herself and the young heir. She had formerly looked upon him as a young fool to be cultivated for his money, and she herself had benefited from this, for when Silverscreen died, Tijen buried some of her jewels with her and gave the rest to Mrs. Hua. This amounted to a legacy worth three or four thousand dollars, and she began to think what she should do with it. With what she had saved out of direct gifts from Tijen, she now had over five thousand dollars. So, when the Revolution came, and a number of Manchus went bankrupt, she bought a curio shop. The price asked was the ridiculous sum of ten thousand, and she beat it down to seventy-five hundred. She told Tijen that now would be a great time for the curio business, because the Manchu aristocracy were selling off their treasures as cheaply as dirt. Second-hand dealers picked up such objects as old incense tripods with encrusted gold from Manchu women at the back door for twenty coppers, and the curio dealers got them from the second-hand men for a few dollars. Mrs. Hua had a sharp eye for business and Tijen promised to give her the sum required to make up the price of the curio shop.

So, now Mrs. Hua owned a shop outside Chienmen and had come

to know some Manchu families. She kept the old employees who were only too glad to hold their jobs. She had adopted a child and had settled down to live a respectable middle-class life. Having had her pleasures in life, and having got so much from Tijen, she now determined to reform him for the sake of her conscience.

Tijen told Lifu that Mrs. Hua had scolded him in the past year, as nobody else could, and he had listened to her as he would not to his own sisters. She had called him a "fool," a "young fool," and again a "damned fool."

"What do you want in life?" she had thundered at him. "You want to enjoy life. Do it! You want women. Get them! You want money. You have it. But get on the good side of your father, or you will lose everything. I know what it is to be disowned by one's family, as that husband of mine was. I know what it is to be poor, to pawn things, to borrow, and to dread the day of paying rent for weeks beforehand. Why do you go out of your way to antagonize your parents and risk being cut off? What if your father does carry out his threat and break up the fortune or give it to a monastery? Get back to your senses, or you are too stupid even to be my friend."

Thus every time he came to her, she lectured him and made him return home early, and he listened to her and decided to stop smoking opium.

．∴．

In the spring of the following year, Mulan went with her husband's family to Shantung for several months. The grandmother wanted to go back and build her own tomb in her lifetime. She had been talking about this constantly for the past half year, for it seemed to lie very much on her conscience. Mr. Tseng had nothing in particular to do and he had not been back home for a long time, and furthermore there was now a railway connecting Peking and Shanghai, and the grandmother wanted to enjoy this novelty. Chinya went with them and stayed until the *Chingming* Festival when he had to return to his office. Sunya and Mulan stayed to the end of the visit, because Mulan's second child was coming, and she could not risk the railway journey back.

While at Shantung, Sunya helped to direct the lay-out of the tomb. The grandmother called in a geomancer and upon his advice had a tall tree cut down because it obstructed the distant view of the Temple to the King of Hell from the site of the tomb. The grandmother wanted to be able to have direct communication with the King of Hell, when she should be lying in her grave.

On May 1, a son was born to Sunya. It was strange that Mulan's first baby was born on the last day of May and this second one on the first day of the same month. In spite of her comparatively small bones, she had no difficulty with either birth, due no doubt to her early marriage. This was the first real grandson Mr. and Mrs. Tseng had, and their joy was great. Mannia's son, Asuan, now a boy of ten, was adopted, and Suyun had greatly disappointed her parents-in-law by giving birth to no child. Mr. Tseng had heard rumors that Mulan, as a modern girl, believed in a practice called birth control. He had resented this, but could not ask even Sunya directly about such a thing, and he had waited impatiently during these three years since Mulan's daughter had been born. Now all the clouds of suspicion were dissipated, and everyone was well satisfied. Mulan had thereby done the greatest, the most important, the most proper thing that a daughter-in-law could do. The new son was called Atung.

The names of the children were chosen by Mulan. She had named her daughter Aman, after the girl of the poet Po Chuyi.

"Why Atung?" asked Sunya.

"In honor of your mother," replied Mulan.

"How?"

"Don't you remember Tao Yuanming's poem about his sons:

'Atung is only nine years old,
He thinks only of pears and chestnuts'?"

"What has that to do with my mother?"

"Well," explained Mulan, "it is a concealed reference. Your mother is called Jade-Pear. If I call our baby Atung, won't he be thinking of pears all the time? 'Thinking of Pears' might be his literary name, if it were not for the taboo."

Sunya explained this to his parents, and they thought it very clever of Mulan. Mulan had been warned by her father not to use the commonplace names. She had secretly laughed at the names of Huaiyu's sons, "Glory of State," "Blessing of State," and such, which showed an entire lack of humor. Her father had given her and her sisters classical names. He had pointed out to her that the best poets and writers gave simple names to their children, which, like all important things in our lives, come naturally and of themselves. He had told her that the poet

Su Tungpo's son was called by the simple word *Kuo,* which might mean "crossing" his father's courtyard as Confucius' son did, or it might more probably mean just "A Mistake." The poet Yuan Tsetsai's son was simply called *Achih,* meaning "Late," because he was born when the poet was already in his old age. In accordance with this, Mulan's younger brother had been named "Afei," or "Wrong" or "Not right," which was about as bad as Su Tungpo's son's name "Akuo." But her father meant by it a reference to a line by Tao Yuanming, "I know today I am right and yesterday was all wrong"—a symbol of awakening. Mulan's father had told her also that there was such a thing as the vulgarity of the educated. In various aspects of life one passed on from the vulgarity of the simple people to the vulgarity of the educated, and only a few ever graduated from the vulgarity of the educated and returned to the simplicity of the vulgar. His Excellency New, for instance, could not have permitted any of his grandchildren to be called "A Mistake." He could not have been satisfied with anything less than "Blessing of the State," or "Splendor of the Court," or "Glory of the Ancestors." Even then this educated rabble had to choose difficult, unknown, and unreadable characters from the *Kanghsi Dictionary* in place of perfectly simple characters, *to avoid being vulgar!*

Mulan dared not expound this philosophy of naming persons to her parents-in-law, for Pingya meant "Peaceful Asia"; Chinya, "Skirting around (that is, embracing) Asia"; Ailien, "Loving Lotus"; and Lilien "Beautiful Lotus." Of these names, she thought Ailien was the best because it was simple and refined. But the best of all was Sunya's name, because it was composed of two simple words that did not quite make sense but did sound very well.

The birth of the boy produced a great change in Mulan. It was not that she loved Aman less, but that she loved Atung more. Unfortunately, Atung had a flat nose like his father, but he had the beautiful eyes of his mother and his skin was extremely light. Sunya noticed that Mulan now became different. It was as though her son were her first child. She became more serious, and less careful in her dress, and for a year or two she lost all interest in her excursions and dinners at little restaurants. Motherhood had leveled her to the eternal type of the average woman. When Sunya suggested going somewhere outside, she always disapproved, and he felt that his place in his wife's heart was dwindling and that he was being supplanted by his baby son.

Mulan was now truly happy, but she was entering a phase which lay entirely outside the mental grasp of her husband. He began for the first time to see her as a mother. The actions of a mother in petting a baby, feeding it at her breast, her way of sitting with one foot resting on the other knee to give support to the baby—an immodest position for an unmarried girl—her whispers, her strange baby talk which he did not understand but the baby did, the transformations of her face and her breasts—these delighted and at the same time mystified him. When Atung was sick with indigestion, he saw Mulan go practically without sleep for a week. He thought he had failed to understand Mulan, but he began to understand woman. He saw that nature had created woman with a more complex mind than man's, to serve the imperious needs of motherhood, which rounded out a woman's mind and personality and made her more realistic than a man. He had thought Mulan a pure spirit of distilled charm, but he saw now that she was also flesh. Yet flesh was also spirit, and the mysteries of the flesh were greater than the mystery of the spirit. So the experience of motherhood in Mulan reached to depths that Sunya could not possibly understand.

He was often irked because she regarded him contemptuously as an amateur when any questions about their son were involved. His suggestions were ignored, and she spoke as if she were a professional authority on the care of the baby. That she was so often right did not make it less unpleasant for him. Why, his wife listened more to Brocade than to him in such questions! Unfortunately the science of motherhood has never been written down by its million authorities, and Sunya had no way of gathering the thousands of profundities of women's lore that Brocade and Mulan and Mannia and all the rest of them had mastered since girlhood. Like all fathers, he felt himself a slightly ridiculous bystander, but soon he grew resigned.

· ·

Now by one of those strange coincidences that do happen, Mulan became the mistress of the girl Dimfragrance, whom she had first known as a fellow-victim of the kidnaper's gang on the Grand Canal thirteen years before.

Mr. and Mrs. Tseng were so pleased with the birth of the grandson that they gave word that another maid should be found to serve Mulan and take special care of this baby. Brocade had helped to care for Aman. Afraid of losing her, Mulan had offered Brocade the opportunity of marrying a young servant in the Tseng home, on the condition that she continue to serve her. Brocade was only too glad to acquire thus both a husband and a secure and comfortable living, especially since Mulan was so kind and their relationship transcended that of the usual mistress and servant. Brocade liked Tsao Chung, an honest and rather handsome lad; and this was well, because servant girls had greater freedom in the choice of their mates than rich men's daughters had. Brocade had therefore married with Mulan's blessing, and Tsao Chung, amazed at his luck in picking up a good wife without spending a cent, came happily to serve in Mulan's court with her. Tsao acted as the man for outside errands, and Brocade as general superintendent of the other servants in the court and nurse for Aman at the same time.

In Shantung, there was no difficulty in finding maidservants, but Mrs. Tseng wanted none but the best for her grandson. Several maids had applied but they were unsatisfactory. Both Sunya and Mulan hated coarse, clumsy country girls. One day Phoenix's aunt came to visit her and told them that on that very morning she had heard that a family in the town was giving up its house and servants and she promised to inquire about its girl servants. Two days later, she came with a girl of nineteen.

Mrs. Tseng asked Mulan to come out and see the girl for herself. The girl was timid, reticent, and shabbily dressed. Having known no kindness, she did not expect any from the world. Her master's family had been on the decline and she had been getting the worst of their poor food and dress. But she was not badly shaped and she looked naturally gentle, and Mulan thought she would take her.

"Have you ever cared for a baby?" asked Mulan.

"I have," replied the girl quietly. She looked as if she were quite uninterested in what was happening to her, feeling that she was only being shuffled by fate from one mistress to another.

"What is your name?" asked Mulan.

"Dimfragrance."

"Dimfragrance!" Mulan said the name over slowly to herself and thought, Where have I heard that name before? Then she recalled that it was the name of the girl who was shut up with her years ago.

"How old are you?" she asked excitedly.

"Nineteen."

"Are your parents living?"

"I have no parents."

The girl began now to raise her eyes to see Mulan, who seemed so beautiful and rich and gentle.

"Tell me about yourself. Where did you come from?"

"*Nainai,*" replied the girl, "I have cared for several babies, and if you like me, I shall call myself lucky to serve you. There is nothing else to say about me. One day for me is just like another."

"But have you no relatives?"

"I was lost at the age of six and I don't know anything about relatives."

"Do you remember where you got lost?" Mulan asked, trying to be calm and almost afraid to hear the girl's reply.

"It was the year of the Boxer uprising, and I lost my parents near Tehchow, and then I was sold to a family at Tsinan. Afterward we came to live in this town."

Phoenix's aunt was standing by with Phoenix. "*Nainai,*" she said, "she is a good girl and very fond of babies. You should take her."

To her surprise, Mulan did not reply, but said to the girl, "Come inside with me." The girl followed her silently. As soon as they were inside the room, Mulan shut the door and took her hand and said, her voice trembling, "Do you remember a girl called Mulan who was shut up together with you?"

The girl thought a moment and said, "Yes, there was another girl who went back to her parents a few days afterward. I think I remember her name was Mulan."

"I am Mulan," said the young mistress, barely able to speak the words, and found herself hugging the girl in tears. It was so sudden that Dimfragrance was stupefied. Luck came always as something unnatural to one used to no luck, and Dimfragrance still refused to believe it.

"Perhaps you have made a mistake. That girl was kind like you, but how could this be?" she asked piteously.

"Of course it was I," said Mulan. "Do you remember the girl was older than you? I was ten then. I was there before you, and do you remember the little cell with a small high window, and the fat old woman? Do you remember that I came from Peking and that I promised to ask my parents to get you out?"

These sentences, falling like hammer blows on Dimfragrance's ears, slowly awakened a series of forgotten memories. She burst out, "And you told the old woman to give me the bowl of date congee when you left!"

Now that she was sure, Dimfragrance fell to weeping as she had never wept before. A servant girl sold to a harsh mistress was usually hardened to stand anything and rarely wept, even when beaten, but kindness was different. She knelt down before Mulan and said almost hysterically, "Good *Nainai,* I will call you my parent. I have been alone in this world, with no friends and no relatives. How is it you were lucky and I was not? You found your parents, but I lost mine. . . ."

She wanted to kowtow to Mulan, but Mulan bent and lifted her up, and mistress and servant sat and stared at each other for a whole minute without words.

"You stay with me and help look after my baby," Mulan said at last. "I will treat you like a sister."

"If it is like this, the days of my sufferings are ended," said Dimfragrance. "I will have to burn incense to thank Heaven and Earth."

Mulan was now ashamed to go out.

"Do you have to go back to get your things?"

"What should I go back for? I have nothing. Only these two hands."

"Then open the door and tell them that you are staying here. Don't say anything else and close the door again," Mulan whispered.

Phoenix and the others outside were amazed, for they had heard the weeping inside, and it was most unusual for one to shut the door in broad daylight in a household, especially with a strange person.

A moment later, Mulan heard Aman's little hands tapping at the door, and asked Dimfragrance to open it. Brocade came in with Aman. She was told the secret and asked to give Dimfragrance some of her dresses.

But for a woman, a secret is either too good to keep or not worth keeping at all, as it has been said. Hardly could she wait till she was permitted to leave the room to tell Mrs. Tseng and the other maids about the strange story. And when they heard of it, they all rushed in and wanted to hear the story from Mulan and Dimfragrance themselves.

"Everything is determined from above," said Mulan. "All my life it has been this way. Just think, if Phoenix's aunt hadn't dropped in to see us, or if she had not accidentally heard about the other family's giving up their house and servants, I might be going back to Peking without meeting her at all, though we were here in the same city."

"Of course it is Heaven's will," said Phoenix. "My aunt said this was how it happened. Her child had dropped a sieve into the well, and she went to a neighbor's family to borrow a rope and hook to get it out. She found another woman there and she stayed chatting and thus she heard of the Ting family's giving up their house. If it were not Heaven's will, how was it that her child had not dropped the sieve into the well a moment sooner or later? Thus one sees that everything is determined above and there is no changing the course of events."

Phoenix's argument made it all the more impressive, and Dimfragrance was looked upon as one especially favored by Heaven to come and serve Mulan.

CHAPTER XXV

*I*N JUNE Mulan returned with her family from Shantung. Her brother-in-law Chinya had been looking after the house in their absence, and Suyun, too, had now come to stay.

Chinya was a steady and rather quiet young man, who worried about small things, and attended to his duties regularly, and he never felt a sense of rebellion against office routine, as Sunya would have. He never inquired into the meaning of existence, that is to say, the meaning of a young man's getting up at a regular hour every morning, going the same distance to the same office, and discussing the same subjects with the same people of the same opinion, passing a document through a department down to the minor clerks and up again to the chief, then on to another department in another ministry, with perhaps a recommendation consisting of four sentences or sixteen syllables altogether, added to the main part which consisted of a quotation from another incoming document, bracketed off by a "Whereas" at the beginning and a "Therefore" at the end—and calling it governing the country. He did not see the humor of it, that the whole process was no more than copy work, since the quotation from the incoming document was the main part both in length and in substance and the recommendation usually consisted of "calling the attention" of the bureau addressed in the document and suggesting that it exercise its "noble judgment" in dealing with the aforesaid communication. The recommendation made by the bureau previously handling the matter was incorporated as a quotation within a quotation, and documents were by no means rare that embodied a quotation within a quotation within another quotation. Thus the formal structure of a typical official document was in outline as follows:—

CONCERNING such-and-such a matter;

WHEREAS this Office has been informed by such-and-such a Bureau to the effect that:

385

WHEREAS the said Bureau had received a communication from such-and-such a Ministry to the effect that. . . . THEREFORE the Bureau had decided to forward it to this Office:

THEREFORE, besides forwarding the same to such-and-such a party, it is considered right and proper by this Office to call your Bright Attention to the above. Whether what is herein proposed is right or not, we pray for your Noble Judgment.

The words "Bright Attention" and "Noble Judgment" are always respectfully written at the top of the page.

The philosophy behind Chinese documentary grammar was suavely expressed by all officials in eight succinct well-balanced words: *Not praying for merits; only praying no demerits.* In another form the same philosophy was expressed as follows—*Do more, err more; do less, err less; do nothing, err nothing.* It was perfect, and a complete guide to official security. That was why the person about to receive the document was always credited with a Bright Attention and a Noble Judgment.

Chinya was honest, sober, and fairly hard-working. But he was not brilliant or naturally sociable. With an influential backing he would normally have risen to be a cabinet minister. But now that his father-in-law had gone out of power, there was little chance of his becoming more than a small bureaucrat. His honesty and caution annoyed Suyun and threw her into dark despair, and at heart she despised him. Besides, he had queer habits. Sometimes after having gone a hundred yards from home, he would return just to see if his umbrella had been left in its usual position on the previous day. If he sent a servant to do an errand, he would repeat his instructions three or four times and then ask him if it was clear, long after the servant had understood, and when the servant had gone out of the door, he would call him back and repeat it once more. If it was a dozen preserved eggs he wanted, he would say both "dozen" and "two plus ten," to the amusement of the maids standing by. Once, going out with Suyun to buy a new felt hat, he walked all the way from the southern end of Morrison Street to the northern end and back again to the first shop he had seen, before he could make up his mind. Suyun told the story to Chinya's mother in his presence, exclaiming, "I didn't believe a man could be so useless."

Mrs. Tseng felt called upon to defend her son and said, "He was always cautious. It keeps him out of trouble. Caution is better than recklessness."

"Anyway, I am not like your brother," Chinya flung back at his wife. "He can tell you anything, promise a man a job next Monday or a dinner next Saturday, and say it with the greatest assurance without even meaning it. The last time I was with him in Tientsin he promised to invite a person to dinner on Saturday evening, and when Saturday evening came, I asked him why he wasn't dining out. He didn't even ring up to apologize or give excuse, and when he met his friend the following week, he did not even mention it. I could never do a thing like that."

"But that is how people get along in this world," said Suyun. "It is because you are too careful of what you say that you don't make more friends. You see how many friends he has made."

On the evening of Mulan's return, Snow Blossom came to tell her a whole series of stories. Snow Blossom had risen to be probably the most important woman servant in the household, and Mrs. Tseng, unable to dispense with her service, had helped her to marry a country lad from her own village, to whom she had been engaged from childhood. Naturally her husband had to be given a place, but being extraordinarily simple-minded, he could not be given higher work than that of a gardener. Mulan had asked Snow Blossom if she was satisfied with her husband, and she said that she had always known him to be simple and thought he would make a more dependable husband than a lot of bright young men in the city. And so in her own way Snow Blossom was happy.

That evening Snow Blossom told Mulan the condition of the household during her absence.

"Third Mistress, you don't know how hard it was to work with the Second Mistress. There would be peace for two or three days and then there was trouble. When she was in a good mood, she would make me and Pien *Tasao* (Mrs. Pien) play cards with her deep into the night, and we had to lose, or else she would be in a frightful temper; and next morning, while we had to get up early, she would lie in bed until midday, hours after Second Master had gone to the office. And the accounts! Don't tell me that a rich mistress has no regard for money. We played for small stakes, but she never forgot a single cent. Last month when I received my monthly expenses, she said, 'Snow Blossom, you remember you owed me sixteen cents the other night. So here is one dollar and eighty-four cents for you.' I was ashamed for her. Now I understand how one becomes the God of Wealth. One day she bought a piece of foreign material at Juifuhsiang's and then after seeing a piece of foreign velvet in another shop, she changed her mind, and next day told Pien to send it back. But the material was cut, and how could the shop take it back? 'Of course, they can,' she said. 'We were always able to send goods back at my home.' Pien had to go and settle it and he had to pay for his own rickshaw, for Second Mistress told him he could walk. The manager of the shop took it back just to please us as old customers, but he said he would have to sell it as an odd piece. She would not buy another piece there because she had seen that piece of foreign velvet in a shop on Morrison Street. Well, she went and bought that piece, and had the tailor make a dress. When the dress was delivered she noticed that the tailor had not been careful and the paste used for trimmings had made a blotch in a corner of the skirt. It was just the size of a thumb and not very serious. But she was angry and made the tailor take away the dress and demanded her money for the material from him. The material cost twenty-eight dollars, and finally, after pleading and begging favor, the tailor promised to pay her fifteen dollars. But he said, 'Young *Nainai,* next time you want a dress made, you had better go to some one else.' There are many little things of this kind."

.·.

The next morning Mochow came with Afei to see Mulan and her new baby. The sisters and brother were very happy to see each other again after the months of separation. Mulan asked how their mother was, and Mochow said that she was well, except that when the weather was changing her wrist troubled her, so that she could foretell a storm. While Mochow was watching the new baby, Mulan asked suddenly if she had seen Lifu lately.

"He comes sometimes to our house and he and Father are great friends," said Mochow.

"And how is Brother?"

"He has reformed and stopped taking opium and he comes home regularly every night. Father and Mother are so pleased."

"Really!" exclaimed Mulan. "Maybe he will come to be a filial son yet. He can be very good when he means to be. Does Father still talk about becoming a monk?"

"He does not mention it now. Of course, he is very pleased and talks more with Brother now. The other day, Father and Brother and Lifu talked until after midnight, the three of them together. Brother says it is Mrs. Hua who has reformed him. Can you imagine! Mother is arranging a match for him with a girl of the Chu family from Tientsin, and he stubbornly refuses, saying that he must marry a girl of his own choice. I hear that he is running after a girl—you know, Huineng, the former nun, who is now a 'red' sing-song girl."

"Do you mean the Huineng who was involved with Tungyu before she entered a convent?"

"Yes, Brother said at the time that he admired the girl greatly for what she did. Mother disapproves, of course. He was so angry about it yesterday after an argument that he walked out of the house."

"What about his affair with Sutan?" asked Mulan, excited by all this news.

"Well, it is a long story. She is married now to a rich merchant's son from the South Seas, a man named Wang Tso. She has made a fool of herself. The other day I met her and her husband. It was a sad sight."

Sutan had become a social derelict. Being a rebel at home and a pioneer among the "modern girls," she had come to live in Peking after her graduation from school. Her brother Sutung, then a medical student at a mission hospital, highly disapproved of her way of living but could do nothing about it. She was enjoying her freedom and had many admirers, for many young men were attracted by her daring freedom and her coquettish type of beauty. She had sometimes come to see Mulan, and had fallen in love with Tijen. The natural question of her possible marriage with him had been raised. Mulan rather disapproved. She had liked Sutan as a school friend, but hardly thought she would be a strong help for her weak brother; nor did she think that her brother deserved her or would make her happy, but she said little of this. But Mochow had actively opposed the marriage at home, and that was the reason why neither Sutan nor Paku ever liked Mochow very much later. In her despair Sutan went off and married the rich, bumptious young man, Wang Tso, who had come up from Singapore to live in a splendid suite at the Hotel de Pékin, and to seek pleasures and a bride. Being rich and proud, he had boasted

389

that he would marry the most beautiful girl in Peking. And so he did, in his own eyes at least. She was pale as a ghost, but extraordinarily beautiful, like an exotic blossom, with seductive eyes like the waters of an autumn lake. Wang Tso had courted her ardently but hardly two months had passed after this marriage before both had found out that it was a mistake.

"I met them one day on Morrison Street, where they had apparently just come out of a hotel restaurant," Mochow continued. "Sutan called to me and intended to introduce me to her tall husband. But he walked straight ahead. He was dressed in foreign style and carrying a cane with a gold ring. Evidently he preferred not to meet any of his wife's friends. Sutan frowned, and before she said a word I understood. 'I must hurry on,' she said. 'Come and see me when you can,' I said. 'No chance of that,' she replied and quickly hastened her steps on her high heels to catch up with her husband, who was standing in front of a shop window, not even looking in our direction. There was no use in her trying to look like a happy bride. Her husband despises her family. He wanted to marry her only as a prize to show off to his friends. Her brother was at the wedding, but no arrangement was made for her mother to come up from the south. Now she seems completely helpless and friendless. When they go out, she merely trails her husband's steps while he walks straight ahead at a pace hard for her to keep up with."

"That marriage will collapse. I'm sure that in a little time they will have to divorce each other," said Mulan. The last Mochow had heard was that the couple had sailed for Manila and Japan.

That afternoon, when Mulan was preparing to visit her parents, a woman servant was sent hurrying from her home, to bring the frightful news that Tijen had fallen from a horse and had been carried home and was at the point of death. Mulan told Brocade to stay with the babies, and went at once, leaving word for Sunya to follow her.

Tijen was just returning to consciousness and crying in pain. He was removed to the hospital where Sutan's brother was working. It appeared from the account of the farmers who brought him home, that he was riding on a powerful mare in the northern suburb. An uncontrolled stallion smelled the mare and came running after her, and she began to run wildly, and Tijen could not stop her. She dashed along a path where a low branch hung across the road. He bent his head as the horse went under it at lightning speed, but the back of his head struck against the tree and he was thrown off and across the road. The doctor said he had a concussion of the brain and compound fractures of his right arm and leg and internal bleeding, and that the shock had been so severe that no operation was possible at the moment.

The father was deeply concerned but controlled himself throughout the evening, while the old mother sat beside her son's deathbed and wept silently. The son came back to consciousness for a while and asked to see Mrs. Hua, and the father obeyed the son's dying wish and sent for her. She arrived and Tijen managed to say, "Father and Mother, I owe you both a debt. I have not been a good son to you, I know. Tell Sister Coral to be severe toward my son Poya and bring him up to be a better man than I am." Then looking at the woman, he said, "Don't misunderstand Mrs. Hua. She is the only true friend I have."

His eyes closed and his voice became inaudible and his breath stopped.

That night Mulan and Sunya heard the father utter the strange remark, "It is well that he died unmarried."

Mulan had intended to return home in any case and stay with her mother after the birth of the new baby, as was frequently done, but now she came home principally to comfort her mother. The mother was now getting old and her hair was almost entirely white, although she was still under fifty. She had loved Tijen to the end, and was now regretting that she had not let him have his wish in regard to marriage. "If I had not tried to stop him from seeing that girl Huineng, probably he would not have gone out riding," she said.

"Mother, this is nonsense," said Mochow. "These things are predetermined. He was fond of riding from his childhood. It was not your fault."

And so the two sisters and the younger brother tried to comfort their old mother and persuade her to eat as usual. Summer had come very suddenly that year, and the sisters took turns fanning their mother with a goose-feather fan, while she lay in bed.

Now that both Tijen and Silverscreen were dead and beyond competition with the living, his family began to think kindly of them both. Time had chastened the hatred even in the mother's heart, and she thought of Silverscreen only as a remote, "ancient" creature, whom Fate had placed across her way, but she held no grudge against her

391

any more. In accordance with the father's order, Silverscreen's remains were removed from her grave and buried side by side with Tijen's in the family cemetery near their country house at the back of the Jade Spring Hill, and Poya was taught to pay respect to these twin tombs as he would to those of a legal father and mother.

The shock of her brother's sudden death was so great that Mulan's milk completely dried up. As Brocade also had a baby about six months old, and her supply of milk seemed inexhaustible, she undertook to wean her own child and to nurse Atung at her breast. For this reason, Brocade and Dimfragrance changed places and Dimfragrance began to take care of Mulan's daughter, Aman.

. · .

The death of Tijen worked an entirely unexpected change in Mr. Yao. Tijen had always been a burden on his heart, even after he had reformed and to all intents and purposes was becoming a good son, coming home regularly, and beginning to take serious interest in the business. There had been still an unpredictable element in him, like that affair with Huineng. He was always self-willed and reckless, and it seemed quite possible that he might get into worse adventures yet. This had given excuse to the father to toy with his idea of breaking up the family fortune and becoming a monk as a gesture of defiance. Now the home was cleared of that threat, and he began to concentrate on his younger son, who was growing up properly and had done nothing wrong.

But his mind turned to this world again with a curious lack of conviction. This man who might have "left the family" and turned monk began to enjoy life with a fervor as if he was riding through thin air. He was in the world and yet out of it. Through his readings and meditations, he had reached a point where he had lost his sense of the ego and the distinction between "self" and "non-self"— the goal of Buddhist sainthood. Since the family was only the ego carried to a higher degree, he had also lost any real belief in the family. Yet this attitude made it possible for him to enjoy his life and his wealth while they lasted with a superiority which few rich men had. He certainly did not take his wealth seriously.

For, to the amazement of his whole family he decided to buy a Manchu prince's garden. It came about like this:

When Mrs. Hua had left Tijen's deathbed, old Yao had told her how grateful he was to her, and that if she wanted anything, she need only come and tell him. She was permitted to attend the funeral, and she showed a great interest in Tijen's four-year-old child, Poya.

Just before the Mid-Autumn Festival, Mrs. Hua came bringing some moon cakes for the child, and said that she wanted to see Mr. Yao. He received her cordially in his study. Having been trained as a sing-song artist she was a perfect conversationalist, and, after discussing the weather in the most leisurely manner of polite talk, she said:

"Uncle Yao, I have come to report to you an interesting piece of news. The position I have today is entirely due to your son and indirectly to you. You must have known about it, and I don't know how to repay you. So when there is really something interesting, I feel that I ought to let you know before anybody else. And this is indeed an exciting opportunity."

"Curios?" said Mr. Yao. "I am tired of them. I have not been buying curios for years."

"No, no, it isn't that. I know you are not interested in curios now. And, Uncle Yao, don't think I have come to do business with you. It is about a garden in the North City, which belongs to a Manchu baron. He is willing to sell it for a ridiculous price, in order to pass the Mid-Autumn. And so I thought, how many people in Peking have the money and the luck to be able to live in a prince's garden except Uncle Yao?"

"Why should I want to live in a prince's garden?" he asked. But the idea piqued his interest.

"For a thing like this," Mrs. Hua rejoined, "one must have both money and the 'luck of leisure.' Many high officials have the money but not the leisure to enjoy a pleasure garden. And leisure is not enough; one must also appreciate such things. Wouldn't it be a pity to let some of those silly-headed metropolitan officials occupy such a place?"

Sing-song artists were as a class the most cynical about the metropolitan officials, because they knew them too well. While trying to entertain them professionally, they knew also all the stories about the officials. In the last days of the Empire, there were still left enough of the cultivated and poetic sing-song girls who despised the officials and were friends with the writers and poets who talked about them. Therefore, Mrs. Hua's remark about the officials showed her taste and refinement.

393

Mr. Yao smiled and said, "How much does he ask?"

"If I mentioned it, you would laugh. Only a hundred thousand dollars. The buildings alone must have cost two or three hundred thousand dollars at the time, and no one can even build such things nowadays. The baron is in need of money and is preparing to give up the residence and go to Tientsin, and that is why he asks so little. He can sell it, I know. If you are interested, I will take you there today or tomorrow."

In Mr. Yao's rapid mind he had already bought the garden. The next day he went to see it with his family. Mulan first heard of it when Coral came over and said, "We are to live in a prince's garden! We are going to see it tomorrow and you must come along."

Parts of the buildings and the pavilions were very old, but the residential houses were in perfect condition. They had been built in the reign of Hsienfeng for a prince, the grandfather of the present baron, and the timber used was solid and massive and expected to last for centuries.

Mr. Yao, having discussed it with his brother-in-law, decided to buy it. The Manchu baron was still very proud and insisted on the round sum. He would not condescend to haggle and Mr. Yao haughtily refused to drive a harder bargain, when the bargain was already good enough in his eyes.

"That Mrs. Hua is one of the cleverest women I ever met," said Mr. Feng on his return. "She must be making at least five thousand out of this deal. I must go into partnership with her. The curio shop is a good business in these days. She was saying that she had no money to buy the baron's curios. What do you think?"

"You can do it if you like," said Mr. Yao. He rather liked Mrs. Hua and if his brother-in-law went into it, the shop would automatically have the backing of his own firm.

"Since we are going to buy the baron's home, it will be easier to sell his curios as genuine," said Mr. Feng. "He will have confidence in us, and it can be arranged on credit."

The decision was made easily. Mr. Yao bought the garden because he had come to regard money very lightly. Mr. Feng approved because it was a good bargain. Afei, Coral, and Mochow were excited because they were going to live in it. And they all thought it well to have a change of surroundings for the mother, who had been very unhappy since Tijen's death.

"What about this house?" asked the mother. "Are you going to sell it?"

"I can give it to Mochow, when she is married," said Mr. Yao. "Or if she wants to come and live in the garden to keep you company we can sell the house—or give it to a school."

. ˙.

Now while things were going fairly well with the Yaos, there were signs of dissolution in the Tseng home. In spite of the wise management of Mrs. Tseng, the preservation of harmony in a large household with grown-up sons and daughters-in-law was a difficult task, successful at times only through good manners and forbearance on the part of all—elements in the art of living at peace with fellowmen in any human community—plus common respect for the head of authority. Mrs. Tseng was able, in spite of her weak health, to keep everybody in his or her place. But good manners and the exercise of forbearance on the part of the other members were beyond her control. The daughters-in-law brought with them their respective home breeding and nothing could change their characters.

Suyun was unhappy, but she was coming back into her own and getting Chinya where she wanted him to be. She loved Tientsin and hated her life in Peking but, after all, Peking was still the capital. It meant power and high politics and the chance to amass a fortune— If only her husband were like her brother! And her brother was coming back to Peking. He was her hero, an example to her of what a man should be; by contrast Chinya was tame and weak and lacking in the manly qualities of push, dash, and daring. How she admired her brother's luck and ability on the Tientsin Stock Exchange! He talked all the time in terms of hundreds of thousands, and here was poor quiet Chinya earning his three hundred a month! It was not enough for house expenses if they had to rent a house. She always had a feeling of helpless rage as she saw her stuttering husband repeating things to servants. But her mother had told her, "Look at your father. I made him!" And it seemed what she needed to do was to take her husband in hand and get her brother back into power to help him. Thanks to her pushing, therefore, Chinya had befriended a jolly young man who was the fifth brother of a director's third concubine, and secured for Huaiyu a temporary job in a government liquidation bureau.

395

The two Tseng brothers were falling still further apart. Sunya was loafing and happy about it; Chinya was working regularly and yet failed to satisfy his wife. He felt often a sense of rebellion against her, but through his good nature or his timidity, he was apparently ready to endure it for a long time yet. Outwardly, he was considered "henpecked" among his friends, but within him brooded a discontent that was not to find expression until he was considerably older. Only when he was annoyed to the limit by Suyun's eternal dissatisfaction with him and with his family, would he answer back by making references to her own "good" family. Once after sulking all morning he went over to Sunya's court and permitted himself to say to his brother, "I wish I had never married at all!"

Curiously it was Suyun who opened Chinya's eyes to the inequality between the brothers.

"Why is Sunya allowed to loaf, while you are working?" she said one day. "You are both born of the same parents, and you both are spending the parents' money. We are all eating and spending from the common family fortune. But while you are earning three hundred a month, he is not doing a thing. Why doesn't he try to get some work? If this continues, it will be better to divide the property. At least we would then have some money of our own to spend and invest as we like. We could ask my brother to invest it for us. He made twenty-five thousand dollars overnight last week just by telephoning to the Stock Exchange. And, although you are the eldest son, Sunya and Mulan are consulted whenever things come up. No matter what the question, you hear Lan-erh this and Lan-erh that. The whole family is bewitched by that female fox-spirit. And if I were not here, you would be still less able to hold your own."

"Hold my own against what and whom?" answered Chinya, piqued by the implication of his uselessness.

"Against them, all of them. Even the servants try to flatter the Third Mistress because she is managing the household. Mannia and she act together. It makes me ill to see them holding their hands together as if they had just met after a long separation."

"This is all in your imagination," replied Chinya. "After all, we are one family. Why can't you make friends with them, too? Why can't we live peacefully together?"

"My imagination indeed! That is why I say you are simple-minded. Didn't you see how the whole family applauded when Atung was crawling on the floor—from the grandmother down to the servants? Really, for a daughter-in-law to give birth to a grandson is like a victorious general returning to the capital."

This last charge of partiality to Mulan was true. By merely producing a grandson, Mulan seemed to have taken an easy lead over the other daughters-in-law. That certainly was not Suyun's fault. But the pressure in an old family was so great that there was no escape from it, and every stir made about Mulan's baby boy was like a silent censure upon Suyun's barrenness. Chinya had heard that the grandmother had said that Suyun was barren, and the grandmother had denied ever saying it, but that did not make it less unpleasant. Mr. and Mrs. Tseng had not said anything, either. But sometimes after lunch, when the family sat around the room, there would be, without any one's instigation, a spontaneous exhibition of Atung. The baby would start to crawl across the floor, and there would be applause and shouts to egg him on from everybody. "Only yesterday he could stand up and walk three steps; today he can walk four!" Mulan would crow in triumph, and there would be showers of praise and roaring laughter at everything Atung did.

Suyun even saw the doctor and asked him what he could do for her to wipe out her shame, but he could do nothing.

. · .

One day, urged by his wife, Chinya spoke to Sunya about trying to get some work. "You could get a job if you tried to. You see how I have helped Huaiyu to get one."

"I know what I am doing," countered Sunya. "And I have seen how you had to cling to the Director's third concubine's fifth brother in order to get that job for him."

"I am telling you as an elder brother," said Chinya. "Our parents are getting old, and all our money and property added together make up only barely over a hundred thousand dollars besides this house. At the rate we are spending, we are eating up six or seven thousand dollars of the capital every year. We are all spending the money of the family and no one is thinking of earning a cent. This is why I tried to get Huaiyu into the government; now that he's in, perhaps he can help us to get some good jobs."

"You had better be careful about that brother-in-law of yours," said Sunya. "He may get you into something that you will regret. He is playing with fire, with that Inging." Sunya, in turn, was expressing Mulan's views.

"What has Inging got to do with us? What harm can she do us?"

"Would you care to have a sing-song artist in our family?" asked Sunya.

"That does not concern us. It is his own affair."

"I don't want to speak against your relatives," said Sunya. "But, as your brother, I would advise you to keep away from him. He is absolutely unscrupulous, and you know it."

Now Inging was a famous courtesan in Tientsin, the toast of the politically disappointed and socially dislocated old gentry who had flocked to the foreign Concessions. She was a woman of great natural charm, about twenty-three or twenty-four years of age, but she was not a courtesan of the old type, having been brought up in the confusing era when sing-song girls began to ape the modern girl students in dress and behavior. With her feminine instinct for attracting men and her natural social abilities that some women are born with, she could do without much learning, and she had also a cold, unemotional scheming ability, which is always frightening in a woman. With her sing-song training, she had no scruples about playing one suitor against another and she was able to get out of any dubious situation with clever or even brilliant subterfuges. The arts of cajoling and humoring men she practiced to perfection, and they seemed part of her daily experience. Men who knew they had been deceived by a clever sing-song girl were nevertheless charmed by her. Since the brother of the Mayor of Tientsin had discovered her and a former secretary of a Viceroy had written a poem about her, she had become one of the "reddest" or most popular courtesans of that city.

Huaiyu was introduced to her by the mayor's brother and the two at once became friends by mutual attraction. Inging knew all about his exploits in the Manchu days, but that only increased her admiration for him. He could tell inside stories of high political intrigue and gigantic schemes costing millions—one of his pet schemes being the opening up and colonization of far-away Heilungkiang through a thirty-million dollar corporation. These talks gained Inging's confidence, if not in his scheme, at least in his imaginative ability. It was clear that her training had prepared her to marry either a powerful, or at least an extremely promising, politician. And after all, she was a woman and Huaiyu was young. The foreign-concession gentry, on the other hand, were either old or ugly, men past their prime, who had feathered their nests and were now thinking only of a safe and comfortable and amusing life, men without imagination and without hope. All of them were tired of their old wives; all wanted a modern girl with her freedom and her ability to parade on men's arms on social occasions, or envied others who had such wives. They all cursed the loosening morals of modern girls, all believed in Confucianism, and all wanted to protect their own daughters and sons from this moral maelstrom of modernity; all believed they could not stop it and all sought courtesans who adopted the names of the ancient cultivated courtesans, but could barely read the stories about themselves in the Chinese newspapers. It was a generation of lost souls, living in the false security of an artificial community called a "foreign concession" under the hypnotism of a new advancing materialism.

Huaiyu dared the jealousy of two powerful older officials, including the mayor's brother, by proposing marriage to Inging as his concubine, and she had consented. The marriage was featured in the Peking and Tientsin newspapers, because she was so well-known, and because the marriage of a son of the former God of Wealth was still a good story. A bizarre touch was added by the fact that Inging herself belonged to the clan of News. By marrying a girl of the same family name, Huaiyu was contravening an age-old custom—a portent of the chaos of moral ideas to which modern China was getting used.

As for Suyun, she was now happy that in her brother's concubine she had found a friend with congenial tastes who was going to make her life in Peking more pleasant for her.

And Chinya kept on believing that his father was partial toward his younger brother and Mulan. He believed, moreover, that some people were born naturally to work and others, more brilliant, were born to loaf and enjoy life, and that he was not one of the latter. He believed that there were men born to good luck and men born to bad luck; and since his marriage to Suyun he had convinced himself that his own life was shadowed by an evil star, and that he must be content with that for the present.

CHAPTER XXVI

THE following spring, the Yaos moved into their new home. As no permanent arrangements had been made for the old house, Mr. Feng said he would stay there with his family. But he had at this time only two sons besides his daughter, Redjade, and the house proved too big for them. Since they would not think of renting part of it, Lifu's family was invited to come and stay with them. Paying rent was of course out of the question, since they had been paying no rent at the Guild, and the proposal was put to Lifu's mother rather as a favor to be sought from her. Since Mr. Yao would not rent it to strangers, would she and her family not come to help occupy the rooms? Mr. Feng went on to say that he was frequently absent on business trips to the south, and his wife would be afraid to keep the house all alone and the presence of Lifu would be a help. So Mrs. Kung and Lifu agreed and came to live there.

The Yaos moved into the garden on the twenty-fifth of March. As it was manifestly improper for them to keep the old name of the garden, Mr. Yao gave it a new name, Chingyiyuan, or "The Garden of Quiet and Suitability." Mulan had suggested several short names, like Garden of Mildness, or Deep Calm, or Plain Simplicity, in accordance with the tradition of great gardens, using a single word to comprise a whole philosophy. But her father thought the name he had chosen more appropriate. It was neither pretentious nor untrue, and therefore affected, as a more poetic name like "The Half-Farmer's Hut" would be. Besides, "suitability" is a fine word, meaning living according to your station in life, and your own nature and character. The choice of a name suggesting domestic contentment, rather than poetic escapism, was comfortably reassuring to the sisters. Mr. Yao began to call himself "Owner of Chingyiyuan." He had one seal made with these characters, and another bearing the characters "The Man of Leisure of a Little Stopping Place by the Peach Clouds," to be used for less formal and more poetic occasions. However, the people of Peking still called the place by its old name of "Prince's Garden."

On the fifteenth of April, Mr. Yao gave a party to the relatives to celebrate the new garden home. Mulan said to Sunya, "I wonder if Inging is coming. I want to see her."

"Of course she'll come. Do you think a woman of that type is afraid of the family?"

Turning to Dimfragrance, Mulan said, "I want you to come, too. You won't believe it, but I tell you there is a room in that garden called Dim Fragrance Studio after you. Isn't that strange?"

Dimfragrance visibly started. She had come now to feel very happy working for Mulan, but some of her old reflexes still remained. At any sudden remark, her body would always shake, prompted by the fear that she had done something wrong. If she happened to be idle at the approach of Mulan, she would at once take up something and pretend to be busy with her hands. Mulan disliked this and would tell her not to be afraid to be seen idle, and Dimfragrance would look up in amazement, and her fear would be allayed only by Mulan's smile. She envied the ease and self-confidence with which Brocade spoke to her mistress, but she found it hard to imitate her.

She had once been surprised to hear Mulan say that Suyun had a maid called Coldfragrance, and she herself was called Dimfragrance, so that it sounded like a pair predetermined by Fate. Now it was a greater shock to hear that a studio in a prince's garden bore her name.

"I don't understand how a prince's studio could be called by such a common name as a maidservant's," Dimfragrance replied.

"It isn't a common name at all," said Mulan. "It comes from a famous poet's line about plum flowers. The studio faces an orchard of plum trees. That is why it is so called."

"I thought 'dim' was a bad word, because I never heard any other girl called by it. I thought it meant 'dim luck' and some one had given me that name just to spite me."

Mulan laughed, and Sunya said, "It is one of the prettiest names you can find."

Strangely, the new pride in her name worked a change thereafter in the girl's opinion of herself. She no longer imagined that she went about with an insulting label and that her life was followed by the "air of the dim moon," at the end of the lunar month.

When Mulan and Sunya were ready to go to the party they went over to the mother's room and found that Mannia's mother, although dressed, was insisting that she should stay at home.

What had happened was this: Cassia was unable to go because she was suffering from the after-effects of a miscarriage. Phoenix was helping to make Mrs. Tseng's coiffure, with Suyun and Mannia sitting in the room, all ready to start. Without looking up, Mrs. Tseng had asked, "Who is going to stay behind to look after the house? Muskrose can only stay in the room to keep Cassia company."

"I will stay if you want me to," said Phoenix.

"Ask Auntie Sun to stay," said Suyun.

If anybody else had said this, or if it had been said differently, it might have been taken as only thoughtless. But Suyun had said things about Mannia's mother before, including a remark that she had no home to go to. This new affront was the last straw, and Mannia for once failed to restrain her anger.

"Why must my mother stay, while others are going?" she demanded. "Who is to stay and who is to go is for the *Taitai* to decide."

At this moment, Mannia's mother had come in, and Mannia had stood up and said, "Mother, we are not invited and so why are we all dressed?"

Mannia's mother was silent, aghast, while Mrs. Tseng, surprised by this sudden temper in Mannia, hastened to explain. "You must not misunderstand. I was asking who was going to stay to keep Cassia company and look after the house. Phoenix said that she would, and then Suyun suggested you should stay. She perhaps did not mean anything, but she should not have said it. Suyun, I think you ought to apologize to Auntie Sun."

Suyun started to speak, but Mannia's mother said, "*Taitai,* I am a guest here and have never complained, because you and cousin have treated me and my daughter always so well. We are poor people and my daughter cannot compare with your second and third daughters-in-law. But even if I am a guest here, I am not homeless. It is because I have this only daughter that I am living with her."

"Whoever said you were homeless?" protested Mrs. Tseng.

"Of course some one did," said Mannia heatedly. "And is it wrong for me to adopt a son? How is it said that one could adopt a hundred sons if one cared to? Is an adopted son therefore not a son? You did not expect a widow to bear a baby, did you?"

Mulan and Sunya came in at this moment and were amazed to hear Mannia's rapid and somewhat comical charges.

"Whoever said all these things?" said Mrs. Tseng.

"Some one must have said them, or my mother and I could not have heard of them," replied Mannia.

"I never said Auntie Sun was homeless," said Suyun. "And if I did say someone had no home to go to, it need not have meant her. I do not have time to waste my thought on others' having or not having a home."

Mrs. Tseng said, "Aunt, you must pardon us. If my second daughter-in-law has said things impolite to you, I apologize for her to you. As for you Suyun, I heard you make that remark today myself. Even if you didn't mean it, was it a proper thing for you to say?"

"What is there strange about staying behind?" said Suyun. "I am willing to stay."

"No, Phoenix will stay. You must come, that is my order," said Mrs. Tseng. "Auntie, don't listen to their childish quarrels. If you don't go, I won't go either."

Mulan had heard this bewildering exchange and saw that Mannia was half in tears. She was angered with Suyun, but she remembered that she was the hostess today and must not break up the party. So she said with restraint:

"Mother, if you will allow me to say something today as the hostess, I insist that Auntie Sun should come with us. Auntie, you must give me this face. If you did not come, I would take it that you did not consider me Mannia's best friend. Besides, today's party is a gathering of relatives. You are, firstly, grandmother's niece, secondly, father's cousin, and, thirdly, my aunt. If you did not come, our party would be incomplete."

Chinya had come in and was listening to Mulan, not yet knowing what it was all about. The father had been listening from the next room, but so long as it was a women's quarrel, he left it to his wife. Now his sons had appeared, and Cassia, who was lying in bed, advised him to go out and set them at peace.

"Chinya and Sunya," he said as he entered, "quarrels among sisters-in-law are common in households. As husbands, you ought to restrain them. Otherwise it will develop from a sisters-in-laws' quarrel into a brothers' quarrel, and that means the downfall of the family. I forbid you all to mention this incident again." Turning to Mrs.

Sun, he said, "Cousin, don't listen to children's quarrels. It is a beautiful day. Forget about this."

So Phoenix and Muskrose stayed behind to keep Cassia company while Brocade and Dimfragrance went along because of the children.

Before leaving the house, Suyun said to her husband, "You stood by to see your wife insulted without saying a word. You heard Mulan's tongue."

"Why didn't you reply to her yourself? I didn't know anything about it," protested Chinya. "And I couldn't make a reply to her, if I did."

"It is my 'dim luck' getting into a quarrel with that ignorant country woman!"

"There you are again. Suppose some one should hear you say that?"

"But she *is* an ignorant country woman. . . . Well, you stand up for your relatives; I stand up for mine. If it weren't for Inging, I would rather not go today."

"We must keep up appearances and observe the rules," said Chinya.

. · .

The party arrived at the new mansion at about half past eleven, a little late because of the quarrel. Afei and Redjade were waiting at the gate into the Garden, for Redjade had come early with her parents to help entertain the guests. Afei was now a boy of sixteen, dressed in foreign clothes and looking very handsome. Happy in circumstances and loved by his parents and sisters, he was lively, charming, good-mannered, but like all boys, perpetually active. Redjade was annoyed by this, for she disliked noisy movements, but she was nevertheless always happy when together with him. A year younger than Afei, she had mentally outstripped him, and in her had sprung up an intense love for this cousin who had grown up with her. She thought him still too childish, but liked him not the less for it.

It was Mulan's idea that the guests should come in that day from the rear entrance, rather than at the main gate on the south. The main living rooms were clustered around the southern entrance and gradually spread out toward the north, leading by an artificial canal and pond through corridors, over bridges, and past various pavilions and terraces into a large orchard. There were several entrances, but the one at the northwest gave a direct view of the peach orchard, with rows of cabbages and a well, and the roofs of the buildings were hidden behind the trees, with occasional glimpses of red-painted balconies and colored girders contrasting with the green foliage. When one entered from this rear gate, it was like going into a farmer's home in the country, with a leisurely approach to the buildings on the south. This gate had been renamed, at Mulan's suggestion, "*Taoyun Hsiaochi,*" or "A Little Stopping Place by the Peach Clouds," because in spring there was a cloud of white and pink peach blossoms in the orchard.

They went slowly because everybody hung behind the grandmother, who was leaning on Damask and Snow Blossom for support. The grandmother was now a very old lady. She was gradually growing shorter because her back was bent, but her pace was not slow for her age. There was no hurry, for the peach flowers were in full bloom, and there was a great variety, the wild peach, the green peach, and the honey peach; and there was also a mixture of plums, apricots, and crab apples, which had already put forth green buds.

"The spring comes early this year," remarked the grandmother. "Usually the peaches bloom in the last third of April. Now I understand why this place is called A Little Stopping Place by the Peach Clouds."

"I thought the clouds resembled the pink of the peach; but it is the peach blossoms that resemble the clouds," said Mannia.

Passing the orchard, they came to the "Keep-Farmer-Company Pavilion" an octagonal pavilion at the end of a winding canal and connected with the buildings by a long promenade corridor along the bank of the canal. A small boat lay at the foot of the pavilion. As the grandmother was setting the leisurely pace, Mr. and Mrs. Tseng and the young people loitered to look at the gray stone panels along one side of the corridor, picturing twenty-four scenes from the *Red Chamber Dream*. Twenty yards beyond, they came to a red-painted wooden bridge, which served to mark, as it were, a tightening up in the general composition of the garden. Standing on the bridge, they saw that the canal widened into a small pond, about forty feet across on the southern side, while a covered terrace with balconied seats all around jutted into the pond with a wooden board bearing three characters in cabbage green, reading, "Terrace of Swirling Waters." A few old women servants were moving about on the terrace, where Mrs. Yao was sitting to welcome the guests. On the right and left, the pond was shaded with overhanging trees, and the corridor became hidden by the leaves and then reappeared again, leading to the terrace.

405

Mulan's father came to welcome them halfway down the corridor, and they followed him to the terrace. It was clearly designed for looking across the pond and the bridge into a vista of rural beauty, and as a lounging place for small summer parties. Into the wooden partition on the south side were fitted four marble panels ten-foot high, inscribed with the calligraphy of Tung Chichang. Several inlaid blackwood tables were laid out, and the tea service of cloisonné pots and cups in square, beveled shapes lent a touch of antique luxury. Lotung's son, who had left his master and come over with Bluehaze, was serving tea with the help of some women servants. Only Coral and Mochow were not there, for they were busy directing the servants inside.

Mulan's mother came forward, and the grandmother extended her congratulations. Mrs. Yao's white hair and general expression revealed that she was now a nervously broken woman, incapable of great happiness. The grandmother needed to rest, and the young people scattered to sit on the balcony seats.

"See the lotus leaves move!" exclaimed Afei. "A fish must be passing under them."

Small bubbles appeared about the lotus leaves resting on the surface of the water like floating pale-green moons on a deep-green firmament, made deeper by the shade of the thick foliage. Drifting moss near the banks turned the water into a greenish-yellow, while in the middle the reflection of the clear blue sky merged with the color of the water and shaded it into the turquoise color known as "precious blue."

Mochow appeared now to greet the relatives, and the grandmother said, "Come over here! I haven't seen you for a long time. You have grown so tall." Mochow quietly went over, and the grandmother took her hands and made her sit on her lap, and Mochow obeyed, although she hardly dared rest her whole weight on the old grandmother. As she was now a girl over twenty and fully grown-up, this was very embarrassing for her. The white plump hands coming out of her rather short sleeves were as if made to hold a baby or an embroidery needle or a saucepan, with that inexpressible beauty of the hands of a young girl physically matured and ready to be wife and mother.

Lifting her wrinkled fingers to pinch Mochow's cheek, the grandmother said:

"Such a pretty child! It is a pity my son didn't give me another

406

grandson, for I would certainly have you as my granddaughter-in-law."
Everybody laughed, and Mochow was ready to die with shame.

"If Mistress Cassia were here she would certainly say that Old Ancestor is getting greedy," remarked Mannia. "She is not satisfied with one daughter of the Yao family!"

"Doesn't the proverb say that the older a person grows, the more greedy he becomes?" replied the grandmother. "But believe my old eyes! A girl with such hands will bring good luck to any family she marries into."

As Mochow could not possibly remain in that precarious position of pretending to sit on the grandmother's lap, she rose now.

"Grandmother hasn't exaggerated," said Mrs. Tseng, intending to pay Mrs. Yao a compliment. "It is gratifying to have a young and responsible daughter-in-law like Lan-erh to take the family responsibilities off my hands. From now on, the family affairs are in the hands of the young people. I am really quite lucky, and have to thank my daughter-in-law's parents for it."

"If my Lan-erh knows filial piety, I am satisfied. But the relatives must control her and not spoil her by indulgence," replied Mulan's mother.

"I think we ought to use the Little Stopping Place by the Peach Clouds as the regular entrance," said Mulan. This started a debate between the sisters.

"Impossible!" said Mochow, "one has to walk over a hundred yards to reach the living rooms. And on rainy days it will be so muddy and inconvenient."

"Why, there is a brick-paved walk," said Mulan. "And if it rains, isn't it the more fun? We can keep some palm-tissue waterproofs at the gatehouse. And we can still keep the side door of the southern entrance open, if mother prefers to use it." Now palm-tissue waterproofs were made of the protecting sheaths around the lower trunk of the palm tree, woven and stitched to serve as raincoats, and Mochow said, "I know you would use one of those fishermen's waterproofs over your silk gowns and like it. Of course it would look fantastic and pretty."

"I shouldn't mind, really," said Mulan.

"That's why I call her Whimsy," said Sunya.

"The question," said Afei, "is whether you want to begin with luxury and end up in simplicity, or begin with simplicity and end up in luxury."

"Exactly," said Mochow. "I quite understand Second Sister; her idea is that we should conceal this luxury and present a simple front. But it is much better to present a luxurious front, while we live an inner life of simplicity within. If you let people pass in and out through the back garden, its atmosphere of seclusion and quiet will be spoiled."

The elders listened silently to the young people's argument, and Mr. Yao thought that in this matter Mochow was more profound than Mulan.

But Mulan went on, "I still don't see. This back entrance gives a better approach and a longer perspective of the buildings. Since we have space, let's enjoy the space. We don't want to step from the entrance right into the living rooms, like a poor man's home. And in the second place, if you don't use it you'll practically never come this way at all."

At this point, Sunya exclaimed, "Look! They have come!" The party looked over the bridge and saw Lifu and his mother and sister coming down the promenade corridor. Afei dashed to welcome them. Huan-erh, now a girl of eighteen, was dressed like a modern girl student in those days, wearing a mauve jacket molded round the hips, black silk trousers, and high-heeled shoes. Lifu was holding his mother's arm; there were certain movements of clinging affectionate intimacy between the son and mother, which were never seen either in the Yao or the Tseng family.

Lifu wore a gown of grayish-blue foreign serge. He at once went up to greet the grandmother and the elders, and then came to speak with Sunya and Mulan. He saw the incredible fact that here was a young woman who had lost none of her youth and beauty after childbirth; her skin was as fine and the corners of her eyes as full and smooth as if nothing had happened. When Lifu approached, Mochow smiled and walked away. The innovation of fiancés seeing each other was still embarrassing for the young people who were not used to it. Mochow was not naturally shy, and she was always dignified, taking Lifu's visits to her home naturally, but in the presence of such a large company, she wanted to keep a little reserve.

"We were debating about the entrance to the Garden," said Mulan to Lifu. "Which do you think should be used, the main southern entrance, or the entrance you came in by?"

"Who were debating?" asked Lifu.

"*Meimei* and I," replied Mulan.

"Don't tell him who was for which," interrupted Sunya.

"Oh, I know," said Lifu. "You are for the Little Stopping Place by Peach Clouds, while she is for the main entrance."

"Marvelous!" said Afei.

"And what do you think?" asked Sunya.

"In rain, I would come by the main entrance; in sunshine, by the Peach Clouds' Little Stopping Place," replied Lifu.

"But isn't there someone who would use the main entrance on clear days and the rear entrance in the rain?" asked Afei, to make fun of Mulan, and Redjade laughed out loud and was very proud of him.

"What is that? Am I going through an examination?" protested Lifu. "Of course there could be no such crazy person."

"Omitabha be praised!" said Mulan.

"But you said Second Sister would prefer the rear entrance?" said Afei again.

"I said she would prefer it in rain and shine, but not in rain only." Mulan smiled with satisfaction, and Mochow was proud of Lifu.

.˙.

Every well-planned home garden was a series of artfully concealed surprises, making every turn an exciting guess and every door the entrance to a mystery. As the party moved on through a door in the partition, they found suddenly that they had been standing on a promontory with the partition dividing it into northern and southern halves. The southern half, named "Mirage Tower," was designed as a stage for theatrical performances, with a landing about five feet below to prevent the actors from falling into the water. The canal curved around the west side of the little promontory and ran east and west in front of the stage for about fifty feet.

Mulan drew Dimfragrance to her and pointed to the hall on the opposite side of the pond, and said, "There is the Dim Fragrance Studio."

Dimfragrance put the child Aman on the ground and stood seeing the unbelievable; and even when the party was leaving, she remained transfixed, looking through a latticed door at the plum trees in the spring sunshine.

"Come," Mulan said gently at last, "We will visit it by and by."

Dimfragrance bit her lip and picked up the child and followed. Coming into the northern half, they saw Redjade standing alone looking into the distance, so absorbed that she did not notice them, and suddenly Mulan realized that Redjade was now a grown-up girl of fifteen. In the distance, Afei and Lilien were talking in the Pavilion beyond the bridge.

"What are they doing there?" Mulan asked.

"He said he was going to wait for Mr. New," Redjade replied. "Come on. We will follow the others."

They went on to a paved garden path, surrounded with shrubbery. Passing through a zigzag turn in the rockery, they came upon the "Meditating-on-Mistakes" or "Self-Examination Hall." This was a fairly spacious residential building, partitioned off by lattice work against bluish-green silk into alcovelike sections, known as "gauze cabinets," which were in the nature of a cross between a magnified bed and a miniature room, sheltered by woodwork and shaded by curtains of gauze, warm in winter and cool in summer, with wall cabinets for holding personal articles, couches, and service stools on which to place tea sets, incense pots, or water tobacco pipes. Of all the residential buildings, this was the farthest back and nearest the garden. It looked out upon the pond on the south, but was so surrounded with trees and rockery that it seemed entirely unconnected with the other parts of the mansion. On its north side was a narrow strip of pebble pavement, blocked off by a white wall, in which a round window with "ancient coin" lattice made of curved roof-tiles, permitted mere glimpses of the fruit trees and rocks beyond. A small vase-shaped side door on the cast led into other enclosed courts, but Mr. Yao suggested that they proceed south to the Dim Fragrance Studio.

They went up some large stone steps to the top of a small mount, where on the level ground there stood a tall fossilized strip of bark, over twelve feet high. By its side was a pine lowering its limbs, as it were, toward the water across a pile of rocks and fine shrubs. The buildings were too near to permit any but their curved roofs being seen at this place, but toward the west could be seen the tower-shaped theatrical stage jutting into the pond. An inscription with the words "Reflecting Russet" chiseled on a rock near by, indicated that this was a place for observing the sunset. As they watched, a kingfisher flew out of a tree and skimmed over the pond, leaving light ripples which disturbed the sky image in the water.

Descending again, they turned west and entered a covered corridor which served as an enclosed bridge, for here the canal turned south. The narrow corridor, with colored glass windows facing the pond, led into a wide hall with an enclosed porch thirty feet long facing the stage, evidently serving as seats where the Prince and his family sat to watch the play. The solid wall rose only two feet from the ground, and the windows were so made that they could be taken down during a theatrical performance. It then appeared that the stage on the promontory, covered by overhanging branches, stood on a foundation of jagged rocks, like a magic tower arising out of the water, and a panel bearing the words "Mirage Tower" was visible. A flight of small stone steps led down to the water's edge. The only thing that marred the beauty of the place and gave it a touch of vulgarity was a clay statue of a fairy boy rising from the middle of the pond before the stage and holding a horizontal scroll with the conventional words of *Chihsiang Juyi,* or "Good Luck and Heart's Desire."

"A good idea this," said Mr. Tseng. "Hearing the sound of flute and singing across the water makes it more enchanting."

Just then Mulan heard laughter coming across the water, which gave the voices a rippling quality. Out from the western side of the stage came the prow of a boat and then the green and pink figures of Afei and Lilien paddling it. The light of the green water shone up on their faces. Lilien was laughing happily.

"How delightful!" exclaimed the grandmother.

"It is a bad thing for the children to have water about the house," said Mrs. Yao, and called to them, "Look out!"

"It's all right," Afei shouted. "The boat has just been repaired."

"I thought you were waiting for the News," Mulan called.

"But they haven't come yet," answered Afei. "When they come, I'll bring them to the front in the boat."

He had paddled the boat close to the porch. "Second Brother, you will be careful," shouted Redjade to him anxiously.

"I know, I know," replied Afei with a smile.

"You don't know how different it looks down here. You people seem to be up in a tower," said Lilien.

"Go back quickly and wait for the guests," said Mr. Yao, "and don't you get into the boat again without an adult. The pond is quite deep."

The wide porch, as well as the hall inside, was provided with tables and seats, so that it seemed they could be used for banquets before or during the play.

"If we wait here for the News," said Mr. Yao, "we can see them coming as soon as they reach the stage. Otherwise, they may not be able to find us easily."

And so the company sat down at the different tables. Mr. Yao was very happy, and turning to the young people, he said, "I will test you. You see the scenery in front of us. The canal encircles the promontory on the west, but the mount encircles the canal also over this side. See who can make the best couplet with the following line:

"Encircling water embraces hill, hill embraces water."

The couplet was difficult because it must repeat three words and must apply to the actual scene, and the tones had to be perfectly contrasted. Now the younger generation, Ailien and Lilien, stood no chance, because they were in a missionary school; even Afei had not learned how to make couplets—an essential training for writing poetry that must begin very early—and Afei and Lilien were still outside and did not come in. There were therefore only Lifu, the Yao sisters, and the Tseng brothers to compete.

Lifu made the first attempt:

"Pond fish pierce shadows, shadows pierce fish."

"Lifu is greedy," said Mulan.

"How?"

"Because you used the word *pierce,* so that you could bring them home on a string and cook them."

"It's you who are greedy yourself," said Coral. "Whoever thought of eating the fish?"

Everybody thought for a moment and Mochow said, "You might change the word into *nestle:*

"Pond fish nestle shadows, shadows nestle fish."

"Good!" exclaimed Mulan. "There's your one-word master"; which referred to a poet who improved the line of another poet by changing one word in it and received the other's adulation. "But you might just as well say:

"Pond fish nestle trees, trees nestle fish."

"There's your two-word master, Brother Lifu," said Coral, who loved to tease Lifu when in his presence.

"That won't do," said Mochow.

"But isn't it true?" replied Mulan. "If the pond fish nestle in the shadows of trees, then they really seem to be nestling in trees."

"You are always fantastic and trying dangerous imagery," said Mochow.

Mulan now offered her own:

"Birds' song resounds (in) trees, trees resound song."

"Good," said Mr. Yao. "One line describes the picture; the other the sound."

Mr. Tseng also smiled in silent approval for he loved these old word games. Then he said to his sons, "Are you two losing before Lan-erh?"

"No use our trying when they are here," said Sunya.

Chinya was thinking of *Turning night into day and day into night,* and he said, "If I could only finish the line:

"Tung hsiao ta tan . . ."

(Whole night reaches morn. . . .)

It was manifestly impossible to use the word *ta* again in *morn reaches night.*

Mochow now said, "How about this?—

"White clouds conceal tower, tower conceals clouds."

"It is not bad," said Mr. Yao. "The first line describes the scene horizontally, and the second line describes it vertically. But it is not quite appropriate; it would be better for a tower situated in a high mountain."

"You don't see the reflections in the water, Father," explained Mochow. "The clouds below are concealed by the tower's shadows."

Now Redjade had been keeping quiet, thinking out her line all this time. Although she was in a missionary school, too, she steeped herself in Chinese by natural inclination and ability.

"I don't know if this will do," she said. Her line was—

"Leisurely men watch actors, actors watch men."

"Who is this?" cried old Mrs. Tseng, quite struck by this unusual approach.

"She is my niece," said Mr. Yao. "She is only fifteen. Good!"

There was no question that Redjade had carried away the honors, and her father was very proud of her. It was not only that the line was perfectly natural and effortless. It was most appropriate to the situation, and behind it was the profound philosophy that the spectators watching the play were themselves but acting in the drama of life watched by the actors across the water. Consequently, afterward

Mr. Yao had Redjade's couplet inscribed on wood and hung in the Dim Fragrance Studio.

To their surprise, Afei now appeared on the stage, followed by Lilien.

"There are knife throwers outside," Afei shouted excitedly across the water. "Shall I call them in?"

"A girl and a boy. Most wonderful to look at!" Lilien called.

Mr. Yao asked Grandmother Tseng if she cared to see the show, and the latter said, "Why not? I have seen knife throwers, but the children will love it."

Mr. Yao gave permission and soon the entertainers appeared on the stage outside the rear gate. Afei had found two Shantung children, a girl about thirteen and her brother about eight, accompanied by their parents. These were street entertainers who wandered from door to door, showing their skill and collecting a few coppers at a time. Their mother walked on a pair of ugly bound feet, with her trousers tied up around the ankles, and a baby tied on her back. The father carried a small ladder and a hand drum. The girl was dressed in an old purple jacket with very broad sleeves—a fashion that had died out ten years earlier. Her feet were bound but she moved about very nimbly. Her face was crudely rouged.

While the party watched across the water, they saw Afei and Lilien talking freely with the entertainers.

"These modern girl students are not at all shy in seeing people," said Mrs. Tseng.

Redjade listened in silence to this comment. Redjade and Lilien were now both in the same missionary school, famous chiefly for teaching the pupils to talk English. Mr. Tseng, in spite of his prejudice against Christianity and all other foreign things, had yielded in this matter and had sent his daughters to a Christian school, since in the government schools discipline had completely broken down because of the chaos of ideas, whereas in missionary schools pupils were at least taught to respect their teachers. And Mrs. Tseng had a better sense of the mode of the times than her husband, and wanted her daughters to be as modern as any. Once in such a school, it was inevitable that their Chinese was neglected. But there was a difference between Redjade and Lilien. Redjade remained at heart a sensitive girl of the old family type, while Lilien took to modern ways as ducks take to water.

The entertainment began with a pathetic version of an ancient comic village dance. The father beat the drum, and the family of four divided into two pairs, standing opposite one another. It was a short song accompanied by movements, at times the women moving forward, and at times the men moving forward and pointing their fingers at the women, with a common refrain:

> *Ter-r-r-r-r-la-ta piao-i-piao.*
> *Ter-r-r-r-r-la-ta piao-i-piao.*

Conceivably, sung by a good chorus it might have been a very pretty little song; but it relied chiefly on its comic effects, the coquettish gestures of the woman and the girl and the flirting of the man and boy, and these were not convincing. But the voices of the young girl and her little brother were hearty and cheerful and good to hear in the spring air.

After the song was finished, the drum beat again, and out the girl came to the little landing below the stage and began to throw three short pointed knives into the air in quick succession, catching them skillfully in her hands. The landing was about five feet wide, but from the side of the spectators, the girl seemed to stand on the very edge and everybody was rather nervous for her. The girl's eyes, however, were looking up steadily at the knives in the air, while she threw and caught them calmly with her hands, apparently without any difficulty.

When she was finished, everybody applauded, and, pleased with the applause, the girl smiled as she retired. Now the father came out and made a bow to the company across the water. He pointed to the water in front and said that he was going to show his skill. Taking his hand ladder and placing it securely on his head, he bent his knees to lower himself, while the little boy prepared to climb up.

"Don't!" shouted Redjade.

"Don't be afraid," said the juggler across the water. Without changing his position, he said, "If *Laoyeh* and *Taitai* think it is good, favor me with a bigger tip." His throat was tense and his voice strong.

Up the boy went, climbing nimbly to the top of the ladder. Resting on the top with the ladder between his legs, he lifted his hands and touched the roof of the tower. The women held their breath, while the boy began to work his way down passing between the rungs of the ladder back and forth, and at one moment suspending his body upside down. It was not an unusual feat, for the boy was light and small, but the effect was exciting. In one of his evolutions, the boy's feet struck the fretwork under the roof and he was thrown off, but quick as lightning, his father threw the hand ladder from his head and caught the boy in his arms. Before the audience had time to be afraid, the boy was safe on the ground. The father made a bow, and the audience applauded. Mr. Yao asked a servant to give the boy a dollar, and the grandmother, touched by the incident, also ordered one of her maids to tip him a dollar, saying that it was hard to be a poor man's son.

Mulan was watching with Aman at her knee and Atung in her arms. When the show was over, she suddenly discovered that Dimfragrance was not in the room, and, going out to look for her, found her sitting alone on a stone bench beneath a plum tree in the garden south of the hall. Dimfragrance, small and thin, was dressed in pink and she sat looking up at the green-studded branches, so that the sun shone with lines of branch shadows on her face, and her braid was hanging down on one side. What was she thinking of?

"What are you doing here that you didn't watch the show, Dimfragrance?" asked Mulan.

Quickly wiping her eyes with the tips of her fingers, she smiled broadly as Mulan had never seen her smile before and replied, "Oh I have been sitting here and just thinking."

"I know what you were thinking of," said Mulan. "The Dim Fragrance Studio of a prince's garden. You see the panel on top there? You can read your own name."

"Yes, but what is the last character?"

"That is 'studio'!"

"It looks like a saucepan cover on top and an earthen stove below with a lump of noodle between."

Mulan laughed. "Perhaps it was built for you, long before this life. Perhaps you were once a young lord here and murdered a maidservant, and that would explain your years of suffering."

Dimfragrance was so happy that again tears rolled down her face. "Well, it's all over!" she said.

"Dim Fragrance—Silent Fragrance—Cold Fragrance—Warm Fragrance," said Mulan. "They are all pretty names. Are you happy now?"

"I must thank *Nainai* for it all. If it were not for you, I should not have known this day."

"It is not me," said Mulan. "It is your luck that brought you here.

Did I know my father was going to buy this garden? You must not think or you will be puzzled. Something is protecting you as something was protecting me when I was lost as a child."

"*Nainai—*" said Dimfragrance, and checked herself.

"What is it?"

Dimfragrance knitted her brow and looked up straight into Mulan's face. "I want to follow you for life."

"How?"

"Like Brocade."

"Oh!" said Mulan.

Now Mulan had already had the idea of marrying Dimfragrance to her husband as his concubine. She was a modern girl and she had all the modern ideas against footbinding and concubinage, but these were ideas in the abstract and manifestly did not apply to her immediate situation. The idea of having a concubine for her husband rather enchanted her. Somehow it was true that a wife without a graceful, helpful concubine was like a crown prince without a pretender. The "rightful" wife's position was set off and enhanced only by the presence of a vice-wife, as a presidency sounds better and is more worth having when there are two vice-presidents.

"A wife without a concubine is like flowers in a vase without green leaves," Mulan had once said to Sunya.

"Whimsy, I thought you were a modern girl," Sunya had replied.

Perhaps it is better to call this simply one of Mulan's many whimsical ideas. Sunya felt that she thought of an assistant wife as an aristocratic luxury, like the jade animals that she loved. And she had a great capacity for friendship, a kind of friendship intimate, informal, sharing joys and sorrows together for life. And she always admired beauty even in other women. There are ideas that are artistically decent, though socially indecorous. Reader, call Mulan immoral, if you like. These things cannot be explained by the rules that the moralists set for us.

Sunya had a weakness for girls, she knew. He had come back from "flower dinners" given by friends, and had told her about the courtesans he had seen, and she was more interested in his description of courtesans than he was himself. He had called her "silly" in this connection, for he was perfectly happy with her—a state of perfection due no doubt to the fact that she placed no restriction on his attending such dinners.

417

There was also Cassia, a perfect example. Mulan could hold her own position as wife with as much ease as Mrs. Tseng did. Her position was in no danger, especially with a girl like Dimfragrance.

When Dimfragrance said she wanted to follow Mulan for life, the latter thought she meant becoming her husband's concubine. Therefore, when Dimfragrance said, "Like Brocade," she merely said, "Oh!" with a suggestion of disappointment, and said nothing more.

She was looking around and standing with Dimfragrance and Aman over an old jar three or four feet in diameter with some large gold fish in it, when she saw Mannia with her son, coming near.

"So you two, mistress and maid, are enjoying yourselves here, avoiding the crowd," said Mannia.

"Why, I have not been hiding myself," replied Mulan.

"The News are here," said Mannia. "I've come away to avoid meeting Mr. New. All their children are here and both the wife and concubine have come."

"Inging? What is she like?" asked Mulan.

"She is all very modern, with the new coiffure and a foreign spring coat and foreign shoes. Like the pictures of modern Shanghai ladies. Indoors she wears a pale pink jacket with a peony stuck in her left shoulder. The funniest thing was, she and Huaiyu came in arm in arm, like a modern couple, while his wife followed with the children behind. And I have something to tell you. *She* is always like that—she made me so angry."

"Who?"

"Suyun. When Inging came in, of course, Suyun was the person to introduce her, and when they came to my mother, she said, 'This is my country aunt.' If you had said it, I would not mind, but not from her. I suppose she is still angry about this morning."

"This is getting to be too much," said Mulan. "It is rude even when said in fun. I will stop her. You wait."

Mulan was all eagerness to see Inging, and she went with Mannia to a side room and watched through a plum-flower lattice.

With the appearance of the New family, the men and women had automatically drifted apart. Huaiyu was with Mr. Tseng and Mr. Yao and Chinya outside. Lifu and Sunya were talking in a corner. Inside, the women were sitting together. Mrs. Yao was talking with Huaiyu's wife, who was surrounded by four children, and Mochow was talking with the children.

418

The presence of Inging, once a notorious courtesan and now a concubine, made the women ill at ease, for family women had a natural antipathy toward women of that class. At the same time, they were very curious to see what she was like.

Inging was sitting with Suyun. She was a woman of apparently great sensual charm, plump and white and lively, and the illusion of youth was enhanced by the peony on her shoulder. She carried herself with complete ease, really unaware of any difference between herself and the family women, or pretending to be. Strange to say, she did not use too much rouge, but her sing-song origin was betrayed by the deep violet silk handkerchief in her hand that she constantly waved in the air as she was talking. And now and then, she would sit with her legs wider open than was good form for family women. Although a concubine, she was wearing skirts just like any fashionable wife. Her pale pink jacket, with high collar and tight short sleeves coming barely below the elbow, showed her plump soft arms. On her finger, Mulan saw a dazzling four-carat diamond. Beside her, Huaiyu's wife, thin and weak from the bearing of children, looked like a discolored old painting, and yet she seemed to be expecting still another child. While Inging talked, waving the violet handkerchief with ease and seeming happiness, the wife looked on like a doomed, mute, suffering animal.

The children, however, all seemed to hang around their mother and to look suspiciously at their father's new mistress. Suyun asked one of them to come to her, and one of the twins came over.

"Come to me," Inging said affectionately and stretched out her hand. The boy, surprised at her demonstrativeness, hung back. But Inging stretched out her white arm and gripped him and imprisoned him in her embrace. Inging tried to play with the four-year old boy, but when his twin brother called him, he broke away and ran back to his mother's side. Abruptly Inging rose and went to join her husband. Huaiyu, who pretended to be modern, immediately stood up, but Mr. Tseng and Mr. Yao remained sitting. Inging and Huaiyu went to the window and stood together looking at the water. Huaiyu offered her a cigarette and lighted it for her, and she put her arm on his shoulder.

"Really, she is without shame," whispered Mannia to Mulan. "She does things we dare not do."

They went in to join the ladies. Seeing Dimfragrance, the grandmother said, pointing to her, "Lan-erh, who is that pretty girl, your friend?"

"Why, Grandma, she is Dimfragrance!" exclaimed Mulan.

"Oh, I am an old fool now," said the grandmother. "I can't remember persons. She is dressed so prettily, like an official's daughter."

This pleased Dimfragrance very much and increased her self-confidence, and from that day on, Mulan saw her grow more poised and sometimes even laugh heartily.

When the company went over for dinner the men walked ahead, while the women and children waited again for the grandmother to lead.

"Asuan, come with me," the grandmother called to her great-grandson, and leaning on Asuan on one hand and on Damask on the other, she began to move along. Mulan noticed that Huan-erh was assisting her mother, and it seemed to her that she never had seen a more truly happy and contented woman than Lifu's mother. By comparison, her own mother, who was being assisted by Mochow, looked like a sad old woman, although she was now mistress of a prince's garden. She was now so broken in spirit that she had completely changed her character and had even lost her old temper.

Following a walk paved with large old bricks, lined on both sides with tall trees, where the spring air was fragrant with vegetation, they reached the banquet hall.

. ·.

The banquet hall was an old building about fifty feet wide and thirty feet deep, supported in front by massive red wooden pillars and with tall doors, eighteen to twenty feet high, beneath a green-base colored fretwork. An old horizontal panel bore the name of the hall, which was "Chungmintang," "Chungmin" being evidently a posthumous title of one of the prince's ancestors. In front was a wide stone yard, with a stone tablet on the west borne by a stone turtle. The tablet had two dragons on top; it commemorated the deeds of the prince and had been presented by the Emperor. Before the hall were two beds of peonies, quiet in the spring sun.

The men were examining the stone tablet when Sunya and Lifu came up and with them was Sutung, Sutan's brother, who had come to know the Yaos quite well. Sutung, a foreign-trained doctor, knew very little Chinese and he looked a little out of place. He was in foreign dress, and was well built, short but square-shouldered, and talked in a quiet, strong voice. Lifu found him looking at the stone turtle instead of at the inscriptions, and poking at the turtle's head with his foreign stick. By nature reticent, he had very observant eyes. Lifu rather liked him.

Turning from the tablet, Huaiyu asked Mr. Yao, "When is your third daughter's marriage?"

"Perhaps this autumn," replied Mr. Yao. Lifu had graduated two years ago and was now teaching, for he had insisted on earning some money of his own before the marriage. Mr. Yao had not objected and Mrs. Yao wished to keep Mochow with her as long as she could.

Huaiyu said to Lifu, "Congratulations! I have heard so much about you. My admiration! My admiration! You will do great things for the country." Lifu was embarrassed as Huaiyu suavely rattled on: "It is a time when our country needs people like you. There are so many things to be done: promote industries, elevate education, open colleges, reform society, clean up politics, and carry out the principles of democracy. In what field isn't there a need for talent?"

Lifu thought this sententious outburst was like the speeches of politicians at college commencements with which he was so familiar. "Reform society" and "clean up politics" were hollow phrases at the politician's tongue tip, which aroused in him a violent dislike. But he merely made a courteous reply.

Four tables were laid, and the Tseng grandmother was seated in the seat of honor at one table, with Mrs. Tseng next below her, while Mr. Tseng occupied the seat of honor at the men's table, with Huaiyu next below him. At the third table of younger women, Mannia's mother was seated highest, while Huaiyu's wife and Suyun sat next to her on one side and Inging sat next below Suyun, thus vindicating the position of the rightful wife. The others grouped themselves naturally, while Lifu, Sunya, and Chinya were seated with the elder men. Lifu's sister Huan-erh was next to Mochow at the grandmother's table, and Mulan and Redjade were with the younger women. At the four tables, Mr. Feng, Mulan, Mochow, and Coral were respectively seated at the ends, acting as the hosts and pouring wine for the guests.

Mulan, as the hostess at her table, soon proposed a toast to Mannia's mother. That the latter was sitting in the seat of honor was a matter of course in accordance with her age, and Mannia was sitting just below her mother, facing Huaiyu's wife, Suyun, and Inging. Some time had been lost before Mannia's mother was willing to assume the seat of honor; she argued a long time that Huaiyu's wife should sit highest. "We see each other everyday," said Mrs. Sun. "Mrs. New ought to be the guest of honor today." But she was overruled by the established tradition of respect for age, since Huaiyu's wife really belonged to the younger generation.

"Here's to Auntie Sun," said Mulan.

"Drink to New *Nainai* first, Lan-erh," said Mannia's mother.

"No, it can't be done," replied Mulan. "First, you are of the older generation. You have crossed more bridges than we have crossed streets. Second, you represent Grandmother's family here. Rudeness to Auntie Sun is rudeness to Grandmother. Whatever people may say, I will not allow them to say that a daughter of the Yao family does not know manners." Mulan stood up to drink the toast, and Suyun sat quiet, but knew the barb was aimed at her.

During dinner, Mulan tried to begin a conversation with Inging, and found that at close range she was even better-looking than at a distance. Mulan was complimenting Redjade on her couplet, and telling it to Inging and Huaiyu's wife who had not heard about the contest before their arrival.

Inging was of the tall northern type, and her voice had a rich, full-grown quality. "I can think of one," she said.

"Change clouds into rain, rain into clouds."

Now the phrase "cloud-rain" was a poetic expression for sexual intercourse. A euphemism, it was permissible in a sing-song house, but not in the present company. Actually it amounted to an insult. Redjade and Mulan understood it, and Redjade blushed, while Mulan looked at her and said nothing.

"What is the harm?" said Inging boldly. "We are living in the modern age."

But no one else spoke, and Inging realized she had shown a fault in taste.

At the men's table Huaiyu was doing the talking, with the zest of a man who completely believed in this world. But his world was largely —even exclusively—the world of politics. It was a good world to live in. Yes, there was the murder of Sung Chiaojen by Yuan but that was inevitable in high politics. The Parliament had been dissolved, but the members of Parliament were fools, easily bought. What was needed was a strong and clean government. Still the Constitution about to be promulgated was a good thing—a bedrock of democracy. There was a possibility the Premier would resign. Changing the cabinet to be responsible only to the President would make for a more stable government. Yes, three millions and a half would easily finance the new oil administration. New bonds of fifty million dollars would be necessary for the Dragon-Boat Festival. . . . (And, Lifu thought, there was not one phase of secret politics, not one high government official that he did not know.)

They went through the dinner as if they had been served with one course of a three-million-and-half oil administration followed by a course of fifty-million-dollar bonds to help those present pass the Dragon-Boat Festival. Huaiyu talked and cleared his throat and spat so loudly that, at moments, conversation at the ladies' tables stopped completely, as if all were about to listen to a great political secret. Even the servants felt as if they were serving at a dinner of cabinet ministers. Only the grandmother remembered to say a kind word for the fish and the goose-fat rolls so delicately prepared by the cook!

Toward the end of the dinner, Lifu became exasperated. Huaiyu was saying:

"We must all unite and support our great Chief Executive, in order to serve our country."

"I don't want to serve our country," said Lifu abruptly.

Huaiyu was horrified. Such a thought was unintelligible to him. It took him so completely by surprise that he was quiet for a second, and then continued, "Our Chief Executive, Old Yuan, would have put the country in order long, long ago, if he had been the Emperor, instead of the Manchus. If he had been born twenty years earlier, he might have become Emperor, and he would have put the country on the road of progress and liberty."

"He might still now," said Lifu, "and put the Republic out of existence."

The atmosphere was charged with danger. Although this was in 1914, there was already a rumor that Yuan was trying to overthrow the Republic and make himself Emperor. No one, not even Yuan's staunchest supporters, had yet dared discuss the rumor openly. Lifu was a staunch Republican, and from the way Huaiyu talked about "supporting our great Chief Executive," Lifu felt he was certainly paving his own way to becoming a monarchist when the time should come.

423

At Lifu's last thrust, conversation came so completely to an end that Mr. Yao rose and broke up the dinner. Pushing back his chair, he said, "I thank everybody."

The guests rose. Lifu's face was red with anger. Mulan came up and smiled at him. But Mochow came close, too, and said in a low voice, "Why did you have to say that to him?"

"I couldn't help it," said Lifu.

CHAPTER XXVII

*S*OON after dinner, Grandmother said she needed a nap, and the elder ladies went in to the front courts with her. The rest of the company scattered to wander about in the mansion. Huaiyu said that he and his family had to leave because of an appointment. For Inging, it had not been a successful party. Although her husband had shone during the conversation, she felt that she had not been accepted quite as an equal of a wife, and the women had not been entirely natural with her.

Having accompanied Huaiyu and his family to the rear gate, Mr. Yao turned back, and came up to Lifu, and to the latter's surprise, said, "You answered him right. Good for you!"

"Father, how can you say such a thing?" said Mochow. "It is better not to offend a person like Huaiyu."

Mr. Yao laughed and said, "Well, I suppose Lifu will be safer in your hands than in mine."

"Didn't it make you angry to hear him talking about supporting *our* Chief Executive and all that rot?" said Lifu. "Millions for this and millions for that, as if he were running the government!"

"What's the harm?" said Mochow. "Let him talk for his part and you listen for your part. Listen to him as you listen to a show."

"But it is officials of this type that are ruining the country. Shining lights of the Republic!"

Mochow, seeing Lifu vehement again, felt as if she were riding a thoroughbred, and knew she had to hold the reins lax sometimes and let him canter a little. So she merely changed the subject by saying, "It does seem that he is not treating his wife properly by flaunting his new mistress so openly in public."

"I wouldn't be in the wife's shoes," said Coral. "He needs some one to tell him straight to his face what people think of him."

Suyun now came to join them, leaving her husband with Mr. Tseng and Sutung, who had struck up quite a lively conversation about Mrs.

Tseng's stomach pains. When she saw Suyun approaching, Mochow said to Lifu, "His sister is coming. Guard your words."

"What an able companion in the chamber!" said Coral. "You are beginning already."

"You don't know my brother's temper," said Lifu's sister. "He doesn't mind his personal things, but he gets excited over things that don't concern him."

"Yang Chisheng's blood, I know," said Mochow.

"I am not interested in politics," said Lifu.

"But you are, more than anybody else I know!" said his fiancée.

"Me? Impossible!"

"Lifu," said Mr. Yao. "My daughter knows you better than you yourself. You listen to her, and you will be all right."

The conversation drifted to Lifu's future. Although he didn't quite know himself, he felt that he wanted to be a journalist, and he wanted to go abroad to study after his marriage. The trouble with him was that he had a facility in expression coupled with an amazing ability for finding out what was wrong in any situation around him, and this resulted in an unusual gift for calling a spade a spade and for pinning vague generalities down with a felicitous phrase. And as human beings are constituted, when a felicitous phrase comes to the mind it has to be expressed somewhere, either orally or in writing. Perhaps Lifu was by nature impatient, intolerant of evil, and especially of sham and hypocrisy. But so much intolerance of evil is merely a matter of seeing more clearly than others where the evil lies. People generally crush a bedbug when they see it, and that crushing of a bedbug is always accompanied by a certain satisfaction. Cleaning up things is a universal pleasure among children, and, even among grown-ups, removing stains or clearing up a blocked-up sink with a stick is always followed by that same sense of satisfaction.

The shouts of girls and boys were heard, among them distinctly Afei's voice; and a kite made in the form of a big cicada was seen struggling to get up in the air to the northeast, but the children were hidden by the flowering trees in the foreground and the artificial mounds beyond. Soon Redjade slowly came through the trees, alone, a slender lovely figure in cream silk jacket and trousers. Now and then she paused to look at a flower and then walked on unaware that they were watching her. Her performance in the couplet competition had greatly impressed them all, including Mr. Yao, and even Coral heard about it.

"What a clever girl Redjade is!" Coral remarked.

"Too clever," said Mr. Yao curtly.

"Why aren't you flying kites with the others?" Coral called.

"I was running about and I felt just a little giddy," Redjade replied, and indeed she was quite pale and panting. "It is the weather," she added. "It is suddenly so warm."

Huan-erh offered to accompany her in, but she said she was all right, only a little out of breath. Huan-erh took her to sit on a stone bench near by. "Here is a nice shade. Keep out of the sun," said Huan-erh.

Redjade had been from childhood delicate and susceptible to colds, and she would easily get a sunstroke if exposed on a hot day. Consequently she had the habit of avoiding the sun, and this gave her a pale white complexion. Her constitution had been undermined by too many bottles of medicine, too much delicate, special food, and too much reading of novels. Ever since the age of twelve, she had taken Tiger-bone-and-Quince Wine, a tonic usually reserved for aged people to strengthen their bones.

She had got up early that morning and come to the garden with her parents, and she had been happily busy in the company of Afei before the others arrived. Then the lunch was unusually late, and there was the excitement of the couplet contest. After dinner, she had forced herself to go about with the active Afei and Lilien and keep up with their breathless pace, and when Afei wanted to fly kites, she forced herself to follow and tried to take part, but soon the suddenly warm weather affected her.

"Who are there?" asked Huan-erh.

"Mulan, Sunya and they."

"What do you mean by 'they'?"

"Afei, and all the children and the Tseng sisters."

Now the company saw Mulan standing on top of a mound holding a kite, evidently to give it a start from the higher altitude, while some one pulled the string from below at a distance.

This was surprising in a respectable mother of two children. "Imagine sister!" said Mochow.

The kite went up a little distance, and Mulan jumped up as if to help it go up. But the kite swung and dived downward.

427

Mulan disappeared in a few minutes and Afei climbed the mound holding the kite and followed by Lilien, who was fighting with him for the chance to send off the kite.

Redjade shivered and was seized with a cough. "You are not feeling well. We had better go in," said Huan-erh.

"Yes, I think I will go in," Redjade said and Coral went in with her.

"That cousin of yours is so frail," said Lifu.

"She never feels well in spring," said Mochow. "Last spring she was in bed for over a month, but she wasn't resting. She read novels deep into the night. Reading too many novels is not good for a young girl. But that is not so serious as her inability to take things easily, and her desire to excel. That is the root of her illness. You hear of 'stupid luck,' but did you ever hear anyone speak of 'smart luck'? It is better to go through this world a little muddle-headed; it is easier and better for long life."

"You agree with Cheng Panchiao?" asked Lifu.

"I do," replied Mochow.

Cheng Panchiao was the eighteenth-century poet-painter-calligraphist who made the famous remark, "It is difficult to be clever; it is still more difficult to *turn* from cleverness to muddle-headedness."

"So you have made that *turn*?" said Lifu.

"So I have."

"Shall we join them?"

When Mochow and Lifu reached the kite-flying party, they found all the children there, Asuan, Poya, Aman, and Redjade's younger brothers, besides Mulan and her husband. Mannia was inside and Little Joy was looking after Asuan and was as happy as could be. Mochow asked Lifu whom he thought was the happiest person there and he agreed that Little Joy was the happiest.

"How old is she now?" asked Lifu.

"Twenty, I think," said Mochow.

"A grown-up girl like that, and still so completely innocent."

"You never can tell," replied Mochow with a cryptic smile; and then as she came near Mulan she exclaimed, "What fun you are having here! I saw you flying the kite, sister. Shame on you!"

"Look at my shoes," replied Mulan, wiping her forehead. "I nearly sprained my ankle coming down that mound. It was Afei's idea. He would not leave his brother-in-law in peace until he had dragged him out to fly the kite for him."

428

"Did you know Redjade was ill?" asked Mochow.

"Is she?" replied Mulan. "We didn't know at all. She was playing with us at first, and we didn't notice her leaving."

The kite was now high in the air, and there was nothing to do except to hold the string and Little Joy held it. When the others went in, Lilien remained playing with Afei and the children.

Mulan said that ever since after dinner, Afei had been hurrying about with Lilien, showing her different things, including the new telephone that had been installed, and Redjade had been trying to keep up with them. They stood around the telephone for a long time and tried to make calls by asking for any number they thought of and then hung up and laughed at the persons who answered.

"The two get along so well. Lilien is so lively. They like the same things, modern things—telephones, cameras, cinemas. Lilien goes to the movies behind her father's back. Redjade is different."

"She likes only Chinese things. But she is cleverer than Lilien," said Lifu.

"A hundred times cleverer," said Mulan.

"Than whom?" asked Mochow, who was close behind.

"We were talking about Lilien and Redjade," Mulan told her sister in a low voice.

"Isn't it sad?" said Lifu suddenly.

Mulan looked up at him. "What do you mean?"

"Those two."

"You mean those three," corrected Mulan. "Well, I suppose it is nothing serious," she said, after a pause.

Mochow had come up now and walked on Lifu's right side, with Mulan on his left, since here the road widened. So the three of them went in and saw the ladies, and Mulan, Mochow, and Ailien went in to see Redjade, who was in bed, with her mother sitting beside her. Huan-erh was also there, talking with her.

After a while, Mulan left to go home. Huan-erh remained in the room with Mochow, for, although studying at a government school, she looked upon Redjade as her little sister. She saw that Redjade's face was still tense with excitement, and lying there, with her head and neck propped up on her pillow, she seemed abnormally thin, although the lower part of her face was round and well molded like a young girl's and her cheeks were flushed with a false glow.

429

"How are you now, Fourth Sister?" asked Mochow of Redjade who was ranked fourth among the cousins.

"I just feel top-heavy," replied Redjade. "It seems that this spring sickness of mine has set in again. People are like flowers and plants. You people are so strong and happy. I think when your trees are bearing clusters of fruit, I shall be like withered petals already floating on the water."

"What words for a young girl of your age to say!" said Mochow.

It was evident that Redjade had read too much poetry and too much romance. Mochow sat contemplating this exquisite creature and she was touched and her bowels yearned toward her. She went and felt her pulse.

"Calm yourself, Fourth Sister," said Mochow. "I have read a few medical books and I think your sickness comes from too much *yang* and deficiency of *yin*. We must have the two principles harmonized and in proportion in order to enjoy health. The *yang* fire goes up and leaves the lower part of your body too light, so that you feel like floating on air. What you need is toning up of your *yin* systems. I think if you will take pearl powder steadily, and use common sense about food and adjustment of the circulating fluids, you will recover quickly. Don't depend too much on medicines; the body needs a great deal of the grain principle for sustenance. Take more congee and vegetables. Our roots are in the bowels, while men's roots are higher up in the heart, lungs and liver. That is why I think women must eat more vegetables and men more meat. But the *yang* and *yin* principles are not merely material, they are also mental. Men have their jobs and women have theirs. Reading too much is bad for us. Everything goes into the head and we get deficiency of *yin*. The earth is *yin,* is woman. Get down to the earth. We women cannot get away from the job of rearing children and attending to food and apparel. Even when a girl is born with intelligence, it is better to dim it a little. Reading history and poetry is all right, but we must not take it too seriously, or the more we read the farther apart we get from everyday life. When you are ill, I should advise you to give up reading novels. Take up some knitting, it is good for a woman."

Redjade listened to Mochow's advice in attentive silence, and was impressed by her sincerity. Mochow continued, "And I have another thing to tell you, Fourth Sister. Better than all medicine is the ability to take things lightly. Generally the more intelligent a man is, the more impatient he becomes. I am not flattering you, and I am fair in saying that your talent ranks above us sisters. But for that reason you ought to be careful of yourself. You have read so many stories of talented girls and beauties; how many of them ended happily? The ancients said, 'Red cheek, harsh fate,' but I say it was not the red cheeks but the clever heads that ruined women. When posterity comes to reckon accounts, it is difficult to say who was clever and who was stupid. In this life, it is better to take things lightly as they come along and not contrive too much. If you can learn to take this attitude, I can promise you that your illness will disappear."

There were tears in Redjade's eyes now. "Good sister, thank you for telling me these things. Nobody ever gave me such sincere advice before."

Mochow stretched forth her hand and put it on Redjade's shoulder and said, "Take pearl powder—the essence of the *yin* principle—for a long time, and you will get well. Now go to sleep."

So saying, Mochow left her.

. ˙ .

Redjade tried to go to sleep, but she could not. The words of Mochow were like a dose of soothing medicine for her, and she began to think of all they meant, and it seemed they suggested a great deal. Then she remembered that while the others had come in to see her, Afei and Lilien had not, and she kept awake. Her thoughts wandered on and on, over all the day's experience. And she said to herself, paraphrasing the saying of the brilliant general in the *Three Kingdoms* about another equally brilliant general, "Since Heaven creates a Redjade, why does it create a Lilien?"

She began to think of the famous beauties of history and romance that she had read about—of Meifei, Feng Hsiaoching, Tsui Inging, Lin Taiyu, Yu Hsuanchi, Chu Shuchen. In most of the tales, there was a stupid, un-understanding man. Afei was not stupid. She knew that Afei loved her, as they had grown up together and played together. But while she was precocious, Afei was not. Neither did he fit the picture of a poet-lover in the ancient romances. If she was the *chiajen* (talented beauty) he was not the *tsaitse* (poet-lover) of the romances. He could not even make a couplet. He spoke the awful school jargon of these modern days. The telephone, the movie, the

431

English words that he and Lilien began to mix in their speech—all of this jarred upon her.

The missionary school where Redjade went was famous for teaching conversational English, but she was too good in Chinese to be good in English, for her heart was never in it. English sounds always seemed to her ridiculous, and she was so sensitive that she was afraid of pronouncing them incorrectly. Hence, though she could easily read and understand English, she never learned to speak it well. A thin-skinned person cannot learn a foreign language well. At school, the students addressed each other by the English word "Miss" and she for one had rebelled against this—as if, she thought, the Chinese language had no way for addressing girls or for girls to address each other.

At last Afei came in belatedly. When the Tsengs were leaving, he wanted to see Mulan and Lilien off, and loitered at the gate, although Mulan said, "You had better run in quickly and see Fourth Sister. She is ill."

Consequently it was about half an hour before Afei came. He stood at the door and called, "Fourth Sister!" There was no reply. Redjade was lying perfectly still, her face away from him. He called again and she did not move. Lightly he tiptoed into the room and seated himself on a chair near the bed and waited silently. All this time Redjade lay motionless, but there was no sound of regular breathing, so that she could not be asleep. Suddenly her shoulders twitched, and Afei heard a low sob. He immediately went to her bedside and called, *"Meimei,* what is the matter?" The sobbing changed into suppressed weeping, and she made a violent movement and hid her face in the pillow. He touched her shoulder and tried to turn her toward him, saying, "I beg a thousand pardons. I didn't know . . ." but before he could finish, she shook him off and said, "Don't touch me. I am not like others who can romp and mingle with boys."

"I won't, then," said Afei, moving away. "See, I am sitting over here. But you must talk to me. When I found you were gone, I didn't know you were ill. *Meimei,* please."

Redjade turned her face toward him now and answered, "How could you know? Others would know long before you did."

Afei looked and looked at her with an expression of love and misery until Redjade was embarrassed. She had not intended to speak to him at all, but now when he did not reply and looked so repentant and miserable, she softened toward him, and said, "Second Brother, you have been out of your mind the whole day. I didn't have the strength to go about with you. Don't you feel tired?"

There was in Redjade's words something that showed she cared for him, and Afei gave her a handkerchief, and Redjade took it and wiping her eyes, said, "You really shouldn't go boating. I was so afraid for you. It is so dangerous."

"Dangerous? There's nothing to fear. Tomorrow I will go boating with you, and you can sit perfectly quiet and I will paddle for you."

"Thank you! You love it, don't you? 'It all looks so different from below,'" Redjade said, quoting Lilien.

"But it was true. It all looked different from the boat."

"Yes, and 'the people on the bank look as though they were in a tower.' You enjoyed it, didn't you?"

"You are wicked," said Afei.

"Honestly, I am not fit to play with you. Why can't you sit quietly like a grown-up and talk of things, like Lifu? You know I do not like noisy movements. I am afraid of the water, ever since I saw that little girl drowned at Shihshahai. . . . But never mind, when I am gone, there will be someone to go playing with you, someone who likes boating and flying kites and the telephone and sports."

Afei came forward and threatened to place his hand on her mouth. "If you say that again, I'll seal up your mouth!" he exclaimed.

She defended herself, and then he tried to tickle her, saying, "You dare? You dare?" and she began to plead for mercy, saying, "Second Brother, forgive me this time. I shan't dare any more." In that moment they were young children once more, playing as they had played since their childhood. Seeing that Redjade was coughing painfully from laughter, Afei relaxed, but Redjade said, "Well, I'm going to tell *Miss* Tseng about it."

He wanted to be lenient toward her as he always had been, because he loved her as his pretty cousin and childhood playmate, with all her faults and temper, admired her for her talent, and was tender to her for her weak health. "A dead duck still has a stiff beak. *Meimei,* you will never let a matter rest until you have won," he said.

"It is all the fault of the catchy and narrow temper of this catchy and narrow mouth of mine," said Redjade. "I tell you, of all our sisters, I admire Third Sister most—she is so wise and sincere and steady."

"But she doesn't tolerate people so well as Second Sister. I like Second Sister better," replied Afei. "Third Sister looks so calm and quiet, but when she starts to scold me, I am afraid of her. I am never afraid of Second Sister. But, *Meimei,* you ought to change your temper yourself." To him Mulan was perfect and he wished Redjade could be like her.

"I know myself, but one's temper cannot be changed," said Redjade. "Third Sister was just here and gave me some very good straight advice."

"What did she say?"

"She told me to take things easily. That was a real 'heart talk.' It is lucky for you that she talked to me first, or I wouldn't be speaking to you now at all."

"Really! Then I ought to go out and thank her," said Afei, pleased to see her reasonable again; and, trying to amuse her, he said, *"Meimei,* everybody admired you for that couplet. I am proud of you. It was really better than all the rest made by the others, including Second Sister's. But I have a better one than yours, if I had been there and had a chance."

"So? Let me hear it," Redjade said.

"Well, it is this . . .

"Sister, I love you, you love me."

She broke into a laugh.

"Shame on you!" she said. "The tones are all wrong. You go to a modern school and you can't even make a couplet. In ancient times, you wouldn't be admitted into the bridal chamber . . . I will tell you a story. It is said that in the Sung Dynasty the poet Su Tungpo had a sister, and his sister married Chin Shaoyu, who could speak English."

"What nonsense!"

"Never mind. On the wedding night, the bride asked the bridegroom to complete a couplet or else he would have to sleep outside in the yard. It was a moonlight night. So she set the line as she closed the door on the bridegroom—

"Closing door, push out moon before window.

Chin couldn't complete the couplet, for he had been to a modern school, and he paced about the moonlit yard, scratching his head. The bride's brother saw him in this position and took pity on him. So he threw a pebble into a jar of water standing in the yard."

"What was that for?" asked Afei.

"Well, he meant to suggest the line—

"*Throwing stone, break up sky under water.*"

"Excellent!" cried Afei.

"Wait a minute. Chin failed to take the cue. And do you know how he got in after all?"

"How?"

"Well, he was a good baseball player. So he took a baseball bat, banged it hard on the door and got in."

Afei blushed. "Why, people didn't play baseball in the Sung Dynasty."

"I swear it is absolutely true. He could even speak English. The poet's sister asked him, 'Where is your couplet?' and he replied, '*Darling*, nowadays we don't learn couplets at school. We only learn to play baseball!'"

"How you can make up a story just to make fun of me!" said Afei, and began to tickle her again, but she promised to behave, for she was most afraid of tickling.

At this moment, her mother came in and was happy to see the two talking happily together.

Redjade told her, "Third Sister advised me to take pearl powder."

And her mother said, "If it's really good, we can pay for it."

"Is it powder from real pearls? How much will a dose cost?" asked Afei.

"It must be a hundred and fifty or two hundred dollars," replied his aunt.

"If Fourth Sister can get strong," said Afei, "what does it matter about the cost? I will go to tell Father." But Mrs. Feng said, "There is no such hurry," and he sat down again.

Afei looked at this pretty cousin of his lying there on the bed, with her face so white and finely chiseled and tinged with the glow of love and excitement. For the first time, a young, strange passion seized him, quite different from the child-love he had always felt toward her before. And Redjade saw that he was staring at her so foolishly, although her mother was present.

"Are you crazy? You look at me as if you were looking at a stranger!" said Redjade.

"No," replied her cousin, "I am just looking at you. Will you always stay like that for me to look at? Your name is Redjade, and you seem

435

to be made of a real piece of jade, but soft and warm. After taking pearl powder, I am afraid you will be like the precious pearl that glows at night."

At this Redjade blushed, and smiled happily and merely uttered one syllable, "You!"

"Look at him," remarked Redjade's mother. "He is sometimes impulsive, but he is all right at heart. I have seen you two grow up together, friends for two days and enemies for three days. Now you are older, and both of you ought to behave better and you, Redjade, must not indulge in your childish tempers. And Afei, you must not drag her about too much. She loves quiet by nature. Let her lie quietly for a few days, and we can slowly build her up and she will be well."

CHAPTER XXVIII

*H*UAIYU's house on Soochow Hutung, near the Legation Quarter, had previously been occupied by foreigners and had been modernized with electric lights, flush toilets, and a telephone. The rooms on different sides of the courtyard had been connected by enclosed corridors so that in winter one did not have to go out into the open to pass from one side to the other. The east was used as a kind of study, connecting with the main rooms on the north, which were occupied by Huaiyu's wife and the children. Inging had her separate court on the west, slightly further back and reached from the court back of the wife's rooms by a four-panel green door. A fountain stood in the middle of her courtyard. They had newly moved in and Huaiyu had furnished both the wife's and the concubine's bedrooms with the same amount and style of furniture. On the east of the second main court was the dining room, where the whole family dined together.

The question of bed was more delicate than that of board. The northern rooms of the second central court were Huaiyu's study and main parlor and were seldom used. There was a small bedroom there which the previous occupants had used as a guest-room, complete with toilet; but Huaiyu never slept in it. It was understood that he was to sleep in the wife's room on the first and fifteenth of every month, and in the Second Mistress' room during the rest of the time. The wife had the youngest twins in the same room with her, and Huaiyu said he needed quiet for his sleep. This arrangement, decided upon by Huaiyu, was satisfactory to everyone. Huaiyu's wife, whose name was Yachin, was satisfied with this nominal respect to her position. When she had learned that her husband was going to marry Inging, she was prepared for the worst and ready to settle down to an arrangement that might be called "peace at any price." She would yield everything so long as her position as wife and mother of her children was left undisturbed.

437

But Inging had come back dissatisfied from the party at the Yao's house. It was her social debut among relatives, and she had been made to feel keenly the position of a concubine. Not only was the wife seated higher at table, but throughout the party, the other women talked with the wife and her children and had turned more or less cold shoulders towards the concubine. Mulan's sisters were polite, but never cordial; and, after Inging's disastrous attempt to make the couplet, Mulan had stopped talking with her so that she was thrown back entirely on Suyun. She left the dinner disgusted with herself. A sing-song girl was always independent and an individualist, not used to the complicated social adjustments demanded in a home. She was determined that it should not happen again.

So on coming home, she went straight to her court and lay in bed, throughout the rest of the afternoon. When Huaiyu asked her what was wrong, she did not reply. Toward sunset, she said she would have her supper in her own room. He decided it was better to let her sulk until she felt better.

When the servants heard that the Second Mistress was unwell, they all came to ask how she was, and the cook took some pains to prepare a special dish to serve in her bedroom.

Now when Huaiyu had returned to take up this house a month before, he had brought Liang, an old servant of the New family, a wideawake man of thirty-five, to be the gatekeeper. Liang had been brought up in Peking and was keenly aware of the possibilities of such a position. He and the other servants were aware also that their master's new mistress was a woman of high reputation in the sing-song world, that they had now two mistresses to please instead of one, although the new mistress was more important, and that they themselves would have the balance of power in the household before long. Liang suggested that the Second Mistress should have a telephone extension in her own room, and this thoughtfulness at once established him in her favor.

There was a struggle among the women servants to serve in Inging's court, and Liang's wife was selected by Inging for good reasons. When Liang's wife came to serve Inging, she said to her, "I see you are an intelligent person, and understand this favor I am conferring upon you. If you and your husband serve me well and loyally, you will be well rewarded." In addition to the Liang couple, there was their young son who ran errands, purchasing fruit, cigarettes, and sundries, and

438

was always very quick about them; and there was the chauffeur, who had more opportunity to drive Inging than the wife who seldom went about. And Inging had brought along her personal maid Wildrose who had been with her for years, and who therefore went about the house with an air of importance. Only the wife's old servant, Tingma, remained doggedly faithful to her mistress.

There was therefore quite a commotion in Inging's court late that afternoon. Inging was excellently served. Wildrose transmitted the orders, and nobody dared defy her. The cook, who was usually a proud person, came personally and stood outside the door to take orders from Wildrose. Only Tingma did not appear.

Inging sent for Liang; and, when he came and stood at the bedroom door, she called him in and he timidly walked a few steps within the threshold. He saw Inging lying in bed, half-covered, and dared not look up, but stood at attention looking at the floor.

"Old Liang," she said, "I have several things to speak to you about. More and more visitors are coming to see the master. You know that in the master's present position, he cannot see everybody. Whoever comes, let me know first, and I will decide. Further, you must have a livery appropriate to our standing. And when the guests come, there ought to be a special man in charge of tea and water and towels. I leave all this to you. In things big and small, there ought to be a head; otherwise when something has to be done, you leave it to me and I leave it to you, and there is utter confusion. We can't go on as we have been."

"Yes, mistress," replied Liang. "You are right. I thought so myself. There are many servants and so many mouths, and there is no head. You spoke of making a livery. Only yesterday I wanted to buy some flowerpots and found it difficult. When Tingma refused to get the money from the Big Mistress, I could do nothing."

"I didn't know it was as bad as that," said Inging, sharply. "If you obey my orders, do you think anyone will dare defy you?"

"No, mistress. When you are willing to issue the general's arrow, I can have anything done according to your wish. I only know one mistress in this house."

Inging smiled and said, "Old Liang, you know how to talk. I wish your deeds were as good as your words. I want to use a loyal servant. I always reward my men well."

"I am honored by your favor," Liang replied. "If you deign to use me, command me just once to do anything, and you will see if Old Liang is not worthy of your confidence."

"Does that mean that if I should order you to kill a person, you would do it?" said Inging with a laugh.

"No, mistress, that I dare not."

"Come here," said Inging with a smile. Old Liang advanced cautiously a few steps and hesitated, but she bade him come nearer to her bed. She surveyed him from head to foot and said, "Suppose I issue a general's arrow-order to put you at the head of the servants, how will you serve me?"

Like a general receiving the Emperor's command, Old Liang went down on his knees, and *po-tung, po-tung,* kowtowed to his mistress, saying, "If madam will thus honor me, I have someone to depend on for life. My wife and my whole family will be at your service."

"Get up," said Inging. "I will speak to the master about it. I really have nothing particular for you to do now. But . . ." She made a sign with her white hand for him to advance and spoke in a whisper, so that the latter had to come close. Old Liang was excited at the air of intrigue. "You know that Tingma. She is an old servant in this house and she is beginning to take on airs. She is the Big Mistress's servant, and I should not like to interfere."

And Inging whispered to Liang what he was to do.

After dinner, Huaiyu came over to see how Inging was and to ask if he should stay over at the wife's side, this being the fifteenth.

"I can go over tomorrow night to make up for it, you know, if you are ill."

"You go to her," said Inging. "I am not really ill, and I shall be well attended here. It is better that I have a little quiet for a night."

"Are you angry with me?" Huaiyu inquired after a moment.

"No, not with you. Sit down, I want to talk to you. Are you going to listen to me?"

"Darling, of course. What is it?"

"When I came to your house," said Inging, "I wanted it to be a home, peaceful and well-managed, like any other official's house. In these few days I have seen that there is great disorder. Some servants listen to this mistress and others listen to that mistress. And when there is really something to be done, there is no one to do it. As the Sage says, the home must be orderly before the country can be at

440

peace. Every servant's duties ought to be well defined, and there ought to be a head of authority."

"Oh, is that it?" said Huaiyu, quite relieved. "You know Yachin can not manage a home. It has been always like this. Shall I make you take control of all the servants?"

"No, you misunderstand me. I have no time to bother with servants. All I want is to see someone put in charge who will have control over the others—like Old Liang, for instance. Otherwise you give an order on this side to a servant, and it will be counter-ordered on the other side. I think Old Liang is a good person."

"Let it be as you wish," said Huaiyu. So the next morning he gave the order that Old Liang was to assume charge of the household service and the other men and women servants were to take orders from him, and he was also to have control of the money for sundry expenses. The result was that the wife began to experience certain petty annoyances. If she sent for someone, that servant was always occupied, and Tingma had to get water and make tea and even go out to buy things herself, if her mistress did not want to wait a long time.

Tingma was angered and puzzled. She had been with the wife for six or seven years; she had helped to bring up the chidren; and she had helped her mistress over many difficulties, so that she was like a mother to her. She had consequently always been the most powerful servant in the home, and the mistress always listened to what she said. She took the children to the parks, and when there were parties she helped to order the menu. Suddenly, this power was taken away from her. And there was that Wildrose, who went about the house as if Tingma didn't exist, and who began to ask her to do things. Tingma grew defiant and had several quarrels with her. The wife was perplexed and did not know what to do.

One day, Tingma came in to her mistress, crying, in the presence of Inging. She had had to go out to buy something, and passing the gate, had grumbled something about the state of things, and Liang heard it and slapped her.

"Mistress, I cannot work here any more," Tingma said, wiping her tears. "They are all against me. Old Liang and his wife and Wildrose are in a league to flatter the Second Mistress. The other servants, seeing that Liang is the power and can reach the Second Mistress' ears, of course try to please her also. The chauffeur willingly does outside errands for Wildrose, but refuses to do anything for me. You see what

441

we are coming to. Really, as the proverb says, a new emperor, a new court entourage."

Mrs. New called Liang for a settlement of the dispute, and he appeared not alone, but bringing his wife and Wildrose.

"Mistress," said Old Liang, "There are so many servants in the household. Since the master put me in charge, everybody has gone about his or her work. Only Tingma won't listen to what I say, relying on having been here before me. When I speak to her, she won't even reply. We are all serving the master and mistresses; why must she be an exception?"

"Does being the head servant mean that you can strike people?" Tingma cried. But before she could continue, Wildrose said, "You had better be silent. It would not sound pleasant if I were to tell everything."

"If we want to reckon accounts, we had better settle it once and for all," said Liang's wife. "Oh, what a lot is in store! We don't mind what she says about us, but it is what she says about our mistress."

"Yes, I heard her say that Second Mistress was a she-fox," said Wildrose.

"I did not say that," said Tingma.

"You did. The cook heard it also," said Wildrose.

"If you want to resign, we can also all resign," said Liang.

Inging, who had been silently listening, now said, "You are all getting out of hand. Tingma is an old servant here, and you ought to let her have her way a little. Tingma, I do not know whether it is true that you said what they say you did. Whether I am a she-fox or not is none of your business. But your eyelashes are starched and glued with rice-soup. I don't care what you say and do among yourselves, so long as you keep me out of it."

Turning to the wife, she said, "Sister, this incident has gone too far. I will not deal with Tingma today and will let it go at that. But we cannot continue to have bickerings and bawlings in the house. In every house there must be respect for a head. If we appoint Tingma to be the head, I don't think she will be able to gain respect and be obeyed by all the servants. Well, then, if she expects to stay here, she must agree with the others and give the house a little peace. What do you say?"

The wife, surprised at this speech, only said, "You have listened to

442

what Second Mistress has just said. Don't let anybody talk of resigning. You must all try to live in peace with each other."

There was no demand for apology from Liang to Tingma for slapping her, and yet somehow Tingma seemed to have been put definitely in the wrong and in everybody's eyes had been let off more easily than she deserved. The Liang group was definitely victorious.

When Huaiyu was told the story both by the wife and the concubine, he thought Inging had been generous and scolded Tingma severely for her gossip and her vicious tongue. From that day on, the situation rapidly became untenable for Tingma. Liang treated her with sneers and contempt. Sometimes near suppertime she would be sent out to buy things and on coming home would find that the other servants had put away all the food. She became very irritable and one day Liang slapped her again and said, "Go and tell the Mistress. Why don't you? Then we will all resign."

Tingma came in weeping and said again to her mistress, "I cannot live in this house any more."

"Tingma, you cannot go. The children are so dependent upon you," said the wife.

"There is nothing to be done about it," Tingma insisted. "I will smash this eight-dollar-a-month rice bowl. I would rather take a three-dollar job and have some peace. But I am worrying about you. When I am gone, things will be worse for you."

She took up the end of her jacket to wipe her tears and the mistress cried with her, and when they heard that Tingma was going to leave, the children also cried.

No sooner was Tingma gone than Liangma recommended a cousin of hers to serve the wife. And the wife and her children began to feel the animosity around them, and dared not even say things in the presence of Lima, the new servant. The husband grew more apart from the children, who secretly hated Inging, and the secret talks between mother and sons against the concubine bound them closer together. These talks in whispers became in fact the real pleasure that Yachin and her sons delighted in and remembered forever afterward. The children not only feared, but also began to hate their father for neglecting their mother, and became their natural selves and were happiest when their father and Inging went away to Tientsin.

..

443

Now Inging was a trained expert in dealing with men. She could be highly entertaining even when she was unwell, and she could be unwell when there was nothing the matter with her. It was in one of those unwell moods that she was most effective. She could be a mature, gracious woman at parties, standing her ground against officials and treating them with an air of easy familiarity; she could also, by a mere change of dress and expression, appear like a small, shy, easily injured, innocent young girl. Men liked both, but Inging knew that the second role was more flattering to all men, and to Huaiyu in particular. Roughly these two different roles were symbolized by two different ways of hairdress; when her hair was done up and she wore skirts and high-heeled shoes, she was the social enchantress, but when she wore braids and a vest and short trousers and slippers at home, she could appear like a young girl of eighteen, and flatteringly helpless.

One evening when she was in that childish mood, lying in bed with her red vest open at the top and munching pears, she seemed worried about something. She munched her pear lazily and seemed to want to say something and didn't care to say it. Holding the half-finished pear in her hand outstretched on the bed, she stopped eating.

Huaiyu saw her plump white arms that were so velvety to the touch and her braid hanging down one side of her breast, as she reclined on the soft pillows. He smelled the fragrance of her body and knew he desired her more than anything else in the world, and he tried to make love to her. But she turned away and said, "Please don't."

"What is the matter?" said Huaiyu, taking her pear away. She curled down to his breast and lay there without saying a word, her eyes blinking. She had lost her proud independence, and was like a small, sweet child, very quiet.

"What are you thinking?" he asked, puzzled.

"Just thinking," she replied lazily.

"Are you angry with me? What is it?"

She sat up a little, and as she spoke, she seemed totally different from the woman Huaiyu saw at parties. In a soft, pleading tone, she said, "Not angry with you, but it comes to the same thing. You have never been a concubine, and you don't know what it is to be one. The other day at the party of the Tsengs, every courtesy was extended to the wife, but not to the one who was a concubine, and I was looked at as if I were a curious animal. Wives side with wives, as officials protect

444

officials. Now I have realized my mistake. After all, there is nothing like one-husband-one-wife, flying by pair and nesting by pair."

"What do you want me to do?" said Huaiyu. "After all, Yachin is the mother of my children. You don't mean I should divorce her."

"I don't ask you to divorce her. Heaven's justice and human conscience! But everyone likes to stand up and sit down as the equal of others. I must not be humiliated before others again. Will you listen to me?"

"I'll do anything you wish."

Her fingers were playing with the buttons on his jacket and she seemed in no hurry to say what she wanted. Her hands roamed over his breast. Seeing her so quiet and troubled, he held her closer. His manly pride was satisfied and he said, "Darling, I'll do anything you wish. I am the master of this house and I want only to make you happy."

In that moment, Inging knew she had conquered. She looked up to his face and said, "I know what I wish, but I don't know whether you can do it."

"Tell me. Tell me. I'll promise."

She rose then and commanded him to sit up, too. "Now sit there and don't move until I have finished," she said, and she went on in her best professional chatter, a mixture of womanly softness of manner and hardness of determination, going at the natural pace of a woman who has her man where she wants him.

"Old Number One, I have chosen to marry you because I believe you are a person one can trust for life. Together we can go far. But you know it isn't easy for me, and to save myself from further humiliation, I will stay with you only on three conditions. Will you promise?"

Huaiyu was curious. "I can't promise until I know what they are!"

"I want you to promise. Don't ask questions, and I'll tell you why after you have promised."

"Well, tell me."

Inging began, "First, in society at least, I must appear as your only wife. I cannot tolerate going about with that woman. Second, at home, I must have control of all money and the servants. I will give Yachin a definite sum for running the household every month. You cannot run a household with two heads, some servants listening to one mistress, and others listening to the other. If she does not cause me trouble, I will be fair to her."

"And third?"

"Don't interrupt until I have finished. Third, I am to have the car at my service, and complete freedom. Thus, we can entertain and go about, and you will soon find out how valuable I can be to you. Now answer me on these three conditions and I will tell you the rest."

"My good mistress," said Huaiyu with an easy smile. "I am at your command. It is not hard for me to promise these three things. The first is easy, because she does not care to appear in public anyway. The use of the car is a small thing, and I don't expect to shut you up anyway. The second, regarding the control of servants, you have already. But control of the money means you are going to control me, doesn't it?"

"Don't be frightened. Will you promise? I will tell you about it afterward."

"Why do you ask this?"

"It'll make me happy, that's all."

"I promise, then, but this is politics in the home. What is my reward for all this?"

"I will make you happy. All promised?"

"All promised," said Huaiyu.

Inging pressed a long kiss on Huaiyu's lips, for she knew now that she held in her hands a man who had become a powerful, but submissive tool for her ambitions.

"You are a wise man," she said. "Honestly, you will see that I, Inging, can do something with you and for you. Since I was a girl of sixteen, I have wanted to marry. But all the men I met were fat, old fools with plenty of money, or pleasure-hunting silly young men. If wealth and comfort were all I wanted, I could easily have married long ago. Sometimes I met nice young men. I fell in love with one young man, madly in love, when I was eighteen, but he was afraid to marry me. He promised to and then he left without saying a word. I think he was married and had a lioness at home. I could neither eat nor drink and kept thinking of him until I gave up. Then I became hardened, and I threw myself upon all those fat, old fools who were willing to pay me handsomely and to buy me jewels and presents, and I gave up all thoughts of marriage. I gave what they wanted, and made them pay for it. You men are strange creatures; the more a girl does not care for a man, the more he runs after her. When I had got all silly ideas of love out of my head, I found it easier and easier to deal with men, and I became more and more sought after. But after all, a sing-song girl had to think of her future. I thought some day I would save up enough money and marry an oil-seller and settle down to small home life and adopt some children. But you know how it is, the expenses were so heavy; all I got had to pass out of my hands again. I could not cut down expenses and enjoy the same prestige, and if I kept it up, I would always be in debt, and I had to take money from the rich old fools to pass the Dragon-Festival and the Mid-Autumn. Then you came. I thought I could do something with you and I hope I have not made a wrong choice.

"Now these conditions I have demanded are all for your own good. If we are to rise in the world, we must go in the world side by side. There must be no problems and worries in the house. The inside must be unified before we can conquer the outside world. Second, you know I have not come to your home just to enjoy a life of ease. If I had, there would not be the other conditions. You know as well as I do that all officials rise through their women, sisters or wives or concubines. Politics is a matter of social entertainment. I am used to this sort of thing and I have helped a few men to get their political appointments on my pillow. For instance, you got this job through the fifth brother of the third concubine of the Director; I can go straight to the third concubine herself. That is all I am after, to go about to help you in social contacts, and I cannot do this and at the same time put up with servants' troubles at home and appear in society as your mistress. I must live up to my reputation. And if you get a mayoralty of Peking or Tientsin and become rich and powerful, who else are to benefit from it but your own wife and children!"

He listened to her attentively and was greatly impressed. "Marvelous! You have thought everything out. My heart and liver, you are so charming and wise. I think my red luck has come."

"But there is to be a fourth condition. Look out!" Inging said, pointing her finger at him. "There is to be no other woman but me."

"I shall need no other woman with you at my side," he said, firmly.

From that day on, Inging constantly went out with her husband in the car without the wife. Her reputation and her social experience and tact made her always welcome with officials and their concubines, who were anxious to cultivate her friendship. At home, she became the head of the family and the servants were more anxious to please her than the wife. The wife now became the business manager of the home, directing the kitchen and the household, but taking orders from Inging.

.·.

A few days after this, Suyun came to visit Inging.

"You ought to have a telephone in your home," Inging said to her. "I can't live without it here. It would be so much more convenient for us to reach each other. And sometimes you miss the best mahjong parties. People can ring you up instantly and we could go out together more in the evenings."

"I don't need to be told this," replied Suyun. "Who does not want to have **a telephone?** But I am not like you, mistress of your own home. Everything has to be approved by the parents, and if I brought up any such idea, it would be sure to be rejected. You know that little fox-spirit is really running the house now." Inging knew that she meant Mulan. "How I envy you! You are free and can go about with your husband wherever you like. If you lived in a big family, you would know what it is like."

"Why don't you move out, then?"

"I have thought of it, but it is not so simple. Number One and Number Three conspire together and when I approach, they become suddenly silent. I have no one to talk with except my own maids. And that stupid husband of mine! He is earning money for the whole family and yet he gets scolded, while Sunya does nothing and is looked up to. I have thought of dividing the property and going out to live alone in a small home like you, but Chinya dares not and says it can't be done."

"Can't you *make* them divide the property?"

"The parents are living. How could I do it?"

"Oh, you simple-mind! Make them do it by making them glad to get you out."

"But you know it can't be done. I would gladly do it if I could. There are family obligations. You don't understand what a big family is like."

"Well, when you want to do a thing, just do it. It is only a case of knowing what you want. You can't waste your young life and make yourself miserable trying to oblige others."

"I wish I had your courage. There is that poor husband of mine to win over first."

"You are a woman. If you can't deal with that husband of yours,

448

you are a fool yourself." Inging lowered her voice and said, "Look at what I have done here. I have got your brother to let me have entire control of the household. Now, you are going to see things happen, or I won't be Inging."

"My husband is what I came to speak to you about. I am sure that between you and my brother we can push my precious husband forward. If the worst comes to the worst, and we cannot separate from the family, we must try to get him a job in Tientsin or elsewhere, so that I can get out of that living hell."

"Don't you worry. I can arrange that. There is that Oil Administration being formed, with American money. The Standard Oil Company has a project to investigate oil possibilities in Shansi. Your brother is working on it himself, and maybe he can get a job for your husband."

"But he is not an engineer," said Suyun. "What does he know about oil?"

"Oh, you fool!" Inging laughed. "The dirty jobs are done by the engineers. Do you think your brother knows anything about oil, either?"

"I'll do anything to get away from that she-fox," said Suyun. "You saw how she insulted me when she proposed the toast to Mannia's mother. That tongue of hers! Somehow I can never find words to answer back. She knows how to worm her way into the parents' favor. And she is using the family's money to win popularity for herself among the servants. The servants squeeze and she knows all about it and doesn't say a thing."

"It seems to me that neither of the Yao sisters is easy to deal with. Her sister is sharp, too. She is so quiet and calm, and yet I would be more afraid of her than of Mulan. The minute I saw her, I felt so. . . ."

The telephone rang. Inging picked up the receiver near her bed and said, "Hullo . . . Chen *Nainai* . . . Oh, it's you! A mahjong party tonight. . . . Fine, I'll be there."

Putting down the telephone, she said, "You see, how convenient it is! It is Chen Fifth Young Master's wife calling about a mahjong party tonight. You had better come with us." Chen Fifth Young Master was the fifth brother of the Director's third concubine.

"I am not free like you. I have to ask permission from the mother."

"That is exactly the point. You just insist on coming out, and raise hell if you don't. Pretty soon they will be glad to have you leave the house."

449

"I wish I had your courage," said Suyun.

"You will have," said Inging.

Suyun went home with a new point of view and a greater determination to win her freedom. She asked permission from the mother to go out that evening, and to her surprise the mother readily consented. There was no trouble whatsover.

So Suyun began to go out more and more in Inging's company, sometimes with her husband, sometimes without. Especially did Suyun enjoy riding in Inging's car, and she would come back late at night. The car impressed the Tseng family who still used a horse carriage. Suyun did not dare to ask them to get a car but she did raise the question of the telephone. She had a good case. Huaiyu's house had one, so why shouldn't they? But Mr. Tseng hated the telephone, a foreign innovation that broke into the privacy of the home. But on this question, Suyun happened to have Mulan's support because the Yao home had one, too, and Mr. Tseng kept quiet when Mulan proposed it as her own idea. The telephone was installed, and Mulan continually talked with Mochow and Afei and her father, but not with her mother, who could use the telephone only when others had made the connection for her. And Suyun would talk for half an hour with Inging, so that whenever there was a call for Suyun, the servants knew it was from Inging.

Soon afterward, Huaiyu got a job for himself in the new Oil Administration, while concurrently keeping his old post. He got a job there for Chinya also, with the handsome salary of five hundred dollars, plus social expenses of six hundred monthly. The offer was so good that Mr. Tseng let Chinya go with Huaiyu to Shansi to work in the Oil Prospecting Bureau at Taiyuan.

The absence of her husband made a good opportunity for Suyun to go away, and she asked permission to pay a long visit to her parents at Tientsin. She was thankful to Inging for giving her this new freedom and for making a great many new social contacts for her. Inging, too, often went away to live at Tientsin, but refused to stay in the New home. The old News did not think of controlling a daughter-in-law like Inging, and she claimed that all the successes of her husband were due to her social activities, and he was independent. She had more social obligations to keep up with there, she said, and a hotel was a more convenient place for entertaining. One could have complete service all the time. This was not unusual. Chinese husbands in the foreign concessions often had a cheap house for a home and entertained lavishly at hotels. People rented hotel rooms for a night of mahjong play; authors rented a small room to get away from the distractions of crying babies at home and to write an article; commercial agents had offices in hotel rooms for negotiations and political agents had rooms there to make arrangements and receive bribes; some prostitutes had permanent rooms to receive travelers. A hotel was always noisy and alive. One could have tea, noodles, coffee, toast, a foreign meal, a Chinese meal, opium, women, at all hours of the day and night, and the flush toilet and enameled bathtubs and white-tiled bathrooms were always so beautiful and hot water was so ready. A hotel was indeed an epitome of the bewildering life of the foreign concession itself.

Suyun was irresistibly attracted by Tientsin hotel life. Every day and every night, she visited Inging. Money flowed like water in the hotel, and it fascinated Suyun. It was good to be modern, to have a telephone by your bedside, to sleep on soft-springed brass beds with mirrors at the heads, to lie on spotless white sofas, to have eternal hot and cold running water, and to have waiters who only took commands and asked no questions. It was good to be free!

CHAPTER XXIX

*M*ochow was now carefully planning her wedding with the help of her sister. She wanted a modern wedding at the Grand Hotel de Pékin but wanted the usual traditional ceremonies and the usual bridal chamber at home as well. The bride was to wear white and a bridal veil, and she wanted Lifu to appear in foreign dress. Redjade and Ailien were to be the bridesmaids, Sutung and Afei the best men, and Aman the flower-girl. Lilien was to play Mendelssohn's *Wedding March*. It did seem that Redjade was as excited about the wedding as the bride herself. She looked so resplendent that day that it elicited a great deal of talk about her and Afei. After the wedding the new couple were to have a suite of rooms in the hotel for the night. The bride would then presently go with her husband to Japan, where he was to study.

Lifu had wanted to go to England, but Mrs. Yao was getting very weak and after long discussions the sisters decided Mochow should not go so far away. Every time she spoke of going abroad, her mother would weep and say that she had not long to live. She was so weak and looked so pathetic that Mochow compromised on Japan.

It had been Mochow's duty to attend to her mother's food and medicine, and at night a woman servant had to sleep in the same room to keep her company. It happened like this. Once Mrs. Yao had heard about a sorceress who could conjure up the spirits of dead relatives and impersonate them. She took a carriage to see the sorceress and came home worse than before, and burned incense before the tablet of Silverscreen's spirit. As usual, the sorceress, without knowing anything about her client, could always address her correctly. Mrs. Yao wanted to speak to her son, but Silverscreen's spirit came instead and with a laugh greeted her as *"Taitai."* Mrs. Yao wanted to stop, but the sorceress was already in a trance and talked on. The manner of speech and the Hangchow accent were so strikingly like Silverscreen's that Mrs.

Yao had a severe shock. Silverscreen commanded her to look well after her young son Poya, for he would grow up into an important person.

"Have mercy upon an old woman," Mrs. Yao pleaded. "I swear I did not mean you ill. I only wanted my son to be happy with you."

"Do not worry," said Silverscreen's spirit. "He is with me. I was so lonely out here that the King of Devils pitied me and gave me permission to transform myself into a mare and bring him here."

"How long yet will I live, do you know?"

"I don't know, *Taitai*. But I have heard one of the devils say that some one else in the family will die before you and then will come your turn."

Mrs. Yao almost fainted, and came back and lay in bed for weeks. Ever since that time, her condition had grown steadily worse. She hired nuns to say prayers to Buddha for her and visited temples, and though Mr. Yao did not believe in these things, he allowed her. Her mind was dwelling more on the next world than on the present, and consequently she had become extremely kind as well as religious. Even living in the prince's garden did not make her happier.

The money on which Lifu was going to Japan to study was to come from Mochow's dowry. In fact, the wedding expenses were borne by the Yao family. Lifu's savings would barely cover a small, modest wedding, and he disliked the grand wedding they were planning, but Mulan insisted along with the others that this was only being fair to her sister.

Mochow was practical. When the question of trousseau was brought up, she said she did not need many things and would rather have cash. Her father did not have too much cash at this time, but he said he would give her ten thousand dollars, besides the wedding which would cost several thousand.

"Father, how can you?" said Mulan. "I had about fifty thousand dollars' worth of trousseau. And Brother Lifu and Sister are both going to study abroad for some years."

"Lifu will be all right," replied her father. "And Mochow is more thrifty than you. Your sister can do more with one thousand than you with two. I was playing with money in your case."

"That is unfair!" said Mulan.

The result was that the father gave Mochow fifteen thousand dollars in cash, a teashop in Soochow worth about five thousand, and several

453

thousand in trousseau, plus the wedding expenses, which brought up the total to about thirty thousand dollars. Mochow was satisfied. She could do more with a sum in cash than with twice the amount in jewels and curios.

Lifu and his mother were now living in Mochow's old home on Matajen Hutung, and the bridal chamber was the one where the sisters had slept in their childhood. Mochow was so familiar with Lifu now that she and Mulan went over to help prepare the room. The bridal bed was an old one carved and varnished, and with surrounding posts and drawers. The third rail at the head was slightly loose, and Mulan still remembered how as a child she had played with it by twisting it around. She stood before it and lingered before the drawer at the end with the painting of two mandarin ducks that had delighted her childish imagination. She remembered the night she was engaged and Mochow was sleeping soundly in the other bed, and she lay awake thinking how her sister was luckier than she. And now her prophecy had come true.

Mr. Fu was at this time living in Peking, having recently accepted the post of a censor in the censorate, and come out of his retirement in Tientsin, where he had been editing old books since the establishment of the Republic. Both Mr. and Mrs. Fu took active part in the arrangements before and after the wedding, and Mr. Fu himself officiated at the ceremony. At Lifu's request, he presented the couple with a pair of scrolls to hang in their bridal chamber and to remember him by. To Mr. Fu's surprise, Mochow said, "Uncle Fu, if you want to write, write the following words:

> "*Yin* and *yang* fittingly complement
> *Luan* and *feng* in harmony sing."

(*Luan* and *feng* referred to the male and the female phoenix.)

"Why such trite phrases?" asked Mr. Fu.

"I want it so," said Mochow. "They are common, but still they are good phrases, aren't they?"

After the wedding, Mochow and her husband settled down in their home for some time before their departure for Japan. The house was the one in which she had grown up, but with the difference that she was now the mistress. Every brick and step and corner was familiar to her. And there were her husband, and her mother-in-law and Huan-erh, living together in a "small family" life—almost too ideal. Her

454

uncle and aunt were living in the southwest court, which had been Mr. Yao's library.

Ever since their talk that day in the garden, Redjade had come to love Mochow with the love of a grown-up, thinking girl, and they had more heartfelt talks about "dimming one's intelligence." One day Redjade said to her, "As for being impatient, I think Lifu is as impatient as myself. He also likes to excel. How lucky he is to have you to guide him, Third Sister!" Lifu himself had come to know Redjade quite well. One day, Lifu made the strange remark to Mochow, "There ought to be Six Cosmic Elements, instead of five. Redjade belongs really to the jade type. She is jade to the bone, pure and proud and hard and brittle." And Mochow replied, "Being jade is both an advantage and a disadvantage. Jade can never be stained, and is hard and also brittle. The best jade ought to have a soft luster. Do you see how she refuses to try to please my parents?" "She *will* be her true self. I admire her for it, though," replied Lifu. It was true, however, that under the influence of Lifu and Mochow, Redjade had learned to restrain herself and grown to be a maturer, more thoughtful girl.

What completely fascinated Mrs. Feng was Lifu's ways with her, so familiar and utterly without restraint. Mrs. Feng was a woman brought up in the old tradition and very careful of her conduct. While living with her sister-in-law, she had never allowed herself to go beyond the rules, in spite of their familiarity. But living with Lifu's family was completely different. It was something hard to define, something new that she could not understand. Lifu had apparently thrown away all rules, and yet was living in accordance with them and was never cheap, however familiar. Lifu's mother always apologized for her son's breaking of the rules of manners, and Mrs. Feng always replied that she was not conscious of any rules of manners being broken. Good manners like many other things were of the spirit, and though Lifu broke all the rules, he was never bad-mannered. He was just being natural. And so the two families lived in harmony together and liked each other.

Actually, Lifu had been greatly influenced by his father-in-law, Mr. Yao, and was an iconoclast in respect to Confucianism, especially Confucian restraint and rules of propriety. Old Yao had made him read Laotse and Chuangtse, and one of the sayings of Laotse that stuck in his mind was this:

Therefore after Nature (Tao) was lost, one talked of character:
After character was lost, then one talked of kindness;
After kindness was lost, then one talked of righteousness;
After righteousness was lost, then one talked of rules of conduct.
Now rules of conduct indicate the thinning out of the innate
    honesty of man
And are the beginning of human chaos.
The Prophets are but the flowering-epoch of Tao
And the beginning of ignorance.
Therefore the man of character stands upon the root-strength
And not upon what is thinning out;
He dwells in the fruit-substance, and not the flowering-expression.
Therefore he takes one and rejects the other.

. ˙.

Mochow was very happy in her honeymoon at home, so happy that she did not want to leave, and almost wished that she could settle down permanently there and begin running the home routine that she loved. She herself had no urge for travel, to see Japan or any other country. In the first month of their marriage, Lifu saw something utterly amazing to him. He had lived with women—his mother and sister—all his life, but now he saw for the first time something womanly, or wifely, the figure of Mochow who simply and silently assumed that this was her home and that she and nobody else was going to run it. She seemed to him to take an inexpressible, because deep and instinctive, delight in giving the cook the food orders for the day, looking after the laundry, washed and unwashed, arranging the flowers every morning, and taking her work basket and sitting near the window in a sunny corner in her room to do her needlework. It meant peace. It meant also Mochow's dream of happiness on earth. This was going to be a clean and orderly home. It just happened so for Lifu.

The fact that he changed into foreign dress for the wedding and for the trip abroad had great consequences. Suddenly he lost control of his wardrobe. He had always been independent and was used to taking care of himself. Now he did not know where his shirts, ties, buttons, handkerchiefs, and socks were; and he felt completely helpless. Mochow, and nobody else, decided where his clothes should be put, and in the packing and unpacking, there had to be changes of place. Lifu, looking for a pair of socks, would get impatient, and Mochow would say with a smile, "Now slowly, slowly," and go herself and get the socks he wanted. They would smell of moth balls. Lifu had never seen such a thing. Moth balls had a strange fascination for his young wife. She was lavish with them—moth balls in the trunks, suitcases, wardrobes, made into little bags and hung or hidden all over the place.

And Lifu's shoes had an even greater fascination for Mochow. She knew how the best foreign shoes ought to look, ever since Tijen had bought them for his trip to England. Before the wedding, the sisters had gone together with Lifu to shop for shoes and they had decided the style and quality that he should have. Now after the wedding, Mochow was dissatisfied and took him one day to the shop, and spent for three pairs of English-made shoes for him the horrifying sum of one hundred and twenty-five dollars.

"Your father calls you economical. I don't believe it," said Lifu.

On the voyage to Japan Mochow, young, beautiful, and modern, made many friends for them that Lifu could not have made if he had been alone. But once, sitting alone in his deck chair, he mentally made the following notes:

He had completely lost control of his own wardrobe.

He had learned that ladies' dresses must be wrapped in special silk scarves, and that nobody must touch them, while ransacking a trunk.

That Mochow had many such plain silk scarves.

That all suits and dresses smelled of the moth ball.

That shoes formed the foundation of a man's personality.

That it was bad manners to bite one's nails.

That it was bad manners to go ahead of a lady in getting into a car.

And that all this modern respect for ladies was a nuisance for gentlemen.

Finally, he was convinced that all these things were not important one way or the other, and that he loved Mochow, but did not understand woman.

Later Lifu learned one more remarkable thing, that Mochow was like a jellyfish that clung to him and enveloped him, adapting its contours softly and flexibly to his wishes and whims and serving as protection for him against the outside world. The infinite patience, infinite adaptability, infinite selflessness of Mochow staggered him. His comfort and his welfare were her law, and he felt as if this woman had staked her all on him and his future.

Lifu, who might have grown into a solitary, bookish spirit, more at home among the trees and the animals and the poor peasants than in the city, and possibly a great rebel against the well-to-do, found that he had a rich and beautiful home thrust upon him, and a wife who was conservative and practical and who planned to give him security and comfort. He felt that he was being bribed, though he was never reconciled to the life of the wealthy. He was never bitter against them, since he had always been lucky, but he always kept his childhood contempt for the class to which he and his mother had never belonged. This showed itself best in his scorn of table manners, his annoyance at having to wash his hands and brush his hair before dinner, his persistence in biting his fingernails in public, and always a certain uncouthness which his wife was trying to polish away.

"Don't put your hands in your pockets," she would say.

"Why not?" he would ask.

"It is not polite, not nice."

"Why?"

"There is no why. It is simply not polite."

And he would argue, "Now you can never convince me not to put my hands in my pockets unless and until you can show me a good reason for it. You can't. Therefore you are wrong and I am right."

Nevertheless, he ceased gradually to put his hands in his pockets because she desired it and because he cared for her. And the bright-eyed Mochow sometimes insisted, sometimes yielded, but always waited patiently and watched for the right moment to speak. There was in Lifu a touch-off quality, a quick sense of rebellion against pressure, and the wise Mochow knew it and pressed only hard enough not to antagonize him. For Mochow could wait. Every time that she yielded, he knew he had been defeated. And the more she knew him, the more she knew that by not antagonizing him she could make him do anything in the end, and so she gradually molded him to her will.

Lifu was now spending Mochow's dowry, and he was as careless of money as she was thrifty. Yet throughout the first year of marriage, she never once made Lifu feel that it was her money, taking it for granted that they now belonged together. Lifu came to think it after all not a bad thing to have married a rich wife. Once he said to her, "If I were Chinya, I would have divorced Suyun instantly." He meant that Mochow was so different and that he really appreciated and loved her, but he thought the obvious compliment to her unnecessary. And so she never openly got credit for helping him with her money, and he never spoke his gratitude directly.

Because her superior wisdom had made life so easy for him, Lifu sometimes thought he himself was only a fool, though perhaps a brilliant fool. She was mature as he was immature. Thus he came more and more to take her point of view, to listen to her advice, to despise his own reasoning and respect her common sense. He valued and cherished her greatly, feeling that she was always dependable and strong like the good earth itself.

Nevertheless, somewhere deep in his soul, he remembered that he was a poor man's son and took pride in this fact and in his independence. He hated the manners of the rich, the false values of society women, as represented by Suyun, and the hypocrisy and crookedness of politicians as represented by Huaiyu. And this hatred was eternal.

.·.

Barely six weeks had passed after their arrival in Kyoto when a letter came from Mulan saying that their mother was dangerously ill, and had lost her power of speech. On receiving a second letter from Coral, Mochow decided to return home at once, although she was extremely reluctant to leave Lifu. She had to go home because it seemed to be her natural duty, for she had been taking care of her mother for years whenever she was sick, and she could not leave it to Coral or to Mulan or to anybody but herself.

This altered their plans completely and she was not sure when she could come back to Lifu. He said that he could take care of himself, and Mochow did not question it, but he suddenly realized how dependent he had become upon his young bride. She said that if she could not leave home, he was to come to her in the summer vacation.

At parting, she wept, for she could not control herself. The last thing she said was, "Take care of yourself, eat well, and don't try to save. If any time you need money, write and tell me."

She found that her mother was considerably worse. She was a pitiful sight, as she pointed to her throat and her chest, and could not speak. Sutung had been consulted and had made a thorough examination, but he could not say what was wrong with her. The servants were agreed that she had been "struck by a ghost"—presumably that of Silverscreen. Tijen's curse upon his mother had come true. And now she could not tolerate near her the presence of the little Poya, Silverscreen's child. She seemed to be afraid of him, although he was her only "internal" grandson. It was hard for the little child to hear that his mother was a ghost, and he became enraged and wanted to defend her against everybody. He knew already that he was the grandson of this Yao family and future owner of this prince's garden, and he meant to grow up to be a great man, to avenge his mother and put her portrait in the center of the Chungmintang. And he hated his grandmother. These thoughts often made the little child very solemn.

Now with both daughters married off and the mother ill, the Garden became a dreary, lonely place. There were at least ten residential courts, and not enough people to fill half of them. So it was decided that they should rent the old house, and Mr. and Mrs. Feng and Mrs. Kung moved over with their families to live in the Garden. Mochow's duties were thus divided between those toward her mother and her mother-in-law, but she occupied a courtyard near her mother, while Lifu's mother and sister lived in another courtyard. Mr. Yao was living with Afei in the Self-Examination Hall. Redjade's court was in front of Mochow's, enabling them to speak to each other through a lattice-window in the white wall of the court, and a great friendship grew up between them.

. ˙ .

In the early summer just before Lifu returned on vacation, Mochow gave birth to a boy. It was difficult labor, and the child took twenty hours to come out of the mother's womb. The family had decided that it would be more convenient to have Mochow at home during the confinement, than to send her to a hospital, but it almost proved fatal. Mulan came over during the delivery and witnessed her sister's torture, so that she thought at times that Mochow's strength was giving out. She kept a pot of Korean ginseng stewing over a stove to strengthen her heart. When all was over, luckily both mother and child were safe, but Mochow's face was like a white sheet and she lay for weeks in bed before she fully recovered, with Mulan attending her all the time.

Lifu came home to find the two sisters together in his room. Lying in bed, with her son by her side, Mochow smiled her welcome to her husband. Lifu bent down and kissed his wife in Mulan's presence.

"You don't know what sister went through," said Mulan.

But Mochow was happy now and showed him the child, saying, "He is your son. I went near death to give him life." She made him sit on her bed and held his hand, and said: "I felt as if my body were on a rack. But it was well worth it. And I felt as if my spirit and my body were being cleansed—and all my sins forgiven through these horrible pains," she added.

"Have *you* any sins?" said Mulan with a smile. "Already she says she would go through it all over again."

"I would indeed, to get another little Fu," said Mochow.

She told Lifu that she would name their son Hsiaofu, or Little Fu.

"It sounds like a street cleaner or a porter," said Lifu.

"I never thought of that. It didn't seem so to me. It means just Little Fu to me. What would you suggest?"

"Call him Hsiaofu, but with '*hsiao*' in the falling tone and not in the rising tone," suggested Mulan.

"That means 'Filial Fu'? It is a name that has been used."

"That, or the 'small' and 'flesh' *hsiao,* meaning 'like father like son,' " said Mulan.

"That is better. After all, to be filial is to be like father," said Mochow.

"The two words *hsiao* were probably related," Lifu remarked.

A woman servant over forty came in, with a cup of dragon-eye tea and Mochow said, "This is Chenma, our new servant."

Chenma gave Lifu a broad smile and said, "Master, I welcome you home. You didn't know what the Mistress went through. Now I shall take care of you while she is still in her bed."

When Chenma had left the room, Mochow said, "There is a most marvelous woman, good-mannered and motherly and so decent. You don't have to tell her to do anything, and since she came everything is in order in this court. She talks to me as if I were her child."

Mochow began to tell them about Chenma, saying, "Her story keeps me awake at night, now that I know what it is to be a mother. You, Lifu, are proud of your mother, but there is a great mother.

"She lost her son during the Revolution," Mochow went on, "and doesn't know where he is, or whether he is dead or alive. When we engaged her, she promised to do everything, on only one condition, that once a month she must have a day off. 'What for?' I asked, and she said, 'To look for my son.' So I promised her, and she came to work with us and has been here for two or three months. She does her work very well, as if it were her home. And then at night she sews and sews, to make clothing for her lost son, although she cannot send it to him. She showed me a great pile of the clothing she has made. She spends all her savings on it. Her son, she says, must be twenty now, but she lost him in her village in Changli district, northeast of Peking, when he was sixteen. He was taken by a press gang and forced to carry luggage for the soldiers in the Revolution. I saw the strong, padded jacket she made for him when he was seventeen, and another bigger one when he was eighteen, and another still bigger when he was nineteen. She packs them up carefully, and takes them out to sun them regularly. She says she knows exactly how tall he is each year, and how long his sleeves should be. Just now she is working on a blue cotton summer suit for him, to have it ready when she finds him, or to send to him, as soon as she knows where he is. And once a month, she gets up very early and comes into my room, her face lit up by hope and says that this is her day off and she is going to find him today. At night she comes home downcast, dragging her tired legs, with her package of clothing still under her arm. She goes all about the city, east city, west city, north city, south city, and outside the gates sometimes."

"But why does she think her son is in Peking?" said Lifu.

"Just because she can't go anywhere else. Principally she goes to the south city because there are so many soldiers there. 'If he is there, I shall know him, even in a crowd of thousands,' she says. She waited for him to come back to the village for a year after the Revolution was over. Then she gave up her farmhouse and said she would come to the capital because the soldiers pass through it. She goes about and stops young soldiers and looks at their faces, and they laugh and ask her what she wants. It seems so hopeless, but I dare not tell her so, for I do not want to take away that hope which keeps her alive. She will never give up as long as she lives."

Mulan's eyes were full, and Lifu sighed and said, "That is what war does, separating husbands and wives and mothers and sons."

"Think of that son!" said Mulan. "To have such a woman for a mother and then to have lost her! I wonder what he is like."

"She never talks about him. She will not discuss him with anybody," said Mochow.

"Maybe he is just a poor fool, dear only in his mother's eyes," said Lifu.

"No, I have a feeling that he must be a very fine boy," said Mulan. "The mother's face has such nobility and strength of character."

"Does she go to pray at the temples?" asked Lifu.

"No, the strange thing is she does not believe in Buddha. She always says, 'Piety is in the heart.' You can see it in her. You never saw a cleaner woman, her hair and dress always so neat. She says, 'Heaven never betrays an honest person.' Sometimes I almost believe that she *will* find him even after these four years."

"We must treat her well," said Lifu, "and make her feel that she is in a real home of her own."

"You will see," said Mochow. "She will treat you like her son and mother you, as she is treating me like her daughter. But you can only pretend to be her son, for this is a matter of flesh and blood that cannot be borrowed or substituted. A son is a son."

Little Fu began to cry, and Mochow turned and fed him at her breast, and felt peace and happiness. The moment was so beautiful, so self-sufficient, so rich, she wanted it to be always like this.

It was a perfect summer. Lifu often rose at dawn from the warm fragrance of his wife's flesh and went out to the cool summer morning air of the garden and felt that he would like to embrace this earth, this existence. Mochow would get up very early to feed her baby and go over to see her mother and father. Her father was an early riser, too, and often the father-in-law and son-in-law would saunter together under the tall trees before breakfast, the skirts of their light gowns made wet by the grass. But as the poet Tao Yuanming said, what did it matter that one's gown was wet, if one had his heart's desire?

Mulan and Sunya and Mannia often came in the morning with their maids and children, and stayed the whole day there in the garden. After having for lunch a light soup of small green hard-crust peas, cooked with refined sugar and dates, the party, including Coral, Redjade, Afei, and Huan-erh, would lounge on the Terrace of Swirling Waters and chat the afternoon away. Mochow, occupied with her baby and other duties, would join them later for tea, while Mr. Yao would usually retire after lunch for repose in the Self-Examination Hall.

Mulan was already teaching her daughter Aman to read and write. The child picked up the characters very easily, and Dimfragrance was fascinated by this pictorial writing and began to learn it for herself. Often while the company were talking, Dimfragrance would take Huan-erh aside and ask her to give her lessons, and she learned very fast.

Sometimes Mrs. Tseng would come and Cassia, too, with her daughters. Cassia was becoming fat, since her long illness after the miscarriage. Mrs. Yao was usually in bed and could not sleep soundly. Still unable to speak, she would sit very long before a statue of Buddha in her room and burn incense and say her silent prayers. They had tried once to exorcise the evil spirit by inviting a Tibetan priest to say the *Dharani Sutra,* but it was of no avail. She could eat and cough as usual, but she had lost the power to be articulate. Sometimes her lips would start to move, but they merely quivered and made meaningless movements and no voice came out.

Mulan suggested that the woman servant Chenma might be of great service if she were transferred to serve the mother. It was a great sacrifice on Mochow's part, but she did as Mulan suggested and immediately her mother improved greatly, because Chenma understood the mother's wishes and could talk to her. In the following years, Chenma became an indispensable and constant companion to Mrs. Yao, and only on days when she went out to search for her son, did Coral and Mochow take her place.

At the end of the summer, Lifu went back to Japan to continue his studies, but Mochow stayed behind with her mother.

$\mathcal{H}$ ER husband being away, Suyun found it difficult and lonely to remain with her mother-in-law, and was spending her time at Tientsin as much as possible. He had arranged that, of the eleven hundred dollars from his monthly salary and expense allowance, six hundred were to be sent to his home at Peking. Suyun had insisted that this was her husband's money and therefore belonged to her, and Mrs. Tseng quietly had the check sent to her when she was not at home. Sometimes, when she returned to Peking, she would go to Inging's house for a night or two, where she would always find herself happily occupied, being often invited out to mahjong parties.

Mr. Tseng hated to see his daughter-in-law going about with a notorious ex-sing-song woman, and he heard rumors that the two were constantly seen together when they were both in Tientsin, and he regretted the match he had made for his son.

"Why don't you stop her?" Cassia said to him.

"She would only cause more trouble at home. You can change the face of a mountain, but you cannot change a person's nature," he replied.

Suyun, however, felt she was doing a great service to the family by pushing her husband forward and making connections for him. "He would have still been a small bureaucrat at the Ministry of the Interior, if we had not taken him in hand," she said to Inging.

"This is only the beginning," said Inging. "The Sixth Mistress of President Yuan can do something big for us yet." The Sixth Mistress was the relative of a well-known Hung and was the president's favorite.

Suyun saw the bankers and retired officials going about in limousines and living in modern villas which cost hundreds of thousands of dollars. She saw their wives, mistresses, and daughters dressed in fashionable modern evening dress, in the theaters, hotel ballrooms, and night clubs, and she knew that was where she belonged. Since Inging had obtained control of Huaiyu's bank account, she had been speculating in government bonds and gold bars through a young man named Chin, who was a great friend of Huaiyu. Suyun heard so much about these operations that the names and rates of interest of the many bond issues became familiar to her. One day over the telephone Inging learned that she had made a clear nine thousand dollars overnight.

"Why don't you come in?" said Inging. "You have your own money. You might have made four or five thousand easily if you had listened to my advice."

"What if I lost?" asked Suyun.

"You cannot lose. Chin is the best-informed man at the Exchange. He buys and sells for the Sixth Mistress, too."

"I only have about ten thousand of my own, and I don't like to risk it. Chinya has not saved a cent, and you know he hasn't a free hand at home."

"Oh, you thickhead," said Inging with a smile. "You said you wanted to come out and live alone. Here is your chance. I have an idea. You play with that ten thousand and if you win, the money is yours. If you lose, tell Chinya and ask him to get money from his father. If he protests, all the better. Then ask for a division of property. Meanwhile, you stand a chance of winning some money for yourself. There is absolutely no risk."

And so Suyun began to take active part in the transactions. At the closing of the first month's accounts she had made fifteen hundred.

"Hurray! We are earning money, too, as well as the men," said Suyun.

"After all you are a daughter of the God of Wealth," said Inging.

And so they had a great celebration that night at Inging's room in the hotel. Chin was a self-made man, very wide awake and a good mixer who had left college after his freshman year. His experience had taught him to be sociable and easy with every person he met. He could joke, he could dance, he knew all the places about town, and he was always willing to oblige a lady. He was a furious smoker, and instead of packages of cigarettes, he carried a tin of fifty about with him in his hand, and would swear that he had just opened it this morning and now it was half gone.

The ladies liked him and called him "Old Chin." His legs seemed to be tireless and he was always in high spirits. He could arrange dinners, reserve rooms, plan outings to the suburbs. Whenever the ladies were bored and had nothing to do in the evening, they could call up Old Chin. He could be reached by telephone and would leave his wife and come to their rooms at any time of the night.

"Hullo! General Wu! What can I do for you? You want me to come right away? All right." For Inging was always known as General Wu at the other end of the telephone.

Then everybody would be in good spirits and the evening would pass off easily and happily.

In Chin's presence Suyun was a different person. Her pride, her social front, her mannered ways were gone. The annoying memory of her home and her chafing at her husband's tame, dull-witted character, were gone. She was once more merely a young woman wanting some fun, and she had found it in Chin's company. Chin said to a friend who criticized Suyun's haughtiness in public, "My dear sir, you do her an injustice. She is a most simple-hearted woman, so easy to please. You don't know the hearts of these society ladies until you have seen them in their under vests and trousers. They are just common souls. Sometimes when I take her home after the theater she seems so tired. She is one of the loneliest souls I know. You can't blame her for wanting a bit of fun. You ought to see her on the right side, which is the night side."

It was true that Suyun's soul stood completely naked before her playtime lover. She was a child once more, playing with her gay friend, and in recapturing that childish happiness she had long lost, she also recovered some of the natural sweetness of childhood. So often does the mere act of being happy make one human again. And only Chin seemed to understand her.

Now when Inging made Huaiyu promise that there was to be no other woman for him, she did not mean that there was to be no other man for herself. This was not unfair, because he had promised too readily as he always did, and she knew him too well, and she made him promise only in the sense that she would not tolerate his going with women with her knowledge. And so the two ladies were often seen together with Chin in the dance halls and theaters and restaurants, which came naturally to Mr. Tseng's knowledge. At the theaters and dance halls they also met many officials from Peking, who came to enjoy themselves during the week ends, as well as a few "generals" in long gowns and a few strange-looking bald-headed old mandarins, with foreign hats and foreign canes but in Chinese dress, who a decade or two ago were prominent Manchu officials and whose names were now so remote that they suggested a past epoch. Suyun could not believe her eyes when she was told by Inging in whispers that this one was a former Imperial Inspector Wu and that one was the famous ex-Governor of Fukien. But it was a motley crowd of old and young. And Suyun was secure in the knowledge that she could have no child.

She wrote to her husband that she was very happy, that Old Chin was a very good fellow, and that she was making money on the Exchange. This frightened Chinya, who feared some trouble, and he moped for a whole day. To his brother-in-law, who was with him in Taiyuan, he said, "Here I am working my head off trying to earn some hard money in this barbaric place, with not a decent hotel or theater, and my wife goes off enjoying herself and playing with my money on the Stock Exchange."

"Don't worry," Huaiyu comforted him. "Those two women can take care of themselves. Old Chin is one of my best friends. He is a gentleman."

"No, I ought to stop her. You know, Brother, I believe in such a thing as a person's good or bad star. Playing on the Exchange is all right for you, because you are always lucky. But I am not one of those lucky persons. Ever since I was born, I feel, I have been under an unlucky star. Luck never comes my way. I am not saying this against your sister, but look at my marriage. What do I get out of it? Look at my brother enjoying himself with Mulan. Something is wrong with me. I am afraid I shall be ruined if your sister continues to speculate."

His prophecy came too true. After two months he heard that his wife had lost ten thousand dollars and had borrowed the amount from her mother, and that he must break the news to his father and somehow return the money.

He was furious and wrote back that he refused to make his father stand the loss, and that he would soon come back to settle with her.

∵

When their grandmother died on September 17 of that year, both Chinya and Suyun had to return to Peking. The grandmother died peacefully one morning without any one knowing, her head slipping off the smooth leather pillow.

Chinya came back much thinner and tanned, and wearing a foreign coat and khaki shorts, which he had taken up through his association with American engineers. His thin legs were shown to great disadvantage in the heavy woolen stockings. His mother was greatly grieved to see him so thin and changed, but he said that his health was good, and that he had begun to like the high mountains of Shansi. He told of his adventures, of falling off a donkey on a mountain path and his great trip with the engineers, and their camp where he cooked his first meal. The experience on the whole seemed to have done him good; contact with nature and with the simple peasants had given him an outlook on life that he had never had before. He said the work was still going on, but according to the engineers there seemed to be little prospect of oil.

The brothers were very cordial in their first meeting after a year's separation. During the first days of mourning for the grandmother, the matter of the ten-thousand-dollar loss was kept in abeyance. But Suyun had already spoken to her husband about it. He could not understand why she had to speculate. After he had met mountain girls and had been impressed by their beauty, their erect carriage, their independence, and their total lack of false modesty, Suyun, whining for pity in her trouble, aroused in him only a feeling of repugnance.

"I told you not to speculate," he said, more firmly than he had ever spoken to her before. "Well, you have your own money, and since you have lost, you can make it up yourself."

His tone shocked her. "The idea!" she said. "I was trying to make money for you, and when I lose, I have to pay for it myself! You have blackened your conscience."

"All right. You account for it to Father. I had nothing to do with it."

But in the following days she talked Chinya into believing that it would be a grave injustice to make her bear the loss alone, and into thinking that the time was come for a division of property, since he had all the responsibilities and none of the privileges of the only money-earning male of the family. It would be a good idea to take this opportunity to force the issue. So Chinya consented to speak to his father about it.

The death of the grandmother and the funeral expenses involved made an occasion for Mr. Tseng to take stock of the family situation. He was at this time suffering from a strange weakening disease, diabetes, identified by the Imperial Physician as 'weakening thirst.' He felt constantly a burning inside, and he suffered from continuous thirst and was often hungry, but he had no appetite and his complexion grew paler every day. The more water he drank, the more he wanted to relieve himself. White tiger stew and ginseng stew proved of no avail. His legs were so weak that he constantly lay in bed or on a couch. When it was recognized that there was a floating substance in his urine, the physicians told him it was a severe form of *hsiaoko* and that his kidney system had been injured. Mr. Tseng was enough of a scholar to know that this was the famous disease from which the poet-lover Szema Hsiangju suffered in the second century B.C. and that the hope of recovery was one or two in ten cases. The physician told him to stop eating rich food and to sleep alone, apart from Cassia. He felt, therefore, very despondent during the whole time.

One evening, Mr. Tseng, lying on his couch in the sitting room, wanted to talk to his sons, and the family was gathered before him. "Chinya and Sunya," he began, "your grandmother is dead and your parents are old. Thanks to our ancestors' protection, we have had a peaceful time for all these years. I have nothing to be ashamed of before our ancestors when I go away. Although I have not much to leave you, there is enough so that you will not starve. In the money shops we have a total cash of not quite a hundred thousand dollars. I have earned this money through years of careful saving, helped by your mother, and I have not extorted money from the people, but took only what came naturally to me as an official in my position. Perhaps compared with other officials in Manchu times, I might call myself corrupt, but compared with these officials of the Republic I must call myself clean." This sally at the modern officials drew a smile from all the children. "Now besides the cash, we have only this house, a silk shop worth ten or fifteen thousand dollars, and land in the country which is not bringing us any income, the tax being so heavy. I want you to know these things. Expenses are heavy and this funeral must cost us at the least several thousand dollars." He wanted to say more but stopped for breath.

Suyun looked at Chinya, and after some hesitation, he summoned up courage to say, "Father, I want to tell you something. Please do not be angry."

"What is it?" asked the father in his best pontifical mandarin.

"Well, while I was away, my 'daughter-in-law' lost some money on the Tientsin Stock Exchange."

This was the first Mulan and her husband had heard of this, and they looked quickly at Suyun, whose eyes were cast down.

"What?" the father exclaimed.

"She has lost on government bonds."

"Addled egg!" the father cried. "Who told you to play with such things—'selling empty, buying empty!' Haven't you better sense than that?" His mandarin tone was like that of a magistrate and Chinya felt like a convict on trial. There was a tense silence.

"How much?" the father asked at last.

"Ten thousand," said Chinya. "She thought she could safely make some money for us."

Mr. Tseng exploded a splutter of sound through his mustache and beard.

Turning to Suyun, he said, "Who told you to speculate and earn money for us?"

"Father," said Suyun, strengthened by her readiness for a complete break, "it is just bad luck; I had the advice of the best informed man at the Exchange, who is selling and buying for the President's Sixth Mistress."

"What is his name?"

"His surname is Chin."

Mr. Tseng sat up and knocked his long pipe on the floor. "You young fool! I had wanted to talk to you; now that my son is here, you might as well know it. Don't deceive yourself by thinking that I don't know all about what you are doing at Tientsin with that Inging and with that Chin. People are already laughing at us for that disgrace. You have a home here, but you could not stay at my house. And you had to go about flirting with young men and make a laughing stock of your husband and my house."

Suyun's face turned scarlet and Chinya was aghast and angry, and he exclaimed, "Father, what are you saying?"

"You may as well know this. The whole town is talking about it. What are you going to do?"

Suyun was now ready to defend herself. "Father, you have been listening to gossip. I have done nothing wrong. Going out with men is nothing strange in modern days."

"Stop!" shouted the father. "If you have no sense of shame, I have. All modern women are *wangpa!*"

Now *wangpa* was the most extreme curse word possible in mandarin.

471

Originally it meant "forget-the-eighth"—shame being the last of the eight virtues—but usage had connected it with "tortoise" and so made it a word of low abuse, which mandarins often used on criminals and servants. The family sat in silent awe before the enraged father, who was panting violently. Stung by this abuse, Suyun covered her head in shame and cried aloud. Cassia assisted the sick old man from his couch and led him, puffing with anger, into the inner room. Upon his disappearance, Suyun suddenly stopped her crying and stood up and walked out of the room. Mrs. Tseng sat in silent anger, while Chinya was confused and bitter and felt that he had lost face before the whole family.

Mrs. Tseng shouted to all the maids to go away. "My son," she said, "this has something to do with the good name of the whole family. Whether the rumors are true or not, you ought to stop them. If I had known the daughter of the New family was like this, I would never have made this match for you. If your 'daughter-in-law' is not more careful, she will send your father to his death."

Suddenly Chinya broke down like a child. He cried so loudly that it seemed as if all his mental sufferings for years, of which he had never spoken and could not tell anybody, were now poured forth in a flood of tears before his mother. Seeing her son so, the mother also cried, and caressing him as if he were a child, she said, "Calm yourself now. I know it is hard for you. I will tell your father to pay the money and make up the loss. If you would rather stay at home, you can resign. We don't need you to go so far away to make money."

Sunya and Mulan also came up to say words of comfort to him, and Sunya said,

"Brother, we will ask Father to give you the money."

And Mulan said, "Brother, you had better go to Suyun now. Try to calm her and tell her that there is nothing at home that cannot be settled. After all, a family is a family. And don't take it too much to heart yourself, but consider it a past affair."

"What is this talk about what she was doing at Tientsin?" asked Chinya.

"We don't know," said Mulan. "Father must have heard about it outside. You had better go to her now."

So Chinya walked out of the room, his head swimming with conflicting thoughts and emotions. He found Suyun crying in bed, and tried to comfort her, but she would not say a word.

Suddenly he was overcome by a wave of anger. "I don't think you need to cry like that," he said. "How about me? What have you done to me? To be laughed at as a cuckold! If Father scolded you, it was only right. You have made a fool of yourself and me. Look at your sisters-in-law. Why can they remain at home, but not you?"

Puffing with a sense of personal injury, he left his wife, and went out and talked with his brother about the business situation of the family.

"I may be a stupid elder brother," he said, "but today's affair is not entirely your sister-in-law's fault. You people won't speak to her. That is why she had to go with Inging."

"Brother," said Mulan, "don't be unfair. No one tried to discriminate against her. You know Second Sister-in-law is hard to please."

"What I want to say," said Chinya, after a pause, "is that she will never be quite happy in this home. Honestly, I tell you, she would prefer to separate from the family and live alone. Now there is grandmother's funeral, and soon I shall be going away again. The parents are old, and if you approve, we can ask Father to divide the property. We will move out, and there will be much less friction."

Sunya looked at Mulan, and she said, "What young couple does not desire to live alone? But there are the parents. As long as the parents are living, no one likes to break up the family. It should not be done."

"But," Chinya kept on, "there is this matter of the loss in speculation. It would be wrong for you to bear part of the loss. And by the way, why don't you, Sunya, try to get some work? Now, I am earning so much a month. Everybody is spending the common money. If I put my earnings into the common fund, Suyun would be displeased, and if I don't, you may think I am selfish."

"That is all right," replied Sunya. "You don't have to feel that way about it. These are all modern ideas. We never had such problems before. What difference does it make? Isn't it all in the family? If we rise, we rise together, and if we lose, we lose together. But I know Second Sister-in-law. As far as Mulan and I are concerned, you can keep all your earnings. And we are only spending Father's money."

The conversation reached no conclusion. But while they were talking, Little Joy ran over, shouting, "Second Master, Second Master! where are you? Second Mistress has hung herself!"

They ran and found Suyun lying on the floor and the room in

473

great disorder. Disgraced in the presence of all the women of the family, she had stood on a stool and put about her neck a braided belt and tied it to a high bedpost and then kicked the stool away. The braided belt had broken and she had fallen to the floor. Cold-fragrance heard the fall and rushed in, saw what had happened and went screaming for help. A woman servant had come and found that she was stunned, but still breathing. Cassia came, but Mrs. Tseng and Mannia hid themselves, trembling in fear. Only when it was found that Suyun was not dead did Mrs. Tseng and the others come to see her. She was put in bed and only after twenty minutes did she begin to groan, with her eyes closed, careless of what was happening around her.

Brocade said to Mulan, "The belt was not really broken. I saw it. The knot had slipped loose."

Mulan looked at her and said, "You had better not say anything at all. We might have been charged by her family with forcing suicide, if she had succeeded."

· · ·

Whether the attempt at suicide was genuine or not, Suyun won a partial victory. A division of property was made, but in accounts only. She did not gain her immediate objective of living apart from the family. Each of the three branches of the family, including Mannia as representing Pingya, was to receive only twenty thousand dollars and some land in the country; and Mannia's son, as the eldest grandson of the family, was to have the silk shop which would provide for his education, while each of Cassia's daughters, Ailien and Lilien, was to have five thousand dollars set aside for her dowry. The Peking house was not divided and would not be so long as the parents lived, but the proceeds of the sale would eventually be divided between Chinya and Sunya only. The parents kept the rest of the money for themselves. On Mrs. Tseng's plea, Mr. Tseng paid Chinya for the ten-thousand-dollar loss out of the common fund, which meant that the burden was evenly distributed between the three branches of the family.

Each branch was to spend its own money or invest it with the parents' advice and approval. Mulan liked the arrangement and she and Sunya began to think very hard what they should do with their share, and they secretly thanked Suyun for it.

474

Chinya had asked for one month's leave to come home for his grand-mother's funeral. But on account of his wife, he stayed for five weeks; and at the end of the fifth week, he got a telegram saying that the American representative at Taiyuan was asking why a grandmother's funeral should last five weeks, and that he had better return immediately.

On the day he departed, he spoke to his brother.

"I am keeping tight hold on my money; she is not going to play with it," he said to Sunya. "I am giving her four hundred a month, and that should be enough. Why a woman should spend four hundred or even three hundred a month I cannot understand."

"Why not? Fifty dollars at mahjong in one night is nothing," said Sunya. "Has she agreed?"

"Whether she agrees or not, she will have to be satisfied. Do you think I am going to be a slave just to let her have money to play with? I have to count every cent I spend myself. . . . You know what it is. We are not like you two. . . . She hates me, I know. . . . Oh, marriage is a *cangue,* it's a *cangue!*"

A sigh broke from the innermost depths of his belly. He touched his collar as if it were a symbolical *cangue* for him, and Mulan and Sunya felt very sorry for him. Suddenly he spoke directly to Mulan:

"If I had a wife like you, I should not mind working very hard and spending it all. At least I should have got some fun out of it. But now what fun do I get out of it?"

"Second Brother," said Mulan, "you understand now why I did not get along with her. We will try again to make her feel more at ease in the home, but there must be a response. Of course, she is a little ashamed of herself now, but soon she will get over it. At least I shall not mention the past."

Chinya sat listening and yet not hearing. "If I—I—" he stammered.

"What?" asked Mulan.

"I am through with her," he cried. "I am through with all daughters of rich families. If I—if I ever had a chance to marry again, you know what kind of a girl I would marry?" He was talking almost to himself. "Out there in Shansi, I have seen so many sweet peasant girls. Any one of them would be grateful if I married her."

"You're not joking?" said Sunya.

"You don't believe it? Why, three hundred dollars a month, even a hundred, even fifty, would make a poor peasant wife crazy with

475

happiness. And she would look after me well, and would be loyal and contented and would work all day. This is no life, continually bickering every day."

"You are not thinking of divorcing her?" asked Mulan, agitated.

"Divorce? Any time she is ready, I am ready. What difference does it make? But don't let her know yet. . . . Do you know the kind of girl I should like to marry?" By his tone, Chinya already seemed free and happy. "I would marry a girl who has had a very hard life. A famine refugee, for instance—one sold as a child, as a slave, and half starved. Then sold again as some one's concubine, and beaten by the wife. Then thirdly . . ." Chinya paused.

"Then thirdly," completed Mulan for him, "thirdly, she ran away into a monastery and became a nun up on Wutai Mountain, dead to this world, and then she met a young man traveling with American engineers and fell in love and decided to marry again."

"That's it! That's it!" cried Chinya, elated. "What a wife such a girl would make! And I would treat her like a queen!"

And when he left, his last words were, "I am really glad to go. Perhaps there is a nun up on Wutai Mountain waiting for me. Who knows?"

Dimfragrance had stood by with Aman listening to this conversation, and Chinya had not noticed her. When he was gone, Mulan looked at Dimfragrance and looked so long that it seemed for once that Mulan was slow-witted and was trying to put together a long train of hitherto unconnected thoughts.

Finally, she smiled and said, "Dimfragrance, will you go to Wutai Mountain, or not?"

Dimfragrance bent her head to feed Aman with the chopsticks.

. ·.

Mulan tried to think very hard about what they should do with their money. Her idea was that with this money Sunya was to find a job. She said to Sunya:

"What can you do?"

"Nothing, Whimsy."

"What would you like to do?"

"We need not go over the whole ground again. I am trained up to be an official. Now I refuse to be an official. Therefore I can do nothing."

476

"Sunya," she said, "please be serious this time. If we leave this money in a bank and get 7 per cent interest, we shall get about fourteen hundred a year, which cannot keep us alive, if we have to pay rent. But the principal thing is that you have to find some work. Now I am a merchant's daughter, and I have some plebeian ambitions. Would you like to hear them?"

"Certainly."

"Well, I want to be a plebeian. No politics. No fame. No power. Just a plain business man's wife—with enough to live on and no great worries. A teashop here, a cloth shop there, and to own a small restaurant where you and I can be sure of the best food. When the old people are gone, we can go and live in a simple house with a small garden, where nobody would want to do us any harm, and when you are free, we can go boating together. You know I have never seen Hangchow yet. It remains in my heart like a dream—having heard mother and Redjade talk about it. Hangchow carp's head is famous. We'll have a house on the Lake. I might yet learn to paint. And there our children will grow up and I will teach them myself. That is not asking much from life, is it?"

"Whimsy, that is asking a great deal. Do you think we shall have that luck?"

"Really, I am not asking much from you. God save us from power and glory! You might be surprised, but I could be a plain business man's wife. I could cook such delicious vegetable soup for you!"

"Well, what shop, then?" asked Sunya.

"My father owns many shops. We might offer to buy a teashop or a medicine shop from him. Any shop will do. Even a fan shop, or one of those famous Hangchow scissors shops. Anything except a pawnshop. I shouldn't be able to stand that."

"What would you do if you inherited a pawnshop?"

"I would return all the goods and close it up! But I like these other shops. The people all seem so busy."

"It is all your imagination, Whimsy. You have grown up in a rich man's house. That is why a small shop seems so poetic."

"Now you can manage a shop, can you not?"

"Of course I could, but what—?"

"We will talk with my father about it."

When Mulan and Sunya went to see Mr. Yao, the latter thought a while and said, "You can have one of my shops in Hangchow if you

477

want it. But you cannot go down south with your parents living. Why not take over the partnership in Mrs. Hua's curio shop? It is doing very well. Last year they made five thousand dollars."

"That is a splendid idea!" said Mulan. "But it belongs to Uncle."

"It can be arranged."

"Do you think Uncle would give his share up?"

"He will, for my daughter and son-in-law," said the father confidently.

"Does she sell old books, too?"

"Most of the curio shops do, but Mrs. Hua's shop doesn't."

The more Mulan thought of the curio shop, the more the idea fascinated her. It was a leisurely job, with very few customers, and those that did come were like antiques themselves, and they would loiter and chat for a whole afternoon. She would meet painters and scholars there, and if she added a section for old editions, she would meet still more scholars and cultivate their friendship.

The thing was done. Mr. Feng said he would keep one-fourth of his present share, since the shop was making good money, but would sell Sunya three-fourths for fifteen thousand dollars, since it was all in the family. Mr. Tseng readily consented, when Sunya spoke to him about it. And so, Mr. Feng took them to talk it over with Mrs. Hua, who was immensely proud that the rich Yao daughter was going to be her partner.

It happened that the very first day in the shop Sunya and Mulan met the old painter Chi there. He was dozing and snoring in a rattan chair, with his great belly heaving up and down and his beard being carried up and down with it. Mulan mistook him for an old employee or a relative of Mrs. Hua and asked in a whisper: "Who is that?"

"That is the great Chi—the painter."

Mr. Chi was not asleep, for he said in a deep voice, with his eyes closed, "Don't sell me. I don't belong to the shop. But I am for sale just for one evening—for two catties of wine and a dish of pickled mutton."

Mulan said, with her low, musical laugh, "I have so long wanted to meet you, Mr. Chi."

"What a voice! What a voice!" said the old painter, his eyes still closed. "There is a voice I should like to paint."

His eyes slowly opened. At the sight of Mulan, he sat up and tried hurriedly to find his slippers.

"Who are you?" he demanded. Before Mulan could be introduced, he continued, "Never mind! I have wanted to paint a lady with a voice like you!"

Mulan was overjoyed, and she said, "Really, are you to be sold for the night? We should like to buy you for tonight with two catties of wine. We will go anywhere you say. Chengyanglou or Chiumeitsai."

The unconventional familiarity of talking with the great painter frightened Mulan after she had extended the invitation, but it suited the old painter very well. And so, after chatting for a whole afternoon in the shop, they celebrated the new partnership that night together with Mrs. Hua and the painter Chi. And that was how Sunya began his first day of business.

CHAPTER XXXI

M R. TSENG wept at his mother's funeral not only for form's sake, but from the bottom of his heart. What with his grief for her and his own illness, and the scandal about Suyun and her attempted suicide, he was very sad. And his sadness was deepened by the troubles of the country and the feeling that the old Chinese world he knew was slipping from beneath his feet.

Sutung, who had come to visit them occasionally, had sometime ago convinced him that he was suffering from the "sugar-urine disease" and that there was a sure scientific cure for it in the Western medicine called insulin. Now Mr. Tseng had never admitted into his body any foreign medicine except quinine which had become so common that it had a Chinese name and was taken for granted. Women are more practical-minded, because they have no vast, unshakable systems of ideas to defend, and both his wife and Cassia suggested giving insulin a trial. He had laughed at the very notion and name of a "sugar-urine disease" until Mulan looked up the Chinese medical books and showed him that Chinese medicine recognized the sweetness of the urine. Then he said, "Of course we knew all about it," but although the Chinese books suggested various treatments they offered nothing very specific. Sutung was able to offer his advice not as a professional "Western doctor," but as a friend of the family. Since his assurances were so emphatic, Mr. Tseng finally yielded and consented to try.

But his pride was terribly hurt. His pride had already been slowly sapped and undermined by many things. He had had to resign from the secure world of the mandarinate and had been made practically a derelict. He had had to submit to his wife's pressure and allow his own daughters to go into a missionary school and learn English, about which he knew and cared nothing. He blamed the failure of the modern government schools on the collapse of the old ideas. He called the modern times "an age without king, without father, and without

480

teacher"—the three symbols of authority and order in human life. He was unable to check up on his daughters' progress in geography, science, and history, and their Chinese was being neglected. They never touched a writing brush, and wrote abominable wobbly characters with a fountain pen. And now Sutung assured him that the West could cure his body when the East had failed! Sutung wore foreign dress and spoke bad Chinese, and he even had difficulty in explaining the disease without resort to strange foreign chemical names. When he came to a difficult point he always said, "There is no such term in Chinese." And yet Mr. Tseng could not help respecting him because he was sober and steady and could talk very intelligently on various topics not connected with Chinese literature.

And now the very country was threatened with foreign conquest.

When Yuan Shihkai was planning to establish his own imperial dynasty, he had approached Mr. Tseng to ask him if he would join his government. The "Society for Planning Peace" was already being organized for a return to monarchy. But Mr. Tseng saw the force of republican ideas, recognized the danger, and tried to avoid Yuan on the ground of his illness. When the President invited him to a private tea party he accepted in order to show the President how really sick he was. It was on this occasion that Mulan, who went with her parents-in-law, had her chance to see Yuan, and she was greatly struck by his resemblance to her own father, in his short build, the rings below the eyes, and the steady presence of spirit and mastery of self that showed in his face. Yuan then saw that Mr. Tseng was very pale and emaciated and released him, to Mr. Tseng's great relief.

Yuan's regime was already blackened by the greatest political disgrace that had ever been forced upon a Chinese government. Under duress, and with a sly hint of Japanese support for his monarchist ambitions, Yuan had accepted the Twenty-One Demands, which would not only take away China's railroad and mining rights, but would even allow Japan to police parts of China and appoint "advisers" in all civil, military, police, financial, and educational agencies. China would thereby be enslaved and turned into a protectorate. There was already Japanese talk of a "common Asiatic culture"—meaning thereby a common market for Asiatic shopkeepers, a great continent subjugated and held by Japanese bayonets for exploitation by Japanese financiers, manufacturers, and other money hunters. Chinese wage earners were to become economic slaves of these foreign money worshipers from a country that had lately repudiated all that was best in Asiatic culture and had become infected with the two greatest evils of the modern world—commercial greed and arrogant militarism.

Mr. Tseng could not reason that far. But he did understand the threat of foreign conquest and enslavement of the Chinese race. These things were apparent to him as far back as 1915. At the outbreak of the World War, Japan had availed herself of European chaos to capture Tsingtao, the German concession, and then extended her grip to the heart of Shantung by forcible occupation of a railway line; and in the Twenty-One Demands, Shantung had been clearly earmarked as the nearest and biggest morsel to be swallowed up by Japan.

As a native of Shantung Mr. Tseng hated all this. So when he saw his mother buried, according to custom, in all the glory of her official mandarin coat and skirts proper to her rank as the wife of a former Manchu Minister, he felt that all his old world was being buried in that coffin with her. And he wept so bitterly that several times he fainted, and Cassia and the servants had to hold him up, and he had to be taken into the bedroom and put to bed where he stayed for days, groaning.

For three months he observed strict mourning, and in the first weeks he even refused to take medicine. Cassia and Mrs. Tseng took turns in serving him, while Mannia and Mulan forbore from stepping inside his bedroom, and only helped in preparing his soup and tea and sat on stools at the curtained door to attend upon him and learn of his progress. Nobody asked Suyun to join in this service and she did not.

Lying there, broken in spirit and body, Mr. Tseng at last yielded enough to try insulin regularly. Sutung's visits were always a comfort to him, and his appetite and health improved until he got to the point of actually talking with some enthusiasm about this modern marvel that had enabled him to recover, and his bitterness against the Western world somewhat lessened.

After a few months he got well enough to go about, and in the spring he decided to transport the coffin and bury his mother in the ancestral graveyard in Shantung, which had been made ready in her lifetime.

He was anxious to leave the capital anyway, because Yuan Shihkai's monarchist plans had become public and rebellion had begun. General Tsai Ao secretly slipped away from Peking, escaping Yuan's vigilance by pretending to debauch himself in sing-song houses, and declared the rebellion on Christmas Day, 1915, in southwest Yunnan. The doom of the Twenty-One Demands was bound up with the fall of Yuan. There were widespread secret plots and conspiracies everywhere, even in Peking itself, and Mr. Tseng decided that he should get out of the way for a while. In the following summer Yuan was defeated and died almost immediately afterward, a broken, disillusioned man.

Some time after Mr. Tseng's return from Shantung, because he was so grateful for his recovery from near death, he said to Sutung one day, with his usual mandarin dignity: "I will make you my son-in-law. You have saved my life. I will give you my daughter."

He did not even mention which daughter, and Sutung did not dare ask.

"Uncle Tseng," he said, "it will be my honor to be related to you."

Sutung took it for granted that it was Ailien that her father meant, for he had seen and talked with Ailien, and thought her a good match; and luckily it was.

Mr. Tseng was so pleased that he said nothing against Sutung's taking his daughter out before marriage and accepted their modern ways and freedom without question. He decided that the wedding was to take place as soon as she was graduated from school, in the summer of 1917.

.·.

Mulan took the occasion of Ailien's wedding in 1917 to take her long-desired trip to the south with her husband. Sutung's mother was living at Shanghai and, being ill, was unable to come north; so it was decided that the wedding should be in Shanghai. Cassia was going with her daughter, as Mr. Tseng was still not well enough to stand the strain of both the journey and the wedding. Sunya offered to go in his father's place, and Mulan seized this opportunity to see Shanghai and Hangchow.

When Afei learned that his sister was going south, he said he wanted to go also. Redjade had suggested this to him, thinking it would be wonderful if they could go together. The two cousins had been enclosed together in this garden home, seeing each other every day, and the spring in the garden and the spring in their own hearts had intoxicated them with an almost delirious love. Afei's mother was too occupied with the salvation of her soul and too much confined in her room to notice it; the loss of speech confined her still more to the more bodily

483

needs of her own self. Curiously, she smoked her water pipe as usual, and the gurgle of the pipe and the blowing at the stem were the nearest to articulate sounds that she could make. Nobody knew what was going on in her head because she could not write. Mr. Yao, while not believing that Redjade was an ideal wife for his son, was nevertheless kind and sympathetic because of her intelligence and tender beauty. He knew, moreover, that any other match for Afei would certainly send the delicate and impetuous Redjade to her death. Redjade's parents naturally encouraged the match, since Afei was heir to the Yao fortune. So the young people had been left very much to themselves.

In the fall of the preceding year, Redjade had been ill in bed for about two months, which made Afei all the more tender toward her, and since that time, she had stopped going to school. It was suspected that she had lung trouble. Illness brought her a strange restlessness and made her all the more eager to cling to life and squeeze from it the last drop of happiness. It made her envy health, but it also made her sentimental over a leaf that the wind had blown into her room. She asked Afei to go out and collect the most beautiful autumn leaves and she kept them pressed in the books on her bedside table. She developed also a habit of fastidiousness about herself and her room, and an abnormal fear of the worms and bugs that sometimes came in on the flowers in her vases. She demanded that the woman servant who served her should wear only new dresses, and her mother had indulged her in this and in all her desires. This spring she was much better and felt a new yearning to visit her childhood home. A trip to Hangchow and boating with Afei on the West Lake, would fulfil her dream of happiness.

Since Afei's vacation began at the same time, he was given permission to go with his sister and Redjade. Sutung went a week ahead to make arrangements for the wedding, while his younger sister, Suchen, being unable to leave before the school closed, was to go with the Tseng sisters who were her classmates. Mochow did not feel the need of travel, and said that her child was too young to stand the hot journey and Lifu would be coming home very soon. So Mochow did not go.

The gay party of modern young people left Peking at the end of June. Lilien, as well as everybody else, took it for granted that Afei and Redjade would be engaged and kept aloof, and Redjade was very vivacious throughout the journey. Mulan was to chaperone Redjade and shared a compartment with her. Redjade refused to eat foreign food on the Blue Express, and Afei kept rushing in and out again to order special fried rice for her. She even made him open her suitcase and take out things for her, and he enjoyed the intimate service.

"How well you are serving Fourth Sister," Mulan remarked. "You are a good girl's companion, too, like Eldest Brother, except that he paid his attentions in the wrong places. You have already wiped the windowsill three or four times this morning. By and by I think you will have to take a broom to sweep the floor for her."

"In fact, I have already done so," confessed Afei with a smile.

Redjade *tsui'd* her, which was to make a motion of the mouth, similar to the English "pfui!".

Mulan made a rather poor chaperone. Afei practically spent all his time in their compartment. Redjade began to show a certain womanly reserve. Still in Mulan's presence Redjade would talk as naturally with him as if Mulan were not present and would adjust his red tie when it was out of order, looking up at him with a proud smile; and, after the tie was adjusted, her white, delicate arm would linger for a moment on his breast.

"Do you still quarrel?" asked Mulan.

"How can we quarrel when I do her wish every time?" said Afei.

"Shame on you!" said Redjade. And then, addressing Mulan, she said, "If I didn't yield to him every time in argument, he would be still worse off. And he doesn't know it himself!"

"My goodness!" said Afei. "Every time she won in her argument, and yet she says she yielded!"

"Have I ever said anything really unkind to you?" asked Redjade.

"No, *Meimei*," admitted Afei.

"Well, I hope only that you two will always be happy together," said his sister.

And so at night, sharing the compartment, Redjade found it possible to open her heart to Mulan and discuss both Afei and her love. She had been afraid that Mulan might use her influence with her father in favor of Lilien, but now she felt that Mulan was willing to help her.

For Redjade was happy and yet unhappy. She was already eighteen and Afei nineteen; yet there had been no talk of engagement on the part of Mr. and Mrs. Yao. Under the circumstances, Redjade considered it peculiar, although naturally she could not have spoken of that strange forgetfulness on the part of Afei's parents. No hint whatsoever had come from them.

Redjade was as happily in love as it was possible for a young girl to be. Afei was now grown to be a tall and handsome young man, well-to-do and unspoiled and very devoted to her, and she was living close to him. Few girls could find love in such ideal circumstances at the period when a girl's whole being demanded some one to love and be loved by. Yet why should neither Mr. Yao nor Mrs. Yao have said a word about the engagement? Did they like her? Or did they merely tolerate her? For Redjade was a talented and therefore independent girl. Lavishing her great love on Afei, and relying upon her charm and talent, she was yet not the type to bother about trying to please others for an ulterior motive. She was too young, too proud, too independent to use any wiles. Whether before Afei's father or his mother, she was still her natural self. The one thing she could not do was to pretend to like someone she did not like, and she did not like Afei's mother. While she liked her uncle, she had that fatal willfulness to show her independence before him, exactly because she might be otherwise suspected of trying to flatter a future father-in-law. Love with her was a purely spontaneous and honest thing, apart from all the machinations which older people connected with it. In loving Afei she went the whole way, sometimes rather too openly even in the presence of elder people; in trying to secure the favor of his parents, she did not do half enough. Still the absence of any open talk of engagement gave her a certain uneasiness of mind.

"I don't know why I am so afraid to lose him," she now confessed to Mulan. "Every time I am with him and our happiness is perfect, I imagine that this is too good to be true, that it cannot last forever."

"That is because you love much," said Mulan. "Love is an immortal wound that cannot be closed up. A person loses something, a part of her soul, when she loves someone. And she goes about looking for that lost part of her soul, for she knows that otherwise she is incomplete and cannot be at rest. It is only when she is with the person she loves that she becomes complete again in herself; but the moment he leaves, she loses that part which he has taken with him and knows no rest till she has found him once more."

Mulan spoke so earnestly that Redjade felt she was giving expression to something more than a philosophy of love in general. She paused and in that silence Redjade, who was in the upper berth, wished she could see how Mulan looked at that moment.

486

"What if one does not meet her lover, or if the lover dies?" she asked at last.

"Who can know such things of the spirit?" Mulan replied. "Perhaps that part of herself never returns and becomes spirit also. The beings of the 'bright world' and the occult world do not seem to have dealings with one another. But if the living lover marries some one else, the *yang* and *yin* balance is somehow restored again, and the immortal wound is healed with a substitute. But it is never quite the same."

Mochow had never spoken of such experiences of love to Redjade, and probably could not; nor had Redjade ever heard anything like it from any other girl.

Mulan went on to speak of Sutan. Now divorced and living in Peking on the money of the divorce settlement, she had refused to come to her brother's wedding and was living very much alone, refusing to go out and see people.

"And yet they were very much in love before their marriage," remarked Redjade.

"Oh, no, that was not love!" said Mulan emphatically.

This surprised Redjade, and she fell asleep in a confusion of thought about herself and her cousin-sister.

. · .

After the wedding the bride was left with her husband, and after some orgies of shopping in Shanghai for silk stockings, Mulan went with Sunya and Afei and Redjade and Lilien and her mother to Hangchow, which was only four hours further by railway. They spent five beautiful days in the old house on the Lake. It was near General Yofei's Temple, facing the road on one side and the lake on the other, so that there were structures built into a quiet corner of the lake and enclosing part of it as a pond.

The city of Hangchow fascinated Mulan completely. It had none of the splendor of Peking; yet it was soft, enticing, exquisite. For it is a lake city, surrounded by tall mountains, capped by temples and ancient pagodas. Seeing Hangchow after Peking is like having a good cup of Hangchow tea after a heavy dinner. Of the beauties of Peking, Mulan had always liked the Eunuch's Bridge and the Shihshahai, its most rural aspects that remind one of the south. Here was Hangchow, the south itself, with the softness and delicacy of the south. The Kunming Lake in the New Summer Palace, built by human labor with the extravagance of the Empress Dowager, was but meant to be a small model of the West Lake, and here was the West Lake itself. Magnificent as the lake in the Summer Palace is, it compares with the West Lake as a shadow with its reality, as a doll with a living pretty young woman. The West Lake, known always as Mademoiselle West, or Hsitse, the most famous ancient beauty referred to by Mencius, suggests to us always a fickle southern woman, smiling on clear, bright days and knitting her brows on cloudy, misty days; and like Mademoiselle West, it is more enticing in the latter mood, when the lake is enveloped in mists. Magic willow-covered islands seem to float on the grayish moistness, and you do not know whether the mountains have gone up to meet the clouds or the clouds have come down to meet the mountains.

Mulan knew now that as one grew a year older, one also became one year wiser. And apart from its natural beauties, Hangchow was, and is, always the Mecca of poets and beauties. It has a tradition older than Peking, for it was the capital of the Southern Sung Dynasty before the Peking Mongol city was built—a tradition, too, more associated with literary, than with political history. Its two long embankments were built by and named after two of the greatest poets of China, Po Chuyi and Su Tungpo, of the Tang and Sung Dynasties. Poets and famous courtesans have lived, reveled, died, and been buried in Hangchow for a thousand years, and their residences and tombs are to be found everywhere. Mulan decided she wanted to come and live here when their parents were dead and they should be independent. It would be the realization of her dream of a peaceful, humble, rural family life.

Mulan took great interest in her father's shops and they spent several mornings talking with the shop managers who did their best to entertain them. The rest of the time was passed in idyllic laziness. At night when the lake was blanketed with a white mist, they would sit in a small boat, enjoying the soft breeze over the lake and listening to other young people in the distance singing serenades on their boats.

And one afternoon they went to the shrine of the Old Man in the Moon, the God of Matrimony, and drew slips of paper which bore oracular verse about luck at matrimony. These were printed on cheap wood blocks and the verse was undistinguished in diction and trite in phraseology. In fun Cassia drew one for Lilien, which ran like this:

The bloom at the branch's tip nods welcome to spring.
The plum vies also with its fragrant neighbor.
Look at the busy bee working all day—
For whom the "sweet," for whom the bitter labor?

"Nobody believes in these things," said Sunya. "The monks make all the money." But for fun also Redjade drew one, which read as follows:

To paint the brows of love in a lady's chamber.
Peonies on the steps breathe happiness.
Take not the real as false, the false as real.
Pass the perfume and all is emptiness.

Redjade tore up the slip with a knitting of her brows and said to Afei, "You draw one."

"Why?" answered Afei. "Why spend a few coppers to give the monks a chance to be impertinent?" And he would not.

But Mulan could not help wondering about the oracle and the meaning of the word "perfume," which made her think of Dim-fragrance.

That night on the Lake, Redjade was unhappy, but Afei and Sunya kept up their spirits as usual. Neither Lilien nor her mother took the oracle seriously. Redjade said that she had seen a boat in the distance with a young man and girl and heard them chattering together and then had seen it suddenly disappear in the mist leaving no trace behind. The story was told of a pair of lovers at the end of the Ming Dynasty who leaped together into the lake, and how on moonlight nights, people sometimes saw a phantom boat with this couple come out to enjoy themselves in the moonlight. The couple never grew old. They kept their Ming costumes; the man always wore pale blue and a scholar's black cap, and the girl with her coiffure on top of her head always wore purple. She would play the flute, for she had been a sing-song girl, according to tradition.

Nobody had seen it but Redjade.

.·.

While in Hangchow they received a telegram from Lifu, who had returned from Japan and was stopping at Shanghai. Sunya telegraphed back asking Lifu to join them, but the reply said that he should hurry home to his family. So they asked him to wait in Shanghai for them and on the fifth day they went back.

Lifu met them at the station, a little thinner, but healthy-looking. That night they celebrated his homecoming at a restaurant.

"What do you study? Tell us all about it?" said Mulan.

"Oh, something about cells, how they grow, and something about bugs," said Lifu, dismissing in a sentence his chosen subject of biology, for unlike other college graduates, he refused to talk about his studies. And he asked, "What is all this about a *coup d'état* by the pigtailed Chang Hsun?"

"We don't know," said Sunya. "We only read of it in the newspapers. It must have been exciting at home. It is said that the Nanhoyuan Street went up in flames."

"I saw in this morning's paper that it was all over, and the Christian General's soldiers are occupying the Temple of Heaven."

It turned out that Lifu was better informed than the others on the recent developments in Peking. The pigtailed General had indeed staged a *coup d'état,* putting the boy Manchu emperor on the throne again, which lasted exactly ten days. Lifu knew that, with Yuan Shihkai dead, the real power was held by Tuan and that the defeat of the monarchist *coup* meant that the much hated pro-Japanese Anfu clique would come to power. He spoke of politics with more conviction and enthusiasm than of his physiology.

The train journey back to Peking in July was hot, and it was decided that they should stop over at the Tseng home in Shantung to see the Taishan, the Sacred Mountain. Neither Lifu nor Afei nor Redjade had yet seen the Taishan. Mulan wanted to see the sunrise from the top of the mountain, and it was decided that they should stay at the summit overnight. They arrived at Tai-an about ten in the morning and they had two hours' rest before the sedan-chair carriers came and urged them to go up immediately after lunch.

If any mountain in China had wide, well-paved, well-graded, and comfortable roads for ascent, it was the Sacred Mountain of Taishan.

Government and private donations had helped to maintain the broad stone pavements in good condition. Emperors for two thousand years had honored the sacred mountain; centuries of poets had sung about it and left their inscriptions on the rocks; history had enriched it with relics; and folklore and the legend of pilgrims had embellished it with an oral tradition. The road was provided with convenient resting places and landmarks, beginning from the First Gate of Heaven, near Where-Confucius-Climbed, through the Second Gate of Heaven midway, to the South Gate of Heaven at the summit.

There were seven sedan chairs and two carriers besides, who brought up their bedding for the night. The day was gray and cloudy, which made it more pleasant for all, especially for the chair carriers. Giant boulders, smoothed through ages by flowing streams, lay in wild disorder along the gullies by the roadside, half submerged in water, like huge buffaloes or hippopotamuses.

Mulan had never gone up Taishan in such gay company. It was the mountain she had seen and quarreled about with Sunya when they were children. Lifu was on his first trip, and Mulan could see the enthusiasm in his face.

From the monastery up, the view began to grow more strange and more inspiring, with green cedars lining the roads and strange rocks like crouching beasts in different postures on the distant peaks. Passing the Water-Screen Cave, they saw a flying cataract above them, spreading a silver screen of water as it fell, and wetting them with its spray. At the Cliff for Resting Horses, the sedan-chair carriers stopped for a while, and Sunya, Lifu, and Mulan walked about and looked back to the distant winding path by which they had come up. The stream in the gully was so tempting that Afei took off his socks and shoes and waded, and his example was followed by the men, while Mulan, Lilien, Redjade, and Cassia loitered on the bank.

"Come down," Afei shouted to them.

Redjade would never have considered going down to the stream, but Lilien looked at her mother and asked if she should.

"Go in," said Mulan, half wanting to go herself.

"I will, if you will set the example," said Lilien.

"Come down, Whimsy. It is cooling," said Sunya.

With a laugh, Mulan, sitting on a boulder, slipped off her shoes and socks and bared her white naked feet, so rarely exposed, and lightly dipped them in the water.

"Mulan, you are crazy," said Cassia with a smile.

"It is good and delightful," said Mulan. "If you didn't have bound feet, I would pull you in, too."

Lilien joined them. Sunya came and led Mulan into the shallow stream, and Mulan laughed and limped and once almost fell, and was quickly pulled up by her husband. There was a great deal of laughter

491

from the amused sedan-chair carriers. Lifu sat on a boulder in midstream with upturned trousers and looked on. He thought it very unusual, for this was long before the day of modern girl bathers at the beaches. One of the chair carriers shouted, "Have a bath, have a bath, lady! Only you city ladies are afraid of the water."

"Lifu," said Mulan, "you ought to telegraph to Mochow to come and join us, so that we can spend a week here." But Lifu only smiled.

Now the chair bearers asked them to start if they wanted to reach the summit before sundown. Sunya thought Mulan took an unusually long time to dry her feet. Lifu, coming up the bank, saw her white ankles, smooth and small, for she made no effort to conceal them. Instead, she looked up and said to Lifu in a low voice, "Help me up!" and he did, piqued by his wayward and beautiful sister-in-law. The perfect naturalness of Mulan made even an awkward situation beautiful, and he thought of her as a strange spirit but congenial to his world of belief.

Redjade, as she stood watching them, remembered what Mulan had said about love.

"How old is your wife? She looks so young!" one of the chair bearers asked Lifu.

"She is not my wife; she is my relative," answered Lifu.

Mulan heard and for the first time blushed a little.

They got into the chairs and started again. Soon they passed the Cedar Cave, which was really a cedar forest, the foliage being so close together that it formed a roof shutting out the sky as in a cave. It was said that Emperor Chiaching had planted twenty-two thousand cedar trees here and created this grove. Mulan wished she could loiter there, but they had already lost time.

After passing the Second Gate of Heaven, they came to the Happy Three. Asked the reason for the name, the carriers explained that after the steep ascent here was an easy level for a distance of three *li,* which naturally made the climbers happy. From that point on, more magnificent views opened before them, and the pine forests on the higher hillsides moved in the wind and sounded like sea waves roaring in the distance. After passing the Eighteen Bends, they came in sight of the South Gate of Heaven, standing like a tower on an almost perpendicular cliff, cut through and provided with stone steps. The sedan chairs were now carried obliquely, so that the carriers in front were on the right and those behind on the left of the steep steps.

Having reached the South Gate of Heaven, they got out of the sedan chairs and walked along the Heavenly Street and to the Jade Emperor's Temple, the highest point of the mountain, where they were to pass the night. A young Taoist monk about seventeen or eighteen came out to meet them, and Sunya ordered supper for seven persons. They all stood on a stone balcony in the stone-paved court which enclosed a rock sprung from the ground which was considered the highest rock of the whole mountain. When they went in to the main room to wait for supper, Lifu asked Sunya, "Are you tired? We should go and see Emperor Chin's Inscription without Words."

"I am thinking only of one thing, our supper," replied Sunya.

"Come on! It is only a few steps from here," Lifu said.

"Come along!" urged Mulan also. "As we passed the Heavenly Street, I turned and saw a most glorious sunset behind us."

But Sunya, being fat and panting from the walk, said he wanted only to sit at ease and relax. Cassia was directing the servant in making the beds, and Lilien and Redjade were helping her. So Lifu and Mulan and Afei went out.

Now they were above the clouds. Mulan, standing at the landing above the Inscription without Words, her hand on her brother's shoulder, looked like a mountain spirit with the hair at her neck flowing out on the high mountain wind, surveying the distant gray knobs that were the hills and the patches of purple and somber green that were the valleys. A wave of changing magic color was sweeping over the land. Toward the west, Mulan saw a sea of crimson clouds lined with gold and silver. It was like the effect of a sunset shining at an angle upon an old man's head. Lifu had gone down the steps and was standing at the foot of the dark square stone tablet, over twenty feet high, two thousand years old and covered with dry, brown moss. As he looked up, he saw the exquisite silhouette of Mulan cast against a sky of lavish colors finely modulated, extravagantly beautiful.

"You see that, Lifu?" said Mulan, pointing to the clouds in the west.

"I see that," he replied.

She came down to the foot of the tablet. It was the tablet of Chin Shih-huang, builder of the Great Wall. After he had conquered the whole of China and established his Empire he went up to Taishan and offered sacrifices to the Sacred Mountain, which was the prerogative of an emperor. How that tablet came to have no inscriptions on it no one quite knows. Some say that he was suddenly taken ill, and the tablet was therefore left unfinished when he died. A more plausible explanation was that the stone cutters were unwilling to perpetuate the memory of the tyrant and did not cut the words deep enough, so that they wore off in the course of time.

Mulan went close to the tablet where Lifu was standing, staring at the moss-covered stone, lost in meditation. She stretched her hand to pull some of the dry moss, and Lifu said, "Don't!"

"This tablet is so huge," said Mulan. Silence.

"And so old," said Mulan. Silence again.

Mulan became silent also. And the three of them sat on a stone slab near by, speechless as the tablet itself, as if they, too, had become inscriptions without words.

Finally, Lifu broke the silence. "It says so much, this Inscription without Words."

Mulan caught the expression in his dreaming eyes. He had read in that wordless tablet the glory of the builder of the Great Wall, the swift disintegration of his Empire, the march of history—the passing of more than a dozen dynasties—a complete chart, as it were, of the centuries themselves. And the dark shape of the silent rock protruded itself upon his mind and hers in that mountain sunset—a rugged challenger of time.

"Do you remember," said Lifu, "how the Chin Emperor was afraid of death and sent five hundred virgin boys to the Eastern Sea to seek the Pill of Immortality? And now the rock survives him."

"The rock survives because it has no mortal passion," said Mulan enigmatically.

Darkness was quickly enveloping them. What had been a sea of golden fleece was now only a sandy gray surface blanketing the earth; and wandering clouds, tired of their day's journey, came into the valleys before them and settled for the night, leaving the higher peaks like little gray islands in the sea of night. So does Nature herself labor by day and rest by night. It was peace with a terror in it.

Five minutes ago Mulan's heart was excited. Now she was calm and strangely sad, the outward excitement having descended into rumbling depths in her belly, hardly perceptible by her head. Dragging her tired legs up the steps, she thought of life and death, of the life of passion and the life of the rocks without passion. She realized that this was but a passing moment in the eternity of time, but to her it was a memorable moment—a complete philosophy in itself, or rather a

494

complete vision of the past and the present and the future, of the self and the non-self. That vision, too, was wordless. Garrulous philosophers would be at a loss to express what that moment meant. Unable to call it by another word, writers have called it only an "experience."

But the night does not always mean peace for men, as it does for rocks and plants and for the dreamless animals. This night of July 16, 1917, on top of Taishan was a strangely exciting night for Mulan. They had a supper of four dishes only: fried eggs, turnip soup, slices of lotus roots, and bean curd with mushrooms; and for cereals they had light congee and a kind of village buns called *manman*. The journey and the keen mountain air made them all hungry and the dishes were cleared to the bottom. But the sound of distant temple bells made it seem a strange supper. After supper, they had a sharply acid mountain tea. Sunya chatted with Lifu about his experiences in Japan, and then they went to bed.

Sunya was snoring in sound sleep, but Mulan dozed off and woke and dozed again. The unusual tea kept her head awake, while her legs and her bowels were fast asleep, and she did not know whether she was awake or dreaming. She felt, half-dreaming, that she was trying to untie a huge cloudy knot which was a riddle, and the riddle was God. While she was struggling with the knot, a gust of mountain wind shook her bedroom window and woke her again. But Sunya was still snoring.

It seemed as if she had hardly fallen asleep before she was wakened by voices and saw pale light breaking in through the crevices of the window panels. She shook Sunya and said, "It is dawn already! We must not miss the sunrise."

"Hang the sunrise!" said Sunya and turned away and fell instantly asleep again.

But Mulan could sleep no more. She heard the noises in the kitchen —the splutter of fuel burning in the stove and the clanging of the dipper against the water jar. She got up and tiptoed to the next room and found Cassia still asleep with the young girls, and woke them. Returning to her room, she lighted an oil lamp and began to do her hair. She looked at the watch; it was only ten minutes to three.

Having finished dressing, she waited until she began to feel drowsy again, but the kitchen servant came to knock at their door.

"Master, Mistress, get up if you don't want to miss the sunrise."

Mulan woke Sunya again and opened the door. A gust of cold air blew in, smelling entirely unlike the air elsewhere. She saw Lifu already dressed and standing in the court looking into the kitchen.

"You are so early," said Mulan.

"I have been up for an hour. It was chilly and I could not sleep soundly. Are they up? We must hurry."

Mulan went in and put on a woolen sweater. Sunya was just getting out of bed.

"Oh, the sunrise, the sunrise!" he said, unsympathetically.

"That is what we came up here for!" said his wife.

Soon the breakfast was ready. "Eat something warm before you go out into the night," said the servant. Mulan asked for warm wine, and she and Sunya drank it, but Lifu did not take any. Having fortified themselves with warm congee, they went out to the Sunrise Peak. Redjade was coughing and Afei took a blanket along and wrapped her in it.

There was only a patch of white light above the horizon of the Eastern Sea. Then a pale pink gradually crept into the white patch, and the mountain tops about them began to be visible. On the north, they saw a winding white band which they were told was the river running toward the sea.

There was no motion in the clouds. Then as the pink deepened into gold, the clouds, as if at a given signal, began to wake from their night's sleep, stretching and yawning. The upper layers began to move and as they moved, the bottom was tinged with a rippling, translucent purple. The clouds moved all together toward the east and piled themselves up into a golden palace in the heavens. The mountaintops below now showed in clearer detail, and the earth, where it was not covered by clouds, lay still in dark slumber. After about a quarter of an hour, a thin glimmering thread of gold began to line the horizon; and in another few minutes two streaks of brilliant light shot up into the sky announcing the approach of the sun, gilding the clouds anew, and brightening the distant ocean surface. The mountain wind increased its speed. Suddenly a segment of intense red rose over the horizon and a shout went up from them all, "There is the sun!" to welcome that majestic, triumphant approach.

"Now it's half up!"

"Look at the sparkling ocean surface!"

"Now it's all up!"

As if at a bound, the huge disc lifted itself above the horizon, and the faces of the watchers were lit up. Mulan looked at her wrist watch. It was only quarter past four.

"Look!" said Redjade. "The clouds!"

For the finger of dawn had touched the clouds clinging to the multitudinous peaks, and as if obedient to the sun and subtly responsive to the mountain breeze, they stirred and no sooner did they stir than they started down the valley, dancing on their way like gigantic white dragons, leaving open to the view wider and wider stretches of the valleys. The earth was awake.

They had been standing in the morning air for half an hour.

"I am cold," said Lilien.

"I am all right now," said Redjade and took the blanket from her body to give to Lilien, and Afei helped wrap it over Lilien's neck and shoulders.

"This time we have seen the earth go to sleep and the earth wake," said Mulan with enthusiasm. "It was worth it, wasn't it?"

"Yes, it was worth it," replied Sunya. "But I feel like going to bed again. My legs are still stiff."

As their party strolled back, another party were just coming out to see the sunrise and were disappointed to be told that they had missed it. The early dawn seemed strangely quiet, except for the noise of their footfalls and the gentle rustle of the morning wind in their skirts.

"How quiet it is!" said Mulan. "We don't even hear the bird calls."

"We are so high up. The birds sleep in the valleys below," said Lifu and added, "It is a pity Mochow didn't see this. She would have enjoyed it."

They went to see the Moyapei, a big rock with Tang inscriptions, and then went in. The sedan-chair bearers who had stayed overnight at the South Gate of Heaven were already there, wanting them to start early in the hope of catching upcoming fares for the same day.

•·•

After an hour's rest and food, they started down. It would probably take only an hour and a half to the foot of the mountain. Sunya, being plump, took a chair, as did Redjade and Cassia, but most of the party preferred to walk down, each with a walking stick to support his steps. It was true, as Lifu had said, that as they went farther down, they began to hear the birds call and twitter in the valleys.

Somehow Mulan and Lifu naturally walked together and talked all the way. It was not only that Lifu had just returned, but that they had so much to talk about, and both of them being light, they kept up a fast pace, so that they constantly had to stop to wait for the others. At the Happy Three, Sunya got down from his chair and walked a stretch with them, and Mulan was carried from the Second Gate of Heaven to the Dismounting Pass. But there she got down again and with Lifu walked so fast that they soon left the others far behind them. Now they were alone. Mulan had never been in a better mood for talking and walking than on that beautiful day walking with Lifu down the hill. She was protected by her love for her sister and by her confidence in Lifu, and at the same time she was delighted to have this unique experience of going with him alone, so that neither suggested waiting for the others. When they reached the Cedar Cave, they felt invited by the cool shade of the grove to rest and wait for the others.

Lifu moved an old stump and Mulan made herself a seat with a handkerchief on one of the roots. She was almost too happy and she fumbled for something to say. At last she said, "Well, this is better than a visit to the Old Summer Palace ruins, isn't it?"

"Oh, yes, we promised to make that trip together," said Lifu.

"You still remember that!" said Mulan smiling.

"I still remember it," he replied.

"Life is strange, isn't it?" said Mulan meditatively resting her face in her hand.

It was a question impossible to answer. "What do you mean?" he asked.

"Well, it is just strange . . . I never thought we were going to have this delightful trip, but here we are . . . these trees." She looked up and around. "And—I don't know—the sunrise which made the earth seem so human—it cleanses you from the inside and makes you want to be kind to everybody who shares this earth with us . . . And your return home. Everything is so unexpected."

Lifu stood gazing at Mulan sitting there talking to him and yet only to herself, talking softly and at ease under the cedars, exquisitely beautiful, her low accent merging with the whispering forest breeze. The breeze blew some of her hair across her forehead and she swept it back with her fingers, but the breeze wafted it back again and brought with it the fragrance of the cedar forest.

498

"You don't call the sunrise unexpected, do you?" said Lifu. "It is expected everyday."

"I do," replied Mulan. "The sunrise is unexpected. . . . And so is your return. . . . You know—three times have I met you on the mountains. . . . The first time when we were young children . . . Now we sisters are mothers and you are a father, and my mother is dumb."

Lifu began to ask Mulan about her mother and her sister and the baby boy, and she told him of the strange malady that had come over her mother.

Soon Redjade's chair appeared above them, followed by Afei and the others on foot; and Mulan rose, half regretting that the moment was so beautiful and yet so short, and feeling that in itself it was perfect. They all came into the grove to take rest, and soon Sunya and Cassia joined them. After they started again, they reached the starting place within an hour, and the journey was so pleasant that they reached the foot of the hill before any one expected it.

That night they took the train and returned to Peking.

The trip left a permanent effect on Mulan. It made her realize that she could always be happy and content merely to be near Lifu. They had seen together the sundown and the sunrise on the mountain, and somehow this made a difference for her when she was living down in the plains. The dark figure of Lifu standing speechless before the Chin Inscription, that walk in the early dawn, and those short minutes of talk in the Cedar Cave were fraught with spiritual meaning. She did not know what that meaning was and could not have expressed it in words, but she knew that through those gloriously captured moments she saw life more clearly than before.

CHAPTER XXXII

LIFU returned to Peking and found Mochow to greet him at the station in a white dress, young, fresh, and beautiful, leading their two-year-old baby with one hand, and welcoming him with the other, but with no more demonstrativeness than a silent pressure which told him he was welcome back to a home of steadfast love. His sister was there, too, and told him that she had transferred to the Peking National University, which had become coeducational since the so-called "literary renaissance."

When he reached home, he first went in to see his mother, who had not changed much, and then to see his sick mother-in-law. The old woman sat smoking her water pipe which gurgled although she herself still could not utter a sound. But nature had been kind; her mind had been dulled and her interests dwindled to certain simple bodily needs beyond which she had apparently no worries and she was no longer restless. Except for her illness, it was a peaceful home, with the sisters Coral and Mochow running it. Mr. Yao was very cordial toward him as he always was, and the father and son-in-law talked for a long time, until he was called by a servant to the bath which Mochow had made ready for him.

Back in his own court, he found his room clean and cool and darkened against the bright summer day. His trunks had already been taken out to the yard and his clothing was being sunned. His child stood studying him with a sharp, wondering look for a long time before he would come to him. The child had just had a bath, Lifu noticed, and there was not a speck of dirt to be found on his head or his body.

His books had been kept exactly as they were on the desk, but beside them he saw some English books lying open, and some well-thumbed copies of *La Jeunesse,* organ of the literary revolution, and copies of the *Renaissance,* published by the students of Peking University.

"Why, are you studying English?" he said to his wife.

"I am studying it with Huan-erh," she said. "I had nothing to do. I went to listen to both Chen and Lin lecture at the University. They are fighting like dogs and cats—you know, about the Renaissance. Now your bath is getting cold."

Lifu went to his bath.

"Lifu, do you want to hear a piece of news?" said Mochow across the room.

"What news?" said Lifu from inside.

"Interesting news."

"What interesting news?"

"Do you remember Mannia's maid, Little Joy? You said she was completely innocent. Well, she had a child by a servant last year and is married to him now."

Mochow heard Lifu laugh inside. "I still say she is innocent," he said.

Lifu had now finished his bath and had come out.

"I was talking with your father about your mother's illness," he said, "and suggested that a shock might cure her—something that would suddenly compel her to exclaim or shout. But it must be a pleasant kind of shock, or she might get worse."

"We really don't know what to do," Mochow said doubtfully.

Lifu picked up a copy of *La Jeunesse*.

"I read every issue of this in Japan," he said.

"It is like a storm over the country," said Mochow. "We had such fun reading the correspondence and listening to the professors exchanging blows in their respective classrooms."

For Peking University was now the storm center of the literary revolution that raged over the issue of using the modern spoken language instead of the classical language in writing. Reading the essays in the modern language, where the classical language had been the rule, was at first like seeing peasant bridegrooms invade a ladies' salon to claim their brides—uncouth, unmannered, horrifying, or direct, amusing, and satisfying, according to the onlookers. The peasant bridegrooms began to unroll the carpets after trampling upon them with their dusty boots, and the ladies tripped and screamed. Among the rustic invaders was a man by the name of Chen Tuhsiu who was the gang leader and who laid violent hands on the ladies, while another was helpful with his profuse use of profane expletives, to the merriment of the revolutionary crowd gathered outside.

Chancellor Tsai, that gentle, courteous old gentleman who could not hurt a fly, had by his policy of tolerance and liberalism turned the university into a home of hostile groups, fighting each other with complete freedom. Peking University was then truly alive, because it was truly liberal. Lin, the translator of Conan Doyle and Sir Walter Scott, was the leader of the classical group. Ku, the old philosopher and wit and a whole-hearted supporter of oriental culture, was another. Lin wrote a long letter calling the vernacular the language of "rickshaw pullers and pickle vendors" and compared the revolution to a deluge and a letting forth of wild beasts into human society. There were four leaders of the "Renaissance" Chen, Chien, Hu, and Liu. Chien, who wore enormous glasses and was afraid of women and dogs, replied by calling the whole classical school "seeds of sin" and "literary bastards." Professor Hu, a young man just returned from America, who talked and wrote in a professorial academic manner with typical Anglo-Saxon "decency" and "gentlemanliness"—claimed that it was not a revolution but a step in evolution, and he supplied to the movement the prestige of the most up-to-date West. Professors Chen and Chien, having been trained in Japan and so being less well-mannered, provided the revolutionary ammunition of fiery denunciation and outright abusiveness that shocked the old and amused the young and created the literary commotion.

Old China was properly shocked. A revolution had to shock people. The blows at the language were not enough, for they were followed by blows at all restraints in poetic form, at chastity, at the encouragement of widowhood, at the family system, at the "dual standard of morality," at ancestor worship, and at Confucianism itself. This created the excitement. One of the leaders delivered an address at the wedding of a widow, championing her right to remarry and calling Confucianism a "cannibal religion," and the radical youth listened gladly. Mixed with some very useful imported goods there was also a lot of incidental cargo, such as college graduates returned from the West would talk about with great enthusiasm. Young China had not only the right to hope, but it actually had a great deal of hopefulness. For a new gospel, the revolutionists offered Amy Lowell's free verse (but went for free verse that was really free and blank verse that was really blank), Margaret Sanger's birth control, "democratic" and "pro-

502

letarian" literature, Ibsen, Oscar Wilde, and John Dewey, free love, coeducation, divorce, and a somewhat belated condemnation of footbinding, concubinage, and "spirit-writing," which was a kind of planchette writing on sand.

"The new school argues badly and the old school can't argue at all," was the way Lifu summed it up.

Opinions in the Yao family were somewhat divided. Too many idols were being overthrown; too many issues were involved. Old Yao was for the change of language, against the overthrow of the family system, but again for remarriage of widows. Coral had survived widowhood long enough to say jokingly, "I will remarry if any one will marry me."

Mochow was for the "single standard" of morality, for *Lady Windermere's Fan* but wholly against *A Doll's House,* and dogmatically against free verse, at least against the kind they were producing. Redjade was against everything advocated by the revolutionists, and most of all coeducation. Mulan was for the change in language, but was for the kind of graceful vernacular that already existed in *Red Chamber Dream,* and not for the "language of rickshaw pullers and pickle vendors" because she was loyal to Lin Chinnan and to her love for old literature. She was for Confucius and against Ibsen, for coeducation, for concubinage, for ancestor worship, and against footbinding.

Afei worshiped the new leaders, as did all Young China. He was against Confucius and for free love, for birth control, and for tennis.

Mr. Tseng called the whole lot of revolutionists barbarians, "forget-eighths," ignoramuses talking about what they did not understand, particularly Confucianism (which was probably true), and of a piece with the political revolutionists who mixed foreign words into their conversation. He was offended, hurt to the soul. He went so far as to extend an invitation to Lin Chinnan to his home, to Mulan's delight.

Mannia was not even allowed to read *La Jeunesse,* but she was shocked at the things they were discussing in the garden—and particularly at birth control.

Professor Chen, the communist, combined the trenchant pen of a pamphleteer with the ardent soul of a radical revolutionist. He had a theory of rectilinear progress, which he propounded in the magazine. The march of time could not be held back. Every decade and every generation moved steadily forward. Who were the intellectual pioneers of China, back in 1898? Were they not Kang and Liang? And yet

Kang the advance reformer of his day was now a discredited monarchist, whose name was recently coupled with the 1917 *coup d'état*.
Who were the great translators and importers of Western thought and
literature in 1908? Were they not Lin and Yen? And yet Yen was
now an opium smoker and Lin merely an interesting old curiosity.
The coming generation must make its way over the prostrate bodies of
the reformers and pioneers of a generation ago. The eras of Kang and
Liang, and of Lin and Yen were gone, serviceable as they had been
in their times. "In the same way," he wrote in effect, "we the pioneers
of today shall be outmoded and shall be thrown by the wayside by the
advancing generation ten years from now. And we shall gladly make
way for those coming behind."

To the youth of that decade, it was incredible that these brave
leaders of ultra-radicalism could ever be outmoded; it was inconceivable
how man could be more radical. Yet in less than ten years, when newer
ideologies occupied the minds of China's youth, Ibsen and free verse
and liberal reformism sounded as hollow and old-fashioned as the
"intelligentsia" they denounced. Only Professor Chen himself became
Trotzkyist and languished in prison.

.·.

Lifu was by nature a radical and he came back to find this radical
China, basically different from the one he had left. But he did not
throw himself into the fray, partly because he was also by nature an individualist and could not go the whole way with any school. It was his
habit to dissent when assent was apparently unanimous. He was also
too critical and clearminded to accept Professor Chien's denunciation
of old literature. Not that he did not like Professor Chien personally,
for he was as naïve and shy as a child—which explained his boundless
hopefulness for everything new and modern. Chien readily accepted
the dictum that Dostoevski was greater than the author of *Red Chamber Dream*, because a returned student had told him so. Professor
Chien was slightly psychopathic—the type that sometimes blossoms
into a genius; he lived in a college dormitory, separately, though not
separated from his wife and got red in the face when talking, while
always retaining a childish grin. Lifu did not worship him, but he
loved him.

Lifu was also restrained in his radicalism by Mulan and Mochow.
The husband and wife often sat together and talked in the lamplight

on these burning questions. The only practical outcome of their discussions was that they must pick up more English—that "open sesame" to the New World. The English Lifu had learned in Japan was shocking. He could read English, but could not converse in it and could not make himself understood half as well as his sister, who had not been abroad at all.

The common sense of Mochow steadily influenced him.

"Why are you against coeducation?" asked Lifu.

"Because girls should not be educated like boys. They have a different purpose in life," replied Mochow.

Mochow preferred to quote examples rather than. to reason out a point. When Lifu talked with her about the vexatious question of "free love" (which then meant merely marriage of persons by their own choice), Mochow simply said, "Look at Sutan!" And there the problem was disposed of for Mochow.

But Lifu was emotionally as much influenced by Mulan's imaginative loyalty to the old as he was influenced by Mochow's common sense criticism of the new. Mulan was still pathetically attached to Lin, the old author whom she had worshiped since her girlhood days. In loyalty to him, she was apt to be severe toward the revolutionists, and this sentimental loyalty was shared by Lifu who knew what beauty in literature meant. Lin was an old man with a light beard, speaking an atrocious Pekinese with a Foochow accent, in a soft, low voice. He did not argue on these topics when he was in the Tseng home. He just felt pleased and comfortable there, and the Tseng home seemed like a citadel of a lost cause, in which things were not argued, but understood. There was a quiet dignity about this which influenced one's judgment, and Mulan and Lifu felt that it would be sacrilegious even to differ in their hearts.

Old Yao alone remained a dissenter, and in his talks impressed on Lifu the necessity for reform.

"Do you believe in all the childish things they are advocating?" said Lifu. "They are striking even at ancestor worship. They want to sweep aside everything old. Why, they even denounce 'good mothers and helpful wives' as a degrading ideal hampering the woman's own development as an individual!"

"Let them do it," said old Yao. "If they are right, they will do some good, and if they are wrong, they cannot do the Truth (Tao) any harm. As a matter of fact, they are often wrong, as in this individualism. Don't worry. Let them fight it out. When a thing is wrong, they will get tired of it themselves after a while. Have you forgotten Chuangtse? Nobody is right and nobody is wrong. Only one thing is right, and that is the Truth, but nobody knows what it is. It is a thing that changes all the time, and then comes back to the same thing."

The old man's eyes shone under his eyebrows, and he seemed like a spirit that knew eternity itself. Lifu had not heard such philosophy even in the college classrooms. Here was something real.

"You take this literary revolution, for instance," old Yao continued. "Many people think it is right. Why? Because there is something right in it. Any movement grows only when the time is ripe and it says something which many feel. Many feel that this Old China must be swept aside, or we shall never make any progress. People are wanting to change. You cannot help that, and you cannot stop them. There are excesses, but people cannot say what is wrong and maintain it for long. A falsehood is not argued out of court; it just rubs off, like bad paint, by itself. Now you yourself want this old China to change. Look at the situation in China today! Look at this government and all its warlords and politicians!"

This reference aroused an old fire of radicalism in Lifu. He was no longer thinking of his own immediate relations, and the system of life which made such a comfortable life possible for him. He conjured up an image of all the queer warlords and politicians—odd specimens of humanity produced by an ugly mixture of all that was worst in the new and in the old. There was not a queerer assortment of creatures on earth than the job-hunting officials who floated then between Peking and Tientsin and called themselves the ruling class of China. If the younger generation of hot-headed youth contained many queer fish, the older generation were queerer fish still. A generation of Republican profiteers, civil and military, taking advantage of the dissolution of the Empire to feather their own nests. Look at their faces! Lumps of animal flesh upon which were stamped sensuality and greed, the drowsy eyes, the dolorous looks, the Japanese mustache vainly trying to make them look modern and dignified. Only let it be said that the sight of them was as painful to old Mr. Tseng, the good mandarin, as it was to Lifu. Look at their feet; how those foreign shoes must have pinched them and made them limp rather than walk, uncomfortable but modern! They didn't know how to hold a foreign cane and hung it from their fingers gingerly as if they were carrying home a string of fish and trying not to let the fish touch their silk gowns. What a sight when, on public occasions, officials would gather for a photograph! They would wear their tophats and single collars! A war-lord would appear in a resplendent uniform to which he was unused, and then curse because he could not reach an itch on his upper arm; and immediately after the photograph was taken he would unbutton his collar and take off his cap revealing a gigantic close-shaved head straight from the Mongolian plains. There would be several smart young men, Japanese-returned students and pro-Japanese Anfu politi-cians, looking frightfully hopeful and frightfully determined to save the nation, with their hair slicked and parted in the middle. Ninety per cent of the Japanese-returned students studied political science. The old warlords studied nothing at all. Some of them could not even write their military orders! All of them respected Confucius, all of them were sentimentally attached to their mothers, and all were addicted to sharks' fins. A great majority of them smoked opium, or should have. A generation of incomplete, frustrated beings, walking hell-bound with foreign sticks, old without the old culture and modern without the modern social consciousness, fishing happily in the muddy waters of the infant Republic.

There was the Dog-Meat General Chang Tsungchang, who received foreign consuls with a black cigar in his mouth and a Russian mistress on his knee; who stood six feet six inches and kept rolls of banknotes in his trousers; who appointed two men on different days to the same magistracy in Shantung and, when confronted by both of them, told them to "settle such a small matter by themselves"; who had neverthe-less a sense of fair play, and made a point of rewarding a husband with an office, if he took his wife.

There was another general by the name of Yang. On passing a gate in his capital at night, he swore "Your mother!" to the sentry instead of giving the password. Captains and lieutenants began to follow his example, so that in that city, the swearword "Your mother!" became a sure password.

Yes, the Renaissance leaders were right. This Old China must be swept aside. Between these warlords and politicians who were pro-Confucius and the new leaders who were anti-Confucius, the latter had Lifu's sympathy. Only it was a little hard on Confucius to have such allies.

.·.

Lifu had returned to a China also restless and torn by civil wars. The sweeping defeat and death of Yuan had only cleared the ground for more strife among the lesser generals. The giant Republic fell by its own weight and was delivered over into the hands of independent provincial warlords fighting interminable wars that the people did not understand. The big warlords fought big wars at longer intervals and the small warlords in far west Szechuen fought small wars at shorter intervals. Some of the Szechuen warlords had private houses like palaces. Taxation grew in weight, ingenuity, and variety to keep ever-growing uniformed hordes, and famines and floods visited the land as if Heaven, too, were in anger. There were wars in Hupeh and Hunan, Kiangsi, Fukien, Kwangtung, changing in combinations so constantly that the people could not follow them. Provincial warlords resorted to declaring their independence whenever the acts of the Peking Government did not suit their pleasure. In the North a split developed within the Peiyang warlords between the "Anhwei clique," headed by Tuan, now the Premier, and the "Chihli clique," headed by Feng Kuochang, now the Acting President.

The recent *coup d'état* of the Pig-Tailed Chang had for the first time brought war home in Peking. With his defeat, new armies marched into the capital. Tienchiao in the South City swarmed with soldiers of all denominations. And the backwash of that unrest reached Lifu's home.

On the day of Lifu's arrival they had forgotten about Chenma.

The next morning Lifu asked, "Why isn't that wonderful Chenma serving us?"

"Didn't you see her in Mother's room?" replied Mochow.

"Yes, I did. Why was she there?" asked Lifu.

"She is serving Mother now. She is all excited these days, and we are trying hard to keep her. She says her son has come back. I asked her how she knew and she said she was sure of it. Since the new soldiers came in, she had been asking for leave to go out in the afternoon or in the night whenever she is free. You know my mother needs attention all the time and we can't always let her go. But she goes out at nine after putting mother to bed and does not return until past midnight. She dresses and goes out, smiling and talking to herself, as if this night she would surely find him. Under her arm she always carries in a blue cloth package a new suit, a pair of white cloth socks, and a pair of new shoes. She asked me to write a dozen slips of paper about her son so that she could post them at street corners. I did it for her, but you know how hopeless it is. She has no idea how big China is!"

"You can't allow her to do this," said Lifu. "She will go insane if she doesn't find him."

"You try to stop her," said Mochow. "I really don't know what to do. The day before yesterday, she came and said she wanted to leave us, and I said, 'You can't. Young Master is coming back today.' And do you know?—her face brightened and she said to your mother, 'Mrs. Kung, if my son returned, he would be as tall as your son now.'"

"I thought she acted strangely toward me yesterday. She took my hand and looked at me for a long while, smiling. I don't know what she was thinking, but she looked at me in a very strange manner."

"She must have held up many young men like that on the street. But you know in most things she is very thoughtful about others."

"We must help her—perhaps advertise in the newspapers."

"We don't know even whether her son is dead or alive."

"What is his name?"

"Chen San. Think how many people are called Chen San!"

"How did you write the placards for her?"

"I wrote down his name and age, the village he came from and the time he was lost, and said his mother was looking for him, giving her address here. I wish the soldiers had never come near Peking, so that she could always hope—and live on that hope."

Lifu looked troubled, almost angry. At this moment Chenma appeared, her dress clean and her hair very neat, holding a great package, and in her look there was passive determination and great strength.

"Well, Master, Mistress, I am leaving you now," she said. "This is my chance. I have waited for him these seven years. Now he may be waiting for me. I must go and see if he is. If I find him, we mother and son will come back, if you will give him something to do in this garden. If I don't, I will say good-by to you. I cannot carry all these clothes I have made for him. I will leave them here in your place."

She spoke slowly and clearly as if she had a great business in mind.

"But you can't go away like this!" said Lifu. "You stay here. We will help you find him."

She shook her head. "I must go to him," she insisted. "I know he is somewhere here. All soldiers have come back."

"How much money have you?"

509

The woman patted her inside coat pocket and said she had two five-dollar bills and two dollars.

Lifu and Mochow looked at each other, and Mochow went and took five dollars to give to her. But Chenma refused, saying that she would not take money for no work.

"We will not force you to stay," said Lifu. "But you know you are always welcome here. Come back and sleep here whenever you wish. And if you find him, bring him to work for us."

Chenma then said good-by and walked away on her bound feet. Mochow saw her to the door and told her to take good care of herself and to return as soon as she could.

When Chenma failed to return that night and the next night and the next, Lifu said he must go and find her. In the afternoon he went to the South City, the section he knew so well from his childhood. Here he felt the bigness of the city and the life of the great common people with whom he really belonged and with whom he had lately lost contact. He walked until his legs were sore. He went through alleys and streets, and stopped to watch children playing in the open spaces and remembered his own childhood. He went to the Amusement Park and to Tienchiao and the open theaters and the tea houses and saw the swarms of humanity at play—grandfathers leading grandchildren, mothers feeding their babies at their breast while they walked along, a few better-dressed young men and women, but most of them lower-class men and women in all shades of plain blue, and everywhere gray-uniformed soldiers. The search seemed futile, and he sat down in a well-known tea house, and talked with a waiter, asking rather idly if he had seen a middle-aged woman looking for her son.

"You mean that crazy woman?" said the waiter. "She often passes this way. She stops young men in the street."

"She is not crazy. She is looking for her son."

"Not crazy? She lost her son in the army in Manchu times and she is still looking for him now. It is like groping for a needle in an ocean. He may be in Tientsin, Shanghai, Canton, or Szechuen if he is still alive at all. Is there any sense in it?" The waiter swung his towel across his shoulders with the gesture of a man closing a topic with gentle satisfaction and good humor.

Lifu paid for his tea, jumped into a rickshaw and went home.

"Of course I could not find her," he said briefly to Mochow.

. ·.

510

Chenma's disappearance left Lifu profoundly disturbed, although he had been served by her only for one summer. Her image remained in his mind and it kept him thinking about war and what it did to mothers and wives and sons.

Several weeks later, Mochow was sitting over her work basket in the cool shade by the northern window, and Lifu was lying in bed resting, with the child sleeping by his side, when Mochow said,

"I wonder where she is now?"

"Who?" It was impossible to tell from the language whether Mochow meant a "he" or a "she."

"Chenma. Could she just disappear?"

"I am thinking of advertising in the papers."

"Why don't you write it into a story?"

"That's it! That's it!" shouted Lifu, jumping out of bed so violently that the child cried out.

"*That's it!* You've waked him up," remonstrated Mochow, going over to take the child up and pat him to sleep again.

"You know I've never written a story. . . ." Mochow raised a finger across her lips and Lifu continued in a whisper, "I've never written a story, but I will write this one. I will put in her real name and his and the name of their village. And who knows?—perhaps the son is living and will chance to read it, that is, if he can read."

"It is really a story—and with your pen," said Mochow. But when she spoke the word "pen," she had a vague feminine instinct that should not have said it. The pen, like the tongue, was a dangerous weapon that often cut its owner.

"I will do my best with it, and make it a tribute to a mother. I will call it 'The Mother.'" He thought for a moment and went on, "Shall I write it in the spoken tongue? You know I have never done that."

"Of course," replied Mochow. "Stories have always been written in the spoken language. But not in this strange, modern jargon that the writers think the common people speak."

Lifu had written only essays in the classical language, and writing in the new medium was a strange experience for him. He worked on the story in that hot summer weather without stop for two days. As he wrote, Mochow wondered greatly, and looked back and forth from his writing brush to the microscope, on another desk, that he had been peeping into ever since his return. She had a feeling that dealing with bugs was a more peaceful occupation than dealing with words. She saw a change in his expression, an increased excitability and a high tension. After an hour of staring mutely into the microscope, he would look calm, and only a little sad and tired.

Mochow came to his desk and read what he had written, and suggested alterations. "Chenma didn't talk like that," she would remark, and he would change the words and go on.

When the story was finished, he sent it off at once to a Peking newspaper. It was published in the literary supplement of the paper and created a sensation. It was hailed by the revolutionary critics as the first success of "democratic literature," and by the older generation as a moving tribute to mother love and a lesson in filial piety. A professor wrote a review, classifying it in the category of "anti-war" literature with some narrative poems of the Tang Dynasty, and offered a poetical version of his own in the manner of Po Chuyi and Tu Fu, written in "pre-Tang form."

But Lifu exclaimed, "Why can't they see that it was not my creation and stop looking at it as 'literature!' Everybody talks about it as if it weren't a real story, as if Chenma weren't perhaps still living. Can no one do something about it?"

As a matter of fact, Lifu had created out of his imagination the peasant boy that he had never seen and had put in the mother-son relationship that was his own. He also described in a vivid, unforgettable scene the taking away of the son by the press gang. In a few succinct sentences he traced the thoughts of the bereaved mother as she sat in her cottage waiting for the son's return through the four seasons of the year. It was these four seasonal scenes that the professor transcribed into glowing lines.

And the spring blossoms came back to her village
But the woman sat sewing by her door.
And the blossoms turned into summer seeds
But the woman looked far over the hills.
Her son came not.

The autumn leaves strayed into her bare cottage
And drifted on the earthern floor.
The shadows of the winter sun sank quivering down the wall,
And on New Year's Eve she made a meal for two . . .
And sat until dawn. But her son came not.

"That poetry is nonsense!" said Lifu.

At the end of the story Lifu described his own thoughts as he had wandered among the crowds of Tienchiao. He saw, not one, but thousands of soldiers, sons separated from their families, crowding there to snatch a temporary moment of pleasure. Were they not all alike? In that mass of humanity, all individual identity was lost. If Chen San's mother could only see that her son was but one of millions of sons torn—separated from their mothers by war! "But Chen San's mother could not see them so and she went her way and disappeared."

Mulan told him that the bitter argumentative ending ought to have been toned down. But Lifu's name as a writer was established. Magazine editors came to ask for his articles, thinking that he could conjure up another story just as good.

Lifu's scientific studies were thus betrayed. He took a position in the Peking Normal University to teach biology, but he was inevitably drawn into a circle of writers, and he began to write the occasional articles that were to cause Mochow many sleepless nights.

· ·

But these were happy days for the Yao family. There gathered in their garden a gay group of relatives and friends, many of them young people interested in literature and considered modern. They gossiped about current events and the different groups of writers that were making so much noise about modern literature.

The Yao sisters were now quite well-known in Peking, being nicknamed the "Four Beauties" or the *Szeshanchuan,* which was the name of a seventeenth-century dramatic sequence by Hung Sheng, portraying four historical beauties. This was usually assumed to refer to Coral, Mulan, Mochow, and Redjade, although some held that Mannia was to be included, rather than Coral. Who originated the title was not known—possibly it was Paku, the young poet just returned from England, who had suddenly flashed into the Peking literary firmament like a comet, dominating every circle where he appeared by his sheer amiability and exotic genius. Paku seemed to breathe a spirit of youth and expansiveness wherever he went and he made every girl he met imagine she was his sweetheart. He comically styled the four men, Lifu, Sunya, Afei, and himself, the "Four Monkey Cries," or *Szeshengyuan,* which was the name of another dramatic sequence portraying four unrelated stories, one of which was *Chih Mulan,* or "The Female Magnolia."

There were many in this coterie of which Mulan was the central spirit. In the spring of 1918, they had frequent parties in the Garden and sometimes organized outings to the Western Hills and other places in the suburbs, such as the Great Wall and the Ming Tombs. Each person contributed a dollar for these meetings, which came once in two or three weeks, although there was no fixed schedule and no fixed organization. Coral was usually the treasurer-manager and Huan-erh the secretary. Besides the four Yao sisters, including Redjade, there were Mannia, Huan-erh, Ailien, Lilien, Sutan, and later Taiyun who was Huaiyu's half-sister. Sometimes Cassia came with her daughters to the meetings in the beautiful Garden which she loved, and the elder ladies, Mrs. Tseng, Mrs. Sun, Cassia, Mrs. Fu, and Mrs. Hua would occasionally have a party of their own.

Among the men there were Sunya, Chinya, Lifu, Paku, and Afei, and of the elder men Old Yao, Mr. Fu, the painter Chi, and the writer Lin (the last two brought by Mulan); and, as these were carefree spirits also and loved young company, they often celebrated the spring flowers with them.

The appearance of Lin Chinnan and Paku in this coterie needs some explanation. For Lin was against the whole modern movement, and Paku was a close friend of the literary revolutionists. Both Mulan and Lifu intensely admired the old scholar Lin and his poetic way of life, and Lin was rather flattered by such a young and beautiful admirer as Mulan. But Paku stood in a category by himself. Lifu was an individualist and had avoided the revolutionary leaders because he could not join the throng shouting Ibsen and Dostoevski and Sienkiewiez in his ears. He kept aloof, though he knew them all. There were so many groups, the French-returned, the Japanese-returned, the English-American-returned, each with its own weekly organ, all coming to fisticuffs with one another, and all very much alive. Once a problem was started there would be a very lively discussion in all the weeklies. All were liberal and progressive and ready to criticize the Government and the Old China. But there was a group to which Paku belonged, consisting chiefly of English and American trained graduates, who wrote dissertations with great display of learning, and carried on the English tradition of "compromise" with the Tuan Government. This was the group satirized by their enemy as the English "gentlemen." Their professorial style, their conservative, half-hearted progressiveness, and their tendency to get in with the Government alienated Lifu. "All of them are going into the Government," Lifu predicted—a prediction which came true. These professorial displays of learning were but the means by which to get a ministership or a councilorship. It showed in their tendency to extenuate and reason and explain what the rulers were doing, essentially from the point of view of the ruling class, as in the case of the question of the Japanese loans which were the government's sole means of survival. Lifu preferred to associate with a group of writers, most of whom had never been abroad, and whose greatest delight was the satirizing of these "gentlemen."

But Paku was different. Brilliant as a writer but with the guilelessness of a child, he did not understand what these different cliques and animosities meant. He even admired Lin, at whom his group were laughing as out-of-date. He made friends with writers, politicians, and young women alike—and particularly with pretty and charming women.

His marriage with Sutan was typical. Sutan, now a divorcee, living and shifting for herself on what was left of the settlement from her former husband, was suffering from tuberculosis. Paku heard that there was such a disillusioned, pathetic divorcee and decided that he must bring comfort into her life. He visited her without introduction, and fell completely in love with her. His poetic imagination transformed her into a reincarnation of the ancient tragic beauties, shut up for life in a "cold palace" by some jealous empress. Though he was capable of loving a great many pretty girls who were fascinated by his white and noble face, he decided to stay close to Sutan. She had lost most of her money in foolish investments and had decided to open a shop selling coal, because she was told that it was a good business. Paku thought she was joking, but when he returned from a trip and found her actually owning a shop selling coal balls and briquets, he was so melodramatically upset that he at once proposed marriage to her, to save this exotic beauty from bituminous coal. In fact he was moved to write a dithyrambic verse on *Beauty and the Coal Balls*. It was through courting Sutan that Paku came to know Mulan and the Yaos.

Chinya often came out without his wife and mixed gaily with the group. He had come back from Shansi a year before because the prospecting for oil had failed and the Oil Administration had been dissolved. His experience had given him more self-confidence and poise, and he now openly neglected Suyun. It was understood between the husband and wife that each was to go his own way. Dimfragrance was always present at the garden meetings, and by much prompting from Mulan, Chinya had developed a kind of talking familiarity with Dimfragrance; and she, taking the situation half-playfully and half-seriously, and conscious of their common hatred of Suyun, never discouraged him.

Among the unmarried girls, Redjade was the most beautiful, and both the old poet Lin and the young poet Paku thought a great deal of her, and under Lin she began to learn old poetry seriously. Living in a garden, stimulated by the company, she began to write a style of poetry similar to the Ming dramas, which also influenced Paku. Her mother disapproved of these exertions, because she was supposed to be suffering from pulmonary consumption and she had to pay for a day of merrymaking by staying in bed for seven or eight days. But it seemed that the garden, the company, and Afei in particular all existed to make for her a happiness too perfect to last.

And so at the tables, where the young men and women mixed together, there was a great deal of talk and pleasantry about love and politics. The eyes of Mr. Yao watched this scene of young romance in his garden with a strange tolerance. His last duty in this life was to see Afei properly married. He was worried about Redjade's health, wondering whether, when he had closed his eyes, Redjade would always remain his son's wife. He was not taking any definite steps for their engagement, but neither did he interfere. Old Yao was waiting to see how events would shape themselves, according to the Way.

CHAPTER XXXIII

ONE day in late spring a strikingly beautiful Manchu girl, introduced by Mrs. Hua, came to offer her service in the Yao Garden as a domestic. Her name was Paofen, or Rare Perfume. When asked where her parents lived, she hesitated and said it was somewhere in the West City. Whether from shyness or embarrassment or some other cause, there was an air of mystery about her. Mrs. Hua came with her and said that a Manchu friend had introduced her at her shop. She said that Paofen came from a very good family, but that she was now compelled to go out to work as a servant.

Paofen was standing before Mr. Yao and Afei and his sisters, her long lashes shading her eyes. Her dress was evidently that of a refined Manchu family; she wore a braid, as all Manchu girls did, which hung thick and black down her slightly bent back, and her long Manchu gown was fashionably shaped instead of coming down in a straight line as of old. On her feet she wore soft-heeled black silk shoes, in which she stood at ease, since her feet, following the Manchu custom, were unbound. She was of such extraordinary beauty that it struck those present as queer that she was offering herself as a common servant. She seemed out of place, for beauty conferred its own right to dignity and honor. This, and her silence about her family, made her doubly mysterious. She seemed also quiet and modest, and her manners were winning. And when she opened her mouth to speak, she spoke mandarin with a natural grace and polish as only a cultivated Manchu could speak it. Mochow whispered to Coral, "I wouldn't dare to go out with such a maid. She would surely be taken as a mistress, and no matter how the wife looked she would be overshadowed by her." Coral stuck out her tongue involuntarily. Afei stared as if his jaws were glued together.

Mr. Yao winced at first sight of her and felt a strange misgiving, as if she was a temptress such as Taoist stories tell about, sent to tempt nim in his old age. While Coral and Mochow were talking with Mrs. Hua and the Manchu girl, a hundred thoughts were passing through his mind. His first thought was the manifest impropriety of employing Paofen except as a high-class maid in a living chamber. But how? In whose court? Was she to serve himself? Or Afei who was living with him? His sick wife? Mochow? Why didn't Paofen's parents marry her off, as they could easily have found her a very good match? What was Mrs. Hua about? Was this one of her machinations? Even if Paofen was really forced by family circumstances to go out to work as a domestic, she seemed the type that was bound to involve men and inevitably herself in trouble. She was what writers described in their books as "Heaven-born *yuwu*"—an untranslatable word meaning a woman of extraordinary beauty, the ruin of homes and a changer of men's destinies. He thought of Tijen. If Tijen had been living, he would have been sure to fall in love with her. In the sixty-odd years of his life, he had never seen a woman as striking as this Manchu girl. Memories floated back across his mind of the girls he had loved in his wild youth. Yes, there had been one comparable to this one—the girl he had wanted to marry but could not. He was surprised that at his age, he was once again personally interested in a beautiful woman.

Paofen stood talking softly with Coral, but with few words, occasionally knitting her brows as if ill at ease in a new position. Her only defect was that perhaps she drooped slightly, but in her, even such a defect seemed harmonious and beautiful.

"In this garden you can always use an extra person," said Mrs. Hua. "And she would be a decoration to any family."

Old Yao was so occupied with his confused thoughts and memories that he did not quite hear her.

"I say, Uncle Yao, that she would be a decoration to any family that employed her," said Mrs. Hua.

"Why don't her parents marry her off?" he asked.

"Well, it's hard to find good matches among the Bannermen nowadays. And her family is not well off now. Otherwise they would not send such a daughter out to earn money."

"She is too—too refined for a maid. We dare not—we cannot use her," he said, oddly stumbling over the words.

"You can't be serious," replied Mrs. Hua with a smile. "If she weren't quite unusual, would I take the trouble to bring her to you? You know I am not running an employment bureau. I found you this

Manchu garden. Did I make a mistake? Now I have found you this charming Manchu maid. You ought really to thank me. Who else has such luck as you have, Uncle Yao? As for her being too good for your family, that is nonsense. It is true that she would be too distinguished for a common home, and her parents probably would not consent; but, when they heard that I would introduce her to work in this garden, they were delighted. Honestly, in Manchu times, she would certainly have been selected to be sent up into the palace." And turning to the girl, she added "Paofen, you'll see this is like living in a palace itself, and the master and his daughters are such charming people."

Mr. Yao was less able to decide about taking this Manchu girl than he had been about taking the Manchu garden. A garden was but a garden, but a beautiful girl was a woman fraught with consequences. A pretty face has ruined an empire.

But all the women were quite charmed by Paofen and enthusiastic about taking her, and Mr. Yao yielded.

Redjade was in bed, and, when she was told by her mother and Mochow about the striking beauty of the new Manchu maid, she asked to see her. Paofen came in and made a dip with one of her knees, which was the regular Manchu curtsy. Redjade asked her about her parents and whether she knew how to read and write, and even joked a little with her.

"Why doesn't a girl like you get married? Why do you come out to work?"

"Thank you for such undeserved praise," Paofen replied in her polished mandarin. "But *meifatse*. Who has the luck like you, young mistress?" *Meifatse* was a common fatalistic phrase meaning, "there is no choice," or "one can do nothing about it."

As Paofen retired, Redjade dismissed a passing sense of jealousy of one whom she knew to be more beautiful than herself. "After all, I am a young mistress and she is a maid," she thought. She did not quite understand why she was assuring herself of Afei's love.

If Mr. Yao had any suspicion of Mrs. Hua's intentions, it was soon dispelled. It was thought best to let Paofen serve Mrs. Yao. Incredible though it seemed, Paofen immediately changed into a working dress and humbly went about her duties, anxious to please, afraid to offend, doing anything she was told to do, and tripping lightly between the

519

kitchen and the mistress' room on her soft flat-heeled shoes. She was really going to work as a servant.

The engagement of the new maid was so exciting that Coral telephoned to Mulan, and she came over with Dimfragrance in the afternoon, and went to her mother's room. The maid was introduced by Coral who told her, "This is the second daughter of our family."

"What is your name?" asked Mulan.

"Paofen."

"You Manchu people are very fond of the word *pao*," remarked Mulan.

"Not necessarily," replied Paofen. "Paoyu, Paotsa are Chinese. Now we are under the Republic, five races in one union, and there is no difference between Chinese and Manchus, is there, young mistress?"

Mulan was aghast. Paofen was not only speaking literary Chinese, with phrases like "five races in one union," but she was making references to characters in the *Red Chamber Dream*.

"You have read the *Red Chamber Dream*?"

"Who has not?" replied Paofen with a soft smile. "You people in this garden are enacting it, too." Suddenly she checked herself. "Young mistress, forgive my rudeness." Paofen did not know why it was that the instant she saw Mulan she dared talk with her as an equal.

"You can read and write, then?"

"I barely know the words *chih* and *wu*, that is all." Mulan knew she was merely being modest. If she could use a phrase like "barely know *chih* and *wu*," she knew a great deal. Paofen continued, "You know we Manchu families had nothing to do. Young men used to ride, shoot, and fly falcons. Young women used to munch melon seeds, play cards, and gossip. Even Manchu girls who didn't learn to read and write would learn much from the theaters and endless gossip. They would gossip themselves into profound scholars."

Mulan was enchanted and thought she had never found a girl other than Mannia so charming as Paofen, and she was more accomplished than Mannia. But she was also mystified. It seems incredible, she thought.

Later, as she talked more with Paofen, she found that she knew the classics and poetry as well. She thought of her brother Afei. Suddenly she remembered the oracle that Redjade had drawn at the shrine of the God of Matrimony, with the line:

Pass the perfume and all is emptiness.

Why, the meaning of her name was *Rare Perfume!*

⸳·⸳

Mulan came several times to talk with Paofen. It was evident that Paofen had known very good Manchu society, and Mulan enjoyed hearing about Manchu family life. Often while talking, however, Paofen would suddenly check herself, which was still more mystifying.

Mulan so much desired Paofen's company that she went and spoke to her father and said that Dimfragrance was ill and she needed temporary help, and asked if she could borrow Paofen for a few days. Although Paofen liked Mulan, she seemed reluctant to go. But she had to go when she was asked.

Then a curious thing happened. Afei had already begun to go in to see his mother more often. Now during the few days Paofen was with Mulan, he came to visit Mulan. She sensed danger and asked him plainly not to be too friendly with the new maid.

"You are as good as engaged to Fourth Sister, you know," she said to her brother.

"I am interested in Paofen merely in the same way you are," said Afei, defending himself.

"But you are a boy," Mulan pleaded.

When Dimfragrance was better, Mulan still wanted to keep Paofen, but she said, "Thank you for being so kind. But I must not. I wish I could serve you for life."

"Why don't you? We can be such friends."

"I cannot."

This attitude of Paofen was inexplicable to Mulan. Had she fallen in love with Afei?

"You know my brother is engaged to his cousin," she said.

Paofen was quick to guess what she implied and her face turned very serious. "Young mistress, you make a mistake. I am here to work as a servant. I have no ambition to climb socially."

"Then why don't you stay here with me?"

"I cannot," she said simply, and Mulan could not understand.

And so after a few days Paofen went back to Mrs. Yao's court, and Mulan went with her, and after leaving her with her mother she crossed over to Mochow's court, which was immediately on its right. Mulan told her sister about Paofen's strange insistence upon coming back to the garden, and told her also what she had noticed about Afei's interest in the new maid.

"Do you see anything strange over here?" she asked.

"Nothing in particular," replied Mochow. "Perhaps he has been going to see Mother more often. That is natural. Young men like to see pretty girls. But Paofen seems to be a decent girl and keeps him at a distance. She is not cheap."

"And Redjade?"

"She is in bed most of the time. Afei comes to see her, too. You know it is awkward at their age. He cannot go in except when others are present."

"Don't you think it is time they were engaged?" said Mulan. "That will settle the question, and Redjade may feel better. We must speak to Father."

The two sisters went over to Redjade's court. Redjade was much thinner these days; her small face, which had been quite round, looked more slender, and her wrist bones and knuckles showed under the skin. Mulan was worried, but kept it to herself for fear of increasing Redjade's self-pity.

As her maid Honeybush assisted her to sit up and adjusted the pillows, Redjade said, "Second Sister, it is good of you to come. You had better come more often, otherwise you won't see much more of your little sister." Her eyes filled and she took a handkerchief to wipe them.

"You are talking nonsense," said Mulan. "I was talking with Third Sister and saying that we ought soon to be sitting at your wedding dinner."

"If this body of mine does not improve, what is the use of such things? What pleasure is it for a bridegroom to see his wedding chamber filled with medicine bottles?"

"You will have some one to attend upon you and serve you and sweep the bedroom floor for you," said Mulan.

"A person is sick and you are still making fun of her, Second Sister," replied Redjade with a smile. Usually she would have added at least, "Wait until I am well and I will settle accounts with you," but now she said no more.

In her heart she was grateful to Mulan, and thought that she understood her best because she understood love, as she had learned on their Hangchow journey.

522

On the table beside the flower vase were some sheets of paper with some small, delicate writing on them. As Mulan's gaze fell upon the writing, Redjade quickly made an effort to take the paper away.

"Don't read it," she cried.

But the paper was out of her reach and Mulan had already captured it. Holding the crumpled paper behind her back, she asked, "What's in it?"

"Just two poems," replied Redjade. "I shall be angry if you read them."

"I want to see how your poetry has improved."

Honeybush said, "Young Mistress was writing this last night under the lamplight. I tried to persuade her not to exert herself, but she would not listen."

Mulan could not control her curiosity and said, "Please let me read it. All is right between us," and she began to read. Mortified and blushing, Redjade turned her face away. Mochow stood up to read it also.

There were two poems on it. The first poem was about her falling hair, and the second poem was about a familiar theme, "longing in the chamber," with a reference to the Hangchow trip.

"Why, these are quite good," said Mulan.

"Sister," said Mochow, "I told you that it is better not to write poetry. It is not good for your health. But you won't listen to me."

"That is not poetry," said Redjade. "I just felt I had something to say and I had to say it. It is just talking to a piece of paper when one is lonely and has no one to talk to."

"You would not think in terms of poetry if you did not write it," said Mochow. "Poetry is an expression for sentiment, but the more you express it, the more the sentiment grows."

"What Mochow says is right," said Mulan. "If we were living in ancient times, I ought to spank you, as your elder sister. It is different now and I might have written it myself. But the best cure for writing poetry of 'chamber regrets' is to marry. Then you will be writing a different sort of poetry."

Redjade's face was red as a peach, and she excused herself, saying, "I really didn't mean to write poems, chamber regrets or no chamber regrets. I just saw my hair on the pillow and started to write some lines, and unconsciously my pen was carried along and I forgot myself. I must beg sisters' forgiveness."

523

There was a tone in her speech which was new. Was it her illness, or was it love, which made her tenderer and less combative? Or was it her consciousness of dependence on Mulan in this matter of her heart?

Coming out, Mulan said to Mochow, "Do you notice the change that has come over her? Usually she would insist on having the better of an argument. But she is so different now."

"I see it, too," said Mochow.

They heard Honeybush calling lightly to them, "Young mistresses, I want to speak to you."

Mulan and Mochow stopped short. "What is it, Honeybush?" they said anxiously.

"Well, it is this," said Honeybush. "I have been attending upon my mistress day and night and I know her better than anyone else can. She does not sleep well and she is losing appetite. The Second Young Master is coming less often to see her, because they both are grown-up already. And the other day when he came she chided him gently. You know that what is wrong with my young mistress is her tongue. She said something about water being clear in the mountains and muddy in the valley. I don't know what it was—but it was something concerning the new Manchu maid, and Afei grew red all over his face, and left, annoyed. Her mother was there, but it didn't make any difference. . . . Well, she wept so long in bed that I must have given her five or six handkerchiefs. And that night she went to bed without taking anything, in spite of my persuasion. You know her temper. . . . Well, what I want to say is that you two sisters ought to tell your brother to be more considerate to her while she is ill. . . . Otherwise, she will grow worse. . . . She is eating only half a small bowl of rice at a meal—she touches the food and then says she has had enough. . . . I beg you to save my young mistress's life."

Honeybush's eyes were wet, and Mochow told her to go back and said, "You tell your young mistress quietly that we are going to speak to our father about making the engagement."

The sisters found their father in the Self-Examination Hall, and Mulan spoke to him about the matter of Afei's engagement.

"Fourth Sister is not so well, you know. It is time that they were engaged," she said.

Old Yao remained silent, thinking, his eyes very distant. Both daughters looked at him and dared not speak more. Then he said, "You still have this idea of *tsunghsi*. It did not work in the case of Mannia, did it . . . ? Wait until she is better."

"Sister Redjade might improve you know, if there is an engagement," said Mulan.

"Better wait a little," he said abstractedly. "When she is better, we will make the engagement."

The daughters were puzzled. Coming back, they entered into a conspiracy to give Redjade some definite hope. So when Mulan left and Mochow returned to her court, she sent for Honeybush and said to her,

"It is an embarrassing thing. But as a maid, you can accidentally let her know that you have heard that the master has consented and as soon as she gets better, there will be a formal engagement. And please try to persuade her that my brother is grown-up and cannot very well see her in bed, and ask her to feel at ease if he does not come to see her."

Mochow would often say to Redjade that Afei was inquiring after her, and Redjade's appetite began to improve. This was in summer, and the rumor was spread that perhaps in the autumn Redjade would be engaged. Redjade understood it to be so.

. ˙.

Paofen was a very good servant. She seldom left Mrs. Yao's presence, except when she was on leave to go back to see her parents. She had learned to read Mrs. Yao's thoughts and divine her wishes. Consequently Mrs. Yao was greatly pleased with her service and liked her. Afei often came to his mother's room; and, because the mother was dumb, the young master and the maid often talked, while the mother watched them with satisfaction, for she seemed to enjoy listening to them. When Afei would rise to leave, the mother would make a motion for him to remain. There was a little of Tijen in Afei, after all, and he was extremely attentive to the young and pretty girl. Often he offered to do a little menial service himself for her, like wiping cups and saucers and running for matches. Honeybush once found them laughing and struggling over a tray of teacups, but she kept it entirely to herself.

In the autumn Redjade had recovered sufficiently to go out for short walks in the garden. One day after supper she strolled past the pond to the Self-Examination Hall to see what Afei was doing. Finding her uncle alone, she greeted him and went out again and wandered alone, disappointed.

Aimlessly she went along under the tall trees until she suddenly saw Afei at a little distance, standing alone at the northwestern corner of the Chungmintang, looking at something. As she watched he disappeared round the corner.

Her curiosity excited, she went along the shaded path and turned the corner of the northern wall. Here was a paved yard with potted flowers in it and at about a hundred paces away was a hothouse with a great number of empty pots piled in rows in front. And there was Paofen standing, talking excitedly with Afei. Nobody else was in sight. Redjade hid behind a shrub, and saw that Paofen was trying to get away while Afei was trying to stop her. Then Paofen stopped and Afei came away alone. Redjade retreated, ashamed to be seen spying on them and too mortified to face either of them. She stumbled down the path which branched off westward at the corner leading to the back of the Keep-Farmer-Company Pavilion. Tears half blinded her and she tripped several times. It was some time after she was sitting in the Pavilion before she realized where she was. Thinking that if she returned past the Self-Examination Hall she would be seen with swollen eyes, or might meet Afei, she waited a while and then retraced her steps to the wooded path and returned to her court.

Now Afei had seen Paofen walking alone in front of the hothouse. Looking carefully, he was puzzled by her movements. Here she was entirely alone, not looking at the flowers, but walking with measured steps back and forth from a point in the center. She would walk four or five steps, then stop and scrutinize the ground with a finger on her lips, apparently thinking and talking to herself, then walk back to the original point. She seemed to count her steps as she went back and forth. Afei was so interested by this that he went along the side of the yard until he was quite near her, and called her name. Paofen looked up startled and saw him about thirty steps away from her, and affected a smile.

"Did I frighten you? What are you doing here?" said Afei as he approached.

"I am enjoying the flowers," replied Paofen.

"But there are no flowers here. The flowers are inside—you were not looking at them."

"How do you know?"

"I saw you from the distance."

Paofen, realizing that she had been watched, said, "I have been looking for a hairpin." Quickly she added, "Why did you come out here? I was only having a little stroll after attending upon your mother all day."

"I am taking a stroll, too," replied Afei. "Why take so much trouble over a hairpin? Can I help you?"

"Never mind," said Paofen, and she started to go away, and he tried to stop her.

"Paofen," he said, "I have never had a chance to be with you alone. *Meimei,* I . . ."

Paofen shot a look at him and said, "Be dignified. What would people say if some one should see us?"

He was persistent, and she said, "Please go and leave me alone. I shall be grateful."

Then Afei obeyed and went away, both unaware that they had been seen.

When Afei returned to his rooms, he was told by his father that Redjade had been to see him.

"You might go and see her," said the father.

When Afei came to Redjade's court she refused to see him. Honeybush came out and told him that her young mistress was too tired to be disturbed.

"Tell her that I came immediately after hearing she had visited me," he said.

Sadly he walked away, puzzled by these rebuffs from two girls, one whom he loved and one whom he admired.

"Why are there girls in this world? They are the most unaccountable creatures," he reflected. His father saw disappointment in his face but said nothing.

Afei did not tell any one that he had seen Paofen near the hothouse, partly because he had no suspicion about what she was doing, partly because he could not tell people that they had met alone. He only hoped that she would come out again and meet him at the same place.

. .

Honeybush came the next day to speak to Mochow. "Third Young Mistress, you ought to come over to have a good talk with her. Last night she went for a stroll after supper and came back with her eyes all swollen. Soon the young master came and she refused to see him. I asked her what had happened and she would not reply. They must have quarreled again, for, after lying in bed for half an hour, she asked me to open a drawer and bring her book of poems, and then she asked me to bring the brass basin; and, throwing the book of poems into it, she lighted a match and burned them. And then she broke down weeping and turned her head away. Third Young Mistress, how was I to speak to her? It hurt me to see her. This morning she woke up early and began to cough. I examined the sputum and there was a clot of fresh blood. I called her mother, and she came with her father and they ordered some medicine. But what is the use of medicine at all? I couldn't tell her parents about last night. It is all the second young master. Young men are so unreliable. . . . I hate him!"

When she spoke with such vehemence Mochow said, "You have forgotten yourself. You don't know whether Afei had anything to do with what happened last night."

"I am sorry, Young Mistress. But you know I am right. It is all that Manchu maid!"

"I appreciate your loyalty to your young mistress. What are we to do about it?" asked Mochow.

"This kind of thing I can only speak about to you sisters. Can't you speak to the Old Master and hurry the engagement?"

The news that Redjade had spat blood caused a mild sensation in the house and the whole family came to see her, even Mrs. Yao, assisted by Paofen. All eyes centered upon Afei and Redjade. But Honeybush stood beside Redjade's bed and fixed her eyes on Paofen and Afei with a gleam of hatred. In the presence of the elders, Afei could not be demonstrative toward Redjade as he wanted to be and he did not say many words.

Redjade thanked them all for being so kind and said she was particularly embarrassed to cause her aunt so much trouble, and her own parents also thanked Mrs. Yao and urged her to go back. When they were about to leave, Honeybush surprised them by saying,

"*Laoyeh, Taitai,* I thank you for coming. . . ."

Before she could say more, her throat choked, her eyes glistened, and she broke down crying; and as she wept she said something about it being already autumn, and then stopped and quoted the proverb that all the world's goods are not equal to having one's heart's desire.

Old Yao was quite touched by this unusual grief of the maid, which seemed to say more than an eloquent appeal by his daughters. At leaving, he said, "I will let you all have your heart's desire (*juyi*)."

And Honeybush smiled amidst her tears and saw them all to the door.

．·．

Three days later, there was a party at the Garden. Paku had arranged for a young American woman, a Miss Donahue, to come and see the Garden, and meet his friend Ku. Miss Donahue was a student of landscape architecture and something of a painter. She had come to Peking in the course of her world tour and had decided to stay, and had been in this city now for over a year. She had taken a large Chinese house with more courts than she could use, had a Chinese cook and a Chinese teacher, and had made friends with a number of Chinese intellectuals. At home she even wore Chinese dress occasionally. Peking life and Peking artists completely fascinated her. Like most foreigners in Peking, and unlike most foreigners in Shanghai, she was very intelligent and highly cultured, for Peking naturally attracted the artistic as Shanghai naturally attracted the money-makers. She had met Mulan and Sunya one day at their curio shop, and Mulan had promised to invite her to her home. Naturally she was also fascinated by Paku, who talked perfect English. Everybody in Peking knew Paku, for he was everywhere. Mulan could barely talk a few sentences of English, and Miss Donahue could talk only a few sentences of Chinese. Mulan had laughed at her name when she was introduced, and Miss Donahue was quite charmed by her informality.

The one person whom Miss Donahue had yet not been able to meet after a year's stay was the old philosopher Ku, about whom the foreigners in Peking constantly talked, and Miss Donahue begged Paku to arrange for them to meet. In general Ku hated young people, whom he regarded as having lost the fine manners of old China. On the other hand, he would admit to his house quite ordinary young men and teach them and talk to them as long as they were reactionary and showed their pride in being Chinese. When Paku begged him to come to the party, he consented for two reasons. First, because there were the "four beauties," including a virgin widow Mannia, who might have walked out of the pages of an ancient novel. Ku had a liking for beautiful girls and was unashamedly partial to them. Paku raved in his usual poetic fashion about Mannia so that Ku came

529

actually to think of the sight of her as a rare privilege. Paku had telephoned to Mulan that she must guarantee Mannia's appearance and she had promised it. Second, Paku had told Ku that the sisters were good reactionaries and that Redjade could write short dramatic sketches in the manner of the Ming *chuanchi*.

Of Mulan and Mochow, Paku spoke to old Ku in his highly poetic manner. "Mulan's eyes are longer, while Mochow's are rounder. Mulan is vivacious like a brook, Mochow is quiet like a pond. Mulan is like liquor, Mochow, like wine. Mulan stirs and stimulates like a day in autumn woods, Mochow soothes and strengthens like the summer morn. Mulan's spirit constantly soars to heaven, while Mochow's spirit is calm and strong like the spring earth."

Redjade decided she must join such an unusual party at all costs, for she wanted to see both the American lady and the old Ku. She rested the preceding day and the whole morning, and at midday had a light lunch, and then another nap. When she got up to dress for the party, there was something like passionate gaiety about her. As she dressed her hair and applied her rouge, she joked and laughed as she seldom did, so that Honeybush felt greatly relieved.

"I am feeling very well," she said. "A very famous philosopher is coming. I have been wanting to meet him for so long. And the American lady is coming too. Oh, I never felt so well before!"

Mulan and Mannia and Sunya came to see Redjade for a while and were surprised at her high spirits. She was so well made up that, except for a slight sallowness around her cheeks, one could not have told that she was ill.

When they heard that Paku and Sutan had arrived with the old philosopher Ku, they all went out to the Terrace of Swirling Waters for tea. Miss Donahue, having acquired the Oriental virtue of leisureliness, had not yet come. Old Yao, Coral, Afei, Chinya, Dimfragrance, and the rest were all there. Only Cassia was absent. The nursing of Mr. Tseng had added a few wrinkles to her face, and she had lost a little of her youthful vivacity. Her daughter, Lilien, also refused to come.

Mannia appeared old-fashioned with her loose coiffure and her comparatively broad sleeves, but she looked amazingly young, and her old-fashioned attire only made her more effective. She had never heard of Ku, and it was entirely to oblige Mulan that she consented to come, after some clever coaxing. When it was her turn to be intro-

530

duced, she held her hands together in front of her chest, made a deep bow and blushed, exactly as she might have done in Manchu times.

"This is the eldest daughter-in-law of Mr. Tseng, and sister-in-law of Mulan," Paku said.

Now although Mr. Ku believed in old China and in the seclusion of women, including footbinding, he talked freely with young women, believing this was his right, first as a man and secondly as an old man. He acknowledged Mannia's greeting with a beaming smile.

"How old are you?" he asked.

Mannia blushed again and, holding her son's hand as if leaning on him for defense, said with a smile revealing her pearly teeth, "I was born in the Dog-year." She retired into the ranks of the young women and looked out from there with the bright look of a badger, amused at this old man with a queue. He was as much a piece of antiquity as herself.

"Are you twenty? That can't be," he said.

Mannia smiled. "I belong to the upper cycle—thirty-two—*tofo* (thanks to your invisible protection)."

"That is her son. He is fifteen already," said Mulan. Asuan came forward and bowed low to the old guest.

"Incredible!" said Ku. "But I believe you. Nowadays ladies do not have such a charming flavor. Do you know how she keeps so young? By staying indoors and having her feet bound. You young ladies, if you go out and play tennis like all these modern girl students, you will be old by the age of thirty."

Everybody laughed. "Tell us more about that," said the young people. Afei was sitting with Redjade and they smiled at each other as the old man went on joking to the amusement of all. But it was not all humor; there was something instructive, too, in all that he said.

Mr. Ku was happy when he was talking to willing listeners, and he waxed more and more eloquent. Mulan remembered that he was the man who had stood up in the moving picture theater and joked about foreign women's dress. She felt like saying something now in defense of the emancipation of women, but she refrained out of respect for his great age. Although he was from Amoy, he spoke mandarin with hardly an accent, being a good linguist. He was the man who made the famous defense of concubinage: You have seen a teapot with four cups; have you ever seen a teacup with four teapots? But he was not talking of concubinage now; he was talking about the physical

531

and moral virtues of footbinding—how it increased woman's charm and improved her figure, and how it was the symbol of modesty and restraint.

"The first thing that gives dignity and refinement to woman is the texture of her skin and flesh—whiteness and softness—and you can attain that natural nobility only through gentility of movement. And you attain that natural, spiritual nobility also by being less seen in public. The moment a woman unbinds her feet and tramps about with palm-leaf feet, she loses that physical and moral distinction of her sex. Foreign women wear corsets to distort their body, which is harmful to the natural processes of digestion. But what is the harm of distorting one's feet? None whatsoever. They have nothing to do with the vital functions. I ask you, would you rather be shot in the leg or in the abdomen? And how it sets up an erect posture! Did you ever see a woman with bound feet who did not walk dignified and erect? Foreign women wear corsets to emphasize the hip artificially; but footbinding, through its influence on posture, develops and promotes the natural growth of the hips, because the center of locomotion is thrown back from the feet to the hips and the blood goes to nourish them."

The young women, particularly Mannia, were ready to die with shame. Redjade, however, listened attentively and was fascinated.

"Do I scandalize you?" continued Mr. Ku. "You ought to be more scandalized by the show windows in foreign shops in Tientsin and Shanghai with their displays of corsets and brassières. No, there is no more intimacy left for women; her whole body is completely exploited, from top to bottom, by this so-called Western civilization. I tell you, distort your feet but do not distort your abdomen. The abdomen is the seat of maternity and must not be tampered with."

Now Miss Donahue arrived. To the great surprise of all she came in a Chinese dress. Dimfragrance giggled until Mulan told her it was impolite. Paku had told the company before she came near what a clever and charming woman Miss Donahue was. If she had a smaller figure, she would be perfect from the Chinese point of view; but judged by Western standards she was not tall. Appearing in a Chinese dress was a thoughtful tribute to the old Chinese philosopher whom she wanted to meet.

Mr. Yao stood up to shake hands with her, and she extended her hand to him, and came to Mr. Ku.

"*Chiuyang,*" said Miss Donahue in Chinese with a foreign accent. She almost got her tones right.

"You speak Chinese, too?" said Mr. Ku in English. "I am most pleased to meet you."

"Just a few words," said Miss Donahue. She turned and, recognizing Mulan and Paku and Sutan, shook hands with them. No matter what she did, her movements were a little too quick in Chinese company and this, coupled with the fact that she was the only foreigner, centered attention upon her. Paku told Mulan to introduce her to the others, and Mulan talked to her in Chinese. When it came to Redjade, Mulan said this was her first cousin, adding the words "most clever" in English, and laughed at her own English.

Mulan called to Paku and said, "You tell Miss Donahue about Redjade."

Paku came over and said, "She is the one who writes poetry and drama."

"Oh, are you the one I heard Paku talk about?" said Miss Donahue. And she sat near Redjade, who understood English but refused to say more than single words. The American woman kept looking at Mannia and thought her like the ancient Chinese ladies she had always seen in paintings.

"Don't let me interrupt your conversation. Talk in Chinese. I can learn more by listening," said Miss Donahue to Mr. Ku in English.

"We were talking about the physical and moral virtues of footbinding."

"How fascinating!" said Miss Donahue.

"You may not like it, though."

"I don't have to agree with you, Mr. Ku. But I am interested in whatever you say."

Just then, Sutan whispered something to Mulan and she whispered it to Sunya, who said aloud to the company, "I have great news to announce to you. Our friends Paku and Sutan are going to be married!"

The news created great excitement and everybody congratulated the newly engaged couple. Sutan had seldom looked so happy as she did on that day. What she had gone through had left her with a forlorn and weary air which gave her added charm. She had been used to talk with a kind of indolent lisp and whisper, but at this moment she was gay and lively as she had been in her school days. She was wearing bangs on her forehead which gave her a girlish appearance when she laughed, and there was a curious liquid luster in her eyes. She was childishly wayward and capricious and today she had come in trousers instead of skirts, although she had been married. Around her shoulders she had a scarf of the violet gauze that Peking women often wore on the street and used to cover their faces while riding in a rickshaw during a sandstorm.

As the days were getting shorter, they were to have an early dinner, after which they could still wander about the garden. Miss Donahue was charmed with the garden, and Paku suggested going about to see it before dinner. She asked Redjade to come along, and therefore Afei as well as Sutan went with them.

After a while, Redjade said she must rest and Afei stopped with her, while the others went ahead. They were at the plum orchard south of the Dim Fragrance Studio, only a short distance from Redjade's own room. There was an intricate rockery, and south of it, a small bridge over a pond. Redjade loitered on the bridge, looking at the black and red gold fish swimming below.

Now that they were alone, Afei said, "*Meimei,* why did you refuse to admit me the other night when I came to see you?"

Redjade shot a glance at him and said merely: "*Yuanchia!*", meaning "predestined enemy." After a pause, she said, "You yourself know best why."

"Honestly, I didn't know and I don't know still."

Afei wondered if she could have seen him with Paofen. He thought of telling what he had seen Paofen do, but he thought that might be awkward. Then he thought that he ought to explain after all why he was out when she came to see him.

"*Meimei,* let me explain . . ." he began.

"Don't explain," said Redjade, cutting him short.

"*Meimei,* you know we will soon be engaged, and we must not quarrel," Afei pleaded, with a note of tenderness.

She did not know why in his presence she was always impelled to say things that were more provocative than she had intended, which she regretted afterward as she thought of him in her own room. Perhaps it was man's comparative simplicity of mind; perhaps there was an instinct in women to subdue the men they loved. Or perhaps it was merely a woman's way of testing her hold on her man. So now she

534

merely said, "You go back to them. I want to go in and have a little rest."

"You are coming to the dinner?"

"Yes, I am coming."

"Shall I come for you?"

"No, I can come by myself."

He stood watching her disappear through the side door, and disconsolately walked back alone.

As soon as Redjade was in her room, she regretted again that she had been so unkind.

．·．

When Redjade came back to the terrace, the party had already left for Chungmintang. As she started to turn back, she heard Afei's voice, and saw Huan-erh's head inside the Self-Examination Hall. Then she heard the American woman's voice.

She was going in to join them and was on the steps when she heard Afei say something about an engagement. She concealed herself behind the little rockery to listen. Afei had been telling them that Paku had decided to marry Sutan because he did not want to see her sell coal, but their voices were low, so that Redjade could hear only snatches of their conversation.

"Men are like that," she heard Afei say. "They would do anything for the girl they love. I would do exactly the same."

"I hear she has an old *laoping*," said Huan-erh.

"What is *laoping*?" asked the American lady.

"It is tuberculosis," Afei said gravely.

"And you would still marry her?"

"I would. Men are like that. . . . Out of pity . . . and serve her for life. . . . She is charming but very willful."

Redjade was too engrossed in her own affair to realize that the conversation was about Sutan. She could hear her own heart pounding with shame, remorse, love, regret, hatred, pride, sacrifice, all in one big dizzy confusion. The party stood up to leave and as Redjade saw them coming out she hid herself; her legs were shaking and unconsciously she grasped a protruding rock for support.

When they were out of the way, she tottered back to the terrace and collapsed on a chair, her cheeks turning now white with anger, now red with shame. Her pride was hurt and her love was injured. He

535

loved her, then, truly. . . . He said so. . . . But he would marry her and serve her for life out of pity. . . . Did he love Paofen. . . ? What was she to do. . . ?

She felt that she must go to the dinner, must see Afei.

The other people were already seated and waiting for her. With a laugh, she looked at Afei and said, "Afei, I have been wanting to see you. I thought I had lost you."

Her cheeks were a bright rosy color, and her eyes shone, and Afei was delighted that she had apparently forgiven him.

At the dinner wine was served. As course after course was brought, Redjade steadily looked at Afei. Mr. Ku was talking about love and modesty. One of the things he said was that it was immoral and demoralizing for a girl to hunt her own man. Modern girls would have no modesty left because the modest girl would have no chance. Men would choose the girls who dared to use their charms. A good girl would rather die of shame than go out and get a man for herself.

Redjade barely heard; her thoughts were too incoherent to follow the talk clearly, but it seemed that Mr. Ku was talking about her, was denouncing her in public.

"Afei, what are you thinking of?" she suddenly cried, beaming at him. "Come, I drink to your happiness!"

The sisters looked at each other as Afei lifted his cup and drank.

"You are ill," said Mochow.

"I am all right," said Redjade. Then she coughed and began to choke. With the cough came wine, mixed with blood.

Mulan rose and insisted that she retire at once.

"When I am so happy? Why do you want me to go away?" Redjade said.

But they made her get up. Mochow and Mulan rose to assist her. Turning to Afei, Redjade said, "Aren't you coming?" and he leaped to his feet. Everybody was puzzled at her sudden behavior, for she had not taken much wine.

Having reached her courtyard, Redjade said, "Third Sister, you can go back. And Second Sister, too. I want to talk to him."

Mulan said to Afei, "Did you quarrel again?"

"No, we are so happy," Redjade answered quickly. "I only want to speak to him."

Mulan whispered to Afei to be very careful and said they would wait on the way for him.

536

He was puzzled by the series of events that he could not understand. As soon as they were alone, Redjade said, "I want you to tell me now all that is in your heart."

It was so unexpected that he was held back for a moment. He looked closely into her face in the dark and pressed her to him and said, "Of course, *Meimei*. You know my heart. I have long given it to you."

"That is all I want to know," she said.

"We will soon be engaged," said Afei.

"Yes."

They went in to her room, hand in hand. "You must lie down, and I will ask Honeybush to come. You are strange tonight."

"No, I am not strange. I just love you. I never loved you more."

He came close again and kissed her ardently and she permitted him. He felt that he was happy as he never was happy before. After a while he went and brought Honeybush to stay with her, and then he left. Redjade's eyes followed him out of sight and then her expression suddenly changed. She sat silent and motionless as a rock for a long time, then gradually she relaxed and the maid saw an expression of peace and calm come over her face. Suddenly she laughed almost hysterically, again and again, until her tears came.

"Don't frighten people like that," said Honeybush. "What are you laughing about?"

"I understand it all now," Redjade said, still laughing.

"Understand what?"

"I should have known."

"Did you have a quarrel with him?"

"No, no!" said Redjade. "Come here, I will tell you," she continued in a whisper. "Do you know that Afei loves me? He said so just a moment ago."

Honeybush thought she understood now why her mistress laughed, and was happy with her.

"He is a good boy, isn't he? *Isn't he?*" said Redjade.

She went to the dressing table to look at herself in the mirror.

"You believe in destiny, don't you?" she asked.

"Yes. Why?"

Redjade did not answer, but sat before the dressing table and began to attend to her make-up again. She had calmed down now and said to Honeybush, "I don't need you now. You can go back. I want only a little quiet."

537

Honeybush asked if she was going back to the dinner with the guests.

"Perhaps. Stay as long as you like. My mother needs you."

Honeybush left her sitting at the dressing table, repainting her eyebrows.

. ∙ .

After an hour Honeybush came back and found that her mistress was not in the room. She had evidently changed into a new pair of shoes, and an eyebrow pencil lay on the dressing table. This convinced her that Redjade must have gone to join the guests. So she sat down and took up some needlework, thinking how strange her mistress had been that evening.

How long she sat working, she did not know; it must have been nearly an hour. The dinner must be over now, and she went to the small kitchen in the courtyard to make some special Yunnan tea that would be good for her mistress's digestion after the dinner. She returned with the pot and put it in the basket to keep it very hot, and went to turn on the light in the court. Coming back into her room, she was mumbling to herself that if her mistress tired herself out by staying up late, she would be ill for another five or six days, when she heard voices.

Honeybush rushed out and met Coral, Mulan, Mochow, Mannia, and Afei at the door.

"How is your young mistress?" asked Mochow.

"Isn't she with you?" Honeybush cried.

"No. I left her with you, didn't I?" asked Afei.

They all ran in, talking in confusion.

"She was very happy," Honeybush cried, "and told me to go back. I went because they were just having dinner and short of service. I left her laughing and smiling, and sitting there in front of the dressing table, repainting her eyebrows. And she had changed her shoes. So I took it for granted that she must have been planning to join you again."

Mulan was suddenly seized with a sense of terror, and Afei, catching it, dashed out through the front door, shouting, "Redjade, Redjade, where are you?" and in a few moments he was back, wild-eyed. "She isn't out there," he shouted. "Where is she?" Then he ran in the dark like a mad man to his uncle's court, asking if she had come that way.

Redjade's parents and two little brothers immediately came back with him.

Where had she gone? Mulan felt sure that something was wrong. She turned up the bedding and found nothing. She saw a writing brush and a white-copper inkcase on the desk. She pulled the brush from its cap and saw that it was still partly moist. She looked for papers, hoping to find some message. She pulled out the drawer and found a package marked "For Honeybush."

"Here is something," she said. The others came to look. It was a jewel box, containing some jade earrings and a beautiful brooch.

"And here is something, too," shouted Afei, as he took up a piece of paper from the drawer.

There was blood on it. The writing was in a shaky hand, and toward the end of the paper there was Redjade's name, about two inches in size, scrawled in blood by a cut finger. All the paper was smeared with blood and marks of tears, which blurred some of the characters.

Mr. Feng snatched the paper and read it, his hand trembling. It was addressed to her parents and written in the classical, balanced style:

> DEAR FATHER AND MOTHER: Your unfilial daughter has received your care and love from childhood and has not been able to repay you. Also due to Uncle and Aunt's love, I have been treated like their own child and surrounded with luxury and comfort. But unfortunately, your little daughter was born weak in health; I have lain in bed for months and years and have taken more medicine than food. Although I wish to continue to live to serve you, I shall only be an obstacle to another's future. Alas! life and death are predetermined and one's destiny is unalterable. I have studied poetry and books since childhood, and I have not been able to escape the tangle of romance. Recently, the Old Man in the Moon has opened my eyes. Once the oracle was revealed, I reached a great understanding. Great as the universe is, how should it miss a little being like Redjade? Enough! parting in life or death is unavoidable, and please do not grieve. I am returning my body to my parents pure as jade. Uncle and Aunt have been kind to me, and thank them for me. Little brothers Tan and Tsien should struggle upward and do their duties by our parents. The sin of your unfilial daughter can only be redeemed in the next generation.
>
> Your unfortunate daughter,
> REDJADE

As soon as Mr. Feng saw his daughter's signature in blood, he knew it was her farewell letter. He had hurriedly glanced through it and was stamping his feet in distress, saying to his wife, *"Pu hao liao!"* meaning that disaster had come, and tears rolled down his face. His wife began to weep aloud. Afei sat dazed and hid his face in his hands and broke down crying. Mannia, holding her son very close, clung with one hand to Mulan.

"Quick! We must find her!" said Mr. Feng, recovering from his momentary shock. "How long ago did you leave her?"

"When I came over to your side for supper," replied Honeybush. "It must have been nearly two hours."

Now others had heard the shouting, and Lifu and his sister and mother came into the room, and Paofen came to learn what had happened and went back to tell Mr. and Mrs. Yao.

Some one suggested that Redjade might have drowned herself in the pond.

She could have hanged herself, but it was unreasonable that she would hang herself anywhere but in her own room. So it was quickly concluded that she must have leaped into the pond. So, while the men and servants went out in all directions to look for her through all the courts, Mr. Yao and Mr. Feng and Sunya and Lifu went straight to the pond.

Among the women who stayed huddled together in the room, it was Mochow who kept her presence of mind. In the general excitement over Redjade's "letter in blood" they had forgotten the package which she had left for Honeybush. The paper wrapping lay on the floor and Mochow saw some writing on it and went to pick it up. On the reverse side there was a brief note, saying only this:

> Tell Afei to proceed according to the oracle of the Old Man in the Moon. I wish him happiness in marriage.
>
> REDJADE

This must have been written first, for there were no blood stains on it.

Outside, the light of the crackling torches held by the servants going all around the pond awakened the birds and cast flaming shadows into the water, which lay in the pale moonlight peaceful and undisturbed, withholding from the terrified spectators a mystery within its dark green bosom. The men talked in whispers, if at all, each occupied with his own thoughts. Only the sounds of the servants across the pond and the call of frightened crows and the screeching of an owl broke the heavy silence.

Lifu silently pointed out to Sunya the wooden tablets, inscribed with Redjade's couplet.

> Encircling water embraces hill, hill embraces water.
> Leisurely men watch actors, actors watch men.

Later on, these tablets were taken down by Mr. Yao's order, as being too pathetic.

The pond was five or six feet deep on the stage side, but twelve or fifteen feet on the studio side. While it was more probable that the girl might have jumped down from this side, dragging was impossible during the night. Only some servants waded on the other side as far as they could go, but work was difficult at that late hour. All agreed that if she jumped down two hours ago, she would be past rescue, and they would have to wait till the next morning. They sat there, waiting for news from other servants who had gone to search the back garden. When these returned and reported finding nothing, Mr. Feng suggested that they should rest for the night and thanked them all. It was midnight when Mannia and Mulan and Sunya returned to the Tseng home with the mystery unsolved. Sunya suggested staying, but they had to leave on account of Mannia's timidity. Honeybush, crying bitterly, was forcibly taken to Mr. and Mrs. Feng's court, where no one slept through that night.

Before dawn Mr. Feng went out again to search for his daughter. Crossing over to the Mirage Tower, he saw in the early daylight a shining black object floating near the foundation of the Dim Fragrance Studio. The more he looked, the more it resembled a woman's shoe. He went over and saw that it was indeed a shoe of patent leather. He ran back to his wife and told her, and Honeybush told him that Redjade's shoes, to which she had changed, were of patent leather. Then it seemed probable that she had jumped into the pond from that side. It was seen now that Redjade could have gone through the western side door and reached the Dim Fragrance Studio, which was deserted the night before, and that she could have leaped through the open window across the two-foot wall on the porch. Mrs. Feng broke into a wailing, crying between her wails that her ill-fated daughter had feared the water ever since she saw that girl drowned at Shihshahai when she was a mere child.

541

It was important that her body be found immediately, before it became disfigured. Now that it was certain that she was dead, outside people were hired to drag the pond, and all the women stayed away from the scene, except Redjade's mother and some old servants. Afei stood waiting inside the Self-Examination Hall, at the corner where Redjade had heard him talking with Huan-erh and the American woman only the afternoon before.

When Redjade's body was lifted out of the water, he quickly turned his eyes away. He could not look at her now. For all the care she had taken to paint herself and to appear neat and beautiful before going to her death, there was only a mud-smeared face and body with the long braid of hair dripping muddy water back into the pond.

CHAPTER XXXIV

*M*ULAN came over with her husband, Mannia, Cassia, and Lilien the next morning and went in to see Redjade's mother, who was crying like a "doll of tears." They comforted her by saying that Redjade had had a happy life and the parents' hearts should be contented, that she had been severely ill in any case and that all things were determined by Heaven. Nothing was said about her love for Afei or about her farewell letter. The women inevitably spoke of her good points and of her long illness, and the more they talked, the more they cried. So Mulan's eyes were quite red when she came over to Mochow's court.

"Something must have happened yesterday," said Mulan. "She had already made up her mind when she came to the dinner. You remember how she looked when she came in."

"According to Afei," said Mochow," he left her very happy."

"Because she knew it was their last meeting," remarked Lifu. "I shall ask Afei exactly what happened."

"I have thought of something," said Huan-erh. "Just before dinner, the American lady and Afei and I were talking in Afei's court after you had gone. As we came out, I thought I saw some one hiding in the rockery, who may have overheard us. It may have been Redjade."

"What were you talking about?" asked Lifu.

"About Sutan's engagement, and we were saying that she had tuberculosis, and Afei said that Paku was marrying her out of pity. Fourth Sister may have overheard us and thought Afei was speaking of her."

The others were silent, thinking, until Mochow said, "You see she was really out of her mind when she came to the dinner. The way she looked and smiled at Afei as if none of us were present. What an unlucky coincidence! It seems to me that Fourth Sister's death is due to several causes, partly from the gods and partly from men. First,

543

because of this unfortunate coincidence that Sutan was just engaged and that she too had tuberculosis; second, because she grew up with too much sentimental romance; and third, because she believes in the Old Man in the Moon of Hangchow!"

Just then Mrs. Hua came in, much excited, for she, too, had heard the news.

"What did she mean by 'proceeding according to the Old Man in the Moon'?" asked Lifu.

"That is a problem," said Mulan after a pause. "I dare not say what she meant."

Mrs. Hua was puzzled by the reference to the oracle at Hangchow, and was informed by the others about the oracle slips that Redjade and Lilien had drawn at West Lake.

"The Old Man in the Moon was an interesting legend," said Mulan, "but she took it too seriously. You can't say there is destiny, and you can't say there is not. She believed in it, and so it became true for her. . . . That caused her death. But it could not have been easy. I may say in your presence that she really loved Afei and she died to make him happy. Her last wish was his happiness in marriage."

"In my opinion," said Lilien, "she has died at the hands of the monks. She was quite distressed that afternoon after reading the oracle. If you believe in the monks, then you are ruled by the monks."

In Lilien's tone there was still a certain bitterness against her dead rival. She had resigned herself to the fact that Afei was to be engaged to Redjade, but she could not like her. Mr. Tseng was already talking of an engagement for her; but, like many modern girls, she had refused and to the great chagrin of her father, had brought pressure upon her mother, Cassia, to prevent the match.

Mulan had read the oracle, *Pass the perfume and all is emptiness,* as referring to either Dimfragrance or Paofen, probably the latter, as Dimfragrance was older than Afei by several years. So far the prophecy had turned out to be true. But the oracle had said nothing about what should come after the "emptiness" for Redjade, nor had it said specifically who was to marry Afei. Redjade's dying wish "to proceed according to the Old Man in the Moon" could therefore be interpreted as one wished. The mysterious figure of Paofen was constantly in Mulan's mind, but in Lilien's presence she preferred to say no more. Instead she sent word to Afei that they wished to see him.

Afei came, looking like a ghost, or like a person struck by a ghost.

544

He did not even greet Cassia and the guests. The ladies took compassion on him, and Cassia said, "Don't grieve too much. The dead one cannot come back to life again."

"What is Father doing?" asked Mulan.

"He is at the Dim Fragrance Studio with Uncle and Aunt. They are dressing her."

Abruptly Afei rose and went to the front court, where he found Honeybush weeping and at the same time trying to gather the articles for dressing Redjade.

"I want to ask you, how did she die?" said Afei.

Honeybush looked up with mingled anger and sorrow.

"How do I know?" she replied.

"You ought to know. How did my fourth sister die?"

"Can't you read her farewell message?" answered Honeybush, and went on with what she was doing. He stood watching this pert maid, who in so many ways resembled her dead mistress. When she had her arms full of her mistress's garments and was ready to go back to the Studio, he stopped her. "Honeybush," he said, "my heart is already broken. Have pity on me. I want only to know what made her seek the short way?"

Honeybush turned and said in a tone of pity, "You men are strange creatures. When a girl loves a man, he forces her to death and then weeps over her. What is the use of it? Can the dead come back alive?"

"Honeybush, you are unfair," he cried. "My intestines are broken and I cannot think. What was wrong? It was not my fault, was it?"

Honeybush said with raised eyebrows, "When you two were good, you were very good to each other. Then you would cause her to shed tears for days and nights. The other day when she came back and burned her book of poems, I knew she would not live long. It seems to me that she owed you a debt of tears in her previous life. She has paid the debt and her tears are dry now. What more do you want?"

"I didn't know that she burned her poems! Why?"

Honeybush's resentment softened a little when she saw him look so miserable, and she said, "She wishes you happiness in marriage. Isn't it clear enough that she died for you?"

Afei broke down crying upon Redjade's bed, and Honeybush left him.

It was Mulan who came over with Cassia and lifted Afei up from Redjade's bed and took him to Mochow's court to rest.

"I have killed her. I have killed her," he said.

Lifu told him what Huan-erh had suggested as a reason for the suicide. It seemed plausible. But Afei sat dazed and confused and unable to think.

Mrs. Hua suggested that they go to see Mrs. Yao, and Cassia and Mulan went over, as was the proper form. Paofen was sitting silently beside the bed where Mrs. Yao lay, looking quite ill, a terrified expression on her old wrinkled face.

"Last night she didn't sleep at all," said Paofen. "At midnight, she wanted to get up and say prayers to Buddha, and she sat there for hours and refused to go to bed."

A change had come over Mrs. Yao. As she could not speak, no one could read what was in her mind. But her hearing was still good, and the person talking to her had to go on guessing what she wanted until she nodded her head. If she raised three fingers, Paofen would ask whether she meant three, or thirty, or three hundred and three dollars. Paofen was quick to read her mind and this had made it easier. At times when she felt better, she would ask Paofen to read to her; but the reading was limited to Buddhist stories of retribution, of providence and of miraculous cures. There were many such religious pamphlets urging people toward faith, warning against killing cows, or recounting "evidences of the work of God," privately printed and distributed by devout Buddhists. Especially did she love the story of Mulien, which she had seen long ago in dramatized form back at Hangchow.

The death of Redjade brought about a change in her. She seemed to be suffering from a great fear and lost sleep, and her condition rapidly grew worse. Because Redjade was a young girl, the mourning and prayers for her were to last only twenty-one days. But when Mrs. Yao heard the drums and bells and cymbals of the monks, she looked as if she were seized with a secret terror. Yet she wanted nuns to come into her court and say prayers for her.

Poya, Silverscreen's child by Tijen, had so far been kept away; but Coral, who was taking care of him, was now constantly in the room. One day Poya, who had grown very tall for a boy of nine, came to find Coral and happened to be seen by his grandmother. She suddenly shrieked aloud and covered her face, and a cold perspiration broke out over her whole body.

To their amazement, she then moaned and spoke. "You are coming to claim my life," she said distinctly.

Quickly Coral sent the boy out of the room, and he left, hurt and bewildered.

"But *Taitai* is talking!" cried Paofen. It had come so suddenly with the shock that neither Coral nor Mochow had thought of their mother's recovery of speech. They went close to the bed and heard her murmuring, "Oh, have mercy upon me. I cannot stand it."

"Mother, you have recovered!" said Mochow with tears of happiness. "You are speaking!"

"What?" said the mother.

"You are talking now."

Although Poya had left the room, he stood just outside listening, and he peeped in again and said to Coral, "Has grandma recovered?"

Mrs. Yao had an uncanny sense of Poya's presence, and before Coral could reply she said, "Oh, send him away! He is coming to claim my life!"

Coral shouted to the boy and he slunk away.

The excitement over Mrs. Yao's sudden recovery of speech was so great that it overshadowed Redjade's funeral ceremonies. But it was like the glow before the sunset. Mulan rushed over, as soon as she heard the news by telephone, to find her father and Coral in her mother's room.

"It is no use," the mother was saying. "My days are near an end. You had better prepare for my last affairs and burn more incense for me at the temples for a safe voyage to the next world."

"What are you thinking? This is all your dream," said Mulan.

"No. This is true. I know it. Silverscreen's spirit told me that after some one in the family should die, my turn would come next. Now Redjade has died and it is my turn."

"Father," said Mulan, "isn't it enough that Fourth Sister has died at the hand of the monks? Must we allow Mother to suffer the same?"

"If she will believe us," said the father briefly.

In the following days her condition rapidly became critical, and from exhaustion and sorrow Afei fell ill also. In obedience to the dying mother's wish, he was moved inside to sleep in the outer room of her court and was attended by Paofen. When he was better, he remained in the same room and often came in, so that he was continually with Paofen in the mother's presence during her last days.

∴

Paofen was so occupied with the mistress' sickness that she had not been able to go home at all. Her father had visited the shop and learned what had happened, and one day some one from her home came to the Garden and asked to see Paofen.

"Ask him to come in," said Afei. "I have never seen your people."

"He is just a servant," said Paofen.

"So you have a servant, too!" said Afei. "I knew you came from a good home."

Paofen was embarrassed, said nothing and went out to see the messenger. She came in again and said that her mother wanted to see her on some important matter at home.

"We will send you home in our carriage," said Afei.

"No, that would not be right. What would the other servants say? I can be back within two hours."

Paofen went home and saw her parents and her uncle.

"You have been in the Garden for three or four months now," said her father, a middle-aged Manchu gentleman. "What is the news?"

"There is no news, Father," replied Paofen. "I haven't been able to do anything about it."

"Why?"

"I have to attend upon the mistress all the time. Now her niece has died, and the mistress herself is critically ill. Who could have the mind to attend to such things?"

"Haven't you been able to locate the place at all?"

"Once I went out after supper, and the young master saw me, and I had to make an excuse. I haven't dared to go out again."

"You must not bungle this affair," continued her father. "And you must not do anything to arouse suspicion. Did the young master suspect anything?"

"I don't think so. Afei is such an easygoing boy. He asked me what I was doing and I said I was looking for something lost. He wanted to help and I told him to go away."

"Who is Afei?"

"He is the young master."

"Why do you call him that?"

"He told me to. He says the distinction between master and servant is ridiculous. He said . . ." Paofen stopped and blushed. She did not know why she blushed and why she talked more about Afei than about others in the family. But she realized that she had said too much.

"Take your time, and go about it cautiously," said her father. "You know this would mean a fortune to our family."

Paofen frowned. "Father, you have given me a hard task to do. I am afraid . . . I would never do it, except for you parents."

Suddenly she hid her face in her hands and cried, "I can't do it! I can't do it! The people are so nice to us, and we are like thieves."

Paofen's parents were very fond of their only daughter, but the father said, "It is not exactly as you say. The treasure is not theirs. They bought the Garden, but did not buy the treasure underground. Otherwise we would not have sent you. Why, it may be worth as much as the Garden itself."

It should be explained that Paofen's ancestor was one of the Manchu army that followed the father of the first Manchu Emperor in his campaign, and a hereditary rank was conferred upon the family for his meritorius service. The rank expired in the mid-eighteenth century, but the family was well-to-do and had occupied important official positions from generation to generation. With the collapse of the Manchu Empire, the family property was quickly used up, through the desire or the necessity of keeping up the standard of living to which they were accustomed. When the Revolution came, Paofen was only eleven years old, but she was precocious and she had grown up with the consciousness of a fast-dwindling family fortune. They were still able to keep servants, but the family was struggling to preserve a false front ("outside strong, inside dry"), and Paofen knew it.

Paofen's father had bought at Mrs. Hua's shop some old bundles which she had purchased along with the curios which had belonged to the Baron, the former owner of the Garden. Paofen's father, who had adopted the Chinese name Tung, was a scholar and interested in Manchu family history and being too poor to buy the curios and antiques, he bought the old manuscripts for two dollars. The bundles contained various odd volumes, some of them manuscripts of poems and travel sketches never published. One night in going over the old volumes he discovered an old diary of the grandfather of the Baron. There was a note concerning the sack of Peking, particularly the burning of the Old Summer Palace and its huge library in 1859

549

by the British and French soldiers. During the sack of the city, treasures had been buried and the old Baron had indicated the whereabouts of the hidden family treasures in his garden. The Baron evidently died soon afterward, or perhaps he had fled with his family and had never come back, for the entries were discontinued. Many of such secret burials of treasures were never heard of by relatives and forgotten. As this occurred a few years after the building of the Garden when the old Baron was at the height of his prosperity and imperial favor, it could easily be conceived that the treasure hidden must have been of great value. Several such treasures had been dug up when Manchu princes' gardens were brought up and rebuilt upon.

Now when Paofen heard her father say that the Yaos had bought the Garden, but not the treasure underground, she said, "But, Father, it is their garden now; anyway, it is not ours."

Her uncle then spoke, "Paofen, all we want you to do is to help verify the location. The rest you can leave to us."

"Don't worry about it now," said Paofen's mother. "I only hope that your work is not too hard on you. You have never worked before."

"That is all right," replied the daughter. "The work is easy and the family are such nice people. You ought to see their daughters."

"I hear from Mrs. Hua that this Redjade was engaged to the young master."

"Yes," said Paofen, hesitantly. "So I heard."

"Why did she jump into the water?"

"I don't know."

And Paofen left her home and soon returned to the Garden.

. .

Soon after Redjade's funeral, Mrs. Yao's condition grew so critical that it was expected she would not survive many days. It was very strange that, after her recovery of speech, she tended to speak only in her native dialect, which puzzled and annoyed Paofen and made it more difficult for her to understand her. She also began to fall into a reminiscent mood and speak of her girlhood home and of Hangchow history. Afei loved to listen to these stories, and he also understood the Hangchow dialect, so that he often explained ambiguities to Paofen. And so mixed with sorrow, there were times of youthful merriment. Honeybush, who was now serving Redjade's mother, was after a long time reconciled to Afei through persuasion and explana-

550

tions by Mochow and Huan-erh that Redjade had overheard and misunderstood a conversation between Afei and the American woman.

One day as Mrs. Yao, lying in her bed, was watching Afei and Paofen together, she suddenly asked the maid, "Have your parents made an engagement for you?"

Paofen bent her head and said, "No."

"I shall remain in this world not very long now," said Mrs. Yao. "You have been serving me during my last days. You know people have said that I hated Silverscreen and interfered with my son's marriage to a maid. It is not true and I have a mind to show them so."

Paofen turned red all over her face and said not a word.

"Don't be shy," Mrs. Yao said. "Matrimony is fixed by Heaven. I see you two thrown together by Fate and getting on so well. Tell me about your home."

"We are poor people," said Paofen, and would say no more.

That talk made the two young people conscious of a relationship that they had been trying to deny to themselves. Paofen began to be very serious and very shy toward Afei, and there was no more of that careless freedom between young master and maid, and she no longer allowed Afei to help in menial service. On the other hand, there was a greater tenderness that could not be hidden when she spoke to Afei. The other girl servants noticed that Paofen began to take more care of her dress than before. Afei ceased to treat her as a maid and refused to have her serve him. Under the circumstances, Paofen was irresistible and sometimes Afei involuntarily compared her with Redjade to the latter's disadvantage—for instance, Paofen never quarreled with him, and was so strong and healthy—and then he was suddenly struck with a sense of guilt for thinking unkindly of his deceased love.

Several struggles were going on in Paofen's mind. First was the thought that she did not seriously think of the mission on which she had been sent here by her parents and had put it completely out of mind. A more important struggle was the natural assertion, before her lover, of the pride of a girl in love. It reached the point where she was willing to tell him secretly something about her home.

"How is it that you have a servant and you yourself come out to work?" asked Afei.

"I have never worked before, you know," replied the girl.

"Then why?"

551

"I will tell you later," said the Manchu maid. "But don't tell anybody else what I have said to you."

Thus secrecy added a flavor to their intimacy.

But it was not only Mrs. Yao and themselves who thought of the obvious. Mulan, Lifu, and Mochow studied the meaning of Redjade's dying wish and concluded that Redjade had Paofen in mind. The protests of Honeybush about Afei's duplicity only made it more certain that it could not be any other person. Mulan thought Paofen a more appropriate match for her brother than Redjade, and with all the old breeding, she was incomparably a better match than the somewhat frivolous and modern Lilien. Cassia, though interested, forebore mentioning the topic so soon after Redjade's death.

Very soon Mrs. Yao began to sink rapidly, and again lost her power of speech while she yet remained conscious. For three days she was not able to take food. Paofen gave her a cupful of ginseng tea; sometimes she took it and sometimes it came up again. Definite preparations were made for her funeral.

On the last afternoon, Mrs. Yao woke when Coral, Mochow, Afei, and Paofen were in the room. The sick old mother opened her eyes and showed by a motion that she wanted to speak and could not. Paofen and the others went close to her. Mrs. Yao took Afei's hand and reached feebly for Paofen's hand. Paofen dared not move. Mochow understood and took Paofen's hand. Mrs. Yao put the two hands together, and her lips seemed to move, but no words came. Then she sank back and never became conscious again. Two hours later she died.

Coral and Mochow, who witnessed this scene, told their father and the relatives.

Mr. Yao once again moved with a rapidity that astounded his daughters. It seemed that he had meditated in his Self-Examination Hall and had calculated beforehand what was to happen. He had a complete plan. He must have already approved of Paofen, or he would not have sent Afei to his mother's room. He told them that this marriage was in accordance with Redjade's wish and his wife's wish, that Paofen would make an excellent daughter-in-law, that she deserved it because she had served their mother on her deathbed—that, in short, it was a "union by Heaven."

Mr. Yao sent for Mrs. Hua. He explained to her the situation and asked her to be go-between.

"How soon?" asked Mrs. Hua.

"Immediately," said Mr. Yao.

Mr. Yao explained to Mrs. Hua that this was his last duty toward his family on earth, that he wanted to see his younger son married off with his blessing, and that if they were not married now Afei would have to wait three years until the mourning was over. Afei had graduated this summer, and he was planning to send his son and daughter-in-law to England, perhaps for three years after the wedding.

A hurried wedding before the last funeral rites was in accordance with the old custom. Thus Mrs. Yao would be honored at her funeral by having not only a son but also a daughter-in-law to follow the coffin in the funeral procession. The wedding ceremonies would have to be extremely simple, and the mourning dress would be suspended just for one day, the day of the wedding, after which the bride and groom would have to go into severe mourning at once.

The formalities of engagement were entered into, and Mr. Yao discovered, not greatly to his surprise, that Paofen's father had been a high Manchu official. He knew they were poor now, and did not suspect any ulterior motives. He only believed that this engagement was a machination of Mrs. Hua's masterly mind, one of her diplomatic triumphs. On the day of the engagement, he said to Mrs. Hua, "You have sold me a Manchu garden. But you have also brought me a good daughter-in-law. I am satisfied with Paofen. I thank you."

Paofen's parents were agreeably surprised. Having a son-in-law as the owner of the Garden was surer and safer than anticipating hidden treasures, with the many possible complications, even of a lawsuit if they should fail, and of a bad name. When Paofen came home to prepare for the wedding, she told her parents and uncle to give up their plan. "If there is treasure, I shall not have to steal it now," she said. And her mother said, "Finding hidden treasure is not so good as finding a good son-in-law."

But Afei was such an easygoing person and was so much in love with Paofen that shortly after their wedding she decided to tell him about the great treasure that might be in their garden. Although she had told her parents that she would not reveal that she had been sent to the Garden for this purpose, she did secretly tell Afei. Afei was amazed, but he understood.

"What were they going to do if you found it?" he asked.

"I don't know. I was merely told to locate it. After seeing that your

553

family was so kind, I couldn't do it, and so there the matter stopped."

She had been afraid of what he might say or do, but to her surprise, he was pleased and said, "Isn't it wonderful? Otherwise, I should never have met you. They have lost their treasure already."

Paofen was perplexed and asked, "What do you mean?"

"I mean you. They haven't found the buried treasure, but they have already lost you, their dearest treasure, to me."

Paofen felt happy and kissed him.

"Shall I let Father know?" Afei asked.

"No, you must not," she said. "It would be so embarrassing for our people."

Still they could not resist the temptation to look for the treasure. "How shall we do it?" said Afei.

"There is a big round slab there," said Paofen. "Say that you want to use it as a stone table top to set in the courtyard, and have it dug up. Then we shall see if the treasure is beneath it."

One day Afei casually asked two gardeners to go out with him and dig up the round slab which was about three feet in diameter. When it was lifted, they saw two jars underneath.

"What is that?" asked Afei, pretending to be as surprised as the workmen were.

"They must have been used for burying treasures," one of the workmen remarked.

"Take them up and see," Afei ordered.

The jars were empty, except that in one there was a small piece of very old brocade and some clods of earth. The treasure had evidently been discovered by somebody already, possibly by one of the former owners or their servants.

Afei and Paofen were greatly disappointed, but she still stood looking at the bottom of the hole where the jars had stood.

"See!" she said, "there is something there!"

They all peered in and saw mixed in the yellow soil, three pearls, the size of large beans, round and glistening. The workmen reached down to get them, and turned the earth about to find more.

"Here is another!" said one.

Finally they recovered five large pearls of equal size which evidently had belonged together and had been spilt into the ground. Paofen took the pearls and regarded them as her property.

They then told the story to Mr. Yao. He thought now that he un-

554

derstood why Mrs. Hua had sent Paofen to serve as a domestic in his garden; but he pretended not to know and merely said, "It is your bad luck. Someone was before you, or you might have found the whole treasure."

"But, Afei," he added, "isn't one treasure enough for you? You have your bride and that is enough luck for any man."

Mr. Yao smiled at Paofen and she smiled to thank him, and this was the close of the whole adventure.

. . .

The hurried wedding of Afei and Paofen had been but a step in Mr. Yao's long contemplated plan for leaving the family. On the evening of their wedding, he had delivered a strange sermon before the gathered family.

He spoke in a sad and yet calm voice. Addressing the newly-married couple and his brother-in-law, his brother-in-law's wife, and his three daughters, he said:

"Tse-an, Pin-erh, Afei, Paofen, and my daughters, events have happened recently in quick succession to our family. Your mother is now dead, and you, Afei and Paofen, are married, and my duties toward the family on this earth are done. You wonder perhaps why I shed no tears at your mother's death. Read Chuangtse and you'll understand. Life and death and growth and decay are the very law of nature. Luck and adversity are but the natural consequences of each one's personal character, and there is no avoiding them. So although parting in life or through death is sad according to normal human sentiments, I wish you to take these things and accept them as part of the Way. You are all now grown-up, and should take a grown-up attitude toward life. If you see life clearly in its natural evolution, you will not grieve too much over what I am about to tell you.

"Afei, I am happy to see you united with Paofen. Remember that she served your mother in her last days and had already fulfilled her duties as daughter-in-law before she married into our home. I am sending you both to England. Paofen, it is your duty to look after my son, for I place him in your hands. Greater honor I could not confer upon a girl than to let her take charge of the destiny of my son and therefore of the future of my family. I have confidence in you and my mind is at peace.

"Let no one shed tears now, when I tell you that I am about to

555

leave this home. As soon as your mother's funeral is over and Afei and Paofen depart for England, I shall leave you. Do not be sentimental. There is no parent in this world who does not sooner or later have to take leave of his children. I shall come back to see you after ten years, if I am still alive. Do not try to search for me; I shall come to you.

"You have heard of people who leave their families to become hermits. There are only two attitudes toward life: 'entering the world' and 'leaving the world.' Do not be frightened by those phrases. I have lived with you and your mother, and have seen you grow up and all satisfactorily married. I myself have had a happy life and have lived up to my human obligations. Now I am ready for a rest. Do not think that I am trying to become an immortal. Perhaps you will not understand these things if I try to explain them to you. I am going out and try to find myself; to find oneself is to find the Way and to find the Way is to find oneself; and you know 'to find oneself' is to be 'happy.' I have not yet found the Way; but I have obtained an insight into the ways of the Creator, and I shall try to reach a greater understanding.

"Redjade has reached an understanding in her own way. Think kindly of her. Remember, Afei, that she died to make you happy. Who but the Way has ordained that matters should turn out so?"

At this point, Redjade's mother and Afei were greatly touched, and there were sobs among the women. Mr. Yao continued:

"During Afei's absence, Mochow and Mulan will jointly take charge of the property with the assistance of your uncle. I shall tell you the details later."

"Where are you going?" his brother-in-law asked when he had finished.

"I cannot tell you. I know that you will be happy and I shall be happy."

Mrs. Feng, as now the eldest woman, tried to dissuade him from leaving the family and begged him to remain. "You could live a completely quiet and retired life at home, even if you wanted to follow the Way," she said.

"No, it is impossible," he said. "Living in a home, one will think of home. These things I cannot explain to you."

Mulan and Mochow knew that when their father spoke with such clearness of mind there was no chance of dissuading him. He seemed to have planned this course for years.

And so a chapter of Mulan's life closed with the death of her mother and the departure of her father into the mountains. He left his family —in his lifetime, instead of at his death. This made the mother's funeral doubly sad and the departure of Afei and Paofen doubly difficult. Time and again Afei and Paofen insisted on delaying their trip, that their father might remain longer with them. But Mr. Yao was adamant and spoke again of his philosophy and gave them a broader vision.

He had made his will. Afei was to be the heir, sharing the property with Poya, the grandson born of Tijen and Silverscreen. During Poya's minority Coral was to represent him, but Afei was to be the head of the family. In Afei's absence, Mulan and Mochow were jointly to represent him and co-operate with their uncle in managing the property. A settlement of ten thousand dollars was given to each of his three daughters immediately after his departure, which they could keep or withdraw as they individually liked.

Mulan brought up her old idea of owning a shop in Hangchow; and this, too, he had arranged. She was to turn over part of her jewelry and sell it at her shop, the proceeds of which would bring approximately twenty thousand dollars, which was to be the payment for the Hangchow teashop. Thus Mulan was to have a teashop in Hangchow, while Mochow already had a shop in Soochow as part of her dowry.

. ˙.

On the day before Afei's departure, he and Paofen prepared baskets of wine and fruit and fresh flowers to sacrifice at Redjade's grave behind their country home near the Jade Spring.

They took Honeybush with them. After Huan-erh's explanation, and after she was shown that this marriage was in accordance with her dead mistress's wish, Honeybush had become reconciled to the new situation. One day she told Afei that, had Redjade not told her on her last night that Afei had been kind to her, she would never have been able to forgive him.

It was a day in late autumn. The three of them proceeded outside Hsichihmen Gate to the Jade Spring. Neither Afei nor Paofen decorated themselves. At the sight of the grave, Afei could not control himself, and Honeybush and Paofen, touched by the bitterness of his weeping, wept with him. He knelt before the grave, and Paofen knelt beside him, while Honeybush arranged the fruit and flowers on the stone before the epitaph and passed the pewter pot of wine to Afei, and then knelt down behind them.

Afei poured the wine to the ground and said the sacrificial prayer, which Paofen had helped him to write. It was in sentences of four words each.

"Oh, Fourth Sister Redjade! Your cousin-brother Afei calls to you. Do you remember how you came to my home as a child, shy and quiet of manners? We played and romped together. Quarreling we loved, and loving we quarreled. How we studied together and you were brighter and taught me many things! How beautiful the good old days, when you and I had little fringes over our foreheads and we were but two innocent, young children! Seeing the flood at Shih-shahai, you were frightened by the drowning of the lotus-picking girl; unfortunate it was that this became an ill omen in your life. Then you and I grew and we moved into the garden home. On the beautiful days of spring and autumn, we roamed the garden in peace and happiness, and flew kites and caught crickets. In the winter nights, I heard you talking and laughing over poetry and romance. At the West Lake in Hangchow, we boated and we sang. I had hoped that we might live together for life, and you had promised me. Unfortunately you were ill in bed, and I was prevented from seeing you, and a misunderstanding arose, resulting in this tragedy. Alas! you have parted from me. In the generosity of your love, you had forgiven me and wished me well. Deep red was your farewell letter, and how shall I forget it? O, Fourth Sister Redjade! Your cousin-brother Afei is calling to you. If your spirit has consciousness, come and taste of this fruit and wine!"

Faint with exhaustion, Afei collapsed and prostrated himself on the ground. Paofen and Honeybush begged him to control his sorrow and assisted him to his feet. He was so unnerved that Paofen hurried him home before sundown lest he should catch cold in the keen autumn air.

The next day, they departed for England. Paofen's parents came to see them off. There was a lump in Afei's throat as he thought that he was saying farewell to his aged father forever.

After Afei had gone, Mr. Yao shaved off his hair, changed into a simple gown and bade formal farewell to his weeping family, forbidding them to follow him and saying that he would revisit them after ten years. Then he took an old walking stick and went out of the home and disappeared.

Book III

THE SONG OF AUTUMN

Therefore all things are one. What we love is the mystery of life. What we hate is corruption in death. But the corruptible in its turn becomes mysterious life, and this mysterious life once more becomes corruptible.

From "The Northern Travels of Knowledge" by Chuangtse.

CHAPTER XXXV

$\mathcal{S}$HORTLY before Redjade's death, the Yao family had received a letter addressed to the "Owner of Chingyiyuan," written in a perfect "small script." The letter was sent from Anking, a little town on the Yangtse River, and the writer said that he was the lost son of Chenma, whose story he had read about in a local newspaper. Peking was then the center of intellectual life, and articles in the Peking weeklies or the literary supplement of a Peking daily were often reprinted by local newspapers all over the country.

Chen San's letter was brief. But enclosed was a letter for his mother more than a thousand words long, giving an outline of his story since he had been forced into army service, describing his escape, his work with various masters and his self-education and his enrollment with the police and saying that he was now a policeman at Anking, and was earning eight dollars a month. The master of the Yao family was asked to read this to his mother if she ever came back. He further said that he was planning to resign and come up and search for his mother as soon as he could get together the necessary expenses for the journey, which would cost thirty dollars.

When Mochow and Lifu read the letter, they were much excited, and Lifu, greatly pleased with this result of his writing, at once sent forty dollars to Chen San by telegraph. They waited eagerly for his arrival, and were curious to know what this son of Chenma would be like.

"Look at his writing, in such a small even hand," said Huan-erh. "How he must have educated himself! I have seldom seen anyone able to write this small script nowadays."

Since the abolition of the imperial examinations, the writing of this small script had become almost an obsolete art. It was a type of writing that required and bred infinite patience, attention to a standard of correct strokes which is equivalent to standard spelling in

563

English, and great calmness of mind. Curiously, the writing of small script was generally encouraged among policemen, and those who wrote a beautiful hand in their daily and monthly reports received quicker promotion.

"Yet he is earning only eight dollars a month, and some of that, I suspect, is in arrears," said Lifu. "Government clerks earning forty or fifty dollars don't write as well as that. And his language is simple and clear with only a few minor errors in the use of the more literary phrases."

Chen San arrived a few days after Mrs. Yao's death, when the family was busy with mourning activities. When he was taken to see Mr. Yao, he at once went down on his knees to thank him for taking care of his mother. Mr. Yao quickly lifted him up and asked him to take a seat, but he remained standing.

He was tall and dark, with a broad forehead and a well-chiseled mouth and a good chin. He was wearing a suit converted from his police uniform, with the buttons changed and the identification labels torn off. As he could not buy a hat and could not wear the old police cap, he came with bare head, which was closely shaved. He stood perfectly erect and his shoulders were broad and strong. In his eyes and the general features of his face, he was the image of his mother. He talked with a clear Hankow accent.

"Your mother was a great woman," said Mr. Yao. "How was it you never wrote to her or sent her word?"

Chen San spoke with controlled emotion. "I did. Somehow my letters never reached her. When the Revolution was over I was in Hupeh and I sent another letter, and it came back with a note that my mother had left home and people did not know where she was. I wanted to come home, but I had no money. I thought that my mother must be dead when every letter I wrote was returned."

"We will help you to find her. Meanwhile you stay with us," said Mr. Yao.

Chen San was a man of few words, and if he felt any emotion about coming nearer to his mother, he did not show it. He was taken to Lifu's court, where Lifu and Mochow and Huan-erh were waiting to see him.

"Tell me what happened to you?" Mochow asked.

"Young Mistress, it is a long story," he said. "In the army, I carried a load of over a hundred pounds. I was quite young then, and we had to march a hundred *li* a day. . . . I have fallen sick and got well again. . . . My legs were swollen and at one time I was without food and work for seven days, ready to die on the roadside until a good village woman gave me food and shelter and saved my life. . . . When I got well, I went to Hankow to pull a rickshaw. Then luck came, and I was hired by a master to pull his private rickshaw. After a few months, the good master left the city, and I changed my masters several times until I decided to be independent and I enrolled in the police force."

"Are you married?"

"No. A poor man has no time to think of marriage," he replied. Then he asked, "Have you a picture of my mother?" and when she replied, "I am sorry we haven't," he looked greatly disappointed and was silent. Mochow had been careful not to show him at once the parcels of clothes his mother had made and left for him, lest they should grieve him too much; but now Huan-erh rose and without saying anything went into the back room and came out holding the blue cloth parcel, and went straight to him, saying, "Here are the clothes your mother made for you."

Her voice was trembling. Chen San stood puzzled and embarrassed by this well-dressed girl so close to him. She untied the knots and opened the parcel for him and looked up at him and stepped away. At the sight of the clothes his mother had made, which he had read about in the story, Chen San suddenly broke down crying like a child, so that his tears wet the clothes. Lifu and Mochow were greatly touched, and after a while Mochow managed to say, "Your mother always wanted to know where to send them to you. You ought to keep them well."

Controlling his tears, Chen San said, "I will never wear them."

They heard sobbing from the next room. Huan-erh had disappeared again. Mochow looked at Lifu surprised, but they went on to speak of other things.

"Will you work with us?" said Lifu. "We will give you leave to go and search for your mother. But you must have a place to work in. I understand you do not want to be a servant."

"I will do anything as long as I can remain here where my mother worked," said Chen San. "I shall be grateful if you will give me something to do. My mother may come back."

Lifu asked him how well he could read, for he had intended to give him some clerk's job. But at his own suggestion, Chen San became a watchman of the Garden, saying that he could handle firearms; and, in fact, he was a marksman, having won a prize at a sharp-shooters' contest in the police corps. They had never needed a watch-man, Mr. Yao said, but he consented.

Chen San went on a trip to his village and came back with the news that his mother had returned there a year ago and gone away again. Usually he had nothing to do in the daytime, and being a will-ing worker, he would come to Mochow to ask if there were any errands for him to do. Lifu gave him books to read and sometimes manuscripts to copy, but told him not to take such extraordinary pains over it as if he were doing embroidery.

Chen San never found his mother. He became very grave and solemn. He refused not only to wear the clothes his mother had made but even to wear any blue cloth material similar to them, and this he did all his life. He brought an expensive leather pillowcase, about two feet long, such as opium smokers used to carry on a journey to keep the pipe and serve as a pillow at the same time, and kept in it some of the clothes and slept on it in his bed. At night, he whipped himself to hard work, poring over the books Lifu had loaned him, when he was not on his nightly rounds, under the lamplight that had shone on his mother sewing at night, as if he were purposely punishing himself. For Huan-erh had given him the lamp his mother had had. In his little room near the entrance, he hung a two-foot tablet with a couplet, written by himself in regular, laboriously formed characters—a quotation from a well-known poem:

> *The trees desire repose, but the winds will not be still;*
> *The son wishes to serve, but his parents are no more!*
> *Respectfully written while burning incense by*
> CHEN SAN

He thought sometimes of the girl who had given him the parcel of clothing and found out after a while that she was Lifu's sister. When he met her in Mochow's court, she would speak to him, but he avoided her as much as possible. Mochow said to Lifu that Huan-erh had been quieter ever since he published the story of Chenma, and she had refused to discuss her mother's proposals for marriage, al-though she was now twenty-two and well past the marriageable age. She seemed to be often brooding with a dark, sad expression. Evidently she had taken an imaginative fancy to this mysterious son of of Chenma long before she saw him, and, now that she had seen him, she was not disappointed.

On the other hand, Chen San refused to have a flirtation even with any of the maids, as if he were a woman hater. Mochow later found out that when he had been a house servant at Hankow, he had been pursued by a maid and had resigned in order to avoid her attentions.

. ˙.

The following spring, Dimfragrance was often morose and moody. This change and certain other conditions had not escaped the sharp eyes of Mulan.

The position of Dimfragrance was something more than that of a maid. Even Cassia and Mrs. Tseng knew that Chinya had taken a fancy to her; but, Suyun being now practically no wife to him, the family had accepted the situation. It was far better than if he flirted outside the home. Dimfragrance had now through association learned all the ways of the rich daughters. She was now usually happy and contented, and sometimes Chinya thought her quite handsome. She was well dressed, except that she dared not indulge in earrings and bracelets on ordinary days and her dresses could not be so well cut as those of the mistresses, it being the custom that maids should imitate their mistresses' dress just enough to be fashionable, but not enough to suggest competition with them. The high-heeled shoes, at this time a privilege of the ladies, were never indulged in by the maidservants of the north. And Dimfragrance always wore a long-sleeved jacket to cover a red mark on her left arm which had been burnt with a hot iron by her former mistress. Through Mulan's example and influence, she had been treated and talked to almost as an equal of the sisters in the Yao home. But she still was a maid and never thought of herself as otherwise. Her hard training and experience made her at first take the more gracious, kinder, way of life with great diffidence. As she became more used to the new environment, she began to accept the normal courtesy among human beings gratefully, but as something more than her due. And she showed her delight at this social elevation by being both more desirous to please others and easier to please herself. Consequently she had never learned the finer sophistication of higher society. Being used to the last seat, she was genuinely happy to be offered the last seat but one.

Chinya's attentions flattered her especially. Since his return, Mulan had several times asked him if he had found the "mountain girl." As he grew more and more estranged from his wife, he came to like Sunya and Mulan more and more and was converted to their way of life. One day, Mulan hinted that Dimfragrance came very near to his ideal of a wife, and he took this hint seriously and began to pay the girl little attentions and found her simplicity of heart a charming contrast to his wife's character. She was long past the traditional age of marriage and should normally have been married off already. This was a problem that faced both herself and her mistress.

At last the courtship became so open that Brocade began to tease Dimfragrance about being a "mountain girl."

One day Cassia said to Mulan, "I see Chinya is very good to your Dimfragrance."

Mulan declined to comment, but asked, "Does Mother know?"

"The other day she was talking to me about it," Cassia replied. "Do you know what she said? She said, 'My poor Chinya. We should not have made that match for him. He has no one to take proper care of him. If he is serious, he should marry. Dimfragrance looks like a contented simple girl. It is better than marrying some girl outside who is a stranger to us.' The Old Person is quite reasonable about it, too."

"What about Father?"

"He doesn't know yet."

"What about Suyun? It looks very complicated," said Mulan.

"Well," said Cassia. "The proverb says, a boy grown-up must marry and a girl grown-up must wed. In my opinion, since it is started it may as well be carried through. Dimfragrance is a good girl and a good asset. Rather than let others have the advantage, let's take it ourselves. I am not saying this because I was a maid myself. But isn't a maid a human being also? I will speak to the father. If Dimfragrance should not marry a young master, then I should not have been married to him. Besides, Chinya has no son, and that argument is enough. And if Father consents, Suyun will have to obey. Who told her not to give birth to a son? But, we should keep it a secret from Suyun until the time comes."

The affair was further complicated when Dimfragrance found her own parents by sheer accident. Lost at the age of six and having gone through what were terrifying experiences for a young child, she had forgotten all about her parents and even her own family name. One day, going to the South City Amusement Park with Mulan, she passed a place which brought back her childhood memories. It was the bank of an ancient canal spanned by a stone bridge. The old trees, with low-hanging boughs stood on the bank and cast their shade over a small black-and-red door. Dimfragrance cried to her rickshaw puller to stop. She got down and looked around, her mind filled with this image of her childhood playground. She was sure she had played on this bridge as a child—she knew the stone rails and slabs so well. The low-hanging branches, the stump, the door, the doorstep, the clay relief above the lintel were all familiar. Trembling with excitement, she said to Mulan, "This is my home! I played under this tree and on that bridge. I am sure of it."

They looked at the doorplate. The family name was Shu.

"Yes, yes!" Dimfragrance exclaimed. "My father was called Mr. Shu. I remember now!"

She felt an impulse to rush in, but trembled so with excitement that she dared not. She knocked at the door, turning round and saying to Mulan, "What if it isn't?"

When the door was opened by a young servant, Dimfragrance turned away and looked at Mulan.

"Is this Shu family?" asked Mulan.

"Yes, what do you want?" The servant surveyed the two young ladies and thought them gentlefolk. "Whom do you want to see?"

"If it is the Shu family, perhaps I want to see Mr. Shu," said Dimfragrance timidly.

"Will you kindly tell him something for us?" said Mulan. "This is Miss Dimfragrance Shu. She is trying to find her parents. Will you go in and ask the master if they have lost a daughter by the name of Dimfragrance?"

The door was shut, and Dimfragrance lived a long moment of suspense.

Soon the door was opened again and out came a bent old man with a long white beard and spectacles. He looked steadily at the grown-up girl and seemed not to recognize her, nor could she recognize him.

"What is your name?" he asked.

"My name is Dimfragrance. Did you ever lose a girl by that name? It was some twenty years ago."

"How old are you?"

"I am twenty-five."

The old man thought for a while, and then said with deep emotion, "Are you my Dimfragrance?"

He hesitated and then extended his shaking arms to embrace her. "My child!" said the old man. He turned round to shout to his family, to come out. But there was no need. A young man and a young woman had rushed out to see the old man and the girl weeping together.

"This is your brother. And this is your sister-in-law," said the father. Dimfragrance greeted them as strangers.

"Where is Mother?" she asked.

"Your mother—is dead—these three years," the father said.

Mulan, standing there with her daughter Aman, was asked to go in with them, and the father led them in, still holding his daughter's hand as if afraid of losing her again.

There was a busy exchange of news, but they had been parted so long that they still talked like strangers. Realizing the situation, Mulan soon rose to take leave, saying, "I will go back now with the child. Brocade will take care of her."

"When shall I come?" asked Dimfragrance.

"You will want to celebrate this reunion," said Mulan, gently. "Can you come tomorrow and tell me all about it?"

The next day Dimfragrance came back and told Mulan about her family.

"Would you want to work with us now?" Mulan asked anxiously.

"I don't know. My home seems so strange to me now. My brother and sister-in-law seemed not pleased with my return."

"If you like, go back for ten or eight days, and see. Aman does not need so much attention now. I can look after her."

Dimfragrance went back but returned in ten days, saying that she wanted to remain with her mistress. Her mother was dead and it was not home for her any more. Her brother was the only surviving son. Her father was old, and her sister-in-law, a capable but vicious woman, was running the house and was annoyed with her.

"She is not treating my old father right," Dimfragrance said. "He wanted a big dinner that night, but she said she could not do it on such short notice. My father insisted on having at least some noodles, and she prepared it, grumbling in the kitchen. He told me secretly in tears that he had an unfilial daughter-in-law. When my brother

570

learned that I was still unmarried he looked troubled, and he said later that my marriage would cost money."

"Are your people well-to-do?" Mulan asked.

"They have some property, but my brother is controlling the money, since Father is so old. He can't see very well, and they give him what they like to eat. We maids here have better food than the masters in my home."

"What does your father say he wants with you?"

"He wants to find a good match for me."

"Will you allow him?"

"No," said Dimfragrance emphatically.

"Will you be afraid of Suyun?"

"Sometimes I think it is better to stay independent than to jump with open eyes into a hell. But if Second Master treats me well, it may be different."

So Dimfragrance remained with Mulan. Her father often came to see her, but her brother never once visited her, being glad to be rid of her so easily.

Two months afterward Mulan saw that Dimfragrance was often nervous and unwell. She suspected something and said to her, "Dimfragrance, what is the matter?"

Dimfragrance looked listless and sighed.

"Tell me, is it Chinya?"

Dimfragrance covered her face in shame and said, "Young Mistress, you must save me. I dared not refuse him."

"Did he say he would marry you?"

Dimfragrance nodded.

"What did he say?"

"He said Second Mistress was no wife to him and he was lonely. He said if I was willing, he would marry me. I was desperate, and afraid my father would make me marry someone else."

"Then it is all right. You need not be afraid of Suyun if he stands by you. *Taitai* and Mistress Chien have already discussed it. Second Mistress has borne no child, and the father will consent, when the ladies approve."

Dimfragrance raised her eyes with a look of great relief. "Young Mistress," she pleaded, "my body belongs to him now and there is no going back. You must help me. If his parents don't approve, I will end this miserable life."

571

"Have no fear," said Mulan. "I have talked with Mistress Chien already."

"I shall thank you all my life. But please keep the secret for me. Don't let anyone know, not even Brocade."

"How old is it?"

"It is a month or two," said Dimfragrance, putting her face down again.

"We must hurry," said Mulan.

· · .

Chinya's romance with Dimfragrance and the estrangement from his wife were reflected in his attitude toward his brother-in-law. He was now back in Peking, working in a Conservancy Bureau, but he had broken away from Huaiyu and his circle, much to Suyun's disappointment. Huaiyu was thrown out of office by a sudden change of events. The death of President Yuan had nullified all Inging's efforts in befriending his sixth mistress. Had Huaiyu not been away at Shansi when the monarchist movement came out in the open, he certainly would have fallen with the monarchists. When Yuan died, he publicly and privately denounced Yuan as an ambitious old man who did not know the spirit of the times and "the forces of democracy." After the Anfu clique came into power Huaiyu associated himself with Tsao, who became the Minister of Communications, and was made a councilor in the Ministry. As those were the great days for the Anfu clique, he held three or four posts concurrently and drew a combined salary of over fifteen hundred dollars a month.

Not satisfied with this, he had still greater ambitions. He saw that in such a time of chaos, the man who wielded the gun and commanded soldiers had the real power. Only by closely joining with a warlord could he become a real ruler of a province, with all the power and financial returns that this meant. As far as the ruling class was concerned, the provinces of China were still extremely "rich," that is, lucrative. Direct control of a province was better than holding a post in the Peking Government. People were seldom aware that the ruler of a distant province such as Jehol could amass a fortune running into tens of millions.

So Huaiyu and Inging set to work on a certain General Wu at Tientsin. The general was fascinated by Inging. Some said that Huaiyu had formally presented Inging to be the General's mistress, which was traditional political strategy; some said that Inging was still his wife; but it made no difference one way or the other, since Inging was openly General Wu's mistress and rode out in his car and stayed in his house for weeks. The scandal had a kind of bravado about it. And with this scandal Suyun was associated, although less conspicuously.

Now at this time, a political storm was brewing in the country, rising out of a student movement against the notorious Anfu clique.

The Anfu clique, made up of intensely active politicians, venal, intriguing, and unscrupulous, but personally pleasant and able, had filled its short rule of about two years with such a record of disgusting activities as to make its name synonymous in modern history with uttermost corruption—such as the Nishihara loans negotiated while Wang Kehmin was the Finance Minister. This is the same Wang Kehmin, whom the Japanese chose later, in 1938, to be their puppet at the head of the government in Peking. In spite of these loans, which were made in the name of some very legitimate measures of reconstruction, such as building railroads, opening mines, famine relief, plague prevention, or buying ammunition, the government was always poor. The bureaus, schools and colleges, and the diplomatic service abroad were constantly in arrears. Every loan was an excuse for establishing a new bureau to accommodate the million sons, brothers, nephews, and protégés of officials, many of whom held concurrent posts elsewhere and had not even to be present at the office.

But the "Renaissance" had now had its effect. The awakening of China's youth to political consciousness took the form of a revolt against the ruling class of Peking and the government that still proceeded upon the philosophy of "being monk for a day, strike the bell for a day"—a ruling class and a government that frankly had no authority over the country, offered no program for a way out of the political disunity and financial chaos, and, worst of all, no hope in China and no faith in themselves.

On May 4, 1919, three thousand students marched through the streets of Peking, burned down the house of Minister Tsao and beat up another pro-Japanese official, precipitated a national strike, and forced a change of government and the withdrawal of the Chinese delegation from the Versailles Conference. This date was the beginning of Young China's direct part in the political events and fortunes of the country.

The movement centered around the question of the return of

Shantung to China by Japan, who had seized Tsingtao during the World War. The Shantung question was left unsolved at the Versailles Conference as a result of the May Fourth Movement and later had to be settled at the Washington Conference of 1921. China had been doublecrossed and sold out by Great Britain and France in a secret treaty promising Japan the province of Shantung even while China herself was their "ally" and had sent a hundred thousand laborers to France during the war. But there was also a secret agreement between the Chinese Anfu Government and Japan making the same promise. A year before, when Japanese money was dropping like gold nuggets from heaven into the hands of the Anfu Government in the form of the Nishihara loans, the Japanese Foreign Minister had bound Chang, Chinese Minister at Tokyo, to agree to cede Japan's rights in Shantung. For the sake of a twenty-million-dollar loan, the Anfu Government had agreed and the Chinese Minister at Tokyo had written four words, "We agree with pleasure" to the conditions. When this was revealed at the Versailles Conference, even the Chinese delegation had nothing to say.

When the news of the betrayal was telegraphed back to China, a storm of national indignation broke over the heads of the Anfu leaders, in particular three persons, Tsao and Chang, the Minister to Tokyo, and another former Minister to Tokyo, Lu, now manager of a Sino-Japanese exchange bank.

On May 3, the news was published in Peking that Shantung had been sold to the Japanese and that the Anfu Government had telegraphed to the Chinese delegation at Versailles to accept the cession of Shantung. There had already been plans for a gigantic student demonstration to take place on the seventh, and the police were at work arresting the leaders. The arrest of a girl student, one Miss Chien, decided the leaders to change the date and convene the demonstration the very next day. At one o'clock, there gathered before Tienanmen students from thirteen colleges and other representatives carrying banners with the slogans, "Down with the Traitors!" "Demand the Return of Shantung!" "Abolish the Twenty-One Demands!" One student, Hsieh, went up to the platform and in the presence of the crowd bit off his finger and wrote with his blood on a white banner the words, "Return us Tsingtao."

But the demonstration ostensibly turned into a funeral procession for the "traitors," Tsao and Chang, for there were a pair of white cloth banners, such as used at funerals, bearing the couplet:

Selling their country for personal position, the tombstones of Tsao's descendants shall bear no words.

Flattering foreigners with determination, the heads of Chang's bastards shall have a price.

The procession had planned to go through the Legation Quarter, but negotiations for permission to enter it having failed, the crowd, balked at its object, surged toward the traitor Tsao's mansion. Tsao was at that very moment discussing further Sino-Japanese negotiations with Chang, who had been called back to become Foreign Minister. The house was rigidly guarded and the doors bolted. Some students climbed over the wall and the guards were won over by the students' patriotic appeal. The back door was opened. Tsao had already escaped, but Chang hid himself in a wooden barrel in a yard, was discovered, dragged out, recognized by his Japanese mustache and beaten. Disappointed at not finding the head traitor, the crowd smashed the doors and windows and furniture, then set fire to the house.

Mr. Fu was at this time the Minister of Education. The Ministership of Education was the "poorest" and most unwelcome of all the cabinet posts, because there was no money and plenty of student trouble, and the Anfuites had left it for someone outside their clique. When the crowd began to disperse, thirty-two students were arrested. There were rumors of their execution and of the dissolution of Peking National University. Negotiations for their release having failed, Mr. Fu offered his resignation together with fourteen college presidents, and finally the students were released.

The development of events proved to be a complete victory for the students. The movement spread quickly and the patriotic cause was taken up by Chambers of Commerce in all the important cities, so that there was a national strike. On June 10, the notorious three, Tsao, Chang, and Lu, were dismissed; and on the twenty-eighth, the Chinese delegation in Paris withdrew from the Versailles Conference.

Huaiyu went to see Tsao at the Hotel Wagons-Lits, whither the latter had escaped. In the face of the national wrath, Tsao and the others decided to take refuge in the Japanese Concession at Tientsin, and Huaiyu went with them with a purpose of his own. Suyun and Inging joined him soon afterward. Chinya asked his wife why she was going, and she answered him, "That need not be your business."

The day after Suyun left, her half-sister Taiyun came to visit Mulan. Taiyun was now a girl of seventeen and was living with her own mother and father in Peking. Amazing as it may seem, her father, old Mr. New, had at the age of sixty suddenly abandoned his wife, taken away most of his money, and, defying her, openly come back to live with Taiyun's mother, Funia, who was much younger. Taiyun herself was an ultra-radical girl, typical of the generation that grew up in the nineteen-twenties. It happens that the offspring of corrupt officials either follow the pattern of their parents, or else become complete rebels and are the most uncompromising denouncers of their parents' way of life. Inspired by the new enthusiasm, Taiyun condemned all the old official life and family life with the thoroughness and conviction of one who had revolted from the inside. As family ties were considered a "feudalistic" idea, she spoke with characteristic frankness about her father, her mother, her half-sister, her sister-in-law, and her half-brother Huaiyu. She was loyal to her father as a simple-hearted man, but she was quite willing to admit the origin of his ill-gotten wealth and to agree that he was one of the corrupt officials who ought to be shot when the revolution should come. She spoke in a coarse, unladylike voice, and wore bobbed hair and a white jacket and a short black skirt coming down barely over the knee—the regular schoolgirl dress. Mulan felt as if she were listening to an incredible family tale.

"Hah!" said Taiyun, "When my brother heard that Chang was beaten up by us students, he hid himself and bolted his door and dared not budge from the place. Next morning he was called by Tsao to see him at the hotel and he shaved off his mustache and disguised himself before he dared to go out. You know Tsao and Chang all have the Japanese *jintan* mustache. That was how some of us recognized Chang even hidden in an old barrel. When he came home, he told my sister-in-law that they might be in danger." (*Jintan* is a Japanese mint drop, bearing on its label a Japanese with his mustache.)

"Which sister-in-law? The wife or the concubine?" asked Mulan.

"Of course I mean my sister-in-law. I call the other only Inging. You should have seen how my brother stammered when he scolded me because I had taken part in the demonstration. He said there was no telling what these students might do, and they ought to move into the

Hotel Wagon-Lits for safety. You know he stammers like my father when he is excited and his large lips move up and down like a fish—our whole family has large lips, including myself. . . . Well, he stammered and spluttered and I just sat there, silently smiling and then he turned upon me and said, 'You boy and girl students who won't study and have no respect for the government!' I said, 'Of course I have no respect for a traitorous government. Do you approve that we should sell Shantung to Japan?' I tried to reason with him. 'What do you know about politics?' he said to me. 'At least I know that selling one's country is wrong. Only those with a blackened conscience approve giving Shantung to Japan.' He was still more angry at me and said, 'It's all you girl students—parading in the streets with boys, like prostitutes. No sense of shame.' I flared back at him and said, '*You* think of course that a girl parading in the streets for a patriotic cause is shameless. However, I don't come from a Tientsin whorehouse.' You should have seen how Inging's face turned, and my sister-in-law looked at me with big, surprised eyes!"

"Did you dare to say that?" Mulan asked.

"What do I have to fear? He can do nothing to me. I don't want any of his money, and I am not looking forward to being a rich lady. I will earn my own living. I never cared for Inging anyway; I call her by name only because I refuse to call her sister-in-law, and it is she that is afraid of me."

"What do you know about this story of Inging and General Wu? Is it true?" Mulan asked.

"Hah!" Taiyun replied. "They call us communists, sharing wives and husbands. It is my brother and General Wu who are communists, for they share a common woman. I don't have to keep it a secret because everybody in Tientsin and Peking knows about it. He presented Inging to General Wu as his mistress, and when General Wu does not want her then he can have her. She boasts about it. One day Huaiyu was telling her in his wife's and my presence that a friend was asking him about the affair and do you know what she said? She said, 'Let them talk. They are jealous. Lots of society women would like to be in the General's favor, but can't.' It is true—you won't believe it—he and Inging would be invited to the General's home for dinner together, and after dinner my brother would excuse himself and smilingly go away, leaving Inging with the General to play mahjong and spend the night. Last spring, she stayed in the General's house for seven or eight days. That was the beginning of it."

"Do you believe that Suyun is in it?" asked Mulan. "You can tell me the truth, between you and me. I must protect my brother-in-law's name."

"That I don't know," said Taiyun. "I know that they go everywhere together in Tientsin."

"And is your sister-in-law remaining in the city?"

"Yes, she is here, keeping the house with her children. Nobody would do her any harm."

Mulan was so amused by this rebel of the New family that she asked her to come and see her more often.

Such was the China of those days. It was impossible to say whether the older or the younger generation was more bewildering. The collapse of all values had come. The old were incompetent and corrupt, and the young were rebellious and uncouth. But the old people had lost hope in China or in themselves, while the young had a tremendous enthusiasm for the future. If the young had not the right to hope and enthusiasm, who had? Having thrown everything overboard, they seemed raw and unmannered. Cultured they certainly were not, but they had warm blood and their hearts were right.

The May fourth incident was but the beginning of a great number of student demonstrations that were to take place whenever there was an urgent national crisis and the too cold-hearted older generation in the government did things that enraged and called forth protests from the too hot-blooded youth of China. As always, the older ones complained that the younger ones would not study, and the younger ones complained that the older ones could not rule. It was in accentuated form the conflict between old and young, and the devastating cynicism of the former automatically bred rebelliousness in the latter. It was only when the Kuomintang capitalized upon this tremendous force of young patriotism and enthusiasm that the Nationalist Revolution succeeded in the overthrow of the Peking regime, later in 1927.

But it was also one of these student demonstrations that changed the life of Mulan and other characters in our story.

· ·

It was inevitable that Mulan should talk with her sister and Lifu about the scandalous story of Inging, and Taiyun also came to visit them at the Garden.

"Why does your brother do these things?" Lifu asked. "He is doing well enough."

"*He?*" said Taiyun, giving the word an accent of contempt. "These dog-officials can never be satisfied unless they make a million. The long-gown man has to depend upon the leather-belt man. He is thinking of a still greater fortune and he has to be some warlord's 'brother-in-law on the female side.'" This *"chiuyeh"* was a term of playful contempt, meaning one who sold his sister or his wife to a warlord for the sake of advancement.

"You can write," said Taiyun. "Why don't you expose him?"

"You must be careful," said Mochow to Lifu.

"I am not afraid," said Lifu. "The whole nation is indignant against that clique."

"But many Anfu people still remain in power. And he is in a way our relative," said his wife.

"You are too feudalistic," said Taiyun. "He is my half-brother, too."

"Do you really not mind?" asked Lifu.

"Mind? I will supply you with all the material."

Mulan looked on and said nothing.

"In principle these dog-officials ought to be completely exposed," said Mochow. "But you ought to make some allowance for his being a relative. You cannot use your own name. Why not let some one else do it?"

"These dog-officials will stop at nothing until some one stops them," said Lifu.

"You are a biologist. Why don't you stick to your bugs and your microscope?" said his wife.

"My bugs?" replied Lifu. "I know only two types of bugs. Type A: one who is already some warlord's brother-in-law; Type B: one who aspires to become some warlord's brother-in-law and hasn't succeeded yet. Those are my bugs—the parasites that are eating up China."

"Lifu," said Mulan, "you have seen little and therefore wondered much. Heavens knows that such parasites are everywhere. You know of the great man who received a decoration from the French Government for promoting Oriental and Occidental culture, and who owed his rise to his presenting a concubine to President Yuan?"

"But that was different," replied Lifu. "He did not present his own concubine, but merely bought the sing-song girl that he knew Yuan loved and made her his present. There is a difference. He was not quite so unashamed."

When Mochow saw that Lifu could not be stopped, they struck a compromise. Lifu was to use a pen name, giving his real name only to the editor. And the names of Huaiyu and Inging and the General were to be cleverly concealed. Inging, meaning "oriole," was to be referred to as "Yenyen" meaning "swallow"—as the two words formed an easily recognized phrase, *inging yenyen* meaning a group of prettily dressed women. Huaiyu, meaning precious stone, was changed into "Pienpo" or "Pien's stone," Pien being an ancient who discovered a big precious stone.

Lifu wrote the story and had it copied by Chen San. He imitated the style of traditional storytellers and indulged in a careful description of the voluptuous charms of Inging. It was not said whether it was fiction or was fact, but the character of Inging was easily recognizable. Huaiyu's Japanese "*jintan* mustache" came out again and again, and it was also indicated explicitly that he was an underling and associate of the traitor Tsao.

The story was published in a Peking paper and some readers guessed, while others knew, that "Yenyen" was Inging.

Curiously enough General Wu laughed over the story, when Inging showed it to him. "It is disgusting!" said Inging. "But it is very complimentary to your charms," said the General. He was secretly delighted to be pictured as a "romantic" person capable of flirting with young women at his age. "I don't see anything in it to object to. And it is only a story."

Huaiyu was the most enraged by this exposure. But he thought it awkward to take open action, as it would be tantamount to admitting himself to be the "Pienpo" of the story. He wrote to a fellow-official in Peking asking him to investigate and demand an apology from the editor—or at least an editorial statement that this was pure fiction and that no reflections were cast upon any contemporary. His friend, however, laughed at the matter and did not take serious action. The friend asked the editor the name of the contributor, and the editor, being a friend of Lifu and Mr. Fu, refused. He said that Huaiyu could bring action for libel if he insisted that he was "Pienpo." Huaiyu could not possibly do this without attracting more publicity to himself, and the editor had the tacit protection of Mr. Fu, who although he had resigned as Minister of Education, still had a number of influential friends. So Huaiyu merely smarted in futile rage and suspected that his half-sister Taiyun had had a hand in it. It was only months later that Huaiyu found out who was the author of the article, and then he swore his vengeance.

Now at this time there were a great number of "news agencies" in Peking, established for the sole purpose of drawing a monthly subsidy from some government group, doing nothing, or existing as regularized and institutionalized blackmail, and all government leaders liked to be on good terms with these agencies. Every new Japanese loan, which was rain in the Peking financial desert, benefited them because the government was careful to distribute the "grease" to all agencies. Some drew subsidies no matter from what source, even from both political sides at the same time. There was such an agency that belonged to the enemies of the Anfu group. On seeing Lifu's story, the agency saw a chance to deal a heavy blow at the Tsao-Chang group and printed a parallel story with the real names of Huaiyu and Inging, but referring merely to a "certain" General. Huaiyu's friend in Peking heard of the story beforehand, as it had become a topic of popular dinner gossip, and tried to bribe the agency, but the bribe was refused.

The whole story came out in many papers in Peking the next day. In the story, Huaiyu's sister Suyun was three times mentioned in a disreputable role. The General was really angry this time, and was persuaded to take action. No good could come of magnifying the incident, but some measure of punishment had to be taken to gratify their sense of vengeance and increase the "face" of the General. The General could not ask Tuan to act directly, because he was of the "Manchurian group," and this group and the Chihli group of generals were now combining in a move against Tuan's Anhwei group of generals. But he wrote a private letter to Wu, the Peking Commissioner of Police, to have the news agency closed. Wu was a close ally of the Anfuites and took action. The news agency was closed down, but it did the editor no harm, for he immediately started another agency under a new name. The only net result was that the Peking gossipers had fresh material to talk about, and the affair of Inging became a national scandal.

Suyun's implication in the scandal had more immediate effects. Taiyun came and told how her father felt on reading the story.

"He was reading the newspaper and his face got whiter and whiter as he read. I was sitting with my mother in the same room, for we had just had our breakfast and had read it before him, so I knew all about it already. 'Here is another paper with the same story, Father,' I said. He didn't want to read it, and threw down the paper with a guttural groan. 'Look at what your brother and sister have done! How embarrassing it is for our family! It's Inging's work, not Huaiyu's, I know.' He saw me smiling and stared at me. 'You little blackguard,' he said, 'what are you smiling at?' I said, 'Father, we must also consider ourselves. My brother's working with the traitor Tsao is no honor, either.' 'How do you know Tsao is a traitor?' he asked. 'If the whole country calls him a traitor, then he is a traitor,' I said. My father looked sternly at me and would say no more. I tried to humor him and said, 'Your children are not all bad. Father, would you approve if I should become a warlord's mistress?' He looked at me in surprise and said, 'No, why?' And I answered, 'I was just joking. You always said that my brother and sister are like their mother.' 'Yes,' he said. 'It is all that old woman's seed. I have nothing to do with it.' He hates the mother of Huaiyu and Suyun. And he went on to berate his old wife, and my mother and I sat still, listening to his detractions against my other mother. Of course my own mother was secretly pleased."

The affair affected Chinya more closely, and directly involved the Tseng name.

"Who wrote that story?" Chinya came to ask Sunya and Mulan.

"Who knows?" said Sunya, and Mulan kept quiet. Dimfragrance also knew about the author, but said nothing.

"I think it was Lifu who wrote it," said Chinya.

Mulan asked, "What makes you think so?"

"I just felt it. He always hated Huaiyu."

"Even if it was he, there was nothing in his story about Second Sister-in-law," said Mulan.

"Don't be afraid," said Chinya. "I will have nothing to do with her from now on. I am thinking of publishing an item in the newspapers, breaking off all relationships with her." He cast a glance at Dimfragrance, who looked up with an expression of triumph that she could not conceal. But Sunya said, "Second Brother, for a step of this kind you have to obtain Father's consent. We are trying very hard to keep this from him. We don't know what he will do when he hears of it. He is so ill."

"That is very difficult," said Mulan. "If he knows that the name of our family is involved, he will probably disown Suyun entirely, as you

582

want to do. On the other hand, he is so weak now that it may hasten his end. Yet if we don't let him know and he finds out about it later, he will blame us, because it concerns the reputation of the family."

"This step has to be taken sooner or later," said Chinya. "If I don't wash my hands of that woman, she will drag me through worse yet. How am I going to face my colleagues when I go to the office? I will divorce her and marry Dimfragrance and not let her be a concubine."

When Dimfragrance heard this she walked out of the room, and Mulan remembered that this marriage must not be long delayed.

"Dimfragrance is also some one's daughter," said Mulan, "and you must marry her properly. In my opinion, you should consult mother and Cassia about it."

Chinya went to his mother and said that he wanted to take Dimfragrance as his wife and was determined to be divorced from Suyun. Mrs. Tseng knew the shame that had been brought upon the family by Suyun's exposure, and she suspected that probably something had happened to Dimfragrance, although Mulan had not yet told her the truth. She thought she might be saving the family a double scandal, and she and Cassia decided to let their husband know about the matter.

Mr. Tseng was at this time very much confined to his bed. Strange to say, the weak Mrs. Tseng was surviving old age better than her husband. Cassia prepared the ground by suggesting that Chinya had no son, and Mr. Tseng seemed disposed to consider some such question.

When Mrs. Tseng went in with Chinya, she said, "I think our Number Two is suffering very much and has no one to attend to his comforts. And the second daughter-in-law also bears no child."

"What do you propose?" asked old Tseng.

"Mulan has a maid, Dimfragrance," said his wife. "We grown-ups have observed her and have seen that she is a suitable girl, without 'strange features' on her face. She will make a good wife to Chinya, and he has consented, too."

Chinya remained silent, relying upon the women to speak for him.

"Then take her," said the father. "Has Suyun consented?"

"Father," said Chinya. "If I marry Dimfragrance, I want to marry her as wife. She is not just a maid. She has found her parents and they are well-to-do. . . . I want a divorce from Suyun."

"Why?" asked the father. "What if the New family won't agree?"

"They must agree."

"Why? What reasons would you give?"

Chinya looked at his mother, and she said, "We didn't like to tell you this, and you must not be disturbed. Consider her as not our relative, and it would be better for the name of our family."

"What is it?" demanded the father.

"We have tried to keep this to ourselves, but it is of no use. Now the sooner we separate ourselves from her, the better it is for our family and for our son. The New family cannot object now, because the story is already in the newspapers."

Mr. Tseng's face turned, and the veins in his temples were swollen. "I knew it," he said. "It is her going with that sing-song girl. What story is in the papers?"

Chinya told his father as softly and briefly as he could the story as it had been published. The father demanded to see the paper, which Chinya handed to him, and his hands shook with infirmity and rage as he pored over the story through his crystal spectacles.

"The New family whore!" he snorted. "What evil luck that the clean name of our family should be blackened with hers! Divorce her without doubt! Just publish an advertisement in the papers. Don't trouble about the New family." After a while, he added. "Chinya, you'd better say that you have had nothing to do with her for years. Put it one, two, three years back. Say that we have had nothing to do with the New family for years. Clear your own name and clear your parents'. No, wait a minute! The advertisement will be in my own name. Bring pen and paper."

There before his wife and Cassia, the father dictated an advertisement announcing his son's permanent separation from Suyun. Then he reflected again and also dictated a letter to old Mr. New, the father of Suyun, calling himself a scoundrel for taking the step, but saying that he could not possibly suffer the "clean, white family name of the Tsengs to be smirched," and praying for his indulgence.

His anger spent, he lay panting and exhausted.

"Chinya," he said to his son, "we have made you suffer by this wrong match. But we never knew that it would be as bad as this. We will now do well by you. Bring Dimfragrance here to let me look at her. We must not make a mistake a second time."

Snow Blossom, listening in the outside room, had heard all the news, and when she heard this she ran herself to congratulate Dimfragrance and to bring her to see the master.

584

Dimfragrance came, followed by Mulan and Sunya. She made a bow to Mr. Tseng and stood with her face cast down while the old master looked at her.

"Can you sew and cook?" said the old master.

"Yes, *Laoyeh*," replied Dimfragrance.

"Can you read and write?"

Dimfragrance blushed and remained silent.

"She has read the Hundred Family Names, and can write the names of all fruits and vegetables," said Mulan.

"Can you faithfully serve my son, taking care of his food and clothing?"

Dimfragrance was too shy to reply to such a question and bent her head further down. But Mr. Tseng thought such shyness and modesty the best answer on the part of a girl. After looking at her lowered face for a moment, he said briefly: "I consent."

"Quickly go down on your knees and kowtow thanks to Old Master," said Cassia.

Dimfragrance went down on her knees and kowtowed on the ground three times.

"You should kowtow to Old Mistress, too," said Cassia.

And Dimfragrance again went down on her knees and kowtowed to Chinya's mother and was then led out of the room by Cassia.

The advertisement was published in the newspapers the next day and a go-between was sent to make formal arrangements with Dimfragrance's father.

It was said to Dimfragrance's father that the bridegroom's father was very ill and wished to see the wedding immediately, the next week. Her brother and sister-in-law, hearing that she was to be a regular daughter-in-law of the Tseng family, were now extremely cordial to her and most anxious to do everything to please her.

Chinya and Dimfragrance were very happy and the next day came to see Mulan and thanked her for her help. This happiness made Dimfragrance beautiful.

"Well," said Mulan, "you are my superior now. You must call me Mulan."

"How can I say it?" said Dimfragrance. "You are older than I. Let me call you elder sister."

"But I have to call you second sister-in-law."

"Don't do that," said Sunya. "Call each other by name, like sisters."

585

"I will call her elder sister; she will call me by name," said Dimfragrance. "It does seem strange. When you first found me at Shantung, I was willing to call you my parent. How strange my life has been! It seems that other people's lives just flow on like a river. Mine goes by sudden leaps and turns like a 'nine-dragon waterfall.' The changes are too fast and unexpected."

"A good person is protected by Heaven," said Mulan. "I have a suggestion. Now that you are a young mistress, you don't have to wear a long-sleeved jacket to hide that mark on your arm. It ought to remind you of your present good luck and make you happier."

But Dimfragrance continued to wear jackets with long sleeves. Chinya loved her and was tender toward her particularly for her past sufferings, and the red mark became for him a symbol of her hard days and he often kissed it. He, too, liked to keep it a precious secret, seen and touched by himself only.

In return, Dimfragrance often smoothed away the knitted lines on Chinya's forehead. These contracted lines had been formed in his last years of unhappy marriage. And by the magic of love, Dimfragrance made them disappear after a time.

CHAPTER XXXVI

ON THE day after his advertisement was published, Mr. Tseng received a letter from old Mr. New, which was more softly worded than he had expected. Of course he could not have taken such strong action if old New were in power, but even now he had expected some difficulties or unpleasantness from Suyun's family. To his surprise and comfort, Mr. New's letter said that his unworthy daughter was to blame for bringing shame upon the two families, but merely mentioned that he might have privately arranged for the separation without publicizing it in the papers. For this made him lose face. Mr. Tseng was so satisfied with the mildness of the letter that he dictated a most polite reply, saying that were it not for the fact that Suyun's story had already been publicized and it had become necessary to clear his family reputation, he would not have published the advertisement and offered his regrets and begged forgiveness.

A harsher letter came from Huaiyu a few days later, enclosing a clipping from a Tientsin paper which was an advertisement on the part of New Suyun, saying in effect that she had been hated by her parents-in-law since entering the Tseng family on account of her natural barrenness, and had been badly treated by her husband's family, that she had been practically living on her own money, and that therefore she desired nothing better than a divorce. This made it appear that it was she who did not want to live with her husband and publicly re-established the balance of face between the two parties. Actually, Suyun was furiously angry at the Tsengs' advertisement, which she regarded as a public insult. But she was persuaded by Inging to regard the matter in a different light. She was told that a woman nowadays did not suffer loss of face from a divorce, that it was senseless for her to keep on with her husband for the sake of social standing, and that she would gain much more freedom through a regular divorce. She acquiesced and the counter-statement was published.

Huaiyu's letter began by defending his sister, saying that no credence could be placed in cheap, irresponsible, and prejudiced newspaper stories. His sister was blameless in her conduct and, of all people, her husband's family should be the last to believe in such inspired rumor. Instead of helping to counteract the worthless rumor, the Tseng family had lent it direct support by announcing the separation just at this moment. He said that there was no justice in this present world of terrible moral chaos, that people turned black into white and white into black. He would refrain from defending his own case. Human nature was mean, but he did not quite expect them to throw a stone after a man fallen into a well. Yes, he would meekly swallow the insult, because he could search his heart without guilt and face heaven without shame. But a day might come when even a dumb roof tile would turn, and he swore that the Tsengs would be the mortal enemies of the News. They might meet again!

The letter made Mr. Tseng still more angry, but he left it unanswered.

From now on, Suyun adjusted herself completely to the new circles of her brother, and Inging remained for years attached to Chin, the stockbroker, though she never married him. Huaiyu became the confidential secretary and right-hand man of General Wu and advised on all moves of the really simple-hearted General. He and his mistress and sister soon left with the General for Manchuria, and did not come back to Tientsin until 1924, with the entrance of Manchurian troops inside the Great Wall.

Huaiyu had in fact abandoned his wife and five children. Taiyun greatly sympathized with Huaiyu's wife and persuaded her mother to take them in to live with them. Old Mr. New loved his grandsons and was very fond of them, and only then did Huaiyu's children begin a normal happy child life. Two years later, old Mrs. New committed suicide by drinking foreign "Lysol," a poor, deserted woman living alone in a small Tientsin alley house. Huaiyu and Suyun were then in Manchuria, and only old Mr. New, Huaiyu's wife and the grandsons came to her funeral. So passed the once powerful Grandma Horse—once the terror of Peking.

∴

Mr. Tseng was considerably shaken by Suyun's exposure and the divorce. After the insolent letter of Huaiyu, to which he had disdained to reply, he cursed Suyun and her brother for days, so that his wife began to suggest that he should have written a reply and got it out of his system, rather than show his temper at home, which would not hurt Huaiyu because he could not know it. But Mr. Tseng suddenly grew worse, and one morning he suffered a stroke. Everybody forgot all about the letter. After his partial recovery from the stroke, the wedding ceremony of Chinya and Dimfragrance was performed before his bed in the presence of a small company of gathered relatives, the bride and groom bowing to the parents on both sides and then to each other, while the other entertainments took place outside in the mansion. The ceremonies were simpler because this was Chinya's second marriage, being known as "re-stringing" (of a violin).

But during the dinner, the mother was the happiest of all, as if this second marriage of her son was the making up of a wrong she had felt and thought about for a long time. Consequently she was the leading spirit of the occasion. Yet she, too, had aged considerably. She still dressed herself neatly, and decently as a woman of fifty should, and her hair was three-fourths a whitish gray. She was a small and beautiful figure to see that day.

What made her happiest was that now she had three daughters-in-law whom she liked, and who seemed to be able to get along with each other, which was so important in a home. After the wedding dinner, Cassia said at the women's table:

"I have never seen a house like this. Three daughters-in-law come into a family like a domestic horse luring wild horses into the fold. The eldest lured the third, and the third lured the second."

The company laughed, and Dimfragrance's brother's wife, looking rather frightened and out of place, giggled.

"Yes," said Mannia, "had it not been for me, Mulan might have flown away. My fast legs caught her."

"No," said the mother-in-law. "Don't take all the credit to yourself. Mulan was discovered by your father."

"No one can deny that it was I who discovered Dimfragrance," said Mulan contentedly.

"Since it is so," said the happy mother-in-law, "you ought to be like sisters to one another. I have an idea. Number Three and Number One have called each other sister since childhood. You might as well all pledge each other as sisters. Mannia, being the oldest, will be the first, Mulan the second, and Dimfragrance, being the youngest, will be the third, although she is the second daughter-in-law. Dispense with the address 'sister-in-law.' "

A proposal like this could not be objected to, when the mother-in-law herself made it. And so Cassia left her seat to pour the wine herself for all to drink and celebrate the pledge of the three daughters-in-law to remain in harmony for life.

Mrs. Tseng got slightly drunk that day.

Mulan's need of feminine friendship was thus filled. Only Brocade was slightly soured by Dimfragrance's sudden promotion, but she contented herself by saying that everybody had her destiny fixed at birth.

Mr. Tseng survived the wedding barely two months. His urine trouble got worse again, and he steadily grew weaker and lay gasping in his bed.

Shortly before he died, he called his sons and daughters and daughters-in-law to his presence and said to them:

"I shall not live long now. After I die, you must continue to live in peace and harmony and obey your mother as you are doing now. Cut down the servants, marry off the older maidservants, and do not try to live on the old standard of luxury. Give me a proper, suitable burial, but do not be extravagant. Keep the house as long as your mother is living, but you can sell it afterward. Times have so changed. Nowadays, you have to hire servants and the wages alone of so many servants in such a house will come to over a hundred a month. And don't forget the principle of 'men attending to the outside and women attending to the inside' of the house. Without co-operation and division of labor, no family can prosper. Mannia, you are the oldest and should be the example; but, Mulan, you are the ablest and should help to shoulder the responsibility for all. Ailien, you are well married and you give me no cause for worry. Lilien, you believe in free marriage and want to select your own husband. I warn you, do not make a mistake, as so many modern girls are doing by falling in love with charming fools or by not marrying at all. Listen to your mother and let us grown-ups make a choice for you, and you will have nothing to regret. . . . These are hard times and the country is in chaos, and you, my sons and daughters, should be very prudent and not get yourselves into trouble. We have had more wars in these ten years under the Republic than in the previous hundred years under the Empire. There will be worse chaos still. . . ."

590

He wanted to say more, but stopped through sheer exhaustion and merely added, "Be careful in everything."

Then he called for his grandsons and blessed Asuan and Atung, the boys, and Aman, the girl. He lay back, stretching out two fingers as if to say that there were only two grandsons after all these years. It was meager consolation for an old man departing from this world.

Then Cassia bent down and whispered to him that Dimfragrance had "happiness" in her body. And the old man smiled and drew his last breath.

There were two reasons advanced for his premature death. Cassia's theory was that Suyun's exposure greatly hastened it, for he had his stroke the third morning after receiving Huaiyu's letter, and he had been seen poring over the newspaper story again and again. Another theory was that the completion of Chinya's second marriage had left him with a sense of satisfaction and readiness to leave this earthly life.

The funeral was a grand affair. Elaborate preparations were made and long notices were given, for the children, out of the loyalty of their hearts, wished to spend a great deal in honor of their father in spite of what he had advised. He was a righteous man and true, self-controlled by discipline and culture. The fact that he had made only a hundred thousand dollars after a life of distinguished career as vice-minister, vice-director, and in other offices, was generally taken as sufficient proof of his integrity, in contrast to some minor Republican officials who could have made that amount in six months. Moreover, the children felt that he had been sad in the last part of his life and had made sacrifices all his life for the good of the family. Condolences from his old colleagues poured in from remote parts of the country, and the Shantung Guild went into great activity. All the old paraphernalia of mandarin authority and ceremony were brought out again and he was buried in his mandarin cap, beads, belt, boots, and gown.

. . .

Mulan went into double mourning because her own mother and her father-in-law had died almost within a year of each other. But nature has its laws of compensation and provides for birth and death in appropriate measure. Contrary to orthodox Confucianism, Mulan conceived in the very month following Mr. Tseng's death, so that the following year her baby came five months after Dimfragrance's. There was a doctrinaire Confucianist centuries ago who entered in his diary an item of confession and self-reprobation for having "sexual union once with wife last night" during the period of severe mourning for his parent. While modern Chinese society had ceased to regard such fine points, Mrs. Tseng was enough of a Confucianist to be secretly scandalized by the two successive births of her daughters-in-law. Moreover, Dimfragrance's baby was born seven months after her marriage, although it being very small, nobody could say anything openly. But more grandchildren were great additions to the family, and Dimfragrance had given birth to a boy, and Mulan had given birth to a girl; and these were signs of life and growth in the family. So in spite of her Confucian conscience, Mrs. Tseng was truly pleased.

What with the death of Redjade and Mrs. Yao and the departure of Mr. Yao to an unknown monastery somewhere in the mountains, the Garden was now seldom a place of youthful merrymaking. Somehow the unnamed club of young people was forgotten by its members and broke up when the fortuitous conjunction of a group of carefree youth no longer occurred. The old had passed away and the young had dispersed or become married. The sisters felt a strange sadness and a sense of sober responsibility. Redjade was dead; Afei and Paofen were married and gone abroad; Paku and Sutan were married and since the sisters were in mourning, seldom visited them now, but started club activities of their own. The old writer Lin had gone south. Miss Donahue still occasionally visited them. Sometimes the painter Chi brought messages from Mrs. Hua at the shop, as he was a man of leisure and loved to sit in the Garden. Mannia had developed an ailment in her breast, but she refused to have any doctor, Chinese or Western, examine her; luckily she was cured in time by a secret ointment made of certain herbs recommended by Mulan's country aunt.

Lifu began to write more and more articles on current politics. Apart from one long, thoughtful article on *Science and Taoism*—developed from a favorite theme of his father-in-law's—he wrote only on current questions. Miss Donahue promised to translate the article into English, but she never finished it. It was a kind of scientific mysticism, based on his sense of the mysteries of life as gained from his intimate biologic studies. He wrote also a short sketch on *Feeling in Plants,* which revised the conventional notion of "feeling" and "consciousness" and extended it to cover a sense of perception of the surroundings common to all animals and plants, such as the definite evidence that the ants feel a coming storm. Conscious life, he showed, certainly was not peculiar to the human being. He also broadened the definition of "language" as merely an expression of feeling of whatever kind, so that he came to believe literally in the "smile" of a flower and the "bitter sigh" of an autumn forest. He spoke of the "pain" of a tree when we break off its branches or strip its bark. The tree would feel the breaking off of a branch as an "injury" and the stripping of its bark an "insult," a "disgrace," a "slap in its face." The tree sees, hears, touches, smells, eats, digests, and discharges differently from human beings, but no less effectively for its biologic purposes; it feels the movements of light, sound, warmth, and air and is "happy" or "unhappy" as it gets or fails to get sunshine or rain. This was all consistent with his Taoistic mysticism, derived from Chuangtse. Then he turned about and belittled human arrogance and its assumption of human monopoly of "feeling," "sentiment," "consciousness," and "language." This was a short sketch, which might have been developed into a fuller philosophic treatise but he never came to do it.

It was a kind of scientific pantheism. Chuangtse wrote: "The Tao is in the ants, it is in the weeds, it is in the broken bricks, it is in the excrements." Lifu told his wife that on the first day of childbirth a mother secretes a yellow antiseptic fluid in her breast to protect the baby. "Call it God, or Tao, or the Way. It is there in the mother's breast. And do not think that such mysteries are found only in the human being. The lowest form of life possesses that instinct for perfect adjustment. Bacteria make use of chemical knowledge that baffles the most advanced chemist, and do it simply, perfectly, and infallibly. The silkworm still produces the best silk, while man sells it for money; the spider still produces the only waterproof, weatherproof, solid glue; the firefly still produces the most efficient light. That is what Chuangtse meant when he said that the Tao is in the ants."

Mochow also came to know something of chromosomes, hormones, and enzymes from her husband's constant talking about them. But his scientific background was reflected in his attitude toward politics also. Intimate scientific knowledge bred in him such a deep admiration of the West that he was naturally progressive in his political viewpoint. This showed in his impatience with the Tuan Government in general and with the ruthless and thoroughly corrupt Anfu politicians in particular.

Mulan often came to visit them to discuss the affairs of business, such as a general retrenchment, consolidation of cash, the effect of floods on tea and medicine supplies in stricken districts. Mochow took a more active part in the business than her father had done and gave parties to the shop employees at festival times, which her father seldom thought of. Lifu suggested the idea of bottling and selling certain well-known tonics like Western patent medicines; but Mulan opposed this, thinking it ridiculous to change their sales method. The people were so used to the familiar look of old herbs that they would not take abstract, unrecognizable pills. Imagine buyers of ginseng no longer able to examine the grain and color and shape of a ginseng root! To sell the ginseng extract would mean converting and convincing the public all over by large-scale advertisements and a completely changed staff, and good-by to the old, smoked signboards, and well-known, well-loved woodblock printed labels, and the fragrance of the medicine shop and the clang of mortar and pestle! Why should they want to sell more tea and medicine than they were already selling anyway? Lifu dropped the subject, because he was not seriously interested in it. It was merely one of his "ideas."

But with the frequent visits of Taiyun, the little group often talked also of current politics. Lifu's own uncle, learning that he was now well off, began to write letters to him asking for money, and sent a son to Peking to be educated at his expense. As Mochow's parents were gone, Lifu came to be less of an "external relative" at the Yao Garden and his cousin was installed in one of the rooms.

This group became active in the student movement. The youth of China in general was in a spirit of revolt against the politically bankrupt Peking government. There was a general conviction that a third revolution was necessary to sweep aside the warlords and give China a really modern government. The Kuomintang party offered a complete program for China's reconstruction and attracted the politically conscious college students. Peking University remained the center of radicalism, and was therefore much hated by the Government. Some of the professors were members of the Kuomintang, and one or two were acknowledged communists. A change was noticeable in the newspapers and periodicals, from a rather amorphous reformism and a vague enthusiasm for everything Western, to serious discussions of social and political problems. More and more strange foreign terms were used. Opinion tended to be more radical. The young and active students joined the Kuomintang or the communists. They criticized the acts of the government openly and defiantly, and the government, conscious of its own weakness and of the strength of public opinion, tolerated them, except that once in a while some public official would make a commencement speech, calling all the youth who did not like what the government was doing "communists" and "agents of the Soviet Republic." Kuomintang members were denounced as "reds" and "dangerous thinkers."

Into this political current were swept Lifu, Mulan, Taiyun, Huan-erh, and Lifu's cousin, and to a less extent, Mochow. Sunya, when he was present, was likely to "sprinkle cold water" on their hot discussions by his wayward, facetious remarks, while Mochow often combined with him to restrain them, and the two were labeled "conseratives." Mochow would often say, "What good will that do?" Huan-erh, a dark and usually silent girl, by no means missed the political consciousness of her generation and often surprised them by her new ideas.

Lifu's colleagues and friends began to visit him at his home, and sometimes meetings were held in the Garden. This group, with its new political consciousness, was as different from the group in the Garden before Redjade's death as it was from the club of artist-aesthetes that Paku and Sutan were starting. Chen San, promoted by Lifu as a kind of domestic secretary in charge of accounts, but still keeping up his duties as watchman by going the round of the Garden once before going to bed, would also appear at the meetings and would be asked to take notes. Huan-erh, having been repulsed in her advances to Chen San, would sometimes argue with him violently and take the opposite point of view on whatever question, with a strange vehemence. Her mother had wanted to marry her off, but Lifu told her that it could not be done with Huan-erh, and that nowadays there was no hurry for a girl to marry even when she was long past twenty. However, there came a time when Lifu noticed a change. The two began to agree on most things, Huan-erh ceasing to take exceptions to what Chen San said and he seeming inclined to approve of what she proposed. He was outwardly still his silent self—seemingly remote from all romantic entanglement. However, he had come to respect Huan-erh. It happened like this:

One day she gave him a book and asked him why he was so silent.

"People are situated differently," was his short reply.

"I understand," said Huan-erh. "I know how I would feel if . . . You know we are all very devoted to your mother."

Chen San never talked to anyone about his mother and remained silent.

"You know she felt and acted as if she were in her own home when she was here, and we want you to feel the same," continued Huan-erh.

She bent her head, for she had suddenly spoken with some emotion, against her own will.

"I thank you, *hsiaochieh,* and I must also thank your brother and mother," said Chen San. "Please do not mind my bad manners. I am used to being alone, for I have been living by myself without a relative in this world, ever since I was forced into the army and separated from my mother. Of course I look at the world in a different way from you."

"You do not know," said Huan-erh, "that your mother was different from you. She was alone, too, but she talked with all of us. She was very good to me, and took care of me as if I were her own child."

Chen San was interested by this and began to ask what his mother did in the home and how she lived. Huan-erh told him how his mother looked after her sister-in-law and her mother, exaggerating a little as to how often she and his mother had talked together, morning and night. "You might do the same, and feel quite as much at home here, you know," she continued. "If you have things to mend, you can send them here, and our women servants will do it for you."

"How dare I? I am only an employee. I would not dare to presume."

"That depends upon how you interpret courtesy," replied the girl. "You know you did not even thank me for giving you the dresses your mother left for you."

He looked at her and recalled the first time he saw this well-dressed girl handing him the parcel, her eyes dimmed and her voice shaking. It seemed to him that her attachment to his mother was genuine.

"What do you intend to do for the future?" she asked suddenly.

"Well, I am a watchman. Without help, what can I do?" he said.

"I know you are a filial son," she said with a serious face. "Your one ambition in life is to repay your mother's debt. But the real way of repaying obligations towards one's parents is to become a good man and rise in society, to the glory of the ancestors. You cannot do this by shutting yourself away from human society and sulking."

When Chen San went back with the book to his own room, he began to think seriously of this girl and what she said. He had no idea that he, a watchman, could have anything to do with the master's sister. But he heard, at the informal meeting of the group, mixed with talks on politics, rambling discussions on ideas about marriage. Most of them tended to think that a marriage ceremony was superfluous, since marriage was based on love. Huan-erh expressed the opinion that a marriage certificate was useful only for purposes of litigation and was therefore unnecessary.

"That is nothing new," said Lifu. "You remember how the painter Cheng Panchiao married off his daughter. One day after supper he took his daughter for a walk and went with her to a neighboring village to visit his friend. There he said to his daughter, 'This is my friend's son. You remain here for the night and be a good daughter-in-law.' Saying this, he took his cane and went home alone."

"All marriage ceremonies are feudalistic," said Taiyun.

Lifu became known as a "communist," or at least an ultra-radical with dangerous ideas, through a strange incident in connection with his sister.

Early one afternoon he asked his sister to go out with him to the Western Hills, saying that the day was beautiful and he wanted an outing, and he bade Chen San go with them to keep them company. They went to a temple in a grove high on a hill and waited until sunset, and then went for a stroll above the temple. It was late April and there was a glorious evening sky. Stopping at the beginning of an ascending forest walk, surrounded by tall pines, he said to them, "Huan-erh, Chen San, I want you to be man and wife. We will dispense with all ceremonies. The trees and birds and clouds and myself will be your witnesses. Go up the aisle of pine trees to the pavilion on top against that beautiful sunset sky and kiss each other and you will have the most dignified and beautiful marriage ceremony that man and woman ever had. There is a room at the temple which I have reserved for you."

"Brother!" said Huan-erh, her dark eyes wide open and staring.

"Do as I say," said Lifu.

"What will Mother say?"

"I thought you were modern," said Lifu. "You said you didn't believe in wedding ceremonies. Do as I say. I know you two love each other."

597

Huan-erh, who had been from childhood hypnotized by her brother, obeyed.

Chen San, completely taken by surprise and confused, merely muttered, "I am unworthy," again and again. But he also dared not disobey. Lifu took his hand and joined it with his sister's and said, "Now, I wish you two luck."

Shyly Huan-erh left her hand in Chen San's and walked up the forest aisle with him. Lifu stood watching them until they came out of the trees and their figures were silhouetted against the evening sky. They stopped under the pavilion. He saw Chen San pause and put his arms around Huan-erh and kiss her lowered face. Lifu thought that if she had turned her face up toward Chen San's, the wedding ceremony would have been perfect as he had conceived it.

It was a wedding in harmony with his Taoistic naturalism—a denial of civilization, a return to simplicity, and a rejection of ritualism, carried to somewhat absurd but logical limits.

When Chen San and Huan-erh came down they could not see Lifu.

"Brother!" cried Huan-erh. "Where are you?"

"Young Master!" cried Chen San.

Lifu was gone. They heard the pealing of the temple bells as they came into the back court of the temple and later learned that Lifu had given money to an acolyte to ring them as he hurried out of the Gate. And so Chen San and Huan-erh spent their wedding night in the temple on top of a hill.

Lifu had told only Mochow of his plan beforehand, but he informed his amazed mother of it when he came back late without his sister. Early next morning the "bride and bridegroom" returned to find themselves greeted with the explosions of firecrackers at the entrance. They looked rather foolish, like victims of a practical joke. Lifu and Mochow went out to meet them and led them into the parlor of his mother's court, where the mother received their ceremonial bow. The mother had insisted, amidst Lifu's great laughter, on sending a servant out early to buy some yards of red silk, and festoons were hung across the doors of Huan-erh's room on one side of the parlor and of the mother's room on the other.

The marriage was so strange that the servants told outsiders about it and the story came out in a Peking newspaper, providing excellent material for tea-house gossip. The discovery of Chenma's son had been kept a secret and had been known only to a few friends, but now the story of his return was mentioned along with that of his unusual wedding.

It was thus that Lifu came to be known as an ultra-radical, and by some as a communist. The wedding was a freakish innovation possible only in a topsy-turvy China where the radicals were now ready to go farther even than the modern West. Professor Chien had at this time denounced the family name as an outmoded anachronism, carrying with it the baneful mentality of the family system and submerging the "individual," and had therefore discarded his family name altogether and called himself "Professor Yiku" or "Doubter of the Ancients."

∴

Afei and Paofen returned from England in the autumn of 1924, having spent one year after his graduation in Paris, where Paofen learned painting. They had no child yet, but Paofen was expecting one. There was a great reunion between the brother and sisters. Afei was more attached to Sunya than to Lifu, because Sunya had been his friend from his childhood and was easygoing, while Lifu tended to be abstract and academic in his talks with him. On the second day, Paofen went back to her parents with her husband and stayed with them for three days. Then they went again to Redjade's grave—only the two of them—and were happy to see that the cypress saplings planted around the grave were growing well.

Lifu was now occupying what had been Redjade's court, directly in front of Mochow's, and was using it for his study and laboratory. Mochow had a superstition about using Redjade's court, considering it "unlucky"; but Lifu would not listen, and she yielded because it was convenient to have his study so close to her own. She had pampered her husband, encouraging him to buy the most expensive works of reference and equipment for his studies, so that he had probably the best private reference library in biology and related sciences in any home in Peking. She had given birth to another son and she forbade all servants and her babies to enter the laboratory when Lifu was at work. Regularly at eleven o'clock, she herself would bring a glass of milk and a few biscuits to him, placing them on his table and leaving again without saying a word. Whenever he worked, at night, Mochow also would not be truly asleep, for she had that faculty, peculiar to some women, of being apparently asleep and yet able to hear the slightest sound, so that Lifu would say she could "hear in her sleep."

Mochow hoped that he would devote himself entirely to the "bugs." And he did sometimes bury himself in his laboratory for weeks. But then his other interest in current events would reassert itself. Thinking that joining his political coterie was a better way of guiding him than keeping out of it, Mochow also appeared at the meetings of the group. She had secret worries and fears for her husband that she could not tell him.

Soon after his return, Afei went into Lifu's study to have a chat with him. It was littered with test tubes, microscopes, scribbled sheets, and half-open volumes lying in great confusion on a large unpainted table.

"Tell me what this war is about?" said Afei.

"Which war? Here in Peking? Or in the Southeast? Or in the South? Or Middle China? Or far out in the West? There are so many wars," replied Lifu.

"I mean this one right here in the North."

"Well, it is all sentimental," said Lifu.

"What do you mean by 'sentimental'?"

"They are fighting for a carcass which is Peking. Peking is still the seat of the 'central government' and the man controlling it can have, when he is dead, an extra four or eight words in his list of titles as enumerated in his funeral notice. There is a little extra revenue, of course, too. But not much besides. It is chiefly a war over the length of their respective funeral notices, to see which dead man shall have a longer smile from his coffin when he hears his honors being read."

"But who is fighting against whom?"

"It will confuse you if I go into the details," said Lifu and he took four articles—two pincers, a pencil, and a piece of blotting paper. He explained rather professorially, "Consider these four as representing the four military factions, and regard the second pincer as a defection or outgrowth from the first. We will call them A, B, C, and D. A, the pencil, is the Manchurian faction. B, the first pincer, is the Chihli faction. C, the blotter, is the Anfu faction; and D, the second pincer, is the Christian General's faction. In the past four or five years since you left, there have been wars among them.

"First A combined with B to fight C; then, A and B, having won the victory over C began to fight among themselves; third, while A and B were fighting a second war, D broke off from B; now, D and A are combining to fight B, with the support of C. I am afraid that

D will be successful this time, and that therefore in a short time A will combine with its present enemy B to defeat its present ally D.

"So the Anfuites went out and came back again with Tuan. Orders for their arrest were issued and then they were pardoned, a year or two afterwards. The Christian General Feng, has just returned to the capital, and now Wu will have to fight both the Manchurians in front and the Christian General at his back."

"Do you believe in the Christian General?"

"Yes! His soldiers never harass the people and they pay for what they get. Feng was ordered to fight the Manchurians; but he was very slow about going, and, when he went, he made his soldiers build roads in preparation for his quick, dramatic return to stage a coup. He has surrounded the President's residence, and the Cabinet has resigned, with the exception of Wang Kehmin, the Anfuite, who has fled and is in hiding."

The result of the war which Lifu described thus bitterly, was that the Chihli General was defeated and a part of the Manchurian army came back, and Manchurian influence began to spread inside the Great Wall. The Dog-Meat General with the big, black cigars and his Russian mistresses was in control of Shantung.

Before long Lifu was inspired to join the Kuomintang. Sun Yat-sen, founder of the Kuomintang, had come up to Peking on December 31, 1924, with the enthusiastic acclaim of the Peking populace, especially the college and school students and teachers. Tragically, he had died in a hospital a few months later. His wife, probably the greatest woman who ever lived in China, was by his side. It was impossible to account wholly for the emotional excitement of the public at Sun's funeral. The Father of the Chinese Republic was dead. Only his return to China shortly after the Revolution of 1911 had brought forth a show of public emotion comparable to the demonstration at his funeral. The widow, clad in mourning, followed his coffin, and the nation mourned with her the loss of a great leader. The old and the young were in tears as they lined the streets to watch his coffin pass. And the government was frightened by this proof of the popular strength of the Kuomintang. Deeply moved by Sun Yat-sen's funeral, Lifu joined the Kuomintang.

This demonstration was followed by the event of May 30, two months afterward, when some nationalist agitators were shot down by British police in Shanghai. The whole force of Kuomintang political, student, and labor organizations was brought into play. Students declared strikes and preached in the streets in all cities, to awaken the masses.

All school work was stopped and there were parades and meetings and pasting of slogans and preaching in the streets every day. Lifu and his whole group joined in the activities, and Lifu's laboratory was turned into a propaganda bureau, piled high with great rolls of paper to be written as placards. Even Mochow was infected with the enthusiasm. Chen San and Huan-erh went out to make speeches to the people in the streets, and Chen San rode his bicycle on all kinds of errands. Mulan did nothing important herself, but came and helped in all sorts of small ways.

The Peking University professors and writers were split into hostile camps. The question raised and debated now was the necessity or usefulness of the mass movement, or of propaganda to awaken the masses. The leaders of the Renaissance were already old-fashioned, and became reactionaries. Having accidentally started the awakening of the masses, they were now not ready to go through with it—frightened by the ghost they had conjured up themselves. With the exception of Professor Chen, the communist, they feared and hated the masses.

There was a weekly, the organ of the "gentlemen," that openly derided the movement. This group of "gentlemen," mostly graduates of British and American colleges, believed as usual in the ruling class, in their superior intelligence and in secret diplomacy, having an instinctive distrust of the masses and thinking that all would be well if national affairs were left in their hands. Their superior intelligence, unhampered by cheap emotional demonstrations of youthful hotheads, would be able to save China both from the warlords and from the imperialists—although they were not quite specific about how it was to be done. One Wusha wrote derisively of the shouting and posting of slogans, saying that after the young boy or girl student had pasted a placard on a wall, his emotion would have had an outlet and his enthusiasm would have evaporated. Another writer, a great "scientist" used to associating with warlords but otherwise a sincere good man, wrote, "Converting one hundred rickshaw pullers is not worth half as much as converting one rickshaw rider," and so drew down a storm upon his head. But he rather gloried in the public disapproval, which was a sign of his superior intelligence. This made Lifu perfectly furious and he wrote a biting article openly attacking the "scientist." There was little choice of words when Lifu was angered; he wrote just what he felt. People thought this was the old animosity between the two groups, represented by the two most widely read weeklies.

Lifu had heard with his own ears something which made him cynical. One of the writers for the rival weekly was writing editorials in a Tientsin newspaper which he thought were brave criticisms of the Anfu Government. At a party, however, his friends remarked that because of his vehement attacks on the government the prospect of his being "taken into the fold" by the government was good; and the writer himself had smiled, apparently taking it as a sincere good wish from his friends.

Lifu said to Mochow, "Those writers are prostitutes. Once in the government, they will be just like the rest. Now they are championing free speech and the free press, but they will be the first to suppress it when they are in power."

"Why are you so hot against them?" asked Mochow.

"Because they are all writing as a means to becoming officials. It is the old tradition: 'To have studied well is to be ready for office' is from the *Analects* itself. They regard it as an honor to drink at the home of a warlord, no matter who he is. They are all hanging around the doorsteps of the government, every single one of them. Like that scientist—why doesn't he stick to his science?"

"Why don't *you* stick to your laboratory?" said Mochow, teasing him.

"It is different," said Lifu. "I am not writing for blackmail. The masses must be awakened."

And he wrote an article called "Literary Prostitutes" full of clear hints as to whom he meant. Only when the article was published did Mochow see it, and she resented it.

"Don't be too prominent," she said to him. "You will single yourself out for attack, making enemies like that for no good purpose. What is the idea of offending persons?"

"I was merely writing a historical commentary on Kung Ting-an's remark about the 'Traders in benevolence and righteousness,'" Lifu defended himself.

"It is far from historical. Everybody can see that," retorted his wife.

This was the most difficult adjustment between them as husband and wife. Lifu considered himself very considerate of his wife, yet sometimes he totally disregarded her, when it concerned a thing he really meant to do. Mochow, yielding in all other points of his personal comfort and even his fantasy, would not yield an inch about this "offensive writing" of his. She was firm and clear as to what her husband should and should not write. She had a definite purpose in life—to stand guard over the welfare of this home and their two sons, and to protect Lifu against himself.

. .

Without the enthusiastic political work of the student class and the great awakening of the masses, the Nationalist Revolution of 1926-27 would not have been possible. But for the success of this Revolution, blood had to be shed and youth had to pay. It brought tragedy to Mulan's own family and suddenly and completely changed her whole life.

Dimfragrance was the last maidservant the family had bought or engaged by contract, since in the later years servants had to be hired by the month and paid monthly wages. When Dimfragrance was promoted by marriage, Mulan had taken an *amah* to help look after her children. Her youngest girl, Amei, was now only five. Atung, her son, was already twelve and, being a boy, ran about by himself a great deal. Aman, her eldest daughter, was now fifteen and growing to be almost a replica of her beautiful mother.

Aman was from childhood a thoughtful girl; in the midst of her play, she would leave the game immediately if her mother called. When Dimfragrance was married, she instinctively took over the duties of looking after her younger sister. To be a "big sister" was not only a phrase in the language, but a definite moral idea with definite duties toward one's younger brothers and sisters. She was now attending a middle school, and was dressed usually as a girl student. She was president of her class. Mulan unconsciously let Aman go through the same training that she herself had received from her mother. Tending children satisfied the natural maternal instinct of a growing girl. Furthermore there was a tie of common sex which Aman felt with her younger sister and not with her brother. So without any definite arrangement, Amei became naturally Aman's charge when she was back from school. Aman also did things to help her mother without being told. Sometimes Mulan had to send her away to play with her brother, but after a while she would return again into the room. A girl was a girl. It sometimes seemed that Mulan was partial to her son, except that she never allowed him to bully the servants or the sisters as her own mother had allowed Tijen to do.

Aman was a happy child, and she had great admiration for her mother. But she was still more fascinated by Mannia and loved to hear stories of her mother's childhood and particularly her experiences when she was with the Boxers. The most remarkable thing was that at her grandfather's funeral, Aman, then only nine years old, had surprised everyone by learning to wail at the coffin with the regular tune and intonation used by the grown-up women. This was the woman's instinct for the great solace of communal mourning, which gave one a sense of union with a social community greater than herself.

At the May thirtieth demonstrations, Aman and Mannia's son, Asuan, had taken part as students. A group brought together by Taiyun was planning a short dramatic sketch to be enacted in the streets, depicting more forcefully than placards the shooting of Chinese by the British policemen at Shanghai. What had most aroused public indignation was the order, "Shoot to kill" used by the police commander and quoted in the affidavit of the policemen, and the fact that the demonstrators had been shot in the back when they were running away. Aman was familiar with this and with slogans such as "Recover tariff autonomy!" and "Abolish extra-territoriality!" She had wanted to take part in the dramatic sketch, but Mulan had told her not to do so. Nevertheless, the group had rehearsals in one of the empty courts at the Garden, and Aman and her mother went to see them. The girl students who were to play the role of the crowd had the problem of how to weep when the police began firing and the students were shot down.

"You must do it with real tears," said Aman to one of them.

"How?" the girl student asked.

"Just before you go on the stage, cut some onions," said Aman.

It was a brilliant idea and everybody laughed and her mother was proud of her.

Such demonstrations, however, were getting to be a real nuisance to the government. There had been several clashes in the Peking streets between the students and labor demonstrators and the police. The arrests of students in demonstrations only caused greater demonstrations demanding their release. In November of that year, a crowd thousands strong had held a "grand demonstration of national revolution," demanding the resignation of the Anfu Government and declaring for a national conference such as advocated by the Kuomintang. Then it had gone, in mob fashion, to raid the houses of the Anfu leaders, many of whom, like Wang Kehmin and Liang Hungchih, were to become in 1938 Japanese puppet heads in occupied Peking and Nanking. Several times the demonstrators openly demanded the overthrow of the Anfu Government. They were able to do this under the secret protection of the Christian General's chiefs, who were in sympathy with the Kuomintang and whose troops were stationed around Peking itself. Tuan was actually ruling in Peking, with a hostile revolutionary populace under his very nose.

In March of the following year an international crisis arose out of an exchange of shots between Japanese gunboats and the Christian General's soldiers. The other factions were now combining to encircle the Christian General and oust him from Peking, as Lifu had predicted to Afei two years before. The Manchurian fleet had planned to attack Feng's troops at Tientsin, and he had laid mines and blockaded the Taku Fort. Some Japanese gunboats fired on the fort and the fort returned fire. The diplomatic body of Peking, representing eight foreign powers, sent Feng a forty-four-hour ultimatum demanding the lifting of the blockade at Taku by noon on March 18, or else "necessary measures would be taken by the navies of the powers concerned." This amounted to foreign diplomatic intervention in favor of the Manchurian forces. Japan demanded an apology from the Chinese government, the dismissal of the fort commander, and fifty-thousand dollars in damages.

On the seventeenth, there were clashes between the guards of Tuan's office and public delegates, several of whom were wounded with bayonets. Tuan and the Anfu leaders seemed to be personally angered and determined to teach the young agitators a good lesson.

On March 18, there was a mammoth meeting before the Tienanmen, with representatives from schools, colleges, labor and merchant organizations, holding tall white banners floating against the clear blue sky, demanding again tariff autonomy and a firm stand against the ultimatum of the foreign powers. A few Kuomintang professors were on the platform.

After breakfast, Aman went to school, having just finished washing her own handkerchief and put a new one in her pocket, as she did every day. Soon Mulan received a telephone call from her, saying that her school was joining in the demonstration today and that she might be late for lunch.

"Be careful," said Mulan to her daughter over the telephone.

"It is all right," said Aman. "Our principal says that the leaders have arranged with the garrison commander for protection. Good-by."

The words rang in Mulan's ears. Her daughter's voice was gay and cheerful.

At quarter past twelve, Lifu telephoned to Mulan and asked, "Is Aman taking part in the demonstration today?"

"Yes. Why?"

There was a pause. Then Lifu said, "Well, never mind," and Mulan heard the telephone click as he hung up the receiver.

Lifu had heard at the last moment from a very private source that Tuan meant business today and it would not be well for the demonstrators. Some had seen armed guards going into the cabinet office where the demonstrators were to present their demands.

Lifu dashed out of his house with Chen San. He took a rickshaw, while Chen San rode his bicycle. He told Chen San to go ahead to look for Aman and get her out of the crowd, while he himself would speak to the leaders. Arriving at Tienanmen, Lifu found that the meeting had already ended, resolutions had been passed, and the procession had passed down Hatamen street toward the cabinet office. He caught up with it at the Pailou, but those at the head had already reached the cabinet office. There were thousands of demonstrators and spectators and the streets were jammed. Lifu forsook the rickshaw and ran ahead along the broad mud sidewalk.

Reaching the entrance to the cabinet office, he pushed his way in through the thousands of students standing in the compound outside. He heard a sharp burst of rifle fire. At the sound of the shots, the students began to scream and surge toward the gates. Then out of corners sprang Tuan's own guards who had been lying in ambush. Armed with bayonets, broad swords, and knives, they blocked the gates, chopping and cutting at the students trying to escape. More firing was heard. The students had been ambushed, trapped, their retreat cut off. There was pandemonium. Lifu saw pitiful young boys and girls being cut and stabbed and trampled on the ground before him. He saw a tall, muscular guard, his jacket off, roaring with laughter as he swung the ancient weapon called "iron whip," which was made of a series of jointed blades, each seven or eight inches long,

607

and the whole about seven feet in length. As the iron whip swung, it scraped away noses, foreheads, hands, and the skin of arms. Still the crowd pressed toward that gate of death, pursued by soldiers with bayonets stabbing and thrusting at them from behind. Lifu was carried along on the border of the throng. He saw a guard swinging a heavy chain in front of him. Leaving everything to fate, he rushed on to his own possible destruction. The metal chain struck his right ankle with a stunning blow and he thought that his foot was cut off, but he pressed along, trampling over some prostrate bodies. The guards now seemed to be almost exhausted themselves and were striking at longer intervals and less heavily at that mass of human flesh, all except the swinger of that iron whip, who, as the crowd became smaller, had more room for action, and who seemed tireless, shouting rhythmically in harmony with the deathdealing rattle of his "whip," as he picked his victims one by one.

Of the crowd of about three hundred who had been able to get into the compound, forty-eight were killed on the spot, and nearly two hundred were wounded. Only a small proportion of about fifty who were luckily sandwiched in the middle and protected by the others were able to get out without injury.

Outside the gate Lifu limped a few yards and fell and got up and limped a few yards more. Wounded boys and girls were lying all about him. Hatamen street was full of awestricken spectators. There was a stream of rickshaws carrying away wounded boys and girls, their bodies and their faces bleeding. The white cloth banners that had floated gloriously in the clear blue sky were now lying on the pavement, trampled and soiled with mud and blood.

Lifu felt a sharp pain and discovered that he still had his right foot, but a stream of blood was reddening his gown and shoes and socks. He called a rickshaw and went home.

Chen San, ahead of Lifu, had reached the gate of the compound and could not get in. He was told that Aman's school group was in front, and probably inside. When he heard the shots and saw the students being attacked, he leaped on his bicycle again and rushed to inform Mulan of what was happening. It was only a short distance from the cabinet office.

The lunch table had been laid, waiting for Aman's return, and Mulan was feeding Amei. When she saw Chen San's face, the bowl dropped from her hand, before Chen opened his mouth.

"What is the matter? Are you dumb?" asked Sunya, who was in the room.

"The guards have fired on the students! I went with brother Lifu to find Aman, but I could not get in."

"Where is she?" asked Mulan.

"I don't know. It is all in great confusion there. The students are trying to get out. I am not trying to frighten you, you know, but I heard such screaming inside——."

"Come with us at once," Sunya cried. "Where is Lifu?"

They set out immediately in rickshaws, hoping to see Aman coming on her way home. When they reached the scene of the massacre, it was like a deserted battlefield. Some of the more timid shopkeepers had closed their shops. The guards, having done their noble work, had completely disappeared. A few relatives were now going inside the gate. An American professor whom Sunya recognized, was trying to find his students.

"A massacre like this," said the American, "would cause an instant revolution in any city in America."

Sunya and Mulan had no time to listen or speak. They walked among the corpses strewn around them. There were about fifteen female corpses besides the thirty or more boys. They lay or leaned against the wall in the most grotesque positions. Sunya saw one corpse sitting upon another, staring at him, and averted his eyes. Then he was startled by a body moving under two corpses. As Mulan looked at one after another of the girl bodies and saw that Aman was not among them, she began to grow hopeful.

Then she saw two new coffins lying around a bend in the yard, near a raised terrace. The authorities had been so thoughtful that they had even prepared the coffins! But two was all they were willing to provide! As she approached, she saw Aman's small body lying in one of the coffins.

Mulan cried out and fell across the coffin.

Sunya bent down to touch his daughter's face and hands. They were still warm. Someone had just lifted her into this coffin beside which she had been shot down. From one corner of her mouth flowed a stream of fresh blood. Sunya lifted the little body and sat on the ground with the body in his lap. Mulan began to wail pitifully, "O my child!"

"Is there any hope?" Mulan asked as she took the child's hands, still warm and soft.

609

Sunya opened the eyelids and they stayed open, motionless. He opened her dress. There was a bullet wound in her neck, and the inside garments were red with blood. The American professor came to them and said nothing, but bent down to look into the eye pupils and listen at the girl's heart, and shook his head and went away.

Mulan sat on the ground, wailing, "My child! My child!" her face close against the child's face, and would not move.

The principal of Aman's school came up to them and tried to say something, but words seemed useless. Another of his pupils had been killed, beside Aman. He did not know yet how many were among the injured. It seemed to him that Aman, being among the youngest, had been at the front of her school group and had been the first to be shot down.

Mulan still refused to move and clung tight to her daughter's body.

Sunya rose and told Chen San to call rickshaws to take them home. Then Sunya, his eyes dulled with sorrow, took up the dead child and the principal and Chen San lifted Mulan up, and they went home.

Mochow and Huan-erh and Coral came hurrying to Mulan and said that Lifu had come home with his ankle severely hurt, so that he could not walk and had to go to bed, and a doctor had been sent for.

That unprecedented massacre from ambush of patriotic and defenseless boys and girls shocked the nation and in exactly thirty-three days brought about the fall of Tuan's Anfu government. On April 20, Tuan resigned and the Anfu politicians went into hiding in the Japanese concession in Tientsin. But in the last days of their reign the Anfuites had left something for revolutionary China to remember them by until they should re-emerge in Peking in 1937-38, backed by Japanese bayonets.

Aman was but a little girl, unwittingly a victim of merciless murderers. But in the revolution which began only three months later, many a young patriot consciously laid down his life that there might be a reborn and regenerated China.

CHAPTER XXXVII

AFTER the first shock of her daughter's death, Mulan became very silent, not replying to questions and not even weeping. The body was laid in the ancestral temple. Mannia came over to to stay at Mulan's side. Her own son, Asuan, had not joined in the demonstration that day, for he was in the Customs College which was managed by the Maritime Customs Service, and the students were under more strict control than those in the purely Chinese colleges. Girls from Aman's school and some delegates from the general student body came to express condolences, but Mulan did not see them.

That evening, Mulan took some soup only after Sunya and Mrs. Tseng insisted, and went to bed very early. At midnight her husband and the servants heard her break out into wailing.

The next day, she did not get up. Her husband heard her mumbling incoherently in her sleep, and she had fever. Her eyes would open for a few moments to look around the room and then close again.

Fate had been kind to her ever since her childhood. She had not felt her mother's death as deeply as her sister had, perhaps because she had been married earlier and it was her sister who had served the mother during her long illness. The departure of her father had touched her more profoundly. Now for the first time, sorrow struck deep into her heart. She did not even feel resentment against those who had killed Aman. Her daughter was dead; that was the only fact that had any meaning; what had led to it was irrelevant.

Her thoughts wandered over the panorama of her childhood and later life; apparently trivial yet significant moments were focused before her in rapid, disorderly succession. She was picking flowers in the garden and Mannia was showing her how to make touch-me-nots into fingernail dye. She was cooking peanut soup in Mannia's courtyard and Mannia was embroidering shoes. Sunya came and she gave him the peanut soup and he was delighted with it. She saw the

Boxer woman, and Dimfragrance in the cell with her, and the scene when she stepped into the boat on the Grand Canal. This picture was extraordinarily vivid to her. Mrs. Tseng was sitting with her three children in the bow, and later Mr. Tseng came out to meet her in his short jacket and socks, with a water pipe in hand. She could see Sunya's broad grin and the pieces of dirty inscribed bones wrapped in a handkerchief in Mr. Tseng's hand. From bone inscriptions, her mind wandered to the collection of jade and amber animals she had loved in her childhood, and to her conversation with her father, just before their flight, about these treasures, and to that lesson about good and bad luck. If one without luck had found the buried animals, they would have been changed into little birds and flown away. But she had them still. There was the exquisite white jade dog, in crouching position, that she so loved, and the little green pig and the elephant. And the two monkeys, one looking for lice in the other's ear, and the other with its eye closed and its mouth open and its head tilted, evidently feeling tickled. For ever and ever one monkey picking the other's ear, and the other feeling tickled! Yes, they lived, they never grew old, they were immortal! Only yesterday Aman had been playing with them. Where was Aman? Was Aman *dead?* The scene was blackened out. Then against the blank darkness before her eyes the shape and color of dry brown moss became visible and she was staring at a huge tablet on which there were no words. It was the Emperor Chin's Tablet, and she was with Lifu, on top of Taishan. Why was Lifu so silent? She wanted to scrape away some of the moss from the ancient tablet, and Lifu said, "Don't!"

That moment of sunset on Taishan when she and Lifu had stood before the wordless stone, had come back to her again and again. They had been talking about eternity and survival, and she had told him that the stone survived the dynasties of emperors because it had no mortal passions. There was the life of passion, and there was the life without passion. Then the earth turned and they turned and made the revolution with the earth, and saw the sun coming up, but they were still standing before the tablet.

Then she was in the cedar grove, in the mountains with Lifu. Oh, that precious brief moment! Lifu was kicking at a stump on which she was sitting, and the forest breeze blew a wisp of hair across her forehead and she swept it back. This gesture with her hair meant something to her, but what it meant she could not tell. She was telling

Lifu how strange it was that three times she had met him in the mountains.

Sunya heard her say in her sleep, "We are now down in the valley. We are now down in the valley."

A moment later, he heard her say, "My inscribed bones! My inscribed bones!"

Sunya thought she was talking in her dreams, but her eyes opened, and she said clearly, "Give me my inscribed bones!"

Her husband went close to her, afraid that she had gone out of her mind.

"What is it you want?" he asked.

"My inscribed bones. They are there in the cabinet outside. I have not played with them for so long."

Worried, he went and brought the inscribed bones that had been part of her wedding trousseau and gave them to her.

Mulan took one of them and said, "They are so old. Four thousand years. Long before we were born."

"Yes," he said stupidly.

"I have never studied them," she said plaintively. "Will you promise to study them?"

"*Meimei*, yes, if it will please you."

"You know they tell of kings who lived so many thousand years ago."

"Are you hungry?"

"No, I am not hungry. Those kings lived, you know—they really lived and married and died."

Sunya feared again that Mulan was out of her mind; tears stood in her eyes.

"Where are my jade animals?" she said, looking blankly at him.

Sunya went again and took the whole collection and brought it to her bed, and Mulan looked intensely at them and played with them one by one.

Her fever held all that afternoon. They gave her a black pill to calm her, and a stew to cool her liver and "loosen" her pancreas, and at last at night she went into a sound sleep.

. ' .

Lifu was confined to bed and would not be able to walk for a week or more, but Mochow came to see Mulan in the afternoon.

She came again the following morning and found that after the night's sleep, Mulan's fever had gone, but she would not talk much. She still spoke of distant things and was not interested in the immediate present. Asked when she would like to have the funeral, she said simply, "As soon as the preparations are ready."

"The student groups would like to know and are preparing to send hundreds of delegates to the funeral," said Mochow.

Only then did Mulan speak sharply. "They want to make a hero of my dead daughter? No, Aman is mine, and I will have no outsiders at her funeral. . . . Sister, you should learn a lesson from this experience of mine. Never allow your children to take part in public matters when they grow up. Keep them for yourself."

Mochow went on and said, "The news today says that the whole cabinet have given their resignations and admit their responsibility for the death of the students. There are telegrams from the south demanding the arrest and trial of Tuan."

But Mulan was not even interested in this. She seemed to have a new sense of values. She got up that day and looked after her younger children as usual, and she had a strange calm and dignity as she went about preparing for Aman's funeral. No one saw her weep any more. Her sadness was something deeper than tears, and she bore her sorrow like a queen.

Her new interest in her jade collection and in the bone inscriptions was more than momentary. She kept them all spread out on her bedroom table again. They were fraught with a spiritual meaning for her, reminders of certain moments of joy and of her childhood, but also reminders of Time and Eternity. It seemed to her that the Moment and Eternity were one. These inanimate objects symbolized immortal life. The inscribed bones stood for kings and queens who had lived four thousand years ago, for the births and deaths of princes, and wars and deaths and ancestral sacrifices in that remote past. Although many of them were in fact oracle bones, their meaning to her was neither religious nor historical; it was philosophical and mystic.

. · .

A few days after Aman's simple funeral ceremonies, Mulan surprised Sunya by saying:

"I don't want to live in Peking now."

He took this to mean that since Aman's death, the city had become unbearable for her. For, after the first week of stern restraint and when the funeral was over, he had seen her each morning and afternoon go away into a room alone for a while and he knew that she went to weep alone, unseen and undisturbed. So he said, "*Meimei,* I know that you find it hard to bear this loss. You will feel better after a while."

"No," she replied. "I want peace. This world is too chaotic. There are wars everywhere, and they are coming nearer to Peking. I want to live simply with just you and the children. No more will I let the young ones go out of my sight. I will teach them myself. . . . Can't we go somewhere—down south to Hangchow—where we can have a simple home by the lake?"

Her tone was earnest.

"But Mother and all our relatives are here, and this house," said Sunya. "Wait a while. We will see."

"I want only to live in peace," she repeated. "Isn't there a place where we can live alone?"

So he said, "We will talk about it more and see what we can do."

As soon as Lifu could walk, he came to see Mulan. His wound had healed luckily without complications, but some of the small bones and tendons had been hurt, and for the rest of his life he walked with a slight limp. He came in now leaning on a stick. Mulan looked up sadly at him and for a moment was silent. Then forcing herself to speak, she thanked him, with deep feeling, for trying to find and save Aman on that day of terror. But he would not speak of himself, only saying that he was sorry that he had not been able to come to Aman's funeral.

He was still bitter and excited and he cried, "Do you know that half a dozen more students have died of wounds in the hospitals? What I cannot understand is some people's attitude toward this murder!"

He had with him the latest number of a weekly paper and showed it to them and said, "Can you imagine? The 'gentlemen' are putting the blame on the student leaders! The writer says that professors and leaders have no right to sacrifice the lives of young students. He says they are responsible for the deaths if they knew of the government's attitude and possible action, and are incompetent if they didn't. He insinuates that some of the leaders are communists. That is exactly

615

what the government said in the order for the arrest of the leaders of the meeting! 'Playing the ventriloquist' with the government! The government, of course, was wrong *also,* this writer says—*also* wrong! The government are not murderers, but are merely also wrong! What a fine judicial, cool-headed, impartial style! Why, I know that the leaders were actually assured by the Garrison Commander Lu that they would be safe. Lu himself did not know what Tuan's guards intended to do. It was a secret trap, an ambush. How could the leaders know that they were leading their students to death? And for this writer to say this now, and extenuate the government's guilt! The blackguard!"

Lifu had worked himself into a rage, so that his face was very red.

"Lifu," said Mulan, "be more careful of what you say. It is getting so nowadays that one can die a patriot and yet be called a fool."

But Lifu answered, "I have something more to tell you. Several days ago, the presidents of the nine government universities held a meeting to draw up and issue a statement on the massacre. Do you know what happened? Four out of the nine university presidents objected to calling the government responsible for the crime. They are politicians themselves. They discussed and debated for two hours on the wording, trying to devise a formula that would not hurt the government's sensibility and yet show they, too, were in some measure horrified, by tossing in a few phrases like 'cruel guards' and 'inhuman weapons.' It was so mild that the government must have been quite pleased. *On the one hand . . . on the other hand. . . .* Oh, that balanced, well-reasoned, judicial point of view! These university presidents are thinking about their rice bowls too!"

Mulan felt worried for him.

"Peking cannot be a good place for you to live in either, can it?" she said. "Living here will only make you more and more angry, especially since you have such colleagues."

"I have already sent in an article about the university presidents and it is a reply to this writer too."

"You have!" exclaimed Mulan. "Does my sister approve?"

"She doesn't know I have sent it."

"Lifu, you should restrain yourself," said Sunya. "These are bad times, and it is better to be prudent."

"Don't you see that this must be the last public act of the Anfuites?"

616

said Lifu. "The whole nation is shocked. This government is dead already. That massacre was its suicide."

"How do you know that a new government will be better?" Mulan asked sadly.

Lifu did not answer, but walked toward the table near the window, where the oracle bones and jade animals were displayed. Mulan's eyes followed him.

"Lifu," she said. "I have a serious word to say to you. Look at those animals. There is more sense in them than in all your writings and your politics. They can give you peace."

Lifu took some of the old bones in his hands and began to examine the ancient inscriptions. In half a minute, his face changed, lighted by a curious new happiness.

"You once said you wanted to go to Tibet," said Mulan, watching him closely.

"I never knew that," remarked Sunya.

"He said it on the first day I met him," Mulan said. "That was a long time ago, wasn't it?"

"What then?" said Lifu, putting the bones down with a smile.

"Why don't you take up a study such as these bone inscriptions? A great work waits to be written about them. I know you love them. I have been asking Sunya to study them, too. Leave politics alone."

Lifu limped back and sat down and talked quietly with them for a while, and then limped away, leaning on his stick.

. .

Now Peking was rapidly falling into a state of anarchy. The combined Manchurian and Chihli troops were pressing closer. The Christian General's troops were still in control of the capital. The Anfu government under Tuan began to plot against them and to welcome the Manchurian-Chihli combination. The plot was discovered, and the Garrison Commander Lu changed his attitude and surrounded Tuan's official residence. Tuan and the Anfuites escaped and fled to the Legation Quarter. As the Manchurian troops pressed closer the Commander withdrew his troops outside Peking to avoid battle. The Anfuites then came out of their hiding. But the Chihli faction chief, General Wu Peifu, sent a telegram demanding the arrest of the Anfuites on the spot and that Tuan be kept under surveillance. In despair, the Anfu officials tried to flirt with the Manchurian faction and sent delegates to Tientsin to welcome the Manchurian "Young Marshal." But he refused to see the delegates. Being thus rebuffed by both sides the Anfuites realized that their political life was ended, and on April 20 Tuan resigned.

Peking was in a curious situation. The government was without a head. The "President of the Republic," Tsao Kun, who had been in prison for some time, issued a telegram of resignation, forgetting that he had already "resigned" once, two years earlier. Tuan had had to invent the name "Chief Executive" for himself instead of "President." Now Tuan had resigned and there was neither President nor Chief Executive.

The Manchurian troops entered the city on April 18. They were the troops of the Dog-Meat General, who was governor of Shantung, but whose power was now spreading to Peking. When his soldiers began to pay for goods with their worthless "Manchurian notes," there was almost a riot. With their dollar bills not worth five cents, they would buy a package of cigarettes and demand change of nine dimes and seven cents, plus the cigarettes. Shops were closed and business was at a standstill. Homes were taken over by the soldiers, and women, children, and old people fled to the suburbs.

The Dog-Meat General was called a man of "three don't-knows." He did not know how many soldiers he had, how much money he had, or how many wives, Chinese and Russian, he had. His gigantic stature, his big, black cigars, and his obscene oaths, combined to give him the effect of a gorilla talking human language. In fact, however, he combined the intelligence of a gorilla with a humble peasant's simplicity of soul. He carried rolls of banknotes and gave freely to any one in distress—a Russian woman or a Chinese farmer. He loved straight, clean deals, and simple language that he could understand, and he was sentimental about his mother. If any literary-minded official used words above his understanding, he would curse and shout, "What are you saying? Us (*tsamen*) don't understand." He loved to gamble at mahjong, but he made the rules of the game as he went along. The only unchangeable rule was that he had to win. If he had a "sparrow," the "sparrow" could eat a "cake," and if he had a "cake," the "cake" could smother the "sparrow." His subordinates all agreed with him, for their losses at the mahjong table were only prudent investments in their general's pleasure. He had a robust, rustic humor, and would roar at his own jest about the "sparrow" eating the "cake." (In this, how-

618

ever, he was not unique. For when President Tsao Kun played mah-jong, he often continued to be banker through the whole night until dawn. This was known in fashionable society as "Tsao Kun continuous banker.")

The Dog-Meat General had come to Peking to "stamp out communists." He did not know what communism was. In the Chinese language, it was often called "share-property-share-wives."

"I'm all for sharing wives, but not for sharing property," he would declare. "The thing is mine. How can it be yours? You take only what is yours. The thing is mine. You come and take it, and if you can take it, it is yours; and if I can take yours, it is mine. But we must be fair to the women. You can't sleep with so many wives the same night. So why not let them sleep with other men?" He did what he preached.

But the Dog-Meat General had come to stamp out communists. He hated them because they had no respect for authority and didn't love their mothers. Another thing he hated was letting family girls go to the public parks. He had a sure instinct that they would become "damaged goods" once they stepped inside a public park. He had forbidden it in the province under his control. In Peking besides fighting communists, he was also trying to keep up public morality and restore respect for Confucius. As part of his anti-communist policy therefore, he also forbade girls to go to the park or to have bobbed hair. Bobbed hair and communism were synonymous.

He dismissed the Anfu commissioner of police and put in his place, his own man, one Li, an ignorant officer of the old type. His method of stamping out communists was that of "killing a chicken as a warning to the monkeys," arresting the leaders as a warning to the others.

The Kuomintang leaders had fled and had gone south to join the Kuomintang Government, which was about to start its northward march to overthrow the warlords. There were two editors, Shao and Lin, who continued to publish outspoken editorials about the chaos and misgovernment. Both were arrested on the charge of being communists. Shao was arrested at eleven in the evening and shot at one in the morning, without trial, and Lin eventually met the same fate. Intellectual Peking was terrorized. There was a rumor that the whole-sale arrest of radical professors and writers was planned and the likelihood was that they would be summarily shot.

Taiyun ran in one day to tell Mochow that someone had seen a black list of fifty-two radical teachers and writers, and that her half-brother Huaiyu had come back. She came to caution Lifu, although according to rumor, his name was not on the list. Most of those whose names were reported to be on it had run away from Peking or had gone into the French and German hospitals in the Legation Quarter, which was a safety zone beyond the reach of the Chinese police. The writers of the opposite group, the "gentlemen," were considered "safe" by the authorities, and with one or two exceptions, their names were not on the list.

Hearing that Lifu's name was not listed, Mochow felt as if a heavy stone had been lifted from her heart. Since his article on the university presidents, she had had a hot argument with him and made him promise never to publish anything without letting her know beforehand. Consequently he had written nothing in the last month.

But she begged him again to take care. "Nobody knows whether this report of the list is correct. And it may be changed or added to. You might be arrested and shot without trial, with no chance to defend yourself."

"But I am not a communist," replied Lifu.

"You don't have to be a communist to get shot. If they dislike you, it is enough. What do you expect in this kind of a world? Think of me and of your children, if you don't care for your own life."

"I know, I know," said Lifu, irked by her openly imposing her will upon him. "I can take care of myself."

She went to his laboratory and ransacked all his notes and papers, published and unpublished. He had no communist books, but there were a number of suspect volumes like Sun Yat-sen's *Program of National Reconstruction,* and copies of the Kuomintang manifesto and the Kuomintang membership card. There was a book of minutes of meetings held in their home, written by different hands, mostly Chen San's. Among the papers, Mochow found various essays on current questions. She saw one defending ancestor worship, and wisely left it with other harmless ones among his scientific papers. That night, Lifu saw her spending the whole evening sorting his papers. She was expecting another baby, already six months in her womb, and she breathed heavily as she sat on a low stool and bent over the papers on the floor. He felt the unspoken gravity of an expectant mother and respected it.

"What are you going to do with them?" he asked.

"Get them out of the way for prudence's sake," she said.

"You can't burn my papers."

"I am not going to burn them. But I shall burn some of these books and the membership card. You know a Kuomintang man can be considered red now and can be shot."

"Be shot, be shot! They can't shoot everybody in Peking. How are they going to shoot all the girls with bobbed hair? The shooting of Shao and Lin was meant only as a lesson."

Nevertheless, Mochow took away the Kuomintang books, the membership card, and the minute book and burned them, together with some volumes she had found in Huan-erh's room. His essays she packed in a parcel and put away.

The next morning, Mulan came over to discuss the situation with her sister. She had heard, too, about the black list and about Huaiyu's return. She promised to take away the parcel of Lifu's articles and keep it in Mrs. Hua's curio shop, and she suggested that it would be better for Lifu to go away for a while until the situation became clearer.

It was eleven o'clock in the morning. While the sisters were talking with Lifu, Chen San rushed in, exclaiming, "The police are coming in!"

The sisters' faces turned white.

"Run out by the back door," Mochow cried.

"What is the use?" said Lifu, calmly. "It certainly is surrounded."

Four policemen came in almost immediately.

Mochow went out to meet them, and asked, "What do you want?"

"We have a warrant to arrest Kung Lifu, young mistress," said the chief officer.

Chen San stepped forward, his hand on his gun.

"Don't be foolish!" shouted Lifu, as he came out.

Then he demanded. "What is the charge?"

"We don't know. That is not our business. You will ask and answer questions at the police court."

"You can't take him," said Mochow. "He is a peaceful citizen. He is a scientist."

"You can explain that to the court," said the officer.

Suddenly they heard Mulan's voice inside crying plaintively, "You can't take him! You can't! You can't!"

"Will you come quietly, or shall we handcuff you?" said the chief.

"I am not a criminal. I will come with you," said Lifu.

The chief then ordered two of the men to go with Lifu, while he and another man remained.

When Mulan heard that Lifu was going, she rushed to the door in tears, and behind her came Lifu's mother and sister. Lifu cast a look of intense concern upon his women relatives weeping together. Then he turned to Chen San and told him to go to Mr. Fu at once and to the painter Chi, who had many influential friends.

Mochow was left standing stunned on the threshold. Her eyes followed her husband as he disappeared, anger surging in her breast mixed with a sharp sense of disaster. But she rose to the occasion, when the chief asked, "Where is his study?" "Follow me," she said calmly and politely.

She led the police to the front court, and into the laboratory.

"What is your relation to Mr. Kung?" the chief asked her.

"He is my husband."

"What is his profession?"

"I told you, he is a scientist, a biologist. He studies trees and insects. Has nothing to do with politics. He works in his laboratory all the time."

Chen San, who had been a policeman, and knew all the ways of police, followed them into the laboratory.

The chief was struck by the great calm of this woman whose husband was arrested. She showed him the microscope, the slides, the samples, and all the papers that she knew were perfectly harmless.

Pulling out the drawers, she said, "These are his writings. Take them along if you wish. I tell you he is innocent."

"You ought to take some books, too, to report as evidence," said Chen San.

"Who are you?" said the police chief.

"I have been a policeman, too."

"What are you doing here?" said the policeman, fraternally.

"I am the watchman for the Garden. What is the charge against Mr. Kung?"

"What can it be but communism?"

"Why should we, owners of such a big garden, want to believe in sharing property?" said Mochow.

"Somebody has spoken against him," the chief said. "I should think Mr. Kung must have a lot of influential friends. That is what he needs." He seemed to be in a good mood now.

622

Directing his assistant to bring along the papers and a few of the books, he said to Mochow, "Madam, I am sorry to have disturbed you. I am only carrying out my official duties. I see that a man with a wife like you is not likely to be a communist. You must ask some influential friends to speak for him. Good-by."

Mochow and Chen San sent the policeman politely away, and went back. They discovered then that Mulan had fainted. Huan-erh and Lifu's mother were trying to revive her by mopping her forehead with a cold towel. Mulan's face was white and her lips were deathly gray. Afei, Paofen, and Mrs. Feng had all come in and there was great confusion in the house.

But Mochow, knowing the need of immediate action, said to Chen San, "Quickly run over to see Mr. and Mrs. Fu and ask them to come immediately. I will telephone to Mrs. Hua."

She bent over her sister and said, "It is overstrain from Aman's death. She has been looking very pale these days." Thus outwardly she explained Mulan's fainting.

Fearing a miscarriage, Mrs. Kung said to Mochow, "You should be careful. You must not be too excited."

"I am careful, Mother," said Mochow. She had always believed in the psychological effects of the mother's thoughts during pregnancy. She avoided seeing monstrosities and deformed people and she did quiet needlework, or read about the deeds of noble men, and tried to think only the best thoughts. She took frequent rests and seemed already to live with the baby before it was born.

But this morning it was more than usual self-control that prevented her from shedding a single tear; it was her sense of the need of action.

There was no telephone at Mrs. Hua's shop, but there was one in the tailor's shop opposite which she could use. Mochow rang up and asked them to call Mrs. Hua, who soon came to the telephone and promised to run at once to tell the painter Chi who lived only ten minutes' walk from her shop.

Paofen came in and said, "My father knows Wang Shihchen. Afei, you had better run over and ask him to get in touch with Wang at once." Wang was an eighty-year-old gentleman who had been an official in Manchu times, but was now bringing the military factions together in a national peace move, and in the absence of a government was the head of a temporary local peace-preservation commission.

Now Mochow turned to her sister again. "Shall we call Sunya?" asked Huan-erh.

"Don't frighten him," said Mochow. "She must just rest a little."

Mulan was coming back to consciousness, and probably heard them, but remained silent. Now Mochow bent over her sister and spoke to her, and Mulan opened her eyes and saw her sister's face close above her.

"How are you now?"

Mulan looked round and saw the others there, and said, "I am better now. My heart has been weak lately."

"You must be very careful," said Mochow aloud. "You have looked so pale these days. Your face looked white when you came in today."

Mulan looked at her sister with eyes of infinite softness, and closed them again.

Mrs. Hua soon telephoned again to say that the painter Chi was not at home, and she had left a message for him. When she was able to sit up, Mulan said that she would stay for lunch with her sister and asked Huan-erh to telephone to Sunya to inform him of Lifu's arrest and ask him to come and discuss what should be done.

Sunya came and saw that Mulan's eyes were swollen and her face still very pale. Mrs. Hua came, too, and she watched the two sisters, for nothing escaped her shrewd eyes; and she inwardly admired Mochow for great presence of mind in this crisis. The painter Chi came lumbering in while they were having lunch and said that he would call on several friends who might be useful. The best man he knew, however, was Mr. Fu, the ex-Minister of Education, who was himself Lifu's friend. The matter looked hopeful when in the afternoon Paofen's father came to tell them that he had seen Wang, and Wang had promised to do his best to get Lifu free. Then Mr. Fu came and said that he had seen Lifu and the police chief, and was sure that there was no immediate danger. Cases of suspected communists would be handled by the police and the military courts, but he said the chief had been properly impressed by Lifu's good connections. Some one had informed against Lifu, but there was no regular plaintiff.

Taiyun came in about six o'clock, and at about supper time, the police came again, but without the chief. The new man in charge was a short, ugly, minor officer with eyes in narrow slits. The order now was for the arrest of Chen San and Huan-erh.

Sunya demanded to know the charge.

624

"We came to get the man and girl we have a warrant for," the officer replied brusquely. "If they are communists they will be shot, and if they are peaceful citizens, of course, they will be released."

Huan-erh's mother began to cry, saying, "What bad luck is this, that they take away my two children on the same day? If they are not set free I shall not want to live."

Sunya tried to calm her. Seeing Taiyun, the short officer said, "Why are there so many bobbed-haired women in this house? Is this a nest of communists? You had better come along, too, and answer a few questions."

"What? Arrest me?" shouted Taiyun angrily. "You running-dog of warlords!"

"Well, well!" said the short policeman. "You *do* want to be arrested. I cannot help you against your will." Turning to his man, he shouted to have both of the bobbed-hair girls, Huan-erh and Taiyun, taken into custody.

"Have you any evidence?" asked Sunya.

"Of course there is evidence," answered the officer. "Do you think we have nothing to do but go about arresting peaceful citizens?"

Chen San's revolver was handed over to the police, and he submitted himself to arrest.

This new development put a sinister outlook on the whole situation, and the family was more than ever worried. Paofen's father had said that Mr. Wang had promised that Lifu would be safe until he had a trial, but they must take no chances in times like these, and it was decided to offer bail that very night. In addition, they had to inform old Mr. New of Taiyun's arrest.

Late that night, after half past eleven, Sunya and Mr. Feng came home with Lifu, who had been released on bail of three thousand dollars because Mr. Wang had written a personal letter to the commissioner of police. But bail was refused to the other three, partly because Mr. Wang's letter had not mentioned them and partly because Chen San looked like a possible communist and the two girls, who had bobbed hair, looked like probable communists. It was unnecessary to explain the irregularities of the police court.

All the women had sat up waiting for news. Mulan was the first to hear Lifu's voice as they came in, and she shouted, "He is back! He is here!" Mochow had not shed one useless tear the whole day, but when she saw her husband's face again she rushed forward and took his hands and allowed herself to cry out of sheer happiness. Lifu explained to them: "Somebody has informed against me through the new commissioner of police. I suspect that it is Huaiyu."

"Why are Huan-erh and Chen San arrested?"

"That is exactly what leads me to think it is a personal affair, brought on by an enemy of the family. It is quite apart from the black list. About three o'clock, I was taken to the court again and the judge asked me, 'Is it true that you married your sister to a laborer?' I replied, 'It is true. I married her to a policeman. Isn't a policeman also a man?' The other policemen standing there smiled at my answer. 'You have been accused of marrying your sister to a laborer and are therefore suspected of having communist sympathies.' 'Your honor,' I said, 'if I had more sisters, I would marry them to some of the policemen in your office. At least they work for their living. I approve of men who earn their living. Is that communism?' The policemen laughed. 'Don't be impertinent,' the judge said. 'We are trying to stamp out communism in this city. Don't try to flatter us.' And so I was taken back into the cell until you came."

"Then it is not so dangerous for Huan-erh and Chen San, either," said Mr. Feng.

"I don't think so," answered Lifu.

"Is there any other charge?" asked Mochow.

"I cannot tell until my trial. There is something about my libeling the authorities. So long as there is a trial, I am not afraid. It is lucky you got Wang Shihchen to help us."

"How are Huan-erh and Chen San?" asked Lifu's mother.

"I saw them before I came out. They are in a cell with a number of young students. Huan-erh was crying, and I told her that what the short officer said was not true and that their case was probably not serious. I told Chen San that his only sin was having been a policeman."

And so with Lifu's return and the prospect of an open trial, the family was greatly relieved, and Sunya and Mulan went home.

Mr. Fu went the next morning to the police court to see about the release of Huan-erh and Chen San. The chief assured him that their case was light and they were not in danger, but refused bail.

Then he saw old Mr. New there, trying to arrange for Taiyun's release. There was no evidence against Taiyun and no one had informed against her.

"Are you this girl's father?" the head officer asked Mr. New.

"Why, yes."

"Then she is also New Huaiyu's sister?"

"Of course."

"I beg your pardon. I will release her immediately. But your daughter looks exactly like a communist. You ought to teach her better manners. It is difficult for us to distinguish who are from good families and who are not."

Old Mr. New profoundly thanked him and apologized, saying, "You know these are modern days, and parents have no control over their children. My daughter is young and ignorant and merely modern."

Taiyun, who was present, would not allow her father to apologize for her youth and ignorance. "What do you mean by good family and bad family?" she shouted at the head officer. "By good family you mean people who are big officials and oppress the people. If you release me because I am Huaiyu's sister, I refuse to go out."

The head officer smiled and looked at Old New.

"She talks exactly like a communist," he said. "For your face, I will let her out. But our prison is full of exactly this type of young people. You will do well to teach her to be more careful with her tongue, or she will get into trouble again, and it will be difficult for me to give you face again."

"Tell me who accused Mr. Kung and his sister," said Taiyun. "Is it my brother New Huaiyu?"

"That is not your affair!" the officer shouted.

Mr. Fu said good-by to old New and Taiyun, and asked the head officer whether Lifu's case would be tried in a regular court, and the officer said, "No."

"When will his case be tried? I should like to be his counsel," said Mr. Fu.

"Your Excellency," said the head officer, standing up and making a deep bow, "don't punish us like that. You know we officers sometimes have embarrassing duties to carry out. If Your Excellency honors the trial with your presence, how dare I sit on this seat? What is the accused to you?"

"He is almost like a son to me," said Mr. Fu.

"I assure you he will have a fair trial. You know that he has offended people and has probably written things against the authorities. We are studying the documents in his case and I assure you that we will arrange for his trial as speedily as possible."

This story Mr. Fu brought back to the family, and Lifu thanked him for the trouble he had taken.

CHAPTER XXXVIII

*F*OUR days later, on May 1, Lifu was summoned for trial. It was to be at a military court, held in private. Relatives were debarred, but Mr. Fu insisted on being present. The head police was the accuser. He had gone through the documents closely and had prepared a report carefully worded so that the charges should not be too serious, owing to Mr. Feng's private arrangements with the police chief. Lifu was put on trial first, while Huan-erh and Chen San were held in the waiting room.

The judge was a small, weak man in military uniform. Mr. Fu took a seat at the side. After preliminaries, the judge read the accusation.

"Kung Lifu, you have been accused of writing against the government, of advocating monstrous theories to lead astray the people, and of having sympathies for labor. You are suspected of being a communist. From the documents found in your possession and elsewhere, I see that you have most confused ideas, sometimes defending Confucianism, sometimes attacking it. We will go through these one by one. First, there is the article you published on March 28, charging the government with inhuman slaughter of students. The language was abusive even against your own educational leaders. I understand you are a professor."

"Yes, Your Honor," replied Lifu. "I condemned and still condemn the slaughter of students from ambush."

"But you seem to be defending the leaders of the demonstration. You know they are communists—or Kuomintang—it is the same thing."

"Your Honor," said Lifu, "I don't know whether they are communists. I do know that the students demonstrated for a patriotic cause, and my own niece, a girl of sixteen, was shot to death. I was a witness at the massacre. But, Your Honor, I did not write against this government, but against the government that you overthrew. General

Wu Peifu himself demanded in a telegram the arrest of Tuan Chijui and the Anfu party, and the cabinet itself resigned. The whole nation has condemned the massacre, not I alone."

"You used the words 'corrupt officials and dirty bureaucrats' and again you spoke of 'usurpation of military men.' You understand that under the Republic our country is in chaos, and we military men are only trying to restore peace and order to the country. Don't you agree, Your Excellency?" With this, he turned to Mr. Fu, and shouted to a servant to pour tea for Mr. Fu. The latter saw that Lifu could defend his own case, and merely nodded politely.

"Your Honor," said Lifu in a somewhat affected literary style, "there are officials, some clean, some corrupt, and there are bureaucrats, some dirty, some honest, even under the best government in times of peace. If I had meant *all* officials were corrupt, I should not have to use the word 'corrupt' at all. If I had meant all bureaucrats were dirty, I should not have needed the word 'dirty.' Certainly this is not insult against all officials."

The judge, who seemed to be a literary man of the old type who had somehow stumbled into a military uniform, looked at the accused and appreciated his somewhat bombastic reply. He merely cleared his throat and began again:

"Your thoughts seem to be most unclear. I see you are a good Confucianist, since you approve of ancestor worship. That is in your favor. But what do you mean by talking about 'Feeling in Trees?' There is an article on this subject written by you some years ago. How can you advocate ancestor worship on the one hand and talk about feeling in trees on the other? It is most contradictory. . . ."

Lifu could not suppress a slight laugh within his bosom. He had not expected this from the judge, who continued, "Do you still hold that opinion?"

"I do."

"I am sorry for you. If you are a good follower of the Sage, you cannot abolish this distinction between human beings and trees and animals, and if you speak of trees as having feeling, you are a communist. I have also read Mencius. The most important distinction between men and beasts is our consciousness—the sense of mercy, the sense of right and wrong. Are you not trying to drag men down to the level of beasts when you give the animals and even trees a 'consciousness'? You speak even of the 'language' of trees and animals, just like the modern school books. The Bear says 'so-and-so' and the Fox says 'so-and-so.' These are all diabolical communist doctrines designed to make men resemble the beasts."

"Your Honor," said Lifu, "if you will allow me to explain, that depends upon how we interpret the words of the sages. Mencius saw King Hsuan of Chi and spoke of extending kindness to the animals. History tells us that the court musicians of the Emperors Yao and Shun moved the birds and beasts to dance. The virtue of the sages touched the birds and beasts. If the birds and beasts had no consciousness, how could they be touched by the virtue of the sages and emperors? And the *Book of Chou Rites* spoke of sacrifices to the spirits of lakes and forests by sinking and burying offerings."

This was somewhat confusing to the judge, who, to tell the truth, had never really understood the *Book of Chou Rites,* which was the most unreadable of the classics. Mr. Fu smiled in satisfaction.

"You will confine your defense to what you yourself wrote," said the judge. Then he went on briskly.

"We are dealing today with the communist doctrines, and not with the ancient classics. The classics are always open to different interpretations. Do you admit you are advocating the theory that men and trees and animals are the same and that men are like beasts and beasts are like men? You know this kind of theory tends to stir up trouble in the hearts of the people."

"I speak as a scientist, Your Honor," Lifu replied. "I merely say that men and beasts are alike in having consciousness, but it is consciousness of a different type."

"So you admit men and beasts are alike! But this is not important; it merely shows how confused your thoughts are and how disturbing they are to the public. There is a graver charge against you. It is reported upon investigation that you married your sister without ceremony on the top of a mountain to a common laborer. Is it true?"

"It is true."

"What is the laborer's name?"

"Chen San."

"What is his profession?"

"He was a policeman in Anking. Now he is secretary in my house and concurrently a watchman."

"Is he still serving as a watchman after his marriage to your sister?"

"Nominally, yes."

"This is most irregular," remarked the judge. "Do you know that you are confusing all family order and distinction between master and servant, exactly as the communists are doing? You are allied to the communists."

"I believe in the equality of man. Mencius said that the sages belong to the same species as ourselves."

"Who were the witnesses at your sister's marriage? Who were the go-betweens?"

"I was the sole witness. There were no go-betweens."

"Isn't this the same as believing in sharing property and sharing wives, like the communists?"

The judge seemed intent on establishing the communist charge.

"I have nothing further to say," said Lifu.

The judge sent for the other prisoners to be brought in to court. Chen San and Huan-erh appeared.

"What is your name?"

"Chen San."

"Who is this woman?"

"She is my wife."

"Is this man Kung Lifu your brother-in-law?"

"Yes, he is my wife's brother."

"I consider your marriage most irregular. Do you, Kung Huan-erh, admit Chen San as your husband?"

"I do."

"What is he doing at your brother's house?"

"He is the secretary-treasurer, and also watchman."

"How do you allow your husband to serve as a servant while you are the master's sister? Are you not ashamed that you married a common laborer?"

"I am not ashamed," replied Huan-erh. "He works for his living. There is no shame in that."

"You are talking the communist language. You had no go-between for your marriage."

"My mother approved. I married him because he was a filial son."

"How?"

"My husband is the lost son of Chenma, who used to work with us at the Garden. She was a great woman, and he is a great son."

"You said you were a policeman," said the judge, addressing Chen San. "Tell me how you came to be employed in the Kung home."

Chen San told the story of how he had lost his mother, and how his mother searched for him and how he came to read Lifu's story and decided to come to the capital, only to find his mother gone. He spoke with great emotion toward the end, and the judge seemed touched. Turning to Lifu, he said,

"Are you the person who wrote that famous story of Chenma?"

"Yes. For the sake of a great mother, and a filial son, please be kind," said Lifu.

Mr. Fu intervened and said, "Your Honor, may I speak of what I know?"

"Certainly."

"This Chen San is a filial son," said Mr. Fu. "His misfortune was that he was born poor. I myself have seen his rooms. He sleeps on the clothes his mother made for him, and he has sworn never to wear the same blue cloth again. He is dutiful and honest. I have seen the couplet in his room:

> The trees desire repose, but the winds will not be still;
> The son desires to serve, but his parents are no more.

Such a good son cannot be a communist."

The judge listened attentively and at the end he wished to make a great gesture. He rose from his seat and extended his hands to Chen San:

"I am pleased to meet a filial son. You and your wife are released."

Chen San and Huan-erh bowed low to thank the judge and smiled happily.

The judge returned to his seat. Assuming a serious countenance, he said:

"Kung Lifu, by your own confession, you have advocated monstrous theories to disturb the public mind. Moreover, you have married your sister to a servant without a go-between and without ceremony, out in the wilds, like barbarians who do not know ritual and ceremony. Your acts are close to communism, although you may not be a communist yourself. Human hearts are disturbed enough in these days, and we must suppress all who are likely to stir up more trouble. I sentence you to a year's imprisonment. In consideration, however, of your appreciation of ancestor worship and filial piety, and in further consideration of Mr. Fu's relationship to you, I am willing to convert it to a three-month detention, if you will promise to refrain hereafter from propagating strange theories and all criticisms of the government."

Lifu's face fell. Mr. Fu stood up to plead for mercy and a further reduction of the sentence, but the judge rose and said politely, "I am sorry, but this is all I can do. He has offended people. If you will guide him, with his knowledge and ability, he can be of real good to society and to the country."

Mr. Fu understood that this had been the judge's intention from the start, and that Huaiyu had demanded some sort of punishment. He therefore merely thanked him for his kindness, and the judge bowed to Mr. Fu and retired.

Left now with Mr. Fu, Huan-erh, and Chen San, Lifu asked his sister to tell his wife and mother not to worry. Mr. Fu said that he would still make further efforts to obtain his early release, but that he need have no worry about his comfort. The guards were sufficiently impressed by Mr. Fu and knew that the prisoner lived in a great Manchu Garden and thus would treat Lifu politely, expecting some handsome tips.

. ' .

The family had gathered to await Lifu's return from the trial. When Mochow saw Mr. Fu come in with Chen San and Huan-erh, her heart sank within her. Huan-erh fell upon her mother's breast crying.

"How is it?" the mother asked.

"Don't be worried, Mrs. Kung," said Mr. Fu. "It is not so bad as we thought. He is temporarily shut up but he will be out soon."

"How long?" asked Mochow, aghast.

"Three months. But we will still work for his earlier release."

"Sentenced on what count?" asked Mrs. Fu, who was present.

"On acts close to communism."

"It is ridiculous!" burst out Huan-erh. "We overheard it from the next room. It is that article about 'Feeling in Trees.' He was accused of monstrous theories."

"I congratulate you on your husband," Mr. Fu said to Mochow. "He had a literary argument with the judge and got the better of it. He quoted the *Chou Rites* and the judge immediately changed the subject!"

So Mr. Fu described the trial and Lifu's self-defense.

"It is all irrelevant," he concluded. "The judge was determined to find him guilty from the start. He was evidently committed to someone—probably to Huaiyu. Luckily, among the papers they found a defense of ancestor worship which completely established him as a noncommunist. No communist would defend ancestor worship. Otherwise he might have got a worse sentence."

Mochow was glad that she had left that paper in the laboratory, but she only said, "I think it is more due to your presence, Uncle Fu. Mother and our whole family must thank you."

"I would say both," said Mr. Fu.

"It is all our mistake," said Mochow. "We should have given the judge a present. We thought it was all arranged with the police chief. It is time to spend a little money now."

Mr. Fu promised to exert further efforts. Mulan sat grimly listening.

"What we can do now is to spend more money to provide for his comforts," said Sunya.

"We spent five hundred on the police. What do you propose now? There are different officials who all have to be given their due," said Mr. Feng.

Stretching his fingers, first four and then eight, he asked Mochow silently, "This or this?" He meant four or eight hundred. "The more we spend the more comfortable it will be for him."

"The jailers are easy to deal with," said Mochow. "The important things are to give him a good room, a good bed and bedding, and good food. But if we are trying to obtain his earlier release, it is not a matter of a few hundred."

"It will not be difficult to spend a total of some thousands this time," said Mr. Feng.

"This is not the time to consider money," said Sunya.

"Bedding is easy," said Paofen. "I have a dozen new silk quilts and blankets that have never been used. When the jailers see that a prisoner has good bedding, they treat him nicely. We must all dress as richly as we can when we go to visit him, to give him face. But, of course, the jailers will then expect more and we must be prepared to pay."

Now that there was a temporary settlement and Lifu's life seemed at least safe, the family accepted the situation more calmly, and began to talk of visits to the prison and ensuring comforts for Lifu. Mulan had said nothing during the whole discussion.

That very afternoon Sunya and Afei went with Mochow to visit

Lifu in prison and gave the jailers some tips. The next day Mulan came to Mochow and drew her aside and brought out seven old round pearls, the size of large beans. They had been mounted on a centipede for hair decoration, and she had broken it up and taken off these seven.

"Sister," she said, "here are seven old pearls. I have not much use for them. I am going to speak to Paofen about it. These match exactly the five big pearls Paofen found. I am thinking of adding these seven and making it a round dozen, and asking Paofen's parents to give it to Mr. Wang. The color and size just match, I remember. . . . Who knows who will be in power before the three months are up? What do you think?"

Mochow looked at the pearls and at her sister, and she could say nothing.

"Sister, is there any question?" said Mulan. "We must save him by any means."

"I was thinking . . . whether Paofen would be willing. Or I would buy them from her."

"There is no question," said Mulan. "Afei certainly will be willing. What are jewels to us in this family?"

There were tears in both sisters' eyes. They went and found Afei and Paofen, and Afei said, "Of course," and Paofen said, "It is a good idea. What are pearls without men? I never thought the treasure would have such great use."

The scheme was properly carried out. As a matter of fact, both the families were still well off, and everybody offered to take out her own money, including Coral and Mannia and Dimfragrance.

That afternoon, Mulan and Mochow decided to visit Lifu and see about his removal to a better room. Afei went with them, and Huanerh wanted to go to see her brother, but her mother said that she had just come out of prison and would not allow her. They took an extra pillow and a thermos bottle and Mochow also took a volume of biology from Lifu's study.

They went first to the warden's office to arrange for a better room.

"He is already in a good room by himself," the head warden said, smiling at the rich ladies. "But perhaps after a few days I may be able to arrange something to oblige you ladies. It all depends on whether some rooms will be vacated. It is difficult, but I will do my best for you."

"I know it is not easy," said Afei, "but if you will make a special effort, we shall be most appreciative."

Usually the head warden would not accompany visitors, but he knew these visitors were rich and lived in a garden, and so he rose to conduct them personally. Inside, they passed an empty cell facing south, where the sun was shining in through the bars. It was unoccupied.

"That is a nice room," said Mochow.

"It will be occupied soon," said the warden. "A person from a very good family is expected to go in there."

Mulan knew that the warden was purposely making a difficulty to be smoothed over and she said, "Our family is not so bad, either," and smiled at him.

"Perhaps it can be arranged for," the warden said. "I will have to consult the others."

They proceeded to Lifu's cell. He was overjoyed to see them. He was allowed to wear his ordinary clothes and looked none the worse for spending a night there. Mulan turned and saw that the head warden had left them with another jailer, but he was still going slowly along the corridor. Mulan hurried after him. He stopped and looked round.

"Have you forgotten something?" he asked.

"No," said Mulan. "You know we would so appreciate having that sunny room for our relative."

Now of the ten big pearls on the silver centipede, she had given seven to Paofen that day, and she had still three left, wrapped in a handkerchief in her pocket. She meant to spend them all. Fumbling in her pocket, she took out two pearls and keeping them concealed in her palm, she pressed them into the warden's hand.

He looked at them lying in his hand and said, "Oh, no, I cannot take your presents, lady. I shall be pleased only to serve you."

"Take them and don't refuse. You must allow us to show our appreciation," said Mulan.

"I will do my best," said the warden with a full smile.

Going back to the cell, she came to the jailer outside, who had been watching her. Pressing the one remaining pearl into his hand, she said, nonchalantly, "The cell is so dark."

"Yes, it has no sunshine," the jailer replied, his hand having already closed on the pearl.

"What were you doing?" asked Afei as she came into the cell.

"I went back to remind the warden of the other room," replied Mulan.

Lifu had heard from Mochow that on the first day of his arrest, Mulan had fallen into a swoon, and Mochow and Afei had just been telling him about the pearls, and Mochow was saying, "Second Sister took out seven of her own to make up the dozen."

"Mulan—" said Lifu as she came in toward him, and then for a moment said nothing more. After the pause, he went on, "I have caused you all too much trouble. Do not worry and grieve on account of me."

"What are pearls and jade if our sister has lost her husband? Everybody is helping, and gladly," said Afei.

"If you know how many persons you have caused to worry and grieve, you ought to be more careful hereafter," said Mochow. "For the present, everybody is helping. Coral has taken out fifty dollars of her own money, and Uncle a hundred, and Mannia also offered a hundred. Chinya and Dimfragrance felt that they were responsible for this family enmity and offered more, but I took only a hundred from them. And Paofen has contributed her pearls."

"Don't mention those things," said Afei. "Second Sister's contribution is the biggest of all."

Touched by all this loyalty, Lifu's eyes dimmed, and he looked at Mulan, while saying, "Thank you all. I hope I shall be worthy."

Just then the jailer came in to announce that a better room had been secured and congratulated them, and began energetically to help remove the blankets, basin, and personal articles. Suddenly a wild howling started in one of the cells near by. The women started in fear.

"It has nothing to do with you, gentlemen and ladies," said the jailer cheerfully as he opened the door. Then they saw two young boys, deathly pale and weaping, being led past them down the corridor.

Trembling still with the excitement, they followed until they came to the vacant room which they had seen, and went in and prepared Lifu's bed and arranged the room. It looked out on a blank narrow yard, paved with broken bricks. Mochow took out twenty dollars and gave them to the jailer, saying, "Serve our master well. We will reward you more in the future."

The jailer beamed with gratitude and assured her that she need not worry.

They sat down to talk about the situation, which was most confusing. W. W. Yen was trying to organize a cabinet and act in place of the President who had "resigned." He was supported by the Chihli faction under General Wu Peifu but opposed by the Manchurian faction under Chang Tsolin. Both the Chihli and the Manchurian factions had appointed rival garrison commanders for Peking. Now they had worked out a compromise and General Wu Peifu's man, Wang Huaiching, had assumed office.

Suddenly they heard a burst of shots, then silence. Looking at each other, they knew that the two pale boys they had just seen taken out had been shot.

. ˙.

After going to the warden's office to thank him, the party went home to discuss the next step. Wang, the old Manchu official, had sent a letter to the military commander, but there was no reply yet. Peking was still in a state of virtual anarchy. China was under the rule of the warlords, and as in the Japanese Government of later times, no cabinet could be formed without the militarists' consent. The militarists were the real rulers, and civilian leaders governed only by their permission. The Peace Preservation Commission headed by Wang was still functioning, pending a government approved by the rival warlords, who were not able to come to terms. Emissaries were traveling between Peking, Tientsin, and Mukden, trying to bring about a compromise. Lifu's freedom depended upon the kind of government that would be set up. If W. W. Yen succeeded in forming a government, his influence could be brought to bear upon the militarists supporting him to sanction Lifu's earlier release. Mr. Wang saw Yen often in those days, and Mr. Fu also knew him personally. But while Wu Peifu supported Yen as the new premier, the Manchurians, including the Dog-Meat General, opposed him. It was rumored that the two factions were coming to agree on a coalition cabinet, but Yen's own position was still too uncertain for him to be of service to the family of Lifu in such a small matter.

Meanwhile, Kao, a professor of Peking University, was arrested. His beautiful young wife went to the Manchurian commander's office to beg for his life. The Manchurian commander bargained for the wife's favors. The wife refused and Kao was shot. The news created fresh consternation in the intellectual circles. Besides, the Dog-Meat General was reported to be nominated as generalissimo of the joint Chihli and Manchurian forces inside the Great Wall and he would be in supreme control of Peking in one or two days. What that simple, straight-dealing medieval warlord might choose to do, it was impossible to guess. There would be less law and order than under the local Peace Commission just as the Peace Commission was less able to impose law and order than the Tuan Government had been.

Mulan, now desperate, and seized with a great fear, was quite unnerved. She did not hear or see anything when she went to her own home, and she ate supper without knowing what she was eating. Then she went into her room and changed her clothing.

"What are you doing?" Sunya asked.

"I am going back to my sister's. I promised to give Lifu the books on bone inscriptions to read, and I must take them to her."

"What? Does she visit the prison so late?"

"It is all right. The jailers are growing fat on our oil," Mulan said.

"Are you going, too? Why are you dressing up?"

"I shall go to keep sister company."

"Then I will go with you."

"Don't bother. Afei or Chen San will go with us."

"You must not get too excited, you know," said Sunya.

Mulan looked into the mirror and saw her own eyes strangely mobile, liquid, glistening with a wild emotion. After arranging her hair she rose and took down from the bookshelf two volumes of *Studies on Yinsu Scripts*.

"Which do you think will be best for his reading?" she asked her husband.

"Take the one by Lo. It is the earliest study of the subject," said Sunya.

When she came to her sister's, Mochow was surprised, and asked, "Why, sister, do you come out so late again!"

"I have brought a book that I promised to give to Lifu. Come with me to the prison."

"But why in this hurry?" Mochow asked.

"I promised to give it to him this afternoon. But we were prevented by Paofen's relatives, and I don't like to break the promise."

"Can we go in so late?"

"I think so. The guards know us so well already."

"Then send Chen San with a message that we were prevented from coming."

"I am dressed already," Mulan insisted, "and I will go in case there is anything he needs. There may be some news at the prison."

"Then wait a minute. I will come with you," said Mochow.

"You must not," said Mrs. Kung. "The prison is dark and difficult to walk in. Suppose you should stumble in the dark. You have two lives in your body, not only one."

And so Mochow did not go, and Chen San went with Mulan.

At the prison, Chen San presented the parcel of books to be delivered.

"It is too late," said the guard. "The warden has gone home, and it is against the rules."

Mulan opened the parcel and showed the guard how harmless the books were.

"No smuggling of goods. Everything that comes in must go through the office," he said.

"May we see him only a short moment?" she asked.

"That cannot be," said the guard.

"Then we will bring it again tomorrow," said Mulan. "But tell the prisoner that we were here."

They turned away and separated at the prison door. Chen San wanted to accompany Mulan home, but she insisted that there was no need and got into a rickshaw. She was suddenly seized with a desire to see Lifu alone, even for a short five minutes. The talk with him in the Cedar Grove had made her life fuller and stronger, and she had seen the sunset and sunrise on Taishan with him and that had meant everything to her. If she could only see him alone at night in prison! If he should be shot, what memories she would carry with her for all her life! Her desire to see him was uncontrollable. After going a short distance, she dismissed her rickshaw and walked back to the prison.

"Here you are again!" said the guard. "What do you want?"

"Please let me in just for a short moment," she said. "I am a woman and cannot steal him away. I have some important news for him."

She pressed a five-dollar note into the guard's hand. The guard looked around, and said, "Quick, then! Come in, and make no noise. Only five minutes."

Mulan followed the guard blindly through a dark hall and down a

641

dimly lighted corridor, her heart palpitating. "What will he think of me? I have no excuse," she thought.

When they came to Lifu's room the guard whispered to the jailer in charge, and beckoned Mulan to go in.

Lifu was reading under a small oil lamp. He was completely taken by surprise.

Facing him, Mulan was ashamed and looked at him almost pitifully.

"Why, Mulan! What is it?"

Mulan made a sign toward the guard and asked him to speak more softly.

"I came to bring you some news," she began.

"Sit down," said Lifu and made her a seat with a pillow.

"We had news this afternoon and were not able to come," she stammered.

"What news?"

Suddenly Mulan stopped. The words refused to come, and tears formed in her eyes. Her lips quivered and suddenly she broke down, covering her face in her hands, crying, "Oh, Lifu!"

She dared not cry aloud for fear of being heard. The guard and jailer silently watched at the hole in the door.

Lifu stood directly over her and dared not touch her. But he bent and said, "What is troubling you? I am all right and quite comfortable here."

Mulan's hands searched for Lifu's and she said with low sobs, "I know I should not be here. But if you should die . . . I . . ."

"What is the news?"

Knowing all that he knew of this sister of his wife's, Lifu could not remain untouched. But he only said gently, "Did Mochow send you?"

Wiping her eyes, Mulan checked herself and remained thinking for a moment. Then she raised her pleading eyes at him and said, "Sister and I were coming to see you this afternoon and could not come. I thought of the book on bone inscriptions and came to bring it to you with Chen San. They would not receive anything from the outside so late, and could not admit Chen San because he is a man. I told him I was a woman and was admitted." She rubbed her thumb and fingers together, signifying tips.

"But what is the news?"

"Mr. Wang has written a letter to the commander. Do you think it is of any use?"

"Is that all?"

"They say the Dog-Meat General will be the supreme authority in a few days. . . . Oh, Lifu, I don't know—I have a great fear for you. If anything should happen to you. . . ." Her voice became inaudible, and she lay back on her seat, all strength and will gone out of her. Then she began to weep again.

The jailer knocked. Mulan rose and took out another bill and went to the door and begged, "Another five minutes, please."

Lifu saw her softly shaded eyes shining in the dim lamplight, her oval face so gentle and yet so heroic.

"I should not be here," she said, "but I could not resist coming to see you. You are not offended, are you?"

"Offended, no! You have done so much for me," said Lifu, controlling himself. "I must thank you for giving your pearls to save my life."

On an impulse, he bent down and took her white hand and kissed it gently.

"You know I would give greater things to save your life. I have not done wrong, have I?" she pleaded.

"Why . . .? Except that people might misunderstand," he replied.

"Lifu, I am thinking of leaving Peking. When you come out of here, you should take your family and leave Peking, too. Bury yourself in your studies. You know your life means so much to my sister—and to me."

The guard knocked again, and Mulan rose and stretched out her hands and held Lifu's, and said good-by.

She left the prison gate and stood for a moment, wavering, turned to the right and walked a short distance. Her legs were limp and her heart was pounding, and she suddenly shuddered. She could hardly support herself and paused for breath, leaning on a lamppost. A passerby paused and taking her for a streetwalker, turned to look at her. Enraged, she walked on. A rickshaw was waiting ten yards away, with a lantern lighted. Mulan set her teeth and called the rickshaw.

"To the commander's headquarters!" she said. Her heart pounded louder and louder, until she thought the rickshaw puller must hear it. Professor Kao's wife had gone to plead for her husband's life; why shouldn't she go to plead for Lifu's? Yet how was she to report herself? What if Mochow should hear of it? What if Sunya should hear?

Above all, how was it going to work out? Yet she was sure of one thing, that Lifu must be released at once, before it was too late.

She got down at the commander's office. The guards asked what she wanted.

"I want to see the commander."

"Who are you?"

"Never mind. I must see him."

The guards looked at each other and smiled. They went in and reported to the commander that a beautiful lady they had not seen before wanted to see him. The commander ordered her to be shown into a room.

Mulan stepped into the room trembling, cold perspiration on her forehead. She tried to calm herself. She knew that she was beautiful, but would the commander listen to the mere pleading of a beautiful woman? Would this new commander act in the same way as the Manchurian commander who shot Professor Kao?

The commander came in and was struck by an apparition of beauty. "Do not disturb," he shouted to the guards, who went out and shut the door.

Mulan went down on her knees and kowtowed on the ground. "Great Commander, grant a woman a humble request."

The commander laughed and said, "Get up. A beautiful woman like you does not have to kneel before me."

Mulan raised her eyes and rose, and the commander motioned her to a seat.

"I am speaking for a prisoner. He is wrongly arrested. He is a professor, but his name is not on the list of radical professors. A personal enemy of his has informed against him, and he is imprisoned for writing an essay on 'Feeling in Trees.'"

The commander listened fascinated to the low musical flow of Mulan's words, so slowly and clearly pronounced with the superior Peking accent.

"What? Arrested for an essay on trees?" roared the commander.

"Yes," said Mulan with a smile, "an essay on 'Feeling in Trees.' The judge called it communist theory."

"How can that be?" said the commander in a pleasant, conversational tone. "Well, tell me. I shall be good to you."

"Well," said Mulan, "this man says . . ."

"Wait a minute, who is this man?"

644

"His name is Kung Lifu, and he is in the First Prison."

"And who are you?"

"Do you mind if I don't answer the question?"

"Ha! ha! So it is to be a secret."

Mulan picked up courage. "May I beg you a favor?"

"Certainly, a charming lady like you."

"Please keep this visit a secret."

"Don't you know the door is locked?" said the commander with a roar of laughter.

"That is not funny, is it?" said Mulan.

"What do you mean?" said the commander, his face changed.

"You know that there was a professor who was arrested a week ago. His wife went to beg the favor of the Manchurian commander. This commander is not a gentleman—you know those Manchurians who come from outside the Great Wall—well, this commander had bad intentions toward the young woman, and the young woman refused to comply and her husband was shot. I know you are different and that is why I have come to you. Everybody says that General Wu Peifu's officers are better educated."

The commander's face gradually changed as he heard this unknown woman delivering this unusual discourse. Mulan continued:

"You know, if it were not for General Wu Peifu, the wicked Anfu party would still be in power. And look at the Manchurian soldiers offering their worthless 'Manchurian notes' to the public! It is like robbery."

Thus Mulan played upon the personal jealousy between the two rival commanders appointed to nearly the same office for the same city by the rival warlords. It could not be said that this commander had exactly noble intentions when he ordered the door locked, but he was susceptible to flattery, and when Mulan mentioned the other commander's "bad intentions," his own intentions became automatically "good." He had just won the fight for the office and felt very pleased with himself. His grin disappeared and he assumed a dignified appearance.

"Strange young lady—I don't know what your name is—you know I am here to protect the innocent."

"Then please protect him. We would be so much in your debt. A note from you would be enough," Mulan said and rose to bow to him again. She was surprised at her own courage. She had come in, in

645

sheer desperation, not knowing how she was to come out again. But now her fears had gone.

The General was amused by Mulan's poise and familiarity.

"Not so fast. If you can convince me he is not a communist, I will set him free, but not before."

"Well, I tell you, this enemy of Mr. Kung is a relation of mine—in fact of Mr. Kung's—and so I know. He is with the Manchurian faction, and the judge is their man. Can you imagine anyone being called a communist for writing an essay on trees?"

"That does not seem sensible. But why was he sentenced?"

"He wrote that trees have feelings like animals, that if we break a branch, the tree feels hurt; and if we strip its bark, it is like a slap on the tree's face."

"That has nothing to do with communism."

"But the judge says he is giving the trees a consciousness, and is therefore dragging man to the level of animals and trees. You believe trees have feeling, too, don't you?"

"I don't know."

"Why, it is nothing new. We all believe that old trees become genii, and no one dares to chop them down. People have seen blood coming out when an old tree is chopped down."

"Why, of course, of course," roared the commander. "Even the rocks of Taishan have spirits. Of course they have feelings."

"Then you will set Mr. Kung free? Please, commander," said Mulan with a consciously winning smile.

The commander asked again about the details, and Mulan replied that Lifu was a scientist and his name was not on the list, and it was all on account of a personal grudge.

"What is the reason for this private grudge you allege?"

"Well, this is all among our family relatives. This New was involved in a scandal, and Mr. Kung, my relative, exposed him. New had also a sister, who was married into our family, and after the exposure, we were forced to divorce her. He wrote my father a letter, swearing revenge, and this is his work."

The commander looked long at her beautiful face with its winning smile and then he swore and said, "You force me to be a good man," and he shouted to the guards, and a guard came in.

"Bring me pen and paper."

Mulan stood over the commander, gave the name and place of the prison, her heart delighted beyond measure. She suggested adding the word "immediately" before the word "release." She very nearly dictated to the commander, and he complied.

Mulan received the slip of paper from him and wanted to go down on her knees, but the commander stopped her.

"Now may I beg a favor of you?" he said.

"How dare I refuse you anything?" Mulan answered.

"Tell me your name."

"My name is Yao Mulan."

"You win tonight. And my congratulations to—er—Mr. Kung. I hope you see that I am here to protect the innocent."

"I shall tell everybody about it," said Mulan.

"No secret, then?" laughed the commander.

"No secret," replied Mulan, with a full, grateful smile.

Putting the paper in her handbag, she said, "Then I must go—and a thousand thanks."

"Must you go so soon?" said the commander regretfully.

"Yes, I must."

The commander accompanied her to the house door and ordered the guards to show her politely to the gate, and then he turned round and cursed at the empty corridor.

At the gatehouse, Mulan asked for the telephone. Excited with her unexpected and complete triumph, she called up her sister.

"Lifu will be free . . . I have his pardon . . . Why, I am Second Sister . . . I am at the Commander Wang's headquarters. . . . Never mind how. . . . Sunya telephoned? Oh yes . . . you call him up for me. . . . I am coming straight to you."

Too excited now to ride in a rickshaw, she called for a taxicab, and when it came she thought of her husband and told the driver to go to her home first. It was just a little past ten o'clock. Sunya had not yet gone to sleep, but was fretting in the room, almost ready to go out and search for Mulan. He had telephoned an hour ago, to find that Mochow had not gone to the prison and that his wife had left it some time ago with Chen San, who had come back alone. Where was she? He had been waiting for three quarters of an hour. Then he had a telephone call from Mochow saying that Mulan was going back to Mochow's place and Lifu was free. Now he saw his wife coming in, all excited, shouting,

"Lifu is free!"

"Where have you been?" he asked.

"Direct to Commander Wang's headquarters. See the grant of release?"

"I thought you went to the prison."

"But we were not admitted. I went with Chen San. . . . Aren't you pleased that Lifu is to be free?"

"Of course. But how did you get this?" asked her husband, examining the writ of release.

"I will tell you the whole story at Sister's place. Come! The taxicab is waiting and Sister must be waiting every second for me. I told her I was going straight to her, then I thought I must see you first."

In the car, Sunya asked again, none too enthusiastically, "How did you get his pardon?"

"By going direct to the commander himself."

"But how did you get him to grant the pardon?"

"Just by arguing with him."

"Was it so easy?"

"Of course. What do you think of me?"

Sunya was silent.

"I have got him out, and you don't even compliment me. Aren't you glad, Sunya?"

Sunya paused and said, "How did you introduce yourself, as my wife or what? How did you come to think of that? And why didn't you let me know first? I was anxious for you and wondered where you had gone."

"I didn't introduce myself at all. I didn't do anything wrong, did I?"

"It was very dangerous, you know."

"I had to do it. Sunya, please, when I left the prison, I had an irresistible impulse. I felt a direct appeal to the commander, by a woman, might be of some use. He is of the Chihli faction, opposed to Huaiyu's. And I was right."

"You little devil!" said Sunya, half approvingly and half insinuatingly.

The car had already reached the Garden of Quiet and Suitability. The entrance was lighted and servants were expecting them. Chen San was at the gate. Sunya told the taxicab to wait.

Mochow met them at the corridor leading to her courtyard. Mulan thrust the paper into her sister's hand and said, "There! It bears the commander's seal." Under the light of the corridor lamp, Mochow read it with tears of delight, and said, "Second Sister, how did you get this?" She started to run ahead of them but only with great effort because of the weight of the child in her body. She shouted to the people inside that Lifu was free.

"Tell us how you did it?" said Mochow.

"Well, after leaving the prison, I thought of how Mrs. Kao went to the Manchurian commander to beg for her husband's life. . . ."

"You did!" said Sunya. Mulan was a little abashed at her own words.

"Well, that gave me an idea. I thought this Commander Wang might be more reasonable."

"I admire your courage," said Coral. "Suppose he hadn't been?"

"Well, let me tell the story. I posed as a strange, unknown woman and asked to see the commander, and was shown in. The door was locked and he was grinning behind his beard and I was terrified. I knew that he hated the other commander who had been appointed to the same office by the Dog-Meat General, and I began by mentioning how his rival had shot Professor Kao. I said the other commander was no gentleman and that he tried to bargain Kao's wife's favors. You ought to have seen his face change. He became so serious and dignified. That encouraged me and I praised General Wu Peifu's officers a little, and when I saw him trying to look very decent, I lost all fear and talked with him more easily. I simply told him that it was a case of personal enmity, and that the informer was a relative of mine and of Lifu's and so I knew. And he said, 'I am here only to protect the innocent.' So I closed in and asked him to save Lifu. I don't know why he was so easy to deal with. Then he wanted me to convince him that Lifu was not a communist, and I told him of his being accused on the evidence of the essay on 'Feeling in Trees.' I knew he was superstitious and so made him admit himself that trees have feeling, by talking about old trees that become genii and shed blood when chopped down. He roared in approval and said, 'Of course, of course, trees have feeling. They can even become spirits!' And so I got it."

The company had been listening intently, and when Mulan finished, Coral said, "It was so easy as all that! Sister, you have really read the *Strategies of Warring Kingdoms* well."

"It does indeed sound like a piece out of *Strategies of Warring Kingdoms* itself," said Afei. "Second Sister always has whimsical ideas."

"Who told my parents not to have me born as a boy?" said Mulan, with quiet satisfaction.

"Mulan, I must give you a dinner tomorrow to thank you," said Lifu's mother.

Sunya had been listening to Mulan's account, at first skeptically, but toward the end he was impressed and saw the others were impressed with him, and now he said proudly, "Mulan deserves a dinner from Auntie Kung and another dinner from Lifu and Mochow themselves. This was like going into the tiger's den to capture a cub." And Mulan looked at Sunya with an expression of relief on her face, like a sky from which clouds have just been blown away.

"But we must let Lifu know immediately. Can we get him out tonight? Can we telephone?" Mulan said.

"With this commander's seal, we should be able to get him out at any time," said Sunya.

"But the warden was away," said Chen San. "We must find the warden first."

Sunya, Chen San, and Mochow went off to the prison in that dark night. Mochow wanted her sister to go, too, but Mulan, having a feeling that she perhaps had already done more than she should, said against her own desires, "No. Sunya, when you go in, you should let my sister be the one to take him the news alone."

So she waited at home with the others for Lifu's return.

Lifu came home about twelve o'clock that night, May 8, two days before the Dog-Meat General became supreme commander of the joint forces near Peking. He had been in prison exactly eight days.

CHAPTER XXXIX

THE following month Mulan suffered from dysentery and had a narrow escape. She was now entering the saddest period of her life. The experiences of the past two months had sapped her vitality, and she had indigestion and was very much thinner. The sorrow of Aman's death left a deep scar upon her, and for nearly a year, she never once recovered her gaiety of spirit.

The family had been completely changed. Only one had not changed, and that was Mannia. She, too, had aged a little, but to Mulan she remained always the same beautiful and kind Mannia whom she had worshiped since childhood. Her adopted son Asuan had now been graduated from the college and was employed in the customs service at Tientsin. He was as fond of Mannia as if she had been his real mother, and he had learned her refined ways and seemed quite different from the other young men of his generation.

Chinya had run away during the scare, fearing trouble for himself after Lifu's arrest, and had come back only when the situation was more settled. Ailien was living with her husband away from home, but in Peking, and sometimes came to visit them; she was now mother of two children. She had made a match for her sister Lilien, who was married to another doctor, so that Cassia had two Western-trained doctors for sons-in-law. Cassia's hair was gray and she had become stouter; but, seeing her daughters well married, she had no worries, and she looked rather young for a grandmother. She did not like to move about, which was her privilege since she had worked hard in youth, but she still talked very vigorously and said things that amused the younger generation. But between her and Mrs. Tseng, the latter was more lovely in old age. Mrs. Tseng was old and infirm, but she still had delicate features and a small, intelligent face which showed that she had been beautiful in her youth. And there was this difference: Mrs. Tseng still painted her eyebrows and powdered her face, while Cassia had neglected these things since Mr. Tseng died.

With the exception of Mrs. Tseng, Mulan's parents on both sides were now gone, and she felt a heavier sense of responsibility. Afei was of age and could take care of himself well enough with Paofen at his side. They had both become very modern since their return from England, and their baby was looked after by a modern nurse.

Lifu had been advised to go down to Shanghai for a vacation, for Peking was full of uncertainties and he could be rearrested at a militarist's pleasure. The Manchurian faction was coming more and more into control.

It was uncertain what Lifu would do. The Cantonese National Army had started on its northern expedition. Taiyun, Chen San, and Huan-erh had already gone to the south to join in the work of the Kuomintang, which was an important element. Mochow stood absolutely firm on the point that Lifu should quit politics and devote himself to scholarly studies. She had great difficulty in restraining him from joining the northern expedition of the Kuomintang; but she prevailed. Mochow had a rocklike determination at times, when she would not consider any point of view but her own, even at the risk of unpleasantness. She had made the decision that her husband could not go into politics, and that was all. Yet it was more or less decided that Lifu's family would move down south.

Mulan lay in bed and thought of herself and those closest to her— Sunya and her remaining two children. The children were yet young, and her mother-in-law was old and infirm, and the family responsibility was upon her head. She wanted to get away and she could not.

Sunya had cooled toward her, and she well knew why. She had deceived him about her visit to Lifu in prison alone at night, for Lifu, fearing a misunderstanding, had not even told his wife about it. But Sunya heard of the pearls that Mulan had given, at the dinner the day after Lifu's release, when everybody was toasting Mulan for her part in the rescue. Sunya realized that to Mulan pearls were nothing from a monetary point of view, even though they were unusual pearls and a part of her dowry. Mulan and Lifu were good friends, he knew, and there was no reason why she should not do her part. But she was clearly too excited, too unlike herself, too concerned, during Lifu's imprisonment. They were as good to each other as usual, but there was something that remained, unspoken, between them.

652

Moreover, Sunya began to care increasingly for money and to involve himself in small business ventures. The curio shop had made large profits and he became more and more interested in bonds and other investments. Now in his middle thirties, he was developing an authoritative, complacent manner, and was never willing to be contradicted. That light-heartedness of his youth, that poetic contempt of wealth and position, were gone. This change in his spirit was somehow reflected in his face, and it pained Mulan. She dreaded to discover some of these dregs in her husband's soul.

Mannia, coming to look after Mulan in her illness, saw them quarrel for the first time.

"I still want to leave Peking," said Mulan.

"Why are you so restless?" Sunya asked curtly.

"I told you I wanted to leave Peking immediately after Aman died."

"You know Lifu is moving away," he said. Mulan swallowed a sob.

Mannia interfered. "You must be kinder to her, when she is so weak."

"Sunya," said Mulan, looking up at him imploringly, "you remember years ago we spoke of giving up this mansion style and going somewhere in the country to live a simple peasant life as obscure people. I said I was willing to cook and wash, with you by my side. I want peace. Can't I have peace?"

"But how can we?" replied her husband. "Mother is living, and she is old. How can we leave her? And how about my brother and Mannia? It is your sentimentality."

"Oh, Sunya, I thought you would understand," said Mulan. Her illness had made her voice unusually soft and low.

Seeing his wife sick and pleading, he said, "All right, I promise. But we cannot leave Mother in her old age."

"I will wait, if you will promise," said Mulan meekly.

"Sunya," said Mannia, "you will not mind my saying something, as your eldest sister-in-law. You are blind. You are the luckiest man in the world, and you do not know it. With such a wife, wanting to live a small home life and cook and wash for you and teach the children—is this ordinary mortal luck? You seem not to appreciate it. You do not know woman. And you do not know what the loss of Aman meant to her."

Sunya now seemed touched and turned to his wife and said, *"Meimei,* forgive me."

653

Then Mannia said to Mulan, "What Sunya says is also right. I do not think, out of filial piety, you should leave mother and go away while she is living."

.·.

When Mulan was well enough to go out, Afei and Paofen gave a party at the Grand Hotel de Pékin. It had a double purpose. Afei had seen that his sister was looking very sad and thin and wanted to divert her mind, and so the party was given to celebrate her return to health. A second reason was that Lifu had come back from his "vacation" and was moving south with Mochow and their mother to live in Soochow, where they had a teashop and where Lifu had found a good house for rent. Since Chinya also had come back, the whole family was invited. Present on the Tseng side were Mrs. Tseng, Cassia, Mannia, Mannia's mother, Asuan, Sunya, Mulan, Chinya, Dimfragrance, Sutung, Ailien, Lilien, and her husband, Dr. David Wang of the Peking Union Medical College. On the Yao and Kung side, there were Mr. and Mrs. Feng, Redjade's two brothers, Afei, Paofen, Coral, Lifu, Mochow, and Poya. It was a great family gathering. Mr. and Mrs. Fu were the only non-relatives in the party.

They were to dine at the hotel and dance after dinner. In the whole party, however, only seven could dance—Chinya, Afei, Sutung, and David Wang among the men, and Paofen, Ailien, and Lilien among the women. The rest would simply watch. Ailien and Lilien, now married to modern doctors and moving in English-speaking circles, were called by their husbands, "Eileen" and "Lilian" respectively. Sutung signed himself "Sutton" and David was David.

This was the first time that Mannia ever had dined at a foreign hotel or had seen a modern dance. If her father-in-law had been living, she could not have gone, but now that he was dead, she had a great desire to see the dancing. For her it was the breaking of all precedents. But she was now a middle-aged woman and therefore regarded herself and was regarded by Mrs. Tseng as beyond the pitfalls and temptations of youth.

As this was in a foreign hotel, Afei and Paofen, being modern, had arranged to separate the husbands and wives at table, that most nonsensical and inexcusable custom of foreigners, who believe so much in romance. Mulan was surprised, but Afei said, "We will be laughed at in this place if we don't." Furthermore, as they were seated at a long, straight table, group conversation such as was natural at a round table became impossible. This talking to the woman next to you and not to your wife was most unusual. David Wang and a few of the men did talk with the women next to them, but others did not. The other women either sat speechless, trying to look at the women at other tables, or to talk across their neighbors to other women, which was most uncomfortable.

Lifu and Mr. Fu sat at one end next to Paofen, while Mulan and Mochow sat at the other end next to Afei. Mrs. Tseng and Mrs. Fu were in the middle opposite each other, and Sunya sat between his mother and Mannia. Dimfragrance sat opposite Mannia near Afei's end of the table. Cassia was seated next to her son-in-law, David Wang.

Mulan was still weak and pale and did not talk much, in spite of the gaiety of the dinner. She smoked a cigarette, but could not enjoy it. Sunya tried to talk with Mannia, but she was all agog and so afraid of making a mistake that she did not respond much, so he talked with his mother and Mrs. Fu across the table.

Now at this time, Chinese women had suddenly discarded their jackets and adopted the so-called "Manchu gown." Mulan and Mochow naturally followed the fashion. Mochow was wearing a white dress but it was made very ample, because her expected baby was already in its seventh or eighth month. Mulan wore a peach dress trimmed with three narrow black lines at the border. It made a complete transformation in her figure and was a revelation even to her husband. Whereas her natural body line had been broken below the waist by the ends of the jacket, now the long gown revealed the natural perfection of her figure to great advantage.

A few ultra-modern women had begun to wear brassières and show off their breasts. Mannia had borrowed a gown from Mulan for the occasion and she looked quite different from her usual self. She was occupied, however, in watching those who wore these modern evening dresses. She would eat a mouthful, then quickly look askance at these women, and as quickly lower her glance for shame, and then look up again. It happened that a tall blonde foreign woman, in a glittering evening gown, walked directly past their table. Mannia was lifting to her mouth with a fork a slight morsel that she had just succeeded in scraping from her meat, when this tall woman passed. When she saw a full naked back only two feet away, directly in front of her, the fork dropped from her hand on the plate with a clang and she gave a mouselike squeak and an involuntary gasp. The foreign woman turned round to look at her, and Mannia, who had always been afraid of foreigners, looked up with fear in her roelike eyes.

Some couples had already begun dancing during the dinner. Mrs. Fu who sat obliquely across from Mannia saw her lips quiver in excitement and wonder; and then saw how she kept her eyes down upon the food in front of her, as if it were immoral even to look at the dancers. Only when dinner was over and David and Sutung began to join in the dancing, did Mannia decide it was proper for her to look. Lilien had a slender figure and she danced beautifully. Coming back to the table, with her face flushed, she saw Mannia watching her with a smile.

Afei came to ask Paofen to dance. Paofen's seat was temporarily vacant, and Lifu signaled to Sunya to come over to it. Lifu had been talking with Mr. Fu about his plans for going south. When he had come in, he had met Sunya and thought Sunya was cool toward him. This was the second time he had noticed it, for on the first meeting after his return, he had also noticed that Sunya had changed toward him. But he was going away and this party was partly in his honor, and it seemed to him Sunya might have said a few more words when they met. Nothing pained him more keenly than to see an old friend become cool, or to meet an old schoolmate after long separation with a great intenseness on his own part and to find that his feeling was not reciprocated. It was like looking at a beautiful landscape that thrilled one, only to find that one's companion was unmoved; but in the case of landscape, the admirer could still keep the thrill to himself. In a friendship reciprocity is the basis of its existence and one feels as if the landscape vanished, or like a child who sees its toy broken. As soon as Paofen's seat was vacated, therefore, he beckoned to Sunya to come and join the conversation between himself and Mr. Fu. Sunya came and chatted with them as usual and Lifu felt better. Mulan's eyes were constantly turning in their direction, while she was watching the dance.

When Paofen returned from the dance and found her seat occupied, she went to Sunya's seat. After a while, Chinya came and asked her to dance with him. She was beautifully dressed that night, and she was the youngest of the women present. Chinya was in foreign dress, for he had associated lately a great deal with returned students, and his slender figure led the shining Paofen in skillful steps.

On that crowded floor was a motley company of Chinese and foreigners, of the new and of the old. Many Europeans were dancing with slim, small-boned Chinese partners. Curiously, many of the pro-Confucian older officials and bankers did not object to dancing, but actually loved it. Two old gentlemen dancing in Chinese long gowns particularly attracted attention. One of them had a rotund body and merely walked around the floor on his flat-heeled shoes. No difference between walking and dancing was observable in his case, except that he had one arm outstretched and one arm around a lady's waist.

When Chinya came near this fat old gentleman, he caught a glimpse of his partner's face, which gave him a shock. Surely, it was Suyun, his own divorced wife! But she had changed so much. They had been separated only seven years. Apparently she had not seen him and she had become lost in the crowd again.

"What is it?" asked Paofen, noticing Chinya's sudden stop.

"It is she!" Chinya whispered, as he resumed his steps.

"Who?"

"My former wife, Suyun."

Paofen had never yet seen Suyun, and she wanted to see her closely. Chinya suggested that they leave the floor, but Paofen said, "What for? Are you afraid of her?"

"No. It is just awkward," he said.

And so they danced on, and Paofen asked him to dance near to the fat old man and his partner. She caught glimpses of Suyun's face, and when they came very near she saw that Suyun was decorated all over with diamonds and was wearing a very expensive dress. Nevertheless, she gave the impression of hunger, for she looked unhappy and dry with the dryness which came from a face no longer capable of joy. There were deep lines about her eyes and her cheeks were sallow. The cheerlessness of her expression, in spite of a sharp gleam still in her eyes, made the vermilion bud of her painted lips almost a joke.

They came closer, and now Suyun saw her former husband. The gleam in her eyes brightened. It was but a moment, and there was no need for them to accost each other. She turned to look defiantly again at the fashionable and strikingly beautiful woman with Chinya. Paofen returned the look and saw the huge diamond brooch on her breast, and an affected smile on her face that was most unconvincing. It was such a smile as would make any one think that happiness and her face could not be seen together.

Paofen whispered to Chinya. "Smile! Laugh! Look as happy as you can."

But they could not see Suyun any more. They came back to the table with the exciting news.

"Are you sure?" asked Mrs. Tseng.

"Of course," said Chinya. "I ought to be able to recognize my former wife. She is dancing with the fat old man in a long gown."

The word went round the table in half a minute and everybody was stretching to see. But their table was in a far corner, and it was hard to see the dance floor.

"Who is the fat old man?" asked Mulan.

Nobody knew. Afei asked the waiter, and the waiter said, "That is General Wu."

"Wu Peifu does not dance," said Afei.

"No, this is General Wu of the Manchurian faction. They have come to Peking and are stopping at this hotel."

"Who is the lady dancing with him?" asked Mulan.

"That is his fifth, sixth, or seventh mistress. Who knows?"

"Is she staying with the general?"

"No, he is staying in the room with Third-and-half, and she stays in an adjoining room."

Mulan, Mochow, and Dimfragrance strained their ears to listen.

"What do you mean?" one said.

"Third-and-half is his favorite concubine. She is sitting there at the other end. She is very fashionable and good-looking."

"Why is she called Third-and-half?" Afei asked.

"Well, she is supposed to be the fourth mistress, but she's somebody else's concubine, really, while she openly lives with him. The three of them usually come to dine together."

"Doesn't Third-and-half dance?" asked Mulan.

"She does," the waiter answered.

"Why isn't she dancing tonight?"

"How do I know?"

Suyun and the fat old man did not dance any more, although Paofen and Ailien and Lilien danced several times in the hope of getting a close glimpse of them.

After half an hour, they saw the general rise from the far corner and walk out of the room, followed by Suyun and another woman whom they agreed was Inging. Suyun as she went out turned once to look in their direction and seemed to have seen them.

Now that the other party was gone, they talked less in whispers, as though the others could have heard them before. Mochow asked Afei to learn from the waiter more about General Wu and the women, and the waiter came and was quite willing. He went away to ask from other waiters and came back to say that General Wu had come to Peking only three days ago. Third-and-half, who shared the room with him, was no other than the famous Inging, who was one Mr. New's concubine but had been presented to the general, and this Inging's husband was now the general's right-hand man. The thin lady was no other than Mr. New's own sister. "Do you wonder that his position under the general is so secure? It is all in the family," the waiter concluded.

"What are they doing here?" asked Afei.

"Just pleasure. They have got rich on opium," the waiter said. "They own one of the biggest opium firms in Tientsin, in the Japanese concession. They have a lot of money and own several hotels in Tientsin where people can smoke opium under the Japanese and the general's protection. My friend's brother works in a hotel in Tientsin and knows all about them. I will tell you a joke. This general has a private car for each of his concubines, and each woman's car is useful in smuggling 'white-flour' (heroin). Women are best for carrying such goods back and forth. They all have simple license numbers, and all the policemen know them by heart, so they are secure. Well, this 'third-and-half' has a license number "303." One day they found some one had painted a mark on it, so that it became "303½" and everybody in Tientsin talked about it. This other thin lady is called the 'White-Flour Queen.' You mark my words. This kind of black money will flow out again as easily as it flows in. She will come to a bad end. But don't tell anyone that I told you."

Afei gave him a dollar bill and dismissed him with a smile. The company sat until about eleven o'clock and then returned home.

.•.

Not only did Mochow insist on her husband's devoting himself to his studies, but his mother and even Mulan agreed that he should never go into politics because he was not made for political life. Surrounded by these three women, he yielded and in the early autumn of

659

1926, when Mochow's new baby was barely a month old, they moved down to Soochow. There, living in the outskirts of the city, in a straggling house on the canal, Lifu lived with his books and his scientific apparatus. But he gave more time to his books than to his laboratory.

In that ancient city of bridges and canals, he buried himself in his studies. No other city was more suited to this purpose than Soochow. The Soochow people were so contented with their own traditional life, with its small talks and "small eats," that they passed a law forbidding modern motor cars to enter the city gates. The city elders even objected, a year later, to having Soochow made the provincial capital and let Chinkiang have that honor, because to be a provincial capital meant the stationing of troops and constant danger of war in the neighborhood. The inhabitants of Soochow wanted to be left alone and were willing to leave the world alone.

In the calm, quiet corners of that old and unperturbed city, one might think that nothing ever happened. But Lifu whipped himself to work with a strange passion and he was often irritable. There was an explanation for this. He was seriously interested in the study of bone inscriptions that Mulan had suggested to him. There was a spell of sheer delight in working upon these ancient pictorial signs, deciphering figures and forms yet undeciphered by other scholars, observing and comparing the variants, and tracing their transformations and evolution into the later forms of Confucius' time. The work was also important because these bone inscriptions represented the earliest known forms of Chinese writing, and often threw light upon the histories of words or of religious practices and caused the theories about them to be modified. No paleographist could be up-to-date without keeping abreast of the new researches in this field. And Lifu had many brilliant suggestions.

But the seriousness of his work did not account for his irritability or for his passion for it. With him paleographic study was strangely emotional, a kind of penance, a method of escape from other passions. First of all, there was that Kuomintang expedition against the warlords. Chen San and Huan-erh, as well as Taiyun, were now with the Kuomintang Army, which was capturing city after city with the help of the young party workers, who went ahead of the marching troops to do propaganda and to win the people over to revolution against the warlords. Huan-erh sent letters from the front, which usually came a month late and bore varying addresses because they were moving northward all the time. Within a few months, the Kuomintang Army had conquered several provinces and had captured Hankow. Shanghai and Soochow were still ruled by an old militarist, Sun, and Lifu had to be careful, because Kuomintang sympathizers were liable to arrest. In Shanghai people were arrested for having in their possession Kuomintang handbills, handed to them by strangers on the streets. When Lifu received a letter from Huan-erh he carefully examined the envelope to see whether it had been censored or tampered with. And the more enthusiastically she described in her letters the Kuomintang victories and their happy comradeship on the way, the more restless Lifu became.

Moreover, against his instinct, there was always before him a picture of Mulan, which constantly disturbed him. He had always a sense that she was waiting for the completion of his work. With all the emotional force of a grand passion, he was determined to write the most through, authoritative, and brilliant study on his subject. Ancient people called this "breaking a dyke to divert a stream"; modern people call it "sublimation." For the first year Mulan's letters to her sister usually closed with the best regards to Lifu, and then these references to him became rarer. He usually asked his wife to send his regards also in her letters to Mulan, but there was no sign that Mulan had read them as coming from him.

Mulan's words constantly rang in his ears: "Write the best and most brilliant book on the subject, even if it takes years." He tried to brush these words and Mulan's voice away from his head, as Mulan had brushed her hair away from her forehead in the Cedar Grove; but they came back again and again, even as the forest breeze had blown Mulan's hair back again and wafted with it some of the fragrance of the cedars.

She had spoken these words to him on the day before he left Peking. Mochow and Lifu had come to see Mulan. Sunya was not at home. It was Mochow's habit to pack their things long before a journey, and so they had now a day free for pleasure. Mulan suggested that before their departure they should go to a corner of Peking that they had not seen for some time.

"What better place than Shihshahai!" she said.

It was the place where Mulan and Lifu had seen the flood years ago, while Mochow was at home, ironing Lifu's clothes, and when none of them was yet engaged. Now they went to the same restaurant and sat on the same balcony. It happened also to be at about the same time of the year, so that the scene was much the same. In the distance were still visible the Drum Tower and the Dagoba of Peihai.

There was not much in anything they said, but there was much in what they felt. Mulan had the habit of fixing in her memory certain moments spent with Lifu. She recalled that when they were last in this place, exactly twenty years ago, her father and Redjade were with them. Where was her father now? He had been gone seven years, and if he was still alive, it would be three years before he came back. She thought of the drowning of Redjade and spoke sadly of it to her sister, with tears in her eyes, and Mochow thought that she was unduly sentimental. Mulan also talked of her own desire to move south and her inability to go on account of her sick old mother-in-law.

It was then that they all talked of Lifu's plans for his studies in the south, and Mulan said those memorable words to him about his work.

Lifu had used no more than the usual formula in thanking Mulan for her dramatic effort to obtain his release, but he felt more and more deeply as he reflected what that adventure implied. He recalled that she had said to him alone that night in the prison, before she went to see the commander, "I would give greater things to save your life." What if the commander had acted as the Manchurian commander had done with Mrs. Kao? Would Mulan have sacrificed even her honor to save his life? Mulan, he thought was never bound by conventional ideas; perhaps she might have done even that! The question could not be asked, but it remained in his mind. The memory of the great test of love could not be shaken from him and it was transmuted and became part of the emotional energy that went into his research.

Both Lifu and Mulan were loyal to Mochow. He often had a haunting sense of guilt when Mulan's eyes and voice came into his mind in the midst of his work. There were hidden recesses of the soul, however, that social disapproval could not reach.

Mochow felt all this, but both toward her sister and toward her husband she acted in such a way that no scandal could touch them. She never showed any sense of jealousy. The meaning of what Mulan said years ago before her engagement, "Sister, you are the luckier one," was quite clear to her now. But she knew her sister and her husband too well and was confident of them both. And so she would often tell Lifu what Mulan was doing when she received a letter from her. The sisters wrote to each other regularly, but Mochow was a better correspondent than Mulan.

Back in Peking, Mulan was living more quietly than ever with her husband and her two remaining children. The ever faithful Brocade and her husband were still serving them. Atung had been sent to school, which was now quite safe because all student demonstrations were stopped after the March Massacre. The Dog-Meat General was in power, and neither teachers nor parents were willing to risk trouble.

Mulan began to settle down to her quiet life with half-contented resignation. Undoubtedly she was less gay. She had convinced herself that to leave her mother-in-law at this period of her old age and infirmity was neither right nor possible. Peking had lost its charm for her, but her own rooms and her courtyard were now as familiar to her as life itself, and once she admitted to Sunya that she would be very sorry to leave them and start an entirely new home in the south.

Now that the prison episode was in the past and Mulan had consented to remain in the north for the present, Sunya behaved as usual toward her. She was quite satisfied with her husband, except for his concern for money, which she called his "worldliness." He was naturally good-natured, and nothing kept him under tension for long. Actually he was an easier husband to live with than Lifu. His character was round, while Lifu's character was square. He was more practical, more objective, less ambitious, and he loved his wife and was good-natured with his children. Lifu considered himself more modern in allowing his wife a greater share in deciding family matters; but he was less evenly cheerful, he talked more in the abstract, and at times his work seemed more important than his home. Sunya often went with his wife on her shopping trips, and took a good-humored interest in her purchases—which Lifu practically never did. Mochow knew her husband's nature well enough, but adapted herself wonderfully to it; she kept quiet when he was excited, and reasserted herself when he was in a mood to be sentimental and yielding. This does not mean that Mulan had a lesser problem in her husband than Mochow in hers, as we shall see later. With all his willfulness and impetuosity, Lifu presented no more complicated problem for his wife than keeping him from coming to harm through his writing.

Now Mulan began to feel a strange love of her own body. When she was bathing at night, she would look with approval at her own arms and legs. She indulged in foreign creams, delicate perfumes, and exquisite toilet soaps. She was bitten with a secret pride in her youth and beauty and with regret that this beauty was perishable. She was yet young and her small bones had helped her to keep her look of delicacy. She had lost none of her lovely hair, and like other women of the time, she began to wear a brassière instead of concealing the roundness of her breasts. From a wet nurse, Brocade obtained for her human milk of which she drank a small bowlful after breakfast and a small bowlful at night because it was said to be good for keeping the smoothness of her skin.

But she knew that beauty of the body could not last forever, and, moreover, she sometimes thought of herself as weak and foolish and through this body a slave to impulses and emotions. She never regretted that she had saved Lifu's life, even at the cost of making herself too conspicuously desperate. But she knew that she had acted impulsively, perhaps foolishly—if also heroically—and she thought herself a weak woman. The stronger her passions, the weaker she considered herself. What would she have done if Lifu had not been her sister's husband? The more she thought of herself as a mortal, the more she admired the translucent, passionless immortality of her jade and amber animals. And since this body gave her both torments and joys, she abandoned herself to its joys to compensate for its torments and explored all its sensations of pleasure. And so she was sometimes ardent toward Sunya. But her sensualism had often an imaginative quality that she could not describe.

Only Brocade knew the full secret, both of her feelings toward Lifu and of her exotic care of her body.

.˙.

Mannia had moved back now to the Calm-Heart Studio, so that the three sisters-in-law could live closer together in a triangle, Mannia in the court behind and Mulan and Dimfragrance in front. Many servants had been sent away since Mr. Tseng's death, some courts were left unoccupied, there were fewer pots of flowers in the house, and the little patch of flower garden in the vacant lot was left to grow mostly of itself. Yet with fewer servants and fewer parties, there was a greater quiet, and Mulan rather liked it. Mrs. Tseng was infirm with secret pains, but she was happy to see the three sisters-in-law and two sons living in harmony by her side. She was always partial to Mulan, and

664

Mulan seemed to be more attached to her than she had been to her own mother.

During her illness, Mannia was occupied with looking after her, and Dimfragrance was for a time in charge of the household. But she still could not exercise authority because she had once served as an equal with some of the older servants. It was not true in her case that one who knew how to obey would know how to command. She could not even stand up for her point of view against her sisters-in-law, and she always ended by saying, "You are right."

To Chinya, she seemed unusually sweet of nature and easy to please, while to her Chinya seemed unusually generous and considerate. She was happy, having given birth to another child, a girl. She had invited her old father to live with her, in the little court between hers and Mulan's, which had once been occupied by the teacher Fang, now long dead. Chinya was temporarily without a job, for the funds for the Conservation Bureau had all been used and the Bureau dissolved, and he shared the fate of all people who hold political jobs during frequent changes of government. But being cautious at business, he had made safe investments in bonds secured on the maritime customs revenue, and these were bringing him unusually good returns.

Mrs. Tseng's secret pains steadily grew more acute. She had now two modern-trained physicians as sons-in-law, and Sutung and David were called in for consultation. They suspected cancer and recommended a series of treatments at the hospital. Sunya and Chinya visited her daily, and the three daughters-in-law took turns staying with her. Her whole attitude toward life had been such that in the hospital as at home, she would suppress her groans, that is, make small groans for great pains, and no groans for small pains. Mulan was the one who was most constantly at her bedside; but Dimfragrance was the one who cried most, for she heard secretly from Chinya that his mother's illness was incurable, and that it was only a matter of time. Once, seeing Dimfragrance weeping, Mrs. Tseng said, "Why should you weep? I am surrounded by my two good sons, three good daughters-in-law, two sons-in-law, and seven or eight grandchildren."

One day when all of her children were there, she said to them, "I shall not live very long now. I really have not much to say. I have had a luckier and happier life than most people. I made the right choice in my daughters-in-law. Only Suyun used to trouble me, but now that is a bygone affair. The house was bought when your father was vice-minister and it does not suit our style of living and our means now. We do not need such a big house. Rent out the main courts, or sell it if you can and get a smaller house. Your father left me some twenty thousand dollars in cash in the banks. Of this, spend not more than two thousand on my funeral. I shall give five hundred to Snow Blossom, for she has served me all my life. We can not keep her now, but help her to find some good position or to set up some small business. Give each of the other servants something, thirty or forty dollars, as you dismiss them. Mulan can decide on that. You understand that he who has generosity has luck. Bury me at Tai-an with your father. Cassia, you need have no worry. The two sons-in-law will look after you well."

And her old eyes looked fondly with tears on her children as they stood around her bed. A few days later, on March 11, 1928, at the age of fifty-nine, she died, with a beautiful and serene smile on her lips.

Burying her in her native city of Tai-an was now out of the question. Her home province had been almost ruined in the past few years by the misrule of the Dog-Meat General. Bandits were spreading over the countryside and all the magistrates were degenerating along with the dissolute governor. It was inconceivable that good men should or could come up and serve under such an illiterate warlord. But the immediate reason why they could not go home was the occupation of the Shantung railways by Japanese sailors.

At the Washington Conference the Japanese had been forced to return Shantung to China. But now the Kuomintang Army, having taken firm hold in the Yangtse valley was resuming its northward march upon Peking. Its advance troops reached Tai-an in April and captured the provincial capital a few days later, and the Dog-Meat General and the Manchurian troops retreated to Tehchow. With the object of blocking the Kuomintang advance and in the name of "protecting Japanese lives," Japanese sailors landed and occupied the railways. Twice they bombed the native city of the Tsengs, and in their worst bombing, at Tsinan, 3,625 civilians were killed, and the damage to property was estimated by official reports as twenty-six million dollars. In addition, 918 Kuomintang members were arrested and imprisoned, and Japanese soldiers and sailors gouged out the eyes and cut off the nose and ears of Tsai Kungshih, the head of the Foreign Affairs Bureau attached to the Political Commission of the army, and then murdered him and his associates in his office. This was known as the "Tsinan Incident," and Japan's violation of the Nine-Power Treaty called forth a proposal from America for mediation, which was opposed by the Japanese.

This savagery was followed on June 4, by the bombing of the car of the Manchurian warlord, Chang Tsolin, by a powerful electrically ignited bomb placed under a railway crossing at which Japanese sentries were constantly on duty. Chang and several of his fellow generals were killed.

All this lawlessness stirred up national indignation and an anti-Japanese boycott, of which Mrs. Tsai, the widow of the murdered commissioner, was a leader. Negotiations over the "incident" were prolonged, and it was not till all Japanese troops were withdrawn and peace restored that Mrs. Tseng's remains were taken to Tai-an and buried by the side of her husband, in the spring of the following year. The Tseng home at Tai-an had escaped destruction, but such atrocities coming so close awakened in Mulan a long dormant political interest and a new anti-Japanese hatred. Even Mannia and Dimfragrance, who had never dreamed of either liking or disliking Japan, now hated Japan.

. .

By the spring, Peking was under Kuomintang rule. Stirred by the assassination of his father, the Manchurian "Young Marshal" had come over to the Kuomintang side, against the repeated threats of the Japanese Army. The Dog-Meat General had escaped to Dairen, the Japanese port in Manchuria, whither the Anfu politicians had fled with their wealth. China was, nominally at least, unified under the Kuomintang, with its new capital in Nanking. And the old name of Peking, meaning "Northern Capital," was changed to "Peiping" or "Northern Peace."

Mulan now revived the old question of going to live in Hangchow. There was the question of the house to settle. They had announced that the main courts were to be rented out. Many houses were being vacated in Peking now, because of the general movement of the official class to Nanking. But one day a new official came to inquire about the house and said that he wanted to buy it if possible. His offer was only for forty thousand dollars, but this was such a rare opportunity that the Tseng brothers decided to accept it and rent a smaller house.

Cassia wanted to go and live with her daughter Ailien. Mulan said

667

that she and her family were planning to live in the south, but that, since the Garden of Quiet and Suitability was half unoccupied, Mannia and Chinya's families might move into it, paying what nominal rent they liked. It would make the Garden more cheerful again and would be better than renting it out.

The idea was accepted. Afei was still living in the Self-Examination Hall. Coral used Mochow's court, since Mrs. Yao's court further inside was occupied by Paofen's parents. No one wanted to live in Redjade's court, as it was considered "unlucky." Dimfragrance and her husband with their children therefore moved into Dim Fragrance Studio. It was then that Dimfragrance sighed happily and said, "Everything seems determined by fate. I had always a feeling that I was going to live here."

The servants in the Garden were mostly new, because Paofen had many Manchu relatives who were unemployed, and she had given them different positions in the household.

Poya was now an overserious grown-up boy of twenty. Coral had been like a mother to him, although he called her "Aunt." Now beginning to assert himself as the eldest grandson of the Yao family, he decided one day that he would move the ancestral tablet of his mother, Silverscreen, into the Chungmintang. An enlarged photograph of his mother, one of many which Tijen had taken, was placed beside that of his father in the center of the hall. He ordered large red candles to be burned continually before the sacrificial table, and often he went himself to pay his respects. This love for his persecuted mother existed side by side with his hatred of his grandmother, whom he had thought of only as a mad and dumb wrinkled old woman, whom he had rarely seen. Having heard his mother referred to as a "ghost" that had struck his grandmother dumb, he believed almost literally in the presence of his mother's spirit.

While the grandmother was living, there had always been a kind of observance of the anniversary of Silverscreen's death, partly to propitiate her spirit and partly in the hope of restoring Mrs. Yao's power of speech. As it was now the twentieth anniversary and Poya himself was twenty this year, he wished to make a special celebration. This pious act on his part was readily approved by all the family, and great preparations were made. Monks were invited, and a lamb and a pig were offered on the altar. There was to be a feast in the evening, and at about six in the afternoon candles were lighted, while prayers were said and the monks struck the wooden fish and bells.

Every one in the two families living in the Garden attended the ceremony. Mrs. Hua, as a close friend of Silverscreen, was also invited. Only Cassia and her daughters were absent. Poya knelt before the tablet of his parents and kowtowed and shed real tears. The grandmother's portrait was included against Poya's wish, only on Afei's insistence. And so, above the portraits of Tijen and Silverscreen were now hung also the portraits of his grandparents. For Mr. Yao had been gone ten years, and there had been no news of him, and this too was an act of pious memory.

The monks were just chanting the Diamond Sutra, when Paofen's daughter rushed in and cried to her mother, "An old monk came in! He looked at me with such big fiery eyes."

"Why are you so excited?" said Paofen. "He is just one of the monks."

"No, he looks most strange," said the child. "I asked him who he was, but he didn't say anything."

"Is he coming here?"

"I saw him going to the Self-Examination Hall. The servants tried to stop him, but he only looked at them with those big eyes and walked along. Mother, he has a long white beard and his eyebrows are all white and bushy—like the God of Longevity."

Now, as they were gathered for the ceremony in the candlelighted hall, the old monk came in and stood silently watching while the prayer was said, and no one noticed his coming. After the prayer, the head priest came forward and made preparations to burn paper money in the courtyard. Some followed the head priest out into the courtyard. Those who remained saw the old monk for the first time. He went to the altar and stood with his palms close together before his chest and with his back to them, muttering a brief prayer. The family stood at attention, expecting him to perform some ceremony, but not knowing what it would be.

Then slowly he turned and, facing the company, said with a calm smile, "I have come back."

Now Mulan had become excited even before he turned around, for from the back she had thought she could recognize her father's head and she had been half wondering if he might not be he. At the sight of his face, with the long white beard and bushy white eyebrows and the powerful eyes, they all gasped.

"It is Father!" cried Mulan and ran to him.

"It is Grandfather!" shouted Paofen.

Afei and Coral rushed after Mulan, and Sunya and Chinya also crowded around the old monk. Hearing the excitement inside, Poya and those who had been in the courtyard watching the burning of the paper money, came hurrying in.

Old Yao smiled behind his white beard and greeted them all, but his eyes looked soft and distant.

Mulan, Coral, and Afei were in tears. Mannia and Dimfragrance hung back, unable to come near. When Poya came forward, old Yao laid his hand on him and said, "This is my grandson, grown so much!" Paofen introduced her two little daughters and they trembled as they looked at their strange grandfather. Mr. Feng came up to speak with his brother-in-law, and it was two old men meeting. Redjade's two brothers, grown young men now, came forward with wondering eyes to see their uncle.

Seeing Mrs. Hua beyond them all, old Yao went toward her and called with a lusty voice, "How are you? So you all are here!" Then he turned and asked, "Where are Lifu and Mochow?"

"They are in the south," replied Mulan.

"Are they well?"

"They are very well," said Mulan. "But you? You look so strong! Where have you been?"

"I have been everywhere."

And when Mulan pressed him, he said, "I stayed at the top of Miaofeng Mountain for a year, and then, fearing that you might come after me, I went on to the Wutai Mountain in Shansi. Then I wandered to the Hua Mountain and lived there for three years. Then I went to Mount Omei in Szechuen. . . ."

"Oh, Father!" shouted Mulan, involuntarily, before he could finish. "Why didn't you take me?"

"I even visited Lifu's native village," said Mr. Yao, calmly. "I narrowly escaped being recognized by Mr. and Mrs. Fu, who were there. . . . I went as far south as Mount Tientai and the Pootoo Islands."

"Why, you were enjoying travel!" said Mulan vehemently and with a suggestion of envy. "I would have followed you if you had let me know."

"How could you?" replied her father. "You young people have to travel by boats and sedan chairs. I climbed the ten-thousand feet of the Hua Mountain on foot, and I walked across Szechuen to Mount Omei and back."

"Did you walk on the water to the Pootoo Islands, Grandfather?" asked Paofen's elder daughter.

"Perhaps I did, perhaps I didn't," said old Yao, so solemnly that with his noble face he seemed to the little girl a mythical saint.

"But," asked Coral, "are there no tigers in the forests and bandits in the country, and wars in Szechuen?"

"I passed a tiger on Hua Mountain," said old Yao with a quiet smile, "and he looked at me and I looked at him and he slunk off. My children, I was traveling partly to enjoy nature and partly to free myself. The two are really the same. Perhaps you do not understand that. The basis of all salvation is the training of the body. You must have no money and no worries, and you must be ready to die at any time. Then you travel like a man come back from the dead, and you look upon every day and every moment as a gift from Heaven, for which you offer thanks. When you carry no money no thief will come near you. But you cannot travel in this way unless you train your body —your hands and your feet and first of all your stomach. You must be able to eat any meal you can find, or go hungry, and you must be able to sleep outdoors or in, and to endure all weather. Unless you have such a body, you cannot be saved."

"But how did you get food?" they asked.

"I begged on the way, and people in villages are kind to an old man. I could lie on a hard rock for the night. At temples, I was always given food and shelter, because I carried a formal, stamped certificate from the Wutaishan Monastery. I carried local medicinal herbs from one place to another and I gave some always to the temples where I stayed. And in the Szechuen forests I saw the silver fungus that grows on old stumps, from which our family has made so much money."

Now the news of the master's return had spread through the entire house, and the servants, old and new, came to see this venerable old man. Paofen's parents also came and greeted him as a "high monk returned to the world." His face was deeply lined and was the color of weather-beaten copper, but in spite of his seventy-two years, he walked with a light step and he spoke in a ringing, if mellowed, voice, and his eyes were as bright as ever. He said that he had trained himself

671

to see in the dark so that he could travel easily on mountain paths at night.

That night there was great merrymaking and toasting even though it was Silverscreen's anniversary. Old Yao, still in his monastic robe, sat down and ate of the fish and chicken as if he were not a monk.

"You are really a 'high monk'?" remarked Paofen's father.

"No," replied Yao. "I was a beggar on the way and often I could not afford to eat vegetables. I had to eat chicken if people gave it to me. What do these things matter?"

When the head priest came in he recognized old Yao and said, "Elder Brother, I did not know you were the old master of this Garden! Did you not stay at our temple on the Western Hills a week ago?"

"Why yes, and my thanks for your hospitality," said old Yao. "I heard then that you were invited to come here and that was why I waited until today." So they all understood how it happened that he appeared at such an appropriate time. Mr. Feng tried to tell him of the condition of the tea and medicine shops, but he did not want to hear anything about the business, and turned away to his grandchildren.

"You are not Grandfather," said Paofen's little five-year old girl, who was bright and mischievous, and, pointing to his portrait in the hall, she said, "There is my grandfather. You are a fairy man."

"Your grandfather went away and now he has come back," Paofen explained.

They told him of Lifu's imprisonment and release and how he had moved away to the south for safety; and, when they had to tell, as one of the reasons for Lifu's conviction, how he had married his sister to Chen San on a hilltop, Mr. Yao heartily said that he liked such a marriage.

Mulan telegraphed to Mochow and the next day received a reply from Soochow, saying that she and her husband would soon come up to see her father.

Mulan and Sunya were already planning to go south to Hangchow. Their goods were partly packed up, and they were temporarily staying in one of the poorer courts in the Garden. Mulan was now faced with the problem of leaving her aged father so soon after he had come back, almost as if it were from death itself. She loved and worshiped her father and could not bear parting from him now. She was happy to have the chance to serve him in his old age, if he would consent. So she went to him and spun out a long argument, saying, "Father, we are going south to live in Hangchow. Do you remember my mother's dream that she had when I was lost? I was the one who was helping you to cross the bridge in your old age. You want a quiet home, and that is exactly what we are going to have. It is too noisy here. And, besides, Hangchow is your old home. Hangchow has the best temples, and if you like we can choose a house near Lingyin. There is no better place on earth for a quiet, retired life."

It was natural for the father to wish to stay with his son. But Mulan said, "Sister Mochow is also in the south, and the classics call a son-in-law a half-son, and two half-sons exactly equal one son."

It was much against Afei's wish, and Mr. Yao asked him, "Why don't you come, too?"

But Afei said that he could not, because Paofen's parents were with him, and he was helping in the Anti-Narcotic Association under his father-in-law, in addition to his work with the shop.

Mr. Yao promised to go with Mulan, but said that he would remain in the Garden until her house in Hangchow should be ready. He telegraphed again to Mochow to wait as he would be coming down to visit her soon. But Mochow came up to Peking alone, because she could not wait to see him, and Mulan stayed to go back with her.

Mochow came about a week later. The sisters had been separated for more than two and a half years, and they were very happy to see each other. Mr. Yao asked many questions about Lifu, but Mulan asked only, "Does he still limp?" and Mochow replied simply, "Yes, he still limps a little."

Mochow was very much loved by all the women relatives, and many dinners were given in her honor. Some of these dinners had the double purpose of welcoming Mochow and saying farewell to Mulan. Mannia gave the last dinner on the evening of their departure. Asuan was present, and told of the difficulties of preventing smuggling of opium and other goods as a result of Japanese consular protection of the smugglers who were both Korean and Japanese. He also told stories of Suyun, who had now many interests in the Japanese Concession, and was called the "White-Flour Queen." Mulan was greatly surprised to hear Mannia speak hotly against the Japanese. Later, she understood.

.·.

After a sad farewell to her sisters-in-law, Mannia and Dimfragrance, Mulan left with her family to make their new home in the south, in

673

the lake city of Hangchow. They traveled with Mochow and went first to Soochow. Mulan was happy and excited because she was about to realize her lifelong dream of a simple, peaceful life in the country, and she was glad to leave forever the luxuries of city life and wealthy society. She could not know that this dream of rural happiness was to carry her into an entirely new and difficult experience.

At Soochow, they stopped to visit Mochow's home. Lifu and his children came to meet them at the railway station. Sunya and Lifu were very cordial to each other, and Lifu, in spite of his limp, insisted on helping to carry Sunya's baggage to the horse carriage. Mulan saw that Lifu was paler than he had been in Peking, and he saw that she was as vivacious as ever, but rather overdressed for Soochow. He appeared in an old cotton gown and old Chinese shoes and he was wearing spectacles, looking very much like a scholar. He declared that he had not worn a foreign suit since he came to Soochow.

They engaged a boat on the canal to take them in a leisurely way to Mochow's home in the western suburb. The canal trip fascinated Mulan and her children. After passing under a whole succession of arched bridges, they came out to a place where the canal widened and the shores became more rural, and there on the bank of the canal was Mochow's house.

Lifu's mother and sister were waiting at the rear gate for them. Huan-erh was now back with her mother, while her husband, Chen San, was serving as a captain with the army. Mulan and Sunya had sent their heavy luggage direct to Hangchow and brought only smaller bags with them, intending to stay only for a night.

Mulan was very eager to see Lifu's study and demanded to be taken to it even before they had their noodles. The Soochow houses had plenty of rooms, and as usual Lifu had an entire court for his study. The room was bare, but well lighted. On a long table against a wall stood a Tibetan buddha two feet high. On the shelves were his old volumes on biology and a great number of old Chinese books, well bound in cloth casings. Some of the titles on the book edges were written very neatly by Chen San, and some, less regular, were in the impatient hand of Lifu. His paleographic studies had carried him necessarily to the related fields of bronze and stone inscriptions, and Sunya noticed volumes like *Hsiching Kuchien* and *Chinshihlu,* as well as piles of early rubbings. In a special cabinet with low drawers, were the oracle bones that Lifu had been able to collect himself, and near the Tibetan buddha lay an enormous inscribed piece that apparently was the shoulderbone of some animal. By a northern window, looking directly into his wife's courtyard, was an unpainted old board which served as his desk, and against it was a shiny brown rattan chair.

Mulan said, "There you sit and work?"

Lifu nodded. "Yes."

She recognized again a broad-necked glass bottle containing cigarette ends and ashes, which she had seen in his Peking laboratory. It was Lifu's idea of the ideal ash receiver, because it gave him the pleasure of seeing clearly through the glass how the ashes accumulated, and because the ashes would not fly about, which more appealed to Mochow. Lifu had remarked once that the idea was original with him, and that it cost nothing.

"Where are your manuscripts?" asked Mulan. "I do not see them."

"They are hidden away in the drawers," replied Lifu.

Now his sister came to call them to have noodles. It was spring, and there was white meat of spring chicken in the noodle. Mulan dipped a piece in soya-bean sauce and ate it and became reconciled to Soochow life at once.

"There is no better chicken anywhere than in Soochow, and no better chicken soup than my mother's," declared Lifu proudly.

"And there is no man better fed and more indulged and pampered at home than Lifu," declared Mochow.

They went on to talk of his work and when it would be finished.

"It is a very large book, and the printing is costly, and I don't know whether anyone will read it, except my wife," said Lifu. "I can't sell more than two hundred copies of it in three years, if it is ever published."

"Is that what is delaying you?" asked Mulan.

"No," said Lifu. "There are some points about which I am still uncertain and need more light. Some of the most difficult and most interesting characters. Do you know that this will upset some texts of the classics themselves? In the first of the *Four Books*, the inscription on Emperor Tang's bathtub was quoted as being: 'Since daily renewed, daily, daily renewed; again daily renewed.' In the light of these inscriptions, it should read: 'Brother's name Hsin; grandfather's name Hsin; father's name Hsin.' Confucius' disciples read the inscription wrong. It must have been the fault of their teacher. It was over a thousand years old by Confucius' time."

675

"You will be called a communist if you have too much of this sort of thing in your book," said Huan-erh jokingly.

"Yes," said Lifu sarcastically, "there ought to be one communist philology, another democratic philology, and another fascist philology." At this time, democracy, fascism, and communism were becoming familiar terms among those who read.

Huan-erh, who was a Leftist, was now a little tired of radicalism and a little bitter. After the Nationalist Revolution had succeeded in overthrowing the old government, the Kuomintang had broken with the communists and begun to suppress them. The Kuomintang had gone Right and the youth of China had gone Left, and communistic thought became an underground movement. Mulan learned also that during the Government's anti-communist campaign, Taiyun had been put into prison and got out again and was now hidden somewhere in the Shanghai International Settlement living with a comrade, Loman, without the ceremony of marriage. It should be explained here that now many of the Leftist writers assumed names that sounded like translations of European names, like "Pakin," which was a cross between "Bakunin" and "Pushkin." "Loman" suggested "Romain." The Pakins and Lomans were, however, more revolutionary than the Suttons and Davids.

.·.

That night, they engaged a large houseboat on which to have dinner under the moonlight on the canal. These boats, formerly used by officials and candidates for imperial examinations going up to Peking on the Grand Canal, were now chiefly used for pleasure trips to Taihu Lake, and as boat restaurants, being famous for the excellence of their cooking. The houseboat reminded Mulan and Sunya of the days of their flight from the Boxer trouble.

The moon was up early, and they were rowed out, not to the crowded Ten-Thousand-Year Bridge, but to the countryside, where the canal was considerably wider, and where the broad land lay in perfect peace in the moonlight. One of the boat women could play the flute. After dinner Mulan wanted only the moonlight and ordered all lights to be put out. Then they went out to sit in the prow, where the ladies sat. Lifu lay down on the shining boards of the deck, and put his feet high up on the rail. Mulan, being for the first time initiated into the intimate beauty of the south, became thoroughly sure that she was right in moving down here. The district around Soochow had none of the grandeur of Peking, but there was a moistness in the air and an enticing softness in the look of the country which was said to be responsible for the beauty of the Soochow women. The effeminate and watery quality of the Soochow dialect itself was in perfect harmony with the many waterways and rice paddies in the district. Coming from the young Soochow boat woman, this dialect enchanted Mulan. Mochow's children, especially the younger one, spoke it also. Of these children Mulan was very fond of the eldest, Hsiaofu. Hsiaofu was fourteen years old, and Lifu said that he could already recognize eight thousand characters, because the father himself had taught him by a new system, based on a more scientific grouping of the characters under similar compounds.

As the night wore on and the party became literally steeped in the atmosphere of pale moonlight and soft feminine sounds, Mulan gradually relaxed, and first inclined on her elbow, and finally lay flat on the deck with her children next to her and Lifu lying beyond. Mochow, however, still sat up for the sake of propriety in the presence of Sunya.

Fireflies flew from the shore and alighted on their garments. One crawled up Mulan's outstretched leg. Her sister raised her hand and struck it, and Mulan cried out, "You must have killed it. You struck so hard!"

Mulan sat up to look at the wounded firefly, which had rolled down to the wooden deck. In a second, its beautiful green incandescence went out.

"Oh, you have killed it!" Mulan cried in anguish.

"What then? It is only a firefly," replied Mochow.

"But it was so beautiful!" said Mulan.

"She often crushes insects like that," said Lifu.

"What is it but a worm?" protested Mochow.

"Sister, you really shouldn't," said Mulan miserably. "Why destroy life like that?"

The episode passed, except Mulan was unhappy for a few minutes and realized she should not lie down again. Lifu began to speak of the difference between fireflies and glow-worms and the mysteries of that phosphorescent, heatless light which they give off and which scientists are unable to produce. From that he went on to speak of electric eels that discharge electricity to kill their enemies, and the listening children sat enchanted.

They returned home about eleven, with the young children already asleep. The next day, Sunya and Mulan said good-by to Lifu's family and departed for Hangchow.

CHAPTER XL

*H*ANGCHOW is the city that was the capital of South China in Marco Polo's time, and of which Marco Polo wrote a glowing sketch, calling it *Kinsai,* meaning "capital." He described it as a great trading center, with a special quarter for Hindu and Persian traders who came from across the sea, and as a city of nine hundred bridges over intercrossing canals. He told of its situation on a lake where princes and their noble ladies bathed after the hunt. He spoke of the inhabitants as a cultured people with gentle manners, a people, however, unversed in the arts of war and held in subjection under the Great Khan. To this day, the people of the city on the lake still retain their simple ancient manners, and the city is popular as a resort for travelers and especially for young people on their honeymoons.

Mulan and Sunya chose a house on the City God's Hill because it was a wonderfully quiet section, away from the fashionable villas along the lake, and yet close to the streets. By going down the hill a hundred yards, one could be already in the center of the city. But Mulan chose the house particularly for the view it commanded. The city lay on a wide strip of land between the West Lake at the front and the great river behind, and from the elevation of the hill one could see on one side a large part of the lake with its willow embankments and on the other sailing boats and steamers going up and down the river. On one side was peace and on the other was movement. Mulan loved to see the sailing boats in the distance. The immediate neighborhood was only sparsely built up. The houses were old, with plenty of vacant ground in front and behind, and the pebbled streets and alleys were crooked, with many ups and downs. Further west on the hill, there were whole stretches of extraordinary perforated rocks sticking out of the ground. These bore marks like sea waves, and doubtless had been submerged in the ocean in prehistoric times, and they formed strange shapes that artists loved to paint.

679

Mulan's house had several courts on different levels and the top court had a two-storied building with a landscape tower. These houses, like most houses in the south, were built of bricks and coated white, leaving, however, the red-painted woodwork exposed on the walls. The house stood by itself, with a neighboring house only on the right, and was shaded by old trees and bamboos at the back and on the left. The tower touched some of the tree branches from the back. When they moved in, Mulan found that the former occupant had been very careless. The walls were disfigured, the staircase up the tower creaked, and mice were running inside the walls. The tower evidently had never been used. She had the staircase repaired and the walls painted. Inside the small stone gate was a brick-paved yard, and there were inscriptions on the stones of the gate. The horizontal piece across the top bore the words *Skirt hill girdle river*, meaning that the house had the hill as its skirt and the river as its girdle. The couplet on the doorjambs consisted of four simple words each, which both Sunya and Mulan rather liked:

Mountain's light, water's color.
Birds' chatter, flowers' fragrance.

Mulan was continually amazed by the light on the mountains, and the color of the lake which changed from morning to night, and the chatter of birds and the fragrance of flowers which changed from spring to autumn. The lake and its surrounding mountains changed their appearance according to the weather, and they were especially beautiful on misty or showery days.

In the hall Mulan hung some paintings from her friend Chi and specimens of ancient calligraphy. The portrait Chi had made of herself she hung in her bedchamber, which was one court higher and to the rear. Her bedchamber looked out on a bamboo bush, which cast a green shade into the room. She had not seen such bamboos in the north, and she loved the delicacy of their fine branches. The peculiar shapes of bamboo leaves and tall slender trunks always suggested to her a smiling slender maiden with a fringe on her forehead. She thought often how the shining, brownish-yellow-and-green surface of the bamboo trunks was a well-known symbol of the gentleman, the straightness of line suggesting independence, the hollow center standing for open-mindedness, and the hard joints standing for the gentleman's integrity.

680

Sunya conceived a couplet and commissioned a famous writer to write it specifically for them, through a stationery shop which acted as the calligrapher's agents. It was this:

The location being rural-secluded, the dweller is mild and aloof,
While the trees grow rugged-sparse, their shadows leaning across.

This inscription was hung in the parlor of the upper court.

Now Mulan had come to Hangchow to realize the dream of a simple rural life that she had often discussed with Sunya ever since the first months of their marriage. Above all, she desired peace—peace in a small family. It might in a broad sense be regarded as an escape. Yet very soon another development nearly destroyed the domestic peace that Mulan had so ardently planned. The way it happened seemed to have a touch of irony in it, and Mulan was later convinced that "men strive, but the gods decide," as the proverb says.

In consonance with her scheme, Mulan adopted an entirely new mode of life. She had brought down only Brocade and her husband Tsao Chung and their one son, who was of the same age as Atung. This son was at first called Ping-erh, which was but a word in the Celestial Cycle of reckoning, but as the sound suggested "a little cake," someone had said as a joke that he might as well be called "a little pie," and the name Kao-erh or "pie," somehow stuck. Little Pie was a boy full of fun, very fond of both eating and talking. Mulan agreed with Sunya that there were to be no other servants but these, since it was quiet they wanted. Brocade was to help with the cooking and sewing, Tsao Chung was to do the heavier work, and the boy was to run errands. Mulan herself would cook and sew and look after the little nine-year old Amei. With Atung and Amei, Mulan had tried to forget about Aman and to be contented.

Mulan herself changed her dress to that of a simple woman. She wore cotton and dispensed with silk. Her cotton gowns were still made in the modern style, but she discarded the brassière and the other beauty aids that had seemed appropriate in the Peking mansion but were out of place here. High-heeled shoes became impossible for house and kitchen work and she bought local Hangchow shoes with low heels. Her hair she brushed straight back and tied behind without fringes and curls. She still presented a striking appearance to those who could appreciate her beauty, but the neighbors little knew that this simply dressed woman had known the highest luxuries of the former capital of Peking.

Sunya went to the shops every morning, for they had now all of the Yao shops in Hangchow, except the pawnshop, and he had a great deal to do. Atung was sent to school and she helped him with his studies at night, as she also taught Amei herself in the afternoons, when she was free. She believed she was sincerely happy.

Only one small thing she missed, and that was the foreign pastry of Peking, the pastries sold at Hangchow being quite commonplace. Also, she had been very fond of her morning coffee. In Peking she had often declared that she was forced to get up from bed when she smelled the fragrance of coffee. Sunya had never cared much for coffee, and now that they were living so simply in Hangchow, he taunted her with being inconsistent in still having foreign coffee, so with a certain loyalty to her ideal, she gave it up and took to congee, and soon got quite used to it.

Sunya never completely shared her view of life. Brought up as a rich man's son, he loved material comforts and the gaieties of social occasions. He was at first amused to see Mulan living up to what she promised and going to work in the kitchen. Then he complained that kitchen work made her hands coarse. But she even thoroughly enjoyed taking a light hoe in her hand to scrape the soot from the bottom of the iron caldron in which rice was cooked.

"Why don't you leave it to Tsao Chung?" he said, when he saw her do this.

"I love it. You don't know what fun it is!" she said, panting.

"But your hands will grow callous."

"What is the harm in that? My children will soon be old enough to be married."

Sometimes in the afternoon, she even went with her children to pick firewood and broke the branches with her own hands, while Brocade watched and smiled. It was all poetry to her, because it was new. It got to the point where she often jokingly called herself "an old peasant woman." She would go to the city and to the movie theaters in a cotton gown, clean but simple, and she felt somehow superior to the middle-class women who were wearing all colors of artificial silk. She was determined that her ideal of life should be realized and she carried it too far before she discovered her mistake through a sad experience.

Sunya liked the good food, the theater-going, and the outings on the lake and to the surrounding mountains. He loved fishing and often went with Atung to fish in the lake. He enjoyed with Mulan the delicious Hangchow fish and shrimps, the shopping, the moonlight nights on the water, and the springtime excursions to Lingyin and Santienchu and the Jade Emperor's Summit.

Yet sometimes Mulan could see her husband was bored. Perfect for her, it was not perfect for him. At Peking there had been "flower dinners" or dinners with a sing-song girl sitting behind each guest which was the usual custom, and Mulan had not minded. She had even spoken of finding a concubine for her husband. But after Dimfragrance fell into the pattern of Chinya's ideal of a perfect wife, she had given up the idea and Sunya had never thought of it either. Now at Hangchow all girl entertainers were forbidden by the law of the city, and Sunya missed some of the Peking gaiety. He often took trips to Shanghai, which was only four hours by train, and then worked better when he came back.

"What is the matter with you?" Mulan asked. "Are you bored with your old wife?"

"Nonsense. I had business to do at Shanghai," he said.

His trips to Shanghai became more and more frequent. On some of these trips, Mulan accompanied him. Once or twice she and her sister arranged by letter to meet at Shanghai, she going north and Mochow coming south. From Soochow to Shanghai was only two hours by train, but Lifu hated Shanghai and seldom came.

When Mr. Yao had come to stay with Mulan, Mochow came with Lifu to Hangchow to see him. Both were surprised at Mulan's complete change. After seeing every detail of her new way of life, Lifu exclaimed with exultation and approval. Mochow, while dressed more simply than at Peking, kept to the middle course and was still well dressed, without Mulan's dramatically rustic effect.

On their return from one of their trips to the temples on the mountains, Mochow said, "I like the openness of this city. Soochow is like a rich and knowing widow inside a great mansion. Hangchow is like a girl of eighteen washing clothes on a riverbank."

"What do you think?" Mulan asked Lifu.

"I like the rich and knowing widow better. There are too many tourists here," he said.

"He is perfectly happy in Soochow," said Mochow.

"How is your work now?" Sunya asked.

"It is about ready. The trouble is that I don't know how I am going to reproduce the ancient signs which occur on every page in the text. If I have it lithographed, I shall have to write the whole text myself, because the slightest modification of the strokes might make a difference. I cannot trust it to others, and I shall be blind if I copy the whole book for print."

"Why not get Chen San to do the modern characters for you, while you fill in the ancient script yourself?" suggested Mulan.

"I might do that," Lifu said. "My sister says that Chen San is getting very much disgusted with the anti-communist campaign and the slaughter of the peasants. He is going to give up and leave the army."

"Lithographing should not cost much," said Sunya. "We will subscribe at least fifty copies."

"Of course. But you should not strain your eyes too much," said Mulan. "The day the book is ready we will give a dinner to celebrate its completion."

It was on this trip that something happened which, though trivial, must be recorded. Mulan knew from visits with her sister that Lifu loved chicken gizzards. So one morning, at about half past eleven, Mulan came in from the kitchen, to the upper court, carrying a plate containing the gizzard from a chicken which had just been cooked for the midday meal. Lifu was alone reading, and Mulan had forgotten to bring a pair of chopsticks. Seeing the gizzard, Lifu looked up and smiled, and was about to use his fingers to pick it up. "Oh, I forgot!" said Mulan. Using her own fingers, she took the gizzard and holding it before his mouth, she asked, "Do you mind?" She put it in his mouth and he ate it. Nobody had seen them. At lunch, Sunya hunted for the gizzard, for he, too, was very fond of it, and asked, "Where is the gizzard?" "It is in Lifu's stomach," Mulan replied. She met Sunya's eyes frankly and laughingly, but Sunya said nothing and he did not laugh.

Soon after Lifu and Mochow went home from this trip, Sunya went to Shanghai for a whole week and, after his return, he was very quiet. Mulan felt this change. Whether or not he was jealous of Lifu's sympathetic approval of her way of life, she did not know. Or was it only the age-old problem of a husband cooling off after middle age, the same problem that faced the wife of the great painter Chao Mengfu in the Mongol Dynasty?

"Sunya," said Mulan, "are you dissatisfied with this city?"

"No. What makes you think so?" he said.

"Don't deceive me," she said smiling. "I am not the wife of Chao Mengfu, and cannot write a poem to change your heart. But I see you are dissatisfied. If you would rather take a concubine, I would not object, but don't let people outside call you a fool."

Now Sunya had never had in his mind the idea of taking a concubine, if only for the fact that now it was not being done and if he did it he would be considered old-fashioned. He was contented with the family as it was, but he did enjoy the modern comforts of Shanghai life.

"Whimsy," he said affectionately, for he had begun to call her Whimsy again since coming to Hangchow, "you are mistaken. It is true that Hangchow life is dull for me. But I just enjoy going to Shanghai for a change. I only go and sit in the dance halls. You know I don't dance. What is the harm?"

"None, indeed," replied his wife. "I want you to be happy. Men are made differently from women. I was wondering if you were getting silly in your middle age."

"Then I will stop going to Shanghai—unless with you," he said.

"No, you can go when you have business to do. I am content here with what I have."

After this talk, Sunya did not go to Shanghai for a whole month, although Mulan began to urge him to go. His mind appeared to be occupied and abstracted, and his wife was the first to notice this; but, although she was worried, she said nothing. He was constantly at the shop and came home late and no longer took Atung to fish in the afternoons as he was wont to do. On Sundays and Saturday afternoons, when there was nothing to do at the shop, he frequently went out alone, saying that he was going to meet his friends. Mulan was sure there was a woman behind this, and debated in her own mind how she was going to meet the situation. It all depended on what kind of a woman it was. Suppose, for instance, that he should have a child by a poor family girl, she would without question openly accept her and the child into the family. She had seen this in her husband's family and she would know exactly what to do. Besides, she was sure of herself as a wife. Perhaps it was not so serious, or perhaps it was nothing at all.

One day Little Pie told Mulan he had seen the master at a restaurant with a modern woman. She was instantly tense.

"What nonsense are you talking?" she exclaimed. "Did you actually see her? What was she like?"

"A very young and pretty modern lady," said Little Pie, "with curled hair and high-heeled shoes, you know, like a lady from Shanghai."

From the next room Brocade heard her son talking and came in and gave him a slap on the top of his head, crying, "I'll pinch your lips! You are lying!"

"No, let him speak," said Mulan. "Are you sure it was your master that you saw?"

Now Little Pie hesitated. "I don't know. I thought I was sure. I saw them going together into a restaurant and I saw only the master's back."

"Did he see you?"

"No. They were walking in the street near the restaurant and then turned in."

"How far away were you?"

"Just a few steps."

Mulan was surprised to find herself not at all excited or angry. On the contrary she felt a kind of relief that there was this clue to the mystery. She knew at least it was a modern and fashionably dressed woman.

"If you breathe a word of this to the children or the others, I will twist your neck," said Brocade and Little Pie was frightened.

"It is all right," said Mulan to the boy. "Don't speak of it to my children or to anybody. But you have done nothing wrong to tell me." She patted him on the shoulder, trying to allay his fear, and added, "If you see them again at the restaurant, just tell me."

Mulan found out the name of the restaurant, which was an obscure, small one. She visited it and tried to find out more details. All that the waiter could tell her was that the woman was probably a painter, because they talked of her paintings. Mulan reasoned that she might be a teacher or a student in the school of fine arts, where there were many modern young ladies, all with bobbed or curled hair. This school was on a little island in the lake connected by embankments with the shore. Then on Sundays she began to propose trips with the family, and sometimes Sunya went and sometimes he didn't. One Sunday she insisted on visiting the school of fine arts. When they were there,

Sunya became nervous and was anxious to leave as soon as possible, professing to be totally uninterested.

Mulan said nothing to her husband about what she knew or guessed. She secretly consulted her old father, who asked, "What would you do if you found the woman?"

"That depends," replied Mulan.

"You are not foolishly thinking of divorce, are you?"

"Divorce? That is what I am afraid of. It would be unfair to our children." Then she added, "I don't think it is so serious as that."

"Well, then," said her father, "my advice is that you go off to your sister's for a fortnight or so, and then I can help you. Use tact by all means, and do not antagonize him. Between us two, we can manage him."

So Mulan went to Soochow, leaving her children at home. She said that she wanted a change, and her husband objected to her going, outwardly, but not earnestly. Mochow and Lifu were glad to have this unexpected visit from Mulan, but they soon saw she was worried, and she confided to them the problem on her mind.

"What are you going to do?" Mochow asked, while Lifu sat listening, enraged.

"I don't know," said Mulan. "Father told me to come away for a time."

"Are you sure it is one of those curly-haired modern girls?"

"I haven't even seen her and I don't know her name."

"Well," said Mochow, "I will tell you that you yourself are partly responsible for this."

"What do you mean?" Lifu interjected.

"I mean, Sister, that you shut Sunya up out there on top of a hill, and you dress yourself almost like a farmer's wife, so that even I was shocked."

"What is wrong with that?" demanded Lifu.

"You don't understand," said the wise Mochow to her husband. "Sunya is different from you, but would even you like it if I did not dress properly?"

"Dress properly?" rejoined Lifu hotly. "What can be more proper than the way she dresses? Must women always dress in silk and trinkets? Must men of forty still look at dolls?"

"Lifu," said Mulan, "most men do. Perhaps sister is right."

687

Lifu began to curse, but Mochow remonstrated and said, "There are many corners of the human heart that you do not know yet."

"I know everything," he flung back. "But I didn't expect Sunya to be so . . . unappreciative."

. · .

The eye of old Yao was all-seeing. It saw everything while he pretended to see nothing. With Mulan away, the old man had a chance to watch his son-in-law, whom he still thought essentially a good husband, though he had his weaknesses. One day he dropped in to the shop which now belonged to his daughter and son-in-law. He casually noticed on Sunya's desk a pale pink foreign envelope such as girl students commonly use. He looked closer and saw feminine calligraphy on it. In the lower corner was a printed design of the archway of the school of fine arts, but the red and green colors seemed to have been hand-painted—a characteristically feminine touch. It bore as the sender's name only one word, "Tsao." The writing was round and soft in the Chao style, but made with unusually thin brush strokes. He left cheerfully after a while, and Sunya had not even seen that his father-in-law had noticed the envelope.

Now the students of the arts school, boys and girls, went about painting in the open along the lake, and old Yao, disguised as a monk, went there for several days, hoping to find out more about this Miss Tsao and perhaps to meet her. One morning, strolling outside the park near the school, he passed three girls who were carrying drawing pads and collapsible stools. They were joking and laughing and he heard one of them call another "Miss Tsao." He turned to look. It happened that two of the girls looked around also, for old Yao, with his long white beard and his high Taoist hat and pilgrim dress, made a striking appearance.

"Young ladies," he said, immediately assuming his old role as a mendicant monk, "will you do a good deed?"

The girls laughed and stopped. The one who had not looked back now turned also to see the old pilgrim. She seemed older and taller and more serious than the others, and she was dressed in a long green gown and high-heeled shoes. As the girls stopped, he advanced.

"Young ladies," he repeated, "won't you do a good deed?"

"Suppose we ask the old pilgrim to let us paint him?" whispered the taller girl. Then going toward him she said, "What do you want?"

688

"Young lady, help a poor pilgrim. I have come all the way from the Huang Mountain to beg for funds to rebuild a temple to the Wenshu Bodhisattva. Won't you give something?"

He held out a contribution book.

"We are students, you know," said one of the girls.

"Never mind. Give according to your ability and the Bodhisattva will bless you."

"Lihua, you had better give, and the Bodhisattva will help you in your marriage," said another girl.

"I cannot give much," replied the tall girl. "Let us pay together thirty cents and ask the old uncle to sit for us for a while." Turning to him, she said, "We can give something, but it is very little. We are painters, and we should like to paint you, if you would come into the shade with us and sit for a while."

Old Yao hesitated.

"Is this a bargain?" he said. "If I don't sit for you, you won't give— is that it? Well, I won't. I hate pictures."

"Don't put it that way," said the tall girl. "Come, I will help," and she took out a twenty-cent piece to give to the monk. "Will that do?"

"The Bodhisattva will bless you," he said taking the coin, and opening his contribution book, he said, "Lady, please write your name."

"Why, for such a small sum?"

"Yes, every copper must be entered here."

"You are a good monk," said the girl. She took out her fountain pen and wrote her name "Tsao Lihua." He recognized the same Chao style that he had seen on the letter on Sunya's desk.

"You are an old saint," said one of the girls. "Perhaps you can tell her what luck she will have."

"I am utterly unworthy," said the old pilgrim politely, but that only increased his air of mystery.

"Now come into the shade by the bank," said Lihua. "You can tell us some stories, while I do a sketch of you. Please, old uncle. I shall not detain you long."

Old Yao saw that the girl was good-mannered and had a "regular" type of face and an intelligent look.

They went to a bench in the shade of the tall willows, and the girls put down their stools and took out their drawing pads.

"What do you want me to tell you?" he asked.

"Tell her about her luck," said one of the girls.

689

"Whose luck?"

"Lihua's. This one."

"Luck in what way?" he asked, innocently.

"In matrimony," they said.

"Is she about to be engaged?" he asked.

Lihua looked at the others as if annoyed.

"Tell him. Do not mind," said the other girl. "He is a stranger."

Old Yao looked at Lihua closely as crimson crept into her cheeks.

"Do you want me to tell your fortune?"

She nodded, her face cast down.

"Give me your hand," he said. Lihua stretched out her palm, and he held it and looked at it. It was a soft hand, with slender fingers.

"How old are you?"

"Twenty-two," replied Lihua.

"Well, young lady, you are in love."

The girls laughed.

"You love a man much older than you. He is well-to-do and rather plump. Am I right?"

The three girls exclaimed with amazement.

"But he is not the man you will marry."

Lihua, whose face had been turned aside for shyness, now looked up steadily into the old pilgrim's face.

"I am sorry to tell you. He is already married," said old Yao.

Lihua drew her hand violently from his grasp.

"It is not true!" she cried.

"Perhaps I am wrong. But you can find out for yourself," he said.

"He is not a seer. He cannot be always correct," said the other girl. Now Lihua looked defiantly at him and said, "Are you deceiving me, old uncle?"

"I am sorry," said Mr. Yao. "As I say, I may be wrong and I hope I am. But be comforted, my daughter. You will meet a better man. He is somewhere not far from here. Wait a year and see whether my words are right or not."

The turn of the conversation so distressed Lihua that she could not make her sketch, and old Yao sat watching her silently, while the two other girls tried to draw his face. When he stood up to leave, he asked, "Do you want your twenty cents back?"

"No. Keep it," said Lihua, her face very serious.

"Tell me," he asked gently, "is this man the first you ever loved?"

Lihua looked up bashfully at him and seemed to signify "yes."

"It is hard on you, my child. I hope I am wrong. Good-by!"

Old Yao changed his dress and went home. It was just noon and no one had noticed his absence. He was surprised at his own success, and wrote to Mulan to come home.

. .

When Mulan returned, Sunya was surprised to find that she had bought some new dresses, silk pajamas and pink slips and an assortment of toilet creams and lotions and several pairs of expensive shoes. She had spent almost two hundred dollars. She also brought home six tins of a famous Mexican brand of coffee.

"Why, Whimsy, you bought these shoes?" Sunya exclaimed.

"I bought them for you. You like to see them, don't you?" said Mulan, throwing the slips and pajamas on the bed somewhat contemptuously.

Sunya wondered what Mulan meant. Outwardly she behaved toward him as usual and pretended not to know anything. She went less to the kitchen, and when he asked her why, she answered, "Oh, I am tired." She had been told by her father immediately after her return about his extraordinary meeting with Lihua. He told her that Lihua looked like a good-hearted girl, and that she had fallen in love with Sunya, not knowing he was married. Mulan had only to wait and watch. Sunya, for his part, had previously felt a little resentful about Mulan's change of dress and had attributed it to Lifu's influence, because Lifu himself had changed into simple dress and at their first visit to Soochow had remarked about Mulan's rich dress with seeming surprise and disapproval. Now he could not account for her noticeable change.

He met Lihua three days after Mr. Yao had seen her. She wrote and insisted that she must see him. Their first meeting had been one afternoon on the bank of the lake while she was painting outdoors. He was struck by her beauty and went near to look at her painting and praised it. He was a good talker, and Lihua formed an acquaintance with him; then they became friends, and almost at once it seemed that they had fallen madly in love with each other. He had never told her that he was married and all she knew was his address at the teashop, which she never visited.

Now they met again at the restaurant. Lihua came in with a sad and serious face. Sunya went up and took off her foreign overcoat and held her hand.

"What is it you must talk to me about?" he asked.

"Sit down and I will speak with you."

They sat down and Sunya ordered some tea, for Lihua had to go back to school for supper.

"Sunya, I want to ask you a question," she said. "You must tell me the truth."

"Certainly."

"How old are you?"

"I am just over forty. I can't be older than that, can I?"

"I thought you were much younger," she said. "Why aren't you married?"

Suddenly confronted with this question, Sunya stammered, and she saw that the old monk had been right and she asked quietly, "Is your wife still living?"

Sunya nodded.

"Why didn't you tell me?"

"I was afraid to lose you," Sunya answered. "I was so happy with you. But, you understand, my wife is a . . . peasant woman—of the old type. She merely cooks and washes for me. You know, she does everything, even picking up firewood. You know we who are unfortunately married to the old-type women wish to have a modern wife like you. I didn't want to tell you."

"Can you show me a picture of your wife?"

"No," he said, shortly. "You are not going to give me up, are you? How did you come to think of asking me this question? What made you want to see me so badly?"

"Well, I met a fortune teller," she said. "He is a monk from Huang Mountain, a man with a long white beard, and he came to ask for contributions, and I gave him twenty cents. Some of the girls teased me and asked him to tell my fortune. He looked in my palm and said that the man I was in love with was married—that is you. And it is the most amazing thing—he said the man was much older than myself and plump. You see, he was right!"

"Are you sure he was a monk?" Sunya asked.

"Of course. He had a regular contribution book from Huangshan and he spoke with a strange accent."

"Tell me," said Sunya relieved, "though I am married, can we not still be good friends? I love you, and you love me, too."

"But are you going to divorce your wife?"

"No, that I cannot do. But we can forget the world and be happy between ourselves."

Lihua heaved a deep sigh. She could not make up her mind. So many husbands of the time—high officials, professors, writers—were giving up their old wives and marrying modern girls. Three of the professors at her art school had divorced their wives and married their students.

So they parted disconsolately. Sunya begged her to let him see her again when they might see more clearly what to do, and she consented.

.˙.

Two days later, to Lihua's great surprise, she received a letter from one who signed herself merely as "Mrs. Tseng," and asked to see her privately. The note was polite and very short, and in a masculine hand unusual for a woman's writing. The characters were about an inch high, in the "grand style," and the long strokes and the sweeping connecting lines between the characters suggested great freedom of spirit. Lihua was amazed. Sunya had told her that his wife was an old-type woman, but the writer seemed well educated in old Chinese, at least.

Lihua was as anxious to see this "peasant wife" of her lover as Mulan was to see his sweetheart. She reasoned that if the wife were merely an ignorant, jealous woman, she certainly would not ask for a meeting, but would rudely tell her to stop seeing her husband. She was mystified and at the same time a little afraid. Her fate was in the wife's hand, and would be determined at their meeting.

Mulan had not given the address of her home, but merely asked that they meet at the top pavilion of the Poets' Club, which was open to the public. Lihua debated a long time in her mind about what she should wear and what impression she should create. The more she studied the writing of the note, the less she could guess how this old-type woman would look, how old she would be, and what approach she would take. The wife must be clever, but clever women were often unprepossessing and masculine in appearance, as her writing indicated in this instance. In any case she must look her best and create a good impression. She decided to go in a simple but dignified modern dress.

From the arts school to the Poets' Club was only a ten minutes' walk.

The club, which belonged to a group of poets and was over a hundred years old, had one of the best locations on the West Lake. A short way from its entrance a series of jagged stone steps, flanked by rockery, led up to the top. The pavilion, occupying one of the highest points of Kushan in the middle of the Lake, commanded a full view on all sides. Behind were the rich villas, separated from the Kushan by the Inner Lake. In front lay the outer lake, with Governor Yuan's islet and another islet called "The Moon Imprinted in Three Ponds." On the opposite shore was King Chien's Temple, a spot known as "Listening to Orioles among Willow Waves." To the right in the distance rose great cloud-capped mountains, and to the left across the Lake lay Hangchow City itself, with its many villas dotting the shore line. Close below in front was the archway near the arts school, known as "Placid Lake Autumn Moon."

Lihua came out of the school at two and reached the club first, her heart beating with excitement. She was there a quarter of an hour before time, and the waiting seemed to her interminable. Then she saw a beautifully dressed young woman coming up. She dared not think that this was the woman she was to meet and would rather have found her an old and plump woman—educated, but coarse in appearance. As the woman came nearer, Lihua was struck by her beautiful, expressive eyes. She looked entirely too young to be the wife of Sunya. Certainly she must be one of the tourists visiting the club.

But Mulan approached and came directly to her, and said very casually, with a smile, "It is a steep climb, isn't it? I am all out of breath. Are you Miss Tsao?"

The question wiped out all hope that this was only a rich tourist.

Lihua stood up and asked, "Are you Mrs. Tseng?" She could not say a word more.

Mulan had come in a rich heavy blue dress that she had made out of an ancient "tribute" brocade of which they say "as if made for royalty." It had been part of her dowry. She had cut it into the most modern molded fashion. Today she was wearing her brassiere, the last word in modernity. Her waist was small, her hair full and jet-black, her eyes liquid and her eyebrows drawn out toward her temples.

"I am old now, and a short climb like that makes me pant for breath," she said. Her tone, by no means hostile, allayed part of Lihua's fears.

694

"Why, madam, you are still so young," said Lihua, instinctively using the word *fujen*, reserved for higher-class ladies and officials' wives.

"I heard that my husband has lately met you, and I wished very much to see you myself," said Mulan.

"Are you really Madame Tseng? He told me . . ." Lihua stopped.

"What did he tell you?"

"Madam, this is very embarrassing for me. But I did not know he was married. That was why I even dared go near him."

"Miss Tsao, I am really glad to meet you. I want to talk with you. You have found out that he is married?"

"Yes, because I asked him. Then he confessed, and he said—well you are so different from what I imagined!"

"I suppose he told you that I was an old peasant woman."

"Well, not exactly. But madam, had I known, I should not have thought . . . I really cannot understand."

"You cannot understand what?"

"I cannot understand a man having a wife like you and . . ."

"Miss Tsao, I am older than you. You do not know my poor husband. Since he is your friend, I want to tell you that he is really a good man. But no husband in the world thinks his own wife beautiful, particularly if he marries a pretty wife. Don't you know the proverb? 'Writing is best when it is one's own, and a wife is best when she is someone else's.' It is a new proverb in Peking."

Lihua smiled in spite of herself, and the very act of smiling gave her courage.

"Are you from Peking? You talk a perfect Peking accent," asked Lihua.

"Yes, we only moved to Hangchow a year ago."

"I am from Peking, too. Where did you live?"

"My father is Yao Sze-an. We lived at the Garden of Quiet and Suitability."

"Are you by any chance one of the famous daughters of the Yao family living in the Prince's Garden? I was in school, and heard of them, but I never met them."

"Yes, I am Yao Mulan, the eldest daughter of the family."

"You are Yao Mulan! But how can this be? Your husband . . .!"

"Well, never mind. My husband evidently thinks a great deal of you. That was why I wanted to see you."

"Really, madam, I thought his wife was a country woman. And you have children. I heard that your daughter was shot in the March Massacre."

"Yes," replied Mulan. "When life is so sorrowful as it is, how is it that we make it sadder still?"

But Mulan did not press the question of giving up Sunya, and Lihua felt too stupid to mention him at all. She only said, "Madam Tseng, if you will excuse this misunderstanding, I shall consider myself lucky to have made your acquaintance."

Mulan replied in the same manner and said that she hoped to see her again, but went no further. Now that she knew more about Lihua she felt thoroughly at ease as they parted. If she did nothing more, this meeting would have been sufficient to stop the affair in a simple, dignified way.

.·.

As Lihua went back to her room in the school, she had not the least doubt that she would have to give up Sunya. The situation, as it had developed, had become worse and worse for her. When she had heard from Sunya that his wife was an old-type woman, she still had hope of continuing the affair, however complicated it might be. Like many modern girls she felt justified in the feeling that where there was real love, as in her case, the man needed and deserved a girl like herself. But now this hope was quite dashed, and she felt partly remorse for her own madness and partly chagrin at being deceived. The following Sunday she received a letter from Sunya and could not decide how to answer it. Should she see him for the last time, and, on seeing him, what should she say to him about the lie he had told her? But she was relieved of the problems of facing him with the truth when she received later the same day a letter signed by Yao Mulan.

It was a moving letter, in which Mulan said in writing what she did not wish to say orally.

DEAR LIHUA *Hsiaochieh*:

What luck and pleasure I had to meet you a few days ago! What greater luck that, after meeting you, I found that you did not disdain to talk with me, but were on the contrary gracious and open-minded, so that we could talk like friends whose one regret was we had not met each other earlier. You have heard of my maiden family and you have seen my husband, and I therefore wish to speak to you from the bottom of my heart.

I was born in a well-to-do family, but I have always held unconventional ideas. Often did I wish to forsake the life of the vermilion door and return to the simple home life of fishermen and woodcutters, helping my husband and teaching my children and wearing cotton skirts. But my parents-in-law were old and I could not fullfil my wish. Only last year were we able to leave Peking and come to live a quiet family life here in the south, realizing thus my heart's desire. I cook and I sew and I shut myself away from society. Sister, if you will believe me, the Mulan you saw a few days ago was not myself. It is true that I am an old peasant woman, or trying to be one. But how can one learn that things do not always happen as one wished?

Now the relationship between husband and wife is not something that can be quite explained to an outsider. All that I can say is that my husband's conduct is partly due to my fault. I have seen husbands forsaking better wives than myself, and so I find it possible to understand him. And I have seen many modern girls fall in love with other women's husbands, and I can understand them, too. I have known passion and the torments of passion. Since you came to know my husband without knowing that he was married, I do not blame you.

But, my sister, you are young, and I hope you will listen to what I say. If you are not yet deeply involved in passion, of course you ought to cut the tangled skein bravely with a sharp knife. The times are changing, and the old ideas of duty and gratitude are being displaced by the idea of love. There are very few couples who remain living in harmony until their hair turns silver. Yet I have studied old literature and the old tradition and desire that such an ideal might be realized. I have still one son and one daughter, and even if I do not consider myself, I have to think of giving them a home and a future.

But if you are already deeply involved in passion, I should also advise you to take this matter in a more leisurely way and not rush into hasty action. Some sacrifice or some adjustment is inevitable under these circumstances. I am willing to discuss this with you. Will you meet me again Monday at the same hour and place? This is strictly between ourselves.

YAO MULAN.

Lihua was somewhat annoyed by this new, unexpected move, which seemed unnecessary. Still, she was touched by the letter, which made it easier to make her decision. What adjustment could be meant here? She wrote Sunya that she could not see him because of school work, and prepared to meet Mulan again at the appointed time.

This time Mulan came dressed more simply. She had a new dress, but one that was not meant to create an effect, and her manner also was easier and more familiar.

"Madam Tseng," said Lihua, "you were very kind to write that letter to me."

"What do you think you wish to do?" asked Mulan.

"I will do just what you say."

"In what way?"

"I shall stop going with him. But I have a mind to tell him what I think about his deception. Of course, he will tell me again that he lied because he was afraid of losing me."

"Thank you," said Mulan, knowing that she had already won. "Do you think it will be easy for you to give him up?"

Lihua now almost felt that she hated Mulan, and said, "Elder sister, please do not make it too hard for me. I was not to blame."

"I know that," Mulan replied. "I asked to see you to help you settle this problem, knowing that it is hard for you and for him. If there is any question to discuss, let us discuss it between ourselves before you see him. You should see that I do not mean you any harm. I wish only to make amends to you for my husband. Do not think I am merely selfish."

"What is the need of saying more?" Lihua exclaimed. "I know that I have to stop. That is all."

But Mulan said, "Are there not things we should discuss? Are you sure it is possible for you to stop, and that your way is all clear?"

"It is quite clear," replied Lihua curtly.

"I was afraid there might be other questions. I am glad to hear you say that you are not worried. You may think I am not sincere. Let me tell you again that I have known what it is when a girl loves a man and loses him. There are such great loves in this world. You know in ancient times there was another solution. A girl who fell in love with a married man was willing to accept the position of a concubine. Today there are few whose love is great enough for this. Now you know I am open-minded. Will you be frank enough to tell me whether, if you had your choice, you would rather cut off this affair or come into the family of the man you love?"

Lihua was now greatly surprised and looked long at Mulan.

"No, I cannot," she said at last.

"I only want you to know that you can choose and not do anything desperate. If you do not believe that I am sincere, you can ask my husband if I did not offer him the chance to have a concubine."

"No, I would rather be free," said Lihua, proudly.

"And we can still be friends?"

"Gladly," replied Lihua.

"What are you going to say to my husband?"

"I shall tell him not to see me any more."

"Wait," said Mulan. "I wish that you and my husband could talk this matter over openly and come to a sensible conclusion. Certainly I shall not be in your way. I have an idea. Don't think me a devil. Will you come to my house, and let me introduce you to him as my friend? We will remain friends, and you will be welcome in my house. You will find the difference, once it is in the open."

At this new suggestion Lihua was a second time surprised. She thought in her heart what an unusual woman Mulan was, but the idea of remaining friends with her and Sunya pleased her, and for the first time she genuinely smiled and said, "I should like to see how he looks when he sees me. But will it not be too embarrassing for him?"

"He has to face it anyway," said Mulan. "We will not be too hard on him. We must both be cheerful."

So they agreed to have the meeting the next Saturday evening at Mulan's home.

With the problem thus solved, Lihua found that she was able to meet the situation with a calm mind, and she began to admire Mulan.

· · ·

Sunya was worrying about Lihua's change of attitude and her refusal to keep the appointment with him. He had no idea that his wife knew of the affair. While he was vexed and despondent, he noticed that she was unusually cheerful, and dressed more carefully than before. On Friday night she changed into one of the new dresses she had bought at Shanghai and went to the theater with him. This made him a little suspicious, thinking that she was trying to win him back. But he had seen her change so many times and carry such whimsical ideas into effect that he was not greatly surprised.

"Whimsy, what new idea has got into your head now? I don't understand you," he said as they went home from the theater.

"Just my whims, Fatty," replied Mulan. "All my life I have lived on whims. Some of my whims work and some of them don't. This cotton-skirt peasant woman idea doesn't seem to work."

"Why doesn't it work?"

"Because it doesn't. Another idea of mine was that you should have a concubine."

"You mean you want a concubine for your own companionship?" said Sunya.

"Well, I had to drop that idea, since your brother took a fancy to Dimfragrance." Suddenly she added, "You men!"

"We men, what?"

"Nothing. You men don't tell your wives what you think."

"What makes you think so?"

"Well, you said that you approved of my adopting this simple life and simple dress, but you don't."

"If I didn't tell you what I thought, didn't I let you have your way? It is always a husband's duty to yield to his wife's whims and notions."

"You won't tell me the truth now—for instance, whether you would like to have a concubine."

"Honestly I don't. Do you think I should?"

"That depends on whether you love a girl enough to be willing to take such a step and whether there is a girl who loves you enough to face the humiliation and the social disapproval."

"What gave you this eccentric idea now? Why should I fall in love with a girl now?"

"Answer me the question, directly. If I chose a girl for you, or if you fell in love with a girl, what would you do? Would you take her?"

"You are most impractical. How could I? It is not being done. And modern girls don't want to be concubines."

"Not even if you fell madly in love with her?"

"What would people say? What would people say?"

"So, I see, there is really no love great enough for this. You men!"

"We men are more practical. What made you think of this tonight?"

"Let's not talk of it any more. I want to tell you something else. Don't you go out to any friends' party tomorrow night. I am inviting a girl friend from Shanghai. I met her in Sister's place at Soochow and asked her to come and see me. You will be surprised."

"Have I ever seen her?"

"No, I suppose you haven't."

The next morning, Mulan told Brocade to prepare a home dinner and secretly told her the plan.

"It is Saturday night, and you can take the children out to dinner outside and to see the movies."

"Please, mistress, let me stay. I want to look at her," said Brocade. "And I must help with the cooking."

"Then I will ask my father to take the children out to the Lake and dinner. Get Little Pie out of the way, too. He can go with the children."

Mulan planned carefully that her husband should not see Lihua until the dinner was ready. Lihua came at seven and was discreetly led by Brocade into Mulan's room. Lihua came in her simple school dress, but was surprised to find Mulan dressed still more simply.

"Why, I hardly recognize you!" said Lihua.

"This is how I dress at home," Mulan replied.

"Now I understand."

"That is why I told you I was a peasant woman, really. But men don't look at a woman's soul. They look only at the coat of paint put over it. That is why. . . ."

"I understand," said Lihua again.

Sunya was now ready and wanted to come into his wife's room, but was surprised to find the door closed.

"Whimsy, has your guest come? I am hungry," he called through the door.

"She is here," Mulan called back. "We shall soon be ready." Turning to Lihua, she said, "He is always hungry," and Lihua smiled. "You go into the back room until I come for you."

Lihua obeyed, and Mulan went to open the door.

"Where is your friend?" asked Sunya.

"She is just getting ready in the back room," said Mulan.

She went to the table and turned the oil lamp a little brighter and stood at the door, and asked, "Are you ready?"

From the darkness of the back room, Sunya saw a girl come out, hand in hand with Mulan.

"May I introduce Miss Tsao Lihua?" said Mulan to Sunya.

Sunya was aghast as he looked at Lihua. He knew that he was in a trap. He tried to stammer something.

Mulan said, "Miss Tsao is a student at the school of fine arts, you know?"

"Yes," said Sunya blankly.

"You can't possibly have met her before?" said Mulan, with a sly smile.

"No—yes—I don't think—" Sunya began.

Then Lihua spoke, "You told me you were married—to an old peasant woman."

He stood there, his face turning alternately red and white, and looked from Mulan to Lihua, and back again. Now he saw that this was prearranged between the two women, and he said brusquely, "Enough of this, both of you. Yes, I have met her, and I have made love to her."

"Mr. Tseng," said Lihua, coming toward him, "it is better that we tell each other the truth. You told me you had an old country wife. If I had not met your wife accidentally, I might still be in the dark. I am lucky to have found this out in time before we got deeper into this affair."

"I admit that I was wrong," said Sunya humbly.

Then, looking toward his wife, the girl said, "But I cannot understand how you could be unfaithful to a wife such as this."

"No one is perfect, you know," he said. "I know I am imperfect, myself—and you should know yourself, too."

Mulan looked up at him quickly, and then steadily, and she knew what he meant, but kept silent. She was afraid to provoke him further, for she had a secret in her heart, sacred and wholly her own, a secret that no one must touch, no one must speak of, no one must hear.

"You have forgiven me," said Lihua to Mulan. "Can you forgive him, too?"

Mulan smiled and held out her hand and Sunya took it and kissed it.

"Thank you," he said. "You have saved me from committing a great wrong."

Then Mulan called to Brocade, and they went out and sat down at a table set for the three of them and had a small dinner. Brocade was amazed to find the three talking pleasantly together. She said that it was like an act in a play at the theater. Sunya still felt uncomfortable, but Mulan talked cheerfully and even playfully about many different things of no importance, and Sunya knew that he had met his match in Mulan.

702

After dinner, when Lihua went into the back room for a moment, he said to his wife with a mixture of amused tolerance and spite in his voice, "You devil!" That was all.

When the three sat talking again in the other room after dinner, and Brocade came in to serve tea, Mulan said, "When my father comes in, tell him to join us here."

Old Yao had shared in planning all Mulan's moves and knew that he was expected to play his role tonight. When he came in, he sent the grandchildren to their rooms, and walked quietly into Mulan's room.

Seeing this old man with his unmistakable eyes and long white beard, Lihua gasped and looked at Mulan.

"Who is this?" she whispered.

"He is my father," replied Mulan sweetly, and stood up to introduce them. "Father, this is one of my best friends, Miss Tsao Lihua."

Old Yao bowed with dignity.

"But you are the monk from Huang Mountain," Lihua exclaimed.

"Yes, yes," said old Yao in his most unperturbed manner. "This is my Huang Mountain."

"But, old uncle—" Lihua began.

He interrupted her. "I know, I know. You young people. When I told your fortune, I was not wrong, was I? But you did not have to wait a year to find it so."

Then old Yao said, "Good night," and turned to Sunya and drew him out of the door.

When they were gone, Lihua said to Mulan, "He was indeed the fortune teller I told you about. What does all this mean?"

"Lihua," said Mulan kindly, "I know that it all seems like a melodrama to you, doesn't it? Well, so it is, and my father is the director behind the scenes."

Outside, old Yao said to his son-in-law, "I know about this whole affair, my son. But it is all right. I too have been a fool in my time. In my youth, I did worse things than you have done. I have only been trying to protect my daughter."

"Thank you, Father," said Sunya. "You have saved me from doing a great wrong, both against your daughter and Miss Tsao."

After Lihua went home, Mulan told her husband the whole story. The more he thought and wondered about it, the more he felt that he had never appreciated his wife more. The experience restored their mutual affection, and Sunya also grew wiser and came to see things in their natural light and to realize what was lasting love and what was not.

Lihua became their friend and often came and visited them, and Sunya himself was instrumental in getting her married to a professor of the arts school.

Mulan wrote to her sister about the episode, and toward mid-autumn Mochow and Lifu came to visit them. They were told the whole story again and even met Lihua, and they were greatly amused.

"Did you tell your sister of this thing?" Sunya asked his wife.

"I did," she said.

"I had rather you had not told," he said. "It makes me look like a fool."

"What is the harm?" she asked. "You are not the only husband who has had such an affair, but others are not always so interesting, nor do they have such a happy ending."

And from that time on, Lifu and Mochow also sometimes called Mulan "Whimsy."

CHAPTER XLI

*L*IFU's book was published in the fall of 1932, soon after the Sino-Japanese War in Shanghai; and, as was to be expected, little notice was taken of it by the general public. The actual work took over two years, and the revisions and preparations for printing took about a year. Chen San gave up his army service and came back to copy the material. It took him a month to change back from handling a gun to handling the brush so that he could write with his usual neatness.

After the completion of the great work, Lifu and Mochow came to Hangchow for a deserved vacation and there was a great celebration. Afei and Paofen had come, too, to visit the old father and to invite him to go up and stay with them. Paofen told them of the sad death of Asuan's bride, who had died after giving birth to a boy, and how Mannia thus again had a baby to bring up, as she had brought up Asuan himself. Paofen also told of the friendship that had grown up between the two widows, Mannia and Coral, both now in advanced age and each with a young man as her son. Coral's charge, Poya, had just graduated from college and was developing a friendship with Asuan. Mannia was talking of making Asuan leave the Customs Service, for she was horrified by the stories he told her of the encounters with gangsters smuggling opium. Should anything happen to Asuan, she would have to bring up the baby grandchild all alone, and she was already too old for this. She was hoping that Asuan would marry again, so that she would have a daughter-in-law also to depend on. Paofen had given birth to no sons, and Mochow had no girls, and they had said they would exchange each her youngest child for the other's, but so far nothing had been done about this.

Chen San and his wife, too, had come to Hangchow. When he heard of Asuan's work, he thought he might join the Customs Preventive Service, too, in order to get out of politics. He was skilled with firearms and a crack shot. Afei himself was connected with the Opium Suppression Bureau and said that he could help to place Chen San, and that Mannia probably would be pleased to have him work near Asuan. Therefore, when Afei and Paofen returned to Peking with old Yao, Chen San and Huan-erh went up with them, and Chen San joined the Customs Service with Asuan.

For the next few years Mulan's life was comparatively uneventful. She and her husband had settled down to a peaceful and contented home life. The episode of Lihua had taught them both a lesson. Sunya said to his wife that perhaps he had been a fool, but then he had been in that state of mind when he knew something must happen. He said that he was no saint and that he had been craving for a change. In fact, he said, what he needed was simply novelty, as he needed novelty in his food. Mulan fully understood. Far from allowing their marital life to drift into a routine, taken for granted with all things happening on schedule, she created novelties in their food, their house, and the pleasures of life, with a mature refinement that continually surprised her husband. There were new concoctions of dates flavored with wine, new combinations of honey dates with ham, new ways of making rich, sauce-flavored minced eel, of "eight-precious rice," of "smothering" chicken steamed with bamboo shoots and Szechuen *tsatsai,* dishes of rich, viscid turtle soup cooked with webbed goose feet, cold slices of hardened boiled abalone eaten as a pastime, sugar-smoked fish and wined crabs and wine-flavored soft-shelled clams. She invented new ways of serving and eating foods and experimented with local hand-made vessels and with the pretty Hangchow bamboo lunch baskets. Recalling the Mongolian way of broiling mutton at a famous Peking restaurant, she had a charcoal fire made on a coarse basin, with a convex wire netting fitted over it; preparing very thin slices of beef and fish dipped in soya-bean sauce, they would move the charcoal basin into the middle of the courtyard and broil the meat over the netting, each person broiling his own piece with a pair of coarse wooden chopsticks, and eating it standing, as she insisted. Copying the southern custom of making "beggars' chicken," she would bring out for a picnic a whole chicken, with the entrails taken out, but the feathers unplucked. She would take a lump of clay and smear the chicken all over with a coating of mud and bake it in an open fire, like baking potatoes. After twenty to thirty minutes, depending on the fire and the size of the chicken, she would take it out, and the feathers would come off with the caked mud, and inside would be a steaming hot chicken, delicate and tender, with none of its juice lost. Tearing the wings and legs and breast apart with their hands and eating them dipped in soya-bean sauce, they found this beggar's delight the best chicken they had ever tasted in their lives. She declared that, after all, the simplest cooking was the best, depending more on nature than on culinary showmanship. A good cook was like a good educator; his duty was solely to bring out the talent of the chicken and show it to best advantage, as a good teacher brings out the talent inherent in a young man. Granted that the original talent was there in the chicken, too much coaxing, stuffing, imposing, and spicing would merely distract from its simple beauty and virtue. The principal thing, she properly observed, was eating things hot, immediately after they were done, for otherwise the process of cooking would go on after the food was taken out of the cooking vessel, because of the heat remaining in it, and the texture of meat or fish or bamboo shoots would be altered, so that a thing perfectly cooked would become overcooked.

All these little things were highly convincing to Sunya, although they might not have been enough to bribe Lifu. The contrast between the sisters was quite evident. Mochow expected less of life and she was married to a husband she worshiped; and, in worshiping and caring for her husband and her children, she found full happiness. Mulan by nature craved the ideal life, but she was satisfied, because she was old enough, with what she could find and with trying to make out of it a life for herself as beautiful as she could. There was more conscious artistry and refinement in this. Culinary pleasures were to her but one of the aspects, although the most evident and the surest, in her search for happiness. In this search, she fell back upon the life of the senses and clung to it, it seemed, out of desperation, or at least out of wise disillusionment. Retreating somewhat from the ordinary housework since the Lihua episode, she now consciously put more style into her dress. She would still change her hairdress as she often did in the first years of her marriage, and would wear trousers or skirts or long gowns as her mood and the season dictated. In summer, for instance, she threw aside the long gown and took to what was the equivalent of pajamas. Spring, summer, autumn, and winter were for her never the same, not mere changes in temperature. Even as her potted flowers changed with the seasons (a new hobby which was shared by her husband) so her own moods, her reading, her occupations, and pleasures changed with them.

. · .

Lifu's book was recognized as the best and most comprehensive work on the subject. While the specialists were not ready to accept his interpretations on all points, they agreed on his thoroughness and his scholarship. Philology was always an honored study because of its bearing on classic scholarship, and his name gradually became known to the professors of Chinese. He was enticed for a short term into the teaching profession in a small college near home, and he took active interest in college reforms. It was not long, however, before he discovered that he was essentially a herbivorous animal, as he called it, interested only in individual pasturing, whereas there were many carnivorous animals, even among his colleagues in the educational profession, who took more interest in preventing others from pasturing comfortably than in pasturing in their own individual fields. He found that it was true that the smaller the college, the more numerous were the politicians and the more turbulent the inside politics. Their pettiness goaded Lifu's soul. He was outstanding above the others in the small-town college, both as a former professor of a Peking University and as an author who had produced an important work. A rumor was circulated by his petty colleagues that the seriousness with which he entered into college reforms indicated that he had the ambition to become the college president. It was such a strange and comic idea to him that he quit the college after the vacation, to the delight of some of his colleagues.

One day in Nanking, however, he chanced to meet Wei Wu, the former Imperial Censor who had impeached old Mr. New, and who was now an important member of the censorship branch of the government. Mr. Wei was now nearly seventy, and had been given this post because of his high reputation. He had followed the fortunes of the New family, and had read of Lifu's part in the exposure of Huaiyu. They began after a while to talk of their mutual interests, and the old man insisted on asking Lifu to come to help him. In Nanking, he had already distinguished himself by impeaching several prominent officials. His duties required a great deal of field investigation, sifting of evidence, and preparation of documents; and he had no especially competent young man as his assistant. At this time the censorate was one of five *Yuan* in the Nanking government, its standing being on a par with the Executive, Legislative, Judicial, and Civil Service Yuan. It was independent of the other Yuan and it had provincial bureaus all over the country. People were free to submit impeachments of dishonest officials, and the bureau would send its officials, traveling openly or in disguise, to investigate cases on the spot.

"I like this work," said Lifu to his wife. "If I am to be associated with government, that is the kind of work I would enjoy."

"I know, I know," said Mochow. "Blood of Yang Chisheng. I don't know what to think. You had better ask your mother. The Yang family blood comes from her."

Lifu went to consult his mother. She was as far different as possible from her ancestor, the Imperial Censor Yang. She had heard of Yang's martyrdom three hundred years ago. But she was persuaded by her son that now it was a republic, and there was constitutional protection of the censors. Lifu assured her and his wife that the censors were completely independent of other officials and were protected by formal procedures in carrying out their duties—this being one of the best signs of the improvement of the government. It would be different from writing criticisms of officials as a common citizen. The mother thought it an honor for her son to be an official; and, since he did not like teaching, he had to have a work or profession. Mochow also thought Lifu was older now and less impetuous. So the wife and mother allowed him to accept the post of a councilor in the censorate, drawing a salary of three hundred dollars a month.

He went to Nanking to assume his duties, and proved to be of great help to old Wei, who came more and more to depend upon him. The censors naturally learned about the worst side of officialdom and often amused themselves by talking about the different officials about to be impeached and deciding when to take action. Before an impeachment was decided upon, there was great excitement in the office, particularly if the official was of some prominence. Lifu enjoyed the detective work, fitting the arrows to the bow, the accurate aiming before the shot, watching the victim as he was hit, and also the sense of justice being done to the people. All impeachments, however, were made under the name of Wei Wu, and Lifu contented himself with doing the ground work.

He frequently traveled back and forth between his home and Nanking, sometimes visiting his family on his trips of investigation. His work progressed successfully; and Mochow, being told the inside stories of corruption and oppression, came to believe that his work was important and of benefit to the country.

Moreover, there were clear signs that the Chinese nation was at last on the road of progress. Civil wars had stopped, internal reconstruction was going at a great speed, the governments' financial position steadily improved with the unity of the country and the stability of the government, and, best of all, there was a new spirit of patriotism and national self-confidence both among the people and the rank and file of government bureaucrats.

. ˙ .

But if conditions in central China and in general were making rapid progress, conditions were fantastic in Peking, which was now being called Peiping. A storm was breaking over the northeast, presaged by signs and portents that no words could describe. The atmosphere was electric, and nerves were on edge and strung to an unbearable tension, such as we feel before the outbreak of a great thunderstorm. Peking was under the semi-autonomous council, created by the Nanking government as a buffer to stay the rush of Japanese from beyond the Great Wall. The so-called "East Hopei Anti-communist" regime inspired and supported by the Japanese in the "demilitarized zone," extended its jurisdiction to Tungchow a few miles east of Peking. A sense of insecurity and imminent catastrophe prevailed in the people's hearts. North China was neither Chinese nor Japanese, neither independent of the national government nor exactly dependent upon it. And the bogus East Hopei Government was a paradise for Japanese and Korean smugglers and narcotic dealers and ronins. A deluge had already broken over the Great Wall, with its rivulets of poison and smuggled goods running over to Peking itself and southward to Shantung and westward to southeast Shansi, giving the first promise of what Japan called the "new order in Asia."

For a war was coming, a war to the death between China and Japan. The powers and foresight of man were as little able to stop it as to stop the rising of a hurricane at sea. People sometimes wonder why there must be wars; only a study of the atmosphere preceding them, such as on the eve of the French Revolution, makes it possible to understand such upheavals. We may try to analyze the cause of the Sino-Japanese War; yet we should be no more than meteorologists reading the interesting violent ups and downs of the barometer before a storm, or seismologists analyzing the oscillation chart after an earthquake. Before the war came, there was "the war of nerves." The "war," in fact, had never been interrupted since the Japanese invasion of Manchuria in 1932. And the "new order in Asia" was already being created in Manchuria and in the East Hopei area in the years between 1932 and the outbreak in 1937. To understand that "new order" and the war of nerves is to understand why the war came as it did.

After going back to Peking, Mr. Yao had no wish to return south. He was seventy-nine years old and was staying with his son Afei and his daughter-in-law in the Garden. In May, 1936, Mulan and Mochow had telegrams from their brother saying that their old father was critically ill and they should come. They went up with some of the children, but Lifu could not go until later, on account of his official duties.

Arriving at their old garden home, they found their father lying in bed, very much emaciated, but with his mind perfectly clear. It seemed that his body had been used up like a machine, and only the spirit remained. His illness began with a cold, caught because he insisted on sleeping with the windows open. Afei had thought it might be fatal. Nevertheless, old Yao seemed to get over it, although he never left his bed again. When he grew better, he still insisted on having good air and good light in his room. His voice was thin and small; he was steadily losing appetite, and with that his bowels failed to function. Lying there in bed, he was happy to see his daughters and Sunya and the grandchildren again.

This reunion of the Yao house was both happy and sad. Nothing is so touching as the reunion of relatives when there are many changes in their lives. Coral had died the previous year; Poya was married to a modern college girl from Shanghai, who had been a basket-ball champion and who had been studying in Peking. Mannia was now a woman of fifty, with her hair half gray, and was assuming the prerogatives of a grandmother. Her son Asuan had upon her insistence married again. As he returned only at week ends from his work with the Customs Service at Tientsin, she was now living with his wife and her grandson, a child of four by Asuan's first marriage.

After seeing her father, Mulan went over to Mannia's court to have a good talk with her.

"Lanmei," said Mannia, "I thought I was not going to see you again. You are fortunate to live in the south. It is not a good life to live up here. I am daily frightened. Asuan is engaged in that dangerous work at the customs. Every week before he comes home, I imagine that something may have happened, and I am happy to see that nothing has so far. And Huan-erh is worried, too, for Chen San is stationed at Changli, because it is his native district, trying to catch the smugglers. As you see, our whole family seems to be involved. Afei is in the Opium Suppression Bureau and is daily making raids, in which the traffickers are imprisoned or fined. My daughter-in-law is quite as worried about Asuan as I am, and we want him to give up his work, but he will not listen. You must help me to talk with him, when he returns next Saturday."

"Why is it so dangerous?" asked Mulan. "I thought Chen San was to work with him."

"No, they have to carry out their duties and seize smuggled goods unarmed, while the Japanese and Koreans daily attack them with stones and sticks, and some even carry pistols. Even if Chen San were with him, what would be the use, since he could carry no revolver?"

"Why is that so?" asked Mulan.

"You talk it over with Asuan. He will tell you the whole thing. The Japanese don't allow our customs officers to arm themselves."

Huan-erh came in at this moment, and, joining in the conversation, she said, "Chen San should be returning home in a week. I have written him a letter, saying that my brother is coming up and that he ought to ask for leave and come to see you all. When is Lifu coming?"

"He said in a week at the time we left. He should be here now in a few days."

"Is my mother coming with him?"

"I don't think so. She will probably stay to look after the house; she is so old," said Mulan.

Mannia drew close to Mulan and whispered, "This is within the family and you must not spread it abroad. Poya is a heroin addict and is trying to cure himself. What if people knew that one member of the family was on the Opium Suppression Committee and another an addict?"

"Isn't there a death penalty for smokers?" asked Mulan. "It is dangerous. Down south so many smokers were shot for taking Japanese 'red pills' this year."

"That is what I fear for him," said Huan-erh. "The anti-opium

712

measures are more and more vigorously pushed. Afei alone makes two or three arrests every week. He says it is already announced that beginning next January 1 addicts will be shot here. The new order is that traffickers and manufacturers will be shot—that is, if they are Chinese citizens, for we cannot touch Japanese subjects. For the smokers, there has been a six-year plan since two years ago. All addicts have to register and enter hospitals for cure or take treatment at home. But after this year, all addicts who go back to the drug after having been cured can be shot."

"Why don't we make Poya take a cure at home?" asked Mulan.

"He is doing it, but it is very troublesome," replied Mannia. "It is heroin and not opium. He said he caught the habit from smoking Japanese Gold Bat cigarettes. It is much more deadly than opium because before he knew it, he had to have more and more, or his eyes would water and he would feel as if all his joints were breaking and he were going to die."

Huan-erh interrupted again. "And do you know who made him decide to cure it? A Japanese sailor! He was walking one day with his wife in the Tungan bazaar—you know it is usually crowded. A Japanese sailor in uniform was walking behind and began to touch her bottom. She turned around, and the Japanese continued. She was frightened and whispered to her husband. The third time the Japanese teased her she shrieked and Poya turned round in a rage. Thereupon the Japanese sailor slapped him in the face and laughed. Then his hatred of Japan descended into his bones, and he realized that it was the Japanese who had made him smoke heroin and he determined to cure it."

"What did he do when he was slapped?" asked Mulan.

"What could he do? Chinese police cannot touch a Japanese. It is extraterritoriality!"

Mulan was shocked.

"I tell you," continued Huan-erh, "this is the new order in Asia. It is so in Manchuria. It has already come to Peking. It is already a land of monsters up here, not of human beings. We women and the children have to be very careful when we go out in the streets. . . . There are thousands of Japanese and Koreans here, and four out of five are narcotic dealers. Some of the places are called 'hospitals,' where quack doctors give you a shot of cocaine for a small sum. When Chen San comes he will tell you some stories from the East Hopei areas."

"Do you think Chen San would be willing to resign?" Mulan asked Huan-erh.

"No, the worse it is for them, the better is the spirit of the men. He calls it their *esprit de corps.* . . . I tell you, this state of things cannot last. Isn't it better that China and Japan should fight now and decide once and for all whether we are to be a free country, or whether our women have to submit to such indignities on our own territory while China is at peace with a 'friendly power'?"

• •

Lifu and Chen San both arrived on Friday. Old Yao seemed to have great inner vitality, and, seeing Lifu, he was able to speak to him for a while. Mulan and Mochow were in the room. After asking how he was getting on with his work, old Yao said to Lifu, "I remember you wrote an essay, *Science and Taoism.* You ought to take it up again and write it into a book. It will be my bequest to the world through you. You should also write *A Scientific Commentary on Chuangtse,* to support the thesis. Make footnotes, drawing upon biology and all modern sciences to make Chuangtse's lines clear to the moderns. He anticipated the infinitely great, and the infinitely small, without the benefit of a telescope or a microscope. Think of what he says about the indestructibility of matter, the travel of light, the sounds of nature, and the measurability and immeasurability of things, and the subjectivity of knowledge. Think of the dialogues between Ether and Infinite, between Light and Nothing, between Cloud and Nebula, between the River Spirit and North Sea. Life is an eternal flux, and the universe is the result of the interplay of *yang* and *yin* forces, of the dominant and the recessive, the positive and the negative. It will be astounding. Chuangtse did not put his ideas in scientific language, but his point of view was scientific and modern."

Old Yao still spoke with great mental force, although his skin and bones were now like a beggar's carcass.

Lifu was deeply impressed, and replied, "Of course I will do it. The famous *Chiwulun* is nothing but an essay on relativity. Chuangtse says, 'The snake envies the wind, and the wind envies the eye,' and all I have to do is to put in a footnote, giving the speed of light per second and the maximum speed of the wind. His theory about the evolution of the species—the evolution of man from horses—is comic, though. But I have thrown science overboard now. I am working on human insects. Every time I see one, I crush it. This is real life."

"You crush insects and sister crushes fireflies," said Mulan with a smile. "Between the two of you, the insect world will go out of existence."

"There are more insects in this world than you two can crush," said old Yao. "I warn you, children. When I am gone, there will be war, the worst yet in China's history."

"What should we do?" asked Mulan.

"It will be terrible for you. What will happen to all of you, Heaven alone knows. But I am not afraid for you, and you must not be afraid."

"Father, do you think China can fight?" asked Mulan.

"You are asking a wrong question," replied the old father. "Japan will make China fight, whether she can or not." He paused for a moment and then went on slowly. "You ask Mannia. If Mannia says China must fight, China will win. And if Mannia says China must not fight, China will lose."

The young people were surprised, but Mulan knew that Mannia was violently anti-Japanese and she understood what her father meant. Lifu smiled and said, "Why do you think so much of Mannia? How about us and Poya and Asuan and the other grandchildren?"

"Do not question my words," said old Yao solemnly. "Just ask what Mannia thinks. You others do not count."

"Why don't we count?"

"Wait and see."

Old Yao was evidently indulging in the oracles and conundrums of which the Chinese Zen Buddhists were so fond.

He was tired now, and Lifu and Mochow went out, leaving Mulan at her father's bedside. When she was left alone with him, he asked her, "How is Tsao Lihua?"

"She is married and has a baby already."

Old Yao smiled. "I did good work, didn't I? When I am gone, you will have to be your own detective," he said.

"Father, he is really all right now," said Mulan.

Old Yao smiled softly through his beard.

"Father, do you believe in becoming an immortal?" Mulan asked. "Taoists always believe in it."

"Utter nonsense!" said her father. "That is popular Taoism. They don't understand Chuangtse. Life and death are the very law of existence. A true Taoist merely triumphs over death. He dies more cheerfully than others. He is not afraid of it, because he is 'returning to the Tao,' as we say. Remember what Chuangtse said on his death-bed when he didn't want his disciples to bury him? His disciples feared that his exposed body would be eaten by the vultures, and he said, 'Above the ground I shall be eaten by the vultures, and under-ground I shall be eaten by the ants. Why rob one to give it to the other?' At least, I don't want monks to say prayers at my funeral."

Mulan was touched and surprised to hear her father's thin laughter at his reference to Chuangtse.

"So you do not believe in immortality," said Mulan.

"I do, my child. I am immortal through you and your sister and Afei and all the children born of my children. I am living all over again in you, as you are living all over again in Atung and Amei. There is no death. You cannot defeat nature. Life goes on forever."

. · .

When Mochow and Lifu had left the room, Mochow said to her husband, "I thought you were to arrive sooner."

"I stopped at Tientsin for one day," replied Lifu. "Playing the detective."

"What detective work?"

"I am not really on leave, but I came up with a secret mission. There is a case concerning someone whose name I must keep secret. It has to do with a raid in Shanghai on narcotic dealers, in which a prominent person is involved. You know there is a busy narcotic traffic between Tientsin and Shanghai. I stopped there to look around and investigate. When I asked for leave they asked me to look into this case and also to make a thorough report on the whole smuggling situation. Not a word is allowed to be published in the Chinese papers about this smuggling in millions, for fear of arousing anti-Japanese hatred to an uncontrollable degree. But the newspapers in London and New York are already publishing long stories about it, because British and American business is being ruined by the unfair competition."

"So you are on a job! How long will it take you?"

"I don't know. As long as necessary, probably a month. For this reason I am not going out to meet people. I want as few people as possible to know that I am in the north."

"You have only to stay at home," said Mochow. "Afei and Chen San and Asuan can supply you with all the information."

"I shall see," said Lifu.

Since Lifu wanted to obtain thorough information on the drug situation he went to see Poya, who was under treatment at home and making determined progress. Poya looked pitiful. The expression on his face was a mixture of fear, craving, hatred, and a kind of dry mental torture. Behind his gaunt sunken cheeks and high cheekbones and deep eye sockets, his great roving eyes showed his high intelligence. His mouth, wide and covered with a stubby mustache, was well set, recalling that of his mother Silverscreen. On a table by his side were many bottles and dishes holding sweetmeats. He told how he formed the habit when he was staying at a hotel at Tientsin after his Aunt Coral died. A hotel waiter induced him to try a Japanese cigarette with the white powder concealed in its tip. He took it out of curiosity, he said, and soon contracted the habit and demanded more and more. He told Lifu that he had seen people buying Gold Bat cigarettes just to take off the tip and smoke it on tinfoil.

"Remember your mother, and you will surely get over it," Lifu said as he took leave. But Poya's expression did not show that he had heard.

The next evening Asuan returned for his week end, and after supper Lifu prepared to have a good talk with him and Chen San. Mannia and some of the ladies were also present. Now, although Lifu did not belong to the Tseng family, Asuan had always secretly admired him, while Afei was always closer to Sunya.

Asked about the general situation, Asuan explained:

"Well, it is this. We customs men, unarmed, are supposed to enforce Chinese law against armed Japanese and Korean smugglers, who are not under Chinese law. We seize their goods as far as we can. Every week this April and May there has been an incident. The railway authorities are having a hard time. Every morning the 'Smugglers' Special' leaves the border for Tientsin, and the goods are dumped at the station, waiting for local distribution or reshipment to Shantung. Usually a few Koreans and Japanese stay to guard the goods. As many as ten freight cars a day are arriving besides the goods that come by trucks. Formerly the Japanese were more courteous, and special freight cars were demanded by their military authorities for transporting smuggled goods. If our railway authorities did not comply, they were charged with 'insincerity in co-operation' and with being anti-Japanese.

But now they don't take the trouble to notify us and demand extra cars. Armed Japanese and Koreans just throw the packages into the second-class and third-class cars and drive out the passengers, damaging windows and seats and beating the coolies in their way. Sometimes freight cars have to be attached or detached at the last minute, and the trains cannot run on schedule."

"What do the railway guards do?" asked Lifu.

"What can they do?" replied Asuan. "The smugglers are under extraterritorial protection, and the railway guards cannot touch them. They just look on enraged. Only this week more than a hundred Japanese and Koreans forced their way into the train and kicked and beat the railway staff and the customs officials because they could not get space. Some of my colleagues were hit on the head. Most of them escaped injury only through the intervention of the guards."

"How is it that you are unarmed?" Lifu asked again.

"It seems a joke, but it is perfectly simple. Last year there was a great deal of silver smuggled out, principally over the Great Wall, where our customs patrols were posted—armed of course. Two smugglers were injured by jumping down from the Great Wall, first a Korean, then a Japanese. Thereupon the Japanese military mission demanded five thousand dollars as compensation for the injured men, and the cessation of customs patrols along the entire Great Wall. They threatened force if these demands were not met. What could we do but comply, to avoid an armed conflict? Thus we lost the vantage points on the Great Wall and had to work cautiously below and to avoid further incidents. You see the East-Hopei Regime is really Japanese, but the Maritime Customs are under Sino-foreign control. So we still carry on our duties, but it is such an insane confusion.

"Last September, the Japanese commander notified the commissioner of customs that owing to political conditions the carrying of revolvers by customs patrols should be discontinued. Then another Japanese commander demanded that the customs preventive vessels should be disarmed and their machine guns taken away from them. A few days later came the further demand that all customs preventive vessels, irrespective of armament, should be removed from the three-mile limit off the shore of the 'demilitarized zone' all the way from the Manchurian border to Lutai, near Tientsin. As if that were not enough, the Japanese naval authorities refused to recognize the right of the Chinese customs service to operate in the twelve-mile limit and to signal to suspected boats to heave to, and gave warning that any interference with a Japanese boat, whether it displayed its nationality or not, would be treated as an act of piracy on the high seas!

"So the whole coast from Shanhaikwan to Tientsin is not only a free port; it's a free coast. Fleets of trawlers and steamers from five hundred to one thousand tons, lie off the shore, and motorboats even come direct from Dairen."

Asuan concluded his long speech, to which every one had listened intently.

"You can't call that smuggling," said Chen San. "It's daylight robbery of the Chinese government revenue by a friendly power. I saw it myself at the coast. One day I counted thirty-eight smugglers' vessels lying off the harbor near Shanhaikwan. Tents and camps are pitched on the coast, almost like a small town. Piles of rayon, sugar, cigarette papers, bicycle parts, kerosene, motor tires, alcohol, wire netting, lie there in broad daylight, each lot marked by a white flag bearing the name of the Japanese transportation company. From there the goods come south by motor trucks, pack animals, and carriers, usually escorted by some Koreans or Japanese. We try to stop them. The Chinese drivers generally run away at our approach, but Koreans or Japanese resist with stones, which they carry in their carts."

"I have heard of nations going to war on account of trade," said Huan-erh, "but I have never before heard of a nation resorting to smuggling for commercial competition. Will the Japanese Empire perish if they don't sell those extra gallons of kerosene and bundles of wire netting?"

"It is no small matter," said Afei. "The smuggled goods are reaching even far up the Yangtse valley and are driving the British and Americans out of business. It is estimated that the loss in customs duties is well over a million dollars a week—nearly two million dollars in the worst weeks of April and May."

"Don't you catch Japanese as well as the Chinese?" asked Lifu.

"We do when we have to," replied Chen San. "We may also catch them by mistake. Sometimes the Japanese disguise themselves as Chinese and even assume Chinese names. But we can usually recognize them by their short stature and their black, bushy mustaches, their bow legs, and their awkward gait."

"These must be the riffraff of the Japanese and Korean people," Lifu said.

"Yes," said Chen San. "This is what happens when a nation sends its lowest class into a foreign country and puts them above the law of that country and gives them official protection."

"What do you do when you seize the goods or arrest Japanese?"

"Out in the country, it is different," Chen San replied. "We turn them over to the Japanese consular police. Then Japanese come and demand the return of the goods, and usually there's trouble. But we are careful. When a consignment is marked 'military supplies' or consigned to the Japanese military headquarters, we know it is morphine, heroin, or opium and we can do nothing. There have been hundreds of cases of seizures in the last year and a half."

"Doesn't the Commissioner of Customs protest to the Japanese authorities?" asked Lifu.

"Ah, that's the crowning touch," said Asuan. "The Commissioner protested, and the military authorities sent him on to the Japanese Consular Police. When we protested to the consular police, do you know what they said? They said that, first of all, smuggling into China is not an offense in the eyes of the Japanese law, and they are powerless to stop it, which means that all Japanese arrested must be set free again, according to Japanese law. And secondly, they said, smuggling is understood to be possible only at a national border, and therefore should be stopped at the Great Wall and not below! This, after they forbade us to patrol the Great Wall!"

"Lifu," said Mannia, "don't you think Asuan should get out of this, or perhaps be transferred to Shanghai or elsewhere? He is my only son to depend on in my old age, and he has a young wife and a baby child."

Lifu looked at Mannia, and before he could speak Asuan answered, "Mother, you don't know. It's the same everywhere, in Shanghai, Amoy, or Swatow. Where there are Japanese, there is smuggling. Besides, I should be laughed at by my colleagues for cowardice. They have a fine spirit, and I cannot leave them. The government is at last taking strict action, and perhaps the situation will improve. What would happen to the customs service if everyone left it?"

"Perhaps you ought to think about it," said Lifu. "You have to think of your old mother and your young wife and child. And you are the eldest grandson of the Tseng family." Lifu was surprised to hear himself advising caution to another young man in such an objective tone. Mannia looked gratefully at him as the family party broke up.

CHAPTER XLII

$\mathcal{N}$ow the strange thing was that old Yao refused to die. A natural reserve of vitality carried him on, and his appetite even improved a little. Mulan and Mochow decided to stay, and Mulan wired to Atung to come up after his graduation.

The smuggling had become national. The Chinese government protested to Japan that the loss of customs revenue for the month of April alone was no less than eight million dollars. No satisfactory reply came from Tokyo. Foreign business in China was suffering, and the Japanese foreign office spokesman at a press conference was showered with questions about the smuggling scandal. The spokesman took the very interesting attitude that the high Chinese tariff was directly responsible for the extent of the smuggling, and furthermore that the fault was in the "lack of zeal" of the Chinese customs staff. In a desperate effort to stop the situation, on May 20, the Chinese Central Political Council decided upon death penalties for any Chinese citizen assisting foreign smugglers.

Now Afei had been making arrests and conducting raids on many narcotic dealers and opium dens in Peking. Emboldened by the new government policy, he had intensified his work. He had written to the authorities asking for the transfer of Chen San to the Opium Suppression Bureau in Peking, and Chen San was now assisting him in his raids.

One day there was a report that a heroin manufacturing plant was to be found in a certain street inhabited mostly by Americans and Europeans.

"Would you like to come this afternoon?" said Afei to Lifu. "We are going to raid a heroin plant."

At five o'clock, Afei and Lifu, with Chen San and armed police, went to the house, which was situated between two high foreign buildings. As this was a foreign residential quarter, where only blue-eyed people passed out and in, no one would suspect a drug plant. Chen San was asked to go into the street behind and post guards at the back door. Being armed with a revolver once more gave him a happy feeling and he constantly kept his hand on the smooth wooden butt.

Afei and Lifu went to the front door with some guards. A disguised guard knocked at the door, and, once it was open, the guards concealed at the sides rushed in and kept it from closing again. The servant opening the door was held by one of the guards and prevented from running in to give the alarm. Such plants were usually unguarded, depending more on secrecy and the protection of the Japanese.

In the courtyard, Lifu saw on the floor rows of objects which looked exactly like cakes of toilet soap. Afei pointed out that these were cakes of heroin, to be packed and labeled "hygienic soap," "Coty Perfumed Soap," "Colgate's," and with other foreign brand names.

A face looked out at them from behind one of the small unpapered windowpanes, and disappeared. The party went directly forward. It was a one-story house with a west wing leading inwards, shaped like a capital "L" and about the size of seven rooms. They pushed the door open and Afei ordered the arrest of all present. Several girls and four men with their mouths muffled by white handkerchiefs, were working at two long boards, serving as tables. On the floor were two stoves. The house was full of an intoxicating and nauseating smell. On one of the tables were jars, bottles, large and small spoons, and the white powder on large pieces of white, crisp paper. Here the girls were working. Men were working at the other table, which was fitted with small wheeled machines with hornlike inlets and outlets for mixing and spraying the powder. Against the wall stood a special machine with an enameled top for pressing and cutting the drug into cakes.

They went into the back rooms and saw piles of labels and an assortment of the most curious boxes, tins, and bamboo vessels, with different labels such as "Moon Cakes of Yukuangtang," "Pickled Mutton of Yuehsengtsai," "Parisian Rose Perfume" and bamboo-protected jars such as were used for packing pickled bean curds and pickled vegetables. At a dark corner of the inner back room, some great sealed earthen jars were standing upon the floor, which Afei said contained the raw powder from which heroin products were made.

At this moment, Chen San came in and reported that a woman had been arrested trying to escape into her car, which was standing at the back door. The chauffeur was also arrested.

"Bring them in and place them with the others in the front room."

The woman was brought in, her arm gripped by Chen San's muscular hand.

"Don't hold me so tightly," she protested. "You will answer for this to the Japanese Legation."

Afei and Lifu were standing in the back room and saw the well-dressed woman being taken across the yard directly toward the front room.

"Why, it is Suyun!" exclaimed Lifu. Now Chen San had never seen Suyun, and Afei had not seen her often because he was small when she was living with the Tsengs and she was absent from home most of the time.

They went back into the front room, where the offenders were huddled together, the girls weeping with fright.

Lifu assured Afei that the woman was indeed Suyun. She was dressed in a cream summer gown and looked pale and thin in that darkened room. Chen San was still holding her by the arm. Lifu kept quiet in the background while Afei advanced to her and asked. "Who are you?" His Cambridge education had given him great poise and dignity.

Suyun had recognized Lifu, but she did not know this person speaking to her, and she said haughtily, "Never mind who I am. Release me, officer. I am quite innocent. I was visiting a friend and came into the wrong house."

Speaking to the chauffeur, Afei asked, "Who is your mistress? Tell me the truth, or you will get it the worse. Clear yourself, and I may pardon you."

The chauffeur looked at Suyun and did not reply.

"The car is a private car, with license 505 of the Japanese Concession in Tientsin," said Chen San.

"How long has your car been standing here?" Afei asked.

"About a quarter of an hour," the chauffeur replied.

"Tell me who you are quickly. It may save you some trouble," said Afei to the woman.

"You will find out who I am if you ask in the Japanese Concession in Tientsin," Suyun answered.

"I warn you; don't be stubborn," said Afei. "According to the

723

new order of the government, you can be shot for this." Turning to the other employees, he said, "All of you can be shot. It is the death penalty now for working with the Japanese in drugging our own people."

When they heard this, the four girls—two of whom were barely twelve or thirteen years old—broke out crying and begged for pardon. They had never heard of the new order. The girls and the men knelt on the floor and begged for release.

Turning to the elder girls, Afei commanded them to stand up and said, "Tell me truthfully who is this woman, and I will pardon you."

"She is owner of this place," replied one girl. "We call her Mrs. Wang. But we don't know her well. She lives in Tientsin and does not often come here."

"What is your personal name, Mrs. Wang?" Afei asked.

Now Suyun, living under the protection of General Wu, had not become a naturalized Japanese citizen. When she heard what Afei said and saw Lifu standing silently in the background, she began to soften and replied, "Let us not pretend any more. We are in fact relatives. Is that not Brother Lifu who stands there? I am Suyun."

"Is this true? Is this true?" exclaimed Chen San.

Lifu still refused to speak, but merely looked at her; and, turning directly to him, she said, "I know you hate me."

"No," said Lifu.

"I should consider all the past as past, if I were you," she said. "Otherwise, when will the feud between our families end? Even if you succeed in getting me this time, there are my brother and others to avenge me."

"Is this a threat?" Lifu asked coldly.

"How dare I threaten you? I am pleading for a reasonable settlement. Tell me who is this officer?"

"He is Mulan's younger brother. I am only accompanying him. This is none of my business."

"I never thought I should meet you in such a place," said Afei, in his official tone. "I am carrying out my duties now. I am sorry, but you will have to come along."

He ordered a search of the documents and confiscation of the goods. The employees again begged for release, but Afei told them they were all to go to the detention house, and if they proved to be only em-

724

ployees and answered his questions truthfully, they might be released.

Now Suyun began to be more and more afraid, and while Afei was out of the room she said to Lifu, "What are you going to do with me?"

"How do I know?" replied Lifu. "You will probably be dealt with according to the law."

"I beg you to release me. Some day I may be able to repay you. What did I ever do to you? You ruined my life. Is that not enough? Must you still push a person to the wall?" Her tone and her face were pitiful.

"I tell you this is the sphere of the Opium Suppression Bureau, with which I am not connected. We never expected to find you here. Why are you in this wretched business?"

"It would be a long story to tell you. If you knew it all, you would understand. If you will not speak for me, won't you allow me to talk to my former husband? Perhaps he will speak for me, for old times' sake. I am an old woman, and I have suffered enough. Don't make me suffer more."

Afei had come back from his search and heard the last words, and was sorry for her. Nevertheless he ordered all to be taken to the detention house. A guarded closed car had already arrived from the bureau to take away the prisoners and the seized goods.

Before getting into the car, Suyun turned and asked Lifu, "Where is my husband?"

"He is here in this city. He is remarried."

"To that beautiful lady I saw one evening, dancing with him in the Grand Hotel de Pékin? Please let me speak to him or to her."

She was shut in with the others and the car pulled away under an escort headed by Chen San.

.·.

The news was received by the families with great excitement.

"We didn't go to seek her, but this time she came to seek us," said Lifu with a smile. "What do you think, Chinya? She is asking to see you and your wife."

"Why should she see me?" asked Dimfragrance.

"She wished it. She said that Chinya might intercede for her—her words were 'for old times' sake.' "

" 'Old times' sake!' " Chinya exclaimed.

"She said she wanted to speak to your wife—the lady she saw dancing with you at the Grand Hotel. Wasn't that Ailien or Lilien?"

"No, it was she," said Mulan, pointing to Paofen, who smiled.

Turning to Dimfragrance, Mulan said, "Would you like to talk with your husband's former wife? It would give her a surprise."

"How can we women interfere with the Opium Suppression Bureau?" asked Dimfragrance.

"I will tell you," said Lifu. "We will have her sent here under guard. And I propose that you three sisters-in-law together have a talk with your former sister-in-law and see what she has to say. She seems to have a long story to tell behind all this, and I want to hear it."

"What are you going to do with her?" asked Chinya.

"I don't know," answered Afei. "This is the first case since the new order from the government. I have not studied the documents yet. It is the death penalty, you know, for people acting in conspiracy with Japanese in smuggling. The same penalty is provided for the ringleader of smugglers who openly resist the preventive agents. She did not resist arrest. But another article provides the death penalty also for any one who evades customs duties in excess of six thousand dollars. It could be proved from this haul that she must have evaded more than that. It does not look pretty, and I have a life on my hands."

"If you are going to kill her, I would rather you did not bring her here into the house," said Mannia.

Now it was suppertime, and they separated for supper, and the topic was discussed at all tables in the different courtyards.

Mochow went in to her father, and he said, "Have no blood on your hands. Bring her here. Perhaps I shall want to speak to her myself."

The next day all agreed that Suyun should have a chance to speak to her husband, perhaps because the ladies could not individually resist the temptation to see her in such circumstances. But since old Yao also wished to see her, she had to be brought to the Garden, by special arrangements. She was believed to be a criminal guilty of a capital offense, and Afei had to give his personal guarantee to the bureau for her return, and to have her brought under guard. At his office he studied the seized documents, which revealed more addresses under her management with the assumed name of "Mrs. Wang of Tientsin." He also questioned the employees and promised to release them on probation, but said he could not do so until the case was over and all clues were examined, as a precaution against the news leaking

726

out. Care had to be taken that no word of the raid should reach the Japanese Legation. Although Afei had found out that this was a purely Chinese concern, there was no question but that the "White-Flour Queen" could be shot, in view of her known co-operation with the Japanese, which could very well be interpreted as "conspiracy." He said that the case must be settled quickly, for otherwise, in view of her standing, complications with the Japanese authorities were bound to arise.

Suyun arrived that afternoon under heavy escort, in chains, and wearing the old black suit provided for criminal women. Her eyes were blindfolded until she was in a room in one of the front courts at the Garden. Opening her eyes, she was surprised to find herself in a room with many of her relatives. Mannia, Mulan, and Dimfragrance she recognized at once. Chinya was standing at a side door, and she could not see him.

Her personal possessions had been taken from her, and now in black and without make-up she looked thin and pale and yellow. There were deep lines in her face, although she was only a year older than Mulan. Keeping her eyes down, she remained silent.

Afei walked up to her, and said, "You want to speak with your former husband?"

"Where is he?" asked Suyun.

Afei turned to Chinya, who refused to come out of the corner, and merely said, "She said she wanted to speak to my wife. Ask Dimfragrance to talk to her."

Suyun looked up but could not see the woman she wanted to speak to. Mulan touched Dimfragrance and said to Suyun, "Speak to her. This is Chinya's wife, Dimfragrance."

Suyun lifted her eyes and showed her surprise.

"Sisters and relatives," she said slowly. "I may as well speak to all of you. If you think of our former relationship when we were all living under the same roof, I want to speak a few words. If you do not think of our former relationship, then I need not say anything at all. If it is money you want, tell me your price, and I will pay. I can pay."

"Don't think we want your money," said Mulan, scornfully.

"I only want my life," said Suyun. "I have lived these years now and I know that money does not mean anything. I know you are happy this day to see me in chains. But if you want revenge, I wish to ask what I have done personally to any of you. I was divorced and disgraced by your family. Is that not enough? You must have a conscience. And do not think that Lifu's imprisonment was due to me. It was my brother. I had nothing to do with it."

It seemed to all that the Suyun they now heard was quite different from the Suyun they had known. But Mulan said, "If you don't care for money, as you say, why are you in this terrible business?"

"Mulan," she replied, "I know you hated me. . . ."

"I never did," interrupted Mulan.

"It does not matter whether you did or not. We are both grown many years older. I am terribly lonely."

Mulan was in turn quite touched, and she seemed not able to remember hating her. But Mannia spoke: "Why do you do such a thing? Why are you working with the Japanese against our own people?"

"If you understood all, you would forgive me, Elder Sister-in-law," said Suyun, suddenly calling her by that relationship. "I have no choice. All my money is in Japanese banks, and if I did not go on, it would be confiscated."

"Then why don't you let them confiscate it?" asked Mulan.

"After all, it is a big sum, and it is the work of a lifetime," replied Suyun with a sigh. "How could I willingly let it go? I have hundreds of people dependent on me for a living. If I gave it up, I would have to leave the Japanese Concession and what would happen to all my houses and hotels? Where could I go alone and penniless at my age? I will tell you, because we were former relatives—whether you recognize me as a relative or not—I am a lonely old woman, nothing but a terribly lonely old woman. What is money to me now? I saw you all gathered at the Grand Hotel years ago, so happy together, and I knew I had taken the wrong path. I don't blame my husband. You are the lucky woman, Dimfragrance, and I wish you luck. But spare me my life."

Now all the ladies were in tears and blowing their noses. Her words took them by surprise. They had thought of her only as a rich, proud, successful, ruthless woman.

"Where is Chinya? Why doesn't he speak to me?"

Now Afei motioned to Chinya and he came forward with his children, who rushed over to Dimfragrance, their mother, and Dimfragrance enclosed her arms over them, partly in protection, partly to give herself courage.

"If you had been satisfied with your lot, you would not be like this today," said Chinya.

It seemed to Suyun now that Chinya had been a good husband to her, but she merely said, "If you have regard for our former relationship as husband and wife, you will speak for me."

"Mother," asked Dimfragrance's six-year-old boy, "why is Father her husband?"

"She was married to your father before me," replied Dimfragrance.

The boy turned to the prisoner and said, "Were you married to my father?"

Suyun could not resist stretching out her hand to touch the child, a child of Chinya such as she might have had under other circumstances.

The child shrunk back, and asked, "Are you Chinese?"

Suyun could not answer.

"Why do you work with the Japanese?" the child said.

Tears rolled from Suyun's eyes and Dimfragrance called her child back to her.

"You are making it very hard for us," said Afei. "We understand you now, but you know your business is killing thousands of people every day. Have you the heart to go on?"

"If you release me, I will promise hereafter to cut myself apart from this work. I will also make a big contribution to the Opium Suppression Bureau."

"Don't you hate the Japanese?" asked Mannia.

"I hate all of them. I hate my work and I hate all the people I work with—Chinese, Japanese, and other foreigners."

"Where is your brother?" asked Lifu.

"He is in Dairen, in this business also. What else can he do?"

Now Afei suggested that his old father wanted to see her.

"Why?" asked Suyun.

"He wanted to talk to you. He is very ill. That is why we have had to bring you out here with all this trouble. Perhaps it is your luck."

Afei asked only the guards and Mulan and Mochow to follow them to his father's room. Here the guards remained outside, greatly wondering.

Old Yao was lying in his bed, and the light of the late spring sun coming in through a window cast sharp shadows into the deep lines of his face.

"Sit down," he said.

"I dare not," said Suyun.

"Sit down, I say," old Yao said again.

"You are only a distant relative of mine," he began, "and I don't know whether you will listen to an old man who has not much longer to live. My son happens to hold this office, and you happen to come under his arrest. This is heaven's will and not man's will. I have told Afei I do not want blood on our family, and I will ask him to deal as leniently with you as possible."

"Thank you, Old Uncle," said Suyun.

"Listen to an old man. Remember the parable: The old man at the fort lost his horse; who could be sure it was not his good luck? What are luck and adversity in this world? Who knows if your arrest today is not your good luck?"

"I don't understand you, Old Uncle," said Suyun.

"All depends upon yourself, if Afei releases you. . . . But I tell you a war is coming between China and Japan before long. And when it comes, remember you are a Chinese."

The old man stopped and did not even look at her.

"Good-by!" he said, without turning his eyes.

They all stepped silently out of the room.

The guards, with Chen San, took Suyun back in the closed car, but Afei gave orders not to blindfold her again. He now had to arrange her release, which was technically difficult. He examined her case carefully and laid it before his colleagues at the bureau and asked for leniency, as the dying wish of his old father. This would be the first case of the execution of a Chinese smuggler in the city, and the commissioners were willing to give it careful consideration. He had to draw up a long report in which he minimized the value of the seizure and stated that there was no resistance at arrest, that the documents revealed that the raided house was purely Chinese, that no Japanese had interfered, and that it was to be assumed the article about conspiracy could not apply in this case. Finally, he submitted the prisoner's promise of repentance and her offer of half a million dollars as a contribution to the Opium Suppression Bureau, and recommended that leniency be shown to her as a Chinese caught in unfortunate circumstances.

When the decision came back from Nanking a few weeks later, Suyun was released.

Mr. Yao died one night in his sleep. It was a simple natural death, a gradual waning away of his bodily vitality. His appetite gradually decreased until he could not take rice congee any more; then he stopped taking even water. Long after he was apparently dead, his feeble pulse was still beating and his eyes refused to close. It was truly a Taoist's death.

Now his son and daughters and daughters-in-law stood and knelt by his bed, weeping, and they bathed his body and changed his dress, putting a new one on him, and laid him in his coffin, according to due form. Afei asked for leave from his office to observe the customary severe mourning of a bereaved son. He left Chen San to work in the bureau because he was only a distant relative of the dead father. Mulan and Mochow and their husbands went into the white dress, proper for mourning, while Mannia and Dimfragrance wore blue which was the color of mourning suitable to their relationship.

The funeral was to take place in a fortnight. Mr. and Mrs. Fu had at this time already returned to their native province, and Paofen's parents took active part in arranging for a great funeral. Miss Don-ahue, who had become a close friend of Paofen because she was a painter, came to express her condolences, and Mrs. Hua and the old painter Chi also came to assist. Afei, as the bereaved son, was not expected to attend to the details, since traditionally a son is thought to be too stricken by sorrow to be able to have a mind for such things, and the funeral was arranged for him by his brothers-in-law.

Lifu, however, still went about his investigation of smuggling. The arrest of Suyun gave him a more intimate view of the narcotic trade than he could have got otherwise. Afei was not too sorrow-stricken to plunge into discussion on this topic with Lifu, for after all his father's death had long been expected. Afei gave Lifu both first-hand informa-tion and official reports from the Customs Service and the League of Nations committee on the opium traffic and reports of the English in-vestigator, Miss Muriel Lester, who described a state of affairs that cre-ated a world sensation. Afei also told him that the American Association of University Women of Tientsin had made an investigation of the drug situation, which uncovered conditions so disgusting and so terrifying in their ramifications that they ordered the whole report suppressed. Lifu, could read English only with difficulty, and consulted Afei for exact translations. Lifu had often made fun of the stiff exterior of the English-returned "gentlemen," and this had been something that kept him and Afei apart. But now they learned for the first time to know each other well, and Lifu overcame some of his prejudice against English-returned students.

He was particularly interested in a report that a foreign physician in Tientsin had bought candy from a peddler near a Chinese School in the Japanese Concession, and that analysis proved the candy to be narcotized.

"I can't believe it," said Lifu.

"I can give you the authority for the report," Afei said. "Near a school or not, what does it matter to the narcotic dealers? There is not a street in the Japanese Concession that is free from drug plants or shops, wholesale or retail, even in the best residential districts. Why then should dealers move away on account of a school?"

"Is this the 'new order in Asia'?" exclaimed Lifu, and Afei heard him curse as he had never heard a gentleman curse before.

Lifu made up his mind to go again to Tientsin and he arranged with Asuan to take him through the Japanese Concession in disguise. Lifu's knowledge of Japanese was an advantage to him in this work.

They saw store after store, housed in modern two-story concrete buildings, called *yang hang* ("foreign firm") with Japanese flags prominently hung over the doors. They went into these houses, called *yoko* in Japanese, and found that they carried no other stock except harmful drugs. In a single block, on Hashidate Street, they found ten or twelve of these *yoko*. Then they walked through other streets where they saw what appeared to be only residences, and Asuan told him this was the district of the big narcotic factories and wholesale firms. Directly in the rear of the Japanese consular police station, where Asahi Road becomes Tungmalu Street, with no effort at concealment, was a cluster of low-class narcotic dens, frequented by the poorest people, clothed in rags.

Lifu could not stand the sight of these human dregs and turned away.

"Would you like to see one of the better places—highest-class or middle-class?"

"Take me into a middle-class one."

They took a rickshaw and went to a house where a nauseating smell assailed Lifu's nostrils as he entered. The rooms were dark. Sitting or lying in different positions on couches were a number of addicts, with Chinese and Korean girls attending them.

"Will you *chou* or *tsa?*" asked one of the girls.

"My friend is a novice," said Asuan, pointing to Lifu. Turning to

Lifu, he said, "There are several ways of taking the drug. *Chou* is to smoke it, and *tsa* is to have it injected—that is cocaine or morphine—and there is a third method called *wen* or snuffing, for older addicts."

"Give us fifty cents worth of the white flour," said Asuan.

They were shown to a couch. A Chinese girl brought a small package of heroin on a special paper and half a box of matches.

"I am merely showing my friend," said Asuan to the girl who stood watching them.

"Would you like me to show you?" said the girl with a smile.

"Don't trouble," Lifu replied and the girl went away.

"In the higher-class places, these girls sometimes have a side business also, if you are willing to spend money on them. There you are put in a special closed room with the girl serving you, and no one else comes in unless you call."

This, however, was a semi-open room, where the girls went about serving the different customers who called them.

"Look at that one there. He is 'shooting the anti-aircraft,'" said Asuan, pointing to a man lying on his back on a couch. He had placed a roll of paper over a cigarette, enclosing the white powder, and was smoking it with his face upward. Some used a small pipe, which consisted of a writing brush handle stuck into the side of a large bamboo joint. Others sat up on the couch and heated a quantity of the white powder with a lighted match under the tin foil, and smoked the purplish-blue smoke as it rose from the heated powder, through a paper mouthpiece.

"That is called *ha,* inhaling," said Asuan.

Some new customers came in, one a mere boy of eighteen. A man attendant went up to him, apparently knowing what he wanted, and the young boy pulled up his shirt.

"The injection is given in two ways, intravenous and subcutaneous," said Asuan. "You see how that boy's back is riddled with needle marks. In the worst cases, the skin gets infected and rots. Intravenous injection avoids this, but it is more dangerous. Cases have occurred of persons dying on the spot after an intravenous injection. So most of the morphine addicts prefer a shot under the skin."

· ·.

Lifu returned to Peking and prepared his report. There was as yet no comprehensive Chinese study of the subject, apart from the reports of the Maritime Customs, and he drew heavily on foreign sources.

733

"The Japanese Concession in Tientsin is the heroin capital of the world," he wrote. "It acts as the exporting center for Japanese opium from Dairen, Mukden, Chosen to the North and South Americas. In Tangshan is the largest heroin plant in the world. A Japanese plant at Kalgan alone turns out fifty kilograms of heroin daily, or fifteen times the world's legitimate needs. Stuart Fuller in his report to the League committee, says, 'Where Japanese influence advances in the Far East, what goes with it? Drug traffic.' He describes the drug situation in Manchuria and Jehol as 'terrifying.' The extension of opium cultivation and traffic is under the careful planning and control of the Director of the Monopoly Bureau of the Government-General of Chosen, according to Japanese newspapers. The opium manufacturers' guilds are given goverment subsidies and are responsible to the Monopoly Bureau for directing poppy-growing and making loans to poppy growers, and for the manufacture and delivery of crude opium."

In his conclusion he wrote, "The principal difficulties in the suppression of opium and other smuggling are the Japanese military authorities, and the extraterritorial treaty.

"If such are the realities of the situation in the Far East, which Japan asks to the world to recognize, then the realities are beyond belief. If this is the national policy of a friendly power, then it is time China had more enemies and fewer friends. If this is the new order in Asia, then all decent human conscience ought to demand a return to the old order of the primitive savages as a more civilized form of living. The Japanese Concession in Tientsin is a poison-secreting tumor on the Chinese body politic, a blot upon Japan's own honor, and a menace to the public health of the entire world. It ought to be swept off the surface of the earth."

· ·

Old Yao's funeral was celebrated with proper pomp and glamour. Since his return the neighbors had called him the *Laohsienjen,* Old Fairy Man, and this was spoken of as the Old Fairy Man's funeral— rather a contradiction in terms. Besides Paofen's Manchu relatives and many old friends of the owner of the big tea and business firm, there were many friends and relatives of the younger generation. Afei's work gave him the standing of an official, and many representatives of the city government took part in the procession, which was about a mile long. Brass bands were very popular for funeral processions at this time and two bands were contributed by different bodies. Old Yao had given instruction that no priests should be allowed to say prayers for his soul. The monks of a temple in the Western Hills, however, insisted on coming to pay their respects. As this could not be refused now, Afei accepted their courtesy, but notified them only to join in the procession. The result was an odd mixture of the old and the new, the somber faces and robes of the priests contrasting with the bright epaulets and uniforms of the professional brass bands playing Tchaikowsky's Funeral March.

When Mulan was coming north she had seen at a railway station two brass bands, sent by two different officials, to play at the departure of a military governor. As the train started, the two bands began to play different tunes simultaneously, in a weird and comic cacaphony. She therefore told Sunya now to see to it that the two bands in the funeral procession should come to an agreement between themselves not to play at the same time, and that one should not begin playing until the other had finished.

The funeral gave Mulan and Mochow a chance to see a number of old friends and relatives. Among them were Sutan, now a widow, and Cassia and her daughters, Ailien and Lilien, who seemed well married and very modern. Taiyun's mother also came. Her husband was now dead, and she told them that her daughter was again in prison at Soochow, having been caught on her way to a secret session of communist delegates agitating for a united front to fight the Japanese.

Asuan had asked special leave to attend the funeral because Mannia had insisted on it, although he was not of the Yao family. The funeral took place on Wednesday, and the next day he went back to Tientsin. He learned that the day before, another gang of Japanese ronin had forcibly loaded a third-class coach on a train at the Tientsin East Station with two hundred pieces of goods and had injured a number of Chinese passengers who were forcibly ejected.

There had been eight or nine such incidents in this month of June and the customs officers were nettled. On Friday evening, news came that a big consignment of goods in six mule carts had been intercepted on the way to Tientsin and taken by the customs men, but had been recaptured by three Japanese and three Koreans who rushed in and overpowered them. Asuan's office asked for volunteers to go out and seize the recaptured goods once more. Some of the youngest and strongest volunteered and Asuan was one of them. The ronin were said to be carrying no arms, and it was thought that a force of twelve should be sufficient. They could carry no pistols themselves, the object being merely to seize the goods and foil the smugglers.

The route of the carts was known, and the twelve men went out to a small village, armed only with ropes. At a village shop one of the men saw some big firecrackers, and they bought a few to provide a scare. At about half-past two one of them with a field glass saw the mule carts coming. On the first cart only one short man, probably a Japanese, sat on top of a pile of goods, while the others were in the last two carts. The question was how to fight the escort in the rear without letting the carts in front escape, and how to make the attack a complete surprise. A party of three was detailed to deal with the single Japanese in front and to hold up the muleteers and their goods, while the other nine divided into two parties to hide on opposite sides of the road and attack the escort. Asuan was with these. They crouched under cover of an old wall.

When the first cart passed, their leader signaled to their men to draw nearer the road. Then he lighted the firecrackers and threw them into the cart. At this signal, they rushed out. The Japanese and Koreans, taken by surprise, began to throw a shower of stones. The customs men jumped up into the carts in the face of the hurled stones and came to close grips.

Asuan was the third to follow the leader, and as he was jumping up into the cart, a two-pound boulder hit him on the head and stunned him and he fell back to the ground. Luckily the other men were already up and the Japanese could not throw down any more stones. One Japanese was armed with an axe, and aimed it at the leader, who quickly struck him down with a blow in his belly and the axe dropped into the cart.

The Chinese muleteers ran off, and the carts stopped. After a short scuffle, the two Japanese and three Koreans behind were overpowered and tied up. The one man in the front cart, being half-drunk and sleepy in the June afternoon, had put up no resistance and submitted to arrest, cursing in unintelligible Japanese.

The leader got down and saw Asuan lying unconscious, his scalp bleeding. He sent his men to engage six farmers to drive the carts to the nearest customs station, and Asuan was lifted into one of the carts. He had received only a slight injury and he was already fully conscious when they reached the station, where his wound was bathed and bandaged up. It was a slight surface cut and not considered serious. The party, excited with success, then escorted the arrested Japanese and Koreans to the Japanese police station and handed them over.

At about half past seven, however, three Japanese entered the customs compound and, after looking through the office window, invaded the officers' quarters. They demanded to know where the seized goods were. When the officer in charge replied that they had been sent on to the head office, one of the Japanese became very abusive and slapped the officer in the face. Then they searched the sitting room and took away the axe. Before leaving, the abusive fellow threatened in his bad Chinese to return and kill the officer should his information prove incorrect.

The next day, Asuan was excused from his morning work, and took the nine o'clock express to Peking and arrived early in the afternoon, before the family expected him.

At the sight of his bandaged head, his wife was greatly frightened and at once called Mannia.

"I told you there would be this day," said Mannia. "Suppose you were killed, how would we mother-in-law and daughter-in-law feel?"

Huan-erh and Paofen and Mochow had heard the news, and they came into the room, and Asuan told them all the whole story. Mulan came in later and heard Mannia talking with agitation, half scolding her son and half cursing the Japanese.

"What is this business you are engaged in?" Mulan heard her saying. "An official—but not an official; a bandit—but not a bandit—going to fight tigers with bare fists. I hate the dwarf devils. Why is it that our officers cannot carry arms, while they can? If it were a war between the two countries, with the ground cleared and the regiments lined up on opposite sides and the knives and spears stacked in parallel formation, that would be like a fair battle. . . ."

"Would you approve of China fighting Japan?" asked Mulan.

"If it is to be like this, a war would be better," said Mannia. "How can one ask Asuan to fight the dwarf devils with his bare hands?"

Mulan remembered what her father had said. "*You ask Munnia. If Mannia says China must fight, China will win. And if Mannia says China must not fight, China will lose.*"

"You believe then that China can fight Japan?" said Mulan, slowly.

"China will have to fight whether she wills it or not."

So Mannia had said it!

It meant, old Yao had said, that a war was coming and it was to be a war to the last man.

"Mannia!" said Mulan. "You have declared war on Japan!"

"What do I know about declaring war?" said Mannia. "I know only if we must go down, let us all go down together, China and Japan too!"

"What do you think, Mulan?" asked Huan-erh.

"How can I know? I wish I could ask my father this question now. But he always said that luck was something inside the character of a man. For one qualified for luck, jars of water will turn into silver; for one unqualified, jars of silver will turn into water. You must have the character to stand that luck. These Japanese have not the character to stand the luck of ruling China. Give China to Japan and she will not be able to stand it."

CHAPTER XLIII

HE war broke out the following year, on the seventh of July. It developed out of the North China situation as naturally as a flood that follows an earthquake. Criminologists assume that two separate crimes have been committed by the same criminal when they find certain characteristic methods used in both. The Japanese plan of conquering China was of a piece with their smuggling policy. It was identical in method, character, and motive; and it was inspired, planned, and directed by the same agency, the Japanese Army.

The Japanese Army merely went on with the same ruthless methods, from the robbing of Chinese Government revenues to the robbing of Chinese territory. Curiously, human psychology tends to regard the stealing of a nation's territory as more honorable, more conscionable, more debatable, than the stealing of a lady's handbag. Chuangtse long ago wrote:

> Steal a hook,
> And you hang as a crook;
> Steal a kingdom,
> And you're made a duke.

The second half of this truth presents a problem usually studied, examined, diagnosed, prognosticated, analyzed, debated, interpreted, defended, quibbled about, and discussed circumspectly in prospect and in retrospect, by a brilliant galaxy of economic experts and international jurists in learned theses, within which the truth still succeeds in evading their observations, like a ghost at a spiritualist séance. Some say they have seen it, some swear they haven't.

But perhaps Mulan was right. The Japanese "luck-character" could not change.

Scientifically, the war might be said to have started "spontaneously." The so-called Marco Polo Bridge "incident" was not even an incident. Japanese troops after night maneuvers in illegal areas went to demand entrance into a guarded and fortified Chinese city at four thirty in the morning in search of a "missing" soldier, and the Chinese were alleged to have fired on them. Afterward the Japanese did not even consistently maintain that the soldier was "missing." But anyone living in China in the year before the war knew that war must come sooner or later. After taking Manchuria, annexing Jehol, pushing quietly into Chahar, and creating the East Hopei Regime, the Japanese now wanted to detach the "five northern provinces," and they thought China would give the territory to them. The Chinese hated the Japanese, but the Japanese loved China's territory, and the more the Japanese loved our land, the more bitter was the Chinese hatred.

And thereupon the two nations started the most terrible, the most inhuman, the most brutal, the most devastating war in all Asia's history.

As a matter of fact, a war of nerves had been going on for years, and Chinese nerves were now on edge. The Chinese had to fight Japan and kill Japanese in order to save themselves from national delirium. The Chinese Government helped to fray Chinese nerves by forbidding any public expression of anti-Japanese sentiment, whether by writing, speech, meetings, or street demonstrations. But the growing and suppressed anti-Japanese sentiment in the people burst forth with the force of a dammed flood. It nearly engulfed Chiang Kai-shek himself in dramatic fashion at Sian. When the Japanese said the Chinese people were anti-Japanese, they were entirely right. But when they said that Chiang Kai-shek encouraged public expression of that anti-Japanese sentiment, they were entirely wrong, for he did not move a finger to give it outlet. If they thought the Japanese could stamp out Chinese hatred and make themselves lovable in Chinese eyes, by waging war and destruction upon the people, that is another problem, and one for Japanese wisdom to solve. Neither old Yao, nor Mulan, nor Mannia, nor the best philosophers of China could help them in that matter.

Objectively considered, the movement toward war since 1932 was as follows: Manchuria was the first Japanese blow. The Tangku Truce after the fall of Jehol in 1933, demanding the "demilitarized zone" on the Chinese side of the Great Wall, was the second. In the spring of 1935, when most of the Chinese Army was pursuing the communists into western China, Japan struck the third blow by compelling the withdrawal of certain units of the Chinese Army from Hopei. Thus the stage was set for the creation of a puppet state, similar to "Manchukuo," out of the five northern provinces, by intrigue with local commanders and the promotion of an "autonomy movement" to declare independence of Nanking. Sadly surprised by the "insincerity in co-operation" of even the provincial authorities, Japan tried in the fall of 1935 to concentrate on Hopei and Chahar alone, but the Chinese Government replied by recalling troops from the west and massing them along the Lunghai railway. Realizing the danger, Japan temporarily abandoned the big scheme and struck the fourth blow by creating the East Hopei "anti-communist" regime, tightening her grip on the Chinese Hopei-Chahar Council and increasing her North China garrison to a strength four times greater than the Boxer protocol powers had considered necessary for the past thirty-six years.

In the fall of 1936, the fifth blow was struck by the seizure of Fengtai, the railway junction near Peking, where all southbound and eastbound trains passed, in spite of its being clearly outside the limit defined by the Boxer Protocol for the stationing of foreign troops. Following close upon this, came the sixth blow in the form of a Japanese-inspired Mongol invasion of Suiyuan, which was for the first time met openly by the Chinese Government troops and repulsed. Then came the seventh blow—the Marco Polo Bridge incident.

Both Taoism and modern science agree on this: That action and reaction are equal. The spirit of Chinese resistance is the reaction; the anti-Chinese acts of Japan in the years 1931-37 are the preceding action. The strength of the Chinese resistance should be understood as a direct measure of the enormity of Japan's acts against a friendly power before the war. Only thus can we understand the war. The best air, land, and sea forces of the greatest power on earth unfortunately cannot bomb and shell Nature's immutable Law of Action and Reaction out of existence.

The war became inevitable now, because both nations were ready for a showdown in North China. While negotiations for armistice were prolonged, sporadic fighting continued. Chiang Kai-shek was conferring at Kuling with military leaders from all provinces to make the momentous decision; Japanese troops continued to pour in unmolested for three weeks to strengthen their positions along the Peking-Tientsin Railway. Within nine days after the incident it was reported that five Japanese divisions, totaling one hundred thousand men, had been sent to China proper and Inner Mongolia. Trainloads of munitions and military supplies had poured into Tientsin and had been distributed to Fengtai and other points. When the real fighting began around Peking, Japanese troops were already entrenched at all strategic points a few miles from the city. General Sung Chehyuan flatly rejected the Japanese ultimatum of July 26 demanding the withdrawal of the entire thirty-seventh division south of Paoting, and then the war started. The Chinese launched a heavy attack on the twenty-eighth, but General Sung dramatically left Peking at eleven o'clock that night, appointing a pro-Japanese mayor, and the resistance of his 29th Army ceased by midnight of the twenty-ninth. Peking was already in Japanese hands.

. ∴.

After their father's funeral, Mulan and Mochow had returned South with their families, and were living at their homes in Hangchow and Soochow when the war broke out. Afei and the others were still in Peking. After the Marco Polo Bridge incident, rumors flew fast in Peking; and, while the Nanking government was trying to reach its great decision, the inhabitants daily prayed for the appearance over the city of Chinese airplanes, but they never came. There were whispered hopes that the city would be saved, and whispered fears that it might not. If there was hatred of the invaders, it was a deep, large, smouldering hatred, tempered with the patience of centuries. When they saw the Japanese planes circling over their heads, they cursed discreetly, secretly.

Most of the people of that ancient capital, the true natives, gossiped imperturbably and even good-humoredly in their homes and teahouses about the coming of war and speculated about its outcome, but they went about their business as usual.

They disliked an invader, but they had seen other invaders before. There was a wild assortment of people living in Peking, old, retired Manchu officials and young patriotic students, chicken-hearted officers and bland, cynical politicians, honest tradesmen and the poorest riffraff working as Japanese spies. But the average man was too civilized to like violence and war, and little inclined to terrorism and riots such as there were in Shanghai. He was mild, reserved, peace-loving, and indomitably patient.

The true inheritors of Peking's ancient culture have proved themselves superior to all attacks of modernism; as their forefathers had lived, so they are living now. There is an atmosphere of contentment in their houses, a suggestion of inexhaustible mental reserve in their outlook upon life, a philosophical detachment from the sense of time in their mode of living, and a wise, good-humored, leisurely style in their conversation. For in old Peking, the moment and eternity are one. What are centuries elsewhere are but short moments in Peking, spanning the generations from grandfather to grandson, carrying on the same tradition of living. For Peking can wait and grows old and yet never grows old. Conquered many times, it has ever conquered its conquerors, and adapted and modified them to its own way of living.

The Manchus have come and gone, and Peking does not care. The white Europeans have come and proved their military superiority in successive sacks of the city, and Peking does not care. Modern returned students in foreign dress and modern curly-haired women have come and introduced new fashions and new distractions, and Peking does not care. Modern tall ten-storied hotels stand side by side with old one-story houses, palatial modern hospitals exist side by side with centuries-old medicine shops, modern girl students live in the same yard with old half-naked Boxers, and Peking does not care. Scholars, philosophers, saints, prostitutes, crooked politicians, traitors, monks, and eunuchs have come to share its shadows, and Peking welcomes them all. Its joy of living still goes on. Its beggars' guilds, opera houses, children's dramatic schools, shuttlecock players' clubs, duck and crab restaurants, lantern streets, curio streets, temple fairs, wedding and funeral processions, still go on for ever.

It was unbelievable that its Temple of Heaven, its Forbidden City and imperial palaces, should be bombed and destroyed. And like a charmed city, of all the cities occupied by the Japanese army, Peking alone escaped unharmed this time.

You cannot talk excitedly about politics or current events in Peking, or your Peking culture is incomplete and you have lived in Peking in vain. What distinguishes the Peking accent from other dialects is not its vowels and consonants, but its calm tempo and its composed tone, good-humored and contemplative, the talkers ready to appreciate the full flavor of talk in forgetfulness of time. This leisurely view is in the very metaphors of its speech. To go shopping at a bazaar is but to *kuang* or "play" the bazaar, and to walk in the moonlight is to "play" the moonlight. The dropping of a bomb from an airplane is but the "iron bird laying an egg," and to be hit by the bomb is but to "win first prize in the aviation lottery." Even to have blood streaking down from a wound in one's temple is but to "hang a festoon of red silk"! Death itself is but to display "a crooked queue," like a dead beggar on a roadside.

But there was at least one in Peking who was excitable, and that was Taiyun, who had been released from prison late in May. Taiyun did not belong to Peking, but to the politically conscious and martial-spirited young China. To her, the war that had now broken out was not by any means a catastrophe, but an inspiring and long-prayed-for chance to fight for national freedom against the hated invader. If one understood the preceding years, one could readily see that the war came as a great mental relief, a restoration of sanity and balance, and a release of stored-up energy. The news that, at long last, a Chinese government was ready to lead the nation to fight Japan was too good to be true. If one understood the national despondency and psychological frustration and fretting in the seven years before, the waiting for a clear national leadership and a firm national policy and the almost futile hope for a national united front of all factions and parties against Japan, one could easily see how the consummation of the united front and the decision upon a war of resistance to the end meant to Taiyun the realization of her fondest dream.

Her enthusiasm was infectious, and it affected her nephews, Huaiyu's children, and even his wife. Huaiyu had come back, and with him Inging, and they were staying in a German hotel. His father was dead, and his children and their mother were staying with Taiyun's mother, whom he called Funia, and he had come back to claim his own children.

One day he appeared at Taiyun's home. He was now fifty years old, and his Japanese mustache had turned white. He was rich and well-to-do and wore a foreign suit and gold-rimmed spectacles, and he had acquired some Japanese mannerisms, such as making a hissing sound through his teeth, or clapping his hands to call for servants.

Kuochang, now a man of thirty, both hated and despised his father. "What do you come back for?" he demanded. "Looking for a chance to come back into power with the Japanese Army, I suppose."

"Young man," Huaiyu said patronizingly, "what do you understand? How can China fight Japan?"

"You don't approve of resisting Japan?"

"I greatly disapprove. It is like a moth flapping its wings against a lamp—suicide. Come here, I want to talk to you."

744

He led his eldest son into another room. Within five minutes Kuo-chang's mother in the outside room heard him shouting inside and then he rushed out, his face red with anger.

"Traitor! Traitor!" he cried.

"What is it?" asked Taiyun.

"He is a Japanese spy and he wants me to be a Japanese spy!"

His father came out, calm and unperturbed.

"*Wangkuonu!*" cried Taiyun, calling him literally a "sell-country slave."

"What's the use of getting excited like that?" said the father. "You have no respect for your father! I never thought you would be such an unfilial son!"

"What? You—my father? My father was dead long ago. Where was he all those years while I grew up? I have already disowned you." Turning to Taiyun and his mother, he said, "He offered me three hundred dollars a month to act as a Japanese spy!"

Suddenly his long-suffering wife, Yachin, began to shout. "Get out of here! Get out! Get out!"

She picked up a glass goblet and hurled it with such good aim that it hit his gold-rimmed spectacles, which dropped to the floor with the broken glass.

"You—!" Huaiyu cried.

"Get out of here!" she shouted again. "Leave us, mother and children, alone. Luckily we haven't starved to death, but don't come near us again."

"Well, well!" said Huaiyu angrily. "This is revolution at home!"

He was advancing toward his wife, raising his gold-ringed stick with a menacing gesture as if to strike her. Kuochang forcibly wrested the stick from his hand.

"Leave here, you, instantly," said the son, holding his father by his collar.

Mortified, Huaiyu turned to go away.

"No law and no heaven!" he exclaimed. "China must perish! China must perish!"

"Here are your spectacles. Take them and get out of here," said the younger brother, and then gave his father a kick behind.

"Rotted egg! Bastard!" shouted Huaiyu as he rolled out into the yard. "You'll see whether you are right or I am right. All working for the country . . ." His mutterings became inaudible.

Suyun was still living in Tientsin, which was practically under martial law. Both in the Concessions and in the Chinese city, passers-by were constantly searched. Japanese soldiers and munitions were being rushed inland. The Chinese railway was used for transporting these men and supplies, and General Sung, in an effort not to aggravate the situation, permitted them to come through. The intense nervousness in Tientsin caused a great exodus from the Chinese city into the foreign concession areas and down to Shanghai. There were many arrests, assassinations, and similar incidents daily in Tientsin. Above all, there was a great spy scare, and frequent deaths, Japanese spies killing Chinese agents, and Chinese agents killing Japanese spies. Corpses floating down the Hai River, a common sight at Tientsin in recent years, now greatly increased in number, and there was public speculation as to the causes. One theory was that, besides the regular heroin victims, Chinese laborers who had been forced to construct Japanese defense works at Haikuangsze were being murdered afterward to prevent the exposure of military secrets.

Now that the Japanese knew the war was coming, the network of their spy system which spread over China was being intensified. The headquarters for North China was at Tientsin, although later Peking had its own head office with a Japanese in charge. The system ramified and extended inland, through Chinese, Koreans, Formosans, and a large number of white Russians. The spy system had been established for years all over China, the secret agents being chiefly traveling salesmen of Japanese patent medicines, narcotic dealers, and others working under cover as photographers or for news and advertising agencies. Employees or servants working in aviation, political, and military bureaus who could be bought were being paid monthly salaries. These spies were trained to take photographs, draw maps, and send secret messages and were provided with cameras, chemicals, and even wireless sets. The object was mainly to obtain Chinese military secrets, maps and plans of defense, and other military information. Only the highest and most intelligent ones, some of whom were women, were selected for the more difficult and more delicate work of making contact with Chinese military officers. To these large rewards were paid for special work, and a staff was provided for them.

One day Suyun, who was still in Tientsin, was called to the Japanese spy headquarters, known as the Special Service Department. This belonged to the Japanese military mission, and was frequently at odds with the Special Service Department of the Kwantung Army, which was headed by the notorious Doihara.

A man of about forty was seated in the office when Suyun came in. He had a full but bony face and a round, close-shaved head. He wore a black mustache, but no spectacles, which was unusual for a Japanese. On the whole, it was an intelligent and pleasant face. He spoke tolerable Chinese and a little atrocious English and Russian.

Suyun knew why she had been sent for. She was a large owner of hotels and estates in the Japanese concession and a narcotic leader of long standing, and the Japanese were confident of securing her co-operation. When she had gone back to Tientsin after her release the year before, her case was well-known to the Japanese authorities. That she had sent half a million dollars to the Chinese Bureau was understood by the Japanese as a form of bribery, the price of her freedom. Since her other establishments in Peking were also raided, they merely thought it was her bad luck, and they had no reason to believe that the Opium Suppression Bureau was well disposed toward her, or she toward the Bureau. She was keeping up her old life as usual, having apparently no alternative and being afraid to act on her convictions. But she took less interest in the business and was contented merely to carry on.

"Sit down, Miss New," said the Japanese officer, most courteously. "We appreciate your long co-operation with us. I have here something for you to do. Before I forget it, I want to express our appreciation of the fact that all of your money is in Japanese banks. . . . Now to business: there are many hotels here under your ownership, and in every hotel, there are dancing hostesses. You will select twelve or fifteen of the prettiest and most intelligent ones and report to me with them for further instructions. This department has need of their service. And we do not forget you yourself. I shall place you at their head. Choose Chinese, Koreans, or White Russians. We will pay two hundred dollars a month each, and up to five hundred for the cleverest ones. . . . And special expenses will be paid. Is that clear?"

All this was not surprising to Suyun, and it was far from welcome; but under the circumstances, she knew that she had to accept or lose her properties or even her life.

"Certainly," she replied. "I shall do my best."

The officer rose and shook hands with her heartily. Suyun responded, but she felt a sense of nausea inside.

She went home and thought anxiously of the problem facing her. Making money on opium was something different. She had drifted into it and could not get out. But now war was coming, a war between the Japanese and her own people.

Was she to consent to act as Japan's spy against her own people? Her hatred of herself, her whole career, and her whole wretched surroundings now became transformed into a hatred of the Japanese in whose grip she found herself. A decision had to be made. Either she was to face confiscation of her property and the wiping out of her whole fortune, or she must submit and turn traitor. The name "traitor" was now met with everywhere and there were daily stories of arrest. And what would be her end? What could she possibly gain by acting for the enemy even if she survived all the risks? Of money she had enough. What if she were arrested and shot? Her nerves were on edge.

Then the words of old Yao came back to her. *"When the war comes, remember, you are a Chinese."* How did that old man know? Was he really a "fairy man"? Even more unforgettable was the question of Dimfragrance's boy: *"Are you a Chinese? Why are you working with the Japanese?"*

She decided that she would pretend to go on until she had a chance to save some of her fortune and escape without attracting attention. She arranged for a number of dancing hostesses, among them only two or three Chinese. One of them flatly rejected her offer and said, "I want money, but to sell my country—I won't." The others were mostly Korean and White Russian girls. The next day she took the girls to the special service department for the chief to look over, and she was greatly complimented by the chief for her prompt work. When the girls had left, he asked her to remain.

"Miss New," he said, "you are an elderly lady and I have perfect confidence in you. A war is coming—you know that. Japanese soldiers will be inside Peking in half a month. We have the city practically surrounded already. We must have the best persons we can get. Your duty will be to report on the political positions of the Chinese officers in the 29th Army. We are trying to secure a victory without bloodshed, or with as little sacrifice as possible. We have already contacts with Chang Tsechung and Pan Yukuei. But as a Chinese woman, you can get inside information that cannot be obtained otherwise. Select the two prettiest girls and present them to Chang Tsechung not as our gifts, but as your own, and work from inside—do you understand?

748

The other girls I shall assign to different work in the Chinese city and the British and French concessions."

Suyun prepared to leave for Peking. She went to her Japanese bank and drew out thirty thousand dollars, not daring to draw more for fear of attracting the attention of the Japanese authorities. She went to Peking with two Korean girls and took rooms at a foreign hotel in the Legation Quarter.

Now Taiyun had heard of her half-sister's arrest and release through the Yaos, and had visited her at Tientsin, praising her for her decision to reform and urging her to quit her work as early as possible. Now in her desperation, she, Suyun, inevitably thought of Taiyun as the only person who could talk with her, for strangely enough, her brother Huaiyu had gone his own way entirely since she had left General Wu. She knew what Taiyun would say, if she asked for advice, yet she could not resist going to talk to her. For Taiyun and Huaiyu's wife and children were the only relatives she had left in the world.

So about the middle of July, she arrived at her sister's house. Huaiyu's wife received her coldly, if courteously. Her nephews did not know what to think of her.

Taking Taiyun aside, she said, "I must talk to you. Our parents are dead, and, at our age, Huaiyu is no longer a brother to me. You know that we have quarreled since his business and mine crossed each other's paths."

"He is here in this city, too," said Taiyun, and she told with a great deal of laughter of the scene they had had at home.

"I am a traitor, too," said Suyun with a smile.

"He who is a traitor does not announce it, and he who announces it is not a traitor," said Taiyun.

"This is serious. I want to talk to you. . . ."

"You, a 'sell-country slave,' too?" shouted Taiyun. "Are you going to bribe me?"

Suyun quickly hushed her. "I want your advice. I have no one else in this world to advise me now. This is the situation I am in. I had rather be dead!"

She outlined her dilemma between losing all her fortune and possible death as a traitor.

"So that is it!" said Taiyun, when her sister ended. "There is nothing more simple. Are you a Chinese or not? That is the only question. Sister, there is only one way to go. How can a Chinese help the enemy

749

to enslave our own people? What could you gain by it, even if you got richer than you are? Most probably you will be shot. Now that you have been honest with me, I may as well be honest with you. There are patriotic anti-traitor societies everywhere, specializing in hunting out and shooting traitors. I am one of them and, Sister, if you really go with the Japanese, I may shoot you myself. Do you want some one to put a bullet into your head?"

Taiyun laughed as she said this, and her manner was friendly, although her words were menacing.

"What do you think I should do?" asked Suyun again, very much worried and frightened.

"Do? Be a patriot! The only question is whether you hate the Japanese or not. Can't you see that every single Chinese man, woman, and child is against the Japs, and that China must certainly win? By all the mothers of the Japanese and Chinese traitors, can't you see that I am happy and you are not?"

Now this was a rather obscene oath and it amused Suyun, and there was something in Taiyun's buoyant spirit that amazed her.

"Can China win?"

"Of course—beyond a doubt. We may all die, but it is better to die with our own people."

"Are you sure you will be happy to die with our own people, if you must?"

"Of course, I am happy. Can't you see?"

Suyun felt a new and strange feeling surging up in her. Happiness had been something quite remote from her, and she had never heard any one say he was happy with such conviction.

"*Happy, happy,*" she muttered the words and seemed to try to see if that little word could ever sound real to her again. Then she said, "Sister, I wish I could remain always with you. I am surrounded by ghosts over there. How I hate the Japanese—and my Chinese associates too!"

"You hate them?"

"I loathe them." Suyun kept quiet for a moment, and added, "I loathe myself."

"Then escape and come over to the Chinese side. Stay with us here."

"Didn't you say you were in the anti-traitor society?"

"Yes, but it is a secret group only. If you will help me, I will go myself with you to Tientsin and put bullets into the heads of some Japanese spies."

Suyun was suddenly seized with terror and broke down, crying and moaning, "I am afraid to die!"

Taiyun's eyes flashed. "Look here!" she said. "Here is a great chance to serve China. I will come with you to Tientsin with some of my group and we will obtain Japanese secrets. I will pose as a spy myself. You will be a great national hero. Why are you afraid to die?"

Taiyun's cheerful courage touched and even infected her sister, and opened her mind to a new world she had not known during the last half of her life. In her spiritual desolation she clung now to her sister, and in her company the great decision was made.

She was to go to Tientsin with Taiyun, Kuochang, and Chen San. Taiyun was to be introduced to the Japanese Special Service as Suyun's own sister. Suyun was to stay in the Japanese Concession and make contact with the Special Service Department and pass on whatever information she could get to the others working in the Chinese city. Meanwhile, she was to draw out her money at intervals from the Japanese banks, two or three thousands of dollars at a time, so as not to arouse suspicion.

. ∴ .

Suyun went to the Japanese office once every two or three days. She secured the help of Liling, the Chinese dancing partner who had refused to serve the Japanese before, and swore her to absolute secrecy. Taiyun was introduced to the chief on the first day. The chief looked suspiciously at her, but Suyun assured him that she was her own sister. Taiyun thus knew all the secret signals and had a free pass through the Japanese sentries.

Strangely, many Japanese spies, including some of the girls Suyun had previously secured, were shot or disappeared mysteriously.

One day when Suyun went into the office she was asked by the Japanese chief, "Do you know anything about the Chinese anti-traitor groups? There are too many incidents among our agents. There must be a leakage somewhere. I warn you to be more careful. By the way, how did you happen to draw out of the banks thirty thousand dollars on July 10, five thousand on July 16 after you came back from Peking, and two thousand on the eighteenth?"

"Oh!" replied Suyun calmly, "these are troubled days. Who is not drawing some cash to provide for emergencies? The thirty thousand dollars was for a consignment of morphine despatched from Dairen. I can show you the bills."

"Well, I am just warning you."

Suyun affected to joke. "Chief," she said, "what about my pay for this work? I must have at least a thousand a month. And what price will you pay me if I succeed in getting Chang Tsechung to rebel?"

"Come, what do you need money for? You are a millionnaire."

"What do you think I work for, if not for money?"

"All right, a thousand a month for you. And extra rewards for special work. Do you think Chang can be bought over for half a million?"

"I will try."

This conversation temporarily allayed the chief's suspicions. But Suyun stopped drawing money from the Japanese banks and only began collecting her bills as much in cash as she could, for all checks went through Japanese banks. And she warned Taiyun not to come again into the Japanese Concession.

Now the situation in Peking and Tientsin was becoming critical. On the twenty-eighth serious fighting broke out, and Japanese planes were bombing Chinese troops at all points between the two cities. Japan rushed more troops to the Peking front.

Suyun passed out the important information that the Japanese garrison was depleted to only slightly over two thousand, most of the available men having been sent to the front. The message was brought to Chen San in the Chinese city by the Chinese girl named Liling.

Acting on this information, Chen San plotted with the Chinese Peace Preservation Corps in the Chinese area, to make a dramatic attack on the Japanese Concession itself. They had knowledge of a mutiny planned to take place at Tungchow on the following day among the East Hopei troops, which had been equipped and trained by the Japanese. Moreover, the news of a Chinese counterattack all along the line and the reported capture of Fengtai and Lanfang decided them to launch the bold scheme of driving the Japanese out of Tientsin altogether.

Fighting began within Tientsin city at two o'clock in the morning of July 29. All day the Chinese city was subjected to heavy shelling and airplane bombing. Nankai University, outside, was heavily bombed and practically razed to the ground. Fires in the city spread unchecked.

At eleven o'clock Suyun received word that Liling, on her third trip to the Chinese city, had been arrested by a sentry and taken to Japanese headquarters. Suyun was struck with terror. The Japanese chief had looked strangely at her the previous day, having apparently received some information from his other service men about her duplicity.

She determined to escape into the adjoining French Concession, and went out in disguise through a back door of her house, carrying only a small bag. She called a rickshaw. Before she could get into the rickshaw, a policeman stepped up and asked her, "Where are you going?"

Suyun gave him the secret signal, showing that she was in Japanese service.

"So you are Miss New," said the policeman. "You are just the one I am looking for. Come with me to the head office."

Suyun was handcuffed and marched off.

"Are you not a Chinese?" said Suyun to the man.

"Yes; but I can't guarantee you your life."

"Let me off, please. We are all Chinese."

"So you are afraid to die for China?" said the policeman. The Chinese police in the Japanese Concession were noted for their height, for their haughtiness toward their own countrymen, and for their corruption, being capable even of extorting a few coppers from waiting rickshaw men.

"Here, take the bag and let me off," said Suyun to the policeman. "There are thirty thousand dollars in banknotes in it."

The policeman took over the bag, and was hesitating and whispering in scared tones to Suyun, looking about them, when a Japanese sentry, just ten yards away, saw them talking together. He came up to question them, and then went on with them. The chance was gone. Suyun began to talk to the Chinese again. The Japanese soldier, not understanding Chinese, slapped her on the face by way of shutting her up. Seeing the little suitcase in the policeman's hand, he asked that it be handed over with the key, and the three walked on in silence with Suyun in the center.

She was smarting under the physical humiliation of the slap. "So this is my reward for serving these Japs," she thought. Her anger rose, and suddenly she lost all fear. She had had a strange feeling when she heard the policeman say, "You are afraid to die for China." She had a confused sense that she was doing a great thing; that on her one side walked a Chinese and on the other a Japanese; and that the Chinese on her right represented China, and she was going to die for China. She knew that her end had come.

At the headquarters, she was asked a few questions and she was defiant. The officer telephoned to the Special Service Department.

"Shoot me!" she interrupted. "I am ready to die. I hate and loathe you all."

"You will be shot right enough," said the officer. "Take her out."

Suyun was shot in the yard.

∴

Taiyun and Chen San and Kuochang wondered when they ceased to receive messages from either Liling or Suyun. Only days later they were told that a Japanese newspaper had published the news of the shooting of the "White-Flour Queen" as a Chinese spy. The Chinese readers in Tientsin were greatly mystified. But there was no time for speculation.

The Chinese Peace Preservation Corps, acting in conjunction with some units of the 29th Army, had broken through the Japanese defenses, and fighting took place in the streets of the Japanese Concession. In the Chinese city, shells exploded and bombs dropped, and the streets were machine-gunned from the air. It seemed for a time that Japan was losing at Tientsin, caught unprepared by the attack near home, after its troops had been sent inland. The Chinese corps, numbering only a thousand, captured the East Station and the Central Station, blocking all Japanese reinforcements to the Peking front. After this, they went on to capture the Japanese camp at Haikuangsze. Finally, they skirted the east bank and were ready to destroy the Japanese airdrome; some of the Japanese had even retreated to Tangku. Late at night, however, Chinese railway employees brought them the news that the 29th Army had begun to evacuate Peking.

"You had better give up," said one of the railway men. "Don't make unnecessary sacrifices. The 29th Army has backed out, and you have no reinforcements coming."

Stunned by the news, some of the corps continued to hold firm, but most of them scattered to fight a retreat. The Japanese re-entered the captured areas and took over the Chinese city, together with the former Austrian and Russian Concessions.

Furious with their disgrace, the Japanese took terrible vengeance upon the Chinese city. Men, women, and children filled the streets in utter confusion, fleeing in all directions, blocked by fires set to many houses by kerosene, stabbed, trampled, machine-gunned from the air. There was in some places sporadic fighting between the enemy and the remnants of the Peace Preservation Corps, many of whom fought until their ammunition was gone and then hurled themselves forward to grapple with Japanese soldiers bare-handed.

In the melee Kuochang was hit by a stray bullet. Chen San tried to assist him, but within fifty yards he dropped dead, and Chen San had to abandon him. His last words were to ask his Aunt Taiyun to comfort his mother and kill his father.

Taiyun and Chen San had now to make their escape across the country. The railway was out of the question, and they must go on foot back to Peking. On the way they met many soldiers on their way to rejoin the main body of troops moving down to Paoting. It was only on August 3 that they heard of the mutiny at Tungchow and the massacre of the three hundred Japanese in that capital of the East Hopei Regime.

Their problem was how to get into Peking again to rejoin their families. Peking, they knew, was already in the hands of a pro-Japanese commission, and all who sought to enter were searched at the gates.

As they walked on, dusty, hungry, and weary, Taiyun heard Chen San curse the 29th Army and all the three generations of its officers, as she had never heard a man curse before.

"But what next?" she asked. "What are you going to do?"

"Do? Carry on!" said Chen San. "If nothing can be done in Peking, perhaps I will join the army at Nankow, or the guerrillas. That will be the best branch of the Chinese Army."

"I will go with you," said Taiyun. "Loman is already in the northwest now. Huan-erh will come too, I am sure. But I have a mind to go and shoot my brother as Kuochang said. That ought to be our first work. He is staying at the German hotel. I'm sure he and his Anfu friends are all flocking back from Manchuria to set up a puppet government."

When they came almost within sight of the city, it was already dark, and they stopped at a village. They knew they could not enter in their present garb. They begged entrance to several homes, but the doors were shut against them.

"What now? Must we pass a night in the open, and get arrested in the morning?" said Chen San with a smile.

Finally an old woman admitted them, after they told her that they were refugees from Tientsin. Chen San and Taiyun had to pose as man and wife.

"You are a good-hearted person," said Taiyun to the old woman. "Will you allow us to pass the night here? We shall leave early in the morning."

The old woman went to the kitchen and warmed up some bean soup.

"You are not soldiers, are you?" asked the old woman. "Oh, a pitiful sight it was! After the soldiers mutinied at Tungchow and killed off all the east-ocean pygmies, they arrested Yin Jukeng and escorted him to Peking to hand over to General Sung. Who would think that the 29th Army had retreated in the meantime? These, our soldiers, were not even admitted into the city. The traitor Yin was handed over to the patrols at the city wall by a mistake. Can you imagine that?"

"Where are those Tungchow soldiers now?" Chen San asked.

"They had to go around and I hear they joined other troops on the other side of the city across the Yungting River," the old woman said. "I am already in advanced age. Only my teeth are still good. If I were younger by ten years, I would go into the mountains and lead a band of guerrillas of my own."

"If all Chinese people were like you, Japan could not conquer China in ten thousand years," said Taiyun, complimenting her.

Now that they knew they were safe, Chen San confessed that he had fought with the soldiers in Tientsin and took out his concealed revolver.

"Was your wife fighting by your side, too? Think of these modern *kuniang!*"

Taiyun looked at Chen San, slightly embarrassed, and replied, "I was working with the anti-traitor group. That revolver is going to shoot a few traitors in Peking before we go out again. Do you think we can get in safely?"

"Not with that revolver," replied the peasant woman. "You will be caught and shot. All the city gates are closed except Hsichihman, and you have to go all the way round to the west-city suburb. I think your wife will not get through easily with her hair and dress."

Then an idea struck them. Chen San would disguise himself as a farmer carrying fresh vegetables into the city in the early morning and Taiyun would go with him to sell the vegetables.

"Look here, Old Aunt," said Chen San. "You must help us. I will give you two dollars, and the revolver too. And I don't think I can go in with these boots. In exchange, you must lend me and my wife a suit of peasant clothes and two basketfuls of green vegetables."

"You will have to pick the vegetables yourself," said the peasant woman promptly. "I will take the money and lend you some clothes. But don't think I want your boots or your revolver. You should have seen, outside the gates, how rifles and revolvers and army clothing lay all along the city wall, for anybody to take. The new police chief sent big trucks to pick them up, and he gave them to the Japanese."

Chen San went out with Taiyun to cut green vegetables, while the old woman looked on through the darkness.

Then the old woman showed them into a dark room, where a small earthen *kang* was to serve as their bed.

"You must sleep here," said Chen San when the woman had gone away. "I will sleep outside on the bench."

"That won't do. She will suspect us," said Taiyun. "Let's go to sleep with our clothing and boots on."

So Chen San and Taiyun lay down to sleep that night together on that little *kang*.

Before dawn the two got up. Chen San could not bear to part company with his revolver and decided to hide it under his vegetables. He discarded his military boots, however, and unable to find a pair of shoes, went barefooted. Taiyun tied up her short hair under an old black cotton cloth and dressed as a peasant woman. They said good-by to the woman when the sky was just beginning to show a light gray and went off on their way, Chen San carrying the vegetables in two baskets hung on a pole across his shoulders.

They were there at the West Gate before it was open. Afraid of attracting attention, they waited at a distance until other farmers carrying vegetables began to arrive. Seeing some women selling live chickens, Taiyun bought two from one of them, and carried the chickens by their legs upside down, as if for sale. Mixing in with seven or eight of these villagers, Chen San took his basketfuls of vegetables in through the gate, while Taiyun followed with the two chickens. At the gate, they were stopped by the new police that had been stationed there by the pro-Japanese commissioner, Pan.

Chen San halted and dropped his baskets on the ground.

The policeman began to search the baskets. Chen San's heart beat

757

fast as the policeman's hands felt for the vegetables at the bottom. Luckily the concealed revolver was in the other basket.

Taiyun, standing by Chen San's side, was desperate, thinking that the next moment the revolver would be in the policeman's hand. She let go one hand and her chicken dropped to the ground and scampered off with a great cackling.

"Oh, my chicken has flown away!" she shouted, and ran after it. Other farmers tried to help her catch the chicken, and in the confusion, Taiyun let the other chicken go, so that there was great laughter and noise among the villagers and the police, as was usual with the Peking populace. One of the policemen even ran about to help capture the chickens.

"Oh, my buddha!" exclaimed Taiyun, affecting the local villager's accent. "If these chickens run away, I shall have to go without rice for three days. Thank you, good sir, thank you!"

The diversion put everybody in good humor, including the police, who passed them all without further search. Chen San returned to his home at the Garden with Taiyun, and they went in and washed and changed their clothes and told the others about the adventure of the morning and the good old village woman the night before. Huan-erh was happy beyond measure to see her husband home safe, for they had heard of the massacre and chaos in Tientsin and had had no news from him for five or six days.

By this time, only Japanese and pro-Japanese papers were allowed to be sold in Peking. Afei and the others had read in these papers of the death of Suyun as a Chinese spy. But they could not understand it until Chen San and Taiyun told them the story of her final redemption.

. . .

Chen San went with Taiyun to her home to take to Yachin the sad news of Kuochang's death. Taiyun gave her her son's last message, but concealed from her the second part about killing his father. The mother had expected some ill news, knowing that men and women had died by the tens of thousands in these days following the fall of Tientsin, and she took it bravely.

After she had composed herself, Taiyun told her and the nephews of their adventures on the way, and of Suyun's death.

"How are things in the city?" asked Taiyun.

758

"You had better be careful," they said. "Peking is now in the hands of traitors. Houses were searched, and Kuomintang flags and books and Sun Yat-sen's portraits were burned."

"Who did that? The Japanese?"

"No, the Japanese did not have to do it," replied Yachin. "The traitor commissioner of police, Pan, did it for them. He disarmed the old police and sent the arms to the Japanese headquarters as his gift, and organized riffraff coolies at twenty cents apiece to welcome the Japanese soldiers into the city. Peking was betrayed."

"How?" asked Taiyun.

"You know, don't you, that there was news of great victories on the twenty-eighth," said Yachin. "All Peking was excited. Then next morning, Kuotung and his brothers got up early to read the morning news about more victories, but no newspapers came. The *amah* coming home from the market said the streets were deserted and the sandbag barricades gone. All the soldiers had disappeared—both Chinese and Japanese. General Sung had left for Paoting in the night. Kuotung went out for a look and passed the police station and saw only a few policemen sitting in the yard, with their heads down and with no uniforms. During the whole day, Peking was like a ghost city. Shops were closed. Straggling and wounded soldiers filled the whole of Hatamen Street. The street cars were still running, with only the conductors clanging their bells, and all the cars empty. The brothers haven't stirred out of the house for days."

"Has that old man turned up again?" Taiyun asked.

"Which old man?"

"That good brother of mine."

"Why should he come here again?"

Taiyun said no more; she did not tell Yachin that she and Chen San planned to kill Huaiyu. The killing was to be the last act of Chen San before leaving Peking. Most of the members of his secret group were eager to join the communists who were now beginning to operate in Shansi. Taiyun was the more anxious to go with him because ever since her imprisonment she had been separated from her husband, Loman.

Chen San and Huan-erh and Taiyun got ready to start immediately after the attack. Huan-erh left with Afei a letter for her brother and mother and came over to Taiyun's house. Taiyun said farewell to her mother, merely telling her that the party was going to the northwest

759

to fight Japan, and her mother knew that she could not stop her. Funia had no other child but Taiyun, and she found it very hard to part with her. Yachin's children called her grandmother since they came to live with her, and indeed they were like her own grandchildren and Yachin like her own daughter-in-law. It happened that Suyun had left ten thousand dollars in cash with Taiyun when she went back to Tientsin, and now Taiyun turned over this sum to her sister-in-law for the support of her mother and of the family.

The German hotel where Huaiyu was staying was in the northeastern corner of the inner city, a short distance from the Legation Quarter. Chen San went there with two other men, all armed with concealed pistols, shortly after eight, for they knew that Huaiyu went out to confer with other Anfuites at night. His car was standing in front of the hotel facing west. Chen San and his associates hid in an alley running north and south.

After a time the car began to move in their direction. Chen San stood at the entrance of the alley, avoiding the headlights. The car was still in first gear and was just beginning to go faster. Hidden at the corner, Chen San drew out his pistol and fired with quick aim. The car careened to the left and ran into a lamppost. The chauffeur had apparently dropped dead at the wheel. Chen San had heard a woman's scream and, by the reflection of the headlights against the wall, he could see a woman's figure in the back seat. He and his men fired six or seven shots into the back of the car and saw the woman's head roll over. Then, since the shots had been heard by passers-by, he told his men to flee back through the dark alley, and followed them.

They ran to Taiyun's house on Soochow Hutung, which was only a short distance and where Taiyun, Huan-erh, and the others were waiting for them.

"It is done!" said Chen San very calmly.

Taiyun's mother watched the three men come in, panting for breath, and wondered.

"What is done?" she asked.

"Nothing," replied Chen San. "All our arrangements have been made to start."

Drawing his wife to one side, Chen San said, "I believe it was Inging, but not Huaiyu. No man that we could see was in the car, except the chauffeur."

Huan-erh whispered the news to Taiyun, who could not suppress a low exclamation of triumph.

The group—four men and three women—decided to take rickshaws to the city gate and march across country to the other side of Yungting River, where many Chinese troops remained.

As their preparations were already made for immediate departure, and they would be unsafe in Peking after the attack on Inging, they decided to let Huaiyu alone. Huaiyu lived to become for a time an important member of the puppet government of Peking under Wang Kehmin, the Anfuite.

Here we must leave Chen San, Huan-erh, and Taiyun. How they got out, lost each other and met again, how they succeeded in reaching northern Shansi and later on, were joined by Asuan, and enlisted with the guerrillas fighting there, blocking the Japanese advance to the northwest, for months and years after the beginning of the war, will have to be left to the reader's imagination. They are of that group of brave, patriotic young Chinese whose spirit prospers best under the harshest physical surroundings and whose good cheer and courage are indomitable.

CHAPTER XLIV

$\mathcal{N}$o news of the murder of Inging was permitted to be published in the Peking newspapers. Most of the Chinese papers were closed down, and a puppet paper, called *Regeneration,* which had been suppressed in June, was now revived. Some copies of the Catholic paper published in the Italian Concession at Tientsin were smuggled through and brought a high price, but the news dealers were subject to arrest for selling it. The puppet paper printed only news given out by Domei, the Japanese news agency, and cables from Tokyo, and editorials about the "New Order in Asia." Peking was cut off from the rest of China, and only the more well-to-do had radio sets, which they anxiously tuned in on the news broadcast from Nanking.

No trace of the murderers could be found by the police. But Huaiyu, both frightened and enraged, had his eye on the Yao Garden.

The following day a group of policemen came to the Garden and made careful inquiries about the occupants, taking down all their names. They were the families of Mr. Feng, Afei, Chinya, and Poya. Mr. and Mrs. Feng and Paofen's parents were old people. Luckily there were no longer the names of Lifu, Huan-erh, and Chen San. After being assured these were all the occupants of the Garden the police left courteously after inspecting the house and made no disturbance.

Afei had heard of the murder, and half suspected that Chen San and Huan-erh were connected with it, but fortunately they were gone. He also suspected that the coming of the police had something to do with the murder, and that they had probably been sent by Huaiyu. He learned later that the police had been to Taiyun's home, but the mother had told them that her daughter was away at Tientsin and had not come back.

Under the circumstances, Afei decided that both he himself and the Garden were in danger: first, because of Huaiyu's return, and, second, because he had made many enemies as head of the Opium Suppression Bureau and could be considered a Chinese government official. He invited Miss Donahue, Paofen's American friend, to stay in the Garden and made a deed turning over the Garden to her, and told her to raise an American flag at the entrance. He knew that she was too honest to take advantage of this, and the deed was a mere formality to satisfy the police in case of trouble. In any event, the presence of a white foreigner acted as a restraint on Japanese looters, soldiers as well as ronin, of whom there were many.

But when the police came to make their report there were also missing from their list the names of Mannia and Asuan's family; for immediately after the Marco Polo Bridge incident, Mannia, being afraid of a Japanese sack of the city, had determined to move out into the country. She thought of the Yaos' villa near the Jade Spring Hill, but Asuan's wife insisted that her relatives' home north of Peking was safer, because it was further away. Old Mrs. Sun, Mannia's mother, had died the previous winter, and so Asuan had set out with his family, his mother Mannia, his wife and his child five years old, to his wife's native village.

The village was about three miles from a station on the railway, and they had taken the train and arrived without much difficulty three days before the fall of Peking. Asuan's wife came from a family by the name of Chu, and the village was known as Chuchiachuang, or "Chu-clan-hamlet." It was only a market town, situated in a hilly district, and the whole village belonged to the same clan. The arrival of Mannia's family was an event in the village. The simple dresses the ladies had traveled in were unbelievable luxuries to the villagers, and the village women gathered to see the city ladies from the "Prince's Garden" in the former capital.

The house they stayed in belonged to a sister of Asuan's father-in-law. The village houses built of mud, were the simplest possible, but this house had the distinction of an enclosed small court in front and a large enclosed threshing yard behind, the lower part of the walls being built of boulders from the hills.

The village aunt gave her niece her own room and moved out to live in a back room, profoundly apologizing for the simplicity of the place. As there was no extra room for Mannia, Asuan said he would sleep out in the sitting room, letting his mother sleep on the same *kang* with his wife and child.

763

The change to the country from the harassing days in Peking was delightful. The village lay peacefully by the hillside, and in the cool evenings Asuan and his modern wife and young child walked to a neighboring stream. All seemed quiet for seven or eight days. Then villagers, going near the railway, saw trainloads of Japanese soldiers going north toward the Nankow Pass on the Great Wall. Still there was no trouble in the village.

Another five days passed, and Japanese troops began to march across the country, mainly following the railway. They began to see farmers and their families fleeing with their pigs, chickens, and other animals from villages nearer the railway line, and some from the suburbs of Peking. These were but the first signs of the general uprooting of life from the North China countryside that was to leave in the most harassed districts not a man or beast and sometimes not even a tree. The refugee women whispered to the village women stories of shame. A man had been clubbed on the head for letting his wife escape the clutches of the Japanese soldiers. The men told of the quartering of troops in their homes, the killing of all their chickens and pigs, the smashing of doors and windows, and the taking of all furniture for fuel. Fuel was scarce in North China, and the first effect of the passing armies was the destruction of everything made of wood.

Now, curiously, the village of Chuchiachuang was spared. Being situated across a stream from the railway and abruptly rising into the hillside, it was out of the way of the marching Japanese troops. There were reports of a big battle around the Nankow Pass, but it was so far away that they could not hear the guns, and only saw the thousands of Japanese soldiers in the distance marching across the country along the railway, accompanied by tanks. At night, sometimes they could see huge bonfires in the distance, and they knew that these were made of the farmers' furniture, weaving looms, and doorposts. Yet Chuchiachuang, lying in the sight of the enemy, slept in peace.

Now new streams of refugees began to come in the opposite direction from the north. They brought tales of the burning of whole villages and the flight of hundreds of women into the mines, hidden there without food for days. And then roving bands of bandits began to appear all over the countryside.

One day, at a time when no soldiers were in sight, Asuan ventured across the stream to a deserted village that had been in the Japanese path and went through the streets of that dead village, which bore every mark of depredation. On a wall he saw a printed proclamation of the Japanese Army written in good Chinese, to the following effect:

PROCLAMATION OF THE GREAT JAPANESE ARMY No. 1

The undersigned Commander H————of the Army of Great Japan orders the following to be proclaimed to the Chinese people: Our Army, in carrying out the mission of the Great Japanese Empire, wishes only to establish peace in the Far East and increase the happiness and welfare of the Chinese people, that our desire of the mutual prosperity and close interdependence of China and Japan may be realized. Beyond this, there is no other objective. This time, stirred by the provacations and the unreasonable attitude of the Chinese Army toward our Army, I, the commander, bore these provocations once and again with great patience, in the hope of not aggravating the situation and of a future settlement. But the Chinese Army has not realized its mistakes or ceased its provocations. Such conduct on the part of the Chinese Army is not only an insult to the honor of the Great Japanese Empire, but also endangers the peace in the Far East, committing the people to ten thousand generations of irrevocable disaster. For this reason, our Army, acting in accord with Heaven's will above and the people's desire below, has decided to punish, on behalf of Heaven, such unkind, unjust, stupid, and stubborn gangsters. But all the people who are not hostile to us will be regarded as our relatives and friends. We promise not to harass the good obedient citizens, but will, on the other hand, provide for their permanent welfare. It is hoped that the inhabitants will remain calm, distinguish between the righteous and the unrighteous, and understand the sincerity of our Army. You are ordered to attend to your regular business without disturbance and to wait for the coming of the paradise. Persons who take advantage of the unsettled condition to create disturbances or help the rebels will be severely punished without pardon. H————

Commander of the Great Imperial Japanese Army
July, the 12th year of Hirohito.

Asuan read this on the wall beside a shop, with its shelves empty, the floor strewn with broken glass and overturned tables, and a half-wrenched doorpost leaning across the threshold.

Reading the proclamation enabled Asuan to understand better a story that he heard a few days later from some refugees from the north. Two surviving brothers from a village told this story:

Someone in their village had put a dot over the word "Great" in an army proclamation. Now the word "great" was shaped like an inverted capital "Y" with a horizontal stroke across its "waist." If a dot was added to its right "shoulder," on the upper righthand corner, it became the character for "dog." The heading of the proclamation therefore read as that of the "dog Japanese Army," and a few of the "great's" in the text itself received also the benefit of such transformation. A troop of forty or fifty Japanese passed, and someone called the attention of the commander to what had been done. The commander sent for the village elder, who knelt on the ground and pleaded that he did not know about it, that he would be responsible thereafter, and that he would kneel down before the proclamation for a day as an atonement. The commander insisted on his producing the culprit, but the elder still pleaded his ignorance.

"Get up!" shouted the commander, "and go and find out. I give you ten minutes."

But before the ten minutes were over, Japanese soldiers were running about the streets with cans of kerosene, setting fire to the houses. The inhabitants tried to escape, only to find that a cordon of soldiers had been posted around the village, shooting anyone who tried to escape. The whole village was burned down and its inhabitants with it. The brothers hid under a pile of debris for a day and a night, before they dared to venture out and escape to tell the story.

Now they began to see also bands of slightly wounded soldiers returning from Nankow. It was said that twenty-five thousand Japanese troops had been massed to storm the pass, and the battle was of the bloodiest. Apparently, the railway could not take care of all the transportation, having enough to do to transport ammunition, heavy artillery, and supplies.

The situation became more menacing. Straggling bands of tired and weary Japanese began to come back over all routes in the neighborhood. Some came directly through the village, and the women began to be afraid. War is war everywhere, but the Japanese attitude toward women, or the whole subject of Japanese sexual life, is a chapter still reserved for experts to study.

Asuan was worried. He insisted on fleeing further away from the routes of the Japanese soldiers. Hearing that there was a well-situated village hidden in an out-of-the-way valley, a few miles off, he left one day to see it and to arrange for sleeping quarters. He found one family willing to take them in after he had offered a good price.

Returning about dusk, he met a stream of refugees from his own village, who cried that Japanese had been there. Fathers carrying old grandfathers on their backs, husbands carrying wounded women, told a wordless tale of woe.

"Where are my family?" Asuan demanded.

"Who knows? Each one ran for his own life," they all replied.

Asuan ran straight to his house. The Japanese had gone. Only a few dogs could be seen, prowling the deserted streets.

He went into his house. In the outer room, a table was overturned. He went into the bedroom. His wife lay naked on the *kang,* stabbed in the abdomen, her life already gone. An unearthly shiver ran down his spine. He saw his child lying prostrate on the floor. He hurried to pick it up. It was a mass of cold, limp flesh. Two diagonal slashes, showing great dexterity, had been cut across the flesh between its neck and its shoulders. Asuan held the boy in his arms, and then, looking up at his wife's bleeding naked body, forgot himself and dropped the child's body. It fell limp to the floor. He had a curious feeling that he was in hell for eternal damnation. It was not a feeling that he himself had escaped, but that he was in the grip of a great demon and that he was utterly powerless. He did not weep. The whole circulation system of his body seemed to have been inverted. Saliva ran outward, and therefore all tears and perspiration ran inwards, leaving his eyes curiously dry and his skin creeping as if immersed in a cold liquid from the outside.

A groan from the back room awakened him from his trance.

He dashed into the back room, and saw his mother Mannia's body dangling from a rope near a window, partly disrobed. He shut his eyes in terror.

A new groan set his hair on end.

"Take her body down and cover her decently," said the voice as if in a great weariness.

He opened his eyes and looked in the direction of the bed. From that dark and curtained corner came the sound of someone moving.

Asuan approached the bed. His wife's old aunt was feebly clutching at the mat.

"Are you hurt?" Asuan asked.

"Take her down," said the voice again, feebly. He looked again at Mannia's horrible position. She whose body had never been seen by the eyes of man now hung there half exposed.

Averting his eyes, Asuan went forward bravely, and, first adjusting her trousers, took his mother down. Now the touch of her still-warm body made him able to cry; it seemed that he was once more in contact with a human world. He looked into the face of his mother, still calm and beautiful in death, and touched her limp, hanging arms, the arms that had fondled him and held him and raised him from childhood; and a flood of tears burst from the innermost corners of his soul, turbulent, uncontrollable.

He did not know how long he sat moaning over the body of Mannia. When his tears seemed to have been exhausted, he thought again of the old aunt, and rose and approached the bed once more.

"Light a lamp," the voice said.

Asuan looked for matches furiously. He went again into the room where the bodies of his wife and child lay, and suddenly became frightened and ran out again into the yard and took a long breath. Then he remembered he was looking for a match and went into the kitchen and took a box and went back into the dark room. Stepping into that room, his tears welled forth again—there was still magic in that dead body of Mannia.

He struck a match to light the small oil lamp. As he lighted it, the world seemed transformed. The match, the lamp, his own hand, all lost their meaning. What was a lamp? What was a flame? What was a human hand? What were those bent knuckles of his fingers? Out of his half-daze, consciousness slowly returned. Yes, he was there. His wife was dead, his child, his mother. He was alone in that room with an old aunt, many miles from Peking. The terrible realization penetrated his brain that he was alone in this world.

He felt a sudden impulse to burn the whole house and die with his family there. But the voice from the bed spoke again.

"Give me a drink of water."

This brought him back to the world. He went into the kitchen and came back with a bowl of water, and went near to his old aunt and moved the lamp nearer to the bed. He saw that her head was bruised. He held her up slightly and gave her the bowl of water to drink.

"Lie back; I will wash your wound," he said.

He went and brought a basin of water, and took a handkerchief

768

and dipped it in the water and washed away the clots of blood on her temple. The old woman shrieked, but he saw that it was merely a surface wound.

"Tell me what happened," he said.

"This disgrace for me, a woman of over fifty," she moaned. "Why didn't they kill me?"

"Nonsense, this is no disgrace," he replied.

"Please tell no one in the village."

"There is no one in the village to tell."

"Where are they?"

"They have all fled. The village is deserted. Tell me what happened." Then she gathered her strength and told him.

"The pygmies came. Who knows when and how? They broke into the house. Your wife was playing with the child in the front yard. A fierce, terrible Japanese soldier came in. Your wife ran in, dragging the child with her, and the Japanese chased after her. She bolted the door, but the soldier forced it open. Mannia and I ran into this back room. We heard screams. Then we heard a clanging of metal and the child's screams suddenly stopped. Then after a while came a scream from your wife. I crept under the bed, but your mother hanged herself. The Jap came in and I was dragged out from under the bed. He was angry and struck me and put me on the bed. After that I swooned off. When I came to, there was not a noise in the house. I saw your mother's body there. You see, even after a woman is dead, he must still make his fun with her. Are your wife and the child dead?"

Asuan nodded in silence. He did not dare enter the room where his wife was. He sat looking at his mother's body lying on the floor. Strange to say, every time he looked at her he received new strength. She did not even look pitiful, but only dead and as beautiful to him as ever. Finally he summoned up all his courage and went into the front room and laid his child by the mother's side and covered their bodies.

"Do you wish to eat?" said the aunt.

"No, I cannot eat," he said.

"Go to the cabinet and take out the piece of ginseng in the right drawer and boil me a stew. I need some strength."

He did as he was told. The actions of cutting, cooking, and preparing the ginseng stew calmed and steadied him but not without a touch of the strangeness of his situation; that with his family lying dead, he was peacefully cooking ginseng stew. Everything seemed strange; every little normal detail seemed as it should not be. He looked at the spluttering fire and was lost in contemplation. Slowly, silently, a decision was forming in his heart.

Going back, he looked again at his mother's body. "I will avenge you, Mother," he said almost aloud to her. "I will kill and kill and kill."

He now lost all fear of death and he lost all concern for himself. He felt a sudden relief in contrast to the oppression he had felt only this morning. He was ready to meet a Japanese and to die at any moment. He was free.

He went out to look about at the neighboring houses. No living being was in sight. Here and there he saw corpses, but he was not afraid. He went farther and heard a noise of scampering feet. Somebody was still alive there. He felt like a healthily alive human being, walking in a ghost land. He went into the dark house and coughed aloud.

There was absolute silence. He was frightened a little at himself.

"I am a Chinese," he called. "Is anyone here?"

He repeated his question into the dark void. "Don't be afraid. The pygmy devils are gone."

There was a noise of moving feet and rustling cloth, and he could barely see the shapes of two figures moving forward.

"Who are you?" a woman's voice asked.

"I am Mr. Tseng, from Peking. The three lives in my family are all dead."

One woman went to light a lamp.

"How did you survive?" he asked.

"We two, mother-in-law and daughter-in-law, hid under a corner behind the kitchen stove."

"You had better go tomorrow to join your relatives in the mountains. The Japanese may come again," he told them, and went back and lay on the floor and slept by his mother's side that night.

The next day, he assisted his aunt and the two women to the mountains, and went back to his dead. He was all alone, in the village. He took a hoe and shovel and buried the bodies in the back court, and he did not finish until it was night.

Then he felt hungry. He entered the kitchen and cooked himself a rough meal. He went out again and sat above the graves of his mother and wife and child.

He could not bear to leave them the next day and he remained two more days—the only living soul in that village of ghosts.

On the morning of the third day, he wept ceremoniously over the graves once more and then started away.

He wore on his two small fingers a ring from his mother and one from his wife, and he took in his pocketbook three tufts of hair from his mother, his wife, and his child.

He made his way to the camp of the guerrillas and joined them, and after this he was always at the forefront of battle and yet was never wounded. His life seemed to be under a charm; his comrades wondered why he fought with such a demonlike heartiness and courage. He did not tell them that the shades of his mother and his wife and child were with him to bid him courage. They did not understand that he was alone and yet not alone.

. · .

In Peking it was impossible to get news of Mannia's family. Since the visit of the police and the moving in of Miss Donahue, things were outwardly quiet in the Garden. Afei and Paofen, however, decided that they had to leave Peking, as it was clear he could be arrested as a government official at any time Huaiyu and the pro-Japanese officials chose. Chinya and Dimfragrance also decided that they would be safer out of Huaiyu's reach.

But apart from such personal reasons, Peking was now for all practical purposes a lost city, cut apart from China, enveloped in an atmosphere of chaos, lawlessness, and bloodshed. The Japanese had not openly taken over the city government, but the puppets were ready to set up a Local Preservation Commission, assisting the Japanese in maintaining local order and doing everything to co-operate with them. Asiatic Cultural Unions sprang up to encourage the study of Japanese. School textbooks were to be changed. Narcotic dens, gradually decreased in the past year, thrived once more. A flood of Japanese businessmen began to come into the city. Most of the Japanese women were dressed either in Western clothes or in Chinese long gowns. The reason given for the latter was that the long gowns were known as "Manchu gowns" and that they were patriotically wearing these to "cement the friendship with Manchukuo." It was noticeable, however, that this change of fashion followed, and did not precede, the Tungchow mutiny, in which three hundred Japanese had been wiped out.

Peking had for the Chinese all the aspects of a "perished city." The old Anfu politician, Wang Kehmin, of the Nishihara Loans fame, was already actively planning with his colleagues to set up a puppet government.

Afei and Chinya discussed preparations for going to Shanghai with their families. Poya, now completely cured of his drug habit, decided that he would remain with his wife. Old Mr. and Mrs. Feng and Paofen's parents said that there was no need for them to leave, and they would remain to look after the Garden with Miss Donahue.

By this time, the war had broken out in Shanghai also, but foreign vessels still plied regularly between Tientsin and Shanghai. Once the families got on board and safely out of Tientsin, they would be out of any personal danger. They knew that, leaving Peking on the train, they would be subject to search, but first-class passengers would be less molested. The class of people most likely to be closely examined and possibly arrested were students and young men between twenty and forty who resembled soldiers in any way. Businessmen as a class were as a rule easily let off. Chinya was near fifty and should be safe. Afei was just under forty, but he took care to dress as a businessman, wear old-fashioned spectacles, carry a water pipe, and look as old as possible, with the help of a little unshaven beard. They were to take business documents from the medicine and curio shops.

Dimfragrance easily passed as a businessman's wife. Paofen looked very modern and much younger; but, traveling in a first-class carriage with a wealthy shop owner, she should be able to pass with her husband and children. Besides, Miss Donahue was willing to take the trip with them and see them safely aboard at Tientsin, knowing that the presence of an American woman had a tendency to remind the Japanese to behave like "civilized" beings.

So in the middle of August they said good-by to the grand old city of Peking. As they drove through the Hatamen Street and saw its familiar shops, Afei and Paofen held each other's hands with restrained emotion. Passing the East-One Pailou, Afei gave the driver instructions to turn west on the Tienanmen Street so that they might get a glimpse once more of the golden imperial roofs.

"Thank God the imperial architecture is still safe. It is always Peking to me," said Miss Donahue in English.

They arrived at the station early in the morning. The train was supposed to leave at eight-thirty. A huge crowd of people, old and young, was milling in front of the station, with a mixture of rickshaws, automobiles, and carriages piled high with luggage.

Entering the station, the passengers had to be searched, irrespective of age and sex, and those waiting outside were held up for a long time. After getting through this examination, they were once more required to open their trunks and bags on the platform. Afei's party got through without great difficulty into reserved rooms in the first-class car. But it was already ten o'clock and the train did not seem ready to move.

Impatient with waiting, Afei got down to walk about on the platform, telling Dimfragrance and Paofen to keep the children strictly inside the car. He saw other passengers still being searched and their baggage examined.

To the passengers whose turn had come, a Chinese guard said aloud, "Open your trunks!" and then whispered in a low voice, "Any objectionable books or articles should be removed." Groups of two or three Japanese gendarmes, with their bayonets displayed, merely looked on.

Walking further on to the third-class coach, Afei saw the passengers standing in line and being individually searched before they were admitted into the car. They stood ready with their jackets unbuttoned. A girl student did not unbutton her jacket, since she had no pockets.

A Japanese gendarme stepped up and, pointing to the girl, said something to a Chinese guard.

"Better yield a little at such times," said a fellow-traveler, an old merchant of fifty.

The girl began to unbutton her jacket with a blush. At the bottom of the inside flap were some characters.

The Japanese gendarme pointed to the characters and asked what they were.

"It is the laundry number at school," explained the student.

Luckily the Chinese interpreter, who was apparently from Mukden, spoke kindly in her behalf, and the Japanese walked away.

It was half-past eleven before the train started. It stopped, however, at every station, even before leaving the Peking city wall; and twice Japanese soldiers accompanied by Chinese guards boarded it again and re-examined the luggage. The first-class cars, however, were gone over only cursorily.

Leaving the city they saw a fleet of ten or twelve Japanese airplanes overhead flying northwest. The great battle was going on near Nankow and elsewhere, and the Japanese were busy transporting military supplies. Consequently, the train was held up at every station until a westbound train passed, loaded with artillery parts, ammunition, and sometimes with carloads of horses leaving a smell of offal. There had been severe fighting along the railway, and the little towns presented sad sights of destruction. Here and there groups of Japanese soldiers squatted on the ground in none too orderly fashion. All the way there were Chinese villages with red sun flags flying on housetops. Trees had been felled at the roadside, evidently for Japanese defenses, but these seemed also to provide excellent opportunities for Chinese ambush, unless they were well guarded by the enemy.

They did not reach Tientsin till half-past seven, a journey of eight hours, whereas in times of peace it took only about two and one half hours.

Passage through the Tientsin Station was most difficult.

"Pass the bridge and keep to the middle of the way, and don't hurry!" the guard cautioned them.

Accompanied by the American woman, they got out of the station without trouble. Just as they were saying to themselves how lucky they were to get through, some guards came up and said, "File to the left." They saw people standing in twos and threes, moving slowly. Four or five Japanese soldiers stood at the left and picked out one passenger after another for more careful questioning. Businessmen, students, men and women, rich and poor, seemed to be chosen without distinction. These had to fall out and stand separately.

When it came their turn, the Japanese soldier suddenly seized Chinya's seventeen-year-old boy and pulled him out of the line. Miss Donahue interfered and spoke to the Japanese, but he merely looked at her and motioned the boy to stand aside. Dimfragrance was trembling. His father threw to the boy a little suitcase containing business documents. The Japanese saw this but did not interfere.

While the party waited anxiously for the return of the boy, he was herded with the others into a near-by office building. His father had cautioned him not to hurry or show fear, and to answer questions directly. He knew that some were immediately released and some were kept for one, two, or three days, while those who showed any evidence of having been soldiers were shot. Anyone leaving the examination and going out in a hurry would be sent back and questioned again.

Chinya's boy was a cautious person. Carrying the suitcase, he waited for his turn patiently, with no sign of worry. When it came his turn, he was taken into a small room where three Japanese sat at three desks with over-serious expressions. A succession of questions was fired at him.

"Are you anti-Japanese?"

"Are you a Kuomintang man?"

"Are you a Blue-Shirt?"

"Are you a Communist?"

"Are you of the Anglo-American clique?"

"Have you read the Sanmin Doctrine?"

"Do you believe in Sun Yat-sen?"

"Do you believe in Chiang Kai-shek?"

"What is your attitude toward Manchukuo?"

"Do you believe in the co-operation of Japan, China, and Manchukuo?"

"Is it fair for China to play one foreign nation against another?"

"When were you born? How many sisters have you? Their ages? Names? Schools attended?"

One by one the rigamarole questions were asked in humorless fashion, and the answers scribbled down most carefully and dutifully. The Japanese officers took themselves very seriously and did not permit themselves a smile. As if anyone would have answered the first questions in the affirmative under the circumstances!

"What is that thing you are carrying?"

The boy opened it for inspection. After conning the documents studiously for what must have been half an hour, the officer motioned to him to go out by a certain door.

He knew he was released. He went down the stairs slowly and came out into the open, to find his family anxiously waiting at the entrance and very happy to see him back alive. Dimfragrance held him as if he had come back from the dead.

They went into the British Concession and took rooms at a foreign hotel. There was no boat available until three days later. Miss Donahue insisted on staying to see them safely on the launch which would take them to the English boat at Tangku. Paofen, however, assured her that they were now perfectly safe; she urged her to go back and thanked her profoundly for her steadfast friendship in times of trouble.

Miss Donahue went back to Peking a day before they sailed because she felt a little anxious about the people at the Garden in her absence. After a five days' voyage, calling at different ports, Afei's and Chinya's families arrived at Shanghai, to the accompaniment of a deafening bombardment on both sides of the river. A fleet of Japanese warships lay in the harbor, shelling the Chinese city, where fires blazed and columns of smoke clouded the sky.

Their ship landed them in the International Settlement, and they went to a hotel there and telegraphed to Mulan and Mochow the news of their arrival.

CHAPTER XLV

W̲HEN the war began, Mulan and her family were spending the summer at Kuling, the mountain resort on the Yangtse.

Amei, now a girl of seventeen, was a student at the missionary college at Nanking. Atung had graduated and was working with the Chinese Government Telegraphs at the Chenju wireless broadcast station near Shanghai, which could send powerful messages across the Pacific to San Francisco. He had asked for six weeks' leave and joined the family at Kuling.

Hangchow was now the center of a great motor highway system which the government had been building up feverishly, connecting almost all parts of China. Over the great river at the back of the city a giant steel bridge for both rail and motor-car traffic, a modern engineering marvel to the villagers, had just been completed. A new railway connected Hangchow and Nanking directly with Nanchang, which was the capital of Kiangsi province and only a short way from Kuling. The new railway lay across mountainous country, but the tremendous work had been finished in a year and a half. The pace of this national reconstruction program was in fact one of the important causes of the war: for Japan, because she realized that she must strike now or never; and for China, because there was born a new spirit of national self-confidence, and therefore of resistance toward Japan's violation of her sovereign rights.

Chiang Kai-shek and Madame Chiang were staying at this time at Kuling, which had become a fashionable summer resort for government officials. Mulan's house was directly above theirs. Although Chiang's house was at the front of its compound, separated from the rear wall by fifty yards of wild hillside, Mulan caught glimpses of the activities of the servants in the house. Its front entrance stood at the beginning of a road, where it was blocked by a mountain gully coming down. The road ran for a hundred yards along the gully until a cross-

777

ing was reached, from which point on it became a more open public road. At the crossing, where sentries were posted, or across the gully, one could see intense activity going on about the house. High military officers from the provinces and important Nanking officials were continually passing in and out, some on foot and some in sedan chairs. For in this house was being decided the future destiny of China, whether she was to sink irrevocably to the status of a protectorate of Japan, or to fight and build herself up into a free, united, and independent state.

On July 17, the momentous decision was made. Chiang broadcast to the country the policy of a war of resistance to the end. He warned the nation, however, of the tremendous sacrifices to be made and the impossibility of stopping midway, which would leave China worse off than if she were to patch up a settlement now.

"That man is the coolest and the most stubborn I ever saw," remarked Sunya. "He has done things that Chuko Liang (in the *Three Kingdoms*) could not do. He had the worst task any man ever undertook in this world, in uniting China. And now that he has done it, he is confronted with a still greater task, leading China to fight Japan. He is like a petrel that finds its natural element in a storm at sea—and perhaps enjoys it, too. He will carry the war to the end if anyone will. I have watched him for these last ten years. He is so gaunt and bony, but look at his mouth! His face shows the most curious combination of stubbornness and wiliness I've ever seen."

"If Chiang is the Chuko Liang, I am going to be the little ferryman in the *Three Kingdoms*," said Atung.

"What?" exclaimed Mulan. Her countenance suddenly fell.

"Mother, what's the matter? Don't you hate Japan?"

Mulan looked silently at Sunya, and he also kept silent.

"Don't you approve? China needs every man," Atung repeated.

But Mulan walked away, her silence unbroken. Nor did she speak again for an hour. She lost her composure and suddenly felt as all mothers feel at the coming of war. For war had come to her very door. Why had she not thought of this? China was claiming from her, her only son.

She discussed it with her husband and an hour later she and Sunya called their son and talked with him.

"Have you decided to go to war?" she asked.

778

"What would be the use of all my education, if I didn't?" he replied. "Why, Mother, I cannot understand you!"

"No, you can't. . . . I am only asking if you have decided."

"I have, Mother," said Atung.

A great struggle was going on in Mulan, a struggle which brought tears welling up to her eyes. "Oh, Atung, you are my only son. . . ." she said, and broke down crying.

Now Sunya spoke. "My son, you are young and you have never been a parent . . ."

"I would rather die myself than see you die. I shan't be able to stand it," Mulan exclaimed.

"Atung, listen," said the father again. "Your mother and I have talked this over. If China calls for you, then you must go. But know that the sacrifice is greater on our part than on yours. A young patriot dies gloriously and cheerfully on the battlefield—he has his friends—but it is his old parents who live to suffer at home. We are not obstructing you. But you ought to consider a little the family."

"What's the use of a family, if one's country perishes?" replied Atung.

"I know all that," the father said patiently. "If I were young like you, I probably would want to go to war myself. But you are the only son, and we have already given a daughter, your elder sister, to the country. Your mother and I are old and we cannot expect another son. From the point of view of an individual and of the state, you ought to go. From the point of view of the Tseng family, your life cannot be easily sacrificed without very extraordinary reasons. Your case is quite special. Suppose the Tseng family becomes extinct. The Japanese want to exterminate us, but the family is our first line of defense. Think of your grandfather and grandmother. How many grandsons have been born to the Tseng family after all these years? Three generations have worked and lived to produce only you and Chinya's two sons. Asuan does not really come of Tseng blood, and we do not know where he is. The Tseng blood must go on forever. You may think this far-fetched, and perhaps you won't understand. But that is how China has survived all these four thousand years. Even in countries with a conscription system, they do not call in the only son of a family until it becomes necessary. . . ."

"Father and Mother," said Atung, his hands nervously clutching the arms of his chair, "I know this is hard. . . . But I have to go."

779

Mulan looked up at him with her tearful face, and said, "Well, go! It is my fate to suffer."

"Tell me, what are you going to do?" said Sunya. "Are you going to enlist?"

"I will enlist and do anything they ask me to do. I must do something."

"Why should you not remain working at the wireless station?" said the father. "It is serving the country just the same, even though it is not going to the front."

Mulan clutched at the idea. "You said you wanted to be the ferryman," she said. "The wireless across the Pacific is just like a ferry. Why don't you do that?"

"Well, I can do that," said Atung slowly. "If it is important for the country."

This seemed like a compromise between parents and son. But as a matter of fact, the wireless station was near Kiangwan, and in the very heart of the battle.

. ·.

Amei was not as brilliant as her elder sister had been. She was less vivacious, but there was an instinct of courtesy and refinement in her which she had unconsciously absorbed from her mother. She also admired Mannia and resembled her in demureness and timidity. Among the modern girl students, she was at once classed with those having a fine family breeding.

Now at this time several missionary women who were teachers at Ginling College, were also passing the summer in Kuling. Amei was very popular with her teachers, and there was one Miss Cunningham who especially took great interest in her. These teachers had been at Mulan's house at Kuling, and Mulan's family had been invited to their homes. When the war broke out in Shanghai on August 13, it was a question whether the colleges were to reopen in the fall. Amei did not wish to miss a term if the college did reopen. Since Atung's leave was about to expire, Mulan was talking of going back to Hangchow to spend a few more days with him before he returned to his office. Miss Cunningham suggested that Amei stay with her and go back to Nanking with her. If college did not open, Amei could conveniently return to Hangchow by the railway. Miss Cunningham was a kind and sweet New England woman, and Mulan rather liked her and agreed to let Amei stay with her.

The day before they were to return to Hangchow, Mulan said: "Atung and Amei, you brother and sister are going to part for some time. I have no idea how long this war is going to last. But I shall be near you, and, Amei, when there is trouble, telegraph me immediately and come home. Never mind about the studies. If the war is over soon, next year I will get a daughter-in-law for Atung. You see how peaceful and quiet it is out here in the country. We can buy several hundred *mow* of farms, and I will see Atung and my daughter-in-law settle down to a farm and bring up grandchildren for me."

She was half joking, but her children understood.

"The war will be over in a short time. We are already attacking Hongkew and driving the Japs down the river," said Atung.

The next day Sunya and Mulan returned with their son, taking a large comfortable riverboat down to Hangchow from a town near Huichow. The voyage was most beautiful, especially through the section known as Chililung. On one side of the bank were two big rocks, called the "Fishing Terrace of Yen Tseling," a famous recluse of two thousand years ago who refused offers of office although he was a school friend of an emperor. The rocks stand now at least sixty feet above the water, and as their boat anchored near the place for the night, Mulan greatly wondered how old Yen could have fished from a terrace so high above the water. They all speculated whether the land had risen or the sea fallen since two thousand years ago, and they were greatly moved by these thoughts. The nights on the riverboat, with the moon above the mountains, and the breeze coming from the river, were indescribably beautiful, and Sunya and Mulan had many of the "little drinks" they loved.

After staying at home with his parents for two days, Atung went back to his office in Shanghai. Soon his parents received a letter saying that the wireless station with its high aerial towers had been among the first buildings to be bombed and demolished by the Japanese, together with the library, museum, gymnasium, and stadium of the new Civic Center of Kiangwan. They had saved what equipment they could and would try to operate their wireless from the International Settlement.

Heavy Chinese reinforcements were sent to the Woosung area, and trench warfare began on a gigantic scale in the Yangtse delta around

Shanghai. War had become general and promised to extend over wider and wider areas. The cities along the Shanghai-Nanking Railway were subjected to frequent air raids, and traveling by train was dangerous. Hangchow itself had already been bombed several times.

Many residents in Shanghai and Hangchow were moving in different directions, Hangchow people fleeing to the Foreign Concessions in Shanghai for safety, and Shanghai people fleeing inland to get out of the spreading war zone.

About this time, Mulan received the telegram from Afei saying that they had arrived at Shanghai and were staying with Chinya's family at the Burlington Hotel. But there was no mention of Mannia and Asuan. Why had they not come? Mulan was greatly worried, and thought of going to see Afei and Paofen and Dimfragrance to get more detailed news.

The situation was so critical by the first of September that Sunya and Mulan decided that Amei must be brought back to Hangchow before it became worse. Travel by rail was still possible, though with certain risks and necessary delays; the motor road would be open in any case. Meaning to take no chances with their daughter's safety, Sunya and Mulan decided that the father should go and bring her home. Mulan said that she would go to Shanghai also, since she was very anxious to get some news of Mannia. Perhaps Mannia had even come with them. At the thought of this possibility, she became very excited.

The evening before they were to start, a letter came from Atung, saying:

> MY DEAR PARENTS: I have enlisted. What would be the good of a family if there were no country? If every son dear to his parents refuses to go to war, how can China fight Japan? Please do not worry. I shall not come back till we have driven the dwarfs back into the sea.
>
> Your son,
> ATUNG.

Mulan was stunned. Her son had enlisted, but when and in what division? Why did he not tell them? She was all the more anxious to go to Shanghai herself, for Atung would be fighting somewhere there. Yet it was just as important to get their daughter out of Nanking before communications became worse. It was a wise action, for had Amei remained at the college at Nanking, which in December was turned into a camp for refugee women, she might have been one of the victims of those atrocities that have staggered the imagination of civilized man, and which must lower the respect of the world for the Japanese people and Japanese army for generations to come.

They went to Shanghai and found Paofen, Dimfragrance, and their families in a comfortable old family hotel, once foreign but now under Chinese management. To her great disappointment, Mulan found that Mannia was not with them, nor did they know what had happened to her sworn-sister or to her family. Mulan became worried.

Mulan stayed with them while Sunya went to Nanking to bring his daughter down. From Shanghai to Nanking was only seven and a half hours by rail, but because of the transportation of troops there would be delays. Mochow had come to Shanghai to see them and had gone home, greatly worried because Soochow would be on the next line of battle in case the Chinese armies withdrew. To move into Shanghai might be safer, but Lifu was a government official, and it would be showing bad spirit for him to move his home; besides, it would be more and more difficult for him to get home. Mulan told her husband to stop in Soochow and see her sister and Lifu and try to persuade them to come to Shanghai once more.

While Sunya was gone, Mulan had time to learn some news about her relatives. The death of Suyun greatly touched her. She heard about the adventures of Taiyun and Chen San and how they had joined the guerrillas in the northwest. They could tell her nothing of Mannia and Asuan's family and feared they might be in trouble, for many refugees had told them horrifying tales of the devastation of the northern countryside and the abuse of women.

Belonging to the upper classes, Mulan's relatives were the least hard-hit by the war so far. But those days in Shanghai were far from peaceful. Bombing planes daily flew over their heads. Bullets from anti-aircraft guns frequently landed on the houses and the streets. Explosions were heard day and night. People gathered on the water-front to watch the artillery duels between Japanese gunboats and the Chinese troops on Pootung, and on housetops to watch the blazing sky over Chapei and Kiangwan. Worst of all, refugee men, women, and children poured over from the Chapei districts, and wandered pitifully in the streets. Yet it amazed these people from Peking to see wealthy men and women still enjoying themselves at theaters and dance halls. It was like being in a different country altogether. The people of Peking were easygoing, resigned, passive, but now at least their faces were sullen, their heads bent, and inside them there was smoldering resentment. By contrast, the rich treaty-port Chinese seemed not even to know that a war was going on, for all that one could see from their behavior. Many were energetic in refugee camp work, in visiting hospitals for the wounded, and bringing relief and comfort to the soldiers, who were ill-provided. But the city as a whole presented the appearance of two clear-cut classes, one enjoying life as usual, happy in the knowledge of foreign protection, and the other the common people, soldiers fighting for their country and the poor refugees bearing the brunt of suffering.

Mulan now took more than a personal interest in the war; she could not forget that her son was out there among the roaring guns. She received a second letter from him, forwarded from home, saying that he was working in the wireless unit at the Yanghong front, and hoped that he might be able to see his parents during a leave, or perhaps she could come and visit him in the field.

On the third day Sunya returned safely with his daughter. Lifu and Mochow also came with their whole family.

Lifu's eldest son, Hsiaofu, was also demanding permission from his parents to go to the war. When Sunya told them that Atung, his only son, had enlisted, it made Hsiaofu's case a foregone conclusion, for Lifu had three sons and could do no less than give his consent. Lifu and Mochow decided to come down themselves with their son and the younger brothers and see if it was possible for the cousins to work in the same regiment, which might help to assuage a little their mothers' anxieties. Hsiaofu, who had just graduated from the Central University at Nanking, was a very fast writer. He was a little short-sighted and wore spectacles, but would be useful in staff work for writing reports and messages.

The fact that Hsiaofu was going to the front immediately made the meeting of the relatives less cheerful than it otherwise would have been. Without anyone saying so, the atmosphere was tense when the sisters were present. Dimfragrance's boy said that he would like to go, too, but his uncle Sunya said, "Leave a seed for the Tseng family. Besides, he is too young."

The problem now was how to send Hsiaofu to the regiment where his cousin was. Lifu took a whole day to make the arrangement.

He came back to the hotel in the evening and told his relatives,

"It's our luck—I found that the colonel of the regiment was a student of mine, years ago in Peking. His wife is living in the French Concession, and I went to see her and she helped me to reach her husband by telephone."

"Did he promise to take special care of our son?" asked Mochow.

"He did. He said he would as far as possible keep the cousins together."

"Did he know of Atung's enlistment in his regiment?" asked Mulan.

"He said he would find out at once."

Now Mochow broke into tears, seeing that her son's enlistment was definite.

"I will take him to the front myself," said Lifu.

"To the front yourself?" asked Sunya.

"Yes. You had better come along, if you want to see Atung. We have to go tomorrow night."

"Why at night?" asked Sunya.

"Because it is the only safe time to go. The colonel will send a car for us. Yanghong is rather far out and ordinary cars are not permitted at the front. An aide will come with the car and direct us."

Mulan sat dazed.

"Lifu," she said suddenly, "can women go, too?"

"I suppose the colonel would let you, but you'll hardly be welcome."

"I have heard of women of the relief association taking things to the front."

"That is different. And they do it at their own risk."

"You'd better not go. There is no use risking your life," Sunya said.

"If my son is not afraid to live there for weeks, why should I be afraid to go for one night? How long will it take?"

"Perhaps a whole night, there and back," Lifu replied. "Of course all lights must be dimmed and the car will go very slowly."

"Is it dangerous?" asked Mulan again.

"You stay here with your sister," said Lifu. "Think of the other lives in your hands."

Then Mulan said no more. A feeling of awe reigned in the family, and all the next day Mochow remained in the room with her son, silently weeping. Mulan asked Sunya to order four wooden cases of oranges to take along for the soldiers.

They ate supper silently. Each one had read the exciting news of the morning, but no one dared mention it. The fighting at the front had been almost the bloodiest since the war began. The Japanese claimed the capture of Paoshan, but Chinese reports said that a single battalion in that seacoast city near Woosung was still holding out, although completely cut off. Two days later a lone survivor came back to report that the entire battalion fought to the last man until all their ammunition was gone.

At ten o'clock a young man in soiled military uniform, but looking very smart with his steel helmet, came into the hotel and announced that the car was ready to take them to the colonel's headquarters. Now the inevitable scene followed. Between their tears, Mulan and Mochow showered Hsiaofu with those mother's words which are so simple, yet so hard for sons to forget. Farewells were repeated over and over, because they could never say enough.

At last Lifu asked his son to get into the car, and they got in after him. Mochow peered into the car, and Hsiaofu stretched out his hand once again to hold his mother's hand until the car jerked them apart.

The aide was sitting in front with the driver. As soon as they passed out of the Concession into the straggling suburbs, the driver shut off his lights. There was no moon, but this was well, for then they were safe from night bombing.

"How can you see like that?" asked Sunya.

"We know the whole way. Our eyes get used to it. We like it. The night is beautiful at the front."

The aide, a bright, cheerful young man, began to tell them many stories.

"Are you not afraid?"

"Afraid?" he exclaimed. "We have been waiting for years for this chance to meet our friends on the other side. And can we be afraid now? Our men were too foolhardy, if anything, at first. They were impatient to rush out over the top and would not retreat under orders. There is a kind of contagion out there. We never had such a chance before. One man's heroism makes another ashamed. There was a boy of nineteen from the country. His mother had just married him to a country girl. He left his bride and came to the front. He always said, 'The Japanese guns shoot 2,000 meters, and our guns shoot 1,500. So we run forward 500 meters and make it even.' He did it, and died."

"Password!" a voice shouted from the dark.

The aide replied. A flashlight shone directly into their car and their faces and went out. All was silence and weird darkness once more.

"How are we going?"

"We will soon be in Tazang," said the aide. "After Liuhong, you will hear machine guns, and after Yanghong you will hear the big guns. Beyond that is the no man's land where they have been fighting the whole day."

After passing Tazang they saw the searchlights of the Japanese warships wheeling about the sky and playing in all directions. Besides the low gurgle of their car engine, they heard only the serene chirping of crickets in the fields.

"I hear there are some Manchukuo troops, our own Chinese, on the enemy side," said Sunya.

"Yes," replied the aide, "but not many. The other day there was close combat. When our soldiers came within forty or fifty yards of the enemy, we heard shouting from the other side in Chinese, 'All are Chinese. Don't come!' They were Manchurians. They shouted, 'You mustn't advance or we will shoot,' and our men replied, 'Hah! Would you like to taste our rifles?' And a tall fellow shouted from the other side, 'Ours are much better.' We saw him fire, but into the air. The next moment a Japanese came up from behind and stabbed him in the back. One of our soldiers pulled his trigger and ended that Jap's life immediately, to avenge our countryman. It is hard on the Manchurians. They are Chinese and they are forced by Japan to kill Chinese."

Now they began to hear the machine guns cackle, louder and louder. Once a minute they saw a sudden glare on the distant horizon, and a booming noise came about ten seconds later, like distant thunder. Streaks of light suddenly illuminated the sky, accompanied by a somewhat musical whistle and then a crash. A sharp whine went past them through the air.

"What is that?" asked Hsiaofu.

"That's just a bullet," said the aide with a laugh.

"Are you afraid?" Lifu asked his son.

"No," said Hsiaofu, but without great conviction.

"You can still go back."

"Certainly not."

"You will see a still better sight, when we reach Yanghong," said the driver.

Now the road lay zigzag with indistinguishable black masses before them, and the driver slowed down to a snail's pace.

"Password!"

The aide again gave the word. Again a flashlight from the dark shone at them.

"Proceed!"

They heard tramping feet.

"Soldiers going up to the trenches."

"In the dark like that?"

"Night is the best time."

In the still darkness they heard the muffled tramp of human feet, but no voices anywhere.

Hsiaofu had brought a flashlight. He could not resist flashing it on the dark moving shape of the column. It was fantastic. Soldiers in helmets and uniforms, rifles slung round their shoulders, moving in absolute silence in the dark—grim, determined men going forward to battle.

Before he could see more, a voice shouted, "Lights out!" And then cursed, "Your mother!"

Hsiaofu at once clicked out his light.

"You shouldn't do that," the aide remarked sternly.

"Look, there is a beautiful thing!" said the driver.

They looked in the direction of his hand, and saw high in the air two lights, one red and one yellow. The aide explained that it was a signal for the artillery.

Shells began to explode now in the nearer distance, each preceded by a hiss and landing with a crash. The earth shook and their car shook with it.

The car began to take many turns and soon they were at the headquarters. The aide led them in, and Sunya, Lifu, and Hsiaofu stood at the door.

It was a small village house. A camp bed stood by the telephone, and there was a lamp under the table by the bedside. The windows were all closed.

The colonel was telephoning.

"What? The whole regiment gone? We will send another. . . . No . . . ? Yes, commander."

Colonel Liu hung up the telephone with a bang and stood to welcome the guests.

788

"I have been expecting you, Mr. Kung," he said. "Sit down, Old Teacher."

Lifu introduced his son and Sunya. "Coming to join us?" said the colonel, giving Hsiaofu a smile. He then sent the aide to the wireless unit to get Atung.

"He has been working without stop for the last twenty-four hours. We are short of men," said Colonel Liu. "Paoshan is doomed, I am afraid. Our men have been sending wireless messages for help, but they are completely cut off. One battalion has held out there, inside the city, for three days. But no help could reach them. Our relief has been wiped out for the third time. I believe the lone battalion is going to fight to the last man." He seemed strangely moved, almost forgetting that they were guests.

In a short time Atung came in, saluting the colonel. He looked different now that he was in uniform. His coat and trousers were soiled, but there was an expression of grim happiness on his face, and a new grown-up dignity in his stride.

"How's your work? Do you like it?" asked Sunya.

"There are only two of us taking turns on the wireless," said his son. "There is no time to think of liking or not liking it. It is so important."

"May I go to the toilet?" asked Hsiaofu, suddenly.

Atung smiled and said, "We were all like that when we first came."

While Hsiaofu was shown outside, Atung saluted the colonel and asked: "May I have a cup of water?"

The colonel went himself to pour half a small cup from his thermos bottle, and gave it to Atung, who drank it slowly, to the last drop.

"Water is precious here," the colonel remarked.

"What can we do to help?" asked Lifu, greatly moved. "We have brought some cases of oranges."

"Oranges are good. Our soldiers suffer more from thirst than hunger. The villagers here have been a great help. But what I cannot stand is the condition of our wounded. Everything is inadequate. The casualties are heavy. Tell people to send us bandages, gauze, medicine, cigarettes."

Meanwhile, Sunya was talking aside with his son. Hsiaofu came back and walked to Atung's side, and Lifu went over to them.

"Look after each other, you two, in sickness and in health," Sunya was saying. "And don't fail to write to us. One can write for the other, if the other is too busy."

789

"Can I learn to serve in the wireless unit, too?" asked Hsiaofu.

Lifu turned to the colonel.

"Take him along," said the colonel to Atung. "At least he can help to watch, if one of you is too tired, or asleep."

"I'll teach him and he is quick to learn," said Atung. "It is not very difficult. George is fat and sleepy."

"Who is that?"

"My companion. A college freshman."

"It's your luck," said Lifu to his son. "Work and learn from Atung, and be to one another as brothers. . . . Love one another as your mothers love each other. . . ."

Even Lifu broke down now. He stopped and took out a handkerchief.

"I must go now," said Atung. "My fifteen minutes are up. It is a busy night. George will fall asleep if I don't go."

Now the two fathers bent to kiss the foreheads of their sons.

"Take six oranges, for the two of you—and for George," said the colonel. "They are from your mother, I understand." Atung's eyes brightened.

The telephone rang again, and the colonel instantly went to it: "Counterattack—five-thirty. Yes, commander!"

Sunya and Lifu said their last good-by to their sons, and told them to come to the hotel when they had leave, and went away immediately, each occupied by his own thoughts. The crickets—"golden bells" and "spinning maidens"—were chirping on the roadside their serene, eternal song of peace. Hearing them, Sunya suddenly remembered the cricket fights he had had with his brothers, Pingya and Chinya, and felt strangely young again. The sky was beginning to lighten when they reached Tazang. It was a night neither of them ever forgot.

They reached the hotel at about four-thirty in the morning. Mulan and Mochow had sat up together all night, waiting for their return. Now Mulan was dozing on the sofa, and Mochow was lying on the bed in all her clothing.

Lifu and Sunya tiptoed into the room. Mochow, as usual, was the first to hear their steps, and sat up. Mulan was still asleep. They whispered together softly. They heard Mulan tossing on the sofa, and suddenly she shrieked, "Atung!"

Sunya rushed to waken her. She was already in tears. She had wept in her dream. Now she looked up, dazed.

"Oh!" she panted. "You are back already. I dreamed—I saw Atung killed, rolling in the mud, and—Hsiaofu was carrying him."

As they comforted her, Sunya looked at his watch. It was ten minutes to five.

They ordered coffee and drank it while Sunya and Lifu told their wives the story of the visit. But Mulan listened in silence. Her heart was troubled.

Lifu sent a hotel boy to get all the morning newspapers and read the news to them, as Mulan listened drowsily.

" 'Counterattack at Paoshan. Chinese recovered some lost ground. Lone battalion pledged to fight to the last man. All night artillery duel between Chinese Pootung forces and the Japanese warships. Continual fighting along the banks of the Whangpoo. Fiercest day of fighting since Aug. 13. President Roosevelt warned all Americans to evacuate China, according to a cable from Washington. . . . The war front in North China stretched 200 miles from Tientsin to northeast Shansi. Japanese said to have 200,000 men now in Hopei province. . . . A total of 61 Japanese planes had been brought down by Chinese aircraft in Chekiang, Kiangsu, and Anhwei between August 14 and September 1. . . .' "

Mulan felt very ill at ease and nervous all that day, hoping for a message from Atung to tell her that her dream was untrue. She told Sunya to send another ten cases of oranges through the Chinese Women's War Relief Association, where Paofen was working.

Mochow said that she and her family must soon return home, for Lifu's old mother was alone and Soochow was unsafe. She talked with Paofen during the day. Mochow's youngest son was of the same age as Paofen's youngest daughter, both being eleven. Paofen had no son and had taken a fancy to Mochow's youngest, and she suggested a mutual adoption. But Mochow said, "There is no need to exchange. They are *kupiao* cousins. Call it a request from our side for engagement. You give your daughter to me as a daughter-in-law."

Paofen consented with a smile. This was said in the hearing of both their husbands, Afei and Lifu.

. ' .

The following day Mulan also planned to return with her husband and Amei to Hangchow. Mochow and Lifu were to take the train for Soochow from a point beyond Chenju, and the sisters and brothers-in-law said good-by. They could not know that they were not to see each other again for a very long time. Mulan also said good-by to Paofen and Dimfragrance, believing that she was to return to Shanghai to see Atung when he should be on leave.

At half-past seven in the morning of September 8, 1937, Mulan went with Sunya and Amei to the Jessfield Station to take their train. It was a misty day, and their minds were clouded, too. Mulan had heard nothing more from Atung. There was a huge crowd of people already waiting, with great piles of luggage. Some refugees were said to have come to the station the day before and slept outdoors, waiting for a chance to get on. Children were lying on trunks and boxes, and some lay beside the road leading to the platform. Chinese and International Settlement police combined to maintain order.

Luckily Sunya and Mulan had not much luggage, and Amei had brought only two small suitcases from Nanking because of the crowding in the train. Sunya gave a two-dollar tip to a porter who promised to get at least two seats for them.

The crowd was pushing and elbowing, but they finally got into a second-class car, the three of them sharing two seats. Even the standing room was taken. Opposite them sat a rich Chinese in a foreign dress of white serge, and a boy of thirteen. The father seemed about thirty-five; his hair was slick and parted in the middle, and he wore spectacles and constantly sniffed with his nose, showing great urbanity and composure and satisfaction with himself. The boy, who called him "Father," was also dressed in a foreign coat and shorts.

An old, greasy-looking business man was standing in the aisle close by. The train moved, leaving the crowd on the platform apparently as great as before. When the car pulled up at Lunghua with a sudden jerk, the old man swung violently and fell against the foreign-dressed boy.

"Haven't you got eyes?" cried the man. The old man apologized.

The train started with another jerk. The old man swayed, but somehow managed to check himself. Timidly, and as if he hoped not to be noticed, he began to sit upon the armrest near the boy. The foreign-dressed man looked at him, took out his handkerchief, and covered his nose in disgust.

Then the old man spoke. "Please, brother, may I borrow a seat? I am an old man."

"Why didn't you come early? Chinese people don't know manners.

792

Suppose a foreigner should see you sitting on the armrest; they would go back to foreign countries and say the Chinese are unclean and disorderly."

Mulan's blood was boiling.

"At such times," she said, apparently to the young man, *"Chiang-chiu hsieh,"* meaning "don't demand too much."

Mulan was wearing a pair of dark spectacles because her eyes were swollen, and the young man could not tell whether she was looking at him or not. He took up an English morning paper, and became immediately transported to a region safe and high above ill-smelling humanity.

This did not bode well for pleasant company on the trip. Mulan sank back into silence. Now the old man did perhaps seem unreasonable—depending on how one looked at it. He had a grandson of five or six who was complaining of standing. He pushed the little boy into a seat beside the boy in foreign dress.

"How do you explain this?" said the bespectacled young man. "Don't you see the rules? 'Seats for two persons in each row.'"

"Please," begged the old man. "He cannot stand the whole way."

Now the young man's son had not really objected, but his father pulled him closer, so that he should not be contaminated.

"What is this?" said Mulan. "Amei, you move across, and let the little boy come over to our side."

The young man looked up in surprise.

"Thank you," he said in English.

Amei went over and sat between the boy and the old man on the arm of the seat. She made a concealed signal to her mother that the old man smelled. The old man's child came over to sit on the inner side next to Sunya.

Now the sky began to grow darker, and there was a light sprinkle of rain. Still outside the windows the green and yellow fields, with their miles of rape flower, lay serene and beautiful in the misty September day.

The shower stopped when the train pulled into the Sungkiang Station. Again there were crowds surging around the train.

The locomotive had been detached and was coming to push the train from behind, since it was not possible to turn round later.

The young man in foreign dress was eating a very cleanly packed sandwich. He told his son the paper was sterilized. Sunya took down a package of apples and cakes and opened it.

Seeing that the child beside him was evidently very hungry, he gave an apple to him. Some one shouted: "Airplanes!"

The young man was just biting his sandwich when he heard this and the sandwich dropped out of his hand. Immediately there was pandemonium. Everybody was trying to rush out of the standing train, with or without luggage. Some jumped down through the windows. Children's cries mingled with women's screams and men's shouts.

The drone of airplanes became louder. Snatching his son, the young man dashed from his seat, looking very pale, cursing and shouting, "My God!" in English. The old man and his grandson disappeared. In a instant the car was almost emptied, with only five or six persons in it besides Mulan's family.

Now Mulan was by nature quick, and Sunya by nature slow.

"What are we going to do?" shouted Mulan.

With unusual strength, she pulled up the shutters on her right.

"Come over," she shouted to Amei. "Crouch down!" Amei crouched to the floor of the car.

Hardly had she said this when they heard a *"zzzzz . . . boom!"* The car almost jumped off the rails. Glasses, lamps, splinters, electric fans flew about. Machine guns made a devilish rattle in the air. A mad howl arose from the refugees outside. A man at the farther end of the car shouted that he had been killed.

The buzzing of the airplanes became fainter and the machine guns ceased. Only the human cries outside were heard.

There was a respite. Luckily, Mulan's family had escaped unharmed.

"Pull up the other shutters!" said Mulan. "We will die here or out-side—it is the same."

Sunya pulled the shutters up, and began to stack up suitcases on the right and left of their seats.

"Hide underneath until it is over," he said. "If a bomb hits us from above, we will die together. But if shrapnel and bullets come from out-side, we have a chance."

Soon cries went up outside again, and then came the drone of the airplanes returning.

Sunya crouched on the side of the center aisle, and Amei and Mulan were crumpled up almost flat beneath their seats; Amei was crying in fear. They drew the suitcases over their heads. A tremendous explosion was heard, shaking the whole train. Evidently the car in front or behind was hit. Then followed the infernal rattle of machine guns in the air. The refugees outside were being slaughtered from above like pigs.

Another bomb hit. Sunya saw part of a human leg fly in through a window and land in the aisle. Somehow it leaned up squarely against a seat with its blood flowing down to the floor. He shut his eyes, seized with nausea.

There was another great explosion with a clang of metal as if the water tank near by had been hit.

After this the droning gradually died away, and they heard people outside say that the airplanes were gone.

With a strange feeling of miraculous luck, Sunya said to Mulan, "They are gone. You lie down. I will look about."

He stood up. A woman at the far end of the car, whose leg had been blown off was crying, "Goddess of Mercy, Savior of the Afflicted and the Distressed!"

He looked out of the window. In the station and in the fields bodies were lying all about, and the lightly wounded were walking about, dazed, trying to find their families and gather their luggage.

"It's all right now. We are safe," he said, and moved away the suitcases which had been their protection.

Mulan got up with Amei. A big blotch on her right trouser leg where Amei's head had lain was completely wet. Amei was still trembling.

"The worst is over, and we are lucky," said Sunya.

They left their car, carrying all their luggage.

"Save my life, good people," came the woman's voice again. "The Goddess of Mercy will bless you."

Sunya spoke to the wounded woman and promised to send help to her.

Outside, the station was like an open-air slaughterhouse. The massacre of students in 1926 had been child's play compared with this. As the newspapers reported later, there were four hundred dead and three hundred injured, all refugees traveling away from Shanghai. Only about fifty escaped uninjured. Eleven planes had raided the refugees and seventeen bombs had been dropped.

One ambulance had now arrived—far inadequate for this appalling disaster. Two cars at the rear of the train were burning, sending up columns of smoke that hung lazily in the gray September sky. Sunya brought assistance to the wounded woman in the car and helped to carry her out to the ambulance. But there was little that could be done for any of the injured.

On the country road beyond the station, they saw the young man in foreign dress lying prostrate, half of his body immersed in a pond, his white serge splashed with water, blood, and mud.

After many anxious difficulties, they arrived at Kashing and put up there for the night. The next day they went on to Hangchow in a hired motorcar.

· ·.

The more Mulan reflected on the danger they had gone through, the more astonished she was at their miraculous escape. She could hardly believe they were alive and safe in their home. And the day after their return, they received a letter from Atung, which greatly relieved the anxiety caused by her dream. Thereafter Atung wrote almost every day, and she came to live for these letters from the front.

This experience of the train journey put a new complexion on plans for the future. She probably would not be able to go to see her son again, even if he returned to Shanghai on leave. Nor would he be able to come to Hangchow.

What lay ahead she did not know. Hangchow seemed safe for the present. Although there were bombings of the city from the air, they were only for creating an effect. While many residents had begun to move inland, the city life went on as usual. Sunya asked Tsao Chung and his son to dig an underground bomb shelter under their rear building.

In the beginning of October, Afei sent her a long letter from Asuan, describing the catastrophe that had happened to Mannia and his family. The letter was addressed both to Afei and to Mulan. As she read the description of the death of Mannia and her family, she stopped to cry and read again and cry again until she reached the last line. The letter was all wet with her tears. She leaned back in her chair, stunned, and the letter dropped to the floor from her hand. Sunya came in and saw her.

"Why, Whimsy, what's the matter?" he cried, frightened.

Mulan pointed to the letter. She could not speak. But she rose, and with dragging footsteps, she went to her bedroom and threw herself upon the bed and wept hopelessly, like one beaten. She lay there the whole afternoon, and though Sunya came to comfort her, she would not be comforted.

That evening, at midnight, she woke up and lighted a lamp, and went to the toilet case and took out the jade peach that her sworn sister had given her at the Tseng home in Shantung. And she hung it close to her breast and went to sleep again. The next day she put an extra blue woolen knot in her hair in memory of Mannia, as a token of mourning. And for many days she remained silent, speaking only when she was forced to.

On October 27, after seventy-six days of heroic resistance, pitting human flesh and blood against superior artillery and aircraft, the Chinese Army began to withdraw, and the cousins at the front were moving north with the staff.

Mochow had moved her family to Nanking to be near her husband. Intensive bombing had made Soochow uninhabitable and the city was in the new line of defense and bound to be subjected to greater bombing and shelling. By November 20, the Chinese Government decided to move its capital up the Yangtse and ordered all its officials not connected with military defense to move their families to Chungking, Hankow, and Changsha. The evacuation of the population began. A huge exodus was moving up the river by every conceivable means of transportation, fleeing from the oncoming Japanese hordes as they had never fled from the worst plague. No population in the world's history ever fled from an invading army as the Chinese fled from the Japanese. It was the beginning of one of the greatest migrations in the world's history.

On the twenty-third, Mulan received a letter from her sister saying she and Lifu and their children would leave Nanking in a week for Chungking. Mulan realized that she would not see them for a long time, and the news that they were going inland set her thinking. What would happen to Hangchow?

Mail still came through from her son at the front, although by circuitous routes. Amei was still keeping up correspondence with Miss Cunningham, through a special foreign mailbag system; and thus some of Atung's letters came in care of Miss Cunningham and were forwarded to a Miss Scranton of the Union Girls' School at Hangchow. In this way Amei began to know Miss Scranton also.

So long as the mails came, Mulan could not make up her mind to flee inland. Hangchow provided easy routes of escape into all points of the interior. Besides, the true character of the Japanese Army had not yet been exposed, and Amei's foreign missionary friends still spoke of their faith in the discipline of Japan's Army, and discredited the stories from North China of Japanese atrocities.

Mulan lived from day to day, awaiting the letters from her son. There was no chance, so far as she could see, of her seeing him until the war was over, or until he was transferred inland. She felt already a bereaved mother, and she began now to understand Chenma's waiting for her son to come home, with the longing that seemed forever part of the mother's life.

As she thought of Chenma, she thought also of Chenma's son, Chen San. And it seemed to her that life had always been so, from the beginning of the world, and she tried to draw a kind of comfort from her father's Taoistic philosophy.

For now she saw herself in the autumn of her life, while it was spring for her son. The song of autumn leaves contains within itself the lullaby of the coming spring and the full melody of the following summer. So do the dual forces of the Tao wax and wane in the alternation of upward and downward cycles, intercrossing. In a true sense, summer begins not at the vernal equinox, but at winter solstice, when the days begin to grow longer and the *yin* forces begin to recede; and winter begins from the summer solstice, when the days begin to grow shorter and the *yang* forces begin to recede in favor of the *yin*. So also does human life go in cycles of youth, maturity, and decay. Chenma had passed, but Chen San was in the full maturity of his manhood. Mannia was gone, too, but Asuan was still carrying on. As Mulan felt her own life entering the period of autumn, she also felt vividly the sense of life and youth springing up in Atung.

And, as she looked back over the almost five decades of her life, she felt that this was true of China also. The old leaves dropped one by one, and new buds sprang up, vigorous and hopeful.

These reflections made Mulan more patient, more resigned, and as the months wore on, her courage returned. Her husband saw that her face had changed, and she looked kinder, if also sadder and older. She had lost the fear of death or of anything that might happen to herself.

. ˙.

The Japanese entered Nanking on December 13, covering themselves with the infamy that made the world's conscience revolt. When they

798

had debauched themselves in a manner that incapacitated them for further advance, the Japanese paused for breath, for a period of months.

The area south of Shanghai on the north of Hangchow Bay, had been under their occupation since the end of October. It seemed that an advance into Hangchow was logical and easy, since Hangchow is at the northern tip of the province, strategically controlling a network of motor highways and a railway into the interior on the south, west, and southwest.

Mulan was still in her languid and resigned state of mind, not caring very much what happened, when rumors began to fly fast that the Chinese troops were about to evacuate and abandon the city. Nobody knew what credence to give to the rumors, until on December 22 the great steel bridge across the river and the electric power plant of which Hangchow had been so proud, were blown up. The retreating Chinese troops were following their "scorched earth" policy of leaving nothing behind for the enemy to exploit to its advantage. The retreat was well executed, and all roads and bridges around the city were blown up.

But Hangchow, the lake city, was once more favored as Peking had been. The destruction there was nothing like what had happened to Soochow, Wusih, and Nanking. No battles were fought over it, and there was no reason to expect great ravages after the Japanese occupation, for it had been left undefended.

On December 24 the Japanese came! Troops straggling in twos and threes, tired and war-weary, filtered into the streets, with no sort of military order or precautions, knowing that there were no Chinese soldiers in the city. They looked soiled and hungry after their days of marching, and wandered aimlessly in search of food.

Here was the great chance for the Japanese Army to demonstrate its discipline and its ability to protect the innocent and let the people carry on a normal life under their rule.

At first, the people were not greatly afraid of the occupation troops. Mulan in her home on the City God's Hill, could hear the singing in the Roman Catholic convent on Christmas morning.

Then evil things began to happen. Frightened women began to seek refuge in foreign schools and hospitals and the convent. Two of the biggest missionary compounds which had intended to take in a maximum of one thousand refugee women and children, were now forced to receive two thousand five hundred each. Corridors, verandas, staircase landings, every empty space a human being could even sit upon, was occupied.

An American resident doctor was driven to write, five weeks after the occupation, "I doubt if one shop or house anywhere was left unmolested. . . . Everywhere terror stalks through the land, and the stories we discounted to our Chinese friends before the Japanese occupation we can only sorrowfully confess do not fully portray the horrors actually experienced . . . now five weeks after the occupation one can hardly walk anywhere in the city without seeing looting openly carried on by soldiers without any evident attempt by the authorities to interfere, and even now hardly anywhere woman is safe."

It was the same monotonously shocking story of greed and lust. Mulan was right: The Japanese "luck-character" could not change.

The hill being a high point commanding a view of the lake and the river, some Japanese sentries were uncomfortably near Mulan's house. Amei knew Miss Scranton, but her school was quite a distance away; on the other hand, the Catholic Convent was in their own neighborhood on the hill. Miss Scranton wrote a letter to the Mother Superior of the convent, asking her to admit Mulan and her daughter and a woman servant for refuge.

So, on December 26, Mulan went with Amei and Brocade into the convent. Men were not admitted, and parting was difficult, but Sunya felt greatly relieved; and, not fearing anything for himself, he went back with Tsao Chung and Little Pie to his house.

On the morning of December 27, Amei went out into the convent garden for a walk after breakfast. Her mother was in the chapel, watching the matin. The morning being bright, the girl went further and further, unconscious of any danger.

Suddenly she saw a head looking over the compound wall from a tree about fifteen feet away. It was clearly a Japanese soldier, for he was wearing an army cap.

Amei screamed and ran. The Japanese jumped over the wall and began to chase her. The road was crooked, and as she ran around one path, the soldier came out from the other side. He missed her by a few feet.

Amei ran with all the energy of her mother's milk, up the steps round a bush. The Japanese tripped on the steps, but he drew close to her again.

"Help! Help!" she cried.

But the Japanese soldier had already seized her and was kissing her forcibly. They were now in the upper yard, near the chapel where the nuns were saying their matin prayers. Mulan was watching the unfamiliar rites and the movements of the Mother Superior, while her mind was trying to gather together the recent sudden and discordant changes in her family and to put them into some sort of connected order. She had been brought up apart from Buddhist worship and the common Buddhist beliefs, which were shared with most women by her own mother. But now she was impressed by this exotic worship of a foreign god, so different from, and yet so similar to, Chinese worship. The tragic happenings of the last few months had brought her nearer that Great Unknown, which her father had called Tao the Unnameable but which she herself thought of only as Destiny. Now as before, whenever she thought of Tao, she thought of her father. The peculiar chanting of the nuns and their pure white faces strangely moved her. Her eyes were moist and she felt herself in the presence of Eternity.

Suddenly she was startled out of this deep reverie by Amei's screams for help, and she screamed out herself. The Mother Superior stopped short her ceremony, gave orders to some of the nuns to go out and see what was wrong, and then went on with the prayer.

Mulan had dashed out at once and four or five sisters followed her. They saw Amei in the clutch of the Japanese, tearing his hair and beating at him helplessly. Mulan threw herself upon the soldier and bit the arm that still held her daughter. Releasing the girl, the soldier turned and struck Mulan's head a blow with his fist. Mulan staggered under the blow. Amei, still screaming, tried to hit back. But at the appearance of the white foreigners, the Japanese walked quickly but calmly away, leaving the mother and girl crying in each other's arms, their hair all disheveled.

The nuns came close and sought to comfort the mother and daughter, muttering soft, sweet syllables in French that they could not understand. Now Mulan, in all her life, had never before been struck by man or woman or even by a beast. Enraged, frightened, and humiliated at this assault upon her daughter and herself, she cursed as she wept, "You three-island short devils! You will not die a good death!" Amei was furiously wiping the spot on her face where she had been kissed, as though she would wipe the very flesh away.

By this time the prayer had been hurriedly finished, and the nuns had come out to the yard, and the Mother Superior led them all into the chapel again. The Mother Superior was a short but big-voiced woman, and beneath her gentle manner, she had great inner strength. She was angered. She held Amei to her breast and spoke words of comfort to her in Chinese. Though the danger was over, Amei was whimpering and shuddering all the more, and her lips were quivering as Mannia's used to do. A Chinese nun came up and began to talk to the mother and daughter in Chinese, and gradually Amei's weeping subsided.

Barely ten minutes later the same Japanese returned with four others and demanded now to see the Mother Superior.

"What do you want?" the Mother Superior shouted at them.

"We must search here for communists and anti-Japanese women. This place is full of them," said one.

"You are not going to," replied the Mother Superior firmly.

There were thirty or forty women in this small chapel and at the sight of the Japanese, they began to hurry away to the inner rooms. The Japanese who had kissed Amei now saw her and Mulan and said, "There they are—the anti-Japanese communists!" Turning up his sleeve, he said, "That woman bit me. It is an insult to His Majesty, the Emperor of Japan. She must be punished."

"You can't take her!" said the Mother Superior, crossing herself and beginning to mumble a prayer.

The Japanese slapped her across the face. Realizing the hopelessness of the situation, the Mother Superior then walked away and without further ado called in French to the sisters to lead the Chinese women from the rear of the chapel and lock the door, while she herself stepped out of the front door and locked it from outside. Thus, the Japanese soldiers were locked into the chapel before they knew it.

The Mother Superior telephoned to the American Mission Hospital and asked for help. In a few minutes an American doctor arrived with a Japanese officer who had happened to be visiting the hospital. The Mother Superior told them the story and led them in, now followed by a few nuns. The officer questioned the soldiers and they replied in Japanese, while the first Japanese rolled up his sleeve again to show where he had been bitten. To their surprise, the officer slapped the soldier without saying anything, and then turned to the Mother Superior.

"Where is that woman and her daughter?" he said in bad Chinese. "I want to see them."

The Mother Superior went in and brought Mulan and Amei out to the officer. He was struck by their beauty and turned a severe look on the accusing soldier, who had evidently told him they were searching for communists.

Conversation proceeded by Amei and the Mother Superior speaking in tolerable English to the American doctor, and the American doctor repeating the English to the Japanese officer. Amei told her own story and the American passed it on to the Japanese officer. The officer seemed to be a good man and to understand, but he was still trying to uphold the dignity of the Japanese Army and he asked a question.

"The officer asks if you are anti-Japanese communists," said the American doctor.

"I hate them!" said Amei, but Mulan said, "We are not communists, but I am anti-Japanese since that soldier assaulted my daughter."

"You are angry," said the officer directly to Mulan.

Mulan understood the word "angry" in English, although the Japanese had said "arn-gli." She now said to the American doctor, who understood Chinese perfectly:

"Will you try to explain to the officer not to expect the impossible? He accuses me of being angry, and that I am. Tell him not to be like Wuyen."

"Who is Wuyen?" asked the American.

"She was the ugliest woman in ancient China. Her name was Wuyen —'No Salt' in English. This No Salt went to the king and demanded that the king marry her and love her. She should have had more self-knowledge."

The American smiled and did not think it quite tactful to translate the analogy. But the officer had heard the words "No Salt" in English, and asked the American what she had said about Wuyen and the American merely said, "She says that Wuyen was pitiful. She was ugly and no one loved her."

The American laughed and the officer laughed also to show that he appreciated the classical reference, although he had missed the point entirely. He thought she had meant that the ugly women had been left unmolested, and he wrote the characters for "No Salt" on his palm to show to Mulan. She smiled a cold smile. The officer also allowed his lips to widen in a half smile. It seemed to the nuns strange that this Japanese officer should smile kindly at a Chinese woman.

"This time you have caught them in the act," said the American doctor to the Japanese. "You professed not to believe these stories."

"We are doing our best to maintain discipline and order," the officer replied. "Our discipline here is really admirable. You should see Nanking, Soochow, and Kashing!"

The officer was apparently trying to do his best, but was unable to check forces beyond his control. Turning to the soldiers, he commanded them in Japanese to get out, and they went out by the chapel door.

"You had better evacuate these women, move them elsewhere. This is an out-of-the-way place and it is difficult for us to keep watch over our men," the officer said as he left.

After this the American doctor decided with the Mother Superior to abandon the convent because of its location. The women were taken by ambulance to the Catholic Hospital, and all refugees were evacuated that very day.

Mulan and her daughter and Brocade returned before noon to their home near by, to the surprise of Sunya and Tsao Chung. Mulan's forehead was still swollen where it had been struck. When they told their story to Sunya, they all said, "How can we stay in Hangchow any longer?" and they agreed to flee inland.

. .

They began to make preparations for the long and difficult journey into the interior. Their property was now worth about a hundred thousand dollars, but all Sunya's shops had shared the fate of others in the city. They had been broken into and robbed by the Japanese soldiers, and the employees had fled, and he could do nothing. He had secured about twenty thousand dollars in banknotes a month before, and this they could carry with them on the journey. Sunya divided ten thousand among himself, his wife, and his daughter; and they sewed it in little cloth bags to their inner jackets. As Brocade's family were to go with them, each was also provided with a hundred dollars similarly hidden. The rest of the money Mulan sewed up inside a quilt. Again, like her old father, Mulan had their better curios and paintings hidden in boxes in the underground shelter, previously dug for air defense, and she also hid a number of jades and pearls in their bags and bedding and on her own body, as well as on that of her daughter. They knew that they must make part of the journey on foot and had no idea whether they could hire any vehicle, and therefore they took no more blankets and clothing than could be carried by

Brocade's husband and her son, Little Pie, who was now a strong young man, of the same age as Atung.

They made arrangements with Miss Scranton to forward their mail, and Mulan wrote a letter to Atung, telling him what had happened to his sister. "In the name of Aunt Mannia and your sister," she wrote angrily, "fight on until these Japs are driven into the sea!"

Since the new steel bridge, which had cost millions of dollars, had been blown up, they decided to flee east and then turn south and cross the river to get to the railway for Nanchang. Normally they would have fled west and taken the railway a short distance from the city, but there was fighting on the west and southwest, and crossing the country on that side was dangerous. Every Chinese refugee was stripped of his money and valuables by the Japanese sentries, on the charge that the goods were looted and must be returned to their rightful owners.

And so, on the morning of December 29, Mulan's family abandoned their home and set out to join the millions of refugees making for the interior of China. There were three men and three women, all grown-up. Tsao Chung and Little Pie carried the larger luggage, while Brocade carried a cloth bundle and Sunya a small leather bag containing the most important documents and valuables. Now Mulan's large, unbound feet stood her in good stead; and, while Amei was slender, she was also well able to walk. Brocade, although a woman, was far from weak, and Mulan and her daughter depended upon her a great deal. As a matter of fact, none of them had any idea of what the journey would be like, for conditions were constantly changing.

Soon they came to a creek twenty feet wide where a bridge had been blown up. The creek was only about one or two feet deep, but Brocade offered to carry Mulan and Amei across so that they should not wet their feet, but her husband said that it was unnecessary for her to do it, and that Little Pie would carry her herself across the creek. So Brocade was taken over on her son's back, and then Tsao Chung and Little Pie carried Mulan and Amei. It was strange that already all distinctions of master and servant had disappeared. Only strength, intelligence, and common loyalty counted. While being carried on Tsao Chung's back, Mulan called to Brocade on the other side:

"Brocade, I ought to thank you!"

"How thank me?"

"For marrying such a strong husband!"

Sunya, already standing on the other bank, said, "Whimsy, you can still joke?"

"Why not, Fatty?" she cried, gayly.

So they went on in good spirits. It was a bright day, and the winter sun made it just right for walking, except that they were overclothed, and soon Mulan and Amei had to take off their outer coats and carry them in their hands. Beyond lay the beautiful country with well-to-do hamlets and tall bamboo groves. In one of these groves, where they took a rest, the bamboos rose to a height of forty or fifty feet.

After a while they came to a village and beyond it to a ferry. The ferryman told them that two miles from the ferry there was a town where they might find some kind of vehicle, if they were lucky. They went on, and soon began to see streams of refugees converging from the east and northeast. In the town no vehicle of any sort was to be had for any price. Rickshaws, motorcars, sedan chairs, pack animals, all had been commandeered by soldiers or hired by people who had already gone ahead. Still Sunya was hopeful that as soon as they reached the trunk highway leading to the Tientai Sacred Mountain they might be able to find something.

So after a little rest they started again, joining the great thickening stream of refugees, all patient and cheerful in spite of tragedy. . . .
Here or there a rickshaw was carrying an old mother or a sick woman. Two brothers were carrying their aged mother lying on a door panel suspended from a pole slung on their shoulders. Sons carried their mothers on their backs, fathers carried young children in a basket at one end of a pole with some bedding and small caldrons hung from the other end. A sick man was tied on the back of a water buffalo.

Thousands of human feet were trudging, trudging, to escape the dreaded invaders. Yet there was calm fortitude in these faces. Few spoke of the past; the future was a blank; they had thoughts only for the immediate needs of the present—whether their shoulders were tired or not, how many miles to the next town, and whether the weather would be good tonight. A stolid mass of trudging humanity, a whole population uprooted from their homes, going with indomitable courage to make new homes in China's interior.

Mulan and her family were carried along with the stream of people, going all in the same direction. Sunya said that as soon as they got to the trunk highway he would see about getting a car, even if they had to pay a fantastic price. But for the present they must go on walking.

806

They camped for the night with hundreds of others in the open, covering themselves with their few blankets and coats.

On the second day they came to a little town, where fortunately Tsao Chung saw a wheelbarrow in a backyard. Sunya went in and inquired and found that the farmer had just returned from a trip to Tientai, and he was able to persuade him to take another trip. And so Tsao Chung was relieved of part of his burden, and Amei and her mother were able to take turns riding on the side seat of the wheelbarrow. A year ago, or even a month ago, a wheelbarrow ride would have seemed poetic to Mulan, but now she felt it to be less an expression of the poetic spirit than a genuine comfort and a relief to her tired legs.

They were nearing the highway now. In the afternoon they saw by the roadside a baby about a year old, sitting crying beside the dead body of her mother, who had evidently died of hunger and exposure. With hardly a word spoken between them, Sunya and Mulan went to the baby together and took her up and put her on the wheelbarrow, and Amei sat with her lest she should fall off.

That night they were able to find shelter in a farmer's house.

On the third day, December 31, they came to the highway. They were near the beginning of the Tientai mountain range, and perpendicular granite peaks stood up here and there out of the plains through which the road ran. Here the highway was broad and straight, and the lines of refugees spread far across the open plains, following the highway like a moving, human Great Wall, seemingly endless, disappearing at the horizon with the highway over a mountain slope.

Before they had gone far on the highway, they came to a place where two gigantic cliffs stood at the sides of the road as if they were the ruins of a gate built by a race of giants. Then they heard a rumble that arose in the distance ahead of them, like thunder. At first, it sounded like the roar of a distant sea; then it became like the rushing of water through a broken dyke. The noise rose and fell in waves and was echoed in the valley. As it drew nearer, it became human voices, like the rending and tearing of gigantic silk sheets in the air. Surprised and frightened, they thought it sounded like an ancient battle or like an army in revolt. The column of refugees moved off the road as in the distance a series of black objects came steadily moving toward them. Then they saw that these were army trucks, filled with Chinese soldiers, lifting their hands high to the cheering of the refugees. The wave of roaring voices rolled toward them and echoed from the cliffs. These were troops going to the Hangchow front.

The army trucks came near, the soldiers standing up proudly in their iron helmets and waving to the people; and, stirred by their welcome, they began to sing a martial song, the refrain of which was:

> We go into battle,
> To fight for home and country!
> Never to come back
> Until our hills and rivers are returned to us!

Mulan's tears began to fall, as everyone around her joined in the deafening roar of applause. The song was gradually lost in the distance and in the receding roar from those who lined the road behind. The refugees near Mulan stood looking back and many still cheered and some wept.

After an hour, the scene was repeated when about fifty army trucks passed. This time several Chinese airplanes flew over their heads, going northward. Again wild cheers went up from the crowds and reverberated in the valley. The granite peaks of Tientai seemed to have joined them, convulsed from the inside, in an almost human assent to the refrain of the soldiers' chorus:

> Never to come back
> Until our hills and rivers are returned to us!

Thus the very mountains spoke.

Mulan felt a sudden liberation, deep and not to be expressed by words. She had felt such liberation once before, on that mid-autumn night some thirty years ago, when she had discovered that she was in love with Lifu. But in that first liberation she had found herself, her personal individuality, while in this present liberation she had lost herself. And it was because of this new liberation that she began to do many things as they went on their way.

Toward one o'clock they came upon two orphans, a girl of fourteen and her brother of nine, begging for food. Mulan thought at once of herself when she had been lost as a child.

"Where are your parents?" asked Mulan.

"They are dead," the girl replied.

"Where are you from?"

"From Sungkiang. All the houses and streets were bombed and set on fire. We tried not to leave. But in the whole town only five old men and some dogs remained, and they couldn't help us. Please, good aunt, my younger brother is hungry."

"And you walked all the way from Sungkiang?"

"Yes. We have begged our way."

The younger child had evidently been a sturdy boy, but he now looked dazed and helpless and seemed to rely entirely upon his elder sister.

"Let's take them," said Mulan.

"How can we?" Sunya asked.

"On the wheelbarrow," said Mulan.

"Good aunt," said the girl, "we can walk; at least I can. But please give us some food."

"Come and ride on the wheelbarrow," said Sunya. The sister and brother were surprised and sat on the wheelbarrow together with the baby.

"*Taitai*," said the wheelbarrow man, "you are a goodhearted person. But if you keep on this way, you yourself won't be able to ride at all."

"It's all right," replied Mulan. "These are the last we will pick up. We grown-ups can all walk."

"Lady," exclaimed the man, "I think I will come inland and work as your servant."

The girl from Sungkiang was really tired, and both she and her brother looked famished. Brocade took out some wheat cakes that they had bought at the last village and gave them to them, and the sister and brother ate without saying a word, as only the hungry eat.

When it was nearing sunset, they came to a stream, and as they were crossing the bridge, they saw a woman lying on the bank below, with her husband and four or five children around her.

"Stop!" cried Mulan.

"What's the matter, now, Whimsy?" asked Sunya.

"That woman is giving birth to a child!" She ran back toward the bank. The wheelbarrow man stopped amazed.

"What is this new whim of yours now? Another child?" Sunya cried after her.

"I am just being sensible," replied Mulan as she ran down the bank.

The woman was lying on the bare ground, and the newborn baby was beside her on a piece of blue cloth. The husband was trying to wipe the blood from the baby's body with an old towel, but the umbilical cord had not yet been cut. The peasant woman was her own midwife and was saying to her husband, "Cover it up first, and leave the placenta and the cord outside. I just need a few moments' rest and I will take care of it by and by."

Now Mulan and Brocade had come near, and Sunya and Amei were standing at a little distance. The husband looked up at them blankly.

"Let me help," said Mulan.

"How dare we?" replied the husband. The woman opened her eyes and saw Mulan, who was wearing an expensive foreign coat, and she said, "Good aunt, I shall be all right after a while. We dare not bother you with this dirty work. But if you can give the baby some clothing, I shall thank you. We were not prepared for this."

Now Brocade knew her mistress well enough, and so when she heard this she ran up the bank and took out a clean inside jacket to wrap the child in.

"Bring the scissors," said Mulan to her.

"Don't use scissors," said the mother. "It is not good for the child. Give me a bowl."

The husband took out a rice bowl.

"Break it," said the woman. The husband broke the bowl. Mulan did not quite understand and asked, "What for?"

"I will cut the cord with the new broken pieces."

"I will do it for you," said Mulan, "you lie down and rest."

Mulan now chose a broken piece of china with a clean, sharp edge, and bent down and performed the operation on the newborn baby, tying the remaining cord into a knot and carefully wrapping the navel with a towel that Brocade brought. The husband threw the placenta into the stream, and Mulan also went to the stream to wash her hands, while the man stood by, not knowing how to thank the unknown good lady before him.

But the mother said, "*Taitai,* you are a kindhearted person. I will give this baby to you, if you will accept. We have too many mouths to feed and we are fleeing in trouble. It is a boy, as you see."

Brocade looked at Mulan and Mulan looked at Brocade; and they both bent to look at the baby.

"Take him," said Brocade. "I will take care of him."

Mulan turned to the mother and said, "Do you mean this? He is a pretty child."

The woman made an effort to sit up and hold her baby, and Mulan passed him to her, and she took him and held him very closely for a moment. Then she looked up at Mulan bravely, and said: "Good aunt, if you will adopt this son of mine, I know it is his good luck. You must have plenty of money. And if I carry him with us, I do not know if he will live. We do not even have enough to eat on the way."

Sunya, watching, saw Mulan kneel on the ground and stretch out her arms to receive the baby. The mother cuddled him to her cheek and then, in tears, handed him to Mulan with a smile. The father said nothing, and the baby's brothers and sisters came to watch their new brother being so soon adopted by the rich lady.

And Mulan rose and unbuttoned her coat and put the baby against her breast to keep him warm and walked up the bank. Sunya went down and asked the parents a few questions about where they came from.

"Tell them our address," Mulan called from above.

"What address?"

"The address of our teashop at Hangchow," said his wife. "Say that we will be coming back when the war is over."

Then she asked Brocade to take ten dollars down to the family on the bank and they went on. The wheelbarrow man was still more amused and said, "Now you have picked up four children in two days. At this rate you will soon have a hundred."

"This is most certainly the last," replied Mulan.

"If all China were like you," the driver said, "the Japs couldn't do anything with us. On my last trip I saw three childbirths like that on the roadside. They can kill a million and we still have four hundred forty-nine million left, and more babies are being born everyday!"

Brocade and Amei now took turns carrying the baby, sometimes riding but usually walking, for the wheelbarrow was already carrying the year-old baby and the boy of nine and the luggage. Mulan thought about what the man had said, and she said to Sunya, "Do you remember what we told Atung? The Chinese blood must go on forever, whether it is ours or that of other families!"

The baby was crying. Mulan had a first-aid kit, and she took some clean cotton and mixed some sugar and water and let the baby suck it out of the cotton.

That night, New Year's Eve, they stopped at a temple at the foot of the Tientai Mountain. The country here was one of the most beautiful districts in Chekiang, seldom seen by tourists until the highway was opened. On the distant horizon, they saw rugged granite peaks rising abruptly, high into the sky, partly hidden by clouds.

The temple was nearly full of refugees. The chief monk, however, learned that they were from the well-known Hangchow teashop and said that he had known their father, old Mr. Yao; he was very cordial and, crowded as the place already was, gave them a room in his own inner courtyard.

Mulan asked for some honey, saying that she wanted it for the baby. The monk gave her three bottles, for honey was a local product here. Brocade offered to sleep with the baby for the night, but Mulan had a strange feeling and said, "No, let me have him for tonight. You sleep with the little one and look after the sister and brother."

"Whimsy, you need a good sleep yourself tonight," Sunya said. "There is the journey ahead tomorrow."

"Let this be my last whim," replied Mulan. "After this I will let Brocade sleep with him."

And at night, when the baby cried, Mulan dipped a piece of cotton in honey and wiped her own breasts with it to make them sweet, and she put the baby to her breast and the baby sucked and went to sleep. Mulan had an exquisite pleasure in this, feeling that even in suckling this one child, she was doing something not for an individual, but something eternal for China, to carry on the life of the Chinese race. And the baby was now a symbol to her of racial immortality, more than her jade and amber animals had ever been.

∴

This was New Year's morning, 1938. Sunya proposed that they should rest a little on this day, and the old monk urged them to stay. And so they had a quiet morning in the temple.

Mulan thought again of her flight from the Boxers and foreign soldiers when she was a mere child and of her entire past. What a world of events had passed between then and now! Her relatives were scattered: Lifu and Mochow a thousand miles ahead of them, in far west Szechuen; Chen San and Huan-erh and Taiyun in Shansi; her brother Afei and Paofen and Chinya and Dimfragrance in Shanghai. And Mannia was dead—although somehow she felt that through this war, Mannia's spirit was still with her. What would not she have given to live over once more her life with all of them! Above all, she thought of her son Atung, in the army with his cousin Hsiaofu, and she imagined them to be like the brave smiling soldiers she had seen on the trucks that had passed them, going to lay down their lives that their children and grandchildren should be free men and women. What an epic story was being lived through by these people of China, of whom she was one!

And on this day, as they rested in the temple, she began to tell Amei the story of her own first flight, and then of Tijen and Silverscreen and Redjade and Aman and Suyun and Mannia, who had now become ancient ones. Above all, Amei loved to hear Mulan tell of her grandfather, old Mr. Yao, whose spirit seemed still to guide and shape their lives.

And through the telling of the story, helped and corrected sometimes by Brocade, Sunya and Mulan and Amei obtained a curious sense of time, like a river ever flowing, majestic, unalterable. And it seemed to them that their own story was but a moment in old, ageless Peking, a story written by the finger of Time itself.

At about noon they heard outside the temple the thundering wave of human voices again rolling towards them. Mulan leaped to her feet.

"Come, let's join them!" she cried. "We must go on with them. Are you all right, Fatty?"

"My legs are still sore, Whimsy, but we will go," said Sunya. "We must reach the railway as soon as we can."

"How far is it now?" asked Mulan.

"Probably four or five days," replied her husband. "I'm afraid it will be hard to get a car. But even if we get one what will be the use? You will soon fill it up with orphans!"

He smiled and rose, calling to the nine-year old boy to walk with him. Brocade carried the one-year old, and Amei carried the newborn baby wrapped in her coat. The girl of fourteen walked along with them. They went to say good-by and give their hearty thanks to the old monk, and he came out with them to the gate.

"Why must you go so early on New Year's Day?" he asked cordially.

"We must try to reach the railway soon," replied Sunya.

"How far are you going inland?" the old monk asked again.

"We do not know yet. Perhaps to Chungking—to see my sister," replied Mulan, and her heart warmed as she thought that there she would see Lifu also. And then to the monk she added, "Perhaps from there we shall all go on together."

The old monk stood at the gate and watched them going down the slope. Only a short distance beyond lay the highway. The thundering noise of many voices rolled nearer.

"Come on quickly and meet them!" the monk heard Mulan cry. He saw her take the baby from her daughter and hurry down.

Below the temple tens of thousands of men, women, and children were moving across the beautiful country on that glorious New Year morning, shouting and cheering as the army trucks passed. The soldiers' song rose once again:

> Never to come back
> Until our hills and rivers are returned to us!

Mulan, drawing near them, was seized with a new and strange emotion. A sense of happiness, a sense of glory, she thought it was. She was stirred as she had never been before, as one can be stirred only when losing oneself in a great movement. She remembered that she had felt the same inward stirring when she watched the funeral of Sun Yat-sen; it was like this but not so powerful, not thus shaking her body and soul. It was not only the soldiers, but this great moving column of which she was a part. She had a sense of her nation such as she had never had so vividly before, of a people united by a common loyalty and, though fleeing from a common enemy, still a people whose patience and strength were like the ten-thousand-*li* Great Wall, and as enduring. She had heard of the flight of whole populations in North and Middle China, and how forty millions of her brothers and sisters from the "same womb" were marching westward in the greatest migration in the world's history, to build a new and modern state in the vast hinterland of China. She felt these forty million people moving in one fundamental rhythm. Amidst the stark privations and sufferings of the refugees, she had not heard one speak against the government for the policy of resistance to Japan. All these people, she saw, preferred war to slavery, like Mannia, even though it was a war that had destroyed their homes, killed their relatives, and left them nothing but the barest personal belongings, their rice bowls and their chopsticks. Such was the triumph of the human spirit. There was no catastrophe so great that the spirit could not rise above it and, out of its very magnitude, transform it into something great and glorious.

And as the scene changed for Mulan, something inside her also changed. She lost all sense of space and direction, lost even the sense